GOD, FREEDOM AND IMMORTALITY

Now I, to confort him, bad him not think of God. I hoped there was no need to trouble himself with any such thoughts yet.

William Shakespeare: King Henry IV Part II

God, Freedom and Immortality

JONATHAN HARRISON

Ashgate

Aldershot • Brookfield USA • Singapore • Sydney

Published by
Ashgate Publishing Ltd
Gower House
Croft Road
Aldershot
Hants GU11 3HR
England

Ashgate Publishing Company
Old Post Road
Brookfield
Vermont 05036
USA

British Library Cataloguing in Publication Data
Harrison, Jonathan
   God, freedom and immortality. - (Avebury series in
   philosophy)
   1. God 2. God - Attributes 3. Knowledge, Theory of
   I. Title
   212

Library of Congress Catalog Card Number: 98-74628

ISBN 1 84014 836 5

Printed in Great Britain

Contents

Prologue

The title of this book is a little misleading, as most of it is about God, and only a little of it about freedom and immortality. Indeed, the amount of space assigned to these three topics is in inverse proportion to the amount taken up in the title by the words for them.

I do not know that bulls ought to be offended because the English name for their species is 'cow', but I may owe my readers an explanation for such things as that I speak of man, where many believe I ought to speak of people, and quite often use the word 'he' when some others say 'she' or 'he or she' or use a plural. This is because I think that words like 'he', 'man' and 'mankind', are ambiguous. Sometimes they refer to human beings of either sex. (I remember coming across a legal document in which a woman in childbirth was referred to as 'he'.) No-one ever supposed that 'He who fights and runs away', 'He who would valiant be' and 'He who runs may read' applied only to males. It is not always that these words refer only to human beings of the male sex. In any case, it is often bad style to substitute 'people' for 'man'. 'People propose, God disposes' or 'People are the measure of all things' sound feeble. And I suspect that too much insistence upon terminological feminism is counterproductive.

These sentiments do not mean that I am an anti-feminist. Indeed, I look forward to a time, and to some small extent try to expedite it, when women are so satisfied and so secure in equal positions as not to want to waste time on such trivialities.

I am indebted to a large number of people, some of them philosophers, but my thanks are mainly due to Jack Smart for agreeing to read the print-out – unfortunately it is too late to take advantage of this – and for many other acts of kindness from which I hope and think that I have greatly profited.

Introduction

This book is divided into four parts. In the *first* I consider some questions in the theory of knowledge, answers to which the other three parts presuppose. It would be possible for the reader to omit this part without seriously impairing his understanding of the other three.

The *second* part discusses and rejects some well-known arguments for the existence of God, but at the same time puts forward the view that the 'existence' of God is not a matter for proof, or even argument, not because we know without argument that he exists, a view which I reject, but because 'postulating' him is not a matter of putting forward a hypothesis. (I later suggest that it is possible to allow the idea of God to play some part in one's life, though a reduced one, without having any religious beliefs which have consequences about the world.) It is therefore possible to a limited extent to be an atheist concerning belief, but a theist concerning attitude and practice.

The *third* part discusses God's attributes, and concludes that we do have a coherent concept of an omnipotent, omniscient, perfectly good disembodied person, though the fact of evil makes the unequivocal existence of such a being incredible, at least so long as his existence is considered as a hypothesis to explain the course of nature.

The *fourth* part considers some ethical problems which the existence of God may raise, and whether what might perhaps be called faith may supply the deficiency of reason pointed out earlier. I conclude in this part that faith, considered as involving a disposition to believe without evidence, or more strongly than the evidence warrants, is a vice, but that there may nevertheless be some merit in inculcating in oneself a religious attitude or way of life. Whether one should inculcate such a way of life in others is more questionable, perhaps because one may take risks for oneself that one is unjustified in taking for one's friends.

I feel I need to make some defence, which once upon a time would have been unnecessary, of the traditional concept of God as that of an omniscient, omnipotent perfectly good person. (To defend the concept from the charge of incoherence is not the same as to claim that there is a God.) If God is to be conceived of as personal – which is one good way of conceiving of him – he must have attributes such as wisdom and power, for even a human being without these attributes would be inadequate. But given that God has them at all, he must have them to a pre-eminent degree. A god who was very powerful without being able to do everything, or who was very knowledgeable without knowing everything, and very good without being morally perfect, or who was ephemeral, would be lacking in something, and it is impossible for God to lack any (appropriate) desirable attribute. (Existence is not one of these.) But given that God is personal and possesses the aforementioned qualities, it follows that he must have created the universe, and be responsible for everything that happens in it, including, as I shall argue, the free actions of men. (Hence determinism and freedom are compatible.) He has this responsibility because he must both know what is happening in the universe and have the power to prevent it. Hence the problem of evil. (Incidentally, I shall reject any form of attempt to reduce statements about the deity to statements about the world which God is alleged to have created. Such attempts confusingly reduce all that is interesting and important about theism to banality.)

That God is transcendent follows from the fact that he is not to be found anywhere in the spatial universe. From this it follows that, if he is personal at all, he must be an immaterial person, though it is in a sense conceivable that he is embodied in the universe in some other way than by having a body. (In what follows I defend the conceivability, though not the wisdom, of regarding God as a disembodied person.)

The absurdity of looking for God within the universe suggests, though it does not prove, that, if God exists, he is a transcendent being outside time, and so is eternal, or, perhaps, sempiternal. He must be a fit and proper object of worship, which may also mean his being eternal. A changing being is too fussy to be properly worshipped.

One might avoid these conclusions if one were to hold that God was not personal. A nonpersonal god cannot be such things as omnipotent or good. But a god who was not personal would suffer from certain limitations. There would be no point in our going to him for help, for he would not be able to give us any. We could place trust only in a personal god. A nonpersonal god could not issue commands that ought to be obeyed. Only if the universe is governed by benevolent personal god can we have any reliance that all things – or even any thing – will work for good. And we could not have a relationship with a nonpersonal god that involved any reciprocation on his part, though his being eternal would also exclude reciprocation. Those who (wrongly) think that it is possible to worship only persons will think that it would be impossible to worship an impersonal god. We could receive help only from the act of contemplating a nonpersonal god; we could not deliberately be given help by one. Though I think we know what the world would have to be like to provide us with evidence for the actual existence of a personal God, even though the world does not provide such evidence, statements about a nonpersonal god are more likely to be unverifiable, and so, perhaps, meaningless. Some of these disadvantages of a nonpersonal god are shared, if I may put the point in an Irish way which I shall try to elucidate in the book, by a personal god who does not exist.

One object of this book is to provide reasons for rejecting what I regard as a wrong view of the deity. This regards the existence of God as explaining the existence of the universe, its genesis and the course of its history, and as leading us to expect to discover or explain certain facts about it. It regards God as an omnipotent, omniscient and benevolent person, who issues commands to man, whom he wishes well, who rewards those who obey his commands and punishes those who do not, and who interferes from time to time for some benevolent purpose in the course of nature. Postulating such a god would be justified only if it explained facts about the world; but it does not.

To avoid later confusion, may I say again that I do not think that rejecting the existence of an onmnipotent, omniscient benevolent person rules out having a favourable attitude to such a person that does not presuppose believing in his existence. Religious devotion, perhaps, does not begin and end with belief, though to disentangle religion from belief is a delicate task which may not be entirely possible, however desirable. One may perhaps feel love or awe of a being whose existence makes no difference to the universe, and contemplate him or meditate upon him whether one thinks he exists or not. One can feel awe of Mount Everest without expecting to benefit from its existence, or thinking that it might intervene on one's behalf. I suspect that it is difficult to accomplish this task successfully with Christianity, which seems excessively cluttered up with doctrine. Even if, as is sometimes said, Christianity is a way of life, rather than a belief, it seems obvious that it is a way of life that presupposes belief.

What I try to put in the place of belief is a god whose 'existence' is not meant to explain anything, but whose sole function is to be an object of love or awe, and a focus of meditation, worship or contemplation. (I suggest in the text that it might be better to say that such a god neither existed nor did not exist than simply to say that he (or it) does not exist.) Since it is immaterial to anything that happens in the universe whether God exists or not, I think that to some extent, what kind of god one contemplates is a matter of personal choice. One may live one's life without worshipping or contemplating anything – many people, if not most, do – but other people find contemplation or meditation necessary or, if not absolutely necessary, something that they find it better to be with or hard to be without. Since contemplation is something some, though not all, find an enjoyable, beneficial and emotionally and aesthetically satisfying activity, perhaps I may be forgiven for trying to find a way of recommending it as suitable for some people, even when it is not accompanied by belief. If religion is not accompanied by belief, different religions may be compatible for, *a fortiori*, they cannot involve incompatible beliefs. They can be compared in other ways than by assessing which is true and which false; for example, by assessing which gives rise to the most emotionally and aesthetically satisfactory concept of a deity that does not involve belief. It may be possible to combine elements taken from different religions.

It would be a great mistake, however, to suppose that such interest as this book has lies only in its conclusions. In philosophy it is not only conclusions that are important, but also the route one takes to acquiring them. Though it may not be entirely true that it is better to travel hopefully than to arrive, at least one should observe and if possible enjoy the scenery on the route to one's destination.

PART I
PRELIMINARY
EPISTEMOLOGICAL
QUESTIONS

1 Meaning and the Word 'God'

(i)   Introduction

It is unfortunate that logic and system demand that the two most difficult chapters, this and the next-but-one, should come early. The reader, however, should not be discouraged by the difficulty of this or any other chapter. For many, if not most, chapters are quite easy, and all are written in such a way as to be understood without recourse to the others. The least central and/or most difficult sections in the chapter are (ix), (xi), (xii), (xiii), (xiv), (xv), (xvi), (xvii) and (xviii), which I have marked with a hash mark (#). The reader is recommended to read the prologue before the book.

(ii)   The Meaning of 'God'

God, in the Western tradition, is usually regarded as an omnipotent, omniscient, perfectly good being, who created the universe, and governs it. He is also supposed to have other attributes such as eternity, aseity, simplicity, unity and, on some views, 'absoluteness'. Alternatively, and more simply, he can be defined as a perfect being, and his other characteristics deduced from the fact that the aforementioned attributes are perfections (if or when they are). A third possibility is that God be defined as a suitable, or perhaps pre-eminently suitable, object of worship, or worshipful contemplation. His other attributes deduced from the fact that he would not be a pre-eminently suitable object of worship if he did not possess them. (The advantage of defining God as a suitable object of worship is that it allows God to be nonpersonal, if a nonpersonal 'entity' can be a suitable object of worship or contemplation.)

The fact that God possesses the aforementioned attributes by definition does not mean that he does not also possess other attributes, but not by definition. For example, he is commonly – and I think correctly – supposed to transcend the universe, and not to be a part of it, but it may be that he does not by definition transcend it. It may or may not be part of the definition of God that he is eternal; being eternal may or may not be a perfection, and it may or may not be necessary to be eternal to be a suitable object of worship. Nor do

7

we *have* to define 'God' so that he possesses certain attributes by definition – though there may often be good reason for doing so. And if there is a god, what attributes he possesses cannot depend upon how people choose to use words.

Usually, to be an adherent of one or other variety of monotheism one has to hold a number of extra doctrines, such as that Christ was God's son, or that Christ was not God's son but Mohammed was his prophet, or that Jews, rather than Christians, are God's chosen people. I shall be concerned with these more specific doctrines, optional to monotheism, only intermittently, and mostly with the Christian ones, since, not surprisingly, that is the one I know most about.

(iii)   Subjectivism, Realism and Relativism

I should at this point make it clear that I am not a subjectivist in one sense of that slippery word. I believe that statements about God are statements about an entity who would exist independently of the existence and nature and beliefs of his creatures. (There is no need to reject idealism for this reason. I am sure that the idealist Berkeley, rightly, thought that it was an objective fact that material objects consisted of ideas (or sensa) in the mind of God, and an objective fact about God's perceptions that men existed and centaurs did not.)

I am not a relativist, in that I think that if one person says one thing and another person says the opposite, one of them must be right and the other wrong. There is to my mind no question of the proposition that God exists being true for one person, but false for another. I have no space to do more than state my point of view about realism, which is that there really are tables and chairs and other people and things existing in space and time independently of people. Indeed, I have neither the space or time, nor much inclination, to say much about any of these rather imponderable and enduring problems. (I shall have to return to them a little in the chapter on God's omniscience, and shall say a little more about relativism later in this chapter.)

(iv)   The View that the Word 'God' is Meaningless

It may seem odd after I have just given a definition of 'God' to raise the question whether the word 'God' is meaningful. But the word 'God' will not be meaningful if the words for the attributes in terms of which this word is defined are not meaningful, or, even if they are, cannot be combined in the way in which they are combined in the definition.

The possibility that the word 'God' might not be meaningful was raised by the logical positivists earlier this century. They were impressed by three facts about God. First was the fact that he was supposed to be transcendent, which meant that we could never come across him in the world that he had allegedly created. Secondly, those who believed in him never accepted any evidence against his existence. No amount of evil, for example, was sufficient to make them say that the world was not created by a benevolent God. Thirdly, they were impressed by the fact that a great deal of metaphysical statements appeared to them – and not without reason – taken on their merits and without reference to any overall doctrine about meaning, not to be meaningful.

According to logical positivists, if there was no way of settling the question whether or not there was a god by finding evidence for or against God's existence, the question must be a meaningless one. They thought that the assertion that there was a god, so far from being false, did not even make sense. Some logical positivists argued that for this reason they were not strictly speaking atheists, for if the sentence 'There is a god' did not make sense, the assertion that there is not one could not make sense either, and atheists are supposed to hold that there is not a god. But they were more like atheists than like theists, for in matters of day-to-day living it would be rational to behave in much the same way if the sentence 'There is a god' is meaningless as it would if it was false.

Strictly speaking, the logical positivists' attack on religious belief is a disjunctive one, to the effect that religious statements are *either* false or meaningless. There is nothing meaningless about the belief that there is an old man with a beard beyond the clouds; but this belief is known to be false. There is nothing obviously meaningless about the belief that we are cared for by a benevolent, omnipotent being who periodically intervenes on our behalf, but there is an enormous amount of evidence against this belief's being true. But if a believer tries to cling to such beliefs, however much evidence there is against them, it becomes doubtful whether it makes any difference to anything whether they are true or not, whether what he believes amounts to anything, whether it is not entirely empty of content, and so whether the words that formulate it make any sort of sense.

Logical positivism was too often asserted as a dogma, whereas one would have expected such a view to arise as the consequence of general considerations about meaning. However, it is not difficult to see how logical positivism could have arisen from such considerations. We learn the meaning of the word 'cat', for example, by learning that there is a correlation between 'cat' and cats. The person who is teaching us says 'cat' in the presence of cats, and does not say it, or says 'No cats' in their absence. Eventually, perhaps with the aid of dissecting cats or seeing one being dissected on one's VDU, we get the idea that there is a certain set of features – including having an inside with a certain function – that an entity must possess to be cat. It may not be necessary for it to possess all of them, or even a specifiable number of them, and some features will have more importance than others, but if it possesses too few features, or two few of the important ones, it will not be a cat.

Words like 'cat' will also have to be given a 'negative connotation by its being conveyed to us that certain features, like laying eggs, exclude their possessor from being a cat. And it should be emphasised that it is not enough, so as to define a word like 'cat' this way, to show someone just one cat. He will have to be shown a number of cats, in order to grasp which features are essential to an animal's being called a cat, and which are merely accidental. Ideally, he will have to be shown a set of cats such that the feature the word being ostensively defined stands for or connotes is the only feature common and peculiar to this set.

All this tells one only how one learns the meaning of a word which already has a meaning, i.e., which already means something to other people, for example, the person teaching you. (Meaning is a three term relation, in that one and the same word can mean one thing to one person, and another thing or nothing at all to another.) But it seems reasonable to suppose that, when our primitive ancestors wanted to draw attention to, say, bears or berries, they made grunts or howls in the presence of bears or berries, and that, if they were successful, they used the same grunt or howl again. Some noises got imitated and used constantly, and others did not, and the ones that did get so imitated came to mean bear or berry. Thus words like 'bear' and 'berry' got 'correlated' with reality, by being used for bears and for berries.

The very set of observations (i.e., observations of cats) that give a sentence such as 'A cat is in the vicinity' its meaning serves to verify the statement that there is a cat in the vicinity. And it seems obvious that if we could not correlate a word like 'cat' with such experiences, but always said it indifferently whether cats were present of not, the word 'cat' would be meaningless. (Obviously, once a correlation between 'cats' and the presence of cats has been established, 'cats' may be used in the absence of cats.) The very experiences – experiences of observing cats – that give the word 'cat' meaning are those which establish the presence of cats when the word 'cats' has come to have a meaning. For this reason, it can be argued, unverifiable statements would be meaningless, just as the logical positivists alleged.

However, the logical positivists did not hold that all unverifiable statements were meaningless. Tautologies such as that people die from mortal wounds did not have to be verified, and it was held that the whole of mathematics and logic was simply one vast set of (disguised) tautologies. It was, indeed, precisely because they were tautologies that we knew that they were true without having to verify them, because tautologies do not assert anything about the world that needs to be verified. One does not need to establish by observation that people die from mortal wounds. And though tautologies are sometimes represented as being exceptions to the verification principle, this is not so. For the words in a tautology, like 'wound' and 'mortal' would have to be meaningful, and for this condition to be fulfilled they would have to be correlated with reality, and so to occur in other sentences, like, in this case, 'Mary was wounded, and Mary died'.[1]

It is true that we can get to know what words like 'cats' mean without ever having seen cats, but then a definition of the word in question will have to be given in terms of other words, and these words themselves will have had to acquire their meaning in some such way as did the word 'cat'. For example, we know what the word 'centaur' means without this word's having ever been correlated with centaurs, for there are none, but a centaur by definition has the head and shoulders of a man and the trunk of a horse, and at some time or other the word 'horse' and 'man' must have been correlated with horses and men.

It should not be supposed that any answers to logical positivists' difficulties about verification can be found by asserting the existence of a god whose existence could be verified, if he chose to make his presence known. For since he has not chosen to make his presence known, the antecedent of the hypothetical 'God's existence could be verified if he chose to make his presence known' would be meaningless, if logical positivism were true.

(v)   **Some Preliminary Reflections on Meaning**

It is a fact which no theory of meaning should ever lose sight of – though some do – that meaning is a 'three term relation', in the sense that a word that may mean one thing to one person may mean another to another. There is no such thing as what a word means, but only what it means to Tom or Mary or to Englishmen. What a word means to Englishmen is just what it means to all or most individual Englishmen.

It does not follow from this that there is anything subjective about our knowledge of meaning. For, that meaning is a fact about 'mind' (or, rather, a fact about people or animals) does not mean that is a fact about mind that is dependent upon the mind that has the beliefs about meaning; it follows only that it is dependent on facts about the mind of the person to whom the symbol in question means what it means. Meaning will be independent of physics only if facts about minds are not physical facts – and they do seem not to be physical facts. It would not follow – though some philosophers have supposed that it does follow – from the fact that facts about meaning are not physical facts, that there is anything 'unscientific' about the study of meaning, or that there is no such things as meaning, or that there is 'no fact of the matter' about what a word means. To suppose otherwise is a manifestation of a physicalist parochialism to which philosophers seem especially prone.

It should be obvious that the difference between seeing a word or sign and understanding what it means and seeing it and not understanding what it means lies in the person (or animal) who sees, or hears or touches or (rarely in the case of humans) smells or tastes, the sign. There need be no connection between the sign and what it stand for over and above this, for any symbol can stand for any object, however unlike the object the symbol is, and whatever the relation between it and the object it stands for. It follows that the relation between a symbol and what it stands for is a conventional one, in that it is because of a human decisions that a word means what it does. It does not follow, however, that the human decision was a deliberately thought-out one. This will be so only in a minority of cases. Nor does it follow that statements about meaning are true by convention.

Visible things (or things tangible or audible or capable of being smelled) are needed to stand for things that are not seen or touched or heard or smelt. The sign 'rain' is needed, for example, to inform someone of, say, the approach of rain, which cannot be seen, by means of something (the symbol 'rain') that can be seen. It follows from this that brain events or entities, however important may be their causal role in sign-using, cannot themselves be signs, for they are not visible, tangible, audible or capable of being smelled; one does not see or touch or hear or smell the relevant parts of one's brain. The whole point of having signs for communication is that signs must be visible to both the person communicating and, when necessary, the person he is communicating with (not necessarily at the same time). The same applies to our use of signs in thought. We could not think with a sign we were not aware of, so could not think with entities in our brains (which is not to say that we could think without brains).[2]

There are three main functions of language, if we neglect its function, which is derivative, of expressing and arousing emotion. Language is used to communicate information – say, information about the whereabouts of food or enemies. It is used to see that the behaviour of some people adjusts to that of others to attain a – usually common – goal. This is done by, among other things, commands, promises and, pre-eminently, by ethical words. The third function is to store information. (Storing information can be regarded as a special case of communicating, i.e., communicating with persons who do not yet exist, or with existing persons at later stages of their lives, or communicating information to a 'later self'.)

(Information, incidentally is abstract. It cannot literally travel along telephone wires or cross oceans, or even be stored in libraries or data banks, though, as a result of electrical impulses travelling along telephone wires or marked books being stored in libraries, pieces of information which were formerly known only to Tom may come to be known to both Tom and Mary, and information that would otherwise be irretrievably lost can be resuscitated when the eyes of a sufficiently knowledgeable person fall upon the ink marks in the books. And what is in the brain is not literally information, but brain cells modified in such a way as to make it true of the person possessing the brain in question that he will behave in ways characteristic of a person possessing that information, if possessing it is relevant to the satisfaction of his wants, e.g. by going meet a train at the time it is due, if he possesses the information that it is due at that time and if he wants to catch it (or rob it).)

Communication need not be by means of physical objects, like printed words, or physical events, like the waving of flags. One could communicate by means of hallucinations or by mental images, including dream images, if one had the power – as a deity would have – of producing them in the person with whom one was trying to communicate. This is because, though a hallucinatory dagger is not a dagger, and the mental image of the Taj Mahal is not a palace, a hallucinatory 'D' is just as good a D as the 'D' on a child's brick, and the mental image of the word 'owl' just as much an instance of the word 'owl' as the same word printed on a page of the *Times*.

I do not wish for one moment to suggest that everything we can say about a thing consists in ascribing to it an attribute or relation, but, to the extent that we are all aware of a world of things which – vastly to oversimplify – possess certain attributes and stand in certain relations to other things, we need words for the things and the attributes and the relations. (It is as nearly as bad a mistake as to think that things must have attributes in order to conform to the fact that our language possesses subjects and predicates as it would be to suppose that apples have cores to conform to the fact that we have apple corers.) Obviously, to the extent that communication is to be possible, we need the same words for the same things, attributes and relations. To the extent that the things we need to talk about, and the attributes and relations we need to ascribe to them, are limited in number, our vocabulary need not be infinite. It does not follow from the fact that we need rules (to see that we mean the same thing by the words we use) that one cannot have meaning without rules. One needs rules to play sophisticated cricket, but a small boy can hit a ball with a bat without any rules at all.

Pace Wittgenstein,[3] words do not have meaning because they 'picture' the world, or have a structure which reflects or is isomorphic with that of the world. It has been remarked that the English sentence 'Tom is tall' contains one word too many – the word 'is' – to reflect the relation between one attribute and one man. One might try to circumvent this by saying 'Tom dark' (omitting the word 'is'), but the relation between the word 'Tom' and the word 'dark' is a spatial one, though the relation between an attribute and an entity that possesses it is not spatial. It does not reflect the relation so well as that between 'Tom beside Mary' would reflect the relationship which holds between Tom and Mary when the former is beside the latter. It is not the case that the word 'Tom' is beside the word 'Mary' – the word 'beside' is between them – but the relation *beside* is not, like the word 'beside' between Tom and Mary. Nor is it the case that the word 'yellow', even if it were beside the word 'Tom', qualifies the word as being tall qualifies Tom.

It would seem at first sight as if the minimum assertion consists of ascribing an attribute to a thing. This means that the minimum sentence must consist of two words – one if the other is understood – one which designates a thing (which may be abstract) and another which connotes the attribute ascribed to that thing. But there must be one word more in a sentence than the words for the thing and the word for the attribute it possesses, because one needs a way of indicating whether one is asserting or denying that, say, Tom is beside Mary, which means that one needs one word more than there are things 'reflected' (which is what English in fact has). In any case, 'Tom is *not* beside Mary', 'If Tom were beside Mary, Mary would be beside Tom', 'If Tom were beside Mary, Mary would be very rude to Tom', 'Some men sit beside some women', etc. cannot reflect the world. For one thing, there is, *pace* Heidegger and Sartre, no such thing in the world as negation or nothingness to be reflected by the words 'not' and 'nothing'. To say that there is nothing in the larder cannot reflect the fact that there is a kind of entity standing in some relation to the larder, for to say this is just to say that there is not anything in the larder.

It would be obviously highly inconvenient, to say the least, to have individual words, like numbers for jokes, for anything we want or need to say. (That the Battle of Hastings was fought in 1066 might then be proposition 9,367,798.) If so, our vocabulary would have to be unlimited. To avoid having to have an enormous number of words it is necessary to have a finite number which, by being combined in different ways, enable us to convey, if necessary, any one of the infinite number of things we might want to assert. In fact this is done by these words being combined in different ways.

That this should be so, however, is not always the result of a clever convention invented by our remote ancestors. It is the automatic consequence of the (aforementioned) fact that we have (a limited number of) words for a limited number of things, attributes and relations, and must combine them to state facts such as that the things possess the attributes and stand in the relations. (Though the number of the attributes and relations may be limited, there is no theoretical limit to the number of individuals whom we might need to describe as possessing them, which may mean introducing new proper names, though the use of demonstrative like 'this' and 'that', and descriptions, may sometimes make this unnecessary.) Sometimes, however special rules are necessary. For example, the fact that we need never run out of symbols for the natural numbers, though these are infinite, is the result not of the fact that we can talk about them in the words (or symbols) that we already have, but because of our ability to form new symbols for new numbers according to a (well-known) rule, exemplified by the series: 0, 1, 2, ... 11, 12, ... 21, 22, ... 100, 101 and so *ad infinitum*.

In order for language to fulfil its function it is essential that it should be unspecific, in the sense that it can give information that is not wholly determinate. It is unspecific, for example, in that it can tell you that there are men in the room without telling you how many men there are in the room nor what kind of men they are or just whereabouts in the room they are situated. We can overcome the difficulty of language being unspecific by combining words; for example, by replacing 'red and round' with 'brick red and two centimetres in diameter'. If language were not unspecific, we would not be able to use very many words at all, for we are very seldom in possession of the specific information that using these unnecessarily unspecific words would have to convey.

There are more facts than there are things possessing certain attributes and standing in certain relations to one another. If the world contained two red balls, one could try to argue that the world reduced to their redness, their roundness and what these characterised (the balls themselves). But we would have the *fact* that there were two red balls, the fact that there was more than one red ball, the fact that there were fewer than three, four, five, etc., red balls, the fact that there were some red balls, the fact that it was not the case that there were no red balls, and so on. We would also have the fact that there were one or more red balls, the fact that, since there were two red balls, the universe is not empty, and so on. Again *pace* Wittgenstein, it is a mistake to suppose that the world is the sum of everything that is the case (even if facts *are* what is the case, which I doubt). Indeed, the world, in the sense of a conglomeration of chairs, tables, constellations and people, does not contain anything of which it makes sense to say that is the case. The world contains Tom, but it does not make sense to say that Tom is the case (or that he is not the case).

Words would be entirely useless were there not some way of relating them to the world. They need to be related to the world in order to that we may know whether, when we use them to say something about the world, we use them to say something true or something false about it. But they also need to be related to the world in order to acquire meaning in the first place. The two activities go hand-in-hand, because, as I have said, the process of showing someone what the word 'red' means by showing him something red would be the same process of demonstrating to him that a thing was red if he already knew what the word 'red' meant.

Words are given their relation to the world by the process of ostensive definition, for example, pointing at something red and saying of it that it is red. (A host of problems, which I have not space to discuss, are hidden in the words 'pointing', 'saying', 'of' and 'it'.) Showing something red to the person to whom one is teaching the word 'red' will not suffice, for he may think it means, for example, 'round'. Ideally, as we have seen, one needs to show him a class of objects which have in common *only* the feature designated by the word one is ostensively defining. (Since it is not always necessary to show someone so many things as this, I suspect that we have an innate and biologically useful tendency to cotton on to the feature to which our teacher is trying to draw our attention without this.) The correlation of most words with the world is not learnt by formal definition, but by people listening to others speaking, and framing and testing hypotheses about what the words they are using mean.

It is not necessary, however, to show someone actual instances of the feature meant by the word that is being ostensively defined. Pictures, television images, diagrams or models will often do. If one had a good enough television set, one could get on perfectly well without coming into contact with any other kind of reality at all. (Pictures, diagrams or models do not themselves have meaning, though philosophers often suppose that they do.) And though knowing what red looks like, so to speak, may be all that is needed to understand the word 'red', more than knowing what a whale *looks* like is necessary to understand a word like 'whale'. Hence showing people whales from the outside is not sufficient ostensively to define the word 'whale'. One would have to have some conception of whales' internal workings, especially of the process of gestation and suckling, which would mean recognising these workings as being a whale's workings, were one to come across them.

But this does not mean that ostensive definition is not good enough, so much as that the ostensive definition in question must not be confined to the outward looks of things. This more elaborate process of ostensive definition presupposes that one knows what causation is, and causal words, though causal transactions *look* just like transactions that are not causal, can only be done ostensively by the person providing the ostensive definition showing his pupil the difference between regular sequences that can be broken by human or accidental intervention and those that cannot (by in some cases trying to break them). Very roughly, if arsenic causes death, taking arsenic is regularly followed by death, and attempts to prevent from dying someone who has taken arsenic fail. Since we may not wish to ascribe attributes and relations only to things, but to talk about these attributes and relations themselves, we need abstract words. (Abstract words, however, are very far from being confined to words for attributes and relations, which philosophers have discussed *ad nauseam*.)

It is not the case that *a priori* sciences like mathematics are, because they are *a priori*, absolved from having ostensively to define the words they use. For example, that two and two are four is a truth which we do not know by observation and experiment, does not mean that the words 'two' and 'four' do not have to be explained by their being correlated with groups of two and four things respectively, that words like 'plus' do not have to be explained by correlating them with the process of (preferably physically) adding two or more groups of things to one another, and that 'equals' does not have to be explained by showing one's pupil actual examples of equality.

What used to be called syncategorematic words – words like 'if' 'and', 'either ... or', 'if', 'so', and 'because' – are also correlated with reality. They are not correlated with reality by showing people ifs and becauses – there are no more such things than there is such a thing as nothingness – but by showing how they modify sentences by being added to them at a legitimately appropriate place. For example, we show that we understand a sentence by knowing what to expect if it is true, and we expect different things when we understand 'There is cheese in the larder' from what we expect if we understand the sentence 'There is no cheese in the larder' and believe what these sentences say. Sentences – those expressing commands, for example – that do not convey information must also be correlated with reality, and are so correlated because they are parasitic upon those that do. For example, the command 'Shut the door' makes sense only because the sentence (which expresses a statement) 'The door is shut' makes sense, and sentence expressed makes sense because the words in it can be correlated with reality. Hence the fact that in religious contexts, among others, words are not used exclusively or even predominantly to make statements does not absolve a philosopher or theologian from the task of explaining how these words come to be meaningful by showing how they are related to a statement that can be attached to (observed) reality.

The moral of this, which reinforces something that has already been said, is that for a word to have meaning there must be some way in which it is anchored to observed reality. Hence there must be difficulty in explaining how a word like 'God', which is a word for something that transcends the world, has meaning. Possible solutions to this difficulty will be discussed later in this chapter.

(vi)   Meaning and Intention

Philosophers have tried to define meaning in terms of the intentions of the person who uses that word. Recourse to a dictionary does show that the word 'means' does indeed have close affiliations with the word 'intends'. And without a doubt, when our first ancestor made a certain kind of grunt to indicate the presence of a cat, he was *intending* this grunt to draw his hearers' attention to a cat. And doubtless too, when nowadays we say something like 'The cat is on the mat' we do say this with the intention of conveying the fact that the cat referred to is on the aforementioned mat. However, now that the words have acquired their meaning, we can usefully use a sentence such as 'The cat is on the mat' with the (successful) intention of conveying the fact that the cat is on the mat only if the word 'cat', in this sentence, means cat, and such words would not have had the meaning they have had they not at some time in the past been correlated with cats. Hence the view that meaning can be defined in terms of intention presupposes the fact about meaning from which the verification principle obtains its plausibility, or such plausibility as it has.

(The view that meaning is intention can admit the fact that meaning is a three term relation because one person may intend (to convey) one thing by a word (and be understood by those who recognise that this is what he intends to convey) while another person may intend to convey something else by it.)

(vii) Meaning and Convention

I do not think that meaning can be defined in terms of observing conventional rules. There are, of course, rules for the use of words like 'cat', but the penalty of breaking them is not that of being misunderstood because we are talking nonsense, but of being misunderstood because we are using words that do not mean to other people what they mean to us. The rules for the use of the word 'cat' govern the use of a word that has meaning apart from convention, and their function is to produce uniformity in an already-existing body of discourse. That is to say, the function of rules of language is more like rules of cricket, which govern certain activities like batting and bowling, which could be done apart from rules, rather than like the rules of chess, without which there could be no such activity as chess. (Moving a piece of wood from one square to another would not count as moving one's king unless there were rules defining a king (in terms of the moves that it was legitimate for it to make). It follows from this that there can be 'private' sets of rules, and that the penalty for breaking the usual public rules is not talking nonsense, but not being understood by others.)

It is not the case that, because meaning is a matter of convention, we could simply, by convention, bestow a meaning on the word 'God'. Or rather, we could, by convention, bestow some meaning, but (a) this would not tell us anything about what we *now* refer to by the word 'God', (b) would not guarantee that 'God' in its new meaning would refer to anything and (c) would not necessarily mean that 'God' in its new meaning stood for anything coherent. (I could by convention introduce a word to mean 'round square', but this would not mean that the new word meant anything coherent.) One would have to introduce the word 'God' by correlating it with something.

(viii) Meaning and Use

According to the view that meaning is use, to know what a word means is to know how to use it. (We show that we know how to use a word by actually using it correctly; it is not necessary to be able to state how a word is to be used in order to use it correctly, any more than it is necessary to have knowledge of mechanics in order to hit a golf ball.) Using a word correctly involves (a) combining it correctly with other words and (b) applying it correctly to things. For example, using the word 'red' correctly involves not saying such things as 'Quadratic equations are red', and not ascribing redness to things that are not red, at least when these are under one's nose. (It is very difficult to draw a line between applying a word incorrectly because you do not know what this word means, and applying it incorrectly, although you do know what it means, but are just mistaken about the nature of what you apply it to; consider the subtle difference between a man who is asked by his wife to fetch magenta paint, and who comes back with pink paint because he thinks 'magenta' means pink, and one who comes back with a tin of pink paint because he mistakenly thought the paint *was* magenta.)

It follows from this that, if there is no difference between two situations, it will be impossible to explain verbally how a word correlates with reality by an expression such as 'Apply the word in this case but not in that' – for example, by saying 'Say "gremlins" in this case, but not in that'. If you cannot say some such thing as 'These accidents were caused by gremlins, but these different accidents were not', or, better, say 'Those are gremlins' while actually pointing to gremlins, it would be impossible to correlate the word 'gremlins' with anything, and the word would be meaningless.

The function of using the sentence 'Dogs bark' is to state that dogs bark. It is also on account of the function of the word 'yellow' that it can be used – by saying, for example, 'Bananas are yellow' – to draw attention to the yellowness of bananas. But these truisms do not explain the actual connection between the words, ourselves and the world which enables us to make use of the sentence 'Dogs bark' to state the fact that dogs bark, or to use 'yellow' in order to draw attention to such things as the yellowness of bananas. Hence the view that meaning is use is not so much false, as unhelpful.

It is frequently pointed out that religious words function not only in statements, but in prayers, commands, exhortation, the language of worship, and so on. But, as I shall argue in my next section, and in more detail in chapter 9, this fact does not mean that the words so used do not have to be correlated with the world.

Holding the view that meaning is use, therefore, does not absolve theologians and philosophers of religion from the task of explaining how the word 'God' acquires its meaning, in spite of the fact that it is a word for a transcendent entity, and defending themselves from the objection that what they say is meaningless because the word 'God' cannot be correlated with anything. One would have supposed that it does this by being correlated with something observed, either in the way in which 'cats' is correlated with cats, or in the entirely different way in which 'electron' is correlated with vapour trails on Wilson cloud chambers. At the very least, theologians and theistically-inclined philosophers of religion should explain why such a correlation is *not* needed.

(ix)   The Meaning of Statements that do not Describe the World

It is true that we do use words for many purposes other than that of conveying information about reality (which is what we use words such as 'The cat is on the mat' for). But this, as I shall argue in more detail in a later chapter, does not mean that words can have a meaning without having been correlated with reality. If I am right, there have to be words in a sentence that have some function other than that of conveying information about reality and that have acquired their meaning by being correlated with reality in the way explained. For example, some religious sentences do not make assertions about reality so much as express prayers ('Give us this day our daily bread'), wishes ('Would that my god would come, unto me'), requests ('Please may I have John the Baptist's head on a charger?') or promises ('I N take thee N'), which sentences have meaning though they make no assertion about reality. For the individual words in this sentence can have such meaning only by themselves being correlated with reality, or by occurring in other sentences which do make (e.g., 'He N took her N to be his lawful wedded wife') assertions about reality. (Someone saying 'Tom took her as his lawful wedded wife' is making a statement reporting the fact that he got married; i.e., reporting the event which Tom actually accomplished by saying 'I take thee ...'. 'I promise ...' does not make a statement, but 'He promised ...' does.)

There is not, however, a neat correspondence between different types of religious activity and the different types of non-propositional expression. Religious activities are alleged to include cosmology, historical narrative, myth and moral discourse, as well as blessing and cursing, confessing and adoring. But there is no especial kind of sentence related to many of these activities, as the type of expression called a 'prayer' is related to a type of sentence also called a 'prayer'. Confessing just consists in making a factual statement about the world, such as that I killed him. What characterises making this statement as *confessing* that one has killed someone rather than *boasting* that one has are the circumstances in which, and the purposes for which, it is made.

Cosmology, myth, and historical narrative are all obviously propositional activities.

There is no class of verbal expressions peculiar to cursing. Ordinary commands ('May your rabbits die') or ordinary performative utterance ('I curse you in the name of the Father, Son and Holy Ghost' or 'Be ye anathema') are the type of sentences we use to make curses. The type of sentence used for blessing is exactly the same as the type of sentence used for cursing. Adoring is a peculiar kind of activity, but there is not a peculiar kind of sentence annexed to it. Most of its verbal aspect consists in making statements of a complimentary nature about the divinity, with the addition of the occasional performative such as 'I adore thee'.[4]

There are enormous problems about moral discourse, but these are not peculiar to moral discourse in religious contexts, and in any case I think the view that ethical sentences do not express statements is wrong. Since the words in all these activities can mean something only if they can be correlated with reality, the view that religious language is non-propositional cannot, without elucidating this correlation, explain how the words in various types of religious utterance acquire their meaning.

If, for a moment, I may pass from discussing meaning to discussing truth, though religious activities such as praying do not consist in making assertions that are capable of being true or false, they would appear to presuppose the truth of such statements. For example, the Lord's prayer presupposes the truth of the proposition that there is a god to hear one's prayer.

Hence recourse to the non-propositional uses of language offers no way of escaping from the task of showing, at least in broad outline, how religious words correlate with things, or provide any answer to the difficulty that, in the case of God, we do not experience – at least with our five senses – anything with which this word can be correlated.

#(x)   **Meaning and Syntax**

Words cannot acquire their meaning simply by being correctly combined with other words according to certain rules. If they could be, then it might be possible for a word to have meaning even though it was not correlated with reality – or correlated only with that part of reality which consists of other words – and so 'God' might have a meaning, though it could not be correlated with reality. Combining words correctly with other words does not guarantee that the person (or thing) combining knows what the word means. Unless a computer that can calculate quite correctly can establish a correlation between, say, the numeral '1' and the number 1, '2' and 2 and so on, its combining these symbols with other words does not tell you whether the computer means one or 10 or 100 by its symbol '1'. For example, without such correlation there is no way of telling whether by '1+1=2' the computer means that one and one are two, or that 10 and 10 are 20, or that 100 and 100 are 200; or rather, without correlation with one or the other there is no such thing as its meaning one of these things rather than another. For it to mean one of them, it would need a scanner, and to be given some way of correlating the symbols with groups of objects having the appropriate number. Similarly, the fact that one can carry on conversation with a computer without discovering that it is not a person does not mean that it knows the meaning of any of the words it uses. It would know what these words mean only if it were given some means of correlating the words with the world, which, without a scanner, it would not have. Hence, a computer without a scanner, or at least without the power to apply words to reality if it did have a scanner, would not know the meaning of any of the words it used.

A computer can be made which can use words like 'rain' or 'today' quite correctly, in the sense of combining them correctly with other words, but unless it can correlate these words with things, the computer does not know what these words mean. One could, indeed, discover quite easily that it did not know what it was talking about, when it used words like 'rain' and 'today', by asking it what the weather was like today. (Its not knowing what the weather was like because it had no built-in mechanism for recognising rain would be quite a different matter from its having such a mechanism, which would work if it had a scanner, or from its having such a mechanism and its scanner's breaking down.) It would be unable to answer not just because it did not have a scanner, but because if it was constituted only to be able to combine words with other words, it would not know what to do with a scanner if it had one.

It follows from this that the word 'God' cannot be shown to be meaningful simply by demonstrating the rules by which it may be combined with other words. Using such rules is a trick that can be learnt quite easily. Academics do it all the time. It must also be shown how it correlates with things.

(xi)   The Meaning of Combinations of Words

The meaning of individual words is conventional, in the sense that it is a matter of (alterable) convention that the English mean snow, and not grass, by 'snow', and mean white, and not black, by 'white'. But once the meaning of each of the words in a sentence has been fixed, there is no room for convention in determining what the sentence as a whole shall mean, in determining whether certain combinations of words are permissible or not, or whether what we use them to say is true or false. Given that 'snow' means snow, 'white' means white and 'is' means is, 'Snow is white' must mean that snow is white. Given that these words mean what they do, and that 'one' (the word for the number one) means what it does, it is not a matter of convention that what is referred to by 'one' cannot be white, but what is referred to by 'snow' can be. It is not a convention, but the nature of one and white, that determine that the sentence 'One is white' does not make sense. And it is not man-made rules, but the nature of things, that make this a sentence that cannot express a truth. And it is also not a matter of convention, but of what actually happens in the world, whether or not words that are combined in permissible[5] ways, express statements that are true. It is not convention, but the nature of snow, that determines that sentence 'Snow is white' expresses a truth, and that the sentence 'The Earth is flat' does not. And given that '1', '2' '+' and '=' mean what they do, it is not a matter of convention that 1+1=2.

Hence there are only rules that determine how words are to be correlated with things. There are no further rules which lay down how, given the manner in which they are correlated with things, they may or may not be combined with one another. 'Superficial grammar' is a matter of convention; 'depth grammar' is not. 'I be going to go over down yonder with she (i.e., with him), look see' is (or used to be) perfectly good Somerset, a sentence which does not obey normal rules concerning nonproliferation of adverbs, or about tenses or accusatives. It is a matter of alterable convention that you use the word 'are' for the plural, 'is' for singular, and also a matter of convention (with certain exceptions) that when in the singular the verb ends in 's'. But, once these rules are fixed, it is not a matter of convention that you cannot combine them to produce a sentence combining a plural noun with the word 'is'.

There are therefore no rules for building up the meaning of wholes from the meaning of parts. Once the meaning of the parts is fixed, the meaning of the whole comes of itself. But the meaning of the parts (including the word 'God' when that is a part) can be fixed only by correlating them, in one way or another, with reality.

#(xii)   The 'Meaning' of Proper Names

There are two theories about proper names. According to the first, they are shorthand for a set of descriptions. Homer, for example, means, among other things, 'the author of the Odyssey'. If this is right, the statement that Homer is the author of the *Odyssey* becomes 'true by definition'.

According to the second theory, proper names, even if they are introduced into language by means of a description, are subsequently simply labels for the thing they name. This has the result that all propositions about Homer are synthetic and none analytic. Even if 'Homer' were introduced into language as a name for the author of the *Odyssey*, the statement that he is its author would, on this view – which I think is the correct one – not be 'true by definition'.

Proper names are normally attached to reality by a process of 'christening'. (The name is not christened, of course, but, in christening something with a name, we introduce the name into language as the name for that thing.) There are two kinds of christening, christening by ostension and christening by description. Each kind can be divided into two, 'christening proper' and 'christening for'. 'Christening for' occurs when a name which has already been used in a christening proper is christened for someone who does not already know what it means. There is no reason why a word that has been christened by ostension should not be christened for, say, Tom by description, or *vice versa*.

If a thing is christened for one by ostension, one is shown Mount Everest, say, and told that it is called 'Everest'. Alternatively, one hears 'Everest' applied to Everest in one's presence, without explicitly being told that that is its name. One then evolves the hypothesis that the person using 'Everest' is using it as name for Everest (by means of a name that has previously been used to christen ('christen proper') Everest, and has become the standard word for Everest). As a result of observing the resulting (in fact, partial) correlation[6] between Everest and 'Everest', one concludes that 'Everest' is a name for Everest, and tests this hypothesis against the subsequent linguistic performance of one's friends. The main differences between the christening of one individual mountain, and the ostensive definition of a word like 'mountain', is that one is rebuked if one applies 'Everest' to any mountain other than Everest, whereas one is not rebuked for calling mountains other than Everest 'mountains' And Everest might change slowly into a hill, and still properly be called 'Everest', but not properly be called a mountain.

The process of christening for presupposes that Everest has already been christened (christening proper) 'Everest'. I imagine the process of christening

Everest for the first time (christening proper), when performed by our remote ancestors, involves someone using 'Everest' to draw attention to Everest, in order to say things about it, and others using this word because he had used it. They would have to establish a (partial) correlation between the presence of Everest and their teacher's use of 'Everest' to be able to do this. The teacher himself would not have learned what 'Everest' meant, but would have decided what it was to mean. Nowadays we could say 'Let's call her Anona', suitably pointing, or referring to Anona with a description that singles her out from other objects in her vicinity. But our ancestors might not have had the linguistic resources to do this.

If a thing is christened by description, one does not have to be aware of the thing one christens. A planet was once christened 'Pluto', although the only reason for thinking that there was such a planet was that its existence was a hypothesis to explain why it was that certain other planets were not in the places were they ought to have been, had the known planets been the only planets.[7] In such a case, the proper name in question is introduced by a description. 'Pluto' was introduced as a name for the planet which was supposed to be causing other planets (in fact, Neptune and Uranus) to behave aberrantly. A thing is christened for someone by description if he is told that it is the name for something which is 'referred to' by a description. (It does not follow that the thing in question exists, though in that case, both the description and the name will fail to refer.)

A difficulty with the view that 'God' is introduced by christening God arises if one is *not* aware of God, as one *is* aware of Everest. If one is not aware of God, it will be impossible either for the person taught or the person being taught to correlate 'God' with some item perceived by both, as 'Everest' can be. (I shall discuss in chapter 13 the view that 'God' acquires its meaning by our being shown God.)

If the word 'God' were introduced by description, this description would have to contain class terms, as 'Pluto is the heavenly body responsible for the apparent aberrations of other planets' contains the class term 'heavenly body'. One could say that God was the creator of the universe. Obviously, for this way of introducing the word 'God' into language to succeed, the words in the description – e.g., the word 'creator' – would have to have meaning.

God could not be a proper name defined ostensively unless our experience were different if there were a god from what it would be if there was not one. 'God' could be partially defined by description, without there being any such difference. But even if the words in the description do have a meaning, this does not imply that there are no problems about the meaning of 'God'. For there to be no such problems, *none* of the words in which 'God' was defined would have to be meaningless. (I argue later (in chapter 2) that 'God' is not a normal proper name and does have a definition.)

It is customary nowadays to call proper names 'rigid designators'.[8] A rigid designator like 'John Stuart Mill' is contrasted with a description, like 'eminent Victorian', which is described as a nonrigid designator. The difference between the two is supposed to be that the description 'eminent Victorian' does not have to designate John Stuart Mill – if James Mill had not taught John Stuart Mill Greek at the age of five, he might not have been an eminent Victorian – but, or so it is said, John Stuart Mill does have to be John Stuart Mill. (If one had said 'John Stuart Mill' might not have been an eminent Victorian, it is still John Stuart Mill who would not have been an eminent Victorian.) In the language of possible worlds, (which I shall discuss briefly in chapter 4) there are possible worlds in which John Stuart Mill is not an eminent Victorian, but in every possible world in which he exists at all, John Stuart Mill is John Stuart Mill.

I shall not explore the problems which rigid designators raise. This is partly because those who hold it offer no very useful views about how the words that they describe as rigid designators attach to the world, or how we know the truth of statements referring to something by a rigid designator, and partly because I think the view is of doubtful coherence. (I shall return to the topic of proper names in chapters 2, 3, 4 and 13.)

#(xiii)   God and Mass Terms

A great deal has also been written recently about what are called 'mass terms' like 'coal' or 'water'. I shall not discuss mass terms for two reasons. First, holding that there are mass terms does not relieve a philosopher of the task of showing how words (for example the word 'God') latch on to experience, which so far as I know those who attach importance to mass terms do not do; mass terms must latch on to experience in some way or other. Secondly, 'God' is obviously not a mass term.

The difference between what can be named by a mass terms and what cannot seems to depend partly on the facts, partly on human interest. For there to be a mass term one would think that there has to be a fairly all-pervasive volume of stuff to be named by the mass term in question. But though coal obviously answers to this description, beef only does this less obviously. What we have a mass term for depends partly on human concerns.

That 'fish' is a mass term, but 'man' not is partly due to the fact that we do not consume men, but do consume fish. If we ate men more often that we do, there might be a word 'man' – resembling 'fish' in a way that the word 'man' which we now have does not – that would enable us to say such things as 'Have some more man?' (as we can say 'Have some more fish'). The subject of mass terms, though interesting, is of no epistemological and little metaphysical interest.

(It may be that 'God' is not as unlike mass terms as one might suppose. Perhaps God is spread evenly throughout the universe, but (unlike water) can be found at any time and place when we need him. Unlike fossil fuels, however, he is replaced as fast as we consume him. But the idea is fanciful.)

#(xiv)   Meaning and Indeterminacy

It ought not to be a matter of controversy whether there is such a thing as meaning. Anyone saying that there is no such a thing as meaning, as Quine would appear to do, would be showing thereby that he did know that there was such a thing as meaning, because he is using meaningful words to express what he supposes to be this fact. But Quine has also held that there is no way of choosing between different views about what a word means, and that when this happens there is no genuine question concerning which of the alternatives is correct. But Quine's argument presupposes that there really is such a thing as meaning; otherwise there could not be two different views about the meaning of a word, between which there could be nothing to choose.

Quine's view is fairly obviously wrong, though I have not space to discuss it here.[9] All I can do is to point out that such a view is not incompatible with the view that words have their meaning by being correlated with reality. Rather, it presupposes it. For the different theories about what a word means, between which Quine says it is impossible to choose, are different theories about how words correlate with reality. Quine's famous example is of the word 'gavagai'. It is impossible, he thinks, to chose between the view that 'gavagai' means rabbit and the view that it means rabbit part. But, if it means rabbit, one would expect people to say 'That is a rabbit', pointing to a rabbit, and if it means rabbit part, to say such things pointing to a rabbit part. If Quine is right, it must be impossible to say which of these is correct, but what is impossible is to say whether 'rabbit' is correlated with rabbit or with rabbit part.

Quine, however, at other times does give an account of meaning that presupposes that words do have meaning, and that they must be correlated with things to have meaning. This is done in what he says, early on in *Word and Object*,[10] about stimulus meaning. In any case, it is poor consolation to a theologian who wishes to hold that 'God' may have meaning, though not correlated with reality, to be told that *no* words have meaning or that it is impossible to choose between competing hypotheses about what a word means. One would suppose the theologian would want to have a firm hypothesis about what the word 'God' meant.

#(xv)   Confrontation and Holism

According to holism (roughly) we cannot understand the meaning of any sentence in isolation, but only if we understand the whole language with which this sentence is part. This view is obviously wrong. But, just as the view that we could not know the *truth* of any statement in isolation from the whole truth – which whole truth obviously no-one does know – had to be bolstered up with a view of degrees of truth, so this holistic view has to be backed up by a view of degrees of meaning. The view that the opinion that I have two arms and two legs is strictly speaking false, because it takes no account of the whole truth, had to be bolstered up by holding that it is as at least more true that I have two arms and two legs than that I have some other number of arms and legs, or fins, or no arms or legs at all. For the same reason, the view that the opinion that the word 'cat' in isolation means furry feline is false, because it is short of the whole meaning of the language, has to be bolstered up by saying that it is much nearer the truth that it means cat than duck-billed platypus. And, in order to know that it is much nearer the truth that 'cat' means furry feline than that it means rabbit, one has to discover that 'cats' is correlated with furry felines, and not with rabbits.

It may be an implication of holism that the meaning of religious discourse should be considered only as a whole; one ought not, on this view, to consider the meaning of religious words in isolation. I think this is an exaggeration. One cannot discuss the meaning of some religious words in isolation from others, but there are other religious words which are isolated from some others. But there is no need for me to discuss this view, because, if it were true that no religious word could be discussed in isolation from any other, this would not absolve the theologian from explaining how a body of religious discourse is as a whole correlated with reality. And this should involve explaining what difference our accepting what is communicated by this discourse makes to the world, or our expectations about the world.

#(xvi)   Defining Meaning in Terms of Truth

A spurious way to avoid the nitty gritty of explaining how words correlate with things, and the especially difficult task, of which I have just scratched the surface, of correlating what might be described as 'abstract' words with 'concrete' things, is the following. (The view has been suggested by reading the work of Donald Davidson,[11] but I wish both to avoid being unfair to him and the time-consuming task of discussing what he actually said, by not claiming that the view is his.) This suggestion, which I shall put in my own way, is that meaning can be defined in terms of truth. For example, since (or so it is commonly supposed) a sentence such as 'Snow is white' is true if and only if snow is white, it follows that, if snow is white, but the sentence 'Snow is white' is not true, then it must be because it does not mean that snow is white. Hence what it is for the sentence 'Snow is white' to mean that snow is white can be defined in terms of that sentence's being (or expressing what is) true.

It would be too difficult, and take me too far from my present purpose, to discuss this view. I shall, however, make the following very brief criticisms of it.

(a) All that can be derived from a consideration of the connection between meaning and truth is the formula that if the sentence 'Snow is white' is true if and only if snow is white, then this sentence must mean that snow is white. It does not tell you that 'Snow is white' *does* mean that snow is white.

(b) Neither the statement that 'Snow is white' means that snow is white, nor the statement that 'Snow is white' is true if and only if snow is white can even be understood by someone who does not already know what the sentence 'Snow is white' means. (Neither the sentence '"God exists"' means that God exists', nor the sentence '"God exists"' means that God exists if and only if it is true if and only if God exists' can be understood by anyone who does not already know what 'God exists' means.)

(c) Truth is not a property of the sentence 'Snow is white', but only of what this sentence is used to assert, viz., *that* snow is white.

(d) Most importantly for the argument in this chapter, the view that 'Snow is white' means that snow is white if and only if 'Snow is white' is true if and only if snow is white no more tells you what meaning means than the statement that p->q is equivalent to -pvq tells you what implication (->) means (or the statement that pvq is equivalent to -p->q tells you what disjunction (v) means). Just as, in the first of these cases, you would need a further account of disjunction and in the second a further account of implication, so, if you define meaning by a statement about truth you need a further account of truth, and if you define truth by a statement about meaning, you need a further account of meaning. The fact that there is the aforementioned equivalence between a statement about meaning and a statement about truth does not mean that one does not have to give an account of how words are correlated with reality. Hence it does not absolve one from the duty of having to give such an account in the case of theistic words.

The bearing of this upon religious discourse is that it is perfectly possible to define the sentence 'God exists' as meaning that God exists if and only if this sentence expresses a truth if and only if God exists. But, since the sentence 'God exists' is being used in the last two words of this sentence, and a sentence is meaningless if part of it is meaningless, this definition of 'God exists' is compatible with 'God exists' being meaningless and, strictly speaking, with it itself being meaningless. And it does not exculpate us from the task of showing how this sentence, and the word 'God', correlate with reality.

#(xvii) Meaning and Truth Conditions

It may follow from the view just being discussed that the meaning of a statement is its truth conditions. (Since it is sentences, not statements or propositions, that have meaning, and statements or propositions, not sentences, that are true or false, what ought to be said is that the meaning of a sentence is the truth conditions of the proposition it expresses.)

The view that meaning is truth conditions derives from the fact that we establish that someone else means red by 'red' by observing that he applies the word to red things. Hence, if he says of red things that they are red, this should mean that he means red by 'red; but something's being red is the very condition which makes his saying that that thing is red true. Hence the view that someone means, say, that this is red if he says 'This is red', if and only if what he says will be true if and only if it is red. Similarly 'That is a cat' will mean that that is a cat if and only if it is true if and only if the animal he is referring to is a cat, and so on for all other meaningful sentences.

The view that meaning is truth conditions has the following difficulties.

(a) The theory has a view about how we know that other people mean cats by 'cats'. We observe a correlation between their saying 'That is a cat' and the presence of cats, which is what makes their statements that cats are present true. But we do not know what we ourselves mean by 'cats' by establishing a correlation between our saying 'cats' and the presence of cats. (Neglecting this distinction is partly what leads to such absurdities as supposing that we ourselves might not mean plus by 'plus'.)[12]

(b) One could not, on the grounds that 'Dogs bark' expresses a truth if and only if dogs bark, tell someone that 'Dogs bark' means that dogs bark, for, unless he already knew what the sentence 'Dogs bark' meant, he would not understand the words – 'Dogs bark' – in which he was being told what it means.

(c) This view does not enable one to recognise a meaningless sentence when one comes across one, because one can admit a nonsense sentence such as 'Some people sleep more slowly than others' by saying that it is true if and only if some people sleep more slowly than others.

(d) The view excludes commands, promises, etc. from having meaning, for it does not make sense to say that 'Shut the door' means shut the door because it is true if and only if shut the door. But commands and promises, etc., do have meaning.

(e) It does not help one to draw a distinction between ordinary factual statements, such as that dogs bark, and moral or aesthetic judgements such as that eating people is wrong. For one can say that just as the truth condition of 'Dogs bark' is that dogs bark, the truth condition of 'Eating people is wrong' is just that eating people is wrong.

(f) We do not normally establish that someone means that that is a cat when he says 'That is a cat' simply because it is true if and only if it is a cat. We need him to say it in the first place in the presence of *observed* cats, so that we may correlate his word 'cat' with cats.

(g) The view that meaning is truth conditions – on the grounds that if someone else says 'That is a cat' in the presence of cats, they must mean that 'That is a cat' – needs to be bolstered up by a subsidiary hypothesis that (1) explains why so often we do not say 'That is a cat' when we do see a cat, and (2) quite often say 'That is a cat' when we do not see a cat. Indeed, we hardly ever say 'That is a table' when a table is visible, and very often make remarks about tables when there are no tables visible. (We need some motive or other to make us say 'cats', even when there are cats, and may have motives impelling us to say 'cats' even when there are none.)

(1) We may know what the word 'cat' means, but not say 'That is a cat' (or even say 'That is not a cat') because we mistake a cat for a canary in a bad light. We may not say 'That is a cat' (or even say 'That is not a cat') because we wish to disguise from our hearers the fact that we know what the word 'cat' means, or disguise from them the fact that it is a cat, or just feel that he would not be interested in this piece of feline information.

(2) There are all sorts of obvious reasons why we may speak about cats when there are no cats present. A theory of meaning needs to make the fact that 'cats' means cats part of a more general view about human linguistic behaviour which explains why people use 'cats' sometimes in the presence but at other times in the absence of cats.

(h) Other problems that this theory simply bypasses are the problem of giving any analysis of the meaning of certain intractable sentences, and of the relation between the statements they express and those expressed by other sentences. To take a common example, it gives no account of the difference between sentences about the average man and those about fat men. It makes no attempt to put abstract entities into some kind of hierarchy by, say, reducing statements about numbers to statements about classes. These problems are all replaced by one excessively easily formula, the truistic formula that a sentence means what makes it true.

It might be replied that to solve these problems is not what the formula is intended to do, but one would have thought that an adequate account of meaning should indicate these problems' existence, and give some outline of the manner in which they might be dealt with. One would have thought that a thorough understanding of the meaning of any sentence would involve understanding its structure and how this resembled the structure of other sentences; how it might break down into more than one sentence (as that someone is an aunt breaks down into her being a parent's female sibling); and how propositions expressed by the sentence were logically related to propositions expressed by at least some other sentences (as that statements about money are related to statements about banks).

(i) The view that meaning is truth conditions makes no inroad on the following important problem: we can correlate some sentences with the states of affairs that make true what these sentences are used to assert because they are sometimes asserted in the presence of those states of affairs. At least sometimes people say such things as 'That is a cat' making it clear that they are speaking of a cat that is visible to both parties. (We have seen that the correlation is far from being simple on account of people not always saying 'cats' when cats are present, and sometimes saying 'cats' when cats are not present.) But this leads to two difficulties.

(1) Saying that we know what 'cats' means because people say 'That is a cat' in the presence of cats is unduly simplistic. Observing a cat is an extremely complex process, involving viewing the cat from different angles and under different circumstances, touching it, feeling it, hearing it, etc. Even an observed cat, like an observed iceberg, is much more unobserved than observed, for it

has a back, insides, liver, lights, kidneys and grey matter, which even that cat itself does not see. The most that is observed is its front surface, and, for reasons that I shall not go into, probably not even that.

(2) The theory does not explain how it comes about that words for things that are never observable come to have meaning. Though the truth conditions of that there are electrons are that there are electrons, one cannot correlate the word for 'electrons' with electrons, but only with the evidence for electrons, viz. the occurrence of vapour trails on the screens of Wilson cloud chambers. But 'There are electrons' does not mean that there are vapour trails, any more than 'There is a cat in that basket' means that miaows are coming from the basket, or that 'There are mountains on the other side of the moon' expresses the propositions about the photographic plates taken by space-probes that are the evidence for these mountain's existence.

(j) It is true that the only way for a sentence like 'Snow is white' not to be true in the event of snow's being white would be for it not to mean that snow is white. (It is also true that the only way for the sentence 'Snow is white' not to mean that snow is white would be for it not to be true in the event of snow's being white.) This may enable one to define meaning in terms of truth. (I suggested earlier that this latter fact might enable one to define truth in terms of meaning.)

But establishing that there is this relationship between meaning and truth is not the same thing as giving an explanation of either the notion of meaning or of the notion of truth. To do this it would be necessary to explain carefully the relation between words like 'that' and what they are being used to single out, by 'red' and redness, to explain such things as how the word 'red' comes to be 'the word for' redness, how it elicits the behaviour that distinguishes a person who sees it and knows what it means from that of a person who sees it but does not know what it means, and to give a detailed account of this behaviour.[13] This the view that meaning is truth conditions does not do. Again, the view that meaning is truth conditions amounts to little more than the view that, for example, the sentence 'Cats miaow' means that cats miaow (since that cats miaow is what makes it true).

(k) In any case, though that 'Snow is white' means that snow is white is equivalent to that 'Snow is white' is true if and only snow is white, I doubt whether this enables us to define meaning in terms of truth. That today is Tuesday may be equivalent to that tomorrow is Wednesday, but 'Today is Tuesday' does not mean 'Tomorrow is Wednesday.'

(l) To return to the matter in hand, the meaning of the word 'God', it does not help anyone who wants to know whether the word 'God' has a meaning, and, if it does, how it comes about that it does, to be told that the sentence 'God exists' means that God exists because its truth conditions are that God exists. And, though it might be possible to argue that someone who does not say 'cats' in the presence of cats does not know what the word 'cats' means, it is not possible to say on the evidence that a person does not say 'electrons' in the presence of vapour trails on the screens of Wilson cloud chambers that this person does not know what 'electrons' means. He might not know that electrons leave vapour trails. But it is likely that refusing to admit evidence for the existence of God is more like the second refusal than it is like the first.

(m) The view that 'God exists' expresses a proposition the truth conditions of which are that God exists (in this case, because it *is* the proposition that God exists) is doubtless, however unhelpfully, true, if 'God exists' means anything at all. But it does not establish that 'God' does mean anything at all.

#(xviii) Chomsky versus Locke[14]

Another highly influential view, at least apparently incompatible with an empiricist theory of meaning, is that of Chomsky. Whereas the view that gives rise to difficulties for theistic statements, viz., that because God is transcendent and perhaps also that statements about him are unverifiable, theistic words cannot be correlated with reality is an empiricist one, Chomsky holds, in opposition to Locke,[15] that we have an *a priori* knowledge of language. One reason for his thinking this is that children would otherwise not have had the time to acquire the knowledge of language that they have.

Since it is obvious that we do not have any *a priori* knowledge of such facts as that 'cat' and not 'chat' is the word for cat – if there was, all people would have the same word for cat – or *a priori* knowledge of the fact that 'Cats have fur' is grammatical, but 'Cats has fur' is not, Chomsky must – and does – hold that the grammar of which we have *a priori* knowledge is not the superficial grammar that one is taught in school. I may well be wrong about this, but I think this amounts to holding that what is *a priori* is not such things as that 'cat' means cat, but such things at that, *given that 'cat', 'mat' and 'is' mean what they do*, 'The cat is on the mat' is a permissible combination, and that 'Mat on the is the cat' is not. (If 'The cat is on the mat' is a permissible combination, the further question arises whether what this expression asserts is true.)

As I said earlier, my own tentative opinion on this question is that there are no rules determining which such combinations of words are permissible and which are not. By this I mean not that these words may be combined in any way one chooses, but that the limits on how these words may be combined are not a matter for legislation. Given the 'first order' rules determining the meaning of 'cat' 'mat', 'is' and 'the', which rules lay down how they are to be correlated with reality, there is no choice about the others. If 'cat' and the other words mean what they do, there is no further act of legislation determining that 'Mat on the is the cat' is not a permissible combination of words (and so does not make sense). Indeed, given that the words 'cat' and so on mean what they do, it is an *a priori* necessary truth that certain combinations are permitted, and others are not. They are permitted by the nature of things, so to speak, rather than by the man-made rules.

Hence there is no set of language rules that presents an exception to empiricism. There are two sorts of rule, the first-order ones the existence of which is a matter of contingent fact, but which present no exception to empiricism because they do have to be learnt empirically. There is another set of 'rules' (second-order rules) that do not have to be learnt empirically, but present no exception to empiricism because they are not contingent matters of fact. Given that 'married' means what it does, and that 'quadratic equations' means what it does, then it is not a matter of empirical discovery, but one of *a priori* necessity, that quadratic equations cannot be married. There is nothing that is both empirical and does not have to be learnt empirically.

However, there is nevertheless this to be said for Chomsky's view, if I am right in interpreting it in such a simple way. The fact that something is *a priori* does not mean that it may not, or mean that it does not, have to be learnt. Children have to be taught the *a priori* necessary truth that two and two are four. Hence it would be a great biological advantage to man if he did not have to learn these *a priori* necessary propositions. Given that it has proved advantageous for man to have a long period of learning, anything that means that more learning can be done in a limited period of time must increase his chances of survival, and so perhaps explain why we have innate knowledge of things that could be learnt *a priori*. Hence Chomsky is probably right in thinking that we have innate knowledge of them, even if he is wrong in thinking, if he does, that this is innate knowledge of empirical truth.

It will be clear that I am using the word 'innate' to mean '*in fact unlearnt*' and *a priori* to mean '*capable* of being seen to be true without recourse to observation'. Hence there is no contradiction in supposing that an *a priori* proposition should be not innate. A proposition that is capable of being known without recourse to observation may nevertheless be in fact known empirically. There is also no contradiction in supposing that an empirical proposition should be innate. For an empirical proposition is one that can be justified only empirically, but this does not entail that we should not believe it before we are justified in believing it. Nature has seen to it that we do not waste time by always waiting upon justification, and I doubt whether we would have survived otherwise. I myself think we have a vast amount of (empirical) knowledge of the behaviour of other people and inanimate objects that is innate, and that such knowledge has enormous survival value.

The existence of innate knowledge is not incompatible with empiricism because empiricism, which will be discussed in my next chapter-but-one, is a theory about the justification of knowledge, not a theory about how it is in fact acquired. Knowledge can be innate – that it is innate is a view about how it is in fact acquired – and still need justification. For example, it seems very likely that we have an innate belief that the future will resemble the past. But the fact that this is innate does not mean that our belief that the future will resemble the past does not need justification. (This may mean that one should speak of innate belief, rather than of innate knowledge.)

It seems to me to be possible that that there is a god is, in some people at any rate, an innate belief. But (a) one still has to show that innate beliefs are not just 'implanted', but also true, and (b) the belief that is innate may be quite a primitive one, to the effect that there is a powerful being above the clouds who will care for one if suitably propitiated. This belief may be correlated with reality, but such correlation simply shows that it is false. If so, innateness is no solution, and we are still left with the problem of correlating the words 'God exists' with reality.

(xix)   Less Crude Account of Confrontation

There are an enormous number of words that cannot be correlated with reality in the relatively simple way in which words like 'cat' can be. 'Beautiful' 'good', 'not' 'and', 'if ... then', 'one', 'times', 'plus', 'time', 'space', 'quadratic equation', 'infinite number', 'equator', 'axis', 'parliamentary government', 'justice', 'influenza epidemic', 'inflation' and so on and so on are all examples. I have said that one should not suppose that words like 'not' and 'nothing' cannot be correlated with reality because one cannot show anyone a not or a nothing, as one can show him a cat. One in fact correlates whole sentences, containing these words, with reality; for example, one correlates the sentence 'There is cheese in the larder' with larders with cheese in them, and the sentence 'There is no cheese in the larder' with larders that contain no cheese (i.e. not larders that contain something called 'no cheese' but larders that do not contain any cheese). One correlates 'There is nothing in the larder' with reality by explaining that it is true when there is not anything in the larder. One can correlate 'and' with reality by correlating the sentence 'There is milk and cheese in the larder' by saying that it expresses a truth if there is milk and there is cheese in the larder, but false if there is milk but no cheese, or cheese but no milk, or neither in the larder. It is not sufficient to do this only in words. One actually has to take the person one is trying to teach to larders which contain the requisite combinations of milk and cheese if one has not already done this with other words.

One can correlate the word 'true' with reality by pointing out that when someone says there is cheese in the larder and there is cheese in the larder, what he says is true (as, when he says that there is cheese in the larder but there is no cheese in the larder, what he says is false). One can correlate 'plus' with reality by demonstrating the operations of combining a group with a another group, and 'minus' with the operation of taking away a class from a class. One can show people what is meant by 'influenza epidemic' by pointing out that many more people have influenza when there is an epidemic than have it at other times of the year. One can explain what an equator is by explaining what it is to be equidistant from two poles, and what a pole is by explaining what it is for a sphere to rotate on an axis, and so on and so on and so on.

This suggests that, since all these words can be defined by showing how they correlate with reality, there is a need to explain how the word 'God' is so correlated.

#(xx)   The Image Theory of Meaning[16]

The above remarks about meaning, which give some semblance of plausibility to logical positivism, square well with what is called the image theory of meaning, a theory which has been undeservedly denigrated.

One reason why the theory has been denigrated is because it has been supposed that those who held it – Berkeley and Hume in particular – thought that words meant or stood for ideas (i.e., roughly) mental images. (It should not be forgotten that words can have meaning without standing for anything, i.e., without standing for any *thing*.)

It has been objected to this that words are signs for things, not ideas of things, and that it is a needless circumlocution to interpose ideas between words and things. The reply to this objection is that those who held the image theory of meaning were not so much giving an account of what words stood for or meant, as giving an account of understanding a word; they held that understanding a word consisted in its conjuring up appropriate ideas. One – though not the only – difference between someone who sees the word 'cat' and knows what it means and someone who does not is that the word can arouse images of cats in the former man, but not in the latter. At least, if it does this it is pure coincidence, and the latter does not know that they are images of what the word stands for.[17]

It would be a difficulty if those who held the image theory of understanding thought that the fact that one could rehearse the experience of applying a word to reality, by having images resembling the objects of the experience one would have if one did this, meant that understanding a word might not be manifested simply by applying this word to reality. If they did think this then, doubtless, they were mistaken. But there is no reason why image theorists should not hold, that, in the absence of the cat, understanding a word manifests itself in imagery of the thing meant, but that in its presence it can be manifested by actually saying of a cat 'That is a cat'. A man's understanding of a word could consists in his having a disposition to combine it correctly with other words, a disposition knowingly to have suitable imagery, and a disposition to apply the word to the thing were he to come across that thing (and have need so to apply it).

Of course, we do not always have images of reality in a manner as simple as that in which we have images of cats. We cannot do this when a word is correlated with reality as are the words listed in the previous section, e.g. parliamentary government. When this is so, we image them by having images which resemble the experiences which would verify propositions they express. For example, the images by which our understanding of 'addition' is manifested can be images of physically adding one group of things to another larger group of things. One understands the meaning of the expression 'parliamentary government' not because one knows what it is like to comes across an entity called 'parliamentary government' – there is no such entity – but because one knows what kinds of experience would verify or falsify statements about parliamentary government. One can have images of such experiences. One knows what is meant by 'inflation' because one knows what it is like for prices and wages constantly to rise, and can have images of finding out that they are constantly rising. One know what is meant by the rule of law because one can have images of men being imprisoned without trial.

The bearing of the image theory of meaning upon theistic words is adverse.

We cannot have an image of God, as we can of a duck-billed platypus or a phoenix, because such an image would be an image of what it would be like to come across God, and we do not come across him. If the existence of God could be verified, we could have images of what it would be like to verify his existence, but this way out is invalidated by the very arguments that were used in an attempt to dispose of logical positivism. The experiences that verify the statement that God exists are one thing, God himself quite another. But it may be possible to defend the view that we do come across God, not with the five senses, but by what some mystics have called 'ghostly sight'. In this case one might say that we never need to think of God by means of images in his absence, because he never is absent. Or one might say that there are ghostly images of God, just as there are sensuous images, and that it is by having these images that one of the ways of understanding the word 'God' is manifested. It could be that it is the difficulty of having ghostly images in the absence of the required ghostly experiences that makes it so difficult to understand what mystics say.

I do not know whether anyone has maintained that the disposition to have mental images is the only way in which the understanding of words manifests itself. If anyone did, his view would be open to the obvious and fatal objection that, as I have said, such understanding also manifests itself in applying words to the things they are for, for example, in applying the word 'cat' to cats. But a view according to which we understand words for things only if we can apply the words to the things would have to hold that we *are* confronted with God, and to show that we understand the word 'God' by applying it to him when we are confronted with him. A very serious difficulty with this view would be that, for a word correctly to be applied to a thing, there would have to be a causal connection between the use of the word and the presence of the thing. It would have to be not just coincidence that we say 'God' in the presence of God, but that we would not be saying 'God' whether God were present or not. But if God is timeless, there can be no causal connection between him and our use of words. Of course, it is open to a theologian to hold that God's causation is different from ordinary temporal causation. But this just brings us back to the problem we started with, the problem of explaining how we know the meaning of words for atemporal causation when we not come across it. I shall discuss possible solutions to this problem later.

(xxi)   **The Meaning of a Sentence not the Method of 'its' Verification**

Logical positivism draws attention to the fact that 'basic words' must be correlated with reality in some such manner as that described above. We know what is meant by 'cat' as a result of being confronted with cats and being told that they are cats, or, more likely, hearing people use the word 'cats' of cats, and just picking up that this is what they are called. Other words then have to be correlated with reality indirectly, by being correlated with or defined in terms of words that are so correlated. (It would be a great mistake to think that the only way in which this could be done is in the way in which we can define 'vixen' as a female fox.) If there is no way in which a word can be correlated with reality, then, according to logical positivism, it must be meaningless.

But it is a great mistake to try do what the logical positivists tried to do and to define the non-basic terms by the *evidence* for what they referred to. The result of attempting to do this is that statements about cats turn out to be statements about the experiences that will confirm them, e.g., miaows coming from a basket, whereas, obviously, the statements that justify one in thinking that there is a cat in a basket – statements about the miaows – are not at all the same as statements about the cat. Statements about the past turn out to be statements about the future; for example, statements about past glaciers turn out to be statements about the future marks on rocks which constitute the evidence for them. Statements about the minds of others turn out to be the statements about the bodies of the owners of the minds, the behaviour of which bodies provided our evidence for their being in these states; for example, statements about other people's pains turn out to be about their screams. Statements about electrons turn out to be statements about the Wilson cloud chambers which enable us to know of the existence of electrons, and statements about remote galaxies turn out to be statements about the behaviour of the measuring instruments that enable us to detect them.

Indeed, in holding the view that the meaning of a statement is the method of its verification, logical positivists may have been confusing verification with confrontation. But it is a very different matter to say that in order to know what 'cats' means it is necessary to have been confronted with cats, and told that the word for them is 'cats', and holding that the meaning of 'cats' comes from the evidence for the existence of cats, such as miaows coming from the airing cupboard and dead birds in the bedroom. And it is not even necessary to be confronted with cats to know what 'cats' means; pictures of cats will often do (though pictures of cats, unlike cats, are no guarantee of the existence of cats. Pictures 'of' mermaids are not evidence for the existence of mermaids).

Of course, we know the meaning of many words without ever having been confronted with the things they stand for, and know the meaning even of words (like 'abominable snowman') that do not stand for anything at all. The obvious way of dealing with this difficulty – which is substantially the way taken by Locke, Berkeley and Hume – is to say that all words do not have to be ostensively defined, but when they cannot be, they must be defined in terms of words that can be so defined. For example, one cannot ostensively define the word 'electron', because one does not come across individual electrons but only with macroscopic objects that are composed of electrons,[18] or with the effects of electrons, but one can ostensively define the words, like 'position' and 'velocity' and the other mathematical terms by means of which the behaviour of electrons can be described.[19] And if one does not come across God, but only his alleged effects, one can ostensively define words like 'omnipotent', 'omniscient' and explain the use of the word 'good'. (I am not suggesting that all the words for the attributes that are ascribed to God can be so defined, but I would be suspicious of the ones that cannot be.)

There were (and are) other problems for verificationists. But I think that certain difficulties directed against logical positivists have arisen over how we come to know the meaning of statements about unobserved objects, others' minds, and the past, which difficulties are quite imaginary. (The verificationists unwisely tried to overcome these difficulties by translating statements about unobserved objects into statements about observed ones, statements about others' minds into statements about their bodies, and statements about the past into statements about the future experiences that would verify them (though they forgot that we are no more aware of the future than we are of the past).)

But, in order to know what is meant by 'unobserved cat' we do not need to have come across a cat that is unobserved; it is sufficient to come across a cat. In order to know what is meant by 'another's pain', it is not necessary to have come across another's pain; it is sufficient to have come across a pain. In order to know what is meant by 'past glacier' it is necessary, at most, only to have come a across a glacier; it is not necessary to perform the impossible feat of coming across a past glacier.

A defect in logical punctuation may have produced the illusion that it is necessary to have come across a past cat in order to know what is meant by 'past cat'. In order to understand statements about past cats all that one needs is to be able to imagine what it would be like to come across a cat which is in fact past, not to imagine what it would be like to come across a cat in the past.

There is a similarity in the description 'knowing what it is like to meet a dead man'. It may mean either knowing what it is like to meet Smith (say) who, it so happens, is in fact dead (which is perfectly possible), or knowing what it is like to meet Smith in the state of being dead, which is not possible. In order to imagine what it would be like to be married to someone else's wife all that is necessary is to imagine what it would be like to be married to Mary (who is in fact someone else's wife). It is not necessary to imagine what it would be like to be married to Mary while she is already married to someone else, which would involve imagining what it would be like to be a party to bigamy. If your aim is to imagine what it would be like to be married, as Tom is, to Mary, then you are not doing this if you imagine what it would be like to be married to Mary while she is still married to Tom, for Tom himself is not married to a woman who is married to someone else.

Similarly, to imagine what it would be like to be in acute pain, as Tom is, it is not necessary to imagine what it would be like to be having an acute pain while Tom is having it, which is impossible. Since Tom is not having an acute pain which someone else is having, but just an acute pain, imagining what it would be like to have the acute pain that is being had by Tom does not involve imagining – as I think Wittgenstein supposes it does – what it would be like to inspect the pain while Tom is having it. All that is involved is imagining inspecting our own pain. And to know what it is like to come across an unobserved object it is not necessary to come across an object while it is being unobserved, which is impossible. All that is necessary is to know what it would be like to come across that object (which is in fact unobserved).[20]

If a logical positivist holds the view that no sentence other than one that expresses a verifiable proposition can have meaning because the meaning of a sentence is the sum total of all those propositions that would verify it, then what he holds is false. If he simply holds that no sentence can have meaning unless it can be shown to express a proposition the truth of which is in some way or other tied to reality, and so can in some way or other be verified, then it may, or may very well, be true. To discuss whether or not it would then be true is too large an enterprise to be undertaken here.

(xxii) Difficulties with the Meaning of the Word 'God': Analogical Meaning, Systematic Ambiguity and Metaphor

I am not suggesting that the process of correlating words with things raises no problems. One difficulty is that words are used not only in the presence of the things with which they are correlated, but also in their absence. (This difficulty is obviously superable, and I shall not discuss it.) The most notorious of the difficulties with correlating words with reality is presented by the fact that we have words for things that we have never been confronted with, and for things that, like electrons, we cannot be confronted with, and even words for things, like centaurs, which we cannot be confronted with because they do not exist. (This difficulty is not a spurious one, as were the difficulties just discussed concerning other minds, past objects, and unobservable objects. Electrons, I suspect, are not by definition unobserved; it just so happens that they cannot be observed because they do not, and perhaps in principle cannot, individually, have effects on our perceptual apparatuses, in particular our eyes.)

The answer to these difficulties has already been suggested; words like 'God', if they cannot be correlated with anything with which we can be confronted, have to be defined in terms of words that can be correlated with such things. (I shall discuss the view that we can be confronted with God in chapter 13) Presumably, then, we show people what 'omnipotent' means by showing them examples of people doing things, and then saying that, as people can do some things but not others, God can do anything. (The word 'anything' can be correlated with reality in some such way as this; someone may take anything if, whatever he takes, he is not rebuked for taking it; whereas if he may take something, but not anything, if there are some things, but not others, that he will be rebuked for taking.) The same will have to be held to be true of words like 'omniscient' and phrases like 'perfectly good'.

However, there is an alternative way of explaining how the word 'God' can have meaning. Since words for God cannot directly be correlated with any observations of God, as the word 'cat' can be correlated with observations of cats, recourse has been had to the doctrine that God must be conceived of analogically, and to the interrelated notion of metaphor. (Conceiving by analogy, which I am discussing here, should not be confused with arguing by analogy, which I shall discuss later (in chapter 7).)

The doctrine of analogical meaning was not originally evolved to explain how words for God could have meaning, so much as to explain why God could both have certain characteristics that were applicable to his creatures, and at the same time not be commensurate with them. His not being commensurate with his creatures seemed to be taken to mean his not having any of the characteristics that his creatures have. It was thought that the difficulty could be surmounted so long as God possessed the characteristics that men possessed in a different sense from that in which men possessed them. The doctrine of analogy was supposed to be a halfway house between saying that words like 'good' were ambiguous, and saying that these words were applicable to men and to God in the same sense. By saying that God was good only in an analogical sense, theologians hoped that they could hold that God was not commensurate with his creatures because he was not literally good, without having to go to the embarrassing lengths of saying that he was not good at all. Here, however, I shall consider the doctrine of analogy not as a way out of the difficulty concerning God's possessing characteristics which men also possess, but only as a way of explaining how words for God have meaning. It may also be necessary to conceive of God by analogy if God is eternal, and if, as I shall argue later, an eternal being cannot literally perform actions.

There have been held to be two kinds of analogy, the analogy of proportionality and the analogy of attribution. The first is most plausible as applied to relations, like being the creator of. Man creates in the primary sense of 'creates'; God creates only in an analogical sense of 'creates'. God's creating resembles man's creating as the foot of a man resembles the foot of a mountain or league table; the first is like, but is not entirely like, the second. A man has a foot in a primary sense; a mountain or league table has a foot only analogically. The second resembles the first analogically because the foot of the league table stands to the table in a relation similar to that in which the foot of the man stands to the man. I suspect that the resemblance in the relations possessed by God and the relations possessed by people resemble one another in that they have the same logical properties.[21] For example, that A stands in the relation of creating to B (i.e., A created B) implies that B does not stand in this relation to A, just as that A stands in the relation of being father of to B implies that B does not stand in the relation of being father of to A (i.e., both relations are asymmetric). As a consequence, the relations of the term used literally and the term used analogically have a similar structure.

But a doctrine of relations presupposes some account of the nature of that which possesses these relations. It cannot be the whole nature of a thing to stand in certain relations and nothing else. For example, it could not be the whole truth about anything that he was someone's father, or that he created something. Nothing can possess relations without also possessing attributes. Hence the analogy of proportionality presupposes the analogy of attribution, which I shall now try to explain.

I suspect that something possesses an attribute analogically (the analogy of attribution) if the word for this attribute is what has been called 'systematically ambiguous'. A word is systematically ambiguous if, though it is ambiguous, it is not a coincidence that it has different meanings, but its different meanings are systematically related to one another. For example, a man can be healthy in what has been called the primary sense, water healthy in that drinking it is the cause of health, and clear urine healthy in that it is a sign of health. The term for the primary sense is that in which the terms for the other senses are defined, and it is obvious, if we are to explain how the words that apply to God get their meaning, that we must hold that the senses in which these words apply to God must be defined in terms of the senses with which we are familiar. These are those in which they apply, non-analogically, to man. (The view of some theologians that it is God to whom systematically ambiguous words like 'good' apply in the primary sense must, therefore, be mistaken. The word 'primary' must or should be used differently in the doctrine of analogy of proportionality and in the doctrine of analogy of attribution. In the former, the analogical senses only resemble the primary senses, whereas in the latter they are defined in terms of them.)

I find the doctrine of analogy by attribution unhelpful. It is important that God should be good in the primary sense. That he should be good or omnipotent or omniscient in the sense that he is the cause or a sign of goodness (or of omnipotence or omniscience) fails to reflect what the ordinary believer demands of him, which is that he should be simply good, as well as omnipotent and omniscient. (Indeed I suspect, for what this fact is worth, that the ordinary believer is content with his being good, powerful and knowledgable, in some quite straightforward non-analogical sense.) That one is not in prison may be a sign of (moderate) goodness, and the state of one's brain a cause of it, but it would be most unsatisfactory to hold that senses like these are the only ones in which God can be good. That God should be good only in the sense in which these impersonal things could be good is to do him an injustice.

Metaphor

Figures of speech, in particular metaphor, are no help with explaining what the word 'God' means. For though religious language is riddled with metaphor, the more fundamental characteristics of God, by reference to which the word 'God' is defined, are not attributed to him metaphorically. God, if he exists, is not metaphorically omnipotent, omniscient and perfectly good. He is omnipotent, omniscient and perfectly good. Hence I shall not discuss the extremely tricky subject of metaphor, important though it is. However, when I think a word applied to God is being used metaphorically (as it is, for example when Christians describe him as 'father', and ought to be when Christ is described as sitting 'on God's right hand') I shall draw attention to the fact.

(xxiii)   God and Microscopic Particles

One serious difficulty with thinking of God as an omnipotent, omniscient, and perfectly good being is that these characteristics need filling out. A being cannot have only characteristics like omnipotence and no others, any more than the only characteristic of a man can be that he is a father or a benevolent despot. A man, to be a benevolent despot or father, must have myriad other characteristics; a date of birth, a mother, a wife, a history, a height, a colour, a weight and a mental and physical constitution.

Sometimes the reasons for thinking that God must have these other characteristics will be inductive. Past experience tells us that men must at least have biological fathers. At other times the reason will be logical. A man cannot have personality alone, without having some specific kind of personality, any more than an object can be red without being some specific shade of red. If the word 'God' is a word like 'father', one would think that God himself must be like a father. But it cannot be the whole truth about a being that he is a father. (In the case of God, we have little idea what such characteristics to attribute to him, or how to find out whether or not he possesses them.)

A similar difficulty arises about the meaning of the word 'electron' and words for other microscopic particles. The spatial characteristics by which the word 'electron' gets its meaning may be defined ostensively by reference to visible, tangible, audible, tastable objects like aniseed balls, capable of being smelled, whereas electrons, unlike aniseed balls, are invisible, intangible, inaudible, and cannot be tasted or smelled. Microscopic particles have spatial and temporal attributes, but no space-filling characteristics like colour. These have got left out. They have the power to affect other particles, but it would be unsatisfactory to define words for them only in terms of words for powers. For the question must arise: 'What is it that has the powers?'

It does not follow from the fact that electrons have no taste or smell that the words for the spatial characteristics of electrons are being used analogically or metaphorically,[22] nor that we do not come to understand what words such as 'electrons' mean from seeing them applied to items which, unlike electrons, we are confronted with. (The same is also true of the most fundamental characteristics, like omnipotence and omniscience, attributed to God.) Words like 'electron' acquire their meaning not analogically, but by subtraction.

Colour, taste and smell are subtracted from our concept of the spatial attributes of electrons in order to produce an idea of a colourless, tasteless, spatial particle.

'God' acquires its meaning by a similar 'subtraction'. The word 'God', though it adds to the ordinary man's concept of, say, power by making God omnipotent, rather than just powerful, also subtracts from this concept by eliminating the other attributes of personality from the deity, as colour and other 'space-filling' characteristics are eliminated by physicists from the ordinary man's concept of microscopic particles. God is a person without a father and a mother, without a height, weight, spatial and (on most views) temporal position, and without all the other characteristics which men must, either logically or as a matter of fact, have. The doctrine of analogy does not answer the difficulty of subtraction.

There are at least two problems concerning the meaning of the word 'God'. One problem is that a being cannot be omnipotent, omniscient and perfectly good without possessing other characteristics as well, and that to ascribe these other characteristics to God borders on absurdity. The other problem, as we shall see later, is that a timeless being cannot possess the attributes by reference to which 'God' is defined except analogically, even if possessing something analogically is possible at all. Since we have rejected the view that God can be omnipotent and omniscient in an analogical sense, we cannot use the doctrine of analogy as a way of holding that God is both omnipotent and omniscient and timeless. Indeed, the view that there can be timeless action is absurd.[23] Since God's omnipotence, omniscience and goodness cannot be made compatible with the view that he is timeless, I shall argue later that at least some religious people need two concepts of God.

It may be that one should have the first attitude to an eternal God, the latter to an everlasting temporal one. Our concept of the second is that of a temporal person or quasi-person who is omniscient, omnipotent and perfectly good. The advantage of having such a concept is that, since the being who answers to it is temporal and personal, it would be possible to have a relationship with such a being. It is easier to have a dialogue with a temporal god than with an eternal one. But even a temporal god would be faced with the subtraction difficulty, that our concept of him takes away from the attributes which an ordinary temporal person has to possess. And since all the evidence that there is is against there being a temporal personal god, this, as I have said, makes it necessary to have some attitude to him short of, or at any rate different from, ordinary belief. (This might be what some Christians sometimes mean by 'faith'.)

The concept of the former is that of a god as a being beyond time. This is aesthetically more satisfactory, as more unitary and more remote from the everyday, and (so?) more awe-inspiring, but, since an eternal being cannot be personal, it cannot give the 'believer' the advantages of having a relationship with a personal god, and is of more doubtful comprehensibility. I believe that it has some attraction for mystics. (I have suggested elsewhere that the question whether the former kind of god exists does not even make sense, but this is a good thing rather than a bad one.)[24]

(xxiv) Conclusions

No theory of meaning which does not explain the correlation of words such as 'God' – or the ways in which such words are defined – with observable things, or at the very least explain why it is unnecessary to give such an account of a certain word, can be considered adequate.

The problem about theistic words is that, because God is transcendent, the word 'God' cannot be correlated with any being with whom we can be confronted – unless it turns out later that we can be confronted with a transcendent being, perhaps in mystical experience.[25] The word 'God' can be defined in terms of words which can be correlated with reality. But the correlation is always with something temporal, whereas God is supposed to be eternal. If God is eternal, too, he can possess personal attributes only analogically, but the doctrine of analogy is of doubtful validity, and one wants God to possess certain characteristics, like goodness, literally. For the purposes for which we need a personal god, we really need God to be literally powerful and good, not only analogically good. It is a further difficulty with our concept of a god who is alleged to be personal that it subtracts from the characteristics which it seems essential that temporal persons have, in the way in which our concept of electron subtracts from characteristics that it seems essential that material things should have.

It seems that the two theological doctrines, the doctrine that God is a supremely good, powerful and knowledgable person, and the doctrine that, if only on account of his eternity, he does not literally, but at most analogically, possess any of the characteristics that human beings possess, are incompatible. But this incompatibility, I suspect, points not so much to the necessity of a doctrine of analogical meaning, so much as to the usefulness of having two concepts of God, a personal god who possesses God's characteristics literally, and an impersonal eternal one, who does not possess these characteristics even analogically. Though the everyday Christian believer needs the first concept (described above, of a personal god), the experience of mystics and perhaps the logic of theologians is more in favour of the second. (It would be suitably pious, but not entirely comprehensible, to suggest that both gods are simply different aspects of one and the same entity.) Some people need both an eternal God and a personal one. I shall say more about this later.

Notes

1   It used to be objected to the verification principle that it itself was neither an empirical generalisation nor a tautology, and so that, if it itself were true, the words that expressed it must be meaningless. What I have just said suggests that the answer to this objection is that the verification principle is what people in those days were pleased to call a tautology, arising from an analysis of meaning, but without the derogatory significance suggested by the word 'tautology'.

2   The reader is referred to Fodor, 1987.

3   See Wittgenstein, 1961.

4   Though someone uttering the words 'I promise', knowing what he is about, in the appropriate circumstances, is promising, regardless of his mental state, it may well be that someone uttering the words 'I adore thee' is only adoring if he is in suitable mental state. (It does not follow from this that someone is the suitable mental state, who is not uttering (even quietly to himself) any words is not adoring.)

5   When I say 'permissible' I am not intending to suggest that this sentence is permitted by human conventions. It is a permissible not in the sense in which a move at chess is permissible if it is permitted by the rules of chess, which are conventions, but in the sense is which it is permitted by the exigencies of needing to win. Apart from the fact that one may be penalised for not observing the rules, what one must do to win is not a matter of convention.

6   I say 'partial correlation' because one does not always say 'Everest' when one sees Everest, and quite often says 'Everest' when one does not see Everest. Such correlation as there is would have to confirm the hypotheses that 'Everest' was the (English) name for Everest.

7   J.J.C. Smart tells me that this ought to be Vulcan, which was postulated to explain the advance of the perihelion of Mercury. There turned out, however, to be no reason to postulate such a planet, as the erratic behaviour of Mercury was later explained by the theory of relativity. Pluto, however, was first hypothesised to explain the erratic behaviour of Uranus, by one astronomer, and Neptune, by another, and was later confirmed by photography, though it did not much resemble the plant postulated. The interesting similarity between Pluto and Vulcan is that in both cases one had to choose between retaining a law and postulating an individual, though opposite manoeuvres were adopted and were successful in the two cases.

8   See Kripke, 1972.

9   I have discussed Quine's view in 'How happy could I be with either, or a gavagai by any other name', in Harrison, 1995.

10   *Loc. cit.*

11   The reader is referred to 'Truth and Meaning' in Davidson, 1984.

12 It is partly through neglecting this fact that Kripke, 1982 has spent rather a long time discussing the possibility that 'plus' might not mean plus.

13 It is sometimes said that an account of meaning should take into account not only the effect of the meaningful word on the person who knows what it means, but also the effect on what it means (the 'entity' it designates or the characteristic or relation it connotes) on this person. I doubt the truth of this, however, because one can explain what descriptions like 'the present king of France' mean by their effect on the person who understands them, but the object of the description 'the present king of France' can have no such effect, because there is none.

14 For a fuller discussion of these matters, the reader is referred to Chomsky, 1966, and to Fodor, 1976.

15 See Locke, 1975, Book I, chapter II, 'No Innate Principles in the Mind'.

16 I have discussed this topic in greater detail in Harrison, 1976, chapter III.

17 He may know that they are images of cats, so long as this statement is not put using the word 'cats', say, by being put in French. To say 'I do not know what the word "cats" means, but I do have images of cats' is pragmatically contradictory, but to say (perhaps of a Frenchman) of me 'He does not know what the words "cats" means, but he does have images of cats' is not.

18 It looks as if one comes across groups of electrons, because chairs and tables are groups of electrons. This may mean that that I have come across a table and that a table is a group of electrons does not entail that I have come across a group of electrons.

19 J.J.C. Smart tells me that electrons are not spatial in any commonsense way. But they must be sufficiently spatial to compose commonsense objects like London, which are.

20 I have argued elsewhere (in Henry Habberley Price, 1899–1984, *British Academy Proceedings*, 1993) reprinted in Harrison, 1995) that it is no more impossible to observe objects which are by definition unobserved than it is to marry bachelors (men who are by definition unmarried). To observe an unobserved object it is no more necessary to observe it while it remains unobserved than in order to marry an unmarried man it is necessary to marry him and leave him in the state of being unmarried.

21 For a discussion of relations the reader is referred to Russell, 1919.

22 But it could be argued that words like 'red' are systematically ambiguous; when applied to light waves, 'red' means 'causes sensations of red', which sensations are red in the primary sense.

23 This view is argued for by Pike, 1970.

24 In 'The Philosophy of Mysticism' in Vol. I of Harrison, 1995.

25 I have discussed difficulties with thinking that this is possible in my 'The Philosophy of Mysticism', *loc. cit.*

2 The Impossibility of Rational Theology

(i) God as a Perfect Being

I now want to pass from considering the meaning of sentences about the deity to the question of whether and how we could know that what they say is true. How could we know that God is omnipotent, for example, or that he is omniscient or perfectly good?

In this section I consider only the possibility of arriving by pure reason at a knowledge of the existence or attributes of a personal God. I am using the expression 'rational theology' rather narrowly to cover only attempts to establish the existence and attributes of God by an entirely *a priori* proof, without any empirical premises. (The ontological argument, the most famous of the arguments that attempt to do this, will be discussed individually later, as will attempts to demonstrate God's existence and attributes using premises that are not all *a priori*.)

The obvious answer to questions such as how we know that God is omnipotent, for example, is that we know this because such statements are true 'by definition'. It is part of the meaning of the word 'God' that any being to whom the word 'God' is properly applied is omnipotent. No being who is not omnipotent can properly be called 'God', because it would be a breach of the rules for using the expression 'God' to apply it to such a being.

It would also follow indirectly that God is omnipotent if God is 'by definition' perfect, and omnipotence is a perfection.

To say that God is a perfect being, however, needs elucidation. It is doubtful whether there can be such a thing as a perfect *being* as such, as opposed to a perfect watch or a perfect man. It is doubtful whether there are perfect members of every class of things. (It may be that there are no absolutely perfect members of any class.) I do not know what a perfect mountain would be, for example. It is even doubtful whether there is such a thing as the class of beings.

A pointer to the meaning of 'God' can be obtained by considering the wishes that there being a God would fulfil, or the needs there being one would satisfy, if there were one. Some of these are the desire for security, desire for protection, the wish to be cared for by a father or ruler, the desire to find a purpose in life by being told what to do, to have rules and ends laid down for one from above and the desire to find a satisfactory object of worship or contemplation. (The fact that one wants there to be a God does not mean that there is not one, only that one ought carefully to scrutinise one's reasons for thinking that there is one.) But though the expression 'perfect being' probably does not make sense, a perfect god would have to be omnipotent, etc., because otherwise he would not be a perfect ruler, and would not fulfil satisfactorily the functions we want or need him to have. When one considers these needs or wants, it turns out that a perfect god is not so much a perfect being, as a perfect master, lord, ruler or father; as such he would have to be omnipotent, omniscient and perfectly good.

It may be also that God is ('by definition') a proper object of worship, and a god, provided he or it was personal at all, who was not omnipotent would not be such an object.

(ii)   Emotive Meaning of the Words 'God' and 'Atheist'

It is part of the function of the word 'God' not simply to connote certain attributes, but to evince certain feelings on the part of the person who uses it, towards what he applies it to. It would be improper to use the word 'God', without suitable qualifications, for any being to whom one has a hostile attitude, or to whom one did not have, to put the matter prosaically, a highly favourable one. Hence those who seem to be complaining about God are not in fact complaining about *God*, but only about the being who governs the universe, against whom one is quite entitled to have a hostile attitude.

Similarly, the word 'atheist' tends to evince an unfavourable attitude to those so described. But the word 'atheist' should be a word for a person who thinks that, as a matter of fact, there is no God. This is a purely factual belief, and there is a case for saying that factual beliefs are all morally neutral.[1] There is no reason why an atheist should not want to believe that there is a God, but feel that, in making up his mind whether there is one or not, he ought not to take his own wishes into consideration.

But in the minds of many, holding this purely factual belief is confused with being against God. But being wholeheartedly against God may be impossible. It will be impossible if we think of God as necessarily supporting us in what we suppose to be our most noble aspirations, for we cannot be wholeheartedly against such a being, though we may not think there is one. One may think that there is no God, but also think that we should fulfil God's wishes, obey his commands, and do what one thinks he would think we ought, if there were a God. It is all the more likely that we should think of God as a being whose wishes we would wish to fulfil because, in thinking that there is a God, we may be partly guided by wanting there to be a being who has just this kind of wish.

An atheist himself cannot think that he is against God, for he must think that there is no God for him to be against. People who think that there is a God can regard an atheist as being (unknowingly) against the entity they themselves suppose to exist. For it looks as if the atheist cannot do certain things which a person who believes that there is a God may think that he must do not to be against God, such as enter into a relationship with him or do what God wants him to do. That one cannot do such things is all the more so if one of the things that one ought to do if there is a God is to believe that there is one.

(iii)   God's Existence Does Not Follow From His Definition

All that follows from the fact that God is 'by definition' omnipotent and perfect is that it would be improper to apply the word 'God' to any being who is not omnipotent or not perfect. It does not at all follow that there is a being to whom it is proper to apply these words. What is implied by the fact that 'God' connotes, among other things, omnipotence, is the truth of the hypothetical proposition that if there is a God, then he is omnipotent. The categorical proposition that there is a being who is omnipotent does not follow from this definition. (I shall discuss what is wrong with the ontological argument, according to which God can exist 'by definition', in my next chapter.)

(iv)   Argument Against the View that Some Propositions about God are True 'by Definition'; 'God' as a Proper Name

If 'God' were a proper name, God could not, contrary to what I have said, possess any of his attributes 'by definition' (see chapter 1).[2]

But 'God' is not a proper name. It is an expression more like 'master' or 'vice-chancellor' or 'father', as used of a particular individual. 'God is good' is more, for example, like 'Masser's in the cold, cold ground', 'Yes, vice-chancellor' or 'Father will not let me go' than it is like a Tom is in the cold,

cold ground or Mary will not let me go. It is not, however, like 'master' or 'vice-chancellor' or 'father' when these are used as class words. They are used as class words in, for example, 'Vice-chancellors are paid more than masters' or 'Fathers are an oppressed race'. Hence 'God' is neither a proper name nor a class word. The word 'God', without word 'the', is like 'omnipotent, omniscient being who governs the universe', also without the word 'the'. It would not apply to a being who did not govern the universe. One can even say that it would not apply to God, if (*per impossibile*) he were to cease to govern the universe. It is not a logical truth that the vice-chancellor of Nottingham University is vice-chancellor of Nottingham University, and one day he or she will not be. But when this person ceases to be a vice-chancellor, it will no longer be proper to address him or her as 'vice-chancellor'. Similarly, if, *per impossibile*, God should not govern the universe, it would be improper to call him 'God'.

There are some logical truths which one can assert because of the definition of the expression 'prime minister of Great Britain'. For example, it is a logical truth that he is head of the Cabinet. Hence there are certain things that must be true of whoever is prime minister of Great Britain, in the sense that the hypothetical proposition that, so long as he (Tony Blair) is prime minister, these things will be true of him. For example, so long as Tony Blair is prime minister, he is head of the Cabinet (from which it does not follow that it is a logical truth that Tony Blair is head of the Cabinet). The proper name 'Tony Blair' can be used of the prime minister of Britain, whether he is prime minister of Britain or not.

(v)   Reasons for Defining 'God' as We Do

It is true that the rules for the use of the expression 'God', as used by ordinary people, are not sufficiently determinate to make the sentence 'God is omnipotent' clearly express an analytic truth. If they knew that the universe had been created by a being who was nearly, but not quite, omnipotent, I am sure that most people would stretch a point and call – though not, I think, properly so – this being 'God'.

But if the word 'God' were used in such a way that God was not 'by definition' omnipotent, there are reasons why we should tidy these rules up a bit, and stipulate that, when we use the expression 'God' we will mean by it 'being who is (among other things) omnipotent'; then, of course, the proposition we use the sentence 'God is omnipotent' to formulate will, 'by definition', be true, and these sentences will express truths because we have defined 'God' in such a way as to make them express truths.

The reason for making God omniscient, say, 'by definition', is not that we discover that the being who governs the universe, if there is one, is discovered to be as a matter of fact omnipotent, omniscient and perfectly good. It is that in trying to create the idea of a perfect 'being' or perfect master or perfect father, we create an idea of one that is omnipotent, omniscient and perfectly good.

It is an odd fact that, though God must possess certain admirable qualities, gods do not have to. If it turned out that there was a rather pedestrian being who governed the universe, he would not be God, but he would nevertheless be a god. In calling this being 'God' we would be expressing an attitude of unqualified approval, which is not expressed by the phrase 'a god'.

(vi)   The Danger of Doing Such Things as Making God Omniscient 'by Definition'

An objection to doing such things as making God omniscient 'by definition' is that, if one proceeds in this way, one can then make any sentence express a true proposition, about God or about anything else, simply by defining the words in it in such a way as to give one the result that one wants. What I describe as 'rational theology' would then simply be a matter of taking rabbits out of a hat when you yourself have already put them there.

When a sentence expresses a true proposition as the result of an arbitrary definition, it is a true proposition despite the arbitrariness of the definition. The trouble arises, however, that when sentences using the word 'God' say what is true because of the way in which one is using this word, they will, if one is using the word eccentrically, seem more eccentric or controversial or important than they really are. This is because people will confuse the truths they really do assert with what these sentences would assert if 'God' were not being used with the eccentric sense that it has been given. There is no need to disagree with the person who says 'God is wicked'. He is, perhaps, simply using the word 'God' in the way in which other people use the word 'devil', and so expressing an uncontroversial truth in a misleading way. (I have heard Jacques Derrida argue that there is no such thing as giving, but he was using the word 'giving' in such an eccentric way that what he was saying was really platitudinous.)

This, however, is only a reason for being cautious with defining words in order to obtain the results one wants, not for not doing it at all. And we have seen that there are reasons for its being quite appropriate to define 'God' in such a way that he is omnipotent, omniscient and perfectly good – provided one does not draw more from the definition than is logically warranted.

(vii) Propositions Cannot be Made True 'by Definition'

Though I have spoken as if propositions such as that God is omnipotent are true 'by definition', this is not strictly speaking true. For example, it is not true that one and one are two because of a definition, even though 'two' does mean that number which you reach by adding one to one. One and one will be two, however one uses the words 'one' and 'two'. What is true as a result of a definition is that the sentence 'One and one are two' expresses the true proposition that one and one are two. And what would happen, if one were to use 'two' to mean three, will be that the sentence 'One and one are two' would express the false proposition that one and one are three, and not the proposition that one and one are two.

Similarly 'God is omniscient' is not true because of the definition of 'God'. If 'God' meant devil, the proposition that we now express in the words 'God is omniscient' would still be true, but would have to be expressed in some other way. Some other word would have to be introduced and defined in such a way as to connote the attributes that 'God' now connotes. Hence, when we say that something is true 'by definition', what we mean is that a word has been introduced and defined in such a way as to make certain sentences containing it express truths. But the truth they express is not true because of the definition. It follows that there are no truths (except some truths *about* words) that are made true by the way we use words. Some truths, such as that two and two are four and that God is omniscient, may be so important that it is just as well that they are independent of human conventions about how words should be used.

(viii) Eternal Truth

It is a corollary of this that knowledge of certain truths such as that one and one are two and that God (if there is one) is omniscient do not depend simply on our knowledge of the way words are used, though we will have to know how words are used in order to know what truths these words express. They are not true by convention and, indeed, are eternally true.

This means that we need a faculty of discerning self-evident truths such as that one and one are two or that God, if he exists, must be omnipotent. The fact that one and one are two can be deduced from the axioms of arithmetic does not mean that it is not self-evident; merely that self-evident truths can be reduced to system. Nor does the fact that a truth is self-evident mean that the truth in question is not a logical truth. That God is omniscient, if 'God' is defined to include every perfection, and omniscience is a perfection, is a logical truth. It should not be supposed that because a truth is true 'by definition', or is logically true, that it is not important. (One could say that the principle that all such logical truths exemplify is the principle that if anything possesses a number of attributes – say omnipotence, omniscience and perfect goodness – it will exemplify any one of them – say omniscience.)

It is my belief that the *only* truths that are self-evident, or are capable of being known *a priori* without observation, are broadly logical or conceptual, and depend on the nature of the concepts expressed by the words in them. It does not follow that *all* such truths are self-evident. Some may not be knowable by human beings at all, though I think they would not only be knowable but self-evident to a being with sufficient intellectual capacity; others can be known because they can be deduced in self-evident steps from propositions that are themselves self-evident.

It is no part of my intention to say that the whole of mathematics consists in self-evident truths. For example, some mathematics consists in deducing consequences from propositions postulated not because they are true but with a view to finding out what follows from them. Here there is no need to hold that the axioms are self-evident, because they are not supposed to be true, but it may be self-evident that the theorems follow from the axioms.[3]

(ix)   Difference Between Theology and Science

I believe that the fact that perfection must be ascribed to God regardless of any investigation of the nature of the universe marks an important difference between theology and science. The business of science is to find out about the world. It would be totally improper for a scientist to define a word in a certain way because he thought that doing so caused a word to signify something more admirable or aesthetically pleasing than would otherwise result. It would be worse if a scientist then concluded that there were things to which the definition applied, or that certain aesthetically pleasing laws obtained, just because they were aesthetically pleasing. And it is just as aesthetically pleasing that objects should fall with an acceleration proportionate to their mass as that mass should be – as is in fact the case – irrelevant to their acceleration, but experiment tells us that the latter is the case. (This being so, it is surprising how often aesthetically satisfying laws are found by scientists also to obtain in actual fact.)

However, it is not at all improper for a theologian to define 'God' in such a way that the word 'God' should apply only to a perfect being. For his object – to anticipate – is not (though he may think it is) to find out about the world, so much as to elaborate a concept of a being who answered to certain devotional, moral and aesthetic requirements. And a personal being who was omnipotent, omniscient and benevolent would meet such requirements more adequately than a being who was not.

It would, however, be as improper for the theologian to conclude without further argument that a being that fulfilled these requirements actually existed. And further, to think we would be justified in calling a being who ruled the universe 'God', if this being was not omniscient and omnipotent and perfectly good, would also be to confuse theology with science. He might be a god with a small 'g', but he could not be God. To worship such a being just because he or it was powerful, even though benevolent as well, would be too much like worshipping an earthly monarch, which would be to bow down to power in a way that should be beneath one's dignity.

(x)   Limitation on the Way in which 'God' Can be Used

There is also another limitation on the way in which we can define 'God' (or any other word, for that matter). The qualities which one decides to confer 'by definition' upon something must fall within the appropriate category. One can decide, for example, whether or not swans should be 'by definition' white, but, if one has decided that they shall be, one cannot then decide that swans shall also be divisible by two. The first choice, which itself is both unlimited and conventional, constrains the other choices one can make, so that one might have made 'swans' refer to something divisible by two, had one first not decided to make the word refer to something white and capable of laying eggs. (This fact is not a matter of convention.)

Similarly, one may have the choice whether or not to define 'God' as a 'spiritual' omnipotent being. But if one does, one does not have the choice of defining God in such a way that he is or is not, say, a good swimmer. It is just a matter of historical accident that the word 'God' means what it now does, and not what the word 'dolphin' now does. But given that one has decided to use the word 'God' for a certain kind of being, there are other ways in which one is precluded from using the word as a result. There are certain attributes which the word 'God' cannot either 'by definition' have or 'by definition' not have. God cannot either be or not be like a train, slow, or like a gazelle, fleet of foot, or like a metal, heavy, or like a quadratic equation, difficult, or like a tune, written in a minor key. The number of attributes which God can either have, or fail to have, is in fact extremely limited.

God is sometimes supposed to be the most real being. There can, however, be no such being, as reality does not admit of degrees. It is an abuse of English not only to say that elephants are more real than phoenixes; it is an abuse of English to say that elephants are real whereas phoenixes are not real. Objects have to exist to be not real, as paste diamonds have to exist not to be real diamonds, and there are no phoenixes to be unreal. (And a *trompe d'oeil* painting can realistically represent a fountain only if it is not a fountain, and a description can be realistic only if it is not a description of a real thing. If it were, it would be accurate or inaccurate, rather than realistic.)

(xi)   The Impossibility of Rational Theology

The fact that some sentences about God, though not all, can be made to express truths as the result of a definition suggests the possibility that rational theology would be rather like Euclidean geometry. One defines the word 'God' to begin with, and then annunciates a number of propositions which are known to be true because they 'follow from the definitions', perhaps together with certain self-evident axioms. In much this way Spinoza thought that his conclusions in the *Ethics* followed from the definitions (and the axioms and postulates) from which he started.

If this kind of rational theology were possible, its possibility would be a fact of the greatest significance. We would be able to answer our questions about God by an application of ordinary logic, the validity of which discipline no sensible person seriously questions. The axioms would be self-evident and necessarily true, and it would be self-evident that the theorems necessarily followed from them.

This method of doing theology, however, has very severe limitations. There must be something wrong with it, if God is an *entity* of any kind, because it looks obvious that one cannot settle what entities exist and what attributes they have by deciding to use a word in one way rather than in another. For example, one may have a chemical substance in front of one, which one may take to be chalk, and be uncertain whether or not it dissolves in sulphuric acid. (If it is chalk, it must so dissolve, but, if it is not, it may or may not do so.) You may think that you can argue as follows; 'chalk' means 'substance that, among other things, dissolves in sulphuric acid'. Hence this substance, because it is chalk, must dissolve in sulphuric acid. To argue in this way, however, is improper, because it begs the question. If 'chalk' means 'substance that dissolves in sulphuric acid', then one does not know whether one may call this substance 'chalk' until one has first discovered whether or not it dissolves in sulphuric acid. If one is in doubt about whether it does dissolve in sulphuric acid, one ought to be just as much in doubt about whether it is chalk, and so one cannot argue from the former to the latter. All you are entitled to conclude from your definition of chalk is the hypothetical proposition that, if this substance does not dissolve in sulphuric acid, then it is not chalk.

Analogously, one may come to think for some reason that the world contains a very powerful being. One may then feel inclined to argue: God is, 'by definition' omnipotent, so this being must be omnipotent. But one cannot legitimately reason like this. Just as one ought not be sure that the substance in front of one is chalk until one has first decided whether or not it dissolves in sulphuric acid, so one should not decide that the aforementioned very powerful being is God until one has first discovered whether or not it is omnipotent. In other words, reflecting on the meaning of the word 'God' does not tell one anything at all about the nature of reality. The most it does is to enable one to decide what reality would have to be like in order to justify one in saying that there is a God. Whether there is anything that can properly have this word applied to it cannot be answered by terminological investigation or fiat, but only by an investigation into what there actually is.

What I have just said imposes a very severe limitation indeed upon rational theology. It means that its conclusions must all be hypothetical. It can tell you that, if there is a God, he will, because he is omniscient, be aware of everything his creatures do, feel or think. It could not, however, tell you whether there was a God who did know everything that his creatures did, felt or thought. It could tell you, in other words, only what are the logical consequences of postulating a God. It cannot tell you whether you ought to postulate a God in the first place. (Similarly, Euclidean geometry can tell you that if there are any objects that travel in Euclidean straight lines, they will never meet, but it cannot tell you whether there are any objects that travel in Euclidean straight lines; that is a matter for physics.)

The conclusions in Spinoza's *Ethics*, even supposing that his reasoning was correct, should then all have been hypothetical and to the effect that if there were any substances, as Spinoza defined 'substance', then they would possess the properties Spinoza ascribed to them. Spinoza cold not tell you whether there were any substances as he defined them. Hence Spinoza could not tell us whether the universe was a substance, as he defined 'substance', but at most only whether, if it was, it would be both God and Nature. Rational theology, without a proof of the actual existence of God, or at least some reason for thinking that there is one, would be at best a science like certain geometries, which told you what would be the case if their axioms were true, but could not tell you whether their axioms were true or not.

(xii)   The Truth of Christianity an Empirical Matter

Not only can God's existence not be deduced from his definition, Christians at any rate must assert a large number of other propositions about God, and these are discovered to be true, if they are true at all, empirically. For example, that God sent his only son to save us cannot be deduced from the possession of any of those characteristics that are part of definition of God, and it is obvious that if God did these things that he did them is an empirical contingent fact. It may be that we know such propositions by revelation, but obtaining knowledge on the testimony of others, of which revealed knowledge is a species, is itself an empirical way of obtaining knowledge.[4]

(xiii)   God as a Completely Adequate Object of Worship

We have seen that not only may one define God as being omnipotent, omniscient and perfectly good, or as being perfect and deduce that he is omnipotent, omniscient and perfectly good because these attributes are perfections, one may also define God as an adequate or completely adequate object of worship (or love, or awe or contemplation). It may then follow (provided God is personal at all) that he is omnipotent, omniscient and perfectly good because a being who did not possess these attributes would not be a completely adequate object of worship, etc.

Though a proper object of worship or contemplation (or love or awe), must, if it is to be personal at all, be omnipotent, omniscient and perfectly good, in fact people worship or contemplate all sorts of other things than this, and appear to find worshipping them satisfactory. I feel that one should be as broad-minded as possible on such matters. But I also suspect that if someone is worshipping something which is not a fully satisfactory object of worship, this must be because he does not realise that it is not. If he himself were to realise that it was unsatisfactory, he would naturally wish to replace it with something better. If he does not replace it with something better, it is due to some limitation on his moral or aesthetic or perhaps religious imagination.

And so, for his worship to find an adequate object, it must, if this object is personal at all, be directed to an omnipotent, omniscient, perfectly good being. But again, this does not mean that there is such a being.

To avoid later confusion, I should say that the definition of God as an object of worship departs from the one that defines him as a perfect father or ruler. For rulers must be personal, but an object of worship does not have to be. Hence, though it may be odd that an impersonal object should be worshipped or contemplated, it would not be proper to rule out a nonpersonal god simply by the definition of 'God'.

(xiv)   God as Neither Existent nor Nonexistent

In what has foregone I have argued that an analysis of the concept of God cannot tell one whether or not there is a God. It is possible, however, that existence is not a proper adjective to apply to God,[5] (or, if you prefer it, and bearing in mind criticisms of the ontological argument that I shall discuss later, to the concept of God). In this case God may neither exist nor not exist.

I shall discuss the view that it is not proper to apply 'existence' to God later in this book. Meanwhile it should be borne in mind that what I say about the existence of God's not following from his definition might have to be modified by the view, with which I have a great deal of sympathy, that God neither exists nor does not exist. Though it could not be true as a result of his definition that he existed, it could perhaps be true as a result of his definition that he neither existed nor did not exist, or that God was not in the right category to have the epithets 'existence' or 'nonexistence' applied to him. In one respect God might be similar to numbers. One might argue that numbers, because of the kind of thing they are, neither exist nor do not exist. Though there are such things as numbers, they are neither to be found in the world nor not to be found in the world. The world is not the place to look for them, and even the idea of looking for a number, except metaphorically, is absurd.

(xv)   Conclusions

God may be defined as being omnipotent, omniscient and perfectly good; as a perfect being; or as a satisfactory object of worship or contemplation. Provided God is a person, and that omnipotence, etc., are perfections, the last two of these three definitions result in same conclusion as that of the first, namely, that, if God exists and is personal at all, he is omnipotent, omniscient and perfectly good.[6]

That there is a God, if existence or nonexistence apply to God at all, cannot follow from his definition. (I shall later suggest the possibility that neither existence nor nonexistence do apply to him.) Knowledge of God, if any, other than that which follows from his definition, is a matter for empirical investigation. I shall argue later that, since there is no way in which such an empirical investigation may be conducted, we do not have such knowledge of God at all. I shall suggest later that the *a priori* activity of exploring our concept of God, and suitably modifying it, is done with a view to different ends and by the application of different criteria from the criteria we use for an explanatory concept. The criteria in theology may be aesthetic and moral, whereas, with an explanatory science, they cannot be.

Notes

1   I have discussed this question in Harrison, 1987.
2   I shall not here discuss the view that proper names are rigid designators because I do not think that to say that 'God' is a rigid designator adds anything of epistemological interest to the more old-fashioned view that 'God' is a proper name.
3   There are also uninterpreted axiom systems, which cannot properly be described as true or false. But it may be necessary to appeal to self-evidence to justify holding that whatever makes the axioms true makes the theorems true.
4   It does not follow that the knowledge so obtained, as opposed to the method of obtaining it, is not *a priori* and necessary – though in this case it is. We may believe empirically, on the authority of a mathematician, that an *a priori* necessary proposition is true.
5   I have also discussed the possibility that God neither exists nor does not exist in 'The Philosophy of Mysticism', in Harrison, 1995.
6   The fact that God is by definition omnipotent and omniscient does not preclude there being some other, possibly necessary, connection between his omnipotence and his omniscience. The fact that a bachelor is by definition unmarried does not preclude there being some necessary connection between his other characteristics and his being unable to marry. Hence what I have said does not preclude the truth of the doctrine of natural kinds – though the idea of God's being a natural kind seems absurd. However, I do not think that there is any truth in the doctrine of natural kinds. Furthermore, though there are empirically

discoverable connections between certain characteristics and others (and some characteristics are more fundamental than others) the connection between such things as God's omnipotence and his omniscience cannot be discovered empirically. The connection is more in our minds, in that we need God to be both.

3 Objections to Empiricism

(i)   Introduction

Most of this chapter, with the exception of section (i), may be omitted by elementary readers who are content to take on trust the empiricism which this chapter defends, and the rest of the book presupposes. Important though the epistemology of religion is, they may prefer to go straight to substantive questions about the existence and nature of God.

The preceding chapter assumed, roughly, the truth of the traditional doctrine that all truths are either on the one hand synthetic, empirical or contingent, or on the other are, in a wide sense, logical or analytic truths, *a priori* and necessary. (I shall explain these terms shortly.) It argued that, though logic could enable you to deduce the logical consequences of assuming that there was a God, it could not tell you that there was a God. In so arguing, it assumed that that there is a God is synthetic, that all synthetic truths are contingent and that they can be known only by observation.

I say 'in a wide sense logical truths' because I wish to include a vast and heterogenous collection of truths which depend on the nature of the concepts involved in them, although they are not in any ordinary sense truths of logic. For example, our knowledge that the king of France cannot be bald if there is no king of France, that truth is eternal, that quadratic equations cannot go hungry, that there are more games of chess than there are electrons in the universe, and that we cannot know a proposition to be true if it is false, all depend only on our understanding the concepts involved in these propositions, e.g. the concepts of chess or quadratic equations. We work out the implications of the statements embodying those concepts, rather than investigate the universe.

(a) The Analytic/Synthetic Distinction

Kant once said that a truth is analytic if its predicate can be abstracted from its subject, as the concept of being female can be abstracted from the concept of being a vixen (which contains it) but the concept of being wily cannot. Since not all propositions assert a predicate of a subject, this definition was

66

later replaced by one that asserted that an analytic truth was one that it was contradictory to deny. (It is contradictory to say that vixens are not female, but not to say that they are not cunning.) But since not all such propositions are in breach of any law of logic – perhaps so much the worse for the laws of logic – I shall say that a proposition is analytic in a wide sense if its truth or falsehood depends not upon empirical fact, but only upon the nature of the concepts involved in understanding the sentences used to assert it, or, what amounts to the same thing, depends simply upon the way in which these words ought to be used. If you hear someone say 'I do not exist', one can reject his claim without further empirical investigation on account of what one knows about the proper use of the word 'I'.

A proposition is synthetic if its truth does not depend solely on the concepts involved in our understanding of the sentence that formulates it.

Whether a truth is analytic or not depends on whether its justification depends on what might broadly speaking be called logic.

(b) The Empirical/A Priori Distinction

A truth is empirical if it is, like the fact that more people say they will vote Labour than vote Conservative or that water expands when it freezes, discovered to be true by observation and, if necessary, by making experiments and noting the results. It is *a priori* if it can be seen to be true without observation, as can that two and two are four, that vixens are female, that if all men are mortal and Socrates is a man, Socrates must be mortal, that numbers are weightless, and that nonexistent people cannot say that they exist.

The empirical/*a priori* distinction is to do with the manner in which a truth comes to be known.

(c) The Necessary/Contingent Distinction

A truth is necessary if, like the truth that two and two are four, it cannot be false.) It is contingent if, like the truth that there are fewer people in Northern Ireland than in the Republic of Ireland, it does not have to be true, could be otherwise, and in some cases, could even (in this case by a suitable immigration policy) be altered. It is sometimes said that the division of truths into necessary and contingent ones has to do with their ontological or metaphysical status, but personally I do not know what this means.

It has been held (by Saul Kripke) that the division of propositions into those which are analytic and those which are synthetic, those which are empirical and those which are *a priori*, those which are necessary and those which are contingent, are three different distinctions, made on three different principles, and he has suggested that they may vary independently of one another in such a manner that the old-fashioned division, which I have just outlined, of propositions into those which are synthetic, empirical and contingent and those which are analytic, *a priori* and necessary, breaks down.

I do not think that Kripke is right about this. Though '*a priori*' 'conceptual' and 'necessary' do not mean the same, it is possible to see how, if a truth does depend upon concepts, it is necessary and *a priori*. It is just because, to take an unrepresentatively simple example, the truth of that vixens are female depends upon the relation between the concept of being a vixen and of being female, that that vixens are female is *a priori* and necessary. The connection between the two concepts – the fact that the concept of vixen includes that of being female – is such that the world cannot make it true that something is a vixen without *ipso facto* making it true that it is female. For this reason it can be seen *a priori* that vixens must be female. Hence it should not be surprising that all and only necessary truths were conceptual, and that all and only conceptual truths are *a priori*. (Kripke has suggested some exceptions to this rule, some of them quite trivial. I shall discuss these suggestions later in this chapter.) It follows from what I have been saying that the truth that all *a priori* necessary truths depend upon concepts itself depends upon concepts, and is itself necessary and *a priori*.

It has been held that all conceptual and straightforwardly analytic truths depend on the meanings of words. There is, however, a sense in which what I shall, following the usual practice, call conceptual or analytic truths depend on the meaning of words and a sense in which they do not. They do not depend, for example, on what, it so happens, 'quadratic equation' means, which is a matter of empirical fact. No quasi-logical or conceptual truths would be altered if 'quadratic equation' were to mean ripe banana and 'ripe banana' meant quadratic equation. The conceptual truths about quadratic equations would just have to be expressed in different words – i.e., in the words 'ripe banana', rather than 'quadratic equation'. But conceptual truths about quadratic equations do depend on the nature of quadratic equations, and quadratic equations is what, it so happens, 'quadratic equations' means. In this sense, conceptual truths do depend on what words mean, i.e., upon that which they mean.[1]

Similarly, the fact that Mary's happiness depends on the man she marries may mean (a) that it depends upon which man she chooses to marry, or it may mean (b) that it depends upon the man she in fact chooses to marry. Conceptual truths depend on the meaning of words in a sense analogous to (b), but not in a sense analogous to (a). But it is only 'accidentally', not 'essentially', that conceptual truths depend on the meanings of words. For that vixens are female depends on the relationship between the concepts of vixen and female, and only indirectly upon the meaning of 'vixen' and 'female', for these, it so happens, are the words for the concepts on which these truths do depend. To take another example, that two and two are four depends on two and four and plus and equals, which are what the words 'two' and 'four' and 'plus' and 'equals' mean, not upon the fact that these words are the words for those numbers. (For the same reason, that two and two are four is not a conventional fact. What is conventional is the fact that 'two' is the English word for two, and 'four' the English word for four. Two and two would be four, whatever 'two and 'four' meant, though it is a non-conventional fact that would have to be expressed in other words if different conventions were adopted for the use of 'two' and 'four'.)

In this chapter I shall consider a number of objections to empiricism, and answer them one by one. (I cannot hope to answer all the objections that have been levelled against empiricism over the years.) Here I shall discuss a selection of these objections which I hope that I have identified correctly as being the most influential.

(Empiricism, incidentally, does not stand or fall by the verification principle, according to which sentences that do not express anything which is either a logical truth or is capable of being established or refuted by empirical methods are meaningless. As we have seen, logical positivists, who hold the verification principle, take the extreme view that every meaningful sentence must express either a proposition that can be empirically verified or one that is logically true. One can be an empiricist without holding the verification principle, provided one holds that no proposition (apart from those that are in a wide sense logically true) ought to be accepted without empirical evidence in its favour. (This is precisely what the non-logical positivist August Compte held.))

(ii)   Two Ancient Difficulties for Empiricism

Two alleged counter-examples to the view that all *a priori* knowledge is analytic or conceptual are (1) that everything coloured must be extended, and (2) that one and the same thing cannot be, say, black and red all over. I suggest the following answers.

(1) To say that something is red is to say of an expanse that it is extended redly, and nothing can be extended redly if it is not extended.

(2) That one and the same thing cannot be both black and red all over can be shown to be an analytic truth if one allows, as one should, negative connotation. When one is taught to use the words 'red', one is taught not only to use it of red things, but to withhold it from things that are not red (including black things). A corresponding assertion is true of 'black'. Hence, if something were red and black all over, one would have to call it red, because that is the correct word for something red, but also to call it not red, because it is incorrect to apply the word 'red' to something that is black. Hence a red and black thing is both red and not red (and both black and not black.) Hence the contradictory of the proposition that a thing cannot be both red and black all over is contradictory, and so the proposition is itself analytic.

(iii)   Objection: *A Priori* Knowledge is not 'Genuine', if Empiricism is True

According to empiricism, the reason why we know certain truths *a priori* is that they say nothing about the spatio-temporal world, or, indeed – or so empiricists have sometimes said – say nothing at all. To take a very simple example, the reason why one knows *a priori* the truth of the disjunctive proposition that either it is raining or it is not raining is that there are only two possibilities, (a) that it is raining and (b) that it is not raining, and that it is either raining or not raining is true whichever of the two holds.[2] And the reason why it is known to be true, in advance of experience, that vixens are female foxes is that when one has said that an animal is a vixen, one has already said that this animal is female.

However, though it is true on an empiricist account that *a priori* knowledge gives one no knowledge of the world except that which can be deduced from knowledge one already possesses, it is false that it gives one no psychologically new knowledge. One's assumptions may sometimes have very surprising consequences.

It is partly empiricists' own fault that they gave the impression that they thought that *a priori* truths could, on their account, give no new knowledge. For they insisted on saying that all such truths were tautologies,[3] whereas such truths are only *like* tautologies in that they point out the consequences of what has already been said. And it is not true – though empiricists like A.J. Ayer[4] have maintained that it is – that *a priori* propositions are simply about words, or record people's determination to use words in a certain way. The proposition that one and one are two is about the number one, not about the numeral '1', and is true however we use the word 'one', though if we were to use the word 'one' in some way other than we do, we would have to use some other words to express the fact that one and one are two. The proposition that the *numeral* '3' refers to the number you obtain by adding one to two is itself not an analytic proposition, but states a brute empirical fact.

Another way of putting the matter is to say that empiricists think that *a priori* knowledge is knowledge only of the consequences of making certain assumptions. It cannot tell you whether these assumptions are true or not. This latter is a matter for experience, observation and experiment. But this does not mean that the consequences of the assumption in question are not surprising or difficult to work out, or that one cannot obtain from a number of assumptions collectively conclusions that one could not have obtained from any one without the others.

(iv)   Objection: Quine has Shown that the Distinction, Essential to Empiricism, Between Analytic Propositions and Synthetic Ones, Breaks Down

It is quite obvious that Quine is wrong, and that there is a distinction between analytic and synthetic propositions. For example, it is obvious that there is a difference between a proposition such as that it is impossible to play a round of golf in as few as 18 strokes, and that it is impossible to play one in as few as 17. A certain amount of empirical information about the physical limitations of golfers, golf clubs and golf balls is needed to know the first. For the second all that it is necessary is to have a full grasp of the concepts of being a round, being a hole and being a stroke. One would have to revise the first if one discovered a Martian golfer who could always hole in one. But there are no circumstances in which one could revise the second. What one could do is something subtly different, e.g., revise the meaning of 'round' so that a round came to mean, say on account of a shortage of land, a sequence of nine strokes instead of a sequence of 18. In that case the proposition expressed by the sentence 'It is impossible to play a round of golf in less than 18 strokes' would come to express a different proposition from the one it expresses now, which former proposition does not have to be revised. It is still true that it is impossible to play what used to be called a round in less than 18 strokes, which fact has not been revised.

Hence it is obvious that there is a distinction between analytic and synthetic propositions, in that it is obvious that some propositions are analytic and some propositions are synthetic. I think that there is also a large class of propositions that are neither analytic nor synthetic. The proposition that vixens are female is analytic, because being female is included in the concept of being a vixen, or because being female is part of what is connoted by the word 'vixen', or because it is self-contradictory to say that vixens are not female. The proposition that vixens are bad tempered is obviously synthetic. But the proposition that vixens suckle their young may be neither analytic nor synthetic, because, since there have been no cases of vixens who do not suckle their young there is no rule of language stating either that 'vixens' connotes suckling one's young, or excludes it. But this does not mean that there is any non-empirical way of finding out facts about vixens. All it does mean is that, if you discover (empirically) that there are some animals resembling female foxes in most ways, but who do not suckle their young, you have the problem of deciding whether or not to specify the rules for the use of the word 'vixen' and 'fox' in such a way as to call them 'vixens'.

Since the fact that some propositions are neither analytic nor synthetic does not mean that there is some other than empirical way of acquiring knowledge, Quine's remarks to the effect that the distinction is blurred do not undermine the empiricism on which this book is based. And Quine himself was an empiricist.

(v)   Objection: Kant has Shown that there are Synthetic *A Priori* Propositions, the Existence of Which is Incompatible with Empiricism

Kant attempted to show that empiricism was false, and that there was synthetic *a priori* knowledge. He thought that it was obvious that we knew analytic propositions to be true *a priori*, and obvious that we could have empirical knowledge of synthetic propositions. But he thought that we also had *a priori* knowledge of such truths as that every event has a cause, which truths were not true by definition – as was the proposition that every effect has a cause – and were consequently synthetic.

He thought that synthetic *a priori* knowledge, unlike analytic *a priori* knowledge and empirical synthetic knowledge, needed a justification (what he called a 'deduction'). He attempted to justify it by trying to show that we could not experience a world to which our synthetic *a priori* knowledge was not applicable; for example, we could not experience a world in which not every event had a cause. We had *a priori* synthetic knowledge when we were incapable of experiencing a world about which the proposition we knew *to be true a priori* was false. This was because experience conformed to our cognitive capacities, rather than our knowledge having to conform to experience, much as the fact that we catch only large fish may tell us more about our net than about the fish in the lake.

This attempted justification was not, for reasons that I shall not discuss, successful. But, even if it had been successful, it would not have shown that we had any synthetic *a priori* knowledge of theology. For – as Kant himself believed – the fact that there was knowledge of synthetic *a priori* propositions did not enable one to know anything about things in themselves, but only about things as they were moulded and distorted by our becoming aware of them. That this was so was a corollary of his justification of synthetic *a priori* knowledge, viz., that experience was, by our coming to know it, modified in such a way as to make certain beliefs about it true; being so modified, it was in consequence mere appearance. Hence we could have synthetic knowledge only of appearance. God, according to Kant, was a thing in itself and, not being moulded by our cognition of him, was unknowable. Hence there could be no *a priori* synthetic knowledge of theology.

(vi)   Objection: Kripke has Shown that the Distinction Between Propositions which are (a) Necessary, Analytic and *A Priori* and (b) Contingent, Synthetic and Empirical, Breaks Down

Saul Kripke has criticised what he regards as the old-fashioned division of propositions into those that are *a priori*, analytic and necessary on the one hand, and those that are synthetic, empirical and contingent on the other. This classification, Kripke thinks, needs to be revised by recognising that there are two further classes of truths.

(a) There is a class of truths that are necessary, though capable of being known only *a posteriori*. Kripke thinks that true identity propositions such as that the morning star is the evening star belong to this class, and are necessarily true, though they can be discovered to be true only empirically. For example, it must be necessarily true that the morning star is the evening star, because it is a necessary truth that everything is identical with itself. But it is an empirical (astronomical) discovery, not an *a priori* truth, that the morning star and the evening star are the same star.

(b) There is a class of truths which, though contingent, are known *a priori*. For example, the metre rod in Paris does not have to be a metre long, because the rod put there might have been some other length. (It might have been some other length because, if the hand of the craftsman who made it had slipped, as it perfectly well might have done, it probably would have been some other length.) Hence it is only a contingent fact that it is the length it is. But, because the word 'metre' was introduced as a name for whatever length the metre rod in Paris has, we know *a priori* that it is a metre long.

I should like to pass the following remarks on these two views of Kripke's.

(a) Kripke's view that identity propositions, such as the proposition that the morning star is the evening star, are necessarily true, though known only empirically, need not detain us, though I do not think that it is true. For though he thinks that identity propositions – some of which previous philosophers had supposed to be contingent – are necessary, he agrees with those who hold the traditional view that our knowledge of them is empirical. Hence he is not offering any extension of our cognitive capacities by attacking the traditional view that they are contingent. For example, though if Kripke is right the identity proposition that Jesus is God, if he is God, would be a necessary truth, we would still have to discover the fact that he is God empirically, and so no difficulties about how we come to know such truths are surmounted. The fact, if it were one, that identity propositions are necessary and *a posteriori* does not offer us the needed extension to our cognitive capacities.

(b) Though Kripke's view about the necessity of certain identity statements would provide no extension to our cognitive capacities, even if it were true, Kripke's view about the necessity of certain *a priori* contingent statements would provide such an extension if it were true; but is not true. Though Kripke thinks (rightly) that the fact that the metre rod is a metre long is contingent, whereas previous philosophers would have supposed that this fact was necessary, he is wrong in thinking that it is a contingent fact that is known *a priori*. Let us suppose that 'umpteen' is a word for the number of cherry stones on our plate, however many cherry stones this might turn out to be. Then however many cherry stones there are on our plate, we will say 'There are umpteen cherry stones on my plate'; but we will not know *a priori* how many cherry stones there will be on our plate. It is just, that, however many of them there are, we will call that number 'umpteen'. Hence the contingent fact that the metre rod in Paris is about 39 inches (a metre) long is not something we know *a priori*. What we do know *a priori* is only the fact that, however long it is, we will call whatever length it happens to have a 'metre'.

(vii) Some Alleged Kinds of Necessity, and Supposed Examples of Necessary Synthetic Truths

The question whether there are necessary statements other than analytic ones should not be confused with the question whether there are kinds of necessity other than the necessity possessed by analytic truths. The answer to this latter question is that there are necessities other than these. Actions can be necessary in the sense that they ought to be done, and events necessary in the sense that they are necessarily connected with other events. Not all statements to the effect that something is necessary are themselves necessary. It is a contingent fact, for example, that those who are born necessarily die, and that one cannot become a member of the Church of England if one is not baptised.

Richard Swinburne,[5] among others, has alleged that there are classes of necessary synthetic statements.

(a) Such propositions as that the number of planets is necessarily greater than four have been held[6] to be necessary and synthetic. This is because two things have been confused (by Quine, whose example it is.)[7] (1) That number which, it so happens, is the number of planets is necessarily greater than four. This proposition is necessary but analytic (and, incidentally, *a priori*). It is true because it so happens that nine is the number of the planets, and nine is necessarily greater than four. (2) That number which, it so happens, numbers the planets necessarily numbers the planets (i.e., there must be that number of planets). That there are that number of planets is synthetic, but contingent; that there must be that number is false. We know *a priori* that nine, the number of the planets, is greater than four, but this proposition is analytic (and, incidentally, empirical). We know only empirically that there are nine planets, but this propositions is synthetic. (We know *a priori* the truth of the proposition that that number which is the number of the planets is not necessarily the number of the planets.)

That the number of gods is one less than two might be held to be a necessary truth, if there were one god, but this would be ambiguous between (a) that number which, it so happens, is the number of gods is necessarily one less than two, which is necessary but analytic, and that there is one god, which is synthetic but not necessary, or not necessary for that reason. (That God is unique by definition would show only that there was not more than one god, not that there were as many as one.)

(b) Swinburne discusses the view that that the author of *Hamlet* wrote *Hamlet* is another necessary truth that is not analytic. But this view is not true. Very roughly, it is ambiguous between: (1) it is necessary that, if 'the author of *Hamlet*' picks out anything, what it picks out wrote *Hamlet*, which is true, but analytic, and (2) if the author of *Hamlet* picks out anything, then what it picks out necessarily wrote *Hamlet*, which is synthetic, but false. (Shakespeare did not necessarily write *Hamlet*.) That the creator of the universe created the universe is ambiguous between (1) it is necessarily the case that, if 'the creator of the universe' picks out anything, it picks out the creator of the universe, which is true but analytic, and (2) if 'the creator of the universe' picks out anything, what it picks out necessarily created the universe, which is synthetic but false. God might have decided not to create a universe. It is not of much interest, for example to be told that if the description 'the creator of the universe' picks out anything, it necessarily picks out the creator of the universe, if it is not a necessary truth that it should pick out anything.

(c) It has been held[8] that statements such as that Nixon is a human being are necessary truths that are synthetic.

This contention should be distinguished from the contention that 'Nixon' is necessarily the name for a human being, which is obviously false. 'Nixon' might have been the name for Nixon's dog. It is rather the claim that, if 'Nixon' names a human being, then what it names is necessarily human. It would follow, if it were true, that Circe could not, as she threatened, have changed Ulysses into a fox. The best she could have done would have been to replace Ulysses with a fox, and call the fox 'Ulysses'. (If she could change Ulysses into a fox, the fox could not be the same man as Ulysses, because he would not be a man at all, but he could be the same animal as Ulysses, and could be the same person if a fox could be a person at all.)

The question whether Nixon is necessarily a man is not the same question as whether men are necessarily men. The statement that men are necessarily men suffers from the kind of ambiguity that has already been discussed; it may mean that, necessarily, if anything is a man it is a man, which is true but analytic, or that if anything is a man, it is necessarily a man, which is synthetic but false. ('A man's a man for a' that' may mean that no adversity can change the fact that, if anyone is a man he is a man, which is incontrovertible, or that, if anyone is a man, no adversity can change him from being a man, which is more dubious.)

It cannot, however, be a necessary truth that Nixon is a man, because this would presuppose that there was such a person as Nixon, which can only be a contingent fact, discoverable empirically. (Existence itself cannot be an attribute necessarily possessed by Nixon, because, as we shall see in a later chapter, existence is not an attribute of Nixon at all.) The most that could be a necessary truth would be the hypothetical proposition that *if* there was man

Nixon, then he would necessarily be a man. (If Nixon existed, then L(Nixon is a man).) The hypothetical proposition that if there is such a person as Nixon, he is necessarily a man might, for all that, theoretically be known *a priori*, but, since it would not tell us whether there was a man Nixon or not, it would be of no importance in telling us anything about the world. So again, no extension to our cognitive capacities is given us by the view that that Nixon is necessarily a man is a necessary proposition.

But, besides not giving us any extension to our cognitive capacities if it were true, it cannot be that that Nixon is a man is necessarily true. This latter proposition cannot be true, because it presupposes the contingent proposition that there is such a person as Nixon, and what must be true cannot be something which would be false in the event of a proposition's being false which might – as it must be the case if it is contingent – be false.

(d) Kripke held that that the table in front of him was not from the very beginning of its inception made of ice was synthetic and necessary. It is synthetic because there is nothing in the definition of 'table' that excludes a table from being made of ice; making a table of ice might one day even become technically possible. But Kripke seems to think that it is self-evident – at least, he gives no argument for the proposition – that, whatever might be true of other tables, the table in front of him could not be made of ice. (It could turn into ice, but that is different.)

I have the same uneasy feeling that two things are again being confused. (1) The first is the proposition that it is necessarily the case that if 'this table' picks out a table that is not made of ice, then the table it picks out is not made of ice. (2) The second is the proposition that if the table picked out is not made of ice, then the table it picks out is necessarily not made of ice. (1) is true but analytic and (2) is indeed not analytic, but is also not true.

Even if Kripke were right, since he is not disputing that it is an empirical discovery that this table is not made of ice, if it were the case that it is necessary that this table is made of ice, this would not remove any empirical limitations to our cognitive capacities; hence Kripke's remarks have no bearing upon the question of the nature of our knowledge of the existence and attributes of God, or upon any other epistemological question.

(e) That root 2 is necessarily a number and that what Tom is talking about is root 2 have been alleged to entail that what Tom is talking about is necessarily a number, which latter fact is supposed to be synthetic and *a priori*. I suspect, however, that the contention that what Tom is talking about is necessarily a number is ambiguous. It may mean (1) that what Tom is talking about is something that is necessarily a number, which will be true if what Tom is talking about is a number, but is analytic, or (2) that Tom is necessarily talking about a number, which is false. Tom is not absolutely fixed on talking about root 2, even though root 2 is necessarily a number.

Earlier in this section I distinguished the necessity of propositions and other kinds of necessity. I held that one could know only empirically that things other than propositions possessed necessity. And even if certain propositions which have until recently been held to be contingent, turn out to be necessary, this does not seem to me to involve holding that there are some propositions that are known *a priori* that were hitherto thought to be capable of being known only *a posteriori*. Hence enlargements of the category of necessary propositions, even if such enlargements are valid and important 'metaphysically', are epistemologically irrelevant, and have no bearing upon the extent of our knowledge of the deity.

What I have said does not mean that God may not necessarily possess certain features (which does not entail that the propositions ascribing these features to him are necessarily true. The proposition asserting that if one revokes it is necessary to forfeit two tricks is not necessarily true). For example, it can be argued that God is a necessary being in the sense that there is no cause of his existence, or in the sense that it is on his existence that everything else depends, or in the sense that he cannot go in and out of existence. I doubt whether these are either senses of 'necessity' or sorts of necessity, but, whether or not God, if he exists, possesses them is a matter of what you regard as being perfections. If you do regard them as perfections, you will regard 'God' as possessing them. But if you do define 'God' so that he possess them, it will not follow that there is a being who possesses them, but only that, if no being does possess them, there is no God.

(viii)   Objection: The Falsity of Foundationalism Means that Empiricism is False[9]

Foundationalism is the view, which one would have supposed to be axiomatic, that knowledge has foundations. As Aristotle said, if we know something by inference, this must be because we know something else, from which we infer it (or by recourse to which we test it), without inference. To hold that we knew everything by inference would lead to an infinite vicious regress, for there would then be nothing suitable from which the propositions that we do know by inference could be inferred. One cannot legitimately infer A from B from C, and then C from A. If the foundations in question are known empirically, which is usually, but wrongly, taken for granted, then foundationalism is an empiricist view. I shall attempt to answer what seem to me to be some of the most important objections to foundationalism.

(a) Alvin Plantinga has said that 'beliefs are properly basic if the subject is justified in holding them even if not supported by other beliefs'. But this is not what a basic belief is. For a belief to be basic it is not enough for it *not* to be supported by other beliefs. It must, over and above this, be supported by something, even if what supports it is not a belief.

A basic empirical belief is in fact one that is supported by inspection, or by acquaintance with what it describes. For example, our belief that we are in pain is a basic belief because we are acquainted with the pain, inspection of which pain is what justifies us in holding that we are in pain. Our belief is confronted, so to speak, with our pain, which is how we know that we are in pain. We do not need to infer that we are in pain from anything else, though others will have to infer or postulate that we are in pain from such things as our words or our groans. Some philosophers hold that such beliefs are *a priori*, because they confuse being non-inferential with being *a priori*. But even if all *a priori* beliefs were non-inferential, not all non-inferential beliefs would be *a priori*. Such beliefs may have been thought to be *a priori* by philosophers who denied (wrongly) the existence of introspection, by means of which we know empirically such things as that we are in pain. Not every basic proposition is known by introspection. E.g., that there is a silver crescent-shaped patch of colour in the middle of my visual field is not known by introspection, as the patch is probably not a mental entity, and probably not a physical one either. There is no reason why the division of things into mental and physical things should be exhaustive.

A basic *a priori* belief is one that is known by the person who knows it because it is self-evident to him. The fact that a belief is self-evident to Tom does not mean that it cannot also be deduced from other beliefs, which may or may not be self-evident. It merely means that Tom does not have to have recourse to these other beliefs in order to know the self-evident belief in question. (In *Principia Mathematica*[10] there is a long proof of the self-evident truth that every proposition implies itself.) And the belief in question may not be self-evident to people other than Tom, and in that case they either do not know it at all, or, if they do, know it on the testimony of others to whom it is self-evident, or because they deduce it from something else which is self-evident to them.

(b) 'Foundationalism' is sometimes defined as the view that knowledge demands indubitable foundations, to which it is objected, wrongly, that nothing is indubitable. But having foundations does not mean having indubitable foundations; some are, others are not. Dubitable propositions can even produce certainty if there are enough of them, as enough sinkable pontoons can produce an unsinkable bridge if there are enough of them.

(c) It is often insisted that it is impossible to separate what is given from the interpretation thereof, but it is overlooked first that it is empirical information that is used to interpret the given, and secondly that if there were no given, there could be nothing to interpret.[11]

(d) Foundationalism may have been rejected because it has been supposed that it implies that there is a class of 'foundational' propositions, and there is no such class. But there is not any reason why what is a foundation relative to one person, time or place should not be 'superstructure' relative to another person at another time and at another place. For example, that I am thinking of philosophy is not something that I need to infer, but it is something that other people do need to infer. (That foundations are relative does not imply that truth is relative, and I do not think that truth is relative.)

(e) The fact that what we experience as the given would not be as it is but for our beliefs about it does not mean that it is not as it is or that it is not given. It means only that its nature is partly psychologically caused, a fact which is not surprising. For example that we see 'causal' and not, as we should (because that is what is there), 'casual' may be the result of our recollection that we wrote 'causal', but this does not mean that we do not see something exactly resembling what we would have seen if we had written 'causal'.

(f) There is no doubt that coherence with other propositions, as opposed to having foundations, does give support to a proposition, but it has to be coherent with other true propositions, and whether the propositions with which it coheres are true or not is an empirical matter. There is no regress involved in holding that that these proportions are themselves true can be further established by the fact that they cohere with yet other true propositions, for which there is empirical evidence, and so *ad infinitum*.

A proposition, to be accepted, must cohere with a web of beliefs, but with a web of beliefs for which there is evidence, and that there is evidence for these beliefs implies that there eventually are foundations.

(g) It has been held that I know that there are people other than myself – indeed, know that I myself exist – without having foundations for this belief. If this were so, there would be no reason why I should not hold that there is a God without having foundations for this belief, either. But obviously, I do have reasons for believing that there are other people. For example, my reasons (foundations) for thinking that there is another person who is in pain are hearing his cries and groans, seeing his bandaged cheeks and because there are what appear to be signs emanating from what appear to be his lips, the natural interpretation of which signs is that he is informing me that he is in pain.

(h) It has been held that we know that Australia exists without there being foundations to this belief. At any rate, it is said, there is very little evidence for the existence of Australia, much less than is necessary to justify us in holding it with the conviction we do. But there is in fact an enormous amount of evidence for the existence of Australia, if one consider one's web of beliefs, and the beliefs that would be displaced if one were to give up the belief that Australia exists. That I would have to revise a belief for which there is evidence by giving up my belief that Australia exists is a reason for believing that Australia exists. My evidence for the beliefs I would have to give up if Australia did not exist is indirect evidence for the belief that Australia exists.

I believe that Australia exists because if it did not exist an enormous disruption would take place to other things I believe. It is not consistent to say that one believes without evidence that Australia exists because of the disruption rejecting it would cause to our other beliefs. For if it disrupts beliefs for which there is no evidence, this is all to the good, and if it disrupts beliefs for which there is evidence, the evidence for them is indirect evidence for the existence of Australia.

(i) It has been argued that foundationalism is self-refuting, because belief in foundationalism has itself no foundations.

A similar argument has been advanced against the verification principle, to the effect that the doctrine that all meaningful sentences express propositions that are either empirically verifiable or tautologies is itself neither empirically verifiable nor tautologous. I think that the answer to this objection, which answer the verificationists themselves did not make, though they ought to have done, should have been that the verificationist principle is in fact a tautology. It is known to be true by careful analysis of the notion of meaning. This reply would have to be coupled with the explanation that what the verificationists called tautologies were not tautologies in a derogatory sense, and could give new information; the whole of mathematics and logic was classed by the verificationists as tautologous, on the grounds that mathematical and logical propositions could not be denied without contradiction, but mathematics and logic certainly give one new information. With this went a whole view of philosophy, according to which philosophical statements, since philosophers are not fitted to deal with matters for which empirical evidence is appropriate, are all a kind of tautology – if one may again use the word in a way that is not derogatory – tautologies which explore the consequences of the concepts that are most fundamental and all-pervading in our life and thought.

But if the verification principle would, if true, be a tautology, then, by parallel reasoning, foundationalism does not need any foundations. It is self-evident, in a sense of 'self-evident' that what can be seen to be true without proof is self-evident, however difficult it is to grasp. Foundationalism does not need foundations, because in fact it is an *a priori* doctrine about how propositions are known to be true, and so is as much a self-evident proposition as the more elementary proposition that if someone knows something, the proposition that he knows must be true.

(j) Many beliefs that are put down as beliefs without foundations are in fact beliefs which we remember. I might be hard put to it to produce reasons for the proposition that the Earth is round, or that the Battle of Hastings was fought in 1066, but in fact I know these things because I have been told them and have not forgotten what I have been told. However, if I believe something on account of memory of what I have been told, I must believe that the person who told me must have had some reason for believing what he told me. I can also remember things that I myself discovered, and have forgotten the reasons for, or remember having thought or done or otherwise experienced things in the past. Things which I believe because I remember them are usually reinforced by other beliefs, though I usually would not be justified in relying on the beliefs that reinforce them were it not that I also remember them. Things that I remember could be classified as beliefs for which I have no reasons, for remembering something is not a matter of inferring it from anything else. But, because the beliefs about the world that I remember must have been empirically acquired, memory is no exception to empiricism. If memory does not help the theologian, it is because I do not know that there is a God because I remember that there is one.

(k) A belief which must be accepted without evidence is not a belief which must be accepted without reason. We are justified in accepting without evidence that things which are each equal to a third thing are equal to one another, but this is not to accept it without reason. Our reason for accepting them is, in the case of *a priori* beliefs, that we can 'see' that they are true.

It has been held that we are justified in accepting without evidence that what is in front of our eyes is a book, because we can see that there is a book in front of our eyes. And it has been held that such things as that what looks like a book at least looks blue, has a word which looks like 'philosophy' on what seems to be its spine, that we have a headache and that we are thinking of our lunch, can be known without evidence. But it is not irrational to accept these things; we are *aware* of the book, the colour it looks, the word, the headache and the thought, and can read off, though not infallibly, their existence and their characteristics as a result of our being aware of them. Empiricist foundationalists have never held that all empirical beliefs are inferred; they have held that they are inferred from empirically known foundations because we are aware of the things about which we report.

(l) It has been supposed that foundationalism must be rejected because it implies the sense-datum theory, and the sense-datum theory is wrong. I shall discuss this objection later.

(m) It has been supposed that it is a basic belief that there are minds other than our own. But in fact we do have evidence that there are such minds, for we can infer it, as we have seen, from their owners' words, their behaviour, their appearance and the state of their owner's insides.

(n) The view that there are basic propositions is only to the point in the philosophy of religion if it could be held that that there was a God is itself a basic proposition. But it is not a proposition like those mentioned, which can be held because they are self-evident, or because we can 'read off' the truth of what they assert from acquaintance with what they are about, as we can 'read off' that something is red because we can see it. And that there is a God is not a basic proposition in the (incorrect) sense that rejecting it would cause us to reject a very large number of well-established beliefs. Indeed, I doubt whether rejecting it would necessitate the rejection of any well-established beliefs. What it would do is to cause some people to make very large emotional and practical adjustments to their lives; but this is a different matter.

(ix)   If Empiricism is True, There is a Barrier of Sense-Data or Sensa Between Us and the World

According to the sense-datum theory, we are not aware of material objects 'directly', but aware only of 'sense-data' or 'sensa' of that object. For example if I look at the sky, I am immediately aware only of a crescent-shaped sensum or impression of the moon, and if I hear an electric drill, I am immediately aware only of the noise the drill makes. It is supposed that, if so, sense-data impose a barrier between us and the world, so that I cannot know of the existence of the world, or perhaps even frame an idea of the possibility of its existence. If I am not aware of the moon, which is about 2,000 miles across, but only of a small crescent-shaped patch of colour, the moon itself might not exist, and it is, on a superficial view, difficult to see how we know anything about it. For the same reason, I cannot know of the existence of the bodies of other human beings, and still less what these human beings are thinking of.

But so far from sense-data imposing a barrier between me and the world, they are what reveal the world to me. I would not see the moon any better if I did not see a yellow shaped patch of colour when I looked at the sky. I would not see the moon at all. There is, indeed, no such thing as seeing the moon naked, unclothed with impressions. Seeing the moon is always, and of necessity, seeing sense-data of the moon, for example a yellow disc or silver crescent. And finding out things about, say, a house – to change the example because one cannot see the back of the moon – is always and of necessity always a bit-by-bit process. We see the front, then a side, then the back. Those who think we cannot work out that a house is a cubical object enclosing a three-dimensional region of space are assuming that our cognitive capacities are limited to inspecting what is in front of us. But if you allow also that in perception there is also involved memory, the ability to place different views of, say, a child's toy brick in such a way as to fit them together to enclose (in this case) a roughly cubical region of space, and the capacity to realise that past repetitions will repeat themselves, then it is perfectly possible to see how we can acquire the idea of a material object from viewing sense-data belonging to it successively.[12] We build up a 'picture' of the objects in our vicinity by repeating the process over and over again.

In any case, rejecting the sense-datum theory does not mean rejecting empiricism. For we are no better off if we accept an alternative to the sense-datum theory. For if there is not a veil of sense-data 'between' us and the things we see by their means, then there is a veil of appearance between us and them. If we see a red car that looks purple in a blue light, what we are directly aware of is a car looking purple; that it really is purple is something that has to be worked out from this; it is not something that is given. Its apparent colour, for example, hides its real colour much as the qualities of the object are supposed to be hidden behind sense-data of the object.

I suspect that many philosophers reject the sense-datum theory because they (wrongly) think that sense-data are something getting between us and the front surfaces of material objects. Even if there were nothing getting between us and the front surfaces of material objects, the sense-datum theory could still be true, but the front surfaces of material objects would then be sense-data. 'Sense-datum' and 'front surface of a material object' would in some cases be different descriptions of one and the same thing (assuming that 'front surface' means 'visible surface'). But this would be no help epistemologically, because the front surfaces of material objects would still get in the way of our perceiving them, so to speak. The front surface of a material object does not come with some such words as 'I am the front surface of a pillar box' written on it, and if it did, there would not necessarily be any reason to believe that it was telling the truth. It is still a matter of further investigation what lies behind its surface, how its front is related to its back and sides, and whether it is a front surface at all, and the epistemological problems this investigation raises are difficult ones.

(x)   Objection: Empiricism Presupposes the Sense-datum Theory; But Sense-data are Private Objects, and Wittgenstein has Shown that it is in Consequence Impossible to Talk about Them

I do not wish to spend much space or time on this objection, as I have discussed it at length elsewhere.[13] Suffice it to say here that there must be something wrong with Wittgenstein's arguments, despite the length of time during which it has been fashionable to accept them, because pain is obviously private, and we can talk about it. There is nothing surprising about our having knowledge of others' pains, though being able to inspect only our own, so long as we do not think that the cognitive capacities of the human mind are limited to inspection, in which case we could know nothing of other people's pains because these cannot be inspected by others. What I have said about pain applies, though less obviously, to sense-data.

We believe such things as that other people are in pain because that other people are in pain turns a partial regularity into a complete one.[14] We observe only a tiny part of the universe, and our only way of knowing about the parts we do not observe is for us to make the assumption that the unobserved part of it, including other people's sense-data in respect both of their nature and location, resembles the observed part. This assumption is an *a priori* beliefs, in that we need to have had it first and find out that it is true afterwards, but it is not *a priori* knowledge, because it is empirically confirmed as we find out that unobserved parts of the universe do resemble observed parts. If anyone objects that we cannot discover the empirically, because one cannot observe the unobserved parts, the reply is that one can observe the (hitherto) unobserved parts.[15] One is no more prevented from doing this than one is prevented from marrying unmarried men by the fact that if one marries one such, he is no longer unmarried. It is necessary to suppose that other people feel pain, etc., for otherwise a partial regularity between such events as tissue damage being followed by pain would not be completed, and would obtain only in one's own case.

Of course, observing reality does make a difference to it, but our knowledge that it does make such a difference itself presupposes that the unobserved resembles the unobserved. For example, it is because we believe that the effect of a warmer object on a cooler one is the same whether it is observed or not that we believe that observing an object cooler than ourselves by feeling it makes a difference to it, by increasing its temperature.

(xi)   Objection: Philosophers like Chomsky have Shown that there is a Great Deal of *A Priori* Knowledge of the World, or at Least of that Part of the World which Consists of Language

The discussion in this section draws upon what has been said about Chomsky in section (xii) in chapter 1. What philosophers like Chomsky have shown is that we have a large number of innate beliefs, rather than that we have innate knowledge. In the case of Chomsky, these are not so much beliefs about words – no Englishman has an innate knowledge of the fact that 'cauliflower' means cauliflower – so much as innate knowledge of the connections between the offices which this or that word – which word will depend on the language that is being used – may or may not fulfil. For example, that numbers cannot wield pickaxes is something we work out *a priori* from our knowledge of that which words for numbers stand for and that which words for implements stand for. We have, so to speak, a 'slot' in our mind which is responsible for our knowing how to use whatever words for a number our language has, but which word we actually use for that number is a matter of historical accident. And there are innate beliefs that are not about 'language'. For example, we have an innate belief that nature is uniform, and (what is not the same) that every event has a cause. I myself suspect that there are enormously many more innate beliefs, both about the behaviour of people and of inanimate objects, than is commonly recognised. I cannot explain in any other way how we adapt so readily to our environment.

But innate belief is not innate knowledge, and innate beliefs have to be shown to be knowledge, or replaced by knowledge, by being justified empirically in the usual way. To return to the example of every event's having a cause, though we have an innate belief that this is so, it only becomes knowledge, if it ever does, by being inductively supported in the usual way. (This is because all evidence for any inductive generalisation is *ipso facto* evidence for the proposition that every event has a cause.)

When it is objected – incorrectly, because to know something without evidence is not the same thing as to know it *a priori* – to empiricism that we must know some things without evidence in order to know other things with evidence, one answer is that, to the extent that this is true at all, we do not have to *know* these things without evidence; it is enough that a true belief in them should be innate. And we would not have survived otherwise.

(xii)   **Objection: Gödel has Proved that not all the Propositions in a Formal System can be Deduced from a Set of Axioms in the Same System**[16]

It does not follow, from what Gödel has proved, that the propositions that cannot be deduced are not analytic. There are many analytic propositions that cannot be proved; they cannot be deduced from other propositions that are known to be true. An example would be that vixens are female. The conception of being analytic and the conception of being provable are different conceptions. Even propositions that can be seen to be true and to be logically true can be sometimes deduced from other propositions known to be true, so their being true (and logically true) does not depend on their being shown to be true (and logically true).

Gödel thought that the axioms of mathematics could be known intuitively. I am inclined to agree that this is so, with certain kinds of axiom at any rate. But the fact that something is known intuitively does not mean that it is not logically true. Indeed, all logical truths (and all *a priori* truths, if there are any *a priori* truths that are not logical) could be known intuitively to a being with sufficient logical insight – say God. Denying that things that are equal to a third thing are equal to one another – one of Euclid's axioms – does seem to involve a contradiction.

It would have to be held that it is only axioms which, like Euclid's, are put forward as being true, that cannot, if they have rightly been put forward, be denied without contradiction. What might be termed 'experimental axioms' which are postulated for the purpose of exploring their consequences, or so-called axioms which lay down rules for the use of the symbols in the system that follows, do not have to be known to be true, and so it is no objection to empiricism that they are not logically true.

(xiii)   It is Not Possible to Deduce all Truths of Mathematics from Axioms of Logic

All this means is that it is not possible to show (in a certain kind of way, and on the (correct) assumption that anything that can be deduced from a logical truth is itself a logical truth) that all mathematical truths are logical truths. Showing this to be impossible does not show that they are *not* logical truths. Perhaps whole subclasses of mathematical truth can be shown to be logical truths, or perhaps they can be shown to be logical truth one by one. It is very difficult to believe, for example, that there is not a contradiction in supposing it to be false that 1+1=2, if '2' just means, as it would seem to mean, 'that number which you obtain by adding one to one'.

The attempt of logicists to define mathematical terms by means of logical terms may be a failure, as may be the attempt to deduce mathematics from logic. But it would not follow from the fact that mathematical terms could not be defined by means of logical ones that there was no logical contradiction in denying mathematical propositions. The words 'sun' and 'east' cannot be defined in logical terms, but this does not mean that that the sun rises in the east is not a logically true proposition, as it will be if 'east' means that quarter in which the sun rises.

Bertrand Russell thought that he had failed in his attempt, by defining numbers in terms of classes, to deduce mathematics from logic, when he discovered the paradox of the class of all classes that are not members of themselves. Since the class of cats is not a cat, there are some classes that are not members of themselves, and so there must be a class consisting of all these classes, viz. the class of all classes that are not members of themselves. But if the class of all classes that are not members of themselves is a member of itself, it follows that it is not a member of itself, because the class that it is a member of is precisely the class of all classes that are *not* members of themselves. On the other hand, if this class is not a member of itself, it follows that it is a member of itself, because the class that it is not a member of is the class of all classes that are *not* members of themselves.

But (a) if this shows anything, it shows that there is a contradiction in the notion of class, which there cannot really be, since we have used the notion of class from time immemorial without problems until philosophers began to reflect on it. (b) If this contradiction were genuine, it would not be created by the attempt to define number in terms of class. It would be there anyway. It may be that it can be removed by having a hierarchy of classes, or by saying that it does not make sense to say that a class is either a member of itself or not a member of itself, from which it follows that there is no such class as the class of classes that are not members of themselves. In any case, the breakdown of an attempt to show that mathematics can be reduced to logic by showing that it follows for certain logical axioms does not show that true mathematical propositions are not known to be true because it is logically contradictory to deny them. Many things that cannot be proved in a certain way are nevertheless true.

(xiv) Objection: Empiricism Gives Rise to 'Atomism', and 'Holism' Shows that Atomism is False[17]

The only kind of holism that is relevant to the question of whether we have any non-empirical way of discovering facts about a transcendent reality, and whether there is any non-empirical knowledge of facts about the world, is the kind of holism which holds that propositions do not stand or fall alone in the face of disconfirmatory evidence, but stand or fall together.

Two views are sometimes confused. There is (a) the view that contrary evidence means revising not just one proposition, but every other proposition in the corpus of scientific knowledge. There is also (b) the view that contrary evidence never eliminates just one proposition, but that it is also possible to revise some other proposition instead; for example that this substance turns blue litmus paper red does not necessarily mean revising the proposition that it is an acid; in principle it might be better to revise the proposition that acids turn blue litmus paper red, or some other proposition, such as that the experimenter was awake when he made the experiment. This second kind of holism is probably true, but does not entail that empiricism is false.

(a) The first doctrine is not true. That this substance does not turn blue litmus paper red may just possibly – though the possibility is remote – mean revising the scientific view that acids turn blue litmus paper red, but it surely does not mean revising views such as that the universe was once corrugated, or that at the time of the big bang its size was less than a centimetre.

This doctrine might be confused with another, which may well be true. It may well be true that for every true scientific proposition B, and for every piece of contrary evidence A, there is *some* set of true propositions which mean that if A is false, B must be false too. For example, this substance's not, as expected, turning blue litmus paper red might, together with some probably enormously large set of true scientific propositions, entail that the big bang did not occur, or not quite in the way it did. This view may be entailed by determinism, the view that for every proposition about the future, there is some set of true propositions which entail that it is true or false. The view is probably true, but does not entail that any of the true propositions in question are not known to be true empirically.

(b) Neither of these two doctrines entail that there are any views that do not stand or fall without empirical evidence. For if it were the case that one could not revise one's belief in one proposition without 'revising' all other propositions, the evidence that would make one need to revise them would still have to be empirical evidence.

There are some propositions in which our belief ought never to be revised. For example, our belief that two and two are four ought never to be revised. Philosophers like Quine sometimes, I think, suggest that they can be because they think that truth is a property of sentences rather than of the propositions that these sentences express. What one can do is to revise the sentence 'Two and two are four', say by changing the meaning of 'four' to 'five', which will make it express a falsehood rather than a fact. But this has no effect on the truth that two and two are four. It just means that, since the word 'four' can no longer be used for the number four, this fact will have to be expressed in different words. When Einstein proved that things simultaneous with a third thing were not necessarily simultaneous with one another, he was not so much setting aside the commonsense belief that they are, so much as redefining, for the purpose of doing physics, 'is simultaneous with' in a more useful way.

(xv)   Objection: Empiricism is Incompatible with the Coherence Theory of Truth, Which is True

It has been held that truth is not a matter of a proposition's corresponding to the facts, but of propositions cohering with other propositions. It may be objected that cohering with other propositions is not enough for truth, but that propositions, to be true, must cohere with other true propositions, which (a) makes the theory circular, and (b) makes it necessary to find out which propositions are true first, and consider whether other propositions cohere with the truth second.

In reply it can be held that one can find out which propositions are true *a priori* because there was only one way of combining propositions to constitute that conjunctive truth that would constitute a true description of the world. Propositions are like the parts of a puzzle all of which could be put together in only one way. But, though God might be able to fit them together correctly, it is absolutely obvious that, when one considers all the billions to the power of billions of propositions there are, and the many times more billions of ways in which they could be combined, man cannot do this. Hence, *faut de mieux*, we have to fall back on empirical investigation. In any case, truth is not a matter of a proposition's cohering with other propositions, but of things being as that proposition says they are.

(xvi)   Objection: All Relations are 'Internal', and so it is Possible to Work out the Nature of the Whole from Knowledge of its Parts

An internal relation is one that (logically) makes a difference to the nature of the things related by it, whether they stand in this relation to it or not. Marriage, for example, is an external relation because a man, so far as logic goes, is just the same in himself whether he stands in the relation of being married to a woman, though marriage, and the nature of the woman to whom he is married, may (causally) make a difference to him. I myself do not believe that there are any internal relations between concrete objects (as opposed to, say, numbers), so I cannot give an example. The doctrine of internal relations, however, is the doctrine that *all* relations are internal.[18]

It looks as if such propositions as that husbands must be married, are exceptions to this statement. However, that husbands are married does not mean that Tom, who is a husband, has to stand in the relation of marriage to anyone. All it means is that, if he did not stand in this relation to anyone, he would not be a husband.

It looks as if, if this doctrine were true, and if necessity went with *a priority*, we could work out *a priori* everything about the rest of the universe from sufficient knowledge of any of its parts. This is because everything is related in some way to everything else, and so a change in the nature of anything in the universe will, if the doctrine of internal relations is true, make a difference to the universe itself and everything else in it.

But even if the doctrine of internal relations were true, we would still have to know empirically the nature of the parts. That is to say, even if we knew *a priori* the hypothetical proposition that if the parts were such-and-such, the whole would have to be so-and-so, we would still have to fall back on empirical knowledge of the fact that the parts were such-and-such.

However, the doctrine of internal relations is not true. It has been refuted by G.E. Moore in a undeservedly (now) neglected paper.[19] I shall put the matter, however, in my own way. That the doctrine of internal relations has been supposed to be true is the result of a modal mistake. It is true that, if a thing (A) stands in a relation to another thing (B) of a certain nature, then anything which does not stand in that relation to a thing of that nature cannot be A. But this does not mean that A necessarily stands in that relation to a thing of that nature. To suppose otherwise is to confuse two contentions. (a) It is necessarily the case that, if A stands in a certain relation to a thing of a certain nature, anything that does not stand in that relation to a thing of that nature is not A. (b) If A stands in a certain relation to a thing of a certain nature then, necessarily, anything that does not stand in that relation to a thing of that nature is not A.[20] The word 'necessarily' governs two quite different propositions in these two sentences. From (b) but not from (a), it follows that A necessarily stands in the relation in question to a thing of this nature.

It might follow from (b) that it is possible to work out from a knowledge of the nature of A everything about the nature of the things to which it is related, but (b) is not true. (b) only seems to be true because it is confused with (a), which is true, but this does not imply that it is possible to work this out. To take an example, if the cat is on the blue Persian mat, then, necessarily, anything that is not on a blue Persian mat is not that cat, but this does not mean that the cat is necessarily on the mat. The poor animal is quite capable of going somewhere else if it wants.

A great deal of the interest goes out of the view that all relations are internal if, as is common these days, necessity is divorced from *a priority*. If a thing necessarily stood in all the relations it did to the kinds of thing it did, and this implied that one could work out *a priori* everything about its relations and the nature of things it stood in these relations to, the doctrine of internal relations would be of enormous importance. But if necessity does not go with *a priority*, it has relatively little interest (but is nevertheless mistaken).

When one says that if one knows everything about the parts, it is possible to know everything about the whole, this doctrine is trivial if knowing everything about the parts includes knowing its relations to the whole, and the nature of the whole to which it is related. Otherwise it is false.

(xvii)   Objection: Empiricism Relies on Induction, and Karl Popper has Refuted the Claim of Science to be Based on Induction

Empiricism does not rely exclusively on induction. If I know by induction that all crows are black, it is not by induction that I know that this, that and the other crow is black. I see that they are. In any case, in order to explain our present knowledge of the world, induction has to be supplemented by memory, the testimony of others, perception and introspection at the very least.

Popper held that scientific hypotheses were not established by induction, but by being subjected to severe tests, which eliminated all but the best of them. But eliminating theories does not show that the theories not eliminated are true. If one of five men might be the murderer, eliminating one increases – given certain empirically justified assumptions concerning, say, the velocity of trains – the chances of one of the remaining four being he, and eliminating four demonstrates that the fifth is he. But that eliminating one scientific theory should increase the chances of the remaining theories being true presupposes that there is a finite number of possible theories.

It is not a necessary truth that there is as much as one true theory. Even if there is a finite number of possible theories, Popper's method presupposes that a theory once refuted in certain circumstances will go on leading to a false result in those circumstances, and for this we need to rely on induction. It is just an empirical fact that being refuted is not good for hypotheses. Indeed, there would have to be a relatively small number of possible hypotheses for eliminating the others to increase by very much the chances of one of the remaining hypotheses being true, and that there is only a limited number of hypotheses is established empirically. There would be no point in eliminating hypotheses for the sake of eliminating them. Eliminating them must also increase the chances of one of the others being true.

(xviii)   Objection: Empiricism Leads to Scepticism

It has been held that empiricism leads to scepticism. It is argued that since every empirical contingent proposition might be false, and what is known must be true, no empirical contingent propositions can be known.

This argument, however, also involves a modal shift fallacy. What must be true is the proposition that if something is known to be true, then it must be true. It does not follow from this that the proposition that is known must be true. For example, from the fact, that necessarily, if Tom knows that his name is 'Tom' his name must be 'Tom', it does not follow that his name must necessarily be 'Tom'.[21] Hence it does not follow from the fact that his name does not have to be 'Tom', which is a contingent fact known empirically, that he cannot know that his name is 'Tom'. Quite obviously, Tom does know this and many other similar things empirically.

(xix)   Objection: Empiricism is Incompatible with the (Correct) Doctrine that there are Real Essences[22]

My remarks about the impossibility of rational theology do not need to be revised in the light of certain modern views about essences. According to these views, natural kinds have real essences, which fact is a different fact from the fact that the words describing them have certain definitions. For example, it may follow from the definition of chalk that it dissolves in sulphuric acid, and not follow from its definition that it is suspendible in water. Nevertheless, it both necessarily dissolves in sulphuric acid and is necessarily suspendible in water, because these are both part of its essence. (It would be necessarily soluble in sulphuric acid, however it was defined.) It is not, however, part of its essence that it is used on blackboards or to chalk billiard cues.

This raises the question of whether God himself has a real essence. If there were such things as essences, it may well be that God, besides being, say, omniscient by definition, is also necessarily and essentially omniscient in some other way. I do not, however, propose to attempt to answer the question whether he is so or not. For though, if God has a real essence, certain of his attributes may be possessed necessarily in spite of the fact that he does not possess them by definition, the fact that God has a real essence would not involve any alteration to empiricist views about what man's cognitive capacities are. For whether things have real essences or not – and I am inclined to think that they do not – we discover *empirically* that these things have the properties that they (necessarily) have, whether these properties are part of their essence or not. It is only necessarily *true* propositions that have to be *a priori*; and chalk's necessarily possessing the property of dissolving in sulphuric acid does not mean that the proposition that it necessarily possesses this property is necessarily true. Indeed, the proposition that chalk necessarily dissolves in sulphuric acid is not necessarily true.

Furthermore, if it is a fact, as we shall see later that it is, that the *existence* of something cannot be part of its essence, then, even if the doctrine of real essences did give us an extension to our knowledge, the facts it would give us would all be hypothetical ones about what would be true of God, if he existed. (One cannot deduce from the fact that it is part of the nature of chalk to dissolve in sulphuric acid that there is such a thing as chalk. Such knowledge would have to be empirical.)

Any criticism of empiricism has to bear in mind the following fact. It is just a 'brute', contingent fact that I exist, that the Battle of Hastings occurred, that the Earth is round, and that Christ was crucified. (Their being empirical contingent facts, of course, does not exclude their having causal explanations.) The question then arises: 'Does the existence of God make any difference to anything that happens in the world'? Either it does or it does not. If it does, no *a priori* proof can be given of God's existence, for no *a priori* proof can be given of the existence of anything which entails a contingent proposition such as that I exist. If it does not, then there is a sense in which the existence of God can have no application to the exigencies of day to day life. For empirical propositions such as that virtue is rewarded, that a person survives the death of his body, that miracles occur and that petitionary prayer is answered cannot be deduced from the presumably necessary existence of the kind of god of whose existence an *a priori* proof can be given.

I myself do not think that there are any real essences. There is just (a) the empirical fact that certain characteristics – those of iron or duck-billed platypuses, for example – go together in clusters, (b) that it is sometimes empirically impossible to separate the elements in the cluster, which means that these elements necessarily go together, and (c) the fact that certain superficial characters of things, like the colour of crows, are the result of other characteristics more fundamental, like their genetic structure, from a knowledge of which latter the former may be deduced.

(xx) Objection: Empiricism Cannot give an Account of Memory and Testimony[23]

An empiricist does not need to give an account of memory, because memory (or one kind of memory) is just a way of holding on to information that has been acquired in some other way, which way may be empirical. (Another kind of memory is knowing things by heart, for example, knowing 'The boy stood on the burning deck'. This involves no exception to empiricism, because empiricism is a doctrine about knowledge of truth, and what we know in this case is not a truth. We can also remember Mary or our way or a place or poem or tune, but these are not truths either.) But that we remember a proposition is not an 'ultimate' justification of it, for this presupposes that we first of all knew it, and how we know it is something that the epistemologist is entitled to enquire into. If empiricism is right, if what we remember is a fact about the world rather than something like a mathematical truth, we can have come to know it in the first place only empirically.

The same is true of testimony. If I accept something on someone else's testimony I must suppose that he himself found out what he claims to know in some reliable way. If empiricism is true, and his claim is one about the nature of the world, this means that he must have discovered by observation what he claims to know, or that it is a hypothesis that is supported by observation. If he has been told by someone else, the same question arises about him.

Memory and testimony are partly accepted because what we remember or are told coheres with other facts about the world. For example, I distrust my memory of where I left my spectacles if they are not where I seem to remember them, or if my memory does not accord with the testimony of others. But the facts with which the deliverances of memory and testimony have to cohere are empirical ones.

(xxi)   Objection: Wittgenstein has Shown that there are Many Functions of Language other than that of Describing the World

It is true that there are many functions of language other than that of describing the world. For example, we use language to give orders, to make promises, to enter into contracts, to worship and to pray. But it is immaterial to epistemology that this is so, because epistemologists are concerned only with how we know things, and, if – as is the case – these other functions of language are not to state what we know, for they then embody no knowledge about which the epistemologist need concern himself. For example, since to give an order or offer up a prayer is not to state anything true or false, there are no truths embodied in orders, and so there can be no epistemology of orders. (Things like prayers and orders *presuppose* truths – as the prayer 'Our father, which art in heaven' presupposes that we have a father who is in heaven, but that is another matter.)

Commands, prayers, etc. may presuppose facts about the world, such as, in the case of commands, that the commander has power or authority over the person commanded, or, in the case of prayers, that the person prayed to has the power to give one what one prays for, but whether these presuppositions are true or not can usually only be ascertained empirically. (There may be certain commands, for example, 'Square the circle', which presuppose a logical or mathematical truth or, as in this case, a falsehood. In any case, in a manner which I shall explain in a later chapter (chapter 6), the nonpropositional use of language involved in such things as worship is parasitic upon the propositional use, which latter only is of concern to the epistemologist.)

(xxii)   Objection: if Empiricism were True, all Existential Propositions Would be Contingent, Which They are Not

All propositions about what the world contains are contingent. But there is a large number of propositions about the existence of abstract entities; such propositions are often *a priori*, but do not tell you anything about the world.

I suspect that there is a subject, which might be called ontology, which tells you about the kinds of things there might possibly be. For example, there are classes, universals, numbers, spaces, times, quadratic equations, square roots, geodesics, novels, symphonies, dances, impulses, axes, influenza epidemics, hurricanes, democracy, and so on through an enormously long list.

There is a peculiar question which philosophers have spent an inordinate amount of time discussing over certain members of the list, viz., whether there are such things. Whether there are such things or not has to be settled in the manner appropriate to the nature of the thing in question. For example, if the question is whether there is a prime number between seven and 11, the question can be settled by finding out whether any number between seven and 11 can be divided by any number other than itself and one. But, after it has been worked out that there is such a number, there is no *further* question, whether this number *exists*. To say that there is no such number is to say, falsely, that no number between seven and 11 is so divisible. To take another example, there is the question whether any two or more things have anything in common, and this question is settled conclusively in the affirmative when it is reflected that there are at least two red things, which entails that they have redness in common. But philosophers write as if there were some further question, which they are fond of discussing, the question whether redness exists. And this question, if the existence of redness is not settled by the fact that A is red and B is red, does not make sense. Having a characteristic in common is not like sharing a car, when there is an entity which two people jointly own. Some questions about abstract objects are empirical, others are not. For example, it is an empirical question whether there are any ways of getting out of a strait-jacket; an *a priori* one whether there is a way of solving the four-colour problem

(xxiii)   Objection: There is *A Priori* Knowledge of Mathematics and Logic, of which Empiricism can give no Account

John Stuart Mill is the only empiricist to have thought that *all* knowledge was empirical.[24] Hume, considered to be the arch-empiricist, divided knowledge into knowledge of matters of fact and of the relation between ideas, and thought that only the latter was empirical. All other empiricists have thought that there was *a priori* knowledge of logic and mathematics, and also of a heterogeneous collection of other propositions such as that nothing can be red and blue all over.

Hence there is what might be called weak and strong empiricism. A strong empiricist thinks that all knowledge is empirical knowledge. (Thus John Stuart Mill was probably the only strong empiricist.) A weak empiricist thinks that only knowledge of nature, or of the way the world goes, need be empirical. We have seen that knowledge of God must be empirical if it is to entail anything about the way the world goes.

Nonempirical knowledge is knowledge, but is not knowledge of the world. That two and two is four tells you nothing about the world, and would be true even if the world did not exist. This is true because all nonempirical knowledge is hypothetical. It does not tell you anything about the world, but only that if one thing is true of the world, something else must be also. Some *a priori* propositions look categorical, but they can be seen to be hypothetical when more perspicuously stated. For example, that two beans and another two beans make four beans does not tell you how many beans there are, but only that if there are two groups of two beans, then there must be a group of four beans. (We understand such words as 'two' and 'plus' and 'four' by being taught how to correlate these words with the world, for example with groups of beans.[25]) This fact shows that 'two' and 'plus' are not *a priori* ideas.

Hence we must distinguish between finding out things about the world and deducing consequences from hypotheses about the world. The proposition that a hypothesis has certain consequences need not be an empirical proposition, but that its consequences are true or false is empirical. (The fact that if the consequences are false the hypothesis must be rejected is also not empirical.) It has been said that framing a hypothesis is not a matter of empirical knowledge, but framing a hypothesis is not a matter of knowledge at all, empirical or *a priori*.

All categorical propositions about the world are empirical, even if hypothetical propositions telling you what are the consequences of statements about the world need not be. More generally, statements about the relations between different empirical statements about the world need not themselves be empirical statements. Hence, even if no logicist account can be given of the whole of mathematics, this fact need not worry an empiricist of the sort I have defined, whom I believe to be the ordinary sort of empiricist, for all such propositions are hypothetical. It would be nice, however, if all propositions other than statements about the world could be shown to be such that it would be contradictory to deny them. But I do not have the knowledge or the ability to do this myself.

(xxiv)   Objection: The Proposition, that all Propositions about the World can be Empirically Verified, Itself Cannot be Empirically Verified

This, as we have seen, is so; but it does not matter, because, if true, weak empiricism is analytically or conceptually true, and so does not need to be empirically verified. (It would be an objection to what I have called 'strong empiricism', but it is not an objection to 'weak empiricism', because weak empiricism is not a claim about the world, but about our knowledge of the world, and because weak empiricists do not think that all knowledge is empirical, but only that knowledge of the world is.) We see that empiricism must be true by reflecting on the concept of knowledge, and the ways in which it can be acquired. It does not just so happen to be true, but is true of necessity. To show that it is true, to the extent of defending it against objections, can be regarded as one of the objects of this chapter.

The claim that empiricism does not need to be justified empirically resembles the claims, whether true or not, that induction does not need to be justified inductively, that the verification principle does not itself have to be verified, and the belief in foundationalism needs no foundations. There is very likely nothing wrong with any of these beliefs. In particular, the verificationists held that all meaningful sentences were either empirical or 'tautologous', so they were perfectly at liberty to hold that, since the verification principle arises from a careful analysis of the notion of meaning, it is in a non-derogatory sense tautologous.

(xxv)   Empiricism and Proper Names

It may well be that statements ascribing some attribute to a thing by referring to it by a proper name are all synthetic (see chapter 1). It involves no objection to empiricism that this should be so, provided all such statements are empirical, which I think they are.

There are two extremely obscure interrelated problems discussed by modern philosophers concerning (a) how much a thing may change and still remain the thing it was, and (b) which of its attributes a thing has necessarily and which it does not. For example, it can be argued that Tom might change by ceasing to have red hair, but not to the extent of becoming an ape, and that, though he does not necessarily have pimples, he does necessarily have the parents he has.

I suspect that it makes no difference to empiricism whether there are any necessary attributes, or which one thinks they are. All that follows, if there are some things we know about John Stuart Mill that are necessarily true, is that there are some necessary truths that have to be known empirically. (I doubt whether there are such necessary truths, but this is because I think that the alleged necessary truths are not necessary, not because I think they are not empirical.)

It seems obvious that, whether or not it is a necessary truth that John Stuart Mill was not born in the eighteenth century, that he was not born in the eighteenth century is a fact discovered empirically – as a first step, by looking it up in a book and finding that he was born in the nineteenth century. Of course, if one knows that he was born in the nineteenth century, one can infer from this that he was not born in the eighteenth, but the proposition that if he was born in the nineteenth century, he was not born in the eighteenth, though necessary, is also a logical truth. It does not follow from the fact that it is a necessary truth that if John Stuart Mill was born in the nineteenth century, he was not born in the eighteenth, that that he was not born in the eighteenth century is a necessary truth.

It looks as if the fact that Ulysses could not have changed into a fox is, if it is necessarily true, something that we could know *a priori*. But in fact Ulysses's inability to change into a fox provides no limitation on what may happen. It does not alter the fact that states that were clearly states of Ulysses might be followed by a series of states all resembling states of Ulysses less and less, and resembling states of a fox more and more, until eventually they get replaced by states which are unequivocally states of a fox. It is just a question of whether the fox is identical with Ulysses, which I suspect is not a 'real' question. There are just as many possible states of the world whether one says that the fox is Ulysses or whether one does not. (I have made the point in chapter 1 that I do not think it makes any difference whether proper names are described as rigid designators.)

(xxvi)   Philosophy is Itself not an Empirical Subject

Philosophers are not known for the assiduity with which they investigate the world. They do not, like physicists and other scientists, make experiments. They do not travel to find out about parts of the world that have not been visited. They do not, like astronomers, look at the cosmos through telescopes. They do not, like botanists and geologists, collect specimens of plants or rocks. They do not, like historians, examine documents mouldering in archives, or like archaeologists, dig up remains. They sit in their armchairs, and think about the information brought to light by the people who do these things.

Hence philosophy must be an *a priori* discipline. It cannot, or cannot by itself, establish any facts about the world, including facts about words, which are just as much empirical facts as any others. It does not follow from this that it does not concern itself with empirical facts, or even that its *raison d'être* is not to aid in discovering the nature of the universe. What does follow is that it is the handmaid, not of science, but of empirical investigation. (It is also to some extent the handmaid of mathematics and logic, although these are not empirical.)

This leaves for philosophy a number of *a priori* functions, which establish conclusions that are both interesting in themselves, and, indirectly, have a bearing upon the conclusions that we come to about the nature of reality. These functions are 'logical geography', or informal logic, which consists in establishing the logical relations between certain propositions, embodying more fundamental and all-pervasive concepts, and certain other propositions. A very simple example would be the proposition that if anyone knows something, what he knows must be true. This is not a matter of investigating the use of words. It is the fact that the proposition that is expressed by the sentence 'Smith knows that it is Tuesday' that entails the proposition that is expressed by the sentence 'It is true that today is Tuesday', not the fact that it is these sentences that express these propositions. (Hence the same fact can be expressed in a language other than English, if it has the appropriate words in which to express them.)

Philosophy has also the *a priori* function of trying to synthesise the views of the world presented by academic subjects which apportion the world among them without leaving any space for philosophy, and of trying to reconcile when the conclusions of the different sciences look incompatible, as they often do.

Philosophy also includes epistemology; that is, that subject whose function it is to find out how the other scientists that investigate the world find out what they claim to know. To a large extent I think that epistemology has to take the scientists' word for it that they do know the things they claim to know, and perhaps also that they find these things out in the way they claim to find them out. But it has to do this only to some extent, for scientists sometimes say the most surprising things. It might be that it is better for a philosopher to study what scientists do, rather than what they say they do. And some philosophers might themselves be sufficiently good at science to have sensible opinions about its methods. Furthermore, philosophy deals with the epistemology of everyday knowledge, on which knowledge there are no experts, of which scientific knowledge is an extension. Epistemology, too, is an *a priori* subject.

There is also ontology, which is another *a priori* subject. Ontology, despite its name, does not aim to tell you what the world contains. It is the function of the geologist to tell you that there are igneous rocks, of the zoologists to tell you that there are no longer dodos, and of the astronomer to tell you that there are black holes. The function of ontology is to tell you not so much what reality contains, as to investigate the structure, if there is one, that all possible realities have. For example, there are individuals, the properties of individuals, classes of individuals, the events that happen to individuals, the numbers of groups of individuals, the dates of the events that happen to individuals, the relations in which individuals stand to other individuals, and so on. The recent science of mereology, which deals with the relationship between parts and wholes, is also an *a priori* subject.[25]

One of the most important functions of philosophy is to refute bad philosophy, which is not produced only by philosophers. Showing what is wrong with arguments that have already been produced is an *a priori* matter (though the fact that these arguments have been produced is empirical and contingent).

Theology is in the same boat as philosophy, insofar as it tries to establish, *a priori*, facts about the existence of a transcendent being. It may be better off than philosophy to the extent that it at least claims to have certain empirical facts that are evidence for the existence of such a being.

(xxvii) Conclusions

We can have only empirical knowledge of the existence and nature of the world.

If God is a personal being who loves us, takes decisions, has plans, feels anger or love, and whose existence has empirical consequences for the world, then his existence can be known only empirically. If he is impersonal, something more like an abstraction, then propositions about him might be capable of being known in an other-than-empirical manner, but he will not be a being who has plans, takes decisions, or is capable of feeling love or anger, or of affecting what happens in the world.

In practice Christian theologians have wavered between the two ideas of God. They have retreated to the latter, esoteric metaphysical one when they wished to claim *a priori* metaphysical knowledge of his existence and attributes. They have relied on the former when they wished to think or represent God as a being with whom one could have a relationship, a being who cared about us, whose providence guided the world and who answered petitionary prayer. But, even with the aid of the doctrine of analogy discussed in the chapter 1, it is impossible to have it both ways. For example, sometimes Christian theologians say that God is love, or existence, or omniscience. (These things, I suspect, are implied by the extremely difficult doctrine that there is no distinction in God between his essence and his existence.) At other times they say that he loves, that he exists, or that he is omniscient. The latter means that he is a person, but that whether or not he exists is an empirical matter. The latter, taken literally, means that God's existence is a matter of *a priori* ratiocination, but that he is an abstraction, incapable of making plans or entering into relationships with people. One can enter into a relationship with an existing being, but not with existence. One can love a loving being, but only in a manner of speaking can one love love. (One can be awed by an awesome being, but one cannot literally be in awe of the abstraction, awe.)

Hence the existence of a personal God can be known only empirically. (I shall consider later to what extent an impersonal God might satisfy the aspirations which have led men to believe in God, and to what extent attitudes to a personal god other than belief (faith) may be justified.)

Notes

1 I have discussed this matter in more detail in 'The Trouble with Tarski, or sentences and Propositions, Pragmatic Contradiction, Analyticity, Linguistic Relativism, Conventionalism, "convention" T and More', forthcoming in *The Philosophical Quarterly*.
2 The point is made in Wittgenstein's *Tractatus Logico-Philosophicus*, though there Wittgenstein appeared to think that all *a priori* knowledge was of this kind.
3 As does Wittgenstein, 1961.
4 For example, in Ayer, 1947.

5   In 1977, especially chapters 13 and 14.
6   By Quine,1960, pp. 195 f.
7   See *ibid.*
8   For a defence of this view, see Swinburne, 1977 chapter XIII.
9   In writing this section I have benefited from listening to Paul Helm's as yet unpublished Stanton Lectures, delivered to the University of Cambridge in 1996. Many of the arguments here discussed are to be found in Plantinga, 1967.
10 By Russell and Whitehead, 1910–13.
11 An attack on the 'myth' of the given is to be found in Sellars, 1963, section 2–4. The myth was defended from earlier criticisms by Price, 1932, chapter I.
12 The best account I know of how this is done is to be found in Price, 1932. See also Broad, 1923, and 1925.
13 Mostly in 'Science, Souls and Sense-data', in Harrison, 1993.
14 I have made out the case for this more fully in 'The Russell/Leibniz Theory of Perception', 1995.
15 The point is argued in more detail in 'Henry Habberley Price, 1899–1984', *Proceedings of the British Academy: 1991 Lectures and Memoirs*, Vol. 80, reprinted in Harrison, 1995,Vol. I.
16 The reader is referred to Gödel, 1986–95.
17 The reader is referred to Fodor, 1987.
18 Whether two things stand in the relation of being similar to one another logically depends on their natures, or what they are like. One would have supposed that whether they stood in the relation of being next to one another did not logically depend upon what they were like.
19 In 'External and Internal Relations', 1919–20; reprinted in 1922.
20 The difference is between (a) L((aRb->(-cRb->-(c=a)) and (b) (aRb)->(-cRb->(L-(c=a)). (a) is true but not important. (b) would be of earth-shattering importance if it were true, but it is not.
21 From: necessarily (if I know my name is Harrison, my name is Harrison) it does not follow that: (if I know my name is Harrison, then, necessarily my name is Harrison). L(aKp->p) is true, but aKp->Lp is false.
22 For further discussion the reader is referred to Schwartz, 1977.
23 Anthony Kenny, in 'Mystical Experience, St. John of the Cross', *Reason and Religion*, Blackwell 1987, p. 96, says that empiricist philosophers cannot give an account of how I know my own name or tie my bootlaces. Knowing how to tie one's bootlaces is not a matter of possessing knowledge, so there is no need for an empiricist to give an account of it. And it is rather obvious that knowing the date of the Battle of Hastings is not *a priori*.
24 See Mill, 1973–4.
25 Some mathematical philosophers appear to think that numbers are defined by something like Peano's axioms. But without correlating words for numbers and words for operations with beans and the process of adding and subtracting them, the words in the axioms would not mean anything, and '0' for example could have indifferently interpreted as meaning 0 or one or 1,000 and the sentences formed express something true, though not the same truth as they express if '0' is taken to mean 0, and so on.

PART II
ARGUMENTS FOR THE
EXISTENCE OF GOD

4   The Ontological Argument

(i)   Kant's Classification of Arguments for the Existence of God

Immanuel Kant[1] divided arguments for the existence of God into three kinds. (1) There is the ontological argument, which has no empirical premises at all. The ontological argument reasons to the existence of God wholly *a priori* from a consideration of the bare idea of God. (2) There is the cosmological argument, which starts from the highly unspecific empirical premise that something or other exists or that something or other is happening. (In the latter case something other than an event must exist for what is happening to happen.) The cosmological argument (unlike the argument from design) is not concerned with the nature of what exists, or the nature of what is happening. It argues from the mere existence of a cosmos, however rudimentary this cosmos may be. (3) There is what Kant, barbarously, called the 'physico-theological' argument (but which is usually called the argument from design, or the argument to design, and might be called the argument to design from the appearance of design). This argument proceeds to the existence of God not from the mere existence of the world, or from the fact that something or other is happening, but from a more detailed (though not very detailed) consideration of the actual nature of what exists or what is happening.

There are, however, other arguments for the existence of God, some of which I shall consider in due course.

(ii)   Introduction to the Ontological Argument

The subject of the ontological argument is vast, and I shall have space only to scratch its surface, though I believe that the most fundamental problems concerning it are here adequately discussed. The ontological argument is an attempt to overcome the limitation, explained in the preceding chapter, on what may properly be accomplished by logic. If the word 'God' includes omniscience as part of its meaning, then the sentence 'God is omniscient' will express a proposition that it is self-contradictory to deny. This will be

107

precisely similar to the fact that, since 'vixen' includes being female as part of its meaning, the proposition that vixens are female will be one that it is self-contradictory to deny.

If so, why can one not maintain that the word 'God' includes *existence* as part of its meaning? If it did, the sentence 'God exists' would also express a truth that it would be self-contradictory to deny. If its meaning does not already include existence, why can it not be made to do this by stipulatively defining the word 'God' so that it does include it?

The ontological argument holds that the word 'God' does in fact connote existence among other things, and so holds that the proposition that God exists is true by definition. That God exists could then not be denied without contradiction. God cannot be anything other than existent, because our concept of the 'predicate', existing, is just part of our concept of the subject, God. If this were so, rational theology would not be limited to deducing the logical consequences of the supposition that there is a God, without its being able to tell you whether or not this supposition is true. Doing rational theology would entitle us to assert that God actually existed.

(iii)   Anselm's Version of the Ontological Argument

Anselm, in *Proslogion*,[2] argues that our concept of God is the concept of a being greater than which nothing can be conceived. What one would be maintaining, if one held that God did not exist, would then be that a being greater than which nothing could be conceived, existed only in the understanding. But a being who existed both in the understanding and in reality would be greater than a being who existed in the understanding alone. If God existed in the understanding alone, it would be possible for there to be a being greater than he. Since the idea of a being greater than God is contradictory, God cannot exist in the understanding alone, and so must exist both in understanding and in reality.

It is a mildly interesting question whether a God who existed in the understanding and in reality would be greater than one who existed in reality without existing in the understanding. If so, it would follow (implausibly) that if there were a God, he would necessarily be thought about (for that is what it means to be in the understanding), as well as that he necessarily exists. But that God is necessarily thought about is palpably untrue. (J.L. Mackie has argued[3] that Anselm himself makes the same mistake as the fool, for it follows from what Anselm has himself said that God cannot exist in the understanding, and so cannot exist in the fool's understanding. Anselm's own premise, therefore, must be false, if what he himself says is true. But the obvious reply is that Anselm thought that there was nothing wrong with a God who exists in the understanding, so long as he does not exist *only* in the understanding, and Anselm did not think that God existed only in the fool's understanding.)

One ought not to confuse the thought of the greatest possible being with having the greatest possible thought. It is possible to think slowly about what is quick, think easy thoughts about a topic that is difficult, to have prolix thoughts about what is brief, and low thoughts about what is elevated. Hence if, when Anselm says that a God who exists in reality would be greater than a God who exited only in the understanding, he is comparing the greatness of God with the greatness of our thought of God, the fact that God is greater than our thought of God is in no way remarkable. There is no reason why our thoughts of what is great should be great thoughts at all. Hence there is no reason why our concept of God should be nearly as great as God, or, indeed, great at all.

It may be that Anselm is confused by his talk of 'existing in the understanding alone'. The understanding is not a sort of place in which God might exist. To say that God exists in the understanding is just to say that he is thought about. And to say that something exists in the understanding alone is not to say that it exists, but only in a funny place. It is to say that that thing is thought about, and wrongly believed to exist.

Furthermore, one cannot compare, in respect of 'greatness', a being who exists in the understanding alone with a being who exists both in the understanding and in reality. The question which of these two beings was greater would be like the question 'Which lives nearer the equator, elephants (who exist both in the understanding and in reality) or unicorns (who exist only in the understanding)'. Since unicorns do not exist, they do not live anywhere – not, of course, in the sense in which homeless people do not live anywhere; a person must exist not to have a home – and so the question whether where they live is nearer to or further from the equator than where elephants live cannot arise. An 'existent being' cannot be compared with a 'nonexistent' one; both terms in the comparison must exist if they are to be compared. I have put the words 'existent being' in quotes because it suggests that beings may be divided into two kinds, existent ones and nonexistent ones, which idea is absurd.)

(It is very easy to confuse the question whether elephants or unicorns live nearest the equator with a different question, which question does arise, and is not meaningless. This is the question whether the place in which elephants live is further from or nearer to the equator than the place (if there is one) where unicorns are supposed to live. Though abominable snowmen cannot live in the Himalayas if there are not any abominable snowmen, and so cannot live either further from or nearer to the equator than elephants, the place where they are supposed to live (the Himalayas) can be either further from or nearer to the place where elephants actually do live.)

To take another example, it is very easy to confuse the assertion that a species of mythical animal lives in the Himalayas (which assertion is incoherent, since, if the animals are mythical, they do not exist, and cannot live anywhere) with the assertion that there is a myth to the effect that a species of animal (abominable snowmen) lives in the Himalayas. This latter assertion is perfectly coherent and is, indeed, true. Similarly, the question 'Is a being who exists in reality greater or not greater than one who exists in the understanding alone?' is also incoherent. There is no being, existing in the understanding, than whom a God who exists in reality can be greater or less great. Both terms in a comparison must exist before the terms in question can be compared, and in comparing a God who exists in the understanding alone with one who exists in reality, one is supposing that only one of the two terms compared – the God who exists in reality – exists.

All one is committed to by saying that God exists in the understanding alone is the existence of people, who either believe or do not believe that there is a God, wonder whether there is a God, address prayers to God, and have a concept of God, however rudimentary. All one is committed to when one talks about Mr Pickwick, a fictional character, is the existence of Dickens, his publishers and his readers. Fictional characters are not, like queer characters, a species of character. To say they are fictional is to say that in reality they do not exist, though in certain contexts people talk and think as if they existed. Similarly, to say that God exists in the understanding alone is to say that God does not exist, but that certain people talk and think as if he existed.

Just as Dickens's concept of Mr Pickwick was not sued for breach of promise, so our concept of God is neither omnipotent nor omniscient. (Neither, of course, does it fall short of being omniscient and omnipotent.) Hence it cannot be compared in respect of these characteristics, or in respect of goodness, with a God who exists in reality (i.e., who in reality exists). (Though the question 'Is the God who exists in our understanding as great as the God who exists in reality?' is incoherent, the question 'Is the God who exists in reality as great as we suppose him to be?' is not. (Presumably he is greater.))

The answer to this question whether the God who exists in reality is as great as we suppose him to be, I think, is that in a way he is, because he is supposed to be as great as it is possible to be, and, if he exists, he *is* as great as it is possible to be. In another way he must be greater than he is supposed to be, because, if he existed, he would presumably have many interesting and desirable characteristics which we did not suppose (or expect) him to have (and perhaps some that we supposed him not to have.)

To sum up, God does not exist in the understanding, literally speaking. What, figuratively speaking, 'exists in' the understanding is our concept of God, and our concept of God can neither be greater nor less great than God. Our concept of God is neither omnipotent nor omniscient nor perfectly good, or rather, it does not make sense to attribute these features to it. Our concept of God does exist, but it is God, not our concept of God, that is omnipotent, omniscient, benevolent, etc.

It has been held[4] that it is to do Anselm an injustice to suppose that he thought that to say that God existed in the understanding alone meant no more than that there was not a God, though some people suppose that there was one. But if Anselm was not comparing the existent God with a God who existed only in the understanding, he must have been comparing God with a God who did not exist at all. In that case, he would have to be holding that the former was greater than the latter. But an existent God could not have a kind of greatness (existence) that a nonexistent God would lack. One must avoid the contradictory suggestion that there might be two Gods, an existent one and a nonexistent one, and that the former be a higher grade entity than the latter. If God does not exist, there will be nothing to have any of God's admirable characteristics. And there cannot be both an existent God and a nonexistent God to be compared.

Presupposed in what I have been saying is the view that existence, as we shall see, is not a feature of anything, and so *a fortiori* not a feature of any two things in respect of which they can be compared. I shall discuss this view later.

(iv) Descartes' Ontological Argument

Descartes puts the ontological argument[5] in a way that, superficially at least, escapes these objections. He escapes them because he does not use the comparative expression 'greater than'.

Descartes' argument goes as follows. God is, by definition, perfect, i.e., possesses every perfection there is to possess. Existence is a perfection. Therefore to say that God does not exist is to say that a being who possesses every perfection lacks a perfection. Hence that God exists is a logical truth, and so God must exist.

If this argument is to be satisfactory, sentences about God must make sense. Furthermore, God's supposed attributes must not be collectively incoherent, as supposing that something might have the attributes of quadratic equations and also be muscular is incoherent. And words like 'omnipotent' and 'omniscient' must also be words for individually coherent characteristics. (Whether they are so is a question which we shall consider later.) Given that these conditions are fulfilled, as we shall assume for the sake of argument that they are, could Descartes' version of the ontological argument be valid?

I have already pointed out that defining 'God' to make it a logical truth that he possesses attributes such as omniscience does not bring it about that there exists a being who possesses these attributes. Indeed, defining 'God' so as to make omniscience one of the attributes that he by definition possesses makes no difference to anything other than the way we use word the word 'God'. By defining 'God' to connote omniscience we do not bring it about that there is a God who is omniscient; we simply behave in such a way as to make it necessary to withhold the epithet 'God' from any being who is not omniscient.

Strictly speaking we do not even by our definition make true the proposition that God is omniscient, for this proposition could be true only if there were a God. The proposition we do make true is the proposition that if there is a God, then he is omniscient.

(But, even more strictly speaking, we may not cause the proposition that we now express in the words 'If there is a God, he is omniscient' to come to express a truth. If we redefine the word 'God' to include omniscience when it does not include omniscience already, then what we do is to cause sentences containing the word 'God', to express a different proposition from the one they previously expressed. Doing this is not necessarily wrong, for a definition of 'God' that includes omniscience will be better for some reasons, as we have seen, than one that does not. But it does not alter the truth of anything, so much as make it necessary to express in different words things that would be true (or false) in whatever words we expressed them. For example, changing the meaning of 'death' to include brain death cannot logically (though causally it may) make anything right that was wrong before, but it may make it necessary to express the same moral judgments in a different way.)

If 'exists' could be treated in the same way as 'omniscient', and God made to possess existence by definition, as he can be made to possess omniscience by definition, the conclusion, parallel to the conclusion 'If there is a God, he is omniscient' would be (if you substitute 'exists' for 'is omniscient') is 'If there is a god, then he is existent (or exists)'. This is both a truism and would remain a truism, whatever definition of 'God' one adopted. It is equally true that if there are any monkeys, they exist. One does not need to evoke a subtle and controversial argument to prove this. (It makes no difference to what I have said about 'existence' whether the definition of 'God' has including existence reports how the word 'God' is used – though I think it most unlikely that 'God' should commonly be used to include existence – or whether it simply lays down how the writer himself intends to use it.)

To this it has been replied[6] that what I have just said begs the question against the ontological argument. If the ontological argument is valid, there is a difference between 'If there is a God, he exists' and 'If there are any monkeys, they exist', which difference my remarks overlook. Though both these hypothetical propositions are by definition true, the antecedent of the latter (that there are monkeys) is only contingently true, whereas, if the ontological argument is valid, the antecedent of the former (that there is a God) is necessarily true. This being so, it follows that we can obtain the conclusion we want, that there is a God, directly from the antecedent of the hypothetical proposition that if there is a God, he exists, though we cannot obtain any such information from the antecedent of the hypothetical proposition that if there are monkeys, they exist. There must be a God, but there do not have to be any monkeys. Neither the former hypothetical proposition's antecedent, that there is a God, nor its the consequent, that he exists, are being asserted in the hypothetical, but that God exists can be derived from the antecedent nevertheless.

(It has been maintained,[7] in defence of the ontological argument, that it also follows that it is illegitimate even to say 'If there is a God, he exists', whereas it is not illegitimate – at least, not for the illegitimate reason about to be given – to say 'If there are any monkeys, they exist', because the use of the word 'if' here suggests that there might not be a God, which the ontological argument shows to be impossible. But his latter point, I think, is just a mistake. You can (truly) say 'If 2+2=4, then 4-2=2' without suggesting that there is any doubt about two and two's being four.)

It is usually – and I think correctly – held, against the ontological argument, that existence would have to be an attribute if God were to exist by definition. But existence is not an attribute. To say that God is omniscient is to attribute something to God. To say that God exists is not to attribute anything to God; it is simply to say that there *is* a God. (That this is so is clearer if we say that there is a God than if we say that God exists. That there is a God does not even look as if it attributes an attribute to God. It would be natural to suppose that 'There is a God' and 'God exists' say the same thing and, if they do, it follows that that God exists does not ascribe an attribute to God.)

Furthermore, if the ontological argument is to be valid, existence must not only be an attribute, but be a desirable attribute (roughly), a perfection. But, if it is a desirable attribute, it must be an attribute, which it cannot be. Though a woman may desire to have a husband who is kind, wealthy and reliable, she can hardly desire to have a husband who exists. To desire to have a husband who exists is just to desire to have a husband. The words 'desires to have a husband who does not exist' do not make sense, whereas the words 'desires to have a husband who is not hard working' do make sense, and sometimes say what is true. To say that she desires existence in her husband is not to say that she wishes the husband she had existed, as to say that she desires kindness in her husband is to say that she wishes the husband she had were kind. If it means anything at all, it is to say she wishes she had a husband. Though she may have to choose between having a husband who is kind and one who is wealthy – though she would prefer to have one who was both of these – she cannot choose between having a husband who is kind and having one who exists.

One reason why existence is supposed not to be an attribute is this. It is sometimes said that a thing must exist before we can even raise the question whether or not it possesses or lacks a certain attribute. Raising the question whether lions[8] purr, for example, presupposes that lions exist, as do the statements that lions do (or do not) purr. That lions exist, however, does not presuppose that lions exist, but states that they do. It would be even odder if to say that lions do not exist presupposes that lions exist, as that lions do not purr presupposes that lions exist (in order not to purr). If that lions did not exist presupposed – as does that they do not purr – that they did exist, then all statements saying that things did not exist would presuppose that they did exist, and therefore presuppose their own falsity. For this reason, though we can say that some lions growl but others do not, we cannot say that some lions exist, but others do not. We can say that there are some lions, but this is not different from saying that there are lions, or that lions exist; it is not to say that some lions exist (though others do not). The expression 'There are all lions' would not make sense, as it would have to if, in the expression 'There are some lions', the word 'some' meant 'some as opposed to all' (as it does in the expression, 'Some lions (but not others) purr')).

It may be pointed out in reply that we can say that some heroes (e.g. Alexander) existed but that others (e.g. Theseus) did not, but were merely mythical. The correct answer to this is to say that these are not statements about heroes, but statements about stories about heroes; some stories about heroes are fact, others are fiction. It is wrong to suppose that nonfictional stories are about real people, but that fictional stories are about a different kind of person, viz., mythical people. (It is obvious that both the historical stories and the fictional stories themselves exist.) It is possible to say that some lions exist but others do not, so long as the context indicates that one is talking about lions in stories, i.e., stories of lions, and indicating that some of these stories report facts about existent lions, and others invent facts about nonexistent ones. For example, the lion in *The Lion, the Witch and the Wardrobe* did not exist, but the lion in *Born Free* did. (Some philosophers, make the mistake of supposing that to say that a remark is about something or other entails that what it is about exists, but a little reflection on the English language should show that this is not so. Both stories about existent lions and stories about nonexistent ones are about lions.)

The ontological argument, to recapitulate, goes: existence is part of the definition of God; therefore God exists. This argument looks similar to the argument: having the attributes of both sexes is part of the definition of 'hermaphrodite'; therefore hermaphrodites have the attributes of both sexes. A slightly different version of it goes: God possesses every perfection; existence is a perfection; therefore God exists. This argument looks similar to – and indeed is formally similar to – the argument: God by definition possesses every perfection; omniscience is a perfection; therefore God by definition possesses omniscience.

The arguments concerning being an hermaphrodite and omniscience really are valid. If, then, one thinks that the ontological argument is not valid, one must elucidate the difference between omniscience and existence, and do this in such a way as to show why this difference allows one to define 'God' to be omniscient, but not to be existent, and to derive from this difference the reason why omniscience can be a perfection, but existence cannot be. Just saying (albeit correctly) that omniscience is an attribute but that existence is not, does not by itself explain why something can be omniscient, or possess other attributes, by definition, but cannot be existent by definition.

(v)   Why One can Define Things to Have Attributes, but Not to Exist

The reason why one can define 'God' to be omniscient but not to be existent is that there is an intimate connection between the features of things, or their characteristics or attributes, and the interconnected notions of description, classification and definition, whereas there can be no similar connection between existence and these notions.

You can *describe* something as having or lacking a certain feature – being tall, for example. You cannot describe something as existing or not existing. Describing a man as tall tells you what kind of man to look for. Describing a man as existing does not. You can describe Smith as tall, dark and handsome, but you cannot describe him as tall, dark, handsome and then add 'and he exists as well'. Smith can be tall, dark and handsome, as compared with another man who is tall, dark but not handsome. But Smith cannot be tall, dark, handsome and existent, as compared with another man who is tall, dark, handsome but, alas, nonexistent.

Descriptions, too, can feature in *directions* for finding things. But knowing that a man exists, unlike his being tall, cannot enable you to pick him out from any other man you come across. All the things one comes across will exist. You can ask to be brought a red apple and complain if you are brought an apple which is not red, but green. But you cannot ask to be brought an existing apple, and complain that you have not been brought an existing apple, but a nonexistent one instead.

Descriptions also feature in *generalisations* about things. One can say that all large men make good husbands, but not that all existent women make good wives (as opposed to nonexistent women, who make bad ones). One can say that all cats except Manx cats have tails, but you cannot say that all cats except nonexistent cats purr. (The nonexistent ones perhaps bark.)

Things like apples may also be *classified* on account of having or lacking certain features (e.g., being green or red, or being a Cox's Orange Pippin or a Bramley) but things cannot be classified as having or lacking existence. Animals can be divided into vertebrates and invertebrates, but they cannot be divided into existent and nonexistent.

Similar remarks apply to *definitions*. Bicycles are by definition a species of wheeled vehicle that is differentiated from others by having two wheels. You could not have a word which stands to 'exists' in the relation in which 'having two wheels' stands to 'bicycle'. You could not have a word, say the word 'exicycle', to mean 'existent wheeled vehicle' as 'bicycle' means 'two wheeled vehicle'. Hence you could not argue that, just as some vehicles are properly called bicycles because they have two wheels and other vehicles are not properly called bicycles because they have more or fewer than two wheels, so some vehicles are properly called 'exicycles' because they exist, but other vehicles are not properly called 'exicycles' because they do not exist. As I have said, one can come across a three wheeled vehicle and say 'That cannot properly be called "bicycle", because it has more than two wheels', but you cannot come across a nonexistent vehicle and say 'That cannot properly be called "exicycle", because it does not exist'. One cannot come across nonexistent wheeled vehicles, or indicate them with the word 'that'. There is, therefore, nothing that the word 'exicycle' could do, and so we not only do not, but could not, have it or anything like it in our vocabulary.

Where attributes are concerned, too, there is very often the possibility of *borderline cases*. We might come across something (a duck-billed platypus, let us say) with most, but not all, of the features that mammals usually have, and then be faced with the question 'Should we decide to call these things mammals or not?' But we cannot come across an animal resembling a mammal in all ways except that it does not exist, and then have to decide whether to call it a mammal or not.

Let us suppose that the universe contains a variety of gods and demigods. We might describe some of these as omniscient, others as not omniscient. We might classify them into those which are omniscient and those which are not. We might invent a special word for the omniscient ones, and say that these are omniscient by definition. What we cannot do is to describe some of these gods as existent, others not, or classify them into those that are existent and those that are not. We cannot invent a word – say the word 'exigod' for gods which have the attribute of existing, and say that exigods exist by definition, and have another word – in actual fact, perhaps, the word 'god' – for other gods, of whom it will not be true that they exist by definition. There would be nothing we could do with a word such as exigod. For what it would do, if this sort of work could be done at all, would be to do the job of enabling us to say 'Well, this god may be an exigod, because this god is existent, but this other one cannot be because it is nonexistent'. But the words 'this other' in the preceding sentence cannot pick out anything. It is only about existent things that you can raise the question of whether or not they answer to a certain description, are members of a certain class, or are correctly called by a certain name. You cannot come across a nonexisting thing in order truly to say of it: 'This does not exist'.

(vi)   Orthodox View of 'Exists'

The orthodox view about the meaning of 'exists', and the difference between it and words for characteristics or attributes, is this. (I shall put this view very much in my own way.) When you say that something is yellow, you are talking about that thing, but when you say that something exists you are, despite appearances, talking about a concept or a universal or a description.[9] You are saying that a concept has something answering to it, that a universal has instances, or that a description has application.

Hence one ought not to try to divide things into existent things and nonexistent things. One simply divides concepts into those which, like the concept of a giraffe, have something answering to them, and those which, like the concept of a centaur, do not. One divides universals into those which, like manhood, have instances, and those which, like phoenixhood, do not. One divides descriptions into those which, like the descriptions of a Mr Major, have application, and those which, like those of a Mr Pickwick, do not. (The fact that there is a description of a Mr Pickwick does not entail that there is a Mr Pickwick, though if something were an attribute of Mr Pickwick, it would entail that there was a Mr Pickwick.)

This way of dealing with the problem about existence is very attractive. One problem some philosophers have had about 'exists', it will be remembered, was this: though one is talking about a banana when one says of some banana that it is not purple, what are you talking about when you say that something does not exist? Something has to exist in order not to be purple. Does this mean that, analogously, that something has to exist in order not to exist?

However, if, when we say that something does not exist we are talking about a concept and saying that that concept has nothing answering to it, our logical conscience may be satisfied, for the concept will exist, even if the entity of which it is a concept does not. Indeed, it must exist to have nothing answering it. By parallel reasoning, the universal must exist in order to have no instances. The description must exist in order to have no application. It is not a difficulty for this view that the concepts, universals or descriptions we are talking about when we say that something or other does not exist must therefore exist, because concepts without application, universals without instances, and descriptions that describe nothing do exist.

If we want, very properly, to push this argument one stage further back and say that not all concepts exist, this want, too, can be satisfied. Not only are there concepts of things, there are also (second order) concepts of concepts. Hence what we mean when we say that a concept does not exist is simply that some concepts of concepts (i.e., second order concepts) do not have any concepts (first order concepts) answering to them.

Difficulties

I am not sure, however, that this tidy-minded theory does justice to all the ways in which we use the word 'exists' and cognate words. For one thing, we have the ostensible class word 'existent' which we use in such expressions as 'All existents are material'. (I am not saying that it is *true* that they are all material.) And what is one to say about the sentence I use when I point to, say, a table, and say (thumping on it) 'Well, that at least exists' (in reply, say, to a philosopher who has said that nothing exists)? Tables are neither concepts, universals nor descriptions. But both the sentences 'That exists' and 'All existents are material' may be degenerate. 'That exists' is degenerate in not have a normal contrary. There is no use for saying (pointing to a table or to nothing at all) 'That does not exist'. And though there is a use for 'All men are mortal, and also many things that are not men' there is no use for 'All existents are material, and also many things that are nonexistent'.

In order to deal with 'That exists' one would have to turn the normal account of existence back to front, and say that though 'Tables exist' means that the universal, being a table, has an instance, 'That exists' (said of a table) means that it is an instance of something. The best I can do with 'Everything is material' is to suggest that it is really about universals, and states that the instances of every first order universal are also instances of the universal 'material thing', or, more simply, that the universal 'nonmaterial thing' has no instances.[10] Even when we say of a particular thing like a table that it exists, we cannot be ascribing to it an attribute or characteristic. If we were, it would be possible to do what we have just said was impossible, point to something and say of it that, because it lacks the characteristic of existence, it does not exist. (It is possible to point to something and say that it lacks the characteristic of being, say, yellow.) Hence the fact that one can say that individuals exist certainly does not enable one to revive the ontological argument. Existence would have to be a characteristic, one which some things had and other things lacked, in order that something (in particular God) could be defined as having it. And, if it were a characteristic, there would have to be the possibility of individuals which did not have it, i.e., of there being individuals which do not exist. This is impossible.

(vii)   Existence and Proper Names

A difficulty with the account of existence just given is that it is perfectly intelligible, and indeed true, to say such things as that Emma does not exist, although 'Emma' is not a name for a concept or a universal or a description. (Whether 'Emma' should be classified as a proper name for logical purposes – it is certainly a grammatically proper name – would depend upon whether proper names by definition must name some existent thing. If they must, 'Emma' cannot be classified logically as a proper name, for Emma did not exist, and neither Jane Austen nor anyone else ever supposed that she did.)

However, the fact that one can say such things as that Emma does not exist, though Emma is not a universal, does not enable one to revive the ontological argument. For (a) one could not without circularity argue that because 'God' was a proper name, there must be a God. One should rather argue that because there was not a God, 'God' could not be a proper name. (b) Rather than to say that Emma did not exist, it might be better to say that there was no such person as Emma. This statement *would* be a statement to the effect that certain characteristics, the ones Jane Austen 'pretended' to ascribe to a woman whom she pretended to call 'Emma', had no instance.

To say that there is no such person as Emma, however, is not quite the same thing as to say that Emma does not exist. If it turned out that there was a woman with the characteristics Jane Austen ascribed to Emma, Emma's characteristics would have an instance, but this person would still not be Emma. For this person to be Emma, Jane Austen, when writing about Emma, would have to have had her in mind, which Jane Austen could not have had, since she did not know of her.

But even if, when saying that Emma does not exist, we are not saying that those characteristics that Jane Austen pretended to attribute to Emma are not instantiated, it is still not possible to argue that there is some contradiction in the proposition that God does not exist. There is no contradiction in supposing that Emma did not exist. Proper names (as opposed to pseudo-proper names) must designate, but there is no contradiction in supposing that 'God' is a pseudo-designator. One could not argue from the existence of the grammatically proper name 'Emma' to that of a woman. All that follows from the fact that there is nothing 'Emma' names is that 'Emma' is what has been called a pseudo-designator[11] – I suggest the expression 'pretend designator' – rather than a normal proper name. In pretending that there is such a person as Emma, Jane Austen pretended to use the word 'Emma' as a proper name of a person she pretended answered to certain descriptions. So, instead of saying that Emma does not exist, or that there is no such person as Emma, one could simply say that 'Emma' does not really designate anyone. Again, one could not argue without circularity from the fact that something is a genuine designator to the existence of what it designates. Rather one should establish first the existence of what a proper name designates, and then conclude that it is a genuine designator. And the same could be true of 'God'. (A word can be a pseudo-designator without those using it knowing that it is.)

Though the question 'Does God exist?' is not the same question as 'Is there a God?' – for the first is about something one is attempting to name with a proper name, and the second is about whether the attributes of 'God' have an instance, it is logically possible correctly to answer 'No' to both questions.[12]

(viii) Malcolm's Ontological Argument

Two Ontological Arguments

I must now consider a number of fairly modern attempts to resurrect the ontological argument. The first of those that I shall discuss was made by Norman Malcolm, in a paper entitled 'Anselm's Ontological Arguments'.[13]

Malcolm thinks that what I have described as his attempt to resurrect the ontological argument is in fact a very old one. It was, he believes, put forward by Anselm himself. Anselm had two ontological arguments, the one just discussed, and a second argument which Malcolm thinks has largely been ignored.

Malcolm agrees with the received view that existence is not an attribute, and so cannot be perfection. Hence he agrees that the proposition that God exists cannot be true by definition, and that in consequence it cannot be necessarily true that there is a God. Hence the statement that there is a God cannot be known to be true *a priori*.

However, Malcolm thinks that the conclusion of Anselm's second argument is not that God necessarily possesses existence, but that he necessarily possesses *necessary* existence. God, he argues, can possess *necessary* existence necessarily (and by definition), even if he cannot possess existence necessarily (and by definition). Though the conclusion of the usual ontological argument (Anselm's first) is that that God exists is a necessary truth, the proposition that Malcolm thinks is a necessary truth is not this, but the proposition that God necessarily exists. This is the conclusion of the second ontological argument. (There are two modal operators in the sentence that God necessarily possesses necessary existence, as the word 'necessarily' occurs twice, not just once, as it does in the sentence 'God necessarily exists'.)

The same is true, Malcolm thinks, of God's other attributes. The property which God must by definition have is not omnipotence, but necessary omnipotence; not omniscience, but necessary omniscience. (It is difficult to see, however, what are Malcolm's motives for thinking that God is necessarily omniscient and omnipotent, rather than just omniscient and omnipotent. For omniscience and omnipotence are attributes, and there are not the same difficulties with holding that God possesses his *attributes* by definition as there are with holding that he is by definition existent.)

Necessarily Possessing Existence and Necessarily Possessing Necessary Existence

One serious difficulty with Malcolm's argument is that it is hard to see how God can possess necessary existence (which Malcolm asserts) if he does not necessarily possess existence (which Malcolm denies). It is a truth of logic that if a proposition is necessarily true, it is true. For example, if it is necessarily true that two and two are four, then it follows that two and two are four. Analogously, if it is necessarily true that God possesses necessary existence, he must possess necessary existence, and therefore exist necessarily. But that is just what the first version of the ontological argument says God does, and just what Malcolm himself denies. So the validity of the second ontological argument entails the validity of the first, which (by contraposition) means that the invalidity of the first must entail the invalidity of the second. In other words, if one thinks, as Malcolm does, that the first ontological argument is invalid, one must think that God cannot necessarily possess existence at all, from which it follows that God cannot possess necessary existence necessarily.

In any case, a type fallacy would be involved in accepting Malcolm's argument. Let us suppose, as I think Malcolm would agree, that for God necessarily to possess existence, 'God' must be defined in such a way that he exists by definition. Then, for God necessarily to possess necessary existence, he must be defined in such a way that, by definition, he exists by definition. But this means that one must use the one word 'God' ambiguously, and so have two concepts of God. 'God' in one sense would be defined so that God possesses existence by definition, in the other sense so that he possesses necessary existence by definition (i.e., possesses existence by definition, by definition).

The second sense of 'God' would presuppose the first, so to avoid the consequent muddle, we would need two words, say 'God1' and 'God2'. 'God2' would need to be defined in terms of 'God1', for 'God2' is applicable to a being only if there is another word ('God1') which is applicable to a being only if he exists. In other words, if, as seems reasonable, you say a being can possess a feature necessarily only if it possesses this feature by definition then, if you accept the old ontological argument, God must possess existence by definition. If you accept the new one, God must by definition exist by definition. But the word which entails by definition existing by definition can have meaning only if there is another word such that this latter word entails just existing by definition. Hence this new version of the ontological argument presupposes the old one. To maintain, as Malcolm must, that (1) nothing can exist by definition, (2) God must, by definition exists by definition and (3) there is, in ordinary religious thought and conversation, the concept of a being who, by definition, exists by definition, is not remotely plausible.

Existence as a Special Kind of Existence

In my criticisms of Malcolm's argument I have been assuming that possessing necessary existence is just necessarily possessing ordinary existence. Malcolm, however (confusingly), sometimes regards necessary existence as what might be described as a special *kind* of existence. Malcolm can therefore suppose that the proposition that God necessarily possesses necessary existence (the special kind of existence) could be true, but the proposition that God necessarily possesses existence be false, because the word 'existence' is being used with different meanings. In the old ontological argument, necessarily possessing existence was just possessing ordinary existence necessarily, i.e., what God possesses necessarily is just what men possess contingently. But in the new version, what God necessarily does is not to possess ordinary existence necessarily, but to possess necessarily a feature which Malcolm *calls* (misleadingly, I think) necessary existence, viz. *independent* existence. Hence Malcolm thinks that what God necessarily possesses (independent existence) is not the same thing as what critics of the ontological argument say God cannot necessarily possess. (Necessary existence, in the sense of independent existence, would be a property of 'things', not of propositions, and so could be possessed by God without its following that the proposition that God existed was a necessarily true proposition.)[14]

God's Necessary Independence

Malcolm reaches his view in the following way. One characteristic which it seems quite reasonable to attribute to God is independence. A man who is independent of food, sleep, a favourable environment, etc., is to that extent superior to a similar man who is not independent of these things. Hence independence is a perfection. Hence a perfect being cannot be dependent on anything. God would be vulnerable if he were dependent, and God cannot be vulnerable. If he were dependent upon anything, it would be possible to conceive of a more perfect being, not dependent upon the existence of anything.

Hence 'God' could be defined so that he is independent by definition, and that God is independent would then be proposition that it would contradictory to deny. And independence, like omniscience, is a perfection, and God by definition possesses every perfection. (I do not know whether Malcolm realises it, but it can be deduced from what Malcolm has said so far only that if there is a God, he is independent. One cannot deduce the categorical proposition that there is a God who is independent. Hence Malcolm has so far not proved that there is an independent God, or shown that it is a necessary truth that there is one.)

Malcolm at this point loses sight of the fact that the object of a proof of the existence of God is to prove that God, in the ordinary sense of 'exists', actually exists, i.e., that there really is a God. To prove that he possesses, necessarily, independence, does not do that.

Malcolm, however, not realising what he has actually proved, goes on to try to show that a being who did not exist necessarily in the ordinary sense would be neither independent nor eternal. He does this in the following way.

Malcolm argues that the proposition that God does not exist leads to contradictions. This is because if God does not exist, then either (i) something must be preventing him from existing, or (ii) it just so happens that he does not exist. But (i) something's preventing God from existing is incompatible with his being omnipotent. And (ii) it could not just so happen that God did not exist; for it would then follow that if he were to exist, he would not always have existed. He would then have mere duration, and not eternity, which, in the case of God, is impossible. (If this argument were valid, necessarily existing in Malcolm's sense – though it looks as if it is compatible with being unable necessarily to possess existence in the ordinary sense – would really *imply* necessarily possessing ordinary existence.)

But there are two mistakes in Malcolm's argument.

(a) The assumption that it would take great strength to prevent an omnipotent being from existing is absurd. A nonexisting omnipotent being cannot be struggling ineffectually to exist against the wishes of some person or being stronger than himself. A nonexistent God cannot be struggling to do anything, for he does not exist to struggle. Hence there is no such thing as preventing a nonexistent God from existing, in the sense of opposing any steps that he might take to bring it about that he exists; if there is no God, there is no being to take these steps. There could be such a thing as taking steps to prevent the eventualities that would bring about God's existence, and if, *per impossibile*, there were such eventualities, taking steps to prevent them would result in God's not existing (if God would otherwise come into existence). (Malcolm argues later, correctly, that God could not come into existence.) But taking such steps would not be to oppose the will of an omnipotent being. Taking steps to prevent the birth of a baby who has not yet been conceived is not to oppose the will of the baby. Indeed, taking steps to prevent God from existing, if he did not exist, could be child's play. For there are no steps we need to take to prevent God from existing, if he does not exist; nor could there be such steps.

(b) The assumption presupposed by Malcolm's argument, that if God does not exist, then, if he were to exist, it would follow that he came into existence at some particular time, is also a mistaken one. If God is indeed eternal, then if there is a God, that there is a God is true at all times, and if there is no God, that there is not a God must also be true at all times. (An eternal God could not exist at some times but not at others.) But neither of these two propositions conflict with God's being eternal. There is a distinction, which Malcolm overlooks, between saying 'if God were to exist' and saying 'if God were to come to exist'. The supposition that God came into existence at some time or other would certainly mean that he is not eternal, and might well mean that he is not independent. But to suppose (in the event of there not being a God), that there is one, is not to suppose that God should come into existence, but to suppose that he existed and always had existed. Hence it is not true that if God's nonexistence is contingent, he cannot be an eternal being (or, more strictly speaking – for a nonexistent being cannot be eternal – that he would not be an eternal being if he existed).

What Malcolm's argument may prove is that God's existence is either necessary or impossible. I shall discuss this contention in the next chapter.

(ix) An Ontological Disproof of the Existence of God

The fact that it is impossible to provide an ontological proof of the existence of God has the consequence that it is also impossible to provide an ontological proof that God does not exist. J.L. Findlay has attempted to provide such a proof in an article in *Mind*.[15] It goes as follows. One of the characteristics that God has, by the definition of 'God', is that he is an adequate object of worship. Any being that did not necessarily exist would not be an adequate object of worship. But (because the ontological argument is invalid) it is impossible that there should be a necessary being. Hence it is impossible that there should be an adequate object of worship, and so impossible that there should be a God.

A conclusive criticism of Findlay's argument is that if the criticisms of the ontological argument are valid, as Findlay supposes they are, existence is not a feature. Hence it cannot be a feature that anything must possess to be an adequate object of worship. Hence an adequate object does not have to possess it.

(x)   God's Existence Necessary or Impossible

Malcolm[16] (and also Hartshorne) have argued that God's existence is either necessary or impossible. They think that to say that God's existence and nonexistence are possible is to assert a contradiction. Either God must exist or he cannot exist. The possibility that he exists just as a matter of brute fact they rule out.

If Malcolm is right in thinking that it is part of the concept of God that he necessarily (and by definition) exists necessarily, then it is right to think that God's existence is either necessary or impossible. Provided that the kind of existence God allegedly possesses necessarily is just existence, then the following argument is valid. Either it is possible to exist necessarily or it is not. If it is possible for a being to exist necessarily, then God, if he by definition exists necessarily, will exist necessarily. Hence he will exist. But if it is not possible for a being to exist necessarily, then the concept of God, as a being who by definition exists necessarily, cannot possibly have any instances. If God's existence implies something that is impossible, viz., necessary existence, then it must necessarily be false that God exists. God's existence must then, if God possesses necessary existence by definition, or if necessary existence is part of the concept of God, be either necessary or impossible.

If you combine this conclusion, that God's existence is either necessary or impossible, with the criticisms of the ontological argument given earlier, which, if they are valid, show that there is no such thing as necessary existence, you must deduce from Malcolm's premises that God's existence is impossible. This suggests another ontological disproof of God's existence. This is: necessary existence is impossible, so if God by definition possesses it, he cannot exist. (If one were to define 'squound' as 'a being who, among other things, is both square and round', it would follow from the definition of 'squound' that there were no squounds.)

Hence it looks as if, for those inclined to want there to be a God, there is both a good side and a bad side to criticisms of the ontological argument. If that God exists cannot be true by definition, which looks bad, it should also follow that it cannot be false by definition either, which looks good. If the proposition that God exists must be contingent, this means that it may be false but, on the other hand, it also means that it may be true. If existence is not a feature, God cannot by definition have it. But, and for the very same reason, he cannot by definition lack it. (I shall, nevertheless, argue at the end of this chapter that God's existence is not an ordinary contingent matter.)

Even if there are senses of 'exist' in which it does not refer to what I have called 'ordinary existence', Malcolm's argument is still invalid. By 'ordinary existence' I mean existence as it is meant in the sentence 'Dodos no longer exist'. Anyone using this sentence would normally be saying that there were no longer any dodos. But it is possible that existence can have a different sense. There are people who live ordinary existences in the sense that their lives are ordinary. If you were to define 'stars' as people whose existence was extraordinary (or who led extraordinary lives), all that would follow would be that, if there were any 'stars', they would lead extraordinary existences; it would not follow that there were any 'stars'. Briefly, if existence is an attribute, then God could possess existence by definition, but it would not follow that there was a God.[17]

If the characteristic that God necessarily possess is some such characteristic as being unable to go in or out of existence, then the statement that God possesses this characteristic will (if possessing it is a perfection) be necessarily true or necessarily false. It will be necessarily true if the characteristic is coherent, necessarily false if (like the characteristic of being round and square) it is not. But there is no reason why it should follow from the fact that it is either necessary or impossible that God should be unable to go in or out of existence, that God's possessing ordinary existence is either necessary or impossible. Hence the necessity of this proposition has no implications whatsoever for God's actual existence.

(xi)   The Necessity of God's Attributes

Are there any features that individuals do possess necessarily, but not by definition? (See the discussion of 'Nixon is human', in section (vii) of chapter

3.) There are certainly some characteristics that individuals do *not* possess necessarily. For example, it is not a necessary truth that Shakespeare wrote *Hamlet*. Perhaps, however, it is a necessary truth that Shakespeare had the parents he did, or that he is not a whale, nor even very like a whale. Perhaps, too, there are ways in which Shakespeare might have been different and still been Shakespeare, but other ways such that, if he were to have been different in these ways, he would not have been Shakespeare. (It should be noted that this is not a question about the features that a thing possesses by definition; there are indeed no features that Shakespeare has by definition, for 'Shakespeare' is a proper name, and so does not have a definition. And that Tom is a bachelor and that bachelors are by definition unmarried does not imply that *Tom* is by definition unmarried, still less that he cannot get married.)

An extreme view is that Shakespeare possesses all his features necessarily. I suspect that people who take this extreme view are committing the modal shift fallacy. They are confusing (a) it is necessarily the case that if Primrose A is by the river's brim, then if this primrose is not by the river's brim it is not Primrose A, with (b) if Primrose A is by the river's brim, then, if this primrose is not by the river's brim it is necessarily the case that it is not Primrose B.[18] (To confuse the two is to make a modal mistake.)

If individuals can necessarily possess properties without possessing them by definition, then that God is omniscient might be necessary on two counts. Firstly, it might be necessary because God is by definition omniscient (partly because omniscience is a perfection, and something that a proper object of worship could not well be without). Secondly his being omniscient might be necessary because, however he is described, he is 'essentially' omniscient.

Whether or not he is necessarily omniscient in the second way does not seem to me to be a matter of much importance. For, as I have already said, his necessarily possessing such characteristics as omniscience would not mean that he existed, but only that, if he existed, he would be omniscient. (For some further remarks about necessity relevant to this discussion, the reader is referred to the preceding chapter.)

Whether or not there is any 'objective' necessity in the connection between omniscience and omnipotence, there is a necessity in our attributing omniscience and omnipotence to God. We have to ascribe both to him in order to produce the idea of a perfect being.

(xii)   Conclusion

The ontological argument, as far as any considerations adduced in this chapter are concerned, is not valid. To think that it is is the result of misunderstanding the function of the word 'exists'. This remark, however, does not conclude the matter, to which I shall return in my next chapter.

Notes

1   In Kant, 1929, Book II, chapter III, Section 3 ('The Arguments of Speculative Reason in Proof of the Existence of a Supreme Being').
2   See Anselm, St.
3   In 1982, p. 51.
4   By Mackie, 1982, chapter 3, Section (b), 'Anselm's Ontological Proof and Gaunilo's Reply'.
5   In *Meditations*, Part IV.
6   By Malcolm, 1960, and reprinted 1968.
7   By Malcolm, *loc. cit.*
8   See Moore's remarks about tigers 'Is Existence a Predicate?', 1936, and reprinted 1959.
9   Or to say that the propositional function 'x is human' is true of at least one thing, says Anthony Blair.
10   The view that one can say of a particular that it exists has been held among other Philosophers by Kripke, 1972.
11   By Ryle, 1947.
12   Proper names being rigid designators would make no difference to this argument.
13   *Loc. cit.*
14   See my 'Hume on Liberty, Necessity, Uniformity, Causation and Unfulfilled Conditionals', 1994.
15   Findlay, 1948. Discussed by Kenny, 1987.
16   *Loc. cit.*
17   In 'The Philosophy of Mysticism' (1995) I discuss there the possibility that God neither exists nor does not exist, i.e., that existence is not appropriately predicable of God. I shall revert to this possibility later in this book (in chapters 29 and 30).
18   (a) is of the form: L((Fa)->(-Fb->(a=b))). (b) is of the form: aF->(-bF->L(a=b)).

5 Possible Worlds and the Ontological Argument

(i)   Statement of the Possible-worlds Theory of Necessity

It is fashionable to put the ontological argument which, of course, concludes that God's existence is necessary, in a manner that presupposes what is called the possible-worlds theory of the nature of necessity. As an example of this kind of ontological argument, I shall consider the influential version that has been put forward by Alvin Plantinga.[1]

In order to understand the possible-world theory one must think of the world as just one among an infinite number of possible worlds, all differing from it by a larger or smaller amount. According to the possible-worlds theory of necessity, the modal notions of actual, possible, impossible and necessary can then be defined in the following ways. (a) To say that something is actual is to say that it exists in this possible world, and to say that something is so is to say that it is true in this world. (b) To say that something is possible is to say that it exists in or is true of at least one possible world. For example, to say that centaurs are possible is to say that there is a possible world in which there are centaurs. (This does not exclude it from being this world, though, in the case of centaurs, it is not this world.) (c) To say that something is impossible is to say that there is no possible world in which it exists or is true. For example, to say that square circles are impossible is to say that there are no possible worlds in which there are square circles. (d) To say that something is necessary is to say that it exists or is true in every possible world. For example, to say that it is necessary that two and two make four is to say that in every possible world two and two makes four. (It is possible to simplify the above definitions a little by defining a possibility as something that is not necessarily *not* the case. For example, something is possible if it is not the case that it exists in no possible world.)

To say that something is contingent without being necessarily true or necessarily false is to say that there are some possible worlds in which it exists and others in which it does not exist. For example, to say that it is just a contingent fact that some men are bald is to say that there are bald men in some possible worlds, but not in all. 'Possible' is being used in such a way that, if something is possible, this does not exclude its being actual or necessary; that something exists in at least one possible world neither excludes its existing in this one nor in all of them. Since if something exists in this possible world it follows that it exists in at least one possible world, that something is actual implies that it is possible.

There are two theories about the nature of possible worlds. According to one, the possible-world language is just an enlightening way of talking. According to the other there is a way in which other possible worlds are just as 'real' as this one. Among those philosophers who have held that the possible-world language are just ways of talking the most eminent is Saul Kripke. David Lewis, on the other hand, thinks that possible worlds are as 'concrete' as the actual world, however concrete that might be.[2]

In what follows I shall show that, if the possible-worlds language is just a way of talking, it is a highly misleading way of talking. But in any case I doubt whether to regard possible worlds as just ways of talking is a possible way of escape for possible-worlds theorists. For statements about possible worlds, to do the job that is demanded of them, have to be true. And how can it be true that there is a possible world in which beggars ride, if, because possible worlds are just ways of talking and do not actually exist, there is no such world?

These possible worlds are not spatially related to this world, and cannot influence it causally. There is no route which you can travel from this world to any possible world. And it should be emphasised that to 'postulate' a possible world is not a matter of science fiction. There is not supposed to be any causal connection between possible worlds and this one. They cannot do anything weird to us by means of antimatter, and we cannot be visited by their denizens. For the same reason, we cannot have any empirical evidence of the existence of philosophical possible worlds, for the merely possible can have no effects on the actual, for the merely possible does not exist.

That there are other possible worlds does not, according to some who hold the possible-world theory, mean that this world is the not the only possible world that is actual. It has been held that the existence of possible worlds is relative. One ought not to say that the possible world in which Harrison does exist is real, and the possible worlds in which Harrison does not exist are not real. The possible world in which Harrison does exist is only real relative to itself, and the possible world in which Harrison does not exist, though only possible in relation to this world, is just as real, relative to itself, as the actual world is in relation to itself. In relation to the other world, it is this world that is merely possible.

(ii)   Brief Criticisms of the Possible-world Theory

Before discussing the possible-worlds version of the ontological argument I wish to make some observations on the possible-worlds theory of necessary truth, which Plantinga's 'proof' presupposes. I believe that the possible-worlds theory of necessity is a philosophical disaster. It has probably produced more confusion than any other philosophical innovation occurring in the Anglo-Saxon philosophical world during this century. Arguments that look valid when stated in the possible-worlds language can be seen to be invalid when stated in the ordinary way, using the (perfectly respectable) notions of possibility, impossibility and necessity. The possible-world theory has been attributed to Leibniz, but I do not think that, when Leibniz said that this world was the best of all possible worlds, he took this remark so literally as to suppose that it implied that there actually existed a large number of possible worlds, all worse than this one. When God chose to produce the best of all possible worlds, he did not choose among worlds, but among specifications of worlds. He chose to actualise the specifications of this world, because these were the specifications which would, if actualised, produce a better world than would actualising any of the other specifications.

Those who hold the possible-worlds theory constantly speak as if it is worlds that are possible, whereas what is possible is that there should be a world of such and such a kind. We have just seen that when Leibniz said that this was the best of all possible worlds, he gives the impression that there are a large number of possible worlds, to each of which this (possible) world is related by the relation: better than. Had he said that this world could not be any better than it is, or that it is not possible for there to be a world better than this one, he would not have given rise to this idea, and posterity would have been much better for it. However, I do not wish to discuss the matter in detail, partly because the topic can become technical, and partly because I have elsewhere treated of it in more detail than would be appropriate here.[3] But one of the worst defects of the possible-world terminology is that it treats 'possible' as a word for an attribute, which can (among other things) belong to worlds. But possibility is not an attribute. A possible child prime minister, for example, is just a child who might become prime minister. It is not the child who is possible, but his being prime minister. Talking of possible children as if they were a kind of child, instead of the children I might have had or would have had, had things been otherwise, makes one think of possible children as something on whom one's actions can have effects, and that in order to do what is best for my family, I ought not only to take into consideration the effects of my actions on the children I have, but on children I did not have, but might have had, had things been different: this is absurd (see later in this chapter).[4] One would not talk or think like this if one did not use the language of possible worlds.

(iii)   Brief Statement of Plantinga's Argument

I shall put Plantinga's argument in my own way. (a) To say that it is possible that there is a God is to say that there is a possible world in which there is a God. (b) To say that God exists necessarily is to say that he exists in every possible world. (c) God is necessarily perfect, or, in Plantinga's terminology, necessarily maximally excellent. (d) Since God is necessarily maximally excellent, he is, by the possible-world definition of necessity, maximally excellent in every possible world. (e) If he is maximally excellent in every possible world, he must exist in every possible world, from which it follows that he exists. (Plantinga does not use this argument as unequivocally as I have here, but prevaricates.) (f) God is also necessarily what Plantinga calls 'maximally great', and to be maximally great is to be perfect or maximally excellent in every possible world. (If a perfect bank is a bank who serves its customers perfectly in every town in which it has a branch, a maximally great bank would be a bank that served it customers perfectly in every branch, and had a branch in every town.) (g) Hence if 'it is possible that there is a God' means that there is a possible world which contains a God, and God is maximally great, God exists in every possible world, and is consequently necessary. (h) Hence if God's existence is possible, his existence is necessary. (i) God's existence is at least possible. Therefore God exists.

(iv)   Criticism of Plantinga's Argument

I should like to make the following criticisms of Plantinga's argument.

(a) It will already be apparent that I do not think it makes sense to say that God is omniscient in a (or every) possible world. Possible worlds are not places in which people, or even gods, can exist. There is no world, for example in which pigs fly. To say that there is a possible world in which pigs fly is just a misleading way of saying that pigs might fly, or that it is possible that they should. It is improper to speak of God's actually existing 'in' a possible world, which suggests that God does exist somewhere, which takes you, illegitimately, half way to concluding that there is a God.

(b) It is difficult to see why Plantinga should not, once he has substituted the statement that God is omniscient in every possible world for the statement that God is necessarily omniscient, then pass directly to claiming that God must exist. For if God exists in every possible world, he ought to exist in this one, and so exist.

But it is a mistake to think that, from the fact that God is necessarily (because by definition) perfect or (in Plantinga's words) maximally excellent, that he is perfect in every possible world. What is really being said when one says that God is necessarily perfect, is that it is impossible for God to be anything other than perfect. Translated into the possible-world terminology, this is to say that there is not an imperfect God in any possible world. From this it does not even seem to follow that there is a God. The trouble is that it is one of the numerous defects of the possible-world terminology that it sometimes lets impossibilities masquerade as necessities. It is doing this when it defines God's necessarily being perfect as his being perfect in every possible world, instead of as his not being less than perfect in any.

The possible-world terminology also disguises the fact that the statement that God is perfect is hypothetical, and asserts only that if there is a God, he must be perfect. If one translates the hypothetical statement into the possible-world terminology, the fact that that God is necessarily perfect is hypothetical is lost, and the unwary will suppose that that God is necessarily perfect implies that there is a perfect God. (The same considerations apply to his necessarily being omnipotent and omniscient.)

(If to say that God is necessarily perfect really did mean that God was perfect in every possible world one could parody a possible-worlds type argument as follows: to say that bachelors are necessarily unmarried (which they are) means that there are unmarried bachelors in every possible world; therefore there are bachelors. Worse, one could argue that, because that centaurs are half horses is a necessary truth, and this means that centaurs are half horses in every possible world, there must be centaurs.)

(c) It would be a simplification of a Plantinga-like definition of 'God' if maximal greatness could be derived directly from maximal excellence. This could be done if existing in every possible world, rather like a bank's having a branches in every town, was a perfection. But Plantinga has done nothing to refute traditional arguments that show that because existence is not an attribute, it cannot be a perfection. Indeed, he seems to accept these arguments. And if, as we have just argued, there is no such thing as existing in a possible world, there can be no such thing as existing in every possible world. There are no possible worlds – which is not to say that no worlds are possible – and so there cannot be numerous possible worlds.

Just because having a branch in every town is an attribute of a bank, a bank can have a branch in every town by definition. God, however, cannot exist in every possible world by definition (even if there were such things) since existence, and so ubiquitous existence, is not an attribute. Because having a branch in every town is an attribute, a perfect bank does not have to exist; all that follows is that if there were a perfect bank, it would have a branch in every town. And for this very reason all that would follow if, because existence was an attribute, God could exist in every possible world by definition, would be that if there were a God, he would exist in every possible world, not that there was a God. And just as a bank has to exist to have a large number of branches, so God would have to exist already to exist in every possible world. If existing in every possible worlds *were* an attribute, God could possess it only if he existed already.

(d) Plantinga says that what he has done is to show that if the existence of God is possible, it is necessary. He does not claim that he has proved that God's existence *is* possible. He does, however, claim that it is not contrary to reason to believe that God's existence is possible.

I dare say that the logical possibility of the existence of God is not contrary to reason, if 'God' is taken in its ordinary (Western) sense as a being with certain attributes, such as wisdom, power, goodness, benevolence, etc. Indeed, it really is logically possible that such a God should exist. But, defined as Plantinga has defined 'God', as possessing maximal *greatness*, which entails existing in every possible world, the existence of God is contrary to reason. For, for reasons already given in the previous chapter, it is impossible for any being necessarily to possess existence, and existing in numerous possible worlds, taken literally, indicates necessarily possessing existence.

Indeed, the possible existence of God, *defined as Plantinga defines 'God'*, *is* contrary to reason. For Plantinga defines 'God' as a being who is maximally excellent and maximally great. To say that God is maximally excellent is just to say that if there is a God, he must be perfect, which is all right, but does not imply that there is a God, but, on the other hand, does not imply that there is not one. But being necessarily maximally great entails existing in every possible world and so existing of necessity. But for a being to exist necessarily is, for reasons already given in the preceding chapter, impossible. Hence, if God is defined in such a way as to exist necessarily, there cannot be a God.

Another way of putting this refutation of Plantinga is to say that, because existence is not an attribute, it is neither possible for God to exist necessarily nor possible for him necessarily not to exist. From this it follows (from the way in which the possible-worlds language has been introduced) that God exists in some possible worlds but not in others. Now we can, if we like, define God as a being who exists in all possible worlds, but, since in fact he exists in only some possible worlds, all that follows from this is that there is no God, so defined. We are back, as we saw in the preceding chapter, to saying that, if God by definition exists necessarily, there can be no God.

(e) The possible-worlds version of the ontological argument is therefore invalid. It only seems valid partly because of a unfamiliar and misleading terminology, which produces confusion and feeds on the imagination in undesirable ways.

(v)   The Ontological Argument, the Course of Nature and Religious Belief

Though the ontological argument is invalid, I do not think that pointing this out ends the matter. Examining the argument carefully reveals important corollaries, concerning not the nature of God, but what is the proper attitude to him.

The ontological argument accords with what I believe to be one important feature of a realistic idea of God; that he (or it) does not reveal his presence in the ordinary course of nature.

If the ontological argument is valid, God is a necessary being, in the sense that the proposition that there is a God is necessarily true. The empirical facts which we all discover in the normal course of living, on the other hand, are all contingent.[5] It must follow from this that, if God is a necessary being, none of these contingent consequences can be deduced from his existence.[6] For example, it cannot be deduced from the existence of a necessary God the contingent fact that I exist, that Christ or Buddha were ever born, that the theory of relativity is true, or that objects attract rather than repel one another. If God is a necessary being, it also follows that his existence cannot imply the occurrence of miracles. For that miracles occur, if they do, would be just one empirical contingent fact among others.

Another corollary of these facts being contingent, and God's being a necessary being, is that there can be no empirical evidence for or against his existence. Since there could be no circumstances in which a being who must exist does not exist, there would be no point in looking for any such circumstances. If contingent consequences could be deduced from the existence of God, God would not exist if these contingent consequences turned out to be false, and so his existence would not be necessary. Hence, if the ontological argument is valid, the course of nature must go on exactly the same whether there is a God or not.

In what might seem to be an odd kind of way, the fact that the ontological argument points to a God who is a necessary being can be regarded as one of this argument's merits. The ontological argument gives one something one needs. In a sense it gives one complete security in one's belief in the 'existence' of God, which is what is wanted. However, it gives this security only at the cost removing any of the expectations that might, on alternative views, have been disappointed, if he had not existed. This is the fact that I try to sum up, perhaps a little eccentrically, by saying that God neither exists nor does not exist.

It is an interesting question whether, given that God cannot be defined as existing, and also cannot be defined as not existing (see above) he might be defined as neither existing nor not existing. It is not true that God must necessarily exist to be an adequate object of worship, but it might be true that only a God to whom the notions of existence were inapplicable could be an adequate object of (silent) worship.

That God's necessity should involve the impossibility of falsification accords with the fact that theists frequently *act* as if it were true that there is no empirical proposition such that it would, if it were true, show that God does not exist. Theists often go on maintaining that there is a God however little evidence there seems for his existence, however much evidence there seems to be against it, and however impossible it is to deduce any verifiable consequences, especially predictions about the future, from the supposition that there is a God. Theists are reluctant, for example, to say that that God does not exist follows from the existence of any amount of evil. Theists may well not give their overt assent to the proposition that there is no possible empirical refutation of God's existence, but in practice they behave in some ways as if they accepted this in fact. If God is a necessary being, their practice, or one aspect of it, is entirely proper.

This invulnerability to contrary evidence is a corollary, too, of the fact that the existence of God is not an explanatory hypothesis, and should not be treated as one. Its function is not to enable us to discover what happens, to account for what happens, or to make predictions about what will happen.

The task of explaining things is much better left to scientists (including historians) of one sort or another. We entertain the idea of a God so that we may worship or contemplate him, and we may contemplate him without drawing any factual conclusions at all about the ordinary course of nature from his existence. Indeed, one might say that to the extent that God is to be contemplated, it is quite irrelevant whether he exists or not.

To contemplate or worship or love or feel awe or have numinous experience[7] of God it may be necessary – though I am not convinced of this – to conceive of him, but it is not necessary to believe that he exists. As I have said elsewhere, it is not necessary to believe that Elizabeth Bennet exists in order to fall in love with her. But if all that is necessary in order to contemplate God is to conceive of him, and no empirical facts have any bearing upon the question whether he exists or not, 'belief' in God does have an invulnerability similar to that which it would have had if the ontological argument had been valid. To the extent that God's only 'function' is to be contemplated, God has the same invulnerability that the ontological argument would have assigned to him if it were valid, but for a different reason. If the ontological argument is valid, nothing can occur that would make it rational to cease to believe that God exists. If his sole function is to be an adequate object of contemplation, worship or love, then, again, nothing that happens in the world can make it rational to cease to believe that God is a satisfactory object of such attitudes.

It also follows from the above remarks about necessity that, if it is necessary that an eternal being should have the attributes he has, no empirical contingent consequences can follow from his having them. If God is benevolent in fact, rather than necessarily benevolent, then consequences about the natural world would seem to follow. (It is, as I have said, and as is in any case obvious, one aspect of the problem of evil that the world is not what one would expect if there was a god who was in fact benevolent.) Hence, if God's being necessarily benevolent is his possessing necessarily that very attribute which he would have if he were just benevolent, but not necessarily benevolent, God cannot be necessarily benevolent, or only in the hypothetical sense that if there is a God, then, necessarily, he would be benevolent.

The only sense in which God might be necessarily benevolent, necessarily omnipotent and necessarily omniscient is the sense that it might be necessary to conceive of God as being benevolent in order to have the idea of a being who is an adequate object of worship. For the purpose of worship, though not for the purposes of expecting one thing rather than another, it may be necessary to conceive of God as being benevolent, omniscient and omnipotent. But I admit that it is rather difficult to disentangle the two.

(vi)   Conclusions

We have thus arrived at the idea of a God from whom no contingent consequences about the world follow. This means that the cosmological argument and the argument from design, which arguments I shall discuss in my next two chapters, must be invalid. For if no contingent consequences follow from the existence of God, no argument that appeals to facts about the existence or nature of these consequences can be valid, for there are no such facts. We shall shortly consider the cosmological argument and the argument from design, and attempt, in the process, to strengthen the view that the existence of God should make no difference, one way or another, to the nature of the universe or of man. (This does not mean that believing in God may not make a very great difference to the person who believes, and so, indirectly to others. It may do this even though the 'believer' thinks that there are no such consequences and that there is no God.)

Notes

1   In his 1974, and 1975. The reader is also referred to his book of readings, 1968.
2   See 1986, p. 81 f.
3   In 'The Impossibility of Possible Worlds', forthcoming in *Philosophy*.
4   David Lewis, in 1986, p. 123 f. considers the possibility that we ought to maximise happiness in other possible worlds than this. He rejects this view (p. 128) not on the grounds that considering the consequences of our action on merely possible people in merely possible worlds is absurd, but on the grounds that we ought only to bother about the consequences of our actions on people in or own possible worlds, as one might hold that we ought to bother only about the consequences of our actions on other members of our own family, country or species. This implies that we could bother about them, but should not, not that the idea of bothering about them is absurd.
5   This has been denied by Kripke, 1980 but his denial extends only to statements about identity, and he is probably wrong even about those.
6   Kripke's criticisms of the traditional distinction between contingent propositions that are known empirically and necessary propositions that are known *a priori* was discussed in the chapter 'Objections to Empiricism'.
7   For more about numinous experience see Otto, 1923.

6 The Cosmological Argument

(i) Introduction

In this chapter I shall discuss the cosmological argument, which is the second
kind of argument in Kant's classification. I shall not consider arguments from
the antecedent probability of a God's creating a universe. Perhaps creating a
universe is just what a certain kind of god would do. But one can imagine
many different kinds of gods who would create universes, for various different
kinds of reason, and some who would not. And the argument, that the universe
was created because it would have been created by an invisible person if
there were one, is, even if it is not supposed to increase the chances of there
being a God by very much, too much like the argument: if I had an invisible
wife, she would clean my house; my house is clean, therefore I have an invisible
wife, to be very compelling. And there is, of course, the counter-argument: if
there were a benevolent God, creating this kind of universe is just what he
would not do; therefore there is not a benevolent God.

There are, I think, two kinds of cosmological argument, the second more
fundamental than the first.[1]

(ii) The First Kind of Cosmological Argument

The first and less fundamental kind of cosmological argument starts from the
fact of motion, or (what is not quite the same) the fact of change. It argues
that this motion or change must be brought about by something, and this by
something else, until one reaches a first cause of motion, which is God. This
argument has several very obvious difficulties, of which I shall mention two.

(a) God is an omnipotent, omniscient, benevolent being who created the
universe. Why should the first cause be God rather than something quite
uninteresting? To show that there was a God, one would need something more
than the fact of motion, which by itself does not enable one to conclude
anything very specific about its cause. From the fact that there is motion the
most one would be able to conclude is that there is a first motion. One would

not even be able to conclude that this motion consisted in an act of a person.

In order to conclude that the universe was brought into existence by a person one would need to appeal to the kind of universe that there actually was. Such an argument would be a form of the argument from design, which we shall consider later. Even if one did need to postulate a god sufficiently wise and powerful to bring about the kind of universe that actually exists, which is very large and complicated, this needs the postulation only of a very intelligent and very powerful god, not one who is infinitely intelligent and infinitely powerful. The conclusion that the world was created by a very powerful and intelligent being would be one of enormous importance, even if he was not sufficiently wise and powerful properly to be called 'God'.)

(b) In arguing from the fact of change to the fact of a cause of that change, one is presupposing that everything must have a cause. However, from the premise that everything must have a cause, it follows that there can*not* be a first cause, rather than that there must be one. Since a cause must precede its effect, and nothing can precede the first cause, the first cause itself can not have a cause. Therefore, if nothing can exist that does not have a cause, there cannot be a first cause.

One way in which every event's having a cause can be reconciled with the existence of a finite chain of causes would be for the first link in the chain of causes to be its own cause.

However, it is not possible for an event to be its own cause. To say that an event has a cause is to say (roughly, for an accurate account of the difficult notion of causation is not necessary for the purpose of this discussion) that there is some other event which is a necessary and/or a sufficient condition of its occurrence; it is to say that if the cause occurs, the effect will occur, or that if the cause does not occur the effect will not occur (or both). Hence to say that an event is its own cause is to say that an event is a necessary and sufficient condition of its own occurrence. But every event is a necessary and sufficient condition of its own occurrence. Hence every event is its own 'cause', in this sense. But if every event is its own condition there is no need to appeal to any other event for its cause; and the cosmological argument will not get started. On the other hand, if one insists, as doubtless one should, that the necessary and sufficient conditions of an event must be other than that event itself, nothing, not even God, can be his or its own cause. In any case, something would have both to exist and not to exist to be a cause of its own existence. It would have not to exist in order for its existence to be brought about, and to exist, in order to bring its own existence about (for what does not exist cannot cause anything).

Therefore, if every event has a cause, there can be no first event. Hence, if God is regarded, though he does not have to be, as a first event, there can be no God.

It is sometimes said that the chain of causes must end in a necessary being of a type which would have been proved by the ontological argument, had it been valid. This is not so. A first cause might be necessary in the sense that it was not causally dependent upon anything else, in which case, if it existed, it would be necessary because nothing that happened could cause it not to exist. But this is not the sense of 'necessary' used in the ontological argument, which is that of logical rather than causal necessity.

If there is no first cause, the series of causes and effects must be infinite. Some have felt that an infinite series of causes is unsatisfactory as an explanation of how anything comes to be happening now. J.L. Mackie (who himself does not accept the argument I am about to state) has likened what is happening now to a railway carriage, which, on the analogy that there is no first cause, is attached to another carriage, and that to another, and so *ad infinitum*, without any carriages being pulled by an engine. An infinite series of causes can also be likened to a hanging chain, in which each link is prevented from falling to the ground by the fact that it is fastened to the link higher up, but where the chain itself is not anchored to anything.

In the universe as we know it, Mackie's series is indeed impossible. Finite trains (running along the flat) must have engines. But infinitely long trains not only would not need engines, they could not have engines, for, if they did, they would terminate in engines, and so not be infinitely long. (If the train was divided into sections, each section being pulled by an engine linked to the last coach in the preceding section, then the train could both have an engine – in fact, an infinite number of engines – and be infinitely long, but then there would not be a first engine.) If it is argued that the train could not move unless it were propelled by an engine, there are two possible replies. For one thing, it is not movement that, according to Newton's laws of motion, needs explanation, but change of movement. (Newton's first law is that bodies not acted upon by external forces continue in a state of uniform motion.) For another thing, one could not establish the fact that even change of movement required a force (such as that provided by a locomotive) unless one could first establish the existence of such a thing as an engine, which fact makes the argument circular.

Consider the ancient conundrum 'Which came first, the chicken or the egg?' In actual fact, chickens and eggs evolved from creatures who less and less resembled contemporary chickens, and produced things that less and less resembled contemporary eggs, so in actual fact neither came first. But in a universe that was not evolving, and so all chickens came from eggs and all eggs from chickens, the answer would be that neither the chicken nor the egg came first. In such a universe every chicken would have been hatched from an egg, and every egg would have been laid by a chicken, and so *ad infinitum*. There would, in this series, be no egg whose existence was not quite adequately explained by its having come from a chicken, and no chicken whose existence was not quite adequately explained by its having come from an egg. Similarly, the universe might be cyclical, and consist of an infinite series of big bangs, followed by the universe's expanding, followed by the universe's contracting, causing another big bang, and so on without beginning or end.

(It has been suggested that the universe is 'circular', and that the first big bang is identical with the last big bang. Since the first big bang happened before the first world war, and the first world war happened before the last big bang, this view would have the unfortunate consequence that, since *before* is a transitive relation, one and the same event, e.g., the first world war, could happen before itself. I believe that, on one view, there was nothing to explode. Nothing existed before the big bang. (I find this difficult to believe.))

A chain could, I think, be an infinite series of links; what could not happen would be that we should properly describe such a chain as 'hanging'. This would imply that there was something from which it hung. But no argument to a first link can be derived from this fact. We would not know whether or not the first link was in a chain that was hanging until we had established without circularity that there was a first link attached to a beam, and so could not argue, from the fact that it was hanging, to a first link.

(iii)   God as an Atemporal 'First' Cause

In any case, if God is himself outside time, and does not change, it cannot, strictly speaking, be that he is temporally the first cause. He would have to be a first cause in some atemporal sense of 'first'. (The expression 'first lady' does not refer to a lady who is temporally first.) Presumably, if there is a temporally first cause, God, if he is an atemporally 'first' cause, brought about this temporal first cause in an atemporal way (if there is such a way). But if God is atemporal, he can stand in no closer temporal relations to the second or later causes (all of which are events in the causal chain) than to the first of them. And, since he is omniscient and omnipotent, he must be equally responsible for all of these causes, and so cannot have caused some but not others. But, if you imagine that there is a god who is atemporally responsible for everything that exists in time, it really makes no difference to the cosmological argument whether the series of changes is finite or not. God could just as easily have atemporally produced an infinite series of events as he could a finite one. In the former case, every event in time would have a cause, so there would be no temporal first cause. There would be a 'first' atemporal cause (God) of the whole time series as a whole which, as a whole, would not have a temporal cause, though every temporal event within it would have a temporal cause.

Perhaps the supporters of this (the less fundamental) form of cosmological argument are thinking, naïvely, in terms of the model of a man getting a ball to roll down hill by giving it a kick. But kicking a ball is just one event in a series of events extending in both directions in time. The kick itself occurs at a moment in time, and it moves an already existing ball, whereas God is not giving a push to an already existing universe. He creates it. Hence, if God creates atemporally, he could just as well have created an infinite as a finite universe. Hence the question whether or not the universe had a beginning in time is quite independent of the question whether or not it was (perhaps atemporally) created.

(The question '*Why* did God create the universe?' suggests that its creation is an event, and that it has an explanation, which, I think, both brings God uncomfortably close to being inside the universe, and suggests that God's creating the universe is itself a chain in an infinite series of causes.)

It is doubtful, however, whether the notion of atemporal causation is coherent. It could not possibly be observed. One cannot so much as imagine what it would be like for an atemporal cause to bring about a temporal event. This makes me suspect that the expression 'atemporally caused' is meaningless. Nor could any verifiable consequence be deduced from the supposition of the occurrence of an atemporal cause. The notion of causation is closely involved with the idea that if one thing (the cause) were not to change, another thing would not change either. But an atemporal cause would have to be eternal, so to suppose that an eternal being might change would be contradictory.

The same, however, is not true of an everlasting[2] being. An everlasting being could change. Even if God were both everlasting and changeless, it could be true that if, *per impossibile*, some change were not to happen to him (say he were not to take some decision which he actually had taken), some change to the universe would not happen; hypothetical propositions with necessarily false antecedents may be true.

(Man's dependence on an eternal being has been likened to the dependence of a theorem upon the axioms from which it can be derived. But though a theorem can be deduced from its axioms, it is not dependent upon them, for the theorem may still be true, even though at least one of the axioms from which it is derived is false. There is, indeed, a sense in which the axioms that are dependent upon the theorems, for the axioms would have to be false if the theorems were false. Pursuing the analogy would then mean that God was in this sense dependent upon the universe, rather than that the universe being dependent upon God.)

The question whether the universe had a beginning in time is an empirical question, and one for scientists rather than for philosophers or theologians to answer (though it is difficult to see how scientists can find the evidence necessary to answer it). If matter, in the form of hydrogen atoms, is being continuously 'created' (or, rather, spontaneously 'springing' into existence, for the word 'created' is question-begging), they may well have been continuously created from all eternity. If the universe started with an explosion, there must have been something in existence before the explosion, for there must – unless something sprang into existence from nothing and immediately started exploding – have been something to explode. And, as we have seen, there might have been an infinite series of explosions, followed by expansions, followed by contractions, followed by explosions, without beginning and without end.

There are arguments designed to show that there cannot have been an infinite series of events before the events that are happening now. Once upon a time it was supposed that the notion of infinity was self-contradictory, on the grounds that if the series of numbers starting with 0 was infinite, the series of numbers starting with 1 would also be infinite, so infinity + 1 would have to equal infinity. This was supposed to be impossible. Again, the number of odd numbers is as infinite as the number of numbers, although there are twice as many numbers as there are odd numbers. In other words an infinite number, if there are any, may equal a number half itself. This, too, and many other similar things, was supposed to be contradictory and so impossible.

It follows that there are as many odd numbers as there are numbers from the fact that two groups must have the same number if every member of the first group can be put into one-to-one correspondence with every member of the second. The class of husbands can be put into one-to-one correspondence with the class of wives, as there is a relation, *being the spouse of*, which is such that it must hold between one and only one thing (a husband) and one and only one other thing (a wife).[3] This means that there must be as many husbands as wives. Since the class of even numbers can be put into one-to-one correspondence with the class of numbers, from which it follows that there are as many odd numbers as there are even numbers. This conclusion, however, is not contradictory, but just an idiosyncrasy of infinite numbers. Indeed, an infinite number can simply be defined as a number that is equal to a (proper) part of itself.

Hence it is impossible to argue that the series of events must be finite on the grounds that, if it were infinite, there would be as many days gone by today as had gone by yesterday, although one more day has gone by today than had gone by yesterday. This would be a consequence of the fact that, if the universe had no beginning, an infinite number of days had gone by both today and yesterday, which fact is in no way contradictory.

People who thought that an infinite series was impossible may have thought, wrongly, that since the series of events has ended (at least in the sense that there as yet are no events after the present event), it must have begun. They may have also have thought, rightly, that if there was no first event, there could not be an nth event (say a 9,877,654,323,640th event after the first event), and have concluded (wrongly) that since the idea of there being no number which is the number of this event is absurd, there must be a first event.

It is true, however, that if there are an infinite number of past events it will not be possible to number events (in days, for example, though as a matter of fact there could not have been any days before the Earth came into existence and started rotating on its axis) from the first event, as we number days from the birth of Christ, for there is no first event. It is true that if there is an infinite number of events, there will be no first event, and so no second or third event, and so no numbers which are the numbers of events, counting from the first. It is not true, however, that there is anything contradictory about this. It is just that one's imagination has to get used to the idea. And the fact that there is no first event does not have any practical importance, for one does not in practice number events from the first event, even if there is one, but from some arbitrary but widely known and locatable event such as the birth of Christ.

It follows from what I have been saying that it is possible for the universe to be either finite or infinite. Whether or not the universe has a beginning and an end in fact is a matter for scientists, not for theologians or philosophers, to decide, though to the extent that reasoning, rather than information, is relevant to the determination of this question, philosophers would be capable of taking some part in it.

(iv)   The Second Kind of Cosmological Argument

The second, more fundamental argument (more fundamental partly because it would apply to any kind of universe, whereas the first would apply only to a universe in which there was change) raises the question 'Why is there anything at all, rather than nothing?' The kind of answer that will, if it will, satisfy us will not be the kind which we explored in the preceding section, viz., 'There are things today because there were things yesterday, and what existed today arose out of what existed yesterday'. This answer is defective, and simply raises the question 'Why were there things yesterday?'

Indeed, if there is an infinite series of events, every event in the series will have an explanation. It will be explained by the event before it, and the event before it by the event before then, and so *ad infinitum*, if the series of events is infinite. But this explanation still, or so it is said, leaves unanswered the question why there is an event-series, whether finite or infinite, rather than no event-series at all.

(I have framed the above arguments in terms of explaining the occurrence of events, rather than in terms of explaining the existence of things. But in fact there may be no difference between explaining the occurrence of events and the existence of things. To explain the existence of a table, for example, is the same thing as to explain the event of a table's coming into existence, and then remaining in existence until it ceases to exist. Hence to ask for the explanation of the existence of the universe may just be to ask for the explanation of the start and continuance of one very long event, perhaps even an infinitely long one (the whole history of the universe), one without beginning and without end.)

Observation is not going to help with the question 'Why is there something rather than nothing?' This question obviously cannot be answered by an empirical scientific investigation. You may discover empirically, by trial and error, such things as what are the necessary and sufficient conditions of the Christmas tree lights working (if they are wired in line. The argument is more difficult if they are not). They work if all the bulbs are working, but do not work if there is one dud bulb. One can discover by experiment which is the dud bulb – supposing that there is only one – by replacing each of the bulbs in succession by a bulb known to be a good one. But you could not discover in this way what are the necessary and sufficient conditions for there being a universe. There is, by definition (because the universe, by definition, comprehends everything that there is) nothing spatiotemporal, analogous to a bulb, outside the universe for the universe to be dependent on. If, *per impossibile*, there were something outside the universe, one could hardly test whether the universe was dependent upon it by removing it and seeing if this obliterated the universe. Both would be too big, and last too long. It is true that one can make statements about the stars without being able to test these statements by experimenting on the stars. One can (for one thing) construct models of a section of the universe minus a certain star, but one cannot construct models of a wholly nonexistent universe to try to find out what would have produced it.

In any case, the same question ('Why does it exist, rather than not exist?') would then arise about the thing upon which the universe was supposed to be dependent. (That it is dependent upon God is the only answer that we shall be interested in here, but it makes no difference if it is supposed to be dependent upon something else.) But to answer this question is in principle impossible. The task of discovering empirically whether there was any connection of dependence between the universe and God would involve (a) annihilating the universe, which would be impossible, and seeing whether anything happened to God, and (b) annihilating God, which would be inconceivable, to see if anything happened to the universe. (I do not think it is an objection to this argument that if we were to annihilate the universe, we would annihilate ourselves with it, and so could not observe the result of annihilating it. Many things can happen that we cannot observe to happen.)

If there were in fact nothing, the question would then be 'Why is there nothing, rather than something?' From the fact that there would be no people to ask it does not show that there is no such question. The people who would ask it, if *per impossibile* there would be any people in a nonexistent universe, would be just the kind of people who would, if there were a universe, ask the question: 'Why is there something rather than nothing?' Both questions are either equally legitimate or illegitimate, but some people are never satisfied. (It is a mistake to suppose that there is anything wrong with a question asking what would happen in certain circumstances, if these circumstances are impossible. *Reductio ad absurdum* argument would be impossible if this were so.)

It follows from the fact that 'Why is there something rather than nothing?' means, in this context, 'Why is there something rather than nothing in this case rather than that?',[4] that the question, 'Why is there something rather than nothing?' is a meaningless question. (If there were nothing, the question would be: 'Why is there nothing, rather than something?', which would be another meaningless question.) These questions are meaningless because, if the question 'Why is there something rather than nothing?' always means, as it does in contexts such as the ones we are discussing, though not in all, 'Why is there something rather than nothing in this case, rather than that', it is meaningless to ask it in circumstances in which there can be no other cases. (If the question was 'Why is there something rather than nothing in the larder?', the question would not be meaningless, but then this larder could be compared with other larders in which there was nothing rather than something. But the creation of the universe must necessarily be unique. Hence the question posed by the cosmological argument 'Why is there a universe' is meaningless.)

One reason why the question 'Why did this thing happen' is meaningless when divorced from the possibility of their being other cases when this thing did not happen, is that answering it involves correlating some other thing with this thing's occurring, and its absence with this thing's not occurring. For example, to justify believing that measles causes spots one has to correlate the presence of measles with the presence of spots, and the absence of measles with the absence of spots. If it so happens that one has never come across any unspotted people, one may still wonder whether the spots are caused by measles, though one will then not be able to answer it. But if it were in principle impossible to come across such people, the question 'What caused the spots?' would not make sense. (In the case of God's motives for creating the universe, the further difficulty arises that, if God is conceived of as timeless, he cannot change, and so no changes in his state – say his state of motivation – can be correlated with the coming into existence of the universe, if it ever did come into existence.)

The fact that the question 'Why?' does not make sense when not involving a comparison with other cases is probably heuristic. We need to know why in one case, rather than in another, one thing happens in the one case but a different thing in the other, because we might need to be able to predict when the one thing will happen, and when the other. Disaster may befall us otherwise. Divorced from a comparison of cases, there is not this need, and no possibility of asking the question.

Even if 'Why?' were not to mean 'Why in this case, but not in that?', answering why-questions would still involve a comparison between two states of affairs. One needs to compare two states of affairs in order to apply Mill's methods.[5] For example, Mill's first method (the method of agreement) is to the effect that if you compare two states of affairs, one of the features in respect of which they *resemble* one another must be the cause of the other such feature, and the other the effect. But if you compare God and the universe, this would demonstrate that, if God is, as is the universe, a complex whole, that part of God which 'agreed' with a certain part of the universe would be the explanation of that part of the universe. However, we are not looking for an explanation of part of the universe, but of the universe as a whole. To apply Mill's methods to the alleged explanation by God of the universe as a whole would be possible only if both God and the universe were members of two wider collections of items, and God and the universe were the only factor in which these collections resembled one another. This way of reasoning would obviously be absurd.

One can, however, instead of asking, as we have been 'Why does such-and-such a thing happen on a particular occasion', ask 'Why does such-and-such a thing always happen?' But in this case one is asking for some law from which it can be deduced, rather than asking for a prior event from which it could have been predicted. For example, Newton explained why this apple fell to the ground rather than that one by some such fact as that the first was unsupported but the second was not. He explained why unsupported apples always fell to the ground by reference to the law of gravity. There can no more be this second kind of explanation of the universe as a whole than there can be the first. For explaining why something happens in the second way can proceed only by producing a law according to which it always happens, and the universe, so to speak, can only have happened once.

When we ask for an explanation of something, it is always against a background where something happened differently in some other place, or at some other time. For example, if one asks why that petrol station caught fire, the question one asks, when made fully explicit, must mean 'Why did this petrol station catch fire, when all those others did not?' The answer must consist in pointing to a factor which was present in the petrol station that did catch fire, but absent in the others. A match was thrown in this one, perhaps, but not in the other ones. If the (different) question is 'Why was this act of match-throwing followed by a fire, whereas all these other acts of match-throwing were not?', the answer may be that there was a petrol station present in the case of this first act, but not in the case of the others. Such an answer is not possible in the case of the universe. Hence the answer to the question 'Why in this case, and not in these others?' depends upon the class of events being considered. The answer depends upon whether you are talking about the class of petrol stations or the class of match-throwings. (Not all philosophers think that it is events that are causes, rather than, say facts, but I do not think that whether this is so or not affects the argument.)

It is inconceivable that there can be any other cases with which to compare the existence of the universe. The universe by definition includes all the cases there are. Hence the question 'Why is there something in this case, but nothing in all these other cases?' does not make sense, because there cannot be any other cases. The question 'Why is there something rather than nothing in that room, but nothing rather than something in that other room?' makes sense. The question 'Why is there something at all, rather than nothing at all?' does not. It is not just that we do not know how to answer it correctly. There is nothing that could conceivably count as a correct answer to it. Hence, though every event in the time series is explained by reference to previous events, the time series itself has no explanation. What follows is that it is meaningless to ask for an explanation of the occurrence of the time series itself.

(v)   From What Motive?

It could be argued that what I have been saying about causes is not entirely true. It is not true when 'Why?' means, as it sometimes does, 'From what motive?' It is true that when the question 'Why?' is asked of an action, it does not always mean 'From what motive?' Though the question 'Why did he do that?' may be answered by mentioning a motive ('Out of spite'), but it can also be answered by mentioning a belief ('Because he thought it would annoy his father'), or by mentioning factors which are neither motives nor beliefs (for example, 'Because he had a tumour on his brain'). But sometimes 'Why?' does mean 'From what motive?'

Hence it might be argued that the question 'Why is there a universe?' means – though it does not have to – 'From what motive is there a universe?' This question obviously does not make sense. The question 'From what motive?' must always mean 'From what motive is some action done?', and the universe is not an action. The question, then, must mean – 'From what motive was the universe created, or made as it is?' It looks as if this question would make sense if the universe were created, and created by the kind of being who is capable of having motives, but if there is no such being the universe cannot have been created from any motive.

One can, analogously to what I have said earlier about causes, make out a case for saying that 'From what motive was this done?' always means 'From what motive did so-and-so do this in this particular case, and not do the same thing in some other similar case?' Statements about motives are always answers to questions ('Why?' questions) when 'Why?' does mean 'Why in this case but not in that?' For one answer to the question 'Why is there a mess in this room but not in that one?' may be that some person had a motive for making a mess in this room, but not in that. (Motives are a species of cause.) Similar questions involving a comparison of cases are 'Why did this person make a mess on this occasion, but not on those other occasions?' and 'Why did this person make a mess, but those other persons not make one?'

But motives themselves have causes, and so the question 'From what motive?' must, like other questions, still be asked against a background. Since motives are a species of cause, the question 'From what motive?' still raises a question of the kind 'Why in this case but not in that?' For the questions will still arise 'Why did Tom have that motive, but Mary not', 'Why did Tom have that motive at that time, but not at another?', 'Why did Tom act on the motive when he did, and not a some other time?', and 'Why did Tom act on that motive whereas there were other motives that he had, but did not act on?' All these questions involve a comparison of cases, and so cannot be asked about the creation of the universe, which is necessarily unique.

There are no other explanations of the way things are than the ones that can be given us by empirical scientists. (The empirical sciences cannot be reduced to physics, and include history.) It is true that the only explanation they can give is one that shows how that things are as they are today arose, according to some law of nature, out of how things were as they were yesterday, and so on. This leaves the whole time series unexplained, but there is no better explanation to be had, and it is a confusion to ask for one.

Even when the question is 'From what motive?', and the universe's coming into existence and being as it is is explained by reference to God's motives, the appearance that one has transcended ordinary scientific explanations is illusory. For motives are acquired by people at certain dates and lost at other dates. There is a causal explanation of how it comes about that they have them, and the motives themselves are advanced as explanations of the actions that are alleged to proceed from them. And the motives occur at the same time as the actions done from those motives, are preceded by the causes of the motives and followed by these actions' effects. Hence explanation of the existence of a universe by reference to motivation is not a different kind of explanation from scientific explanation, and is not exempt from the criteria by which scientific explanations stand or fall. Explanation of the universe as a whole by reference to motivation is just bad scientific explanation. It cannot be used to explain the existence of a universe, or why one thing rather than another should happen within it. Motives cannot occur outside the time series, and so cannot be used to explain the time series as a whole.

'Why?' and 'How?'

'Why?' questions used to be contrasted with 'How?' questions, and it used to be said that science could tell us how things happened, not why they happened. This superficial view is simply not true. Science does tell us how things happen – for example, how the internal combustion engine works – but it also tells us why things happen. For example, it can tell us that the reason why our car will not start is that there is no petrol in the tank; and also tell us why it will not start if there is no petrol in the tank. It is not true that all 'Why?' questions are about motives, and not true that science cannot answer questions about motives. One of the objects of the science of psychology is to do just that.

(vi)   Explaining Away the Contingency of the Universe

The more fundamental version of the cosmological argument, which we are now considering, is often put in the following way. It is supposed that it is just a contingent fact that there is a universe, i.e., the universe is contingent. It is further supposed that the existence of contingent beings demands explanation, and that the only way to explain them adequately is to show that their existence necessarily follows from the existence of a being whose existence is itself necessary. This necessary being is usually supposed to be God, though it is not obvious why. (A criticism of the cosmological argument that involves a criticism of the very notion of necessity will be found at the end of this chapter.)

Let us suppose that the common philosophical view, that questions about whether something is necessarily so (as opposed to simply being so) cannot be answered by observation, is correct (which I believe is true of the kind of question at issue). The answer to the question whether a contingent being demands a necessary one cannot be an empirical question. Hence the considerations (given above) that show that the question 'Why is there something rather than nothing?' is meaningless, if it is considered as an empirical one, do not apply to giving an explanation of mere contingency.

The second more fundamental version of the cosmological argument can be elucidated as follows. No explanation of anything is fully satisfactory unless it shows that the thing to be explained (in this case, the existence of the universe) has to be as it is, i.e., that it is necessary that it should be as it is. Once we see that the thing to be explained must be as it is, the mind is fully satisfied, and feels no need to look further.

There are difficulties about this (more fundamental) version of the cosmological argument.

(a) It may be that, if the ontological argument is valid, all other proofs of the existence of God are unnecessary, and that if it is invalid, all other proofs are impossible. (This remark applies also to the argument from design, which will be considered later.) This is because there is no need to appeal to any empirical premises to prove that there is a God, if his existence follows immediately from his nature, which it must do if his existence is necessary. On the other hand, if the ontological argument is invalid, there cannot be any necessary beings; hence it must be impossible to demonstrate the existence of the universe by recourse to one, which is what the cosmological argument tries to do. Such arguments all depend upon the belief that the contingency of being needs explanation, when in fact, since all being is contingent, contingency is inescapable.

In reply to this argument, let me say that I do not think that the function of the first version of the cosmological argument is to prove the existence of a being that is necessary in the sense of 'necessary' used in the ontological argument. The second version of the argument, however, does need a necessary being, and it may well be that the only way in which a being can be necessary is in the sense demanded by the ontological argument. (No beings, apart from 'abstractions' like numbers, can be necessary in this sense.) If so, the above criticism does apply to it.

(b) If there were a necessary being, and its existence did necessitate the existence of contingent beings, the latter would then not be contingent beings at all (for what is necessitated by what is necessary must itself be necessary). Hence it looks as if the conclusion of this form of cosmological argument (that the universe is necessary, and so fully explicable) contradicts its premises (that the universe is contingent, and so needs explanation).

It might be argued in reply to this difficulty that there are two kinds of necessity, derivative and non-derivative. For example, the necessity of Pythagoras's theorem, since it can be shown necessarily to follow from necessary truths, is derivative. The necessary truths from which it follows (e.g., the necessary truth that things which equal a third thing equal one another) are non-derivative. Hence, the fact that the apparently contingent facts to be explained by being necessarily derived from God's necessity turn out to be themselves necessary, does not mean that they do not require to be explained by another necessity.

I doubt, however, whether the distinction between derivative and non-derivative necessity can be sustained. For example, it is a necessary truth that every proposition implies itself, but the necessity of this is shown to be derivative (in, say, *Principia Mathematica*).[6] It is to some extent an arbitrary matter which necessary truths are used as axioms and which as theorems. Hence, I suspect that (in the kind of mathematical system that is relevant) whatever is derivatively necessary could also be non-derivatively necessary.

So a better way of putting the argument would be not to say that the human mind is always dissatisfied with contingency, but that it is always dissatisfied with apparent contingency. (This allows the facts such as the existence of the universe, which the cosmological argument derives from necessary truths, to be themselves necessary.) The human intellect does not like brute facts, facts which just are so, but do not have to be so. Consequently, it tries to show that there is no possible alternative to things being as they are, and is satisfied when it is shown that these things are not brute facts. In particular, the human intellect is not satisfied with the apparently brute fact that there is a universe. It wants to be able to show that there has to be one.

These conditions for achieving such complete intellectual satisfaction would be fulfilled if it could be shown that there has to be a universe because (a) there has to be a God and (b) it has to be that, if there is a God, there has to be a universe. The trouble with (a) is that, if the criticisms of the ontological argument are correct, there cannot, as we have seen, be a necessary being, and so it cannot be true that there has to be a God. The trouble with (b) is that it is difficult to show how the existence of God does necessitate the existence of the universe. Did God *have* to create it, for example? This might conflict both with God's supposed freedom not to create the universe if he wished, and be inconsistent with his omnipotence. Furthermore, if the criticisms of the ontological argument are valid, all existential propositions must be contingent, and so no explanation which shows that the existence of the universe is only apparently contingent is possible. The existence of the universe really is contingent, not just apparently so.

In any case, the cosmological argument requires both the necessity of God, and the necessity of the hypothetical proposition that if there is a God, there must be a universe. The latter proposition cannot, however, be a necessary truth, even if it is true at all. For God and the universe are quite distinct and different existences, and in that case there cannot be any logical passage from one to the other as there can be, to take Descartes' example, from the existence of a mountain to that of a valley; for mountains and valleys are not distinct existences.

The existence of the universe is contingent. If there was reason for thinking that it cannot be just a contingent fact that the universe exists, then there would be just as much reason for thinking that every fact about it must be necessary. If contingency is unacceptable, little contingencies are just as unacceptable as big ones. It is just as contingent a fact about me that I was born on 22 September, for example, as it is that there is a universe. But not only is the universe not necessary, all the details of the universe *are* also not necessary.

In any case, the ideal of explanation which enables one to see the necessity of what is to be explained is taken from mathematics, and cannot be transferred to facts about the world, or to the fact that there is a world. Where some mathematical explanations are concerned, you can show that the fact to be explained has to be so. For example, if you want to know why the square on the hypotenuse of a right angled triangle is equal to the sum of the squares on the other two sides (Pythagoras's theorem), you are satisfied if you can be shown that this fact necessarily follows from other truths,[7] and it can also be shown, or if not shown, just seen to be self-evident, that these other truths are necessarily true. If this fact cannot be shown to follow necessarily from Euclid's axioms, or Euclid's axioms do not have to be true, it has not been adequately shown *why* the square on the hypotenuse of a right angled triangle equals the sum of the squares on its other two sides. It is this kind of explanation that mathematicians are looking for when they ask why no more than four colours are needed to colour a 'map' in such a way that no two adjacent 'counties' have the same colour.

But if one is explaining why one's car will not start, which is not a mathematical fact, it is impossible to achieve necessity. Perhaps it could not start because there was no petrol in the tank, and it cannot start without petrol. There was no petrol in the tank because I forgot to put any in, but then I might not have forgotten, and it has to be explained why I forgot. Showing that one thing is so because another thing is so can only show that each thing is conditional upon what went before, and leaves open the possibility that the whole series might have been different from what it was.

I do not wish to deny that, if there is no petrol my tank, my car *cannot* start (necessarily does not start). I establish this experimentally, by trying to start the car without petrol and finding that I invariably fail. Necessary connections are just those connections that cannot be separated by attempts to separate them. But that this is so is just another empirical contingent fact. Since it is just a brute fact that my car cannot start without petrol, the human mind is not satisfied. But one's dissatisfaction, again, is just the result of looking for a mathematical type of explanation in a case when this is inappropriate.

Furthermore, if to explain something is to show that it follows upon another thing in accordance with a law of nature, there is always the further possibility that the law of nature might have been different. If you explain the law, in its turn, by deriving it from another law, there is always the possibility that that other law might also have been different. You might look for yet another law, but you cannot go on deducing laws from other laws, *ad infinitum*. At some point or other you have to end with accepting that it is just a brute fact that the laws of nature are as they are.

(vii) The Cosmological Argument and Probability

It is sometimes said that the cosmological argument, though it does not amount to proof, at least leaves its conclusion more probable than it would be without it, or even that it leaves its conclusion more probable than not. But a proof, in the sense in which the cosmological and the ontological arguments purport to be proofs, are all or nothing matters. They are either all right or all wrong. If an attempted proof is flawed, then it does not increase the probability of its conclusion at all.

An ordinary inductive argument might increase the probability of its conclusion. If we were trying to prove that Smith was the murderer, we might think that, though we had failed to prove this conclusion outright, we might at least claim to have left it more probable than not. Whether we had or not would depend upon the circumstances. But with what attempts to be an apodeictic proof, this is not so. It increases the probability of its conclusion only in the way that a mathematician might with reason suspect that its existence shows that he is getting nearer than he was before to finding a proof that is apodeictic. And it is very doubtful whether theologians and metaphysicians are any nearer than they were to finding such a proof.

Indeed, there is a sense in which the existence of God cannot have a probability. The probability that the next time we toss a coin the chances are that it will fall heads uppermost is determined by the fact that out of a long run of tosses, about half are usually heads, together with further factors such as that the longer the run, the more closely the proportion of heads to tosses approximates to a half. Hence we could say only that the existence of a universe made it more probable that there was a God if, out of a large number of universes, more than half were created. But it is in principle impossible to do this. (a) There can only be one universe, (b) If there were any others, we could not observe them. (c) The major premise of our argument, that out of a long series of universes more than half have been created, could be established only if we could establish that more than half of them had been created. This latter makes circular the argument we are considering, and dependent upon other arguments for the existence of God.

The same remarks apply to the contention that the initial conditions which result in there being a universe like this one are so improbable that these conclusions could have been produced only by God. The initial conditions of the universe, if *per impossibile* they could be probable at all, can be neither more nor less probable than the conditions that exist at the moment, and so will, if such facts needed explanation at all, need explanation just as much as its present state. (If the universe were infinite, which seems to me to be likely, it would have no initial conditions.)

It has been supposed that there is another sense of 'probability' (or another kind of probability) in which we can say that the probability of a hypothesis is increased by the evidence for it, although the probability of the hypothesis in question does not concern the relative frequency of events in the past. For example, that the most probable explanation of a death was that the deceased was murdered by Tom cannot be established in so simple a way as can the fact that the probability of the next toss of a coin's being heads is a half. However, frequencies do enter into such a conclusion, though in a less direct way. We need to know the frequencies of handkerchiefs finding their way to places without having been dropped there by their owners, the frequencies of guns going off without their triggers being pulled, of suspects getting from Paris to London in less than half an hour, and so on. Even when we argue that something can be ruled out because it involves an impossibility, we are simply discounting it because it involves something with a frequency that is necessarily nil.

None of these ways of arguing can be used to increase the probability that there is a God. In order to use them, that God created a thing would have to be one of a number of alternative causal explanations of that thing, which it can be only if the alternatives are, like Tom, within the same spatial system as the fact to be explained.

If we were simply considering the probability of something being produced by an invisible, powerful being who existed within nature being responsible for any event, the probability of this could in principle be assessed. (It would, in fact, be nil.) But there is no such thing as the probability of a God spatially and temporally outside the universe being responsible for the universe as a whole. For there cannot in principle be the connections between an atemporal existent outside the universe and events in the universe that would give rise to any probabilities. (To consider this matter further would be to anticipate the treatment of the argument from design in the next chapter.)

The view that there is no such thing as the probability of the universe is not the same as the view that the universe is unique, dismissed by Richard Swinburne on pp. 117–8 of *The Coherence of Theism*. The universe is in fact unique in some respects, and not unique in others, for example in being a spatial entity and having material parts, which is true of many things. The point is not that the universe is unique, but that its coming into existence is not one of a series of events, like a coin's falling head uppermost, such that events in that series occur in a certain proportion of the occasions when an event within the universe, for example a coin's being tossed, occurs. (This could be put by saying that the universe's coming into existence is non-probable, rather than probable or improbable.)

Some people express surprise that the conditions the universe was in when it started are such as to produce a universe just like this one.[8] We ought rather to be surprised – since the universe is just like this one (since it is this one) – if the ultimate conditions which produced it were not such as to produce this one. If one could imagine oneself existing before the universe started, surprise that it was as it was would also be misplaced, because, in advance of any previous experience of universes, we would have no reason to expect one kind of universe rather than another. I am not suggesting that we should not be puzzled by the fact that reality is as it is. But the answer can only be that reality is as it now is because it was as it then was, and that it was as it then was because of what it was like before then. If the whole process had a beginning – which I myself do not believe – there can be no explanation of why it was as it was at the beginning. That it was created so by God only gives rise to the question 'Why was it created so by God?'

(viii) The Argument From the View that Every Possible World Exists[9]

If it should seem very, very improbable that there should be a universe just like this one, one's puzzlement might be somewhat diminished if one were to conclude that every possible universe existed. Indeed, it must be a logical truth that every possible universe does exist, for possible worlds are supposed to exhaust all the logically possible alternatives. Hence, or so it might seem, it is no longer surprising that what exists is this one.

But, if one thinks that an explanation of the existence of the universe is necessary at all, which I do not, there is still something left to explain. It may be true, if every possible world exists, that it is not surprising, and needs no explanation, that this possible world exists. But it might still be regarded as surprising that we inhabit this one of all the possible worlds, and the fact that every possible world exists would not explain it. For, or so it could be argued

– though I think that this rebuttal is, necessarily, as spurious as the argument rebutted – the questions would still arise 'Why do I inhabit this possible universe, rather than any of the others', or 'Why is this the possible universe that is actual (or actual relative to me), rather than any of the others?' Hence one spurious question unanswered gives rise to another spurious question unanswered.

There could be no possible scientific reasons for postulating these other universes, for they could be explained only by their effects on this one, and, since they are different universes, and in their own spaces and times, these effects will be by definition nil. To postulate the existence of an infinite number of universes to allay anything so philosophically problematic as puzzlement about why the universe exists would seem to me to a piece of almost unimaginable hubris, were it not that whether they exist or not could not conceivably make any difference to anyone, since, *ex hypothesi*, their existence can have no effects on this universe. I suspect that this is just anther case of the philosopher's qualifying all what seem to be his most daring speculations in such a way as to make them innocuous. To say that an infinite number of possible worlds actually exist looks daring, but when one points out that it would make not the slightest bit of difference to anyone whether they existed or not, any appearance of recklessness is immediately cancelled.

In any case, the argument presupposes that every possible world exists, and every possible world does not exist. For example there does not exist both the possible world where gremlins are instantiated, and the possible world where gremlins are not instantiated. There is only this possible world, where there are no gremlins. To say that there are possible worlds in which there are gremlins should just be another way of saying that it is possible that there should be gremlins. And the fact that it is possible that there should be gremlins would do nothing whatsoever to show that the existence of this world, in which there are no gremlins, is not improbable (if it could be improbable at all). But in any case it does not make sense to say that the existence of this world is improbable.

(ix) 'Existential Puzzlement'

Pascal was, in fact, born into seventeenth century France. He might express astonishment at not having been born into fourteenth century Italy or into nineteenth century England. But what if he had been born into fourteenth century Italy or into nineteenth century England? He now would (or could with just as much reason) express astonishment at not having been born into seventeenth century France. Hence his astonishment is something that it is impossible to appease, and misplaced in consequence.[10] The only explanation of how it comes about that the world contains me is of the kind that explains how it comes about that it contains my father and mother, how they met, and so on and so on. It is usually known, or is in principle ascertainable, what this explanation is.

(There is a sophistical answer to the question why the world contains me, which is that whoever I am I would still refer to myself by the pronoun 'I', so it is a necessary truth that I am the person I am, born at the time I was; hence there is nothing to explain. But it does not follow from this that the person I refer to with the word 'I' must be the person it refers to, any more than that it follows from the fact that the word 'here' refers to any place I happen to be that I must be at that place. And, of course, an explanation is needed of how I come to be where I am.)

(x)   Christianity and the Size of the Universe

The universe seems too large, and our planet too tiny a part of it, for God to be sufficiently concerned about it to have sent his only son to redeem it. There is an analogical argument to the effect that a planet resembling ours will have life on it as our does. The argument may not be strong in the case of any given planet, but when it is considered that there are billions of galaxies and billions of stars in each galaxy, the chances that there is not life on some of them seem to be remote. I understand that it is not known that there *are* any planets on stars outside the solar system, but again, when it is considered how many such stars there are, the chances of ours being the only one with planets seem even more remote. To think that we might be the only planet with life on it seems to me to be an example of a parochial belief in one's own uniqueness which a wider experience and more imagination would dispel. My guess is that almost every star like ours has planets, and that all the planets of a similar construction within certain ranges of temperature, etc., have life of one sort or another on them, and that life very unlike life as we know it may be on some that we think are not capable of supporting life. In fact, I guess there is life on millions and millions of stars. The odds that man is the 'highest', or even the most intelligent, form of life in the universe seem to me to be small.

A Christian, I suppose, might then think that there might be other incarnations on other planets to serve their inhabitants as ours does us. What modification to traditional Christology this view would necessitate I am not sure. There would, for example, be problems about how many bodies Christ could have, and their numerical identity with one another when it is considered that they cannot be spatio-temporally continuous. I would be inclined to recommend the resurrection of an old heresy (Docetism), according to which the body of Christ was not a flesh and blood body, but a kind of phantasm. But what I say here is obviously highly fanciful.

(xi)   Philosophy, Theology and Cosmology

The chances that philosophers or theologians – who appear to produce, without empirical evidence, conclusions of substance about the universe by sitting in their armchairs theorising about life and the world – obtaining the right conclusion about the universe are remote. They often appear to those hungry for novelty to obtain such conclusions because they employ a judicious confusion of platitude and paradox. The paradox gains credence from its confusion with the platitude, and the platitude gains a heady excitement because it is confused with the paradox. Hence two things, neither of which are interesting – one because it is obviously false and the other because it is obviously true – are mixed together to form a piece of sophistry which looks both true and new.

(xii)   Conclusion

My conclusion is that the cosmological argument is invalid. It does not succeed in showing that the existence of the universe is explained by the existence of God. Indeed, there is and can be no explanation of the existence of the universe, considered as a spatiotemporal whole. That there is a universe is just a brute fact that we have to accept. There can be an explanation of how each section of this spatiotemporal whole came to be as it is. This explanation would always consist in referring to some other sector of the universe. But the question 'How did the universe as a whole come about?', rather than how individual items in it came about, does not make sense.

I myself, however, think that postulating a God not only does not explain, but should not be supposed to explain, the existence of the universe. To suppose that it should is to confuse cosmology with theology, or to regard theology as an ersatz form of cosmology. The function (or one of them) of theology should be more to elaborate a satisfactory concept of God than to explain the universe, a matter which is strictly not its business. And I suspect that part of the business of theology is (among other things) a matter of finding a concept – or perhaps more than one concept – of God which satisfactorily meets (without producing false belief) a legitimate human need, rather than discovering facts about an independently existing entity. A long history of unsuccessful attempts to do the latter does it no credit.

Addendum: The Necessity of Necessity

The eminent philosopher Willard van Orman Quine has argued[11] that there is no such things as a necessity that cannot be reduced to mere universality. If he is right, the apparent contingency of the world cannot be explained away by the necessity of God, because there is no such thing as necessity. But he is not right, though I shall have space to argue against him only very briefly.

(a) I think it is Quine's view not that the word 'necessity' is meaningless, but that nothing in fact possesses it. But one could argue that there must be such a thing as necessity, because the word has been introduced into our language by our being shown examples of it, for example, that two and two must be four, and that people cannot avoid dying.

(b) I think that Quine may think that there is no such thing as necessity because he thinks that there is no such thing as a unrevisable proposition, and because he thinks that necessity would imply that there were.

But (1) it does not make sense to say that propositions either can or cannot be revised. What does make sense is to speak of revising one's belief that a proposition is true. One can do something to one's beliefs, whereas there is a sense in which one can do nothing to propositions. Now it may be that, with the help of drugs or hypnosis, one might be able to cause oneself to disbelieve propositions such as that two and two are four or that we have to die. (Indeed, the statement, about any proposition, that someone believes it, is never a logical truth.) But to make oneself disbelieve certain things would often be of doubtful sanity, and would in any case not show that the proposition one made oneself disbelieve was not a necessarily true one. Schoolchildren manage to doubt quite easy necessary truths with the greatest of ease. Whether it is possible to disbelieve a proposition is one thing; whether or not it is a necessary proposition is quite another.

(2) One reason why Quine thinks that no proposition is immune to revision is, I think, that he thinks, wrongly, that truth is a property of sentences rather

than of propositions. This may make him think that one has revised the truth of the proposition that if a equals b, and b equals c, then a equals c, when all one has done is to invent a mathematical system in which the symbol for equality is not a transitive relation. But to do this is not to 'revise' the proposition that if a equals b and b equals c, then a equals c, but to make the sentence 'If a equals b and b equals c then a equals c' express a proposition different from, and possibly compatible with, the one it expressed formerly. More technically, the words 'If a=b and b=c then -(a=c)' give an implicit definition of '=', and fix its meaning in such a way that it is no longer a word for a transitive relation. This means that the relation it is now a word for is a different relation, with different logical properties, from the relation it formerly stood for. This means that its truth has, without extra premises, no bearing upon the truth of the proposition it formerly expressed, and so the truth of the former does not supplant the truth of the latter.

(c) Quine holds that all necessity is *de dictu* and none of it *de re*. (This, of course, is a different view from the view that there is no such thing as necessity, though Quine may confuse the two views.) However, Quine's treatment of the difference between *de dictu* and *de re* necessity is unsatisfactory.

(1) If by *de dictu* necessity, Quine means that necessity which is the property of words, the reply is that that kind of necessity which belongs to two and two's being four is a not property of the words 'two and two are four' but of the proposition that two and two are four, and this proposition is not a conglomeration of words, though it is expressed in words. (Actually, I think descriptions, like propositions, are also not so much words, but put in words.)

(2) It is obvious that there is some necessity that is not a property of either propositions or words. For example, to be saved it may be necessary to believe the creed, and to live on tins on a desert island it may be necessary to have a tin opener (unless the tins have widgets), but neither believing the creed nor having a tin opener are words.

(d) Quine may be suspicious of the notion of necessity because he thinks that in some contexts necessity is opaque. He thinks this because he thinks that that the number of the planets is necessarily greater than seven depends on how many planets there are, which he thinks (rightly) is a matter of contingent fact. However, how many planets there are determines which number the description 'The number of planets' applies to, but does not determine whether the number it does apply to is necessarily greater than seven. If there were six planets, the words 'The number of planets' would refer to a number which is not necessarily greater than seven (because the number it would then refer to would be smaller than seven), but this is not because it would then refer to a number (nine) which possesses its necessity only under a description, but because it would refer to quite a different number, the number six. Quine is confusing the statement that that number which, it so happens, numbers the planets is a number which is necessarily greater than nine (which is true) with the statement that there are necessarily nine planets (which is false). He can make this confusion because 'The number of the planets is nine' may mean either.

(e) We have seen that revisability, whatever that may mean, would not imply lack of necessity. In any case, not everything is revisable. That not every belief is revisable is partly just a matter of common sense. But it is a difficulty for revisionism that, necessarily, at least some beliefs must be unrevisable. For example, if acids turn blue litmus paper red, and one seems to observe that this piece of litmus paper has not turned red, one must revise either one's belief (1a) that this is an acid, (1b) that acids turn blue litmus paper red, (1c) that this is litmus paper, or (2) that this has not turned red.[12] But being able to reject any one of these beliefs is not unlimited revisability. Unlimited revisability would involve the possibility of accepting (1a) through (1c) and rejecting (2). One may do this, but one does it by accepting something else, namely the proposition that if one accepts that (1a) through (1c) and rejects (2), the former cannot entail the latter. The process can be repeated *ad infinitum*, but wherever one stops along the line, one must stop at a proposition one has not revised. Hence, even if any belief could be revised, it is not possible that all beliefs should be revised.

(f) Quine may think that everything is 'revisable' as a result of the following confusion. It may be true of every proposition that circumstances could arise which should make us alter our beliefs that it is true. One can easily conceive of circumstances which, if they arose, should make us revise our belief that the Earth is flat. But this does not mean that circumstances might arise which should make us revise this belief, for we may be and are quite rightly completely confident that such circumstances will not arise. Indeed, the fact that we know that the Earth is flat, which we do, entails that no such circumstances can arise.

Notes

1   These are not the same two kinds of cosmological argument distinguished by Richard Swinburne, 1977, p. 116. They correspond to a distinction between Aquinas's first and second way on the one hand, and his third on the other.

2   For the distinction, between eternity and everlasingness, see the chapter on God's eternity.

3   See Bertrand Russell, 1919, chapter VIII.

4   A similar view has been put forward by Peter Lipton, 1993.

5   See John Stuart Mill, 1996, Book 3, chapter 8.

6   By Russell and Whitehead, 1910–13.

7   Euclid's axioms are perhaps a bad example, on account of the existence of non-Euclidean geometry.

8   The surprise has been well expressed by Parfit, 1992.

9   The reader is referred to the symposium between Ingwagen and Lowe, 1996. Incidentally, the question 'Why is there a universe?' might mean 'How does it come about that there is a universe?' But there could be no such thing as the coming about of the universe, as all comings about would have to be within the universe.

10   This argument is taken from Edwards, 1967.

11   See 1966, especially p. 76.

12   Despite what people say about the web of belief, I cannot think of anything else that is relevant, though the belief that everything is irrelevant may also be a belief that could be revised.

7 The Argument from Design

(i) Statement and Some Preliminary Criticisms of the Argument from Design

The argument from design starts from the premise that the universe as a whole has those features which it would have if it were designed, and concludes from this that it is in fact designed.

This argument commits the fallacy of affirming the consequent. It is logically possible for its premise to be true and its conclusion false, i.e., for the universe to have all the features of being designed, but not to be designed. That it commits this fallacy, however, need not worry anyone. All inductive arguments commit the fallacy of affirming the consequent. For example, the argument: he would have spots just like this, if he had measles; therefore he has measles, commits this fallacy. (The inductive argument: 'Tom, Dick and Harry have been observed to be mortal, and no-one has been observed not to be mortal, therefore all men are mortal', is also invalid (by the standards of deductive logic) because it involves the fallacy of illicit process (the fallacy of passing from information about some members of a class to a conclusion about all members of that class).) The problem of induction arises precisely because the premises of an inductive argument do not entail its conclusion, which means that it is logically possible for its premises to be true and its conclusion false. Since no-one is foolish enough to await a philosophical solution of the problem of induction before he does natural science, it would be unreasonable to await such a solution before doing natural theology.

The conclusion of the argument from design, viz., that the universe is designed, is a long way short of its being designed by an omnipotent, omniscient benevolent God. (We have seen that the cosmological argument is faced with a similar difficulty.) Though the being who designed the universe would obviously have to be personal (for designing things is an activity that only persons can engage in) and enormously powerful and intelligent, he would not necessarily have to be omnipotent and omniscient. Perhaps this being produced this rather unsatisfactory universe because it was beyond his power either to think of or to produce a better one. And economy would suggest that we do not postulate an omnipotent, omniscient God if the phenomena could be explained equally well by postulating a very powerful and very knowledgable one.

Hume points out[1] that the argument from design does not even show that the universe was designed by a single being, rather than by a committee, each member of which is in charge of different areas. (Perhaps, even, the members of the committee do not cooperate, or there is a very small committee consisting of one benevolent god and one malevolent one, as the Zoroastrians supposed.) Hence a further stage in the argument is needed to show that the being who designed the universe is God, in the sense of an omniscient, omnipotent, benevolent being. The argument from design does not by itself establish this. (One conclusion that might be drawn from the fact of evil, which I shall say more about later, is that evil shows that the being, if there is one, who designed the universe is either not totally benevolent, or does not have the knowledge and power to design a universe in which there is no evil.)

(ii)   The Argument from Design as an Analogical Argument

The argument from design can be put in such a way as to be an analogical argument. An analogical argument reasons that because one thing is known to resemble another in respect of certain features, then it will also resemble it in respect of certain other unknown features. (Arguing by analogy must not be confused with conceiving by analogy.) For example, it can be argued that, because a certain planet is known to resemble the Earth in a large number of other ways it will also resemble Earth in having life on it. The argument from design can be regarded as reasoning that because the universe as a whole resembles in several known ways certain things that are known to be designed, it must also resemble these things in being designed. Archbishop Paley[2] used the example of a watch. Because the universe is known to resemble a watch in that both the watch and the universe possess features normally associated with being designed, he concluded that the universe must further resemble a watch in having what the watch, but not the universe, is known to have, a designer.

The features that all things that are known to be designed have in common, over and above their being designed, however, are rather difficult to specify, and it is doubtful whether there are any. The features of things that are designed, unless the designer has made a botched job of it, are those features which a thing must have in order to further the ends of the designer (or someone hiring the designer, in which case the end of the designer will be to satisfy the person hiring him, by furthering the ends of the latter). But these ends can be so various that the things designed to satisfy them may have nothing in common over and above the fact that they further the designer's ends, whatever ends they may be.

This does not mean that we cannot infer that a thing is designed until we know what ends the designer had in mind. What it does mean is that, in postulating that something is designed, we are postulating a designer and his ends simultaneously. For example, we are postulating a watchmaker who wanted to sell objects like this to people who needed to tell the time, or a God who had in mind the creation of mankind. It does not follow from this, however, that we can never know that something is designed without knowing the purpose of the designer. We may think that something is designed, without knowing its purpose, if it resembles objects that have been designed more than it resembles objects that have not. But our ability to do this presupposes that we have been able first to identify other objects as being designed, and for this we will have had to postulate a purpose as well as a designer.

(iii)   Paley Picked an Example Especially Favourable to his Case

I do not know quite what is shown by the fact that Paley seems to have picked, from the class of human artifacts, one (a watch) most favourable to his case. But human beings do not only make machines like watches. (And it is question-begging to describe the universe as a machine. Machines are made by man to produce some result, if it be only entertainment. It ought to be shown that the universe is designed to produce some result, before it is described as a machine.) Human beings also use tools. But the universe as a whole is not really very like a tool. Human beings paint pictures and write symphonies and novels, but the universe is not very like a picture or a symphony or a novel. They make omelettes, but the universe is not very like an omelette. Nor is it much like a bridge, or a building, or a vehicle, or a club, or a constitution, or a novel, or a piece of music, or a limited liability company, all of which are designed.

Nor, perhaps could it be like the aforementioned things. There would even be some incoherence involved in supposing that it was like some of them. How could it be like a hammer, when it is an essential part of the meaning of 'hammer' that one can take it what it names (a hammer) by a hand – or a tail or some other part of the hammerer's anatomy (if it is not a human hammerer)

– external to the hammer, and with it the hammerer must hit something like a nail, which must also be external to it, into some external receptive material? But there is nothing external to the universe. Nor could the universe be like an omelette, for even if it could have an external cook to make it, it could have no external people to eat it. It might be the case that all there was, ever had been and ever would be in the universe was one object resembling a hammer. But though this thing would be just like a hammer, could it really be a hammer, when, *ex hypothesi* (because the universe is by definition the sum total of everything that there is), it cannot have been constructed by anything else in the universe, and there are no nails, or anything like nails, to hit with it, and no bits of wood, or anything like bits of wood, into which to hit the nails?[3]

It is part of the very concept of human artifacts that the features of a designed object are dependent upon a context. If so, the universe as a whole cannot be like them, since it, again by definition, is not set in any wider context. The notion of having a (useful) purpose, for example, is 'context-dependent'. For something to have a useful purpose, it must have effects, which consist in events causally connected to things that happen later than any act consisting of using the thing that has the purpose. For a carburettor, for example, to have a purpose, it must produce certain later effects upon an engine. Hence the universe could not consist of a carburettor and nothing else, for in that case there would be no engine. So perhaps, though things within the universe can have a purpose, the universe as a whole (logically or conceptually) cannot have one. The universe could consist of something which resembled a carburettor, but it would not be a carburettor unless its function was to mix air with petrol vapour in order to make it suitable for driving an engine, and this, in a universe in which, *ex hypothesi*, there could be neither engines nor engine drivers nor passengers outside the universe, it could not be.

If this is so, the universe could not be like a watch. For it is an essential part of the notion of a watch that it tells the time. To tell the time is to enable someone to know how much of the day has elapsed by means of a uniform motion which is proportionate to the movement of the Earth round its axis. The Earth moves one twenty-fourth of the way round its axis whenever the hour hand on a watch moves one twelfth round the dial. The universe itself could not do this, for there is nothing outside the universe for it to move proportionately to.

No-one, so far as I know, supposed that the universe, if it was like a clock in that it was constructed for some purpose, had the purpose of telling the time. But if having a purpose implies producing some result, aimed at by the designer, at later date, the universe cannot have a purpose, for all (temporal) results are the results within the universe of what happens within the universe, and all dates are dates within the universe. Hence the universe as a whole cannot produce a result at a later date.

There are, however, some members of the class of human artifacts that do not have purposes; works of art, for example. They do not necessarily have any ulterior aim, though they may have one. They are produced for the immediate satisfaction they give us, or for their own sake, or produced by some people on account of the immediate satisfaction they give to others. Perhaps there is no logical difficulty in the universe's being produced for the immediate satisfaction it gives. But all satisfaction is the satisfaction of some person or being. All such beings, with the exception of God, who transcends the universe, are within the universe. Hence, though the universe as a whole cannot give satisfaction to them, they cannot have created it for this satisfaction, for the universe could not be created by a part of itself. If it could be so created, a part of itself would have had to create itself, which implies that that part of the universe existed before the universe was created. But the universe could not give satisfaction in the ordinary way to any being outside the universe, even were such beings possible. For ordinary satisfaction is a causal result of achieving something we aimed to do, and of contemplating something that is as we aimed it to be, and is therefore both a consequence of the attempt and result of the contemplation. But all consequences or results must be consequences or results within the universe.

(iv) Further Ways in Which the Universe is not like an Artifact

The analogy between the construction of a watch and the alleged construction of the universe has been questioned by Immanuel Kant on the following grounds.[4] There are (at least) two important unlikenesses between the universe and the known results of design. (a) The watch is made out of preexisting materials, while the universe is supposed not to have been; God, in creating the universe, is supposed to have created the materials, not just, like a human builder, to have arranged them in one way rather than in another. (b) A human designer makes use of already existing causal laws, whereas the being who designed the universe would be as much responsible for the laws that governed it as for the things it contained.

(a) All human creation can perhaps be regarded as either as rearrangement of already existing materials or the altering of already existing things. When we build a house, we arrange bricks in a way in which they were not arranged previously. When we make a cake, we impose a form on the molecules in flour, milk, eggs, butter and sugar that they did not have before. If we write a symphony, we move ink from our inkwell to manuscript paper, and arrange the ink molecules in certain unusual ways. When we play a symphony, we arrange for groups of molecules (musical instruments, lecterns and musicians) to be collected together in one place, and cause them to make the molecules in the air around them, and so indirectly the ear drums of the audience, vibrate in a way in which they could not have been vibrating before. This results in appropriate modifications to the relevant parts of the brain to which these ears are attached. When we write a novel, we do much the same thing with printer's ink, or the ink molecules on a typewriter ribbon or print, and make broadly similar changes in publishers, printers, book sellers and readers. A preexisting object, for example, a book, will have been caused to be moved by a reader from one place (in a library or book shop) to another place (in our sitting room). If matter can be transformed into energy, and *vice versa*, we may be able to create matter, but this would involve annihilation of energy, so that the total, mass plus energy, can neither be created nor destroyed.

Some philosophers suppose that in some cases we actually do create something, over and above rearranging printer's ink and pieces of paper and cardboard. A novelist actually creates characters, like Pickwick or Macbeth or Pierre Bezukhov, who did not exist before. Pickwick and Macbeth and Pierre Bezukhov, since they are fictional, cannot themselves consist of arrangements of molecules.

(It has been considered a difficulty for various theories (including Frege's and Russell's), according to which statements 'about' nonexistent objects are false, that propositions such as that Lear had three daughters are true.[5] But I suspect that thinking that fictional characters (though writers' creations may be places or events, as well as people) present a difficulty for these theories involves failing to distinguish between the sentences in Lear as used by Shakespeare (or someone reading Shakespeare) and as used by a literary critic or an examination candidate. The first fail to refer to anything, and so are neither true nor false. The second are true or false, but are simply about what Shakespeare said.)

It is, however, a mistake to regard artistic creation as being like God's creation. It is a mistake suppose that a novelist's creating a character literally consists in his causing some person or thing to exists that did not exist before. There is no such entity as Macbeth. All there is is Shakespeare, his actors, his publishers and printers, his audience and readers, and the fact that the latter find it amusing to entertain thoughts or propositions that make an apparent reference to certain people (e.g. Macbeth) who in fact never existed. Shakespeare and other writers do cause ideas to exist in people's minds that did not exist before, but God's creation does not consists solely in the creation of ideas, but of things. (It is arguable – and is indeed frequently argued, but wrongly – that these ideas are themselves no more than rearrangement of molecules in the brain.) God's creation cannot be like the 'creation' of fictional entities, because the universe is not fiction.[6]

Though thoughts do come into existence and are not rearrangements of already existing neurons, the creation of thoughts is not a good model for God's creation. For one thing, we do not exactly create our own thoughts, which to a very large extent our outside our control. For another thing, there is no such thing as people's creating another person's thoughts, and though doubtless God is not limited by our limitations, man's creating other men's thoughts cannot be regarded as an analogue on which God's creation can be understood, let alone argued to, for it simply does not occur. What does occur is our communicating our thoughts to others, with a view to modifying theirs.

(b) Not only does man, unlike God, make the things he designs from preexisting materials. Causal laws are also presupposed in human construction, but not in God's. Though men (at least in a sense) made the mainspring of the watch (though not, of course, the materials out of which the mainspring was made) men did not make the law (concerning elasticity) that coiled springs tend to return to their original shape. They make cakes, but not the laws which determine what happens to a congealed mass of butter and flour when subjected to moderately high temperatures. They turn men into corpses, but do not create the causal laws that determine what happens when a bullet enters a young man's brain. But God not only must have made the materials as well as giving them a certain arrangement; he must also have 'made' the causal laws which govern their operation. He, unlike human beings, decided that the universe should be governed by certain causal laws and not others.

More serious is the fact that God's creation, as it would have to be if it created both the materials and the laws, is timeless – for time cannot exist until they are created – whereas human creation takes place in time. And one can raise a further serious difficulty for the argument from design – as one can for the cosmological argument – by asking oneself the question: 'What would one see if one saw the creation of the universe? What would be the difference between watching a universe coming into existence, and watching it being created by God?' If there would not be any discernible difference, does it even make sense to suppose that there is any difference between the universe's being created and its springing into existence? And, if not, why not just say that it sprang into existence?

(v)   The Argument from Design as an Inductive Argument[7]

An argument from analogy is very like an inductive argument. The difference is this. Where an analogical argument is concerned, as we have seen, we just have two or sometimes more individuals (we will assume that there are two) that are known to resemble one another, and it is argued that, because they are known to resemble one another in certain known ways, it is also likely that they will resemble one another in certain unknown ways. For example, because a document resembles one known to be written by a certain scholar in respect of certain features it may be concluded that it, too, is by that scholar.

But this is just what we are doing when we use an inductive argument, except that, in that case we have more instances and fewer common features. That is to say, in an inductive argument we have a premise to the effect that a large number of things resemble one another in one or a few respects, whereas in an analogical argument we have a premise to the effect that two (or at any rate only a few) things resemble one another in a large number of respects. But the conclusion of both arguments can be the same.

The conclusions will be the same if the conclusion of the inductive argument is that *one* or a *few* other things possess the characteristic that these things are not known to have. They will not be the same if the conclusion is that *everything* of a certain kind possesses a certain feature. If there can be as many resemblances in an analogical argument as in an inductive one, then the only difference between an inductive argument and an analogical one is that the inductive argument cites more instances. If we argue that because this, that and the other duck have been known to lay eggs then this animal, which resembles a duck in a number of respects – because it is a duck – will also lay eggs, then we are arguing from a known resemblance to an unknown one, which is just what we are doing when we use an analogical argument.

Hence you could produce an inductive, as opposed to an analogical, argument to the conclusion that something had been designed. You could argue that because a large number of things with certain features are known to have been designed, then something else, which has the same features must also have been designed. For example, you could argue that because this, that and the other watch, which are known to have been designed, possess certain features, such as hands that move uniformly round a figured dial, then this new object, which also possesses these features, must also be designed. (Such an argument where watches, which are things we find in the universe rather than the universe itself, are concerned would be an inductive argument that was in principle perfectly satisfactory.) Hence one might wish to maintain that the argument that because this, that and the other watch has been observed to be designed, the universe, which possesses the features of a watch, must be designed too is also an inductive argument that is perfectly satisfactory.

But the second, theological, argument, allegedly inductive, is very unlike the first, genuinely inductive argument. For one thing, its conclusion, that the universe is designed, cannot itself be empirically verified or falsified, whereas the conclusion that this watch, which we have just come across for the first time, has, like other watches, been designed, can be tested in an obvious way (by some such thing as by actually identifying the watchmaker, coming across records of him, or actually observing watchmakers making watches). For another thing, there is no element of temporal prediction in the latter argument. (Nor is there retrodiction, as there would be if we were making statements about the *past* construction of watches, as in this case usually we would be). There is a great deal of difference between arguing that because carbon hydrogen and oxygen have been correlated with life, we can predict, retrodict or just dict, rightly or wrongly, that life has occurred, is occurring or will occur (on some other planet also containing carbon, hydrogen and oxygen, in some remote galaxy) and arguing that because a, b, and c (which cannot be correlated with God's activity because this activity is unobservable) have occurred, something (namely God's activity) must occur at no date at all.

(vi)   The Existence of God Regarded as an Hypothesis

I have said that the argument from design can be regarded either as an argument from analogy or as an inductive argument. It makes no difference which. It can also be regarded as treating the proposition that there is a God as a hypothesis. As I have said one argues to the truth of a hypothesis in the following way. If a given hypothesis – say, that where there is no water there can be no life – is true, certain consequences (say, the absence of life) will obtain. These consequences have been observed to obtain (life is absent). Hence the hypothesis which entails them is true. (We decided earlier not to worry about the fact that this argument is invalid by the standards of deductive logic.)[8]

If the consequences deduced from a hypothesis (or a conjunction of hypotheses) are false, then either the hypothesis (or at least one of the conjunction of hypotheses) must be rejected. (For example, that this object does not turn red does not entail that what has been tested on it is not an acid. What it does entail is that either this is not litmus paper, or that this is not an acid, or that acids do not turn blue litmus paper red.) On the other hand, if this hypothesis (or these hypotheses) are true, this goes some way to making it rational to accept it (or them). The more consequences, in more varied circumstances, are confirmed,[9] the more likely the hypothesis becomes. This may be because, since the number of viable hypotheses is limited (the number of hypotheses that are not viable may be infinite), eliminating one increases the probability of those remaining. The more times a hypothesis is confirmed, the more likely it is to go on being confirmed.[10] (The consequences deduced from a hypothesis do not have to be propositions the truth of which is not already known.)

It may well be that deducing correct consequences from a hypothesis does not by itself strengthen it. What strengthens it is the fact that, every time you test a hypothesis and find that the consequences deduced from it are correct, the circumstances surrounding the test are bound to be slightly different in some known or unknown way. (If the consequence deduced from the hypothesis was not previously known, this helps eliminate the possibility that the inventor of the hypothesis was not cooking his results.) Hence repetition is an inferior kind of experiment. Just testing whether another favourable consequence can be deduced from a hypothesis is like experimentally testing a hypothesis by varying the circumstances, since the circumstances will probably vary. But the elimination is done incidentally, instead of being the experimenter's main purpose.

(vii)   Two Kinds of Hypothesis

There are two kinds of hypothesis: (a) those postulating laws or the truth of generalisations; and (b) those postulating the existence of individuals.

(a) You may (for example) frame the hypothesis that two kinds of event are uniformly connected, for example, that heavy objects uniformly fall faster than light ones, or, alternatively, that all objects in a vacuum accelerate at the same rate. (When Boyle first suggested the possibility that the volume of a gas might vary with its temperature, he was putting forward a hypothesis. This was a hypothesis to the effect that there is a law, which hypothesis has subsequently been confirmed by numerous later scientists. Now that it has been adequately confirmed it is called Boyle's law, not Boyle's hypothesis, but the content of the hypothesis, that the volume of a gas varies with its temperature and inversely with the pressure on it, is the same as the content of the law.)

(b) You can frame the hypothesis that the universe contains (a possibly unobserved) object, e.g., a magnet in my pocket, which would be responsible for the apparently aberrant behaviour of a compass needle in my vicinity, or a ferret in Tom's pocket, which would explain his aberrant behaviour. You can put forward the hypothesis that there is a hitherto undiscovered planet responsible for apparently aberrant behaviour in other planets. The presence of the measles virus is a hypothesis to explain why some children feel ill and have spots.

Perhaps some hypotheses fall into both categories at once, or, at any rate, perhaps one can frame both kinds of hypothesis simultaneously for mutual support. For example, you might postulate both that the universe contains some unobserved entities, e.g., electrons, and also postulate that the laws governing their behaviour are such-and-such, or one might postulate both that Tom is the murderer, which he could be, given the truth of the hypothesis that the corpse's being unusually cold would delay *rigor mortis*.

Since a God is an individual, not a law, if that there is a God is a hypothesis, it must be of the second kind. It may, however, be that in this case we are putting forward both kinds of hypothesis simultaneously. Perhaps, since you cannot observe the laws which govern divine behaviour, if there are any, you are putting forward both the hypothesis that there is a God, and the hypothesis that he operates in accordance with certain laws. Ordinary people tend to regard these as the same laws as those which govern human psychology – for example he is often supposed by ordinary people to be, like us, angry when provoked – and I do not know that the learned have anything better with which to replace this view.

(viii)   The Argument from Design is not Valid

Though the fact that hypotheses and the conclusion of analogical arguments and inductive arguments are not entailed by their premises is not necessarily an argument against accepting them, so long as they satisfy the criteria of valid deductive argument, whether these arguments are in fact valid by these criteria is another matter. I believe that the argument from design, judged by the criteria of inductive argument, is in principle not valid.

It is not an adequate reason for accepting a hypothesis that certain true propositions can be deduced from it. One could deduce the proposition that I will recover from the proposition that there is a God who loves me, but this does not mean that my recovering is good evidence for the existence of a God who loves me. If true propositions can be deduced from a hypothesis, it may explain the phenomenon to be explained, but it could be that it still ought to be rejected in favour of an hypothesis – for example that patients with such illnesses always do recover – that explains the phenomenon better. It is not enough that a hypothesis explains the phenomena that have been hitherto known, in the sense that the occurrence of the phenomena can be deduced from the hypothesis. It must be possible to test the hypothesis by finding out whether it will explain certain new phenomena, including those which are artificially produced by experiment, if experiment is possible. If an experiment is not possible, it must be its difficulty, like that of experimenting on remote galaxies or performing illegal operations, that makes it impossible. It must not be because the supposed hypothesis, as is said to be the case in many of Freud's hypotheses, in principle cannot be tested.

It is a very serious difficulty with treating the existence of God as an hypothesis that no-one has ever been able to use it to make any reliable predictions about the future course of our experience that could not otherwise have been predicted. If a hypothesis cannot enable one to make such predictions then, regarded solely as a hypothesis, it is likely to be excessively vague and possibly also vacuous. It is, however, an essential characteristic of a genuine hypothesis that one should be able to deduce consequences (not necessarily new consequences) from it, which consequences can (in principle, though in practice it may be difficult or impossible) be checked by observation.

This does not mean that two hypotheses from which the same consequences can be deduced are equally acceptable. For example, one hypothesis may be more economical than the other. But there is a great danger that the two hypotheses that entail the same consequences do so because they are the same hypothesis put into different words, or because one of the hypotheses contains elements that are superfluous. For example, the hypothesis that we have evolved by natural selection and the (less economical) hypothesis that we have evolved by natural selection presided over and directed by a deity may have exactly the same consequences. In this case the extra element in the latter (that the process is organised by God) is, since nothing can be deduced from it which cannot be deduced from the former, redundant. Less plausibly, it says just what the former says, but in a more elevated vocabulary.

I should add that I believe that the postulation of an unobserved individual or event is always made to complete a partial regularity. We postulate unobserved fire when we experience observed smoke because otherwise there would be only a partial regularity between smoke and fire. We postulate unobserved backs to the houses whose fronts we observe because otherwise there would be only a partial regularity between houses having fronts and having backs. We postulate others' pains because otherwise there would be only a partial regularity between cases of tissue damage and pain. (In our own case we only postulate the tissue damage to complete the regularity; there is no need to postulate our own pain.) We postulate others' thoughts because otherwise there would be only a partial regularity between the occurrence of words and their being produced by someone to whom they mean (usually) what they mean to us. Were there no other people with thoughts like ours there would be a lot of words about the place not connected with any thoughts, for they are not connected with our own thoughts.

If there were no other people with goals like ours, there would be a large number of cases of apparently purposive behaviour that were in fact not done from a purpose, and the partial regularity between such behaviour and such goals or purposes would be incomplete. If there were no planets going round stars other than ours, a partial observed regularity between the presence of stars and the presence of planets would be incomplete. Indeed, our knowledge of unobserved parts of the universe is obtained by a process of sampling it, and assuming that, where there is no reason to suppose the contrary, there are unsampled parts that fit with the sampled parts to produce an overall regular whole. But into this picture, and this account of obtaining knowledge, God, because he is not part of the spatio-temporal world, cannot fit.

(ix)   Design and Uniformity

This latter point needs reinforcing. Whenever one argues to a part of unobserved space and time from one's knowledge of an observed part of it, one is postulating something to complete an observed incomplete regularity. One has often observed a conjunction between fire and smoke, but the observed regularity is incomplete, because sometimes one observes fire without observing smoke, and at other times one observes smoke without observing fire. (One does not, of course observe the absence of smoke or the absence of fire, or there would not be so much as a partial regularity.) When this happens, one postulates unobserved smoke or unobserved fire in order to complete the uniformity. One assumes that the bit of the pattern one cannot see resembles the bits one can see.

But spatio-temporal regularity can be completed only by postulating other spatio-temporal bits, bits that are part of a unified spatio-temporal whole. For example, the postulated smoke will have to be in the spatio-temporal vicinity of the fire, i.e. just a little after in time and usually just a little higher up in space. Hence neither inductive argument nor completing partial regularities can be used to make it likely that there is a transcendent deity, because his acts of will cannot stand in any spatio-temporal relations to the events they are postulated to explain.

The case is no different when the argument is one from design. The design that is known to have caused the watch occurred earlier than the watch, and in the vicinity of the place where it was when it was made. Since God is a non-spatio-temporal being – or at any rate a non-spatial one – the design that caused the eye cannot have occurred before and close to the eye. If God were a spatio-temporal being, the difficulty would be slightly different. It would then be a problem why we do not *observe* this spatio-temporal being actually creating the watch. (It fairly obviously follows that a creator of the universe cannot be a spatio-temporal being.)

It is frequently maintained that the existence of God does not so much complete uncompleted regularities, as explain the fact that there are regularities at all, that is, explain the fact that nature is uniform. That nature is uniform is in that case sometimes adduced as a manifestation of the goodness and wisdom of God. God made nature uniform because he knew that man would not be able to find his way about a world in which events occurred in a manner that was not uniform.

I do not think, however, that it is possible to argue from the existence of regularity to the existence of God. One could obtain the necessary premise only if there were several universes, some of them regular and others not, and it was known that what was common (and peculiar) to the regular ones was that they were all created. But there can be no more than one universe, and if, *per impossibile*, there were several, a being who created only the regular ones would not, properly speaking be God, but some lesser entity, for God must have created all of them. If God had created all of them, then he would have created some irregular 'universes' and some regular ones, so nothing would follow about the existence of God from the regularity of this particular universe.

Where the normal hypothesising of individuals rather than laws in other than religious contexts is concerned, the argument for the hypothesis is based not on regularity, but upon apparent irregularity. There is an apparent irregularity in the behaviour of the compass needle, which irregularity is shown to be merely apparent, and not real, when one postulates an unobserved magnet.

There is an apparent irregularity in the behaviour of the planets, which is shown to be only apparent when an extra, hitherto unobserved, planet is postulated. (Postulating this other planet enabled astronomers to maintain that Kepler's law was correct, i.e., to maintain a regularity in spite of the behaviour which, without this other planet, would have meant that Kepler's law must have been wrong.) If these things – the compass needle and the planet – had gone on behaving in their usual regular ways, there would have been no need to postulate either the magnet or the unknown planet.

Similarly, the existence of God is sometimes postulated as a means of explaining away an apparent irregularity. Eyes, it is argued, are not what, from one's knowledge of past regularities, one would expect if nature did not contain a designer. Eyes without a designer, like watches without a maker, and Kepler's laws without an undiscovered planet, would involve an irregularity. But if you postulate that nature contains a designer, everything is, or so it is supposed, just as regular as one would expect or hope it to be. That man needs food, and there is food of precisely the kind he needs, is far too improbable a fact not to need an explanation, and it can be explained either by God's creating man in such a way as to be a being capable of making use of the materials there are, or of creating materials suitable for nourishing man, or in both ways at once. (Materials are food only if they are capable of nourishing man or some other living organism.)

The trouble with this way of arguing to the existence of God, as Kant pointed out, is that it does not lead one to postulate a being who has created the universe, so much as a lesser being within the universe who must have been tinkering with it. Just as someone must have been tinkering with a stream if there is a dam in it, and we must postulate someone to dam in order to explain away an apparent irregularity in the behaviour of the stream – streams have not previously been observed to dam themselves – so someone must have been tinkering with nature, if it contains eyes (for eyes, or so it was supposed, are not the sort of thing one would expect from nature unaided). But a god who simply tinkers with the course of nature would not be an omnipotent, omniscient creator, and a being who was an omnipotent, omniscient creator might perfectly well have produced a universe which, unlike a clock that perpetually needs winding, did not need tinkering with. God's handiwork might have been so perfect that he had covered up his own traces, so to speak, so that the universe, though in fact designed, showed no signs of being designed. But in this case, he would have created a universe in which there was no evidence for his existence.

(One should beware of the argument: a wise God would leave no traces of his having created the universe; there are no traces of the universe having been created by God; therefore the universe is created by God. It resembles too closely the argument: if my wife were a spy, she would not have told me that she was; she has not told me that she is a spy; therefore she must be one.)

One must concede that, if it could be shown that man was created by a very powerful being, which is the kind of thing that a design argument could in principle demonstrate, this would be a conclusion of the utmost importance, even if this being is not a transcendent God. But the idea that man was created by a mind that is not divine, and which was a part of the universe, is absurd. Such a creature could be observed, but it is not. I find it very difficult to put the following point, which I comprehend only obscurely, but postulating an imperfect being to give a pseudo-scientific explanation of things, and evolving the idea of a perfect being who does not have to explain anything, are two quite different things. I can see some justification in doing the latter, but doing the former, in this scientific age, is ridiculous.

(x)   Evolution and the Argument from Design

While there was no alternative explanation of the phenomenon of apparent design, which the argument from design attempts to explain, the argument from design was bound to seem very convincing. Design is enormously too improbable to have no explanation at all. It could hardly be coincidence that the eye was adapted to enable us to see, the ear to hear, the stomach to digest, the fingers to manipulate objects with, and so on. When less was known about nature, it seemed quite plausible to argue: the eye is not what one would expect from nature left to itself, therefore nature must have been interfered with (or improved upon) by a God, who produced the eye, etc., which nature could not have done by unaided. God was postulated to explain away an apparent irregularity, but in a wrong way.

We have already seen that such an argument will prove only the existence of a God who is part of nature, as a watchmaker is a part of nature. It will not prove the existence of a transcendent God. In any case, it is now known that nature could have produced and did produce the eye by itself.

In the beginning there were replicators. These, not surprisingly produced other replicators. Because they came to be more and more numerous, and were competing for a limited means of subsistence, not all the offspring could survive. Since the offspring did not exactly resemble either their 'parents' or one another, the characteristics of some gave them a better chance of surviving than those of others. Hence they became more numerous, and some of the others extinct. The ones that survived passed on their characteristics to their offspring, often in a more successful form. (For example, if having a long neck is an advantage to a giraffe, the longer-necked giraffes will survive more readily, and pass on their long necks, or even longer necks, to their offspring. Hence the necks of giraffes will (until length of neck gets to be a disadvantage) get longer and longer.)

Up to a point, evolutionary change is like repeatedly passing objects through a sieve which will weed out smaller and smaller particles. The sieve will not only change over time, the kind of sieve it is will be determined by the nature of the objects that pass through it. For example, predators as well as prey are constantly being changed by evolution. The particles passing through the sieve will not be the same as those that met the obstacle, but their offspring.

This theory, which is now in broad outline so successful that it is folly or bigotry (or both) to doubt it, gives an explanation, of the adaptation of man and other living organisms to their environments, in which design plays no part. Scientists sometimes complain that it is not a matter of chance, but of causal necessity, that certain variations survive at the expense of others, but 'chance' in this context means 'undesigned' not 'uncaused'. An accumulation of very tiny chance (undesigned) variations produces large differences because of the enormous amount of time available for them to do this in. For example, a tiny fold of skin that breaks an animal's fall may eventually turn into wings.[11] (The statement that the liver is for cleaning the blood is a true statement that is not incompatible with its not having been designed for that purpose by an intelligent being. It means that that is its function, not that that is its purpose.) In any other planet in any other solar system sufficiently resembling ours – and there must be billions of them – something similar to the evolution of planets and animals on this planet, including man, would be bound to happen. When one speaks of the survival of the fittest, the word 'fittest' has no moral implications; it simply means 'best able to survive'. Naturally, having those characteristics that enable it to survive is good for the animal possessing it, and a certain amount of altruism will enable the altruistic animal itself to survive, as well as enabling other members of its species – and, indeed, other species – to survive. This is partly on account of the fact that what strengthens its society will usually strengthen it.

It can now be seen that God did not provide food because he saw that men would need it, or provide eyes to help them to find it. It is rather the other way round. Food (or substances that became food and drink when there were men to want and need them) existed before men, and men evolved as the sort of beings that needed them because food and water were there to be had. Again, God did not create water because there was man to need drink. There was water before there was man, and man grew up to need water because he had to evolve to need what substances there were. (He could hardly have evolved to need substances that were not there.) Had there been only petrol, it is possible that man (or a being like man) would have evolved to run on petrol.

If evolution was God's way of producing man, then either he interfered with the process of evolution (which would involve miracles) or he did not. If he did not, then his handiwork would have been undetectable, and so no evidence for his existence. On the other hand, the idea that he did interfere by producing miracles is absurd. Would it not be just silly to suppose, for example, that God helped evolution along by miraculously producing some baby giraffes with longer necks than would have occurred in a purely random way? And the fact that there is no verifiable difference between a natural and a God-controlled evolution has made some philosophers think that there is no difference between the two hypotheses, as there is no difference between catching a man with the head of a fish and no arms or legs, and just catching a fish.

It is possible to explain the origin of man himself without recourse to the hypothesis that he or his ancestors were specially created. The hypothesis that he was specially created is an inelegant one. The conjunction of a scientific theory of the creation of the universe as a whole, coupled with a theological theory of the special creation of man at a particular point of time within it, makes the whole affair look like botched job. It is attractive to man's conceit rather than to his intellect. If giraffes could write books on evolution, they would doubtless propound the hypotheses of the special creation of giraffes. But if the origin of man can be explained by the occurrence of certain groups of molecules with the capacity of inaccurately replicating themselves, this is an elegant and scientifically satisfactory explanation of the origin of man. Man and giraffes, like Topsy, just grew.

Evolution theory in the form of sociobiology can also explain man's having his tendencies to behaviour, including his tendencies to social behaviour. Just as insects have instincts which regulate their very complicated social life, so human beings have morals. It seems likely that instead of man's morality being a divinely ordained and enforced set of laws intended for man's welfare, as some theologians have supposed, man's morality and his disposition to adhere to it have evolved over a long period of time because having it is of advantage to the individuals and societies that possessed it. (What is of advantage to society tends to be of advantage to its members, since they need society.) Moralities which are conducive to the survival of those who possess them have survived at the expense of those which are not by the latter's being eliminated (just as necks that are conducive to their possessors' survival have survived at the expense of those that are not).

I shall not consider this question in detail, partly because I have treated of it elsewhere.[12] But it is worth pointing out that it does not follow from the fact that man's morality and his altruism, such as it is, has been brought into existence by its being of advantage to individual members of his species that their morality is selfish or their altruism only apparent. The bee who makes the sacrifice perishes, but it is conducive to the interests of queen bees to perpetuate bees who sacrifice themselves to protect queens. Hence the altruism of workers is perpetuated because it is of advantage to queens. Just as it is of advantage to bees that other bees should sacrifice themselves by stinging intruders to the hive, so it is of advantage to man to love other men, and especially their children, even to the extent of sacrificing their own interest to theirs. It is of advantage to individuals to live in a society where such sacrifices are prevalent, because most people will gain more from the sacrifices of others than they will lose by their own sacrifices. (I am not suggesting that they make the sacrifices for this reason. They do not.) The individuals making the sacrifice may gain symbiotically – sometimes because others will make reciprocal sacrifices – by doing so, since what strengthens his community more often than not strengthens him. The theologian Bishop Butler pointed this out in his sermons[13] many years ago.[14]

Regularity and Personal Explanation

A special case of arguing from the fact that man is well adapted to his environment to the existence of God deserves more consideration; it is the argument from the regularity of nature. It has been suggested that nature is regular because in that way man will be able to find his way about, and use the regularities to achieve his purposes, like melting iron and making cakes. But man grew up to make use of the regularities because they were regularities, just as he grew up to understand them because there are those regularities that he had to understand – because they were there – in order to survive. Man was made for regularity, not regularity for man. Furthermore, God did not create a regular universe in order to enable men to grow in goodness. It is rather that what men regard as growing cleverness must consist (among other things) in dealing with the regularities that they find in nature.

It has been held[15] that explanation by the actions of people can do what scientific explanation cannot do, including explaining why there is a regular universe rather than an irregular one. However, personal explanation is just a species of scientific explanation. For in considering what God would or would not do, for example whether he would or would not make a uniform universe, we have to use regularities about the psychology of human beings. Swinburne – though he is certainly not alone in this – puts himself in God's place, considers what kind of universe he would produce if he were God, points out that this is just the kind of universe that actually exists, and concludes that there is a God. But, in order for this procedure to be successful, there must be some evidence that God's mind does work like this, in fact like ours. (We may build into our definition of 'God' that he is like us – at least to the extent of being, as we often are, benevolent, but much more so – but building this into God's definition (as we he seen elsewhere) just passes the problem from how we know that God, not defined in this way, is benevolent, to how we know that a God, defined in this way, exists.)

And it is not just a case of finding evidence that there is a God like this. Explanation by reference to the purposes of God puts God firmly within the universe, and subject to the very regularities which postulating him is supposed to explain. For in giving him motives from which issue his act of creation, we make him just as bound to the rules which govern motivation as are his creatures. Hence a God with motives must be within a regular universe, and so cannot explain it from 'outside'. But a God inside the universe could not properly be described as 'God' at all.

(xi)   Is Evolution Compatible with God's Existence?

On the other hand, I do not think the theory of evolution, though it undermines an argument for the existence of God, is in itself any more incompatible with the existence of God than is any other scientific theory. Evolution, in other words, might have been God's way of bringing man into existence, though, if so, this hypothesis does not explain anything that is not equally well explained by the theory of evolution itself, without this redundant extra embellishment. It is not so much that the theory of evolution provides one with a reason for disbelieving in the existence of God, so much as that it removes a reason for believing in his existence.

However, though the fact of evolution provides us with no reason for believing that there is a God, particular details of the evolutionary process, for example, the amount of pain and waste and the number of false starts that it seems to involve, may give us some reason for disbelieving in God. I will discuss this difficulty later, when I write about the problem of evil (chapter 20). And the theory of evolution may remove any reason for thinking that there is something sufficiently special about man to make it reasonable to suppose that God created the universe for him or created man in his own image. Men and animals alike are the result of the same processes and subject to the same laws. Whether the existence of God needs man to be something special in this way I am not sure. (Christianity, on account of its doctrine that Christ was sent to this relatively insignificant planet to redeem one species of animal that happens to live here, does need man to be special, which he is not.)

It has been plausibly supposed that the idea of a God especially concerned with the welfare of man is parochial. Though producing a universe like ours would be child's play to an omnipotent, omniscient being, is it not unduly anthropomorphic to think that some being produced the universe in such a vast scale just so that there should be man? The size of the Earth is just a fraction of a fraction of a billionth of the size of the universe. In order to think that God is especially concerned with the Earth, man must have an exaggerated idea of his own importance.

But perhaps this difficulty can be met by enlarging our idea of God. His aim, perhaps, was not to produce man, but to produce intelligent life in numerous parts of the universe, or to produce a universe with intelligent life in it. Perhaps, even, he made himself incarnate in all of them, though perhaps some of his creature on other planets needed this dispensation less than we. There is, however, no more empirical confirmation for this supposition than for the more usual view that his object was to create only man, and I regard the idea as fanciful.

(xii)   Some Miscellaneous Problems

I feel that this, though not a good place, is nevertheless the best place to consider some problems that some people find of great importance to them. In my experience, to worry excessively about these problems is a symptom of being neurotic. But then, not to be somewhat neurotic is not to be human.

'Why am I Here?'

People sometimes ask the question 'Why am I here?' They seem to feel that, if they knew why they were here, the answer to this question would not just be intellectually satisfying, but would give them some purpose in life. If they knew why they were here, or what they were for, they feel that they would then know what they ought to do. For example, if they feel that they were here to worship God, because God created men so that they might worship him, then they ought to worship him.

This raises the ethical question: given that there is a God who demands certain things of me, does it follow that I ought to do the things he demands? Obviously, it follows that I ought to do them only with the addition of an extra ethical premise, viz. that I ought to do those things which God wishes me to do.

This premise is questionable. It could be justified only if moral attributes are included in our conception of God's nature, and whether we could attribute suitable moral characteristics to God solely as a result of examination of the world he is alleged to have created is very very doubtful. The amount of evil the world contains would suggest that, if there is a god at all, we cannot.

However, there is no answer to the question 'Why am I here?' We would be here for some reason if there were a personal God, who put us here for some reason; but either there is no god, or the kind of god that we ought to worship is not the kind of god who has motives or purposes.

What is the Meaning of Life?

Some people ask whether there is any meaning to life. The answer to this question partly depends on what is meant by 'meaning'. If 'meaning' connotes, as sometimes it does, purpose, intention or plan, the question can be answered in the affirmative only if there is a God or some similar entity, capable of having plans, who created the universe, and me along with it, and had certain ends in view for myself and others when he created us. We have seen that this is not very likely.

If there is no meaning to life in this sense, this does not mean that we cannot give our lives import by choosing certain satisfying and not excessively undemanding goals – though some people seem to like their goals to be excessively demanding – and trying to realise them.

It has been held that only words can have meaning, and for this reason held that this question really ought to be reframed as the question: 'What is the meaning of [the word] "life"?' This question is of only academic importance, and certainly not the one which people who raise the former question are trying, however unsuccessfully, to ask.

But it is not true that only words can have meaning. A red sky at night can mean (be a sign of) a fine day tomorrow. Mary can have been meaning (intending) to write to her mother for a long time now. Tom may have meant (intended) his shot to have landed on the fairway. A politician's remarks may not mean very much (i.e., be of little importance, as well, perhaps, as not making much sense and being no reliable sign of any intention on his part to do what his words would suggest he was going to do). It is possible that the sense of 'meaning' in which words have meaning can be defined in terms of the sense of 'meaning' in which people intend things, or intend to do things. 'Snow is white', for example, may mean that snow is white if and only if most people, when they say 'Snow is white' intend to use this sentence to communicate the fact that snow is white.[16]

Since life's having a meaning implies that humans, and perhaps also the universe, were brought into existence by some being who had a reason for bringing them into existence and who expects something of them, the upshot of this chapter is that it cannot be shown that human life does have any meaning. It follows from what I have been saying that the world as a whole cannot make sense or mean anything. For to establish that something has meaning one must establish a connection between it and what it means. But though this connection can be established between one part of the universe and another part, say between smoke and fire (when smoke means fire) and (less reliably) 'smoke' and smoke (when 'smoke' means smoke), it is in principle impossible, for reasons already given, to establish a connection between the universe as a whole and anything else. For there is nothing outside the universe to be correlated with it and, if there were, there would be no possibility of varying the universe and seeing whether this thing outside the universe varied with it, as one can remove a cat, and see whether this stops people saying such things as 'Look at that cat'. Hence, if a meaning could be found within the universe, it would have, for reasons already given, to point to a person (a 'meaner') within the universe tinkering with it, not to a transcendent God. There is no reason to suppose that there is any such being over and above the people who we know in the usual way to exist, and perhaps other people on planets like ours in remote galaxies, and every reason to suppose that there is not.

It can be argued that God may have so constructed me that I am happy only if I do what he intended me to do. But it is not true of all men, though it is of some, that they can find happiness only by doing what some other being intends or wants them to do. Indeed, it may well be that to look at life like this is immature. One wants the universe to tell one what to do, so to speak, as one has been used to being told what to do by one's parents or teachers. But life need not be like some grand game of football, or army manoeuvres, where what I must do is play my part in an overall plan in which I myself have no hand. Personally, I hope, as well as believe, that it is not.

Life, if it has no purpose, would not be 'a tale told by an idiot'. It would not be a tale at all. Though it would signify nothing, it would not signify nothing in the way the words of an idiot signify nothing. They should signify something, but do not; the universe does not signify anything, but there is no reason why it should. One has, if life has no purpose, a free choice about what do with one's life. But this choice is free only in that one has no superhuman being to constrain one in making it. It is not free in the sense that there are no moral constraints, and those further constraints imposed by the desirability of living both prudently and wisely. If one does not live wisely, one oneself suffers whether there is a meaning to life or not. One could, if life has no meaning, nevertheless devote one's own existence to a noble cause of one's own choosing. But some people can be perfectly happy with much more mundane ambitions. Some appear to be perfectly happy just enjoying themselves, though I myself think to be happy in this way is more difficult.

'Who am I?'

Some people seem greatly concerned with the question 'Who am I?' It surprises me that, unless they are suffering from amnesia, they do not know who they are. I myself do know who I am. I am a retired professor of philosophy called 'Harrison'. They may think that there is some deeper meaning to this question, but questions do not usually have deeper meanings, and those who think they do are, by and large, confused.

However, these people may want some information which they think they lack. They may wish to supplement their knowledge of their name, their parents, their marital status, their employment and aspirations, by certain facts such as their position in the cosmos, and feel that, if only they knew such facts, this would help them to decide what to do with their lives.

To a large extent this desire raises questions already discussed. There is no information about the universe other than that discovered by empirical scientists, and this (with the exception that there may be help to be gained by religious techniques such as contemplation) does not presuppose having beliefs other than scientific ones, and does not tell you what to do. But, of course, the fact that there is only scientific information does not lead to the conclusion that it does not matter morally what we ought to do. Though moral rules will not be enforced by God, if there is no God, many of them will be enforced by society, and man is so organised that – with the possible exception of a few psychopaths – he cannot be happy without living a moderately good life. I suspect that an attempt to live a perfect life would be so strenuous and so unsuccessful that a person with a very strong desire for such perfection would often be miserable.

(xiii) Conclusion

I conclude that the argument from design is invalid. There could at best be a being within the universe who interfered with it, not a God who created it, and there is no reason to suppose that the universe is interfered with. (I shall discuss interference by miracles later.) This by itself does not prove that there is not a God, but (faith, which I shall discuss later, apart) one should withhold rational assent from that for which there is no evidence. Without evidence it is much more likely that Tom is not the murderer than that he is, as there are more ways of Tom's not being the murderer (for example, Mary, Jane, Dick or Harry's being the murderer) than of his being it. Generally speaking, affirmative propositions are more specific than negative ones, so they are, evidence apart, more likely to be false than their negative contradictories.[17]

The fact that the argument from design is invalid, however, just shows how absurd it is to treat the existence of God as an explanatory hypothesis, or for theologians to try to do what only scientists of one kind of another can do properly, and explain how things came to be as they are.[18] As I have said, one proper function of theology, whatever theologians have supposed its function to be, is to evolve a satisfactory concept (or perhaps more than one concept) of God. This is a useful and important occupation. Explaining things is not a theologian's business, and, *qua* theologian, he is no good at it; he should not quarrel with scientists, whose business it is. He can only bring his subject into disrepute when he tries.

Notes

1   In his *Dialogues Concerning Natural Religion*, 1935.
2   See 1802, especially chapters I–VI.
3   Putnam has argued (1981, chapter I) that a figure that resembled a portrait of Winston Churchill but was produced by ants, would not be a portrait of Winston Churchill. The works of Shakespeare, if they had been produced by the random typing of monkeys, would

not be a collection of plays, but a collection of marks on paper that happened to resemble plays.

4   In 'Transcendental Dialectic', 1929.

5   See, for example, Read, 1994, p. 127 f.

6   The reader is referred to Ryle, 1971.

7   The reader is referred to J.M. Keynes, chapter XIX.

8   Karl Popper, 1959, has also held that induction does not justify hypotheses, which are in fact justified by strenuous but unsuccessful attempts to refute them. But (a) the probability of any hypothesis would be increased only by eliminating its rivals provided that there were not an infinite number of possible hypotheses; (b) it is just an inductive fact that refuting hypotheses is not good for them, and that a hypothesis once refuted goes on being refuted in the same circumstances.

9   The more varied the circumstances in which the hypothesis is tested, the more rigorous the tests will have been, and so the less likely it is to fail further tests.

10   This is not realised by Popper. See 1959.

11   See Dawkins, 1986.

12   In 1971, 1992 and 1995.

13   *Loc. cit.*

14   The reader is referred to Ridley, 1996.

15   For example, by Swinburne, 1977.

16   This view is very roughly that put forward by Grice, 1968, reprinted 1971.

17   A.J. Ayer has pointed out that it is often not clear whether a proposition is affirmative or negative. For example, 'Mount Everest is the tallest mountain in the world' looks affirmative, but is equivalent to 'There is no mountain in the word higher than Mount Everest', which looks negative. He suggests that one should arbitrarily decide to call a proposition 'affirmative' if it is more specific than its contradictory. Applying this criterion makes 'There is no mountain in the world higher than Mount Everest' affirmative.

18   The view that religious 'statements' – if he held that they were statements – were not hypotheses was suggested by Wittgenstein, 1966. Unfortunately, Wittgenstein (a) does not explain what they are if they are not hypotheses, and (b) confuses the view that they are statements which are not hypotheses with the view that the function of religious sentences is not to express statements at all, but to do something else instead. What else is again unclear.

8 God and Morality: Ethical Arguments for the Existence of God[1]

(i) What an Ethical Argument is

By an ethical argument for the existence of God I mean an argument for his existence at least one of the premises of which is a moral judgment. This may be a very general moral judgment, for example, one to the effect that men have some duties or other. Alternatively, it may be a judgment to the effect that man has certain duties, which he would not have had were there no God. It is then concluded, *via* a valid argument (in the form of the *modus tollendo tollens*), that, since he would not have any duties, or, at any rate, these duties, if there were no God, there must be a God.[2] (This kind of argument does not try to deduce the existence of God from ethical premises alone.)

(ii) Three Views of the Relation Between God's Commands and Man's Duties

Whether it is possible to have an ethical argument for the existence of God having as its premise simply the fact that we have duties depends upon what is the correct view to take of the relationship between God's commands and man's duties. There are, I think, three main views about the nature of this relationship, though each of these views is capable of a certain amount of modification and refinement.

(a) According to the first, the notion of duty must be analysed in terms of what God has commanded.[3] From this it would follow that the proposition that some action is a duty is identical with, and so equivalent to, the proposition that God has commanded his creatures to perform it. To say that an action is a duty, on this view, is just to say that God has commanded us to perform it, or allocated us the task of performing actions of this kind. To say that an action is wrong is to say that God has prohibited actions like this. It is just as, if being a bachelor is correctly analysed into (1) being a man and (2) being unmarried, the statement that someone is a bachelor just is the statement, or is equivalent to, the statement that he is an unmarried man. It would not be improper to say that they were the same statement put into different words. For this reason I shall call the theory we are discussing the terminological theory of the relation between God's commands and man's duties.[4]

(b) It may be held that the only thing that *makes* an action a duty, and its omission wrong, is the fact that God has commanded it. That God has commanded a certain kind of action makes not to perform that action wrong, just as, or so it is commonly supposed, the fact that I have promised to do something makes it wrong not to do it. Since this is a theory about what makes right actions right, I shall call it the normative theory.

(c) It may be held that the only reason why God commands certain actions is that they are already duties, and the only reason why he prohibits others is that they are already wrong. Since this is a theory about God's policy of action, I shall call it the psychological theory.

(iii) Difference Between the Theories

The difference between these three theories is as follows.

(a) The terminological theory is not itself a substantive moral theory, but a second order theory about the correct analysis of the notions of being a duty or of being wrong (or about the meaning of the words 'duty' and 'wrong'). It does not by itself tell you what actions are duties, or what actions are wrong. If it is true, however, it follows that the statement that forgiveness is a duty is equivalent to the statement that God has commanded us to forgive one another. From this it would logically follow that it would be wrong not to be kind to one another, given that forgiveness is what God has commanded. These 'two' facts would be the same fact put into different words.

(b) The normative theory is a substantive first order ethical theory about that characteristic that is common and peculiar to all duties, i.e., that tries to identify that feature (if there is one) that only duties possess, and that all duties have in common. It is, indeed, a formulation of the supreme principle of morality, from which principle, if it is correct, all other derivative principles of duty must follow. It holds that that characteristic that is common to actions that are duties, and which is not also possessed by any actions that are not duties, is that God has commanded us to perform the former. It holds, further, that the *reason why* these actions are duties is that God has commanded them.

(c) The psychological theory, if you can with propriety speak of God's psychology, is a theory about God's strategy vis-à-vis commanding some actions and prohibiting others. Hence I shall call it the psychological theory. It is a view about the reason why God commands some actions, and prohibits others. It maintains that God has adopted as his policy of action that of commanding those actions which are (already) duties. God, according to this theory, has adopted the policy of commanding certain actions because they were man's duties antecedently to his having commanded them. It may be supposed that his doing this is the result of his goodness.

(iv)   The Impossibility of Holding More than One of These Three Theories

It is impossible consistently to hold more than one of these three theories: (a) is incompatible both with (b) and (c). If to say that an action is a duty is to say that God has commanded it, as on the terminological theory it is, then the two apparently different notions, of being a duty and of being commanded by God, must be in fact be identical. Hence it can hardly be the case that the action is a duty *because* God has commanded it (as would be the case on the normative theory) or that he has commanded it *because* it is a duty (as would be the case on the psychological theory). If one thing is so because another thing is so, these two things must be different things. One and the same thing cannot bring about itself.

The normative theory (b) and the psychological theory (c) must also be incompatible, because if the only reason why God commands certain actions is that they are already, antecedently to being commanded, duties, the only the reason why they are duties cannot be that God has commanded them.

(v)   Other Differences Between the Two Theories

(a) There are also other differences between these three theories. No specifically moral insight is necessary in order to know that being commanded by God is identical with being a duty. All we need to know is the meanings of certain words (in English, words such as 'duty', 'commanded' and 'God') or to be in possession of certain concepts, and a certain amount of logical acumen, say that small amount of logical acumen which would be necessary to see that if you maintained that something was a vixen but not a female fox one would be contradicting oneself. (The word 'duty' would be related to the expression 'commanded by God' as the word 'vixen' is related to the expression 'female fox'.) We need to know that what is meant by saying that an action is a duty is that God has commanded it, or we need to have that one concept which, it so happens, is in English expressed by the word 'duty' and, it also so happens, by the expression 'commanded by God'.

(b) We would, however, need moral insight, whatever this may be, in order to know that whatever God commands is made a duty by its being commanded by him, which is what is held to be the case by the normative theory. (Other duties would be derived from the fact that being commanded by God made something a duty. For example, if we had, on this theory, a duty to forgive one another, or to treat all men as brothers, this would be because God has commanded forgiveness or brotherly love.)

(c) In order to know that the psychological theory was true, we would need to have knowledge of the fact that God makes it his rule to command right actions. (It would seem natural to deduce this fact from the fact that God is, by definition, perfectly good.) It seems hardly likely that a morally perfect being would command any actions which were wrong (though I shall argue later that God might command us to perform some actions which, before he commanded them, were neither right nor wrong). We would also, on the psychological theory, need moral insight into what actions were right, antecedently to being commanded by God, if one was to have one of the premises needed in order to make inferences about what actions God actually commanded. I would have to know that helping the poor was right, in order to be able to infer that God commanded it, if the psychological theory is correct. (It is worth reminding the reader that all that follows from the definition of God as perfectly good is that if there is a God, he commands us to perform actions that are antecedently right; that he exists to command them cannot be deduced solely from the definition.)[5]

(vi)   Implications of the Theories for God's Omnipotence

The three theories, all of which might be regarded as excessively anthropomorphic, also have different implications for God's omnipotence.

On the Terminological Theory

On the terminological theory God would have no control over the fact that, given that the words 'commanded by God' and 'duty' mean what they do, the notion expressed by the words 'commanded by God' was the very same notion as that expressed by the word 'duty'. He could no more alter this than he could alter the fact that the number which you get by adding two to two is the same number that you get by subtracting four from eight. There would, however, be no limit to the actions that he could command.

On the Normative Theory

On the normative theory, God would have control over what actions he commanded, and so, by commanding some actions rather than others, he would cause them to be duties. He need have no control, however, over the fact that whatever actions he did command would be duties. He would have no control over the truth of the hypothetical proposition that if God were to command an action it would be a duty, if knowledge of morality is knowledge of *a priori* necessary self-evident truth. He would be like Midas, who could decide what things to turn into gold, but could not help it that whatever he touched did turn to gold.

On the Psychological Theory

On the psychological theory, God would have no control over what actions were duties. He would, however, have the power to decide whether or not to command those actions which were duties. (It has been argued, as we shall see later, that if God is perfect he must decide to command morality, for he would not be perfect if he did not. I do not accept this argument. It is rather like arguing that no bachelor has the power to get married, because he would no longer be a bachelor if he did.)

However, his having no control over what actions were duties would not detract from his omnipotence, if the fact that certain actions were duties is a branch of necessary truth (which I personally and unfashionably think it is). God's omnipotence is not limited by the fact that he cannot alter necessary truth (though it would be limited if he could not alter contingent truth.)

Indeed, the nature of morality would have to be something beyond God's control if he were not to be taking away with one hand what he was giving with the other, by making it his policy to command only such actions as were antecedently right. In allowing his will to be guided by the moral law he would, like King John, be giving us a charter against his commanding such things as human sacrifice. But if he could make human sacrifice right, this charter would be of no avail. He could 'cheat' by deciding to make human sacrifice right before he decided to command it. It would be as if a king decided to be subject to the law, as were his subjects, and then made a law bestowing special exemptions for offences committed by kings.

(vii)   Epistemological Differences Between the Theories

On the assumption that there is a God, the difference between these three theories is just an academic one, and will have no bearing upon what we actually ought to do. All and only those actions which are right will then be commanded by God, on all three theories. But there are important differences, already hinted at, between the accounts of the manner in which we come both to know what actions are duties, or what actions are commanded by God, implied by each of these three theories, whether there is a God or not.

(a) Since, on the terminological theory, statements about duties just are statements about God's commands, we know what our duties are in just that way, if there is a way, in which we know what God commands, by reading the Bible let us suppose, or by praying for guidance. (Should sentences purporting to be about God be meaningless, statements about our duties must also be meaningless.)

(b) On the normative theory we will know by moral insight, whatever that may be, the truth of the hypothetical major premise that if God commands an action, that action must be a duty; knowledge of what actions God actually does command must again be arrived at in whatever way, if there is a way, in which we arrive at the theological knowledge of which knowledge of what God commands is a species.

(c) On the psychological theory, we will know what actions are duties independently of knowing what actions God commands, and may even infer what actions God commands from an antecedent knowledge of our duties, together with the extra premise that if an action is a duty, then God will command it. We will know the truth of this extra premise, if we do, in whatever way we know the truth of theological propositions, if there is a way.

Though if there is a God, the difference between these three theories will be just an academic matter, if there is no God there is bound to be an enormous difference between the demands put upon us by them. On the psychological theory, everything which is a duty if there is a god could still be a duty if there is not one, but on the terminological theory and the normative theory no actions can be duties, if there is no God. On the terminological theory this is because to say that an action is a duty is to say that it is commanded by God, and, if there is no God, all such statements will be false. A nonexistent God cannot command anything. On the normative theory, it is because the only thing that makes an action a duty is its being commanded by God, and, if there is no God, nothing is commanded by him.

It is worth emphasising that only on the terminological theory and the normative theory does it follow, as many people suppose that it does,[6] that if there is no God, we may do as we please. On the psychological theory (the most plausible of the three) this does not follow.

(viii)   Argument to God's Existence from the Existence of Duties

It is at this point, perhaps, that we ought to consider the ethical argument for the existence of God, which has as its premise the fact that we have duties. It argues, as we have seen, that, since we do have duties, but would not have duties if there were no God, there must be a God.

The trouble with this argument is not that it is not valid. It is. But more is necessary for an argument to constitute a satisfactory proof of its conclusion than that it be valid. Its premises must be true, and, not only that, there must be some way of showing that they are true which does not involve establishing the truth of the conclusion. Otherwise the argument is circular, i.e., begs the question.

But though on the psychological theory we could establish that we had duties without first establishing that there was a God, it is not true that we would not have duties if there were no God. Some actions are duties – on the psychological theory, simply because they are acts of kindness, for example – not because God has commanded them. God, if he exists at all, commands them because they are duties. Hence one of the conditions for the acceptability of the above argument will be fulfilled, but not the other.

On the other hand, though if the terminological theory or the psychological theory were correct, it *would* be true that we would not have any duties if there were no God, there would be no way of establishing that we really do have duties, unless we first establish that there is a God. If, as would be the case if the terminological theory were true, to say that an action is a duty is to say that God commands it, we must first establish that God exists before we can establish that we have any duties. And if, as is the case if the normative theory were true, the only reason an action is a duty is that God commands it, we again cannot establish that we have any duties unless we first establish that there is a God (or establish what our duties are until we discover what he commands).

I shall consider more complex arguments for the existence of God later in this chapter.

(ix)   Respective Merits of the Three Theories

(a) The terminological theory, in the manner in which we have stated it, is quite implausible. Those numerous people who maintain, without any awareness of inconsistency, that men have duties although there is no God, show that what we mean when we say that an action is a duty cannot just be that God has commanded us to do it.

Further, those who hold the terminological theory are themselves inclined to speak as if it were a substantive moral truth that it is our duty to obey God's commands. But if the terminological theory gives us a correct definition of what it is to be a duty, the fact that God commands us to do our duty cannot be a substantive moral truth, for all anyone who held that it was our duty to obey God's commands would be saying would be that to obey God's commands is to obey God's commands.[7]

The terminological theory also has the disadvantage that it makes moral judgments about duty into purely factual judgments about what God has or has not commanded. The terminological theory is not naturalistic, in the sense that it turns moral judgments into judgments about the nature of the world. God is supposed to transcend the world. It is naturalistic in the sense that it leaves out all that is morally distinctive about moral judgments and makes them morally neutral. They would, on this theory, be morally neutral because you can say that an action is commanded by God without revealing whether or not you are morally for or against its being done. The terminological theory, therefore, must be false.

(b) Nor can the normative theory be right in thinking that the only reason why any action is wrong is that God has commanded us not to perform it. Some actions are wrong because they hurt other people, for example, and will be wrong for this reason whether there is a God or not. It would be possible to maintain that actions are only derivatively wrong because they hurt people. They are ultimately wrong because God has commanded us not to hurt people.

But it does seem to be the case that actions are wrong because they hurt people, and not just because God has commanded us not to hurt people. Many would hold that it would be wrong to hurt people, even if God, perhaps *per impossibile*, had commanded it.[8] Hence the normative theory, too, must be false.

(c) The psychological theory allows that an act can be right for reasons other than that God has commanded it. It also enables one to say what the first two theories have difficulty in saying, that God is good because his will is governed by an antecedently existing moral law. It has difficulties, however, over accommodating God's omnipotence. That God's will is directed – as it is on the psychological theory – by God's desire that he and we should conform, and that we should conform to an antecedently existing moral law, means that you can say that God is good for the very same kind of reason that men are good. But, since as we have seen, there would be very little point in God's will being directed by the moral law if he himself decided what that law should be, the psychological theory leads to the conclusion that the moral law must be independent of his will, which seems to limit his power. Indeed, if we hold this theory, the most natural answer to give to the question of how we know the difference between right and wrong is to say that moral judgments are a species of self-evident, necessary, *a priori* truths.[9]

If so, we know the truth of the ultimate principles of morals in the same way that we know that things that are each equal to a third thing are equal to one another, with the exception that, unlike this truth, the principles of morality can be denied without contradiction. They are a species of synthetic *a priori* truth. But in that case God cannot do anything to alter them, and the moral law is independent of his will. Any other theory would make a mockery of God's will supposedly being guided by the moral law. If moral judgments, for example, were just empirical judgments about what actions were against a society's rules, then God could decide, because he can cause his creatures to make certain rules rather than others, what these rules would be, which means that his will would be guided only by a law which he had himself decided upon, which is tantamount to his will's not being guided by the moral law at all.

On the terminological theory and the normative theory there is no reason why God should not be able to make right such things as human sacrifice simply by commanding them. It has ben held (by Kant, for example)[10] that a God whose will is not controlled by a moral law would have absolute power, but no goodness, and so be a monster.[11] However, a God who was sufficiently benevolent might create, from benevolence, a moral law pretty much like the one we think we have now. There is a sense in which God could be described as good – the sense in which a benevolent man may be described as good – without suggesting that he is benevolent only from a sense of duty. God, however, on these two theories, would himself bring it about that benevolence was good.

Indeed, the saying 'Amo, et fac quod vis' might apply to God, as well as to his creatures (to the extent that it does apply to them). Hence the difficulty with the terminological theory and the normative theory, that they take away God's morality, may have an answer.

So may the difficulty with the psychological theory, that it diminishes God's omnipotence. For one can argue that the idea of making or altering the moral law, unlike the idea of making or altering the positive law of one's country, does not make sense. It does not make sense because if anyone were to ask us to try to do him a favour by making adultery right instead of wrong, we would not have the faintest idea what he meant, or what to do to alter it. It can scarcely be a limitation on God's omnipotence that he cannot do something that cannot meaningfully be described.

(x)   Modified Versions of the Theories

It may be possible to improve on these theories, partly by combining elements from each of them.

Modified Version of the Terminological Theory

It may be possible to elaborate a more plausible version of the terminological theory. It could be argued that to say that to omit an action is morally wrong is one thing. To say that it is a duty is another. An action is a duty only if it is a task allotted to a person by his superior, which is not true of most wrong actions. Some such tasks are allotted by worldly superiors, but others are supposed to have been allocated to one by God. One will not have these latter tasks if there is not a God, but there are many other duties, i.e., those given by those in authority over one, which one will have whether there is a God or not. To hold that to say that an action is a duty is to say that it is a task allocated to one, perhaps by God, is not as implausible as to hold that to say that an action is morally wrong simply means that it is prohibited by God.

I suspect that this theory must distinguish being morally wrong and being an action that ought not to be done from being a duty, because certain tasks allocated to one by a superior – shooting protesting students, for example – may be tasks that it would be morally wrong to carry out. It could then even be that every wrong action involved neglecting a duty imposed upon one by one's heavenly superior, for it then may be that God has allocated to all men the duty of obeying the moral law. But, even so, though the class of morally wrong actions would then be coextensive with the class of actions that one could not perform without failing in a task that God had imposed upon one, an action's being morally wrong would still be one thing, and its being a duty imposed upon us by God another. We would still, in most cases, have to find out what duties God allocated to us by first finding out what was morally right, and inferring from this that, since this is what God wanted us to do, he had made it our duty. It is not an objection to this theory that God might have allocated to us certain tasks, over and above that of obeying (and perhaps enforcing) the moral law.

A Modified Version of the Normative Theory and the Psychological Theory

It is also possible to combine a modified version of the normative theory with a modified version of the psychological theory, by dropping the claim made by the normative theory, that the *only* reason why an action is right is that it is commanded by God, and the claim, made by the psychological theory, that the *only* reason why God commands an action is that it is antecedently morally right. It could be that, though in the first instance, all actions are duties for some reason other than that they are commanded by God, God then commands us to perform all those actions which are duties, and then these actions become duties on two counts, rather than upon one. They are duties in the first place because they are, say, acts of kindness, and then, because God commands us to perform acts of kindness, also right because we have a duty to obey God's commands. That we have a duty to obey God's commands, on this view, is not the supreme principle of morality.

It could even be that, though some actions are commanded by God because they are duties, other actions are duties solely because they are commanded by him. Some actions would then be right in the first place for some reason other than that God has commanded them, and then become also right because God commands them. Other actions would be right only because God has commanded them. Killing (other) people might be an example of the first class of actions; killing someone might be wrong in the first place because it is murder, and in the second because God has forbidden murder. Not working on Sundays, not baptising our children, copulating with people without having undergone the prescribed religious ceremony, or eating pork, might be examples of the second class of actions, and wrong only because God has prohibited them. The distinction I am drawing would correspond to that made by lawyers between acts that are *mala in se* and acts that are *mala prohibitas*. Some actions – for example, killing people – are wrong whether they are prohibited by law or not. Other actions, say bringing bottles containing white or red liquid from France to England without telling anybody, or parking where there is a double yellow line painted on the road, are wrong only because they are prohibited. Usually these actions are commanded for some reason supposed to do with human welfare, for example that of raising money for various supposedly necessary governmental purposes. The actions God commands could then be divided into two classes, those which would not be wrong if God did not exist and so did not command them, and those which would be wrong whether he existed or not

(It might seem reasonable to suppose that God prohibits the actions that are not antecedently wrong because he sees that the welfare of his creatures is furthered by such actions being prohibited. One day a week's rest, for example, might be good for people, physically, mentally and spiritually. It could be argued that a day's rest would in this case be right anyway, but there could be advantages in a law which compelled even the unnaturally energetic to take a holiday with others, and other advantages in everyone taking a holiday on the same day. It could also be that some of the actions which appear to us to be wrong solely because God has prohibited them are in fact also wrong for some other reason, and that God prohibits them for this reason, though only God can see what this reason is.)

In that case, if God, for some reason best known to himself, were to command some actions that we, antecedently to our being commanded, had a duty *not* to perform, we would be faced with a conflict of duties. This is the situation Abraham thought he was in when he thought God commanded him to sacrifice Isaac, or Agamemnon when he thought he had a duty to the gods (and fellow soldiers) to sacrifice Iphigenia in order to obtain a favourable wind. God could not have commanded Abraham to sacrifice Isaac if he cannot command what is antecedently wrong, but Abraham would still have had a conflict of duties if, *per impossibile*, God had been able to command what was antecedently wrong, and so had commanded him to sacrifice Isaac. And Abraham could have had a conflict between what he supposed were his duties if he had thought, however wrongly, that God had commanded him to sacrifice Isaac.

(It does not, follow, as some philosophers have supposed, that all the alternatives open to Isaac or Agamemnon were wrong. All the alternatives may have involved doing some evil, but then perhaps it would have been right for them to choose the least evil alternative. If both alternatives were equally evil, it might have been right to adopt one or other of them, no matter which. The fact that there are important matters involved does not mean, if the preponderance of evil on either side is equal, that one might not perfectly well decide the issue by tossing a coin.)

(xi) The Psychological Theory Correct

My own view is that (given that there is a God and that he is personal) the psychological theory (modified in the way suggested above) is the correct one. There are some actions that God commands because they are antecedently right for reasons other than that he himself has commanded them; if there is a God, however, it may well be that he has also commanded certain other actions which are not antecedently right.

It could also be that there are some antecedently right actions which God does not positively *command*, though I cannot think of a reason why he should not command them. There is a perfectly good reason why the law should stop short of prohibiting all antecedently wrong actions, for enforcing morality is expensive and inconvenient, involves interference with people's privacy, is often counterproductive, and infringes people's preference for going to the devil in their own way, a merit which may not commend itself as much to the deity as it does to some earthly potentates. However, it presumably costs God nothing to prohibit absolutely every wrong action and, if there is a God, we have no privacy from him anyway.

I think the psychological theory is the correct one because I think that it is obvious that when we say that some action is wrong or a duty we are not saying that God prohibits or enjoins this action. Man would need morality whether there was a God or not. It is needed to prevent men from performing actions which are disruptive of society, and to facilitate cooperation in enterprises for which interest or inclination, without morality, provides no adequate motive. My endorsement of the psychological theory does not mean that I think there is a God. It simply delineates what would be the relations between God and morality if there were a personal God. The psychological theory is preferable to the normative theory because it is difficult to believe that to cause people to suffer would not be wrong even if there were not a God to prohibit such behaviour.

(xii) Some Further Remarks on the Bearing of the Existence of God (and of an Afterlife) upon Morality

If there is a (personal) God, this is likely to make some difference to the way men ought to behave. As we have seen, he may prohibit some actions that would not be wrong had he not prohibited them, and if we have a duty to respect his prohibitions, we then ought to omit these actions, actions which we would be under no obligation to refrain from performing if he did not prohibit them. For example, we might be under an obligation not to fornicate that could not be justified without recourse to the fact (if it is one) that God has prohibited it. If he commands actions that are right anyway, we would then have a more stringent obligation to perform these actions, though we ought to do them whether he commanded them or not. For example, we might be under an obligation to love one another even if such behaviour were not rewarded in heaven, but it might be more incumbent upon us to be loving if loving actions were so rewarded.

If either the terminological or the normative theories are true, this may make a great deal of difference to our moral beliefs. If the psychological theory is true, we will be justified in attributing to God our own moral beliefs, which beliefs will sanction practices that are by and large useful to mankind. There is a great danger, on the terminological and the normative theories, of totally harmful moral beliefs being acted upon and enforced, because men think that God's supposed commands ought to be obeyed blindly, for good or ill. I should put among these the prohibition of anaesthetics, suicide, contraception, homosexual intercourse, euthanasia, and many others. Prohibition of blood transfusions could go on the list if it could be taken seriously. Prohibition of eating pork deprives those who observe it of harmless pleasure. (Not everyone, even among those who are not pigs, thinks that eating pigs is harmless, but that it hurts pigs is not the reason for the prohibition.) Prohibition of fornication, even in moderation, and divorce may have to be added. On the psychological theory, our beliefs about what God commands are more easily altered in the light of changing knowledge and circumstances, or changing and possibly more enlightened beliefs about the harmfulness of the actions prohibited.

If God is capable of being affected by human action, then we might have an obligation to do such things as please him, and if he loves us, we might have an obligation not to give him pain by behaving in ways that hurt him even if he is not capable of intervention. If he responds to petitionary prayer, we might have a duty to pray for things which we and other men need. If he rewards the virtuous and punishes the vicious in this world, then prudence, which is in any case an important virtue, will reinforce an obligation not to behave badly which we would have even if the action in question were not punished. If there is an afterlife and we are rewarded or punished in another world, this will mean that we have an even more stringent obligation, on account of prudence, to avoid vice ourselves, and not to lead others into temptation, on account of an even more serious risk of their coming to harm.

On the other hand, if there is not a God, or not a personal God, or not a God who can be affected by what we do on Earth, then we will find that some of the actions – for example, observing the Sabbath or not eating pork – that religious people think are obligatory are actions which it is not necessary, and may be positively harmful, to perform. Even thinking that harmless actions are obligations is a nuisance, for one has more obligations that one can easily fulfil anyway, and attempting to discharge unnecessary obligations wastes time and energy.

Belief in an afterlife may be a bad thing, for it can encourage unrealistic behaviour. For example, if there is an afterlife, especially one in which all or most of us will be happy, it will not be so much of a disaster, and perhaps not a disaster at all, to obliterate everyone on Earth in pursuit of a mistaken morality. However, it could not be obligatory to obliterate the Earth rather than perform a wrong action, for an action that might be right in normal circumstances is not likely to be right if the end of the world results from performing it, unless there is a heaven to redress the balance. Some who thought it would have been better to be dead than red may think this only because they think that death is not permanent, in which case their belief in an afterlife could, were it effective, be disastrous.

It may be, however, that I am here taking a rather naïve attitude to the next world. If, as I have argued, the existence of God is unverifiable in this world or in the next, then it follows that the consequences of good or bad actions are the same whether there is a God or not, for discovering that one had been punished by God for performing a wrong action would be a form of verifying his existence (just as being punished by one's earthly father for behaving badly is a way of verifying *his* existence). Indeed, if whether or not there was place for life after death depended upon whether or not there was a God, one's getting to this place at all would be a way of verifying God's existence. Hence, if God is a necessary being, and if faith is therefore different from ordinary belief (as I shall argue later that it is), it follows that the existence of God and the existence of an afterlife are logically independent of one another. God's existence, in this case, cannot enforce morality in any other way than by our conceiving of ourselves as being watched over by a God, whose being displeased if we act wrongly may reinforce what favourable attitude to morality we have.

In an earlier chapter (chapter 4) I have pointed out the attraction of the idea of a God who is a necessary being, understood in a certain kind of way. We have seen that no empirical consequences could be deduced from the existence of a necessarily existing God. It looks as if a God from whom no empirical consequences can be deduced can have no bearing upon morality. For morality involves two things, a belief about what one ought to do in such and such circumstances, and a belief that these circumstance obtain. For example, it involves the moral belief that one ought not to sleep with other men's wives, and the factual belief that Mary is someone else's wife. But one certainly cannot deduce facts about the circumstances, such as who is married to whom, from the existence of a necessary being. Nor, so far as I can see, could one deduce facts such as that if the circumstances are such-and-such, then one is under and obligation to do so-and-so. Contemplating God however, might strengthen one's resolve to behave in an appropriate way, at least if one contemplated him with that end in view.

A surprisingly large number of people regard morality as the whole of religion. It seems to me to be very far from being the case that this is so, and the people who hold it are surprisingly blind to a realm of experience, having nothing to do with morality, of a personal God which, whether veridical or not, is certainly there to be explored. I have argued elsewhere that the question whether or not this experience is veridical is a question that it is not clear, and of exaggerated importance.[12]

I am not sure, however, that our believing in God always does reinforce morality. Many people turn to God for relief from excessively high moral standards, and sometimes hope that God may forgive them for actions for which they cannot forgive themselves. (I have nothing against this.) If there is a God, and he has delegated to others the power of absolution from sin, we may sometimes be more ready to sin than we would be if we had not been absolved. If we think there is a God, and that he loves us, we may think he takes a fairly lenient attitude to our sinning. Those who have been brought up to the rigours of the Christian ethic without the consolations of the Christian religion may take a more serious view of sin, possibly at some cost to their mental health, than those who have been brought up to both.

(xiii) Some More Complex Ethical Arguments for the Existence of God

If you had a duty to achieve things that could be achieved only with God's cooperation, then it would follow, by an argument in the form of the *modus tollendo tollens*, that there was a God who did cooperate. For example there is the argument: I have a duty to make the world a better place; I would not have such a duty were there not a God to see that my efforts were not totally unavailing; therefore there is a God. This is a perfectly valid argument. However, I do not have a duty to make (i.e., to succeed in making) the world a better place, so much as (at most) a duty to try to make it a better place, and I can at least try to do this without God's cooperation. And if I really could not make the world a better place without God's cooperation, it needs to be explained why the conclusion is not that there is a God, but, on the contrary, that since there is not a God, I do not have such a duty.

We have seen that all arguments for the existence of God using ethical premises suffer from the defect that, if there were a duty that we would not have if there were no God, we ought first to establish that there is a God before concluding that we had the duty. That we would not have a duty to rescue someone if we could not swim, we do have a duty to rescue him, therefore we can swim, is a perfectly valid argument. But it would seem we ought to find out first whether a man could swim before we blamed him for not rescuing someone, rather than the other way round. (When there is a way of first concluding that a man has the duty to rescue someone – say because that he has this duty has been established by a tribunal which we believe to have gone into the question – it would be in order to conclude that he could swim. But the tribunal itself could not have concluded that the man could swim from the fact that he had the duty.)

Many claim that they would find it difficult to do their duty if they did not believe in God. I suspect that this is more of an argument for *believing* in God than an argument for the *existence* of God. Many people frequently do what they consider to be their duty although they claim not to believe in God.

Kant's Ethical 'Argument' for the Existence of God

Kant thought that it was impossible to prove the existence of God by reason. He thought, however, that the existence of God was what he called a 'postulate of pure practical reason'.[13] Regarded as an argument for the truth of the proposition that there is a God, Kant's argument is quite extraordinarily bad.

So regarded, it consists in holding that God must exist because his existence is a necessary condition of the existence of the *summum bonum*, which is virtue combined with happiness. Without God, virtue might exist and without God happiness might exist, but there would be no reason why they should be combined in the same person. However, since it is not necessary that the *summum bonum* should exist, considerations concerning it provide no reason for thinking that God does.

It may be, however, that Kant regarded a postulate of practical reason more as something that we needed for action rather than for thought. A postulate of practical reason would then be a proposition which we need to act on or believe in order to be good, rather than a proposition that can be deduced from our having certain duties. If so, Kant himself would not even have thought that he had produced a reason for thinking that there was a God.

(xiv)   Ethical Arguments for Immortality[14]

Ethical arguments for the existence of immortality suffer from the same fundamental defects as ethical arguments for the existence of God. They take the form of arguing that we have some duty that we would not have if we were not immortal, and arguing that, in consequence, we *are* immortal. This again is a valid argument in the form of the *modus tollendo tollens*; the trouble is that there is no way of showing that its premises are true without first showing that its conclusion is true. For example, if we were to argue that we have a duty to bring into existence goods that are permanent, and that no goods would be permanent if men were not immortal, the obvious reply is that, since men are not immortal, we have no duty to bring into existence goods that are permanent; otherwise we would have a duty to do the impossible.

It is, I think, very sad and discouraging to think that no good is permanent. But it would not follow from this fact that it is not a good thing that we should try to make the world as good a place as we can, for as long as conscious life exists on it. This period, though only tiny (if not infinitesimal) in relation to the total duration of the universe, is likely to be enormous in relation to the normal length of a human life.

The immortality of the soul was another of Kant's postulates of pure practical reason. Kant is often represented as arguing that since we have a duty to be perfect, and becoming perfect would take an infinite time, we must have that infinite time (for *ought* implies *can*). His conclusion rather should have been that we could not have a duty to make ourselves perfect if perfection takes an infinitely long time. In any case, to say that perfection takes an infinitely long time implies that it can never be achieved – infinitely long periods do not have ends – though perhaps we could approach perfection asymptotically (as the series one-half, three-quarters, seven-eighths, and so on, approaches one).

I would again suggest that Kant did not think that he had proved that it was true that we were immortal, so much as that he had shown that it was necessary to accept it and to act as if it were true. Something on which it is necessary to act, perhaps, is just what a postulate of *practical* reason is.

(xv) Conscience as the Voice of God

Conscience is sometimes regarded as the voice of God, though whether it can be that when it is so fallible and so conditioned by education, formal or otherwise, I do not know. If we are to know that God exists through the deliverances of conscience, this presuppose that we are directly aware of God's commands, which fact, if it were one, would presuppose that there was a God, and that we were immediately aware of him.

Otherwise the existence of God is a hypothesis to explain why we have consciences, which would presuppose either that they also have a normal explanation, which makes the theological explanation superfluous, or that conscience is miraculous. The statement that conscience is the voice of God either implies that it is not susceptible to a normal scientific explanation, or it does not. If it does, then God must suspend normal scientific law when he determines what conscience shall dictate, which is to say that every pronouncement of conscience would be a miracle. It would follow from this that God's existence was not unverifiable, for we would need to postulate him in order to explain why our consciences pronounced as they do, and so his existence would be verified to the extent that the hypothesis that he was responsible for the deliverances of conscience could be shown to be adequate. I am against such hypotheses, for the reason already given, that the God one would have to postulate would have, implausibly, to be part of a causal chain.

It is most unlikely, however, that the deliverances of conscience cannot be explained in a normal scientific way. Conscience is biologically necessary in order to impel men to perform actions for which they otherwise would not have a strong enough motive. And to some extent conscience can be explained by social conditioning, though some people's consciences transcends their conditioning (perhaps as some people's mathematical ability transcends the conditioning they received from their teachers). These people's consciences transcend their conditioning in that they do not always approve of actions that they have been taught to approve of, and sometimes approve of actions which they have been taught not to approve of.

The fact that the deliverances of conscience can be explained would not show that they are irrational. There is doubtless an explanation of why Einstein formed the theory of relativity when he did, but this does not show that he arrived at it only irrationally. What would show something to be irrational is not that it has causes (and so can be explained), but the fact that the reasons for believing it are not among its causes. If they were not among its causes, it would be believed whether there were reasons for believing it or not, and so would be irrational. It is a characteristic of some beliefs' being irrational that there is a very close connection between it and the cultural environment in the place where those who have it were brought up. This is obviously true of religious beliefs

I say 'some beliefs being irrational', for the fact that there is a very strong correlation between beliefs about the geography of a place and living in that place does not necessarily show that these beliefs are irrational. Those who live in a place are more likely to know about its geography than those who do not. And the fact that there is a close correlation between what one believes about computers and whether or not one has lived in the vicinity of the Massachusetts Institute of Technology does not show that the belief of those who have been to this important centre of indoctrination are irrational. And some beliefs about morality peculiar to a given place are not irrational because the circumstances obtaining at that place may demand different moral standards from those that obtain in other places.

It surprises me how few people allow reflection upon the fact that it is only because of an accident of birth that they hold the beliefs they do (a belief in Christianity or communism or Buddhism, for example) to temper the firmness with which they consider that these beliefs are rational. On the contrary, it would seem that, for very good psychological reasons, the more irrational beliefs of a certain kind are, the more, rather than the less, firmly they are held.

(xvi)   God's Goodness

It would be difficult to give an account of God's supposed moral perfection on the terminological and the normative theories of the relation between God's commands and man's duties, because to say that God is morally perfect most naturally implies that his will is, as doubtless ours ought to be, guided by an antecedently existing moral law, and on the terminological and normative theories there is no such law. Saying that God is morally perfect suggests that he always does what he ought, though he, unlike us, may never want to do anything other than what he ought.[15] It is likely that this way of speaking is too anthropomorphic.

It would, however, be a mistake to think of God as having every moral perfection. It would indeed be absurd to attribute to God most of the characteristic traits that are virtues in men. For example, he can hardly be industrious, prudent, considerate, courageous or polite. This may be because he would, unlike us, have no need of these virtues (or that we do not need to attribute them to him), though that is not to say that he does not approve of our having them; we ourselves do need them. The virtues which it is most natural to attribute to God are those characteristics that are virtues in parents and rulers; benevolence, love of those for whom one is responsible, justice, mercy, helpfulness, reliability and administrative competence to a very high (or infinite, if this means anything) degree. It is natural to attribute only these virtues to him partly because, unlike ourselves, he has no private life. No flesh and blood person could have only those virtues, and not other character-filling qualities, so our idea of God is an abstraction in much the same way that physics was once supposed to be an abstraction. Physics is an abstraction because the primary qualities are treated independently of the secondary ones, though in fact any actual being may well have to have both.

Nor does God have superiors to obey, creditors to pay, or wives to keep or placate. This is a further reason for regarding the deity as an abstraction from the idea of a complete man, with the more lowly and mundane characteristics left out. Those who wish to enter into a more intimate relationship with him, however, may wish to attribute to him virtues other than the administrative and paternal ones, which they will consider virtues, for example, the ability to reciprocate affection.

It is an attraction of Christianity that it allows some of us to have a more full-blooded idea of the divinity than we might otherwise have had. God the Son can have characteristics which it would be absurd to attribute to God the Father. Many people would feel deprived if they had only the more austere concept of the latter. In this way, as in some others, Christianity can allow its adherents to have the best of both worlds, which is one reason why it is so popular. This is suspicious, if the aim of a religion is to provide one with a theory of the universe which aims at correct explanation. There is no reason why the truth about the world should be in any way appealing. If it is religion's function merely to provide its believers with an image they can worship and that comforts them and helps them to live more satisfactory lives, then the fact that Christianity is so appealing is less suspicious. Indeed, its being appealing is a positive merit.

I must say, however, despite my own philosophical preference for the psychological theory about the relation between God's commands and man's duties outlined at the beginning of the chapter, I myself sometimes hanker for a God who is beyond good and evil. Constantly worrying about the difference between right and wrong, which difference, one sometimes hopes, may seem less important if one is a divine distance away from it, is one of the things which one sometimes goes to religion to escape from. From a religious point of view, one may look upon being good as the discharging of a divine duty to care for children of God other than oneself. But another common religious attitude to morality regards being good simply as a means to acquiring that peace of mind that is necessary for successful religious contemplation and devotion, and to having a satisfactory relationship with the divine. Too much attention to morality may be counterproductive, and bad for one's health.

Though we think of God as being perfect, as by definition a personal God must be the kind of God that intervened in the course of nature and was responsible for it would be a morally indifferent kind of being. He would be responsible for much good, but also for an enormous amount of evil. That it exculpates him from this responsibility is one advantage of a God who does (and cannot) so intervene, so he also cannot intervene to help us. If such a God helps us at all, it is more as the presence of our mistress rather than that of an armed ally helps us at the scene of combat.

(xvii) Acting as if There were a God

It is sometimes held that we ought to act as if there were a God, even if either there is not one, or if we have no reasons, or have less than adequate reasons, for thinking that there is one. (It is sometimes held that this is what faith consists in, but this is a question I shall discuss later.)

If acting as if there were a God involves acting as if certain propositions that could be deduced from the existence of God if there were one were true, and these propositions are false, then acting as if there were a God must be a bad thing. For example, religious people sometimes tell one that one ought to live each day as if it were one's last, though, of course, most of us have good reasons for believing that this is not our last day. If this injunction were taken quite literally, living each day as if it were our last would be an absurd thing to do, for it would involve not insuring our lives,[16] not sowing seed for crops in the autumn, or writing away for a mail catalogue that would take more than a day to reach one. Perhaps, however, we ought to act in one day, but not in another, as if this day was our last. We ought to get our lives insured because we know perfectly well that this is not our last day, and also get our lives insured because our final state depends on our leaving no duties undone, and this would be one of them. But this presupposes that there is a final state, which itself can be a factual deduction from the existence of God, and, in any case, it could be that we would be defrauding the insurance company if we then insured our lives.

Let us suppose both that there is not a God in fact, and we think we have no reason for thinking that there is, but nevertheless think that if there were a God, one would have a duty to go into a convent or become a monk. To do either of these things would be absurd if one thought that there were not a God. It is not just that we would act imprudently if we acted as if there were a God, from whom verifiable consequences flowed, but there was not one. We could also act contrary to the interests of others if we acted in such a way. For example, we might refuse to give a patient euthanasia, on the grounds that God himself would decide whether to let him die.

On the other hand, it would also be impossible to act as if there were a God if no empirical contingent consequences about the world could be deduced from the existence of God. One could then never be in a situation in which one ought to do one thing if there were a God, but another thing if there were not. For one could be in such a situation only if something would be true of the empirical world if there were a God, which would not be true of it if there were not one. For example, if there were a God who punished the wicked, one ought to behave in a way different from the way one ought to behave if there were not; but if there were a God from whose existence no empirical consequences followed, one ought to behave in precisely the same way whether there were a God or not. Indeed, a person acting as if there were a God would, on this theory, be doubly foolish. He would be wrong in thinking that empirical consequences did follow from the existence of God, and wrong in thinking that he ought to act as if these consequences were so, even when they were not so. It follows from this that the consequences for action (though perhaps not for thought) of the believing in the existence of a God from whom no empirical consequences followed are the same as those of atheism. But I shall return to this topic in the chapter on faith (chapter 28).

(xviii)   Evolution and Theological Ethics

It is my personal opinion that we have the moral codes we do because our having them is conducive to our survival. This fact should not be held against them. I shall not elaborate upon that opinion, as I have expounded and defended this view elsewhere.[17] It does not follow from it that we ought to ignore our moral codes. Nor does it follow that our beliefs that we ought to do certain things are irrational, nor that we ought to be strong and ruthless. One of the features of men's moral codes that are most useful to him is the fact that they demand that men aid other men in distress, care for their (own) wives and children, be loyal to their community, be brave in time of war, and provident and industrious in times of peace.

It is not a difficulty with this view that many items in our moral codes demand sacrifice of the individual to others. Such behaviour is conducive to the survival of the community, and so of the individual who makes the sacrifice, as it is also because he usually gains (over a long period of time) more from being helped by others than he loses in having to help them. For one reason, this is because what he loses is the superfluities which he gives to others when they are distressed; what he gains is the necessities that he is without when he is distressed. Law performs many of the functions of morality, but does not make morality unnecessary, for enforcing morality is not always practicable or desirable. Furthermore, lawbreaking cannot always be detected, but one's conscience can see what policemen cannot, and may refuse to exonerate one where a jury may wrongly acquit one.

One conclusion from this is that there is no necessity to resort to divine intervention to explain our having moral codes, or our having the moral codes we do. Hence, if when one says that morality is given by God, one implies that there was or is some breaking-in by God upon the natural chain of events, this view is unwarranted. There is no more need of divine intervention to explain human morality than there is to explain the human eye. And if one wishes to maintain that morality is produced by God, and evolution is his way of doing it, the reply again is that if there is no verifiable difference between evolution producing morality and evolution producing morality under the surveillance of God, then the latter hypothesis is redundant. (Oddly enough, not only is there no need of God to explain morality, there is no need of God to explain an apparently God-given morality. For a morality that appears to be the voice of God is likely to be more effective than a secular morality, and therefore it would not be wholly surprising if evolution were to favour it.)

Being conducive to our survival explains why we do not have certain features rather than why we do. We do *not* have certain features because they are *not* conducive to survival. Factors other than their being conducive to our survival are necessary to explain why we do have a morality, just as other factors than evolution theory are necessary to explain how it comes about that we have toes. If the shape of something is partly determined by its having been pressed into a mould, something is necessary to explain the force which pressed it into the mould.

In the case of morality, the positive force producing it is probably something to do with the demands of our parents and society being what is called 'internalised'. What actually happens, I think, is that when we perform, or are tempted to perform, an action of which our parents and/or other members of our society disapprove, we tend to feel guilt, and to imagine their witnessing our action and condemning us for it, even when we know perfectly well that they do not and may be cannot know what we have done. One manifestation of this may be the feeling (not the belief, though a belief may not result) that a god, who shares our community's morality, is looking down upon us disapprovingly. It does not follow from this that there is not such a god, but that there is cannot be established by our having the feeling. I myself see no reason why the broad outlines of morality may not be congenital.

(xix)   Divine Command Theories, Relativism and Objectivism

I shall describe the terminological theory and the normative theory of the relationship between God's commands and morality as 'divine command theories' because on each the rectitude of an action is determined, though in different ways, by the commands of God.

A question often discussed is whether a divine command theory of morality is or is not compatible with relativism. Relativism is the view that it might be true for me that infanticide was right, but true for someone else that it was wrong. I do not count the view that what is right for one person or community may be wrong for another person or community as a form of relativism (a) because it is platitudinous, which relativism is not, (b) because this is itself is a non-relative fact – if two different people are saying that something can be wrong for the same community they cannot both be mistaken – and (c) because the different rules that certainly apply to different communities may well be deducible from one absolutely true ultimate rule – which I myself think is utilitarian – that applies to all communities. My own view is that relativism is probably not compatible with a divine command theory, but that this is no objection to such a theory, since relativism is false.[18]

It looks as if a divine command theory might be compatible with relativism, since, if it is true, God might have commanded some actions for some people but other actions for others. Nevertheless, it would remain true that for absolutely everybody everywhere that it would be right to do what God commands, which is not a relativist view. In any case, a just or rational God might be held not to command some things for some people but other things for others unless there was some reason for it, in which case there would have to be some difference between the people to justify the fact that different things were expected of them. It would then not be the case that something was right for one person but the same thing wrong for a precisely similar person. That different things are right for different kinds of people is not a relativistic view.

There is also the question whether a divine command theory implies that moral judgments are objective. I am very far from being sure what is meant by 'objective', but I shall assume that, at the very least, a judgment is objective if there is something independent of the judgment itself and the person making it, about which the person making it can be mistaken. In that case a divine command theory ought to hold that moral judgments are objective, for it ought to be held that the existence and nature of God is independent of our beliefs about him and our attitude to him.

On a divine command theory one can be mistaken about the morality of an action in two ways. One can be mistaken in thinking that God does command it, and mistaken in thinking that, if he does, this makes the action in question right. This would be analogous to a doctor's being mistaken about the factual judgment that a medicine would save someone's life and about the moral judgment that, if it would save his life, he ought to administer it. I think it would be absurd to maintain that the doctor could not be mistaken on the first question, and not enormously adventurous to maintain that he could be mistaken on the second. The same should be true of the moral judgment that something ought to be done because God commands it.

But I suspect that people who hold a divine command theory of morality are absolutist in wishing to maintain, naturally enough, that anyone who does not hold such a theory is mistaken. About this they are right. (Indeed, it seems to me that anyone who holds any theory should think that anyone who holds another theory, incompatible with that theory, must be mistaken, on pain of holding that two contradictory propositions can both be true.) There is no such thing as being true for me but false for you.

(xx)   Conclusions

I should end by reminding the reader that this chapter is written on the assumption that God is a personal God, endowed with human qualities, in particular the qualities of a father and administrator. If that is what God is, then this chapter maps out the abstract logical relations between him and morality. If God is not personal, I would not expect there to be any relations between God and morality, over and above the fact that we might get help to do what we suppose is right by contemplating God, if we want any such help; good behaviour may also (sometimes) produce a tranquillity of mind which is alleged to facilitate this contemplation. But the two divine command theories are excessively anthropomorphic, as is the psychological theory, if its holders think that there really is a personal God who enforces an antecedently existing morality.

The fact that there is no personal God, however, does not mean that one should not intermittently bear in mind the possibility that there might be one, to the extent of considering what would be the attitude of such a being to one's actions if there were one, and to draw what solace, strength and inspiration that may be obtained from contemplating him. Nor does it mean that it is not advantageous to encourage an imaginative encounter with him. The attitude of such a being morally is likely to be only one's own morality writ large, but writing it large may have its advantages.

I also feel that there are (at least) two strands in one's attitude to the divinity, a moral one and a devotional one. The moral strand regards God as approving of and enforcing morality, blaming us when we transgress, sometimes forgiving us, helping us to overcome temptation, and strengthening us in any virtuous resolve. In many people, this idea of the divinity supplants all others, and in extreme cases God and morality are identified. In contrast to this useful but Martha-like divinity there is another (or another aspect of the divinity) who demands a worship and contemplation which we ourselves may need to give, perhaps at the expense of a too enthusiastic adherence to morality.

A God from whose existence no empirical consequences flow cannot enforce morality in any way other than metaphorically, by the effect on us of our contemplating him. (Even a life after death where the virtuous are rewarded is an empirical consequence of a sort, and so cannot be deduced from postulating an unverifiable God.) For an undetectable God cannot intervene to reward the virtuous and punish the vicious, for he cannot intervene at all. Intervening would be an empirical consequence of existing, and there are none.

Notes

1   I have discussed this matter (see 1971 and 1994, chapter IX) and regret that it is necessary to repeat much of the argument that is given there. The reader is also referred to the section 'Mysticism and Ethics', 1995.

2   Ethical arguments for the existence of God bear some resemblance to ethical arguments for human survival. These are ably considered in Broad, 1925, especially chapter XI.

3   This view was rejected Joseph Butler in one of his sermons (Sermons II and III, 1897). It was criticised by Plato in his dialogue 'Euthyphro'. Peter Geach, 1969, criticises Plato's criticisms of this view, and is in his turn criticised by myself (1993).

4   I was tempted to call it the identity theory, but this expression already has a different use. It should be noted that the identity between what is a duty and what is commanded by God is, if this theory is correct, a necessary analytic identity, like the identity between being triangular and being three-sided. Robert Merrihew Adams, 1979 argues that the identity is synthetic, and, as allegedly is the identity between the morning star and the evening star, necessary. But all identities between characteristics either necessarily obtain or necessarily do not obtain, and they are all analytic. For example, the identity between the morning star and the evening star is synthetic, whether it is necessary or not, but that between the characteristics of being a morning star and being an evening star would, if it obtained, have to be analytic. In any case, the objection to the terminological (or identity) theory is that being wrong and being prohibited by God are not identical, not that they are not analytically or necessarily identical.

5   If God is morally perfect, there is a sense in which he must do what is right. It is argued in this chapter that this sense is not incompatible with his being able to do what is wrong. I have also made the point in Harrison, 1976. All that it means is that it cannot be that he will do what is wrong. The point is also made in Morris, 1987.

6   For example, Jean-Paul Sartre (see 1948).

7   This type of argument was made famous by G.E. Moore, 1903, especially chapters I and II.

8   Adams suggests that wrongness should be identified as contrary to the commands of a loving God. In that case, if God is not loving or does not exist, it will follow that nothing is wrong, because then nothing would be contrary to the commands of a loving God. It seems obvious that many things would be wrong whether there were a loving God or not.

9   As has ben held, among others, by Richard Price and W.D. Ross. I have discussed this view in 'Does moral epistemology rest on a mistake' in Harrison, 1993.

10   In Kant, 1947.

11   The point is made by Immanuel Kant, *loc. cit.*

12   In 1995, *loc. cit.*

13   See Kant, 1929.

14   There is an excellent discussion of ethical arguments for immortality in chapter 11 of Broad, 1925.

15   He would be, I suppose, what Kant called a Holy Will; see 1947, Section II.

16   Those more cynical than myself might suggest that it would then be appropriate to insure one's life for a very large sum of money, but I do not suppose one would have the time.

17   In 'Sociobiology and Ethics' in Harrison, 1993b, and in chapter XI, Harrison, 1971 and 1994a.

18   The reasons why I think so have been set out in Harrison, 1971, chapter X and in 'The Wrongheadedness of Moral Relativism', 1993b.

9 Theology without Propositions

Logical positivism was the view, formulated in the verification principle, that sentences can be meaningful only if they express propositions that can be empirically verified or are tautologous or logically true. If it is both the case that logical positivism is true, and that religious assertions are unverifiable, then religious words cannot be meaningful. Even if logical positivism is not true, there is serious difficulty about explaining how sentences expressing assertions about a transcendent God can be meaningful, when sentences containing the word 'God' cannot be correlated with the entity they purport to be about. This chapter will discuss (and reject) one way of circumventing this difficulty about the meaning of sentences about the divinity, which would, if it were successful, also remove any difficulty concerning our knowledge of the truth of such assertions.

When Wittgenstein wrote the *Tractatus*[1] he held (very roughly) that the only meaningful sentences were ones which expressed statements about the world (or statements constructed from such statements by means of disjunction, conjunction, implication or equivalence (see Glossary)). Hence the conjunction or disjunction of two factual statements would itself be a factual statement. Logical truths, e.g., either there will or there will not be a sea battle tomorrow, were not factual statements, but were constructed from factual statements in such a way that they could not assert anything false. They would be true however the world went. Mathematics could be reduced to logic.

It followed from this that there were no such things as philosophical statements. The function of philosophy was to make people see that when they attempted to make any statement other than a factual statement they were abusing language and talking nonsense. Doing philosophy was supposed to be therapeutic and cure people of thinking that there were any problems other than those that could be settled in the 'normal' quasi-scientific way. If this therapy was successful, this would enable 'the fly to get out of the fly bottle', i.e., it would stop people from being perplexed by questions which could not be answered by an ordinary investigation of the world, but were in fact meaningless. (Whether the fly wanted to get out of the fly bottle is another matter.) It was not possible to say anything that was not about the ordinary world, and that of which one could not speak, one must remain silent. (This suggests, intentionally or otherwise, that despite what Wittgenstein himself said, there is nevertheless something above the world, something of which one must remain silent.) Hence it would appear that Wittgenstein agreed with those philosophers who held the verification principle that metaphysics and theology were meaningless.

By the time Wittgenstein came to write the *Philosophical Investigations*[2] he had substantially changed his view.[3] He held there that numerous items of language had functions other than that of making 'factual' statements about the world, and it would appear that he thought that theistic sentences had one of these functions. It would cast no doubt on the credentials of a sentence to say that it did not express a truth of science or mathematics, for it might be that it did not have the function of expressing a truth at all. Using words was like playing a game (a 'language game'), and there were many different games that words could be used to play, over and above that of making statements. Though Wittgenstein did not so far as I know explicitly say so, to use the verification principle to eliminate large areas of discourse was to assume that there was only one kind of thing one could do with words, viz., express truths of logic, mathematics or science (using the word 'science' in a wide sense to include common observation of the world, including history).

It is not clear from what Wittgenstein said, however, exactly what the function (or functions) of theistic sentences was, and how attributing to them this function enabled us to explain how theistic sentences were meaningful, and did not conflict with the aforementioned 'scientific' descriptions of the world. Hence in the remainder of this chapter I shall discuss these questions in my own way.

It would be consistent with Wittgenstein's view to hold that the function of religious language is not to express statements at all. (This view has been more popular with ethical statements than with religious ones, the leading exponents of the view being A.J. Ayer and R.M. Hare.)[4] And it has been supposed that it is possible both to accept the view that sentences that do not express verifiable propositions are meaningless, and consistently to allow that theistic language does have meaning, if one is prepared to pay the price of holding that the function of theistic language is not to express propositions at all. The verification principle, it could be held, is a criterion for whether sentences whose function is to express propositions are meaningful. It does not apply to other kinds of utterance. Indeed, it will not even be, strictly speaking, true to say that these types of utterance – e.g. 'Shut the door' – to which the verification principle does not apply, are unverifiable. It is rather that it does not make sense to raise the question whether they are verifiable or not.

Propositions are those things – like that the cat is on the mat – which are capable of being true or false, believed or disbelieved, doubted, wondered about, asserted, denied and reiterated. It can be true that the cat is on the mat, believed that it is, doubted whether it is, asserted or denied that it is, and if someone says that it is, one can agree or disagree with what he says. This sets propositions apart from utterances like commands ('Shut the door'), requests ('Please pass the salt'), prayers ('Give us this day our daily bread'), expressions of wishes ('Oh to be in England'), or performative utterances,[5] which include vows ('I N take thee, N ... to be my lawful wedded wife' or 'I name this ship the "President Clinton"'), about which none of these things can be said.[6]

Theistic language is certainly not confined to enabling those who use it to make assertions. Most of the Lord's Prayer is in the imperative mood, as one would expect a prayer to be. Even if a person uttering these words had no father in Heaven, those sentences in the Lord's Prayer which were in the imperative mood would not be false.

However, imperatives, though they cannot be false, may be misapplied. One will be misapplying the imperative 'Shut the door' if one issues it when the door is not open, or the object one is referring to is a *trompe l'oeil* painting which one mistakes for a door. One will be misapplying a performative sentence when one says the words 'I name this ship the "Margaret Thatcher"' if the object in front of one is not a ship, or if one has been asked to name it the 'Anthony Blair', or pronounce the words 'I baptise you', mistaking a pig for a baby. One will be misapplying the promise 'I'll pay you back tomorrow' if one addresses it to a waxwork in Madame Toussaud's, or if one has not borrowed any money. One of the most obvious ways of misapplying a nonpropositional utterance is by its presupposing beliefs that are false. The words which, if uttered in certain circumstances, result in someone's becoming a saint, do not result in his becoming one if they are not pronounced by an appropriate person, in the correct form, and about a person who exists and is correctly identified. (They do result in his canonisation if he does not have the attributes which are usually looked for before it is decided to make him a saint. I suspect the word 'saint' is used ambiguously as a word for a person who has the attributes which deserve canonisation, and for someone who actually has been canonised.)

Certainly many sentences, some of those in the Bible, for example, do not make assertions. This means that, where these sentences are concerned, the question of their truth does not arise. (Hence the doctrine that everything in the Bible is literally true would have to be modified so that it became something like: (a) everything in the Bible that is capable of being true or false is true; (b) utterances that are not capable of being true or false are never misapplied and never presuppose anything false.)

But though much theistic language is incapable of being true or false, most of it is so capable. And language that is not intended to be true could look very foolish if the beliefs it presupposed were not true. The prayer 'Our father, which art in Heaven, forgive us our trespasses', for example, presupposes, though it does not assert, that we have a heavenly father. The prayer would be misapplied if we did not have one.

The Benedicite (which starts with the sentence 'O all ye Works of the Lord, bless ye the Lord, praise him, and magnify him for ever') does not contain a single statement. Nevertheless, though nothing which it asserts can be false, for it does not assert anything, saying or reciting the Benedicite would seem to presuppose that there is a Lord, that he can hear what one says, and that he possesses certain characteristics which make it appropriate to worship him. But if discourse about the deity that is nonpropositional presupposes that there is a deity, and that there is a deity is a proposition, then all the problems raised by the verification principle remain with the proposition that God exists, this most fundamental of all propositions in the philosophy of religion. And maintaining that a very large amount of discourse about the deity is nonpropositional will not help. To circumvent the verification principle, all of it must nonpropositional. Otherwise one still has the problem of explaining how the words in the sentences that do express propositions, of which the proposition that God exists would appear to be one, have meaning.

The question is not at all the same as the question whether theistic language is poetic or figurative. The antithesis between language which states facts and that which is poetic and/or figurative is a false one, for much language is undoubtedly both. Language which is poetic and figurative can serve to express statements or propositions. Conversely, language which is neither poetic nor figurative may express things other than propositions. 'Please pass the salt' is neither poetic nor figurative, but does not state a proposition.

> On either side the river lie
> Long fields of barley and of rye
> That clothe the wold and meet the sky

is poetic, but is not figurative, and does express a proposition, which would fail of reference if Tennyson was not referring – as he probably was not referring – to some actual river. (His words, of course, would be no worse for this.)

We have seen that much nonpropositional theistic language presupposes, even if it does not assert, that there is a God, and many theistic sentences appear to make the assertion that God exists quite explicitly. It is therefore necessary for the proponent of nonpropositional theology to explain why the appearance that there are theological propositions is delusive, and what nonpropositional function theistic sentences that appear to express statements really have.

I do not think that the first question can be answered. The appearance that religious sentences express propositions is not delusive. On the second question, I cannot see what the nonpropositional theorist can do other than maintain that a person who says some such thing as 'God exists' is really simply exhorting others to do such things as live a good life, love one's neighbour, and forgive his enemies. Such exhortations are doubtless valuable, but say nothing an atheist might not readily endorse. He would not be able to disagree with the exhortations, since exhortations do not assert anything. A philosopher would have no problem about explaining how such sentences were meaningful because the words 'forgive', 'enemies', 'charity' and so on are not themselves theistic words. In the sentences which here replace 'God exists', no mention is made of God. If mention were made of God, we would be back with exactly the same problem we started with.

The problem of showing how, on the nonpropositional view, sentences about the deity have meaning is here solved rather by eliminating the word 'God' than by holding that they are nonpropositional. It is solved by the fact that the only things mentioned in the exhortations (say) which replace the supposed statement that there is a God are unproblematic words for ordinary things, like 'forgive', 'enemies', 'charity' and so on. The difference between a believer and an atheist would then be constituted simply by the fact that the believer chooses to express, by using the word 'God', virtuous aspirations that even the atheist might harbour. The atheist could simply formulate the same exhortations in a more mundane way.

If one does not eliminate the word 'God', one is not miraculously exempted from explaining how it is that a string of words is intelligible simply because it is in the imperative mood. You cannot make sense out of nonsense simply by maintaining that, when properly understood, it will be seen not to express a proposition. The intelligibility of 'The door is shut' and 'Shut the door' must, indeed, stand or fall together. Hence if the intelligibility of 'God exists' is in question, one does not vindicate it by saying that 'God exists' is really a command, a command to live one's life with constant reference to God, or constantly to behave as if God existed. For if the sentence in the indicative mood, that there is a God, is meaningless, so must be the command to live one's life as if there were a God. The same problematic word, 'God', occurs in both. So if there are considerations (say, the verification principle) which mean that the proposition is unintelligible, these considerations must mean that the command is unintelligible also.

So far, indeed, from its being the case that you can use non-indicative sentences to explain how apparently indicative sentences have meaning, it is the other way round. An imperative sentence like 'Shut the door' can have meaning only so long as corresponding indicatives like 'The door is shut' have meaning. The imperative sentence 'Since it is not brillig, go and ask the slithy toves to gyre and gimble anywhere but on the wabe' is meaningless, because the well known indicative sentence corresponding to it ('Twas brillig, and the slithy toves did gyre and gimble on the wabe') is meaningless. If the indicative sentence 'The universe is governed by a good God' does not have meaning, then it follows that the imperative 'Live your life as if the universe were governed by a good God' also does not have meaning.

I do not think it makes any difference to what I have been saying if it is held that the nonpropositional sentences into which apparently propositional theistic discourse must be translated are not imperatives, but some other kind of nonpropositional utterances. For example, 'Would that more people lived as if there were a God' is not an imperative, but it could only be meaningful unless its 'corresponding' indicatives were meaningful. 'I promise to live as if there were a God', also does not express a proposition. Its function is to enable the person using it to make a promise. But it could not be a promise that it was possible to make unless sentences about God in the indicative mood made sense. Even if it is held that different units of theological discourse must be translated into different kinds of nonpropositional utterance, for example some into commands and others into promises and yet others into expressions of wishes, the case is no better. If none of them have meaningful indicative sentences corresponding to them, all of them must be meaningless. Nonpropositional theology must, therefore, be dismissed both as a solution of the problem of allowing meaning to the sentences with which we attempt to talk about God, and also as, *ipso facto*, a way of evading the question how we know that these statements are true.

Notes

1 Wittgenstein, 1961.
2 Edited by G.E.M. Anscombe and R. Rees, translated by G.E.M. Anscombe, Blackwell, 1953.
3 There is a discussion of Wittgenstein's views about theology in Hudson, Lutterworth Press, 1968.
4 In Ayer, 1936, and Hare, 1952 respectively.
5 Nicholas Lash, 1992, especially III 1, has taken the view that 'I believe ...' as it occurs in 'I believe in God, the father almighty ...' is that species of performative utterance which is a promise. This cannot be so. It is a feature of what are normally called 'performatives' that anyone accomplishing the performance in question by saying, e.g. 'I promise', is being reported by anyone saying 'He is promising' or 'He promised'. That he did in fact promise is entailed by the fact that he said 'I promise ...' in appropriate circumstances – say not in a play or under duress, and knowing what the words he was using meant. It is not characteristic of belief that someone saying 'He believes' is reporting the fact that the person he is talking about has said 'I believe' in appropriate circumstances. He could, in fact, say 'I believe ...' without believing, and believe without saying 'I believe ...'. However, in a wider sense of 'performative', saying 'I believe' could be a performative utterance, for said in a Christian church, saying it does accomplish the performance of committing the speaker, even though the performance cannot be described by saying that the speaker believes.
6 This way of escaping the verificationist dilemma, in this case posed by the fact that moral judgments also appear to be neither verifiable nor meaningless, has been more popular in moral philosophy than it has, so far as I know, in theology. See Ayer, 1936, chapter VI.

10 Deistic Phenomenalism: A Reductionist Account of the Existence of God

(i)   Phenomenalism

Phenomenalism is a theory of the meaning of statements about material objects, and about what we are thinking when we think that there are such things. It was first put forward, though in a schematic way, by Bishop Berkeley in *The Principles of Human Knowledge*. Berkeley (sometimes) held that material objects were no more than bundles of perceptions or ideas.

Since unobserved objects could hardly be bundles of human ideas, they presented Berkeley with a difficulty. He sometimes resolved this by holding that to say there was an unobserved table in the next room or an unobserved tree in an uninhabited quadrangle was to say that God perceived the table or the tree. Such things as trees could then be reduced to God's perceptions, a view which I shall christen deistic idealism. At other times Berkeley held that to speak about unobserved tables or trees was to say that a finite being would perceive the table or the tree if he were suitably situated in the next room or the quad.[1] This view has come to be known as phenomenalism. It has been suggested by philosophers as eminent as John Stuart Mill[2] and defended in this century by the late A.J. Ayer.[3] It has recently become unfashionable for a number of reasons, one of which has been the regrettable rejection of the sense-datum theory which it has been thought to presuppose.

(Very roughly, according to the sense-datum theory, we do not see the moon 'directly', but only a silver crescent which is a sense-datum of the moon. I should emphasis that it does not follow from this that we do not see the moon, any more than it follows from the fact that we cannot kick a wardrobe without kicking some panel of a wardrobe that we cannot kick a wardrobe. It would be absurd to complain that we cannot kick the wardrobe because there is always some panel getting in our way, and it is absurd to complain that we cannot observe the moon because there is always something like a silver crescent or yellow disc getting in our way.)

According to phenomenalism, all statements about material objects may be translated, without loss of meaning, into statements about the perceptions of observers. All there is to the parts of my desk that I cannot see, the unobserved magnet in my pocket, the inside of the Earth, and remote parts of this and other galaxies, is the fact that one would have suitable perceptual experiences if one were to take the appropriate steps. Such steps would be looking in my pocket, delving into the Earth, travelling into space, and so on. There is not, according to phenomenalism, anything to these objects over and above the fact that we can have experiences of them if we take appropriate steps. John Stuart Mill put this by saying that material objects were simply permanent possibilities of perception.

If I may put the view in a way that is picturesque, but I hope not too misleading, Calcutta, when unobserved, is nothing but an empty patch in space. But, though this region of space is empty, any normal person who goes there and keeps his eyes open will have experiences of seeing a large city, teeming with life. Calcutta, then, is nothing over and above observers' experiences of seeing Calcutta. The experiences will spring into existence in the vicinity of this region on my arrival there. But since observers can reliably obtain such experiences whenever they care to make the journey, Calcutta really does exist. All one is claiming, when one says that it exists, is that it is possible to obtain the experiences. This is what makes all the difference between Calcutta, which exists, and Valhalla, which does not. There are recipes for obtaining the experience of seeing (and hearing, feeling, smelling and touching) Calcutta, but no similar recipes for obtaining similar experiences of Valhalla.

The most extraordinary thing about this very daring theory is that the body of the observer is no exception to the general principle that all statements about material objects are statements about the perceptions observers would have. To say that I have a liver or even a brain, for example, is to say that if my body – mention of a body would have to be eliminated in a full reductionist account – were cut open, observers would have the experience of seeing my liver or my brain. I myself might be one of these observers if my head were cut open and I was provided with mirrors.

Descartes imagined a malicious demon, who gave men all the experiences of perceiving a material world although there was not one. (He did this to show that, though the demon might make me mistakenly believe that the external world existed, I myself would have to exist in order mistakenly to believe this.)[4] According to Berkeley, God did just what Descartes' malicious demon did. But though Descartes' malicious demon deceived us, God did not; his producing experiences in a regular way was a manifestation of benevolence, not of malice. In any case, he thought that all there was to a material world was the fact that perceptions of it would turn up as expected, and this is all the ordinary man – though not the natural scientist – was claiming when he said there was one.

(ii)   Deistic Phenomenalism

This suggests the view, that might be called deistic phenomenalism, according to which statements about the existence of God might be translated into or reduced to statements about the experiences of religious people. God, to parody the remark of John Stuart Mill's quoted above, would be a permanent possibility of religious experience.

This theory is a species of reductionism or naturalism, because if it is true statements about the deity are reduced to what would appear to be something else, i.e., to statements about the natural world. There are kinds of reductionism other than deistic phenomenalism. A very crude form of reductionism would be to regard statements to the effect that God exists as asserting no more than that evil will eventually triumph over good. I know Quakers who try to reduce statements about God to statements about the inner light. Some people think that the only way that God can work is through the hearts and minds of men, and then go on to say that all there is to the existence of God is men's thoughts of God working in their hearts and minds. One is a reductionist if one believes that all there is to confrontation with God is the experience of being so confronted, and that the question whether this experience is a veridical one does not arise. This kind of phenomenalism, however, is not the only possible form of reductionism or naturalism.

It is notoriously difficult to describe the perceptual experiences in terms of which statements about God would, on a view like this, have to be analysed. (Some people, indeed, hold that these experiences are ineffable, but fortunately this seldom stops those who have them from talking about them. But not all experience of the deity is perceptual.)

I suspect that there are three kinds of religious experience that are relevant.

(a) Some religious experiences may be classified as visual 'quasi-hallucinations' of one kind or another. (I use the word 'hallucination' without meaning to prejudge the issue whether such experiences are genuine communications from God. I call them 'quasi-hallucinatory' simply because they are not produced in the normal way by light waves from the perceived object falling upon one's retina.)

We might then believe that God was communicating with us *via* hallucinations. (Joan of Arc believed that God was talking to her with voices that were in fact hallucinatory, though she may not have realised that they were.) That we have these experiences because God is communicating with us by means of them, is not likely to be something read off from the experiences, so to speak, but is a theory about the experiences. It requires our interpreting them.

(The view that God is communicating with us by means of these 'hallucinations' is not, therefore, correctly classified as a view to the effect that we know without argument that God exists. That God exists is in that case a hypothesis to explain the experiences. God, according to this theory, uses the experience as a sign of something. We are aware of the sign itself without inference, but that it is a sign is a theory about it, not something of which we know immediately.)

(b) Some people, perhaps most, have felt a sense of the immediate presence of the deity. (I have classified such experiences differently from hallucinations, as it is arguable that they are non-sensuous.) The 'naïve' account of such an experience would be that the experience is one thing, and its object, God, another. A deistic phenomenalist, however would have to hold that all that is meant when we say that there is a God is that it is possible to obtain a sense of his presence, either because such experiences happen spontaneously, or because we use the appropriate recipes for acquiring them. Such experience is 'objective', if that is the right word, in that it may reliably be obtained by any person who cares to use these recipes, though doubtless some people are better at acquiring it than others. But, on this view, all there is to the deity is the fact that it is possible for people to obtain these experiences which would normally be said to be experiences *of* the deity. There is, if deistic phenomenalism is true, nothing to the deity over and above the experiences.

(c) The most common type of religious experience, however, consists not in perceptual experiences, but in the feeling of certain emotions, such as reverence, awe, devotion, love, gratitude, fear and so on. Such experiences are emotional reactions to beliefs that would normally be regarded as beliefs about the deity. If deistic phenomenalism is true, all there is to the deity is the fact that we can obtain such experiences if we wish (as we can go to Calcutta, if we wish).

(iii)   Objections to Deistic Phenomenalism

The view which I have christened 'deistic phenomenalism' is open to serious objections.

(a) It is necessary, if deistic phenomenalism is to be even remotely plausible, for the religious experiences in question to be non-discursive, or something other than emotional reactions to a belief. Otherwise there would be a possibility that such experiences were simply emotional reactions to false beliefs. A philosophical theory, according to which statements to the effect that God existed are true, because they are true statements about the experiences of people who falsely believe that God exists, would be both circular and self-contradictory. It would be circular because we would have to understand statements about the divinity in the first place, in order to know what it was that people are falsely believing to exist (viz., that there is a God). It would be contradictory because, if such people falsely believe that there is a God, there must be no God (for if there were their belief would be true), whereas, if statements to the effect that God exists are just statements asserting the existence of the experience of people who believe in him, then, according to the theory, such statements must be true, for they really do have the experiences. Hence such statements would be both true and not true. However, it may be that not all religious experience is emotional reaction to a belief.

(b) Ordinary phenomenalism is a theory about the existence of material objects. Such phenomenalism would be much less plausible as a theory about the existence of other minds.[5] To say that there is such a person as Smith cannot simply be to talk about one's own experiences and the experiences of other people of Smith. To do so would be nearly as bad as reducing someone to something in someone else's dream. It might even be the case that other peoples' experiences would have to be reduced to statements about mine, and mine to statements about those of others, which procedure would be obviously absurd.

As God can hardly be supposed to be a physical object, and may naturally be supposed to be a 'mind', an attempt to reduce statements about him phenomenalistically would be open to the objection, already given, to the possibility of a phenomenalist account of other minds.

(c) Deistic phenomenalism reduces statements about the deity to statements that even an atheist can believe. For even an atheist can believe that people have and reliably obtain experiences of the deity, though it is likely that he does not value them.

(iv) An Alternative to Deistic Phenomenalism

Perhaps one may value religious experience without making any ontological claims. Statements about an infinite mind cannot just be statements about the experiences of finite minds. There are, however, experiences that finite minds can obtain, and which some regard as valuable, both for their own sakes and because of the heightened capacities they believe result from having them. For example, experiences involved in certain types of prayer are supposed to be valuable in themselves, and to increase the capacities of the person praying, regardless of whether the prayer is answered. That one can obtain religious experience, on a view like this, is an important fact about the world, and one does not have to neglect religious experiences just because one thinks that they are not experiences of an infinite divine mind which exists independently of the experience. In such a way it would be possible to believe that religious experience exists, is valuable, and can be obtained by those willing to take the trouble, and also believe that nothing that could be described as 'God' is an item among the furniture of the world, or even out of it.

Such a view would enable one to combine, as some forms of Buddhism also make possible, academic atheism with living a religious life. There would be no 'artificial' divine sanctions attached to living such a life. If you did not live it, you would miss the tranquillity and detachment and breadth of vision to which it is alleged to be conducive, just as if you did not take exercise you would not attain health. This would not be a punishment for sin, so much as the natural and inevitable consequences of failing to take the necessary means to a valuable end.

(v) Deistic Phenomenalism Compared with Other Forms of Reductionism and Naturalism

What I have called deistic phenomenalism could be regarded as one form of religious reductionism or naturalism. Other forms of religious reductionism hold that propositions about the deity are propositions about the world that have not necessarily anything to do with people's experience.

An example would be the claim that Hell is a state of mind. That people are in a certain state of mind, say one in which they suffer from intolerable remorse, and a sense of irredeemable failure and separation from God, is a fact about the natural world. That there is such a place as Hell purports to be a statement about what may happen to people at some date in the time-stream later than this, and perhaps, more plausibly, also about their whereabouts in a place that transcends the natural world. The view that, when we think we are believing in the one, all we are really doing is believing in the other, involves a reduction of one class of statement to another less problematic. It is very common for philosophers to attempt such a reduction; normally, as in this case, a reduction of problematic entities to entities that are not problematic. For example, material objects have, as we have seen, been reduced to sense experiences, statements about the past to statements about the present, and statements about the 'hidden' minds of others to statements about their overt behaviour.

I think religious reductionism is totally without plausibility. Someone who holds that Hell is a state of mind is not translating the traditional view of Hell into other statements. He is rejecting it in favour of a much less controversial claim. The claim that men do suffer from a sense of separation from God, and that they may do so as a result of their wickedness and disobedience, is totally uncontroversial and uninteresting, whereas the claim that the some men go to Hell is both important and highly controversial. The same goes for reductionist accounts that translate statements about the deity into statements such as that good will triumph over evil, or that there is more good in the world than ill. This is clearly not what people mean when they say that there is a God, and is something an atheist might agree to with complete consistency.

Matthew Arnold said:[6]

> 'Tis God himself becomes apparent, when
> God's wisdom and God's goodness are display'd,
> For God of these his attributes is made.–...
>
> God's Wisdom and God's goodness! Ay, but fools
> Mis-define these till God knows them no more.
> Wisdom and goodness, they are God! – what schools
> Have yet so much as heard this simpler lore?

My own sympathies, however, are with the fools. For one thing, if wisdom and goodness are attributes of God, there must be a God, over and above wisdom and goodness, to possess these attributes. And to say that there is a God is to do much more than to enunciate the platitude that one ought to be wise and good. Oddly Arnold reveals that he himself did not believe what he himself said, for the remark that God did not know the definitions could not be true, or even make sense, unless God is being regarded as a person. Wisdom and goodness are not in an appropriate category to fail to know wisdom and goodness; only a person could do that.

(vi) Conclusions

Talk about the deity is talk about a being who transcends space, and possibly also time. To reduce statements about such a being to statements about the natural world he may have created is virtually indistinguishable from atheism.

Notes

1   Scientists claimed that, over and above this, our perceptions were produced by an underlying invisible 'substratum' of entities, i.e., what philosophers call 'matter'. Berkeley thought that these, precisely because they were invisible and intangible, would not be missed if they did not exist. Indeed, he thought that we did not know what we were talking about when we claimed to be making assertions about them.
2   In his *An Examination of Sir William Hamilton's Philosophy*, chapter XI, 'The Psychological Theory of the Belief in an External World'.
3   In Ayer, 1964, chapter 6, 'Phenomenalism'. Ayer does not there regard phenomenalism as completely satisfactory.
4   This argument is discussed in detail in Harrison, 1989.
5   John Stuart Mill, in chapter XI, 'The Psychological Theory of the Belief in an External World', 1979.
6   From 'The Divinity', Arnold, 1950.

11 Religion without Belief

I started the chapter on nonpropositional theories (chapter 9) by considering the Wittgensteinian view to the effect that there were many more tasks – issuing commands, for example – that could be performed by words other than that of expressing propositions, and that theistic sentences performed some of these. The view I shall consider in this chapter may also have been suggested by Wittgenstein,[1] though, if it was, I doubt whether he clearly distinguished it from the former view. The two are not compatible.

The view I am thinking of is to the effect that a person who holds as a religious tenet that there will be a last day of judgment, for example, is doing something different from believing that there will be one. If so, he is, when he expresses his 'belief' out loud, presumably doing something different from making the prediction that there will be a last day of judgment; he is not doing what he is doing when he predicts that there will be a last day of summer.

I shall call this view the 'nonbelief' theory. It was held by R.B. Braithwaite.[2] According to the nonbelief theory, though the function of ethical words really is to express propositions, the attitude that it is proper to take up to these propositions is not one of belief. There are two ways in which this theory may be developed, which I shall call its non-reductive and its reductive versions. The non-reductive view leaves statements about God as statements about a transcendent being, but holds that they are not meant to be believed. The reductive view tries to reduce such statements to statements about the natural world, statements which are also not meant to be believed.

According to this version of the 'nonbelief theory', religious language resembles the language of fiction, both in that it is not intended to formulate anything that is to be believed and in that religious propositions – and this is where it differs from non-reductionist views – are propositions about the natural world. Most, if not all, fiction, which is also not meant to be believed, is about natural entities like people, or at any rate animals or androids or whatever. The difference between the sentence occurring in one of Jane Austen's novels, 'Mr Bennet had four daughters' and the sentence 'King Henry VIII had seven wives', is not that the second expresses something capable of being true or false but the first does not. The difference is that the hearer is normally expected

236

to believe the second, but not the first. (It is in principle possible for fiction to be about non-natural entities, though I do not know of any; I would count Greek gods as natural entities.) If Richard Braithwaite[3] held that statements about the Trinity are statements about three Lord Shaftesburys, he will not only be holding that statements about the Trinity are not meant to be believed, he will also be giving a reductionist account of these statements, for English lords are not transcendent entities, though some of them may think they are. The different possibility that the story of the three Lord Shaftesburys is a parable will be considered later.[4]

Braithwaite himself thinks that thinking about, without believing, the stories is not enough to make a man a Christian. He must be committed to leading an 'agapeistic way of life', devoted to the general good, and perhaps, though Braithwaite does not say so, also be helped in leading this life by entertaining the stories. But (a) I think Braithwaite exaggerates the extent to which Christianity is agapeistic, though it may be unkind to say that Christianity holds that God is love but Heaven help the man who does not recognise the fact. (b) One could lead an agapeistic way of life without being a Christian, because one associated leading this life with, say, Buddhist stories. (c) Braithwaite thinks he is able to reduce the element of belief in Christianity still further, because he thinks (I think wrongly) that to believe that one ought to live an agapeistic way of life is simply sincerely to intend to live one.

Both forms of the nonbelief theory may help square religion with science in the following way. (a) Theistic beliefs do not have to be scientifically established, because they are not meant to be believed. (b) It can be consistent to hold them together with apparently incompatible scientific beliefs, because, though science is to be believed, religion is not. (This would enable one to hold as a scientific fact that there will not be a last day of judgment, but as a religious tenet that there will be, though I cannot persuade myself that doing this is commendable.) (c) Exactly the same account can be given of the meaning of words in fiction, which is not meant to be believed, as can be given of the same words in the science of history, when they are meant to be believed. (d) Since it may be argued that faith ought to be acquired, holding that the proper attitude to religious propositions is a mental attitude quite distinct from belief does have the advantage of explaining why it may be possible to acquire religious 'beliefs' oneself, or inculcate them in others, without the risk involved in fostering or inculcating ordinary belief against the evidence. I shall have to return to the topic of nonbelief theories in the chapter on faith (chapter 28).

The nonbelief theory has, despite what some consider to be its advantages, the following difficulties.

(a) It may give an account of the attitude of mind to religious propositions of some very sophisticated people. As an account of the attitude of mind of the ordinary believer it is not remotely plausible. The ordinary believer does believe religious propositions. It might be better if he had some attitude other than belief, but in fact he does not. (Braithwaite includes asserting the stories as part of the proper religious attitude to them, but he himself cannot consistently assert them, for he holds that they are not true. I hesitate to say that asserting things you do not yourself believe is usually considered to be wrong.)

A possible answer to this objection is that the ordinary believer is mistaken in thinking that his attitude to religious propositions is one of belief. For example, he does not test them empirically, as he does ordinary beliefs about matters of fact. If he does test them, it is by how satisfactory it is to live his life in accordance with them, whatever 'in accordance with' may mean, rather than by how they square with the empirical facts. (Living one's life in accordance with them, perhaps, is to go through life constantly imagining them – in the way we go through some of our lives constantly dwelling on the fate of the nonexistent characters in a novel we are reading – and gaining support, moral guidance and encouragement from doing so.)

Another possible variant on the nonbelief theory is that though the ordinary believer does believe religious propositions, in fact it would be much better if he did not believe them. He might then not only be able to foster religious 'belief' without the risk of fostering falsehoods, but also be more tolerant of people who have different beliefs from his own. It might then be possible for him to think that he and they – or even he himself at different times – can without inconsistency live their lives by different and inconsistent 'stories'. If a religious 'belief' is a belief, one must believe that those who have beliefs incompatible with one's own are mistaken. But if the 'theoretical' side of religion is a matter of having certain propositions in mind, rather than believing them, the religious person can perhaps accept that other people may find it satisfactory to 'live by' propositions which he does not find it satisfactory to live by. He may think that there is room for both ways of living, in a way in which there would not be room for both sets of beliefs; two incompatible ways of living may both be good, though two incompatible propositions cannot both be true.

It is not always clear whether nonbelief theorists hold that the proper attitude to religious propositions is not one of belief, or whether it is their view that, though the proper and usual attitude is one of belief, those sufficiently sceptical may be allowed to satisfy themselves, *faut de mieux*, with an attitude which falls short of belief, and continue to call themselves 'Christians'. Presumably holders of the nonbelief theory ought to say similar things about religions other than Christianity.

(b) The account of the meaning of sentences, such as 'God exists', that the reductive form of the nonbelief theory presupposes, is not remotely plausible. It is not remotely plausible to suppose that we know what (the main) religious sentences mean because we know what it is like for them to express what is true, in the same way that we know what the sentence 'The Battle of Hastings was fought in 1066' means because we know what it would be like for it to express what is true. We know what 'battle' means because we know what it would be like to come across a battle. But if we do come across God, it is not as we come across battles and other things in the natural world. Our knowledge of God is not on a par with our knowledge of Harold or William.

We have seen that either religious assertions have a simple meaning, as they do on the reductive form of the nonbelief theory, but are not true, or an esoteric one, as on the non-reductive form, and are then difficult to elucidate. In Richard Braithwaite's parable of the three Lord Shaftesburys – each of whom represents a person in the Trinity – one either imagines these persons as each being like an English earl – the reductionist form – or one thinks of them as three transcendent entities – the non-reductionist form. Doing the first enables one to understand them, but it would be absurd to believe them. There were and are not three Lord Shaftesburys. Doing the second presents one with the problem of what one means by the word 'God', in precisely the form it had to begin with, and so does nothing to elucidate its meaning. That one should neither believe religious assertions, nor disbelieve them (nor, I think, suspend judgment about them in the way one might suspend judgment about a dubious historical claim) beside being advice that most people will not take, does not help one at all with giving an account of what the sentences formulating them mean, and how we know that what they say is true.

(The nonbelief theory does not by itself actually say whether they are true, false, or neither, or give an account of how we know them to be true, if they are true, or false, if they are false. Likening them to fiction suggests that they are not straightforwardly true, but leaves it an open question whether they are false or just not true without being false. I do not know that Braithwaite himself brings out carefully enough the fact that, on his view, none of the propositions towards which we are expected to have the attitude he substitutes for belief are true.)

(c) One feels that holding that the propositions expressed by sentences such as 'God exists' are not to be believed is second best to holding that they are to be believed, and are true. One holds the nonbelief theory only because one thinks that there are insuperable difficulties in the way of holding that crucial religious statements are true. Furthermore, if we like to dwell, for the solace it gives to sinful men, on the proposition that Christ died for our sins, it is difficult to see how dwelling on this thought can give much solace unless one really does believe that he died for this reason, and was in fact successful in his objective in, in the next world, saving man from the consequences of sin.

(d) If statements such as that the sheep will be separated from the goats at the last day of judgment are on a par with statements such as that Elizabeth Bennet had three sisters, and are not meant to believed, problems arise about how one reconciles them with thinking that there will be no last day of judgment. This will be especially difficult with the statements Christ is said to have made about himself for, if there was no such person as Christ, none of them can be true.

(e) There is a difficulty about the relationship between a Christian's remark that Christ died in a successful attempt to save us from sin, and the apparently incompatible remark of a non-Christian to the effect that he could not have done, because there is no God to reward Christ's sacrifice by forgiving man for sin. I cannot see why if Braithwaite is right, the Christian should not simply agree with the atheist, for, since he does not believe that Christ actually died for our sins, there is no reason why he should disbelieve an atheist's remark that he could not have done.

(f) The nonbelief theory has difficulty in explaining how Christianity can be a historical religion. If Christian doctrine is not meant to believed, it will not matter whether or not it is supported by facts, historical or otherwise, and so it will not matter whether or not the Bible is true, or even whether or not Christ existed. A piece of writing does not have to be true to consist in or suggest stories.

(g) I suspect some people[5] – perhaps including Wittgenstein – confuse the true statement that the change that takes place when someone is converted to Christianity need not be a change in his beliefs, so much as a change in his attitudes and his way of life, with the false statement that the difference between being a Christian and not being a Christian is not even partly a difference in belief.

Addendum: Belief, Parable and Myth

The failure of the nonpropositional view discussed in an earlier chapter (chapter 9) does not mean that an investigation of 'non-scientific', non-historical non-factual literature may not help us to understand theistic language. Indeed, most of the language of poetry or fiction consists of sentences that express propositions.

Sometimes literary productions attempt to convey a truth by means of statements none of which are themselves true. Fiction, the overt content of which is not true and is not meant to be believed, may somehow or other convey latent morals that are true and are meant to be believed. The individual statements in the parable of the prodigal son, for example, are fiction, not history. Nevertheless, the parable of the prodigal son conveys what is commonly supposed to be a latent truth, a truth about the attitude of the deity to those who return to him after a (metaphorical) absence.

There need not be any problems about the meaning of the overt sentences which convey the latent truth. We have seen that these will have meaning just like any other sentences, say, sentences about ordinary fathers and sons. There may, however, be problems about the meaning and truth of the overall message that the individual statements are meant to convey. If the purported fact that is being conveyed by a parable is a fact about a transcendent being, the fact that it is conveyed by a parable does not absolve a philosopher or theologian from answering the difficulties concerning both meaning and truth to which the transcendence of this being may give rise. These difficulties are not removed by holding that religious language expresses parable.

The Events Recorded in the Bible Regarded as a 'Concrete Parable'

We could draw the same moral from actual events as we can from a parable describing these events. But to be a 'concrete parable', these events would have to be deliberately produced with a view to our enlightenment, that is, as something like a play with a moral, acted out on the stage. (On the stage, of course, the actions do not do most of the things they pretend to do, but if the events recorded by the New Testament are a concrete parable, they must actually have occurred, and not just have been acted)

God could cause a real father to behave in the way that the father in the parable of the prodigal son was described as behaving, with a view to communicating the same moral as that conveyed by the parable. There would then have to be some sign that God was doing this with this end in view. With a concrete parable (which, in the case, we are discussing would be the events described in the New Testament) the question arises 'Who is it that is using the parable to convey a truth, if it is not God himself?' But this person cannot be God himself, because he (God the father) is on this view one of the 'protagonists' in the concrete parable. The prodigal son could not himself have written the parable of the prodigal son, because he was only a character in a story. And one of the events recounted as actually taking place and supposed to be a part of a concrete parable, is that Christ died for our sins. But Christ's dying for our sins cannot be a way of expressing in concrete parable the fact that he died for our sins. The truth expressed in a parable cannot be the truth of the parable itself.

Christian Doctrine as a Parable

The nonbelief theory should not be confused with the view that Christian doctrine (as opposed to the recorded events themselves, which gave rise to the doctrine) is a parable. The theory that Christian doctrine is really a parable, the parable of the three Lord Shaftesburys, for example, is not a version of the nonbelief theory, though the two may have been confused, and I think Braithwaite himself confuses them. The truth conveyed in the form of parable must, contrary to the nonbelief theory, be meant to be believed.

The view that Christian doctrine itself is a parable (as opposed to being expressed in metaphor) about a father who sends his only son to redeem the world that the father has created and which has ungratefully turned away from him, is not tenable. To suggest that Christian doctrine is itself a parable is to abandon it. In a parable the events described have not happened and are fiction, but Christians usually suppose that the events recounted in the story of Christ really did happen, and that the story is true. Regarding the New Testament as itself a parable would imply that these events did not take place, for a parable itself is a species of fiction, although the message communicated by the parable is supposed to be true, and is meant to be believed.

One might suggest that a parable might raise possibilities that were meant to be considered, as well as truths that were meant to be believed. But if this is what the New Testament does, a question arises about the writers of the New Testament story. They, one supposes, wrote these stories as they did because they thought they were telling us what actually happened. But if one is reporting facts one cannot be creating a parable. For a parable is written as it is with a view to putting forward a moral, not with a view to recording truth. There may be lessons to be learned from the story of Napoleon, but this story cannot be a parable, for the very reason that its writers were aiming at recounting what Napoleon actually did, not at getting over some important fact by inventing a story which communicated it.

The view that Christian doctrine is a parable should not be confused with the view that what it asserts, it asserts in metaphor; what is asserted in metaphor is intended to be believed.

Christian Doctrine as Myth

The view that Christianity is a parable should not be confused with the view that Christianity is a kind of myth. Christianity may be a myth, but this is not a view that a Christian can hold, as myths, by definition, are not true. It is not that one needs to have a special kind of nonbelief which enables one who has this attitude to Christianity to call himself a Christian. Ordinary crude disbelief is enough for myth. If Christianity is a myth, there is no need to give, as does the nonbelief theory, a special account of that attitude that some Christians wish to call belief, for, if it is a myth, there is no need of belief at all. And saying that Christianity is a myth does not do justice to the fact that Christians think they are entitled to gain consolation from thinking (i.e., believing) that they are watched over by a benevolent God, that the course of events in the world is guided by providence, and that there is a way in which they will never die. To gain consolation from these things, one has to believe them.

To What Extent is Belief Necessary to Religion

At the risk of labouring a point that I shall argue later (especially in chapters 28 and 30), let me say that, though there are some religious attitudes that presuppose belief, there are others that do not. If I am right, it is possible to have the latter attitudes, or to indulge in certain religious practices (perhaps contemplative prayer) without the belief that there is a God. The view that one can indulge in certain religious practices without religious tenets is not at all the same as the view that religious tenets are necessary, but that holding a religious tenet does not consist in having a belief.

I have elsewhere put the view that one can contemplate, meditate and possibly pray without the necessity of belief as, to anticipate, the view that God neither exists nor does not exist. God does not exactly not exist, because it is possible to contemplate and meditate upon him. On the other hand, he does not exactly exist, because his 'existence' has no effects on the world; there are only the effects of the act of contemplation itself. This way of putting the matter is contradictory as it stands, but in matters bordering the mystical, contradiction is supposed to be venial. Perhaps you could also say that God both exists (in a way) and does not exist (in a way). I prefer the former way of putting the matter, as it suggests that the question whether there is a God or not is somehow misplaced.

I hesitate to suggest 'There is a God who does not exist' as a way of expressing what I want to say, as this would be to treat existence as an attribute, which I have elsewhere (in chapter 4) said that it is not. Perhaps one ought to stick at saying that though God does not exist, it is nevertheless possible and laudable to worship or contemplate him, and that it is laudable to meditate upon him; this is certainly the most economical way of putting the matter. But I have a hankering for the more theatrical way – that God neither exists nor does not exist – favoured by some mystics. (I shall return to this subject later in this book (chapters 28 and 30).)

Notes

1   In Wittgenstein, 1966. There is a discussion of Wittgenstein's view in Phillips, 1971.
2   See Braithwaite, 1955.
3   *Loc. cit.*
4   The view that Christian doctrine is a set of stories has also been held by Lash, 1992. He says '… the way things hang together in the Christian scheme of things has more in common with the oneness of a story with a single plot than with the oneness of a catalogue or list of objects of belief'. (Some may think that these are not exclusive alternatives.) Lash also appears to hold (with some reservation) the view that the creeds are summaries of these stories, much as, I suppose, 'The story so far' is a summary of the story so far. Presumably, however, he thinks they are true stories (though he also likens them to myths, which have to be false).
5   It may be that Wilfred Cantwell Smith, 1979, provides an example of this confusion.

12 Minor Arguments for the Existence of God

(i)   Arguments for the Existence of God that Fall Outside Kant's Classification

There are many arguments that fall outside Kant's classification, useful though it is. One of them, the ethical argument, I have already discussed. (The 'argument' from direct experience also does not fit into Kant's arrangement (because it is not an argument). I shall discuss it later (in chapter 13).) I have space to consider these arguments only briefly, and my list is certainly not exhaustive.

(ii)   The Argument from Received Opinion

The argument from received opinion is not of any great value. It would once have been possible to argue from the received opinion that the world was flat, or that the sun went round it.

The argument from received opinion is not a species of what is misdescribed as an argument from common sense. It is not a matter of common sense that there is a God, as it is a matter of 'common sense' that there are material objects, minds other than our own, that the universe has been in existence for some considerable time before today, and will remain in existence for some considerable time afterwards. To say that such things were a matter of common sense would be to put them on a par with the opinion that one should change one's wet socks if one wishes to avoid a cold.

There are two kinds of scepticism, which I shall call ordinary scepticism and philosophical scepticism. Philosophical scepticism which extends to such matters as scepticism about the existence of material things, is absurd, and so must rest on bad argument. Though the task of finding out what is wrong with these arguments is often difficult – though the process can be philosophically enlightening – there must be something wrong with the arguments, because it is absolutely certain that there are material objects, that there are other people, that two and two does equal four, and that we are aware of a world in space and time which extends before and after the present place and moment. These things are much more certain than that highly abstruse and sometimes sophistical arguments for philosophical scepticism are valid. The function of epistemologists is not so much to justify such things as a belief in the existence of material things, as to elicit the principles or techniques which ordinary people actually use successfully to justify such beliefs. It is not just a matter of common sense that there are material objects, as it is to put money by for a rainy day. Perhaps one could say that it was a matter of 'deep' common sense.

What I shall call 'commonsense scepticism', on the other hand, is simply a disposition not to accept theories without proper scrutiny. In this sense, it is not a matter for misplaced scepticism that there is a God. The belief that there is a God can be dispensed with as the 'commonsense' belief that there are material things cannot be. Intellectually, indeed, it is easy to dispense with it, as it plays no central part in our scientific knowledge of the world. It is emotionally and practically that dispensing with it is for some people difficult.

A question that needs to be answered, however, is how it can be that so many people believe that there is a God if there is not one. The answer could be that most people want to believe that there is a God, probably because as children they were cared for and protected by their parents, and immaturely cannot get out of the habit of believing or half-believing that, in a way, they still are.

That the belief that there is a God is the result of wishful thinking does not mean that such belief is false, though it may mean that the believer has no reason for thinking that it is true. But, though many things that we believe, just because we want to believe them, are true, the fact remains that, if we believe them just because we want to, these beliefs are unfounded.

However, what many people have is not so much a belief that there is a God, but a sense of the presence of God, and having this sense of presence, since it is not a belief, cannot be a case of wishful thinking (i.e. wishful believing), though thinking that this sense of presence is veridical might be. It is possible to have belief in God without a sense of his presence, and also possible to have a sense of the presence of God without believing that there is one. A sense of the presence of God would seem to me to require a different explanation from an explanation of the belief that there is one. For one thing, one may have a sense of God's presence although one does not wish to have it; one may even try to get rid of it, partly because it may impose demands on one that one does not want to meet, or because one is convinced that what it appears to tell us is false. Whether this sense of presence provides those who have it with a good reason for believing that there is a God will be discussed in the next chapter. I suspect that many people believe that there is a God because they have a sense of his presence, rather than the other way round.

It may be that Freud has explained the sense of the presence of God as a kind of superego. This superego should not simply be regarded as conscience, however Freud himself regards it. It is a personalised conscience; we feel the moral demands it makes on us as if they were coming from a person or quasi-person superior to ourselves. Over and above this we can go to its object for solace, companionship, worship, contemplation and many other things, not simply to be reminded of our duty. And it may, at least sometimes, just be there, without making any demands one at all.

Given both that belief in a God who makes moral demands and that having a sense of his presence is prevalent, there are evolutionary explanations of why they should survive. (An evolutionary explanation of something's survival is not the same thing as an explanation of how we come to have it. It is rather an explanation of how its alternatives came to be eliminated.) One's conscience, which often appears as the voice of God, will, by and large, demand that one obeys society's laws, which are, also by and large, conducive to that society's survival. I imagine conscience usually demands that one obey society's rules because by and large one's parents did.

The apparent demands of God and one's conscience are not always conducive to the survival of the individual who pay attention to them, but over a long period of time most individuals will gain more by the sacrifices made as a result of others paying attention to them than they will lose by having to pay attention to them themselves. Hence most people, though not all, will gain more than they will lose from universal obedience to conscience. It does not follow from this that believing in God, perhaps as a result of a sense of his presence, is irrational, though it may follow that it would have survived even if it were not rational. Nor does it follow from the fact that our consciences have evolved by a process of natural selection that we should pay no attention to our consciences, whether they appear in the form of personal demands or not, though it will certainly follow that these demands should not be obeyed uncritically.

Many people have to live with a sense of the presence of God, and it may not be possible for them to pay no attention to it. (I have already suggested that a sense of the presence of God is by no means entirely a matter of being aware of the demands of duty, and may sometimes not involve morality at all. Sometimes God may be a respite from morality.)

(iii)   The Argument from the Idea of God

Some philosophers have thought that there must be a God to explain how we have so excellent an idea as our idea of God, for something can proceed only from something better than itself, and nothing is better than our idea of God than God. But there does not seem to be anything very wonderful about our acquiring an idea of God. There are naturalistic explanations of our having it. And it is just not true that something can proceed only from something better than itself. If this were true, a man could proceed only from parents better than himself, and could not be dependent upon microorganisms which are worse than himself. The idea of God may be the idea of a wonderful being, but this does not necessarily mean that it is a wonderful idea.

Artists and writers can produce things much more interesting or beautiful that those we find in life. The idea of God might be regarded as the result of similar artistry. Living one's life in accordance with such an idea may also be a work of art, but this fact would give no support to the belief that there was a God – though perhaps some support to the view that we ought to live as if there were the God which one's own artistry, combined with that of others, has created.[1]

(iv)   Newman's 'Proof'

John Henry Newman has argued that our belief that there is a God resembles our belief that Great Britain is an island, which belief, of course, we are justified in accepting with complete certainty. I shall mention, and when necessary discuss, the points of resemblance and divergence between the two beliefs in my own way. Newman's argument for the existence of God is not only worth considering in itself, but also because it is connected with one of Alvin Plantinga's, which is more recent.[2] But since I have discussed Plantinga's argument in chapter 3, I shall make only the following comment on Newman's.

Newman thinks that we are justified in accepting the existence of a God who is the object of love on weaker evidence than we would be justified in demanding on some more neutral matter. Newman here confuses acting on a proposition with believing it. If we have a lot to gain if something is true, and very little to lose if it is false, it is appropriate to act as if it were true, while this would not be appropriate if we had only a little to gain if it were true and a lot to lose if it were false. But this is a matter of acting on a proposition not of believing it, and one can act on a proposition, and sometimes ought to, without believing that it is true, if there is enough to gain by so acting. For example, one may rationally propose to a woman who is most unlikely to accept one if one thinks that one would be very miserable without her, but one's case is not expedited by coming to believe that one will be accepted, nor in this case is it necessary to believe that one will be accepted in order to be accepted. In this case, indeed, belief that one would be accepted might make one rejected.

Belief in God may make an enormous emotional and practical difference to the believer. But this fact is not a reason for thinking that belief in God is true, as is the enormous difference that not believing that Great Britain is an island would make to our intellectual beliefs, so much as a reason for going on believing in spite of the fact that it is not true, or that there are no reasons for thinking that it is not true. And believing things in spite of having no reason for thinking that they are true may be reprehensible. (Acting as if a proposition one does not believe is true – i.e., acting in the way someone who did believe it would act – is not a case of not acting on the beliefs one has. If one bets on a horse that one thinks will lose, this is just a special case when the beliefs one has that there is little to lose by betting and much to gain by winning produce the same action as believing that it will win.)

(v)   Aquinas's Fourth Way

Thomas Aquinas's 'five ways' do not necessarily fit neatly into Kant's classification, but most of them are so close to the arguments that do so fit, and which have already been discussed, that I shall not consider them independently, except for one, his fourth.

Aquinas thought that because beings could be arranged in respect of excellence, there must be a being that was most excellent, which was God. However, (a) beings cannot be ordered in order of excellence. It is difficult enough to order mammals in order of excellence, and if you include not only other members of the animal kingdom, but vegetables and minerals as well, to order everything by excellence is quite impossible. Are igneous rocks better, or worse, than sedimentary ones, for example, and which of them is better or worse or neither than microbes? (b) If you could arrange beings in order of excellence, the question would arise whether you were ordering existing beings in order of excellence, or whether you were trying to find a scheme of ordering that would include all possible beings, even those that did not exist. If it is the former, putting existing things in order of merit does not justify one in adding without reason to their number. If it is the latter, it would follow, from the existence of such a scheme, only that God would be the highest of possible beings. It would not follow that there actually was a God.

The argument in principle is of the form, discussed in chapter 3, of completing a partial regularity with extra items which are such that they would turn the partial regularity into a complete one. It fills in the missing links in the great chain of being. In particular, it fills in the apparently missing top or highest link, which is supposed to be God. There is, however, no such chain, and what little ordering there is is entirely anthropocentric. Furthermore, filling in missing links in a intellectually respectable way is filling them in when there is the possibility of empirical confirmation of the existence of the postulated missing link – for example an other side to the moon or an unobserved fire esponsible for the observed smoke. But in the case of God, nor such empirical confirmation is possible.

(vi)   The Argument from Beauty

If there were a God, it might well be that he would create a world that was beautiful – but not perfectly so (in order, it is alleged, that we should have some opportunity for improving it). There are, however, reasons for thinking that we would find fairly beautiful any world in which we have evolved to be as much at home as we are in this one.[3] And it is not always possible for us to improve it in the ways in which it is not beautiful.

(vii)   The Argument from History

The argument from history to a Christian God is that the history of God's chosen people, culminating in the birth, teaching, crucifixion of Christ and the founding of his church makes probable, or at any rate increases the probability of, this process having been produced or presided over by God. This argument rests heavily on miracles. One could demythologise the miracles, but there would need to be real miracles to provide real evidence for the existence of God. There are much more plausible explanations of these events than that they were produced by God, if this is meant to be an alternative to a naturalistic explanation.

If the theory is that there is a naturalistic explanation of these events, but that God presided over and guided this natural order, the theological explanation duplicates the naturalistic one, and so (inelegantly) makes God scientifically redundant. And the events relied upon are on such a small scale compared with the immensity of the universe that it is difficult to believe that thinking that the course of history has anything to do with certain especially favoured men is more than the result of wishful thinking on the part of Jews (in the first part of the period) and Christians (in the second) to believe that they have been so singled out. An omnipotent personal God no doubt could have produced a universe as immense as ours is simply as a backdrop to the aforementioned events. Whether he would have is another matter.

(viii)   The Argument from Miracles

The argument from miracles is that miracles do occur, and are evidence of systematic interference with the universe in such a way as to provide evidence for the existence of a benevolent God, much as stones being hurled in the direction of young women was once supposed to be evidence for the existence of an invisible malignant poltergeist. But the evidence that miracles occur is very dubious, and the ones allegedly recorded are sporadic, haphazard and, compared with the enormity of the universe, on a tiny scale.

(ix)   The Argument from Providence

The argument from providence is like the two above arguments, in that it is alleged that an examination of nature shows that nature goes on as if man was cared for by an intelligent being, and concludes that he is so cared for.

There is a great deal of evidence that man is so constituted that the things he needs are to hand, that he has roughly the abilities that he needs, and that his desires for the most part – though certainly not always – prompt him to perform actions that are to his own good and the good of others. For example, he wants to eat certain substances, and they are good for him. He wants to copulate, and copulation propagates his race. He (usually) loves his children, which causes them to be brought up. He seeks his own economic welfare, and this, according to Adam Smith (not without justice, though Smith exaggerates) leads him, by the guidance of an unseen hand, to perform actions which are also of benefit to others as well as to himself. (It does not follow from this that a love of food or women, or pity for those in distress, just is a desire to perform actions that are conducive to the survival of oneself or others, though these are these desires' effects.)

According to some theologians, the facts mentioned in the previous paragraph are evidence for the existence of a God who arranges things in order to care for us. Empirical investigation, however, indicates that there is always a natural explanation of how allegedly providential events come about. If the hypothesis was that these events are due to the activity of a person in the world, an alternative explanation would rule it out. In the case of God it is suggested that this hypothesis is not ruled out, but that God disguises his benevolent work by his arranging nature so as to make it seem as if our welfare were automatically produced. But in this case the hypothesis that there is a God is again redundant and uneconomical. And to argue: if there were a God there would be no signs of his intervening; there are no signs of his intervening; therefore there is a God, would be absurd.

It is sometimes said that nature is arranged so as to give man the opportunity for helping others, exercising courage and self-discipline, and so on. But it is in fact the other way round. Nature is arranged as she is, and on account of the way she is arranged we need courage and self-discipline and to care for others. Hence nature has tended to select in favour of those who have these virtues. And nature has not been made regular to enable man to find his way about in it. Man has come to be the kind of animal who can make predictions on the basis of past regularities because that is the kind of being he needs to be in order to find his way about an already regular world.

(x)   Argument from Consciousness

It has been argued that the fact of consciousness is inexplicable except on the hypothesis that there is a God.

Consciousness, however, does not seem to be so inexplicable. It can be divided into consciousness of other things and people, and consciousness of one's self. The former is obviously useful to man; no organism could survive long without some knowledge of what was in its vicinity. Thus consciousness could have evolved, and probably has evolved, because of its survival value.

But it is also useful to man to be able to review his thinking and conduct in order to adjust them when they are unsuccessful. Hence self-consciousness, too, would be favoured by natural selection. (Natural selection would not favour unbridled egotism, which would destroy the communities that men find essential to life.)

It is not, however, consciousness and self-consciousness as such that are held to need deistic, as opposed to ordinary, explanations, so much as a particular view of them, namely, that non-reductionist view which regards consciousness as something other than a combination of physical entities. These physical entities existed long before any non-physical consciousness emerged from them, which must tempt one to think that consciousness, when it emerged, must consist just of those entities combined in new ways. But even if consciousness is a phenomenon irreducible to atoms – as I think is obvious despite the efforts of philosophers who try to tailor the facts to suit their theories, rather than accommodating the theories to the facts – it could still be explained as something that automatically results when atoms are combined in certain ways.

Some regard this as *a priori* impossible, but if Hume is right, as I think he was, in thinking that anything may cause anything, they must be mistaken. Consciousness cannot be explained by laws of physics, if the concepts involved in statements about it cannot, as I think they cannot, be defined in terms of the concepts of physics. But this does not mean that their occurrence is not reducible to law, for there are many laws other than physical laws. Hence their occurrence may be both regular and explicable, though the law that explains them will be a heterogeneous law, containing both phenomenological and psychological concepts, describing consciousness, and physical ones. (Some regard this as unsatisfactory, because it rules out the possibility of a theory of everything, but I do not think a theory of everything, as opposed to a theory of everything physical, is possible.)

Explanation of consciousness as resulting whenever physical particles get combined in certain ways is much preferable to explanation by the action of God. One reason for this is that we have other reasons for thinking that there are physical particles, but it is doubtful whether there are other reasons for thinking that there is a God. (One should not forget that, even if consciousness is in principle reducible to physical particles, it would be nevertheless as impossible in practice to deduce all – and perhaps impossible to deduce any – statements about psychology or sociology from those of physics as to deduce when one's car would break down from quantum theory.)

One might regard causing physical entities to assume the necessary configurations as God's way of producing consciousness – compare the view that God produced man, but evolution was his way of doing it. But if consciousness was regularly produced by the configurations, postulating a God at all would be redundant. The physical entities alone would suffice.

(xi) The Argument that the Good has a Tendency to Create Itself

I feel not the slightest sympathy with the above argument. In order to create itself, the good would have not to exist – for if it existed already, it would not need to create itself – and the nonexistent cannot create anything. If, *per impossibile*, the good could create itself, there is not the slightest reason to suppose that it has created our universe. Our universe is not the very same thing as the good, and, indeed, is not particularly good. People's ideas of the good create things – i.e. people, on account of their ideas of good things, sometimes create things – but if God, on account of his idea of what would be good, created the universe, the argument would then reduce to the argument from design, which we have already rejected.

(xii) Conclusion

None of the arguments stated above are valid.

Notes

1   I am indebted for this idea to Don Cupitt.
2   See Newman, 1985 and 1843. See also Plantinga, 1967.
3   I have argued in more detail for a similar view in Harrison, 1971.

13 The 'Argument' from Religious Experience[1]

(i)   The Possibility that We Know of God by Direct Acquaintance

What I shall call the argument from religious experience is, strictly speaking, not an argument at all. It makes the claim that religious experience involves having direct awareness of God. If there is such an awareness those who have it do not have (though they nevertheless may) to arrive at their knowledge, if they have any, that there is a God as a result of some process of argumentation, any more than we arrive by argument at our knowledge of the existence of the things we perceive. These people will know that there is a God because they can 'see' him. 'See', of course, is being used in a metaphorical sense. They do not see God with their eyes, though they do apprehend his existence in some way analogous to seeing. (Mystics frequently claim that they have a non-sensuous awareness of God. Sometimes they describe it as 'ghostly sight'.) Others less well-favoured may not themselves have this direct experience of God, and may, if direct acquaintance is the only way of arriving at knowledge of him, have to content themselves with accepting facts about his existence and nature upon the testimony of those who do have it.

If this view is right, of course, those who have religious experience do not have to come to know that there is a God because this is the conclusion of a valid non-circular argument with true premises. It is unnecessary to prove the existence of that of which one is immediately aware. But though it may be improper to argue for the proposition that God exists, it does not follow that it is improper to argue for (or against) the proposition that the proposition that God exists is not (or not only) a matter for argument, or to consider whether what purports to be awareness of the deity is veridical. That, indeed, is what we shall shortly proceed to do.

255

(ii)   Religious Experience and Testimony

Of course, those who have no religious experience may accept, and those that do have it supplement, their own religious experience with the testimony of others. There is no fundamental principle that testimony ought to be accepted (though we are so constituted as to accept most testimony in fact, and most testimony ought to be accepted). Testimony ought to be accepted if it fits into a coherent picture of the world, which is for the most part itself built on testimony, and such testimony as does not so fit ought to be rejected. If we are in doubt about whether it so fits or not, we ought to suspend judgment. I have suggested in 'The Philosophy of Mysticism'[2] that the question whether or not it fits does not arise.

(iii)   Direct Experience and the Verification Principle

If there is such a thing as direct awareness of God, this could explain how the word 'God' and ancillary words can make sense, to some people at any rate. These words can make sense because those who are immediately acquainted with God have the experiences that give them meaning, just as others have the experience of seeing the colours and shapes and objects and happenings that give meaning to the words for these colours and shapes and objects and happenings. On this view the word 'God' can be ostensively defined for us, like words like 'horse', by our being shown an (or the only) instance.

It matters little whether you say that religious propositions do not need verification, because in religious experience we are immediately aware of the entity they describe, or whether we say that they have verification, because they are verified by our having the experience they describe. In either event, if religious experience is a direct awareness of a deity, the verificationists should have no difficulty about allowing sentences containing the word 'God' to be meaningful. What the verificationists were against, I think rightly, was allowing sentences to be meaningful when they appeared to be saying something that made no difference, either directly or indirectly, to anyone's experience. If there is a direct awareness of God, his existence would, on this view, make a difference to our experience. There would, however, be a problem about explaining how sentences about the deity are meaningful to those who do not have the experience in question.

(iv)   Religious Experience as a Way of Attaching Meaning to the Word 'God'

If we were to have direct experience of God, we would not need to know of his existence by means of argument. (a) Direct experience of God might provide a way of ostensively defining those characteristics in terms of which 'God' is defined, as we learn the meaning of 'furry' by being shown furry things like cats. (b) Direct experience might, if 'God' is a proper name (see chapter 2), be a way of fixing its reference.

(a) Some of God's characteristics, for example omnipotence, can partially ostensively be defined, without having recourse to immediate experience, by reference to things we come across in the normal spatio-temporal world. (I say 'partially ostensively defined' because we do not come across omnipotent beings in this word, but only powerful ones.) This means that it is not necessary to have immediate experience of God to define 'God' by some of his characteristics. But there may be other characteristics, like those ascribed to the One by some mystics, which one cannot come across in the world. To understand words like these we would need to be aware both of them and the entity possessing them. It seems doubtful whether some of the characteristics attributed to the One by mystics could be understood by people who did not have the mystics' experience.

(b) It may be that a difficulty with holding that 'God' can be introduced into language by our being shown God is that 'God' cannot be the word for God unless there can be a causal connection between the presence of God and the uttering of 'God' by a person using this word with a view to telling someone what it refers to. But if God is eternal, there cannot be such a connection, because causation implies change.

However, it may be that all that is necessary for so defining 'God' is that there should be a causal connection between the presence of God and the uttering of 'God', and God, even if he is eternal, is not always present (not because he changes, but because we do). God, like Everest, is not the only thing that is present, and is, as Everest is, sometimes hidden by darkness or by clouds, not always 'visible'. And God might be everlasting rather than eternal, in the sense that temporal predicates do not apply to him. In this case there could be a causal connection between God and the word 'God'. I do not myself, however, find the view that God is only sempiternal satisfactory.

That we learn the reference of 'God' by being shown God, or by 'seeing' God, is not, if God is personal, a view that I myself can consistently hold, because I have rejected the view that a personal God can be the object of immediate experience. I rejected it partly on the grounds that one cannot have immediate experience of dispositional characteristics, partly on the grounds that we can have immediate experience only of the contents of our own mind. (I would add that this does not show that mystical experience cannot be a veridical awareness of something, but only that it cannot be awareness of an omnipotent, omniscient, personal God. However, the object of mystical experience, assuming that there is just one, might not have any dispositional characteristics, and if it is not a mind, we do not have the difficulty, as with the view that we can be acquainted with it, that we cannot be acquainted with minds other than our own.) I have also rejected the view that 'God' is a proper name. (It does not follow from the fact that 'God' is not a proper name that we are not acquainted with God.)

One of the differences between a word for a characteristic like 'omnipotence' and a word like 'Everest' is that one can learn a word for a characteristic by applying it to different individuals, while with a word like 'Everest' one is taught not to use it for a different object even though it possesses the characteristics that Everest possessed. In order to do this with 'God' one would have to 'see' God on at least two different occasions, and know that the entity one 'saw' on the first occasion was identical with the entity one 'saw' on the second. In the case of an impersonal God, I cannot think how this is possible. With a material object like Everest one knows that the object one sees on one occasion is the same as the object one sees on the second occasion because it satisfies the hypothesis that it has taken a route through space and time from the place of the first to that of the 'second'. (A limiting case of this would be its not having travelled at all.) With a non-spatial non-temporal being like God this is not possible. I think that those who think that there is only one God think this because it is not satisfactory to think of there being more than one. One does not think there is one God because of an observed identity, as one has observed that there is only one Taj Mahal. (Strictly speaking, one does not observe that there is only one Taj Mahal, but that there is only one is a hypothesis to explain an exceedingly complex collection of facts, such as that if one were to carve one's name on it, one would find the carving there when one returned by 'suitable' route after an interval. That there is only one Taj Mahal is partly a matter of piecing together various palace-like views in the simplest possible way. I doubt whether this could be done with God.)

If God were a person, and in consequence – since we cannot be acquainted with the minds of persons other than ourselves – that there is a God is a hypothesis, that the God we communicate with on one occasion is the same person that we communicate with on another would be another, more specific hypothesis. Hence if God were a mind (or better, a disembodied person with a mind), that the behaviour that manifests the presence of a mind on one occasion is the product of the same mind as that which is manifested by mind-manifesting behaviour on another, is a hypothesis to explain such things as why we do not have to tell this person the same thing more than once. However, the behaviour appropriate to the existence of a divine mind is not forthcoming, so the question whether it indicates the existence of the same or of different disembodied persons does not arise. (The way of establishing identity that I was considering could work only if the disembodied person in question were a temporal or sempiternal entity (see chapter 18).)

If an entity were the non-personal non-spatio-temporal object of immediate mystical experience, I cannot think how we could decide whether a mystical object that we were aware of on one occasion would be the same or a different object from the one we were aware of on another occasion. One might think that one should say that it must be a different object if it appeared to have different characteristics on the two occasions, but I suppose it could reveal a different aspect of itself without having changed. But if its characteristics make it a satisfactory object of contemplation, perhaps it really does not matter whether it is the same thing or a different thing – or even whether the question makes sense – so long as it has the desired characteristics on both occasions.

If 'God' were a word like 'vice-chancellor' – as I have said I think it is – we would neither need to fix its reference nor to give it meaning by means of immediate experience. If 'God' were, as I have suggested, a word like 'Masser' as it occurs in the sentence 'Masser's in the cold cold ground' there might be no need for one to be acquainted with its object in order to know what the word meant, though such acquaintance might be necessary to demonstrate God's existence.

(We have seen that there is a modern view to the effect that proper names are rigid designators, in the sense that they designate the same thing in all the possible worlds in which the thing they designate exists, but I doubt whether accepting this view makes any difference to what I have said.)

(v) Whether Religious Experience is Discursive or Contemplative

The suggestion that some may know of God's existence without argument raises the question whether religious experience is discursive or what, for want of a better word, I shall call 'contemplative'. If it is discursive, then religious experience consists in an emotional reaction to a belief. One believes that God exists, and that he has certain properties, and in consequence one has such emotions and attitudes as reverence, fear, awe, love, etc., for him. However, on this view, the fact that one feels the emotions can have no tendency to justify the beliefs which (partly) give rise to them, or even to show that the sentences formulating these beliefs fully make sense. If the beliefs are true, then the emotions I feel may be appropriate, and if the beliefs are false, the emotions may be misplaced. (I shall consider later whether, if there is not a God, it follows that all the emotions and attitudes which he evokes must be misplaced.) But the bare fact that I have the emotion can have no tendency to show that the beliefs on which the emotions are based are true ones. To take a simple example, I may hear in the night a noise which I take to be made by a burglar, and feel frightened or angry in consequence. But the bare fact that I feel fear can have no tendency at all to show that my belief that the noise I hear is made by a burglar is true. For all the fact that I have the feelings shows, the noise might have been made by the cat.

If, however, religious experience is contemplative rather than discursive, then the situation is different. Just as we cannot contemplate our navels unless we have a navel and can see it, so we cannot, or so it would seem, contemplate God unless he both exists and we are aware of him. (This contemplation does not have to be contemplation of a personal God.) The possibility must not be forgotten, of course, that experience which seems to the person who has it to be contemplative may not be so in fact. And it is not necessary, if our knowledge of the existence and attributes of God is to be non-inferential knowledge, that religious experience should never be discursive. What is necessary is that it should sometimes be contemplative, i.e., that it should be contemplative for some of the people some of the time.

(vi)   The Analogy Between Religious Experience and Perceptual Experience Misplaced; No Experience of Others' Minds

The analogy with ordinary perception is not necessarily helpful to those who think that they know without argument that God exists because we perceive him. For though, on some theories of perception, we know without inference that perceived things exist, on other theories an inference is involved in our knowledge even of the existence and properties of things which are under our noses. (The truth is probably that perception is neither inference nor immediate awareness (though it involves both).)[3]

However, to repeat a point made more briefly in the preceding chapter, the comparison that I have been making between contemplative religious experience and perception, whether it is helpful or not, seems to be misplaced. We perceive material objects. But a personal God is not a material object. He is at least more like a mind or a disembodied person, and some would say he was a mind.[4] Hence we should expect our knowledge of him to be more like our knowledge of others' minds, or of their thoughts, feelings and mental capacities, than it is like our knowledge of the existence and properties of material objects.

Unfortunately, however, there does not seem to be any such thing as direct non-discursive awareness of the existence, or of the thoughts and feelings, of minds other than our own. We often, though not always, know both that we ourselves think and feel, and what we think and feel, non-discursively, without argument or inference, because we are often immediately aware of our own thoughts and feelings. To suggest that we knew that we ourselves were thinking about a philosophical problem because we had concluded, after a careful consideration of the arguments, that we could come to no other conclusion than that that is what we must be thinking about, would be ridiculous. But we do not seem to know what people other than ourselves think and feel, or that they exist, in the same kind of direct way. In normal (non-religious) situations it is absolutely essential, if one is to know that someone else exists and what he or she is feeling and thinking, to see him (or hear or touch or observe him with a suitable instrument) or to see things, like his letters or his diary or his image on a television screen, or to hear other things, if only on the telephone, which we also believe to have been produced by the activity of his body. (Our own knowledge may be augmented by the testimony of others who have 'perceived' his body in one or other of these ways, even though we have not.)

It is not necessary to see a person's (or animal's) body. He could talk to us from behind a screen, or we could hear him making a party political broadcast on the radio. We could even read his letters to the *Times* newspaper or listen to recordings of his voice or watch video recordings of his doings long after he was dead. But it seems quite obvious that, if we are unable to see his body and to watch it exhibiting various kinds of purposive behaviour, to see him blushing or paling, to hear his groans or to hear or see spoken or written words emanating in some way from his hands or lips, we simply would not have the ghost of an idea what he was thinking and feeling, or even that there was such a person at all. We could accept this person's existence and facts about him on the testimony of others. But then, we could not know of the existence (and beliefs) of the person testifying without having knowledge of the testifier's body or of emanations therefrom, and the testifier himself could not know of the person concerning whom he was testifying without such knowledge. (Our awareness of the words embodying the testimony would be a moderately remote effect of the existence of the person testified to, and so could itself be regarded as an indirect emanation from him.)

(Hence even if the Bible were the word of God we would not, in being aware of the marks on paper which recorded this word, be aware of God's thoughts, but of physical entities (words) from which we inferred God's thoughts as a hypothesis to explain how these entities got there. (I am not suggesting that fundamentalists would themselves suppose that that the Bible is the word of God was a hypothesis.))

It is sometimes supposed that telepathy provides us with knowledge of another's mind which is not obtained by seeing his body, or by hearing or seeing the noises or marks on paper or whatever which emanate from it. However, it does not appear to be the case that telepathy does provide us with such knowledge. All that seems to happen, when and if telepathic communication occurs, is that the contents of one person's mind are affected by another's in a manner which cannot be explained in the usual ways, e.g., by sound waves travelling from the vocal chords of one person to the ears of another. Tom thinks or has images which he thinks he can identify as images of the card which Mary actually sees, though Tom himself cannot see what this card is, and Mary does not tell Tom what card she is seeing. It is not that Tom is aware of Mary's experience, so much as that Tom's experiences are (allegedly) causally connected with Mary's experiences in some paranormal way, and that Tom is able to infer, from knowledge of his experience, the nature of Mary's.

This is shown to be so by the fact that one needs to check in the normal way that one in fact has telepathic powers, e.g., by someone's actually looking at the card that Mary claims to have clairvoyant knowledge of, and seeing whether or not this card is the one that she says it is. Telepathic experiences are not, if they occur, self-authenticating, as an experience would have to be if it is to give us knowledge not obtainable in any other way. If telepathy consisted in immediate knowledge of the thoughts and feelings of others, such checking ought not to be necessary.

It has been held (very roughly, by behaviourist philosophers) that all there is to others' pains is their groans, that all there is to others' intentions is their purposive behaviour, that all there is to others' communications is the symbols in which these are embodied, and that thoughts are nothing over and above the brain processes which have been discovered to be intimately connected with them. This view has never struck me as being even remotely plausible. It is just obvious, really, that Tom's being in pain does not even remotely resemble his groaning or his neurons firing; that Mary's pondering upon whether or not to move her rook is quite different from her moving her rook, even from her moving her rook intelligently. These activities are obviously different from the brain processes with which they are in some way or other intimately connected. The thoughts that Tom commits to paper are both quite different from the written words in which his thoughts are embodied and from the neural activity that is intimately connected in some way or other with his thoughts.[5]

Hence a passage of thought of some kind must be involved in first perceiving someone's body and believing as a result, that he has certain thoughts and feelings, for example, hearing him screaming and seeing him writhing, and concluding that he is in acute pain. Some kind of inference (or at least passage) of some kind is necessary if one is to pass from one to the other; one cannot have direct acquaintance of others' thoughts and feelings. But in that case, if knowledge of God's mind is remotely like our own, our knowledge of it could not be direct. And such indirect knowledge, if any, that we have of it would, if it resembles our knowledge of finite minds, have to involve a direct knowledge of God's body, or of events resembling written or spoken words emanating from him.

(Distinct from the view that pain and such can be reduced to groans, etc. is the view that pains and such can only be described by means of groans and such. This view does not seem to be true. Indeed in describing what I myself feel as a pain I am not making use of a description which refers to anything physical (or anything *else* physical, if pain itself is physical). Whether there is any sense in which God may have a body I shall discuss in a later chapter (chapter 20).)

(vii) The Impossibility of Having Direct Acquaintance with Dispositional Properties like Omnipotence

There is this further reason for thinking that we cannot have direct acquaintance with a personal God. To be a person it is necessary to have certain dispositional properties. Just as salt has to have the dispositional property of being soluble in water, a person has (and must have) the disposition to respond to certain stimuli in certain ways. To be a person it is necessary that one should sometimes feel pain if someone attempts to hurt one, to have plans, which involves reacting in certain ways to certain contingencies if they rise, to have beliefs, which involves a disposition to act in way which would get one what one wants if these beliefs were true, and to feel emotions, which involves a disposition to behave in certain ways in certain situations if they were to arise. For example, if the emotion is jealousy, one's being jealous involves a disposition to take hostile action towards the people of whom one is jealous if the opportunity arises.

But the possession of dispositional properties cannot be established by acquaintance or direct awareness. We do not know even of our own mental dispositions by immediate acquaintance. One must experiment and note the results. In the case of salt, we find out that it has the dispositional property of being soluble by putting it in water and seeing whether or not it dissolves. In the case of people, one must, in order, say, to find out what they believe, note how they behave in certain circumstances when these circumstances arise. If these circumstances do not arise, one has to produce them artificially, and see what happens. The simplest and most ethical way of doing this is to ask them questions and note what they say, but there are more devious ways. Not all of these are verbal. One can test whether or not someone believes the cup is poisoned by inviting him or her to drink from it, and observing whether he or she does so.

Direct acquaintance will tell you nothing, for direct acquaintance with a dispositional property is impossible. All we can be acquainted with are the manifestations of these dispositions. But claims about a personal deity involve such things as his being omnipotent and perfectly good. Being omnipotent and perfectly good are dispositional characteristics, and involve a disposition to do certain things in certain circumstances, if those circumstance arise, for example obliterate the universe if it displeases beyond one a certain point, or to help people if they are sufficiently in need. Since these characteristics are dispositional there is no way in which that there is a God who possesses these characteristics can be established by direct acquaintance. To say we know of him by direct acquaintance is much too easy a way of solving the problem of our knowledge of a personal God.

(viii)   Direct Awareness and God's Morality

If God is by definition good, claiming that we know by direct experience that he exists involves claiming that we know by direct awareness that he has certain moral attributes. This would again involve the difficulty, just discussed, for the view that we are directly aware of God, for moral characteristics are usually dispositional, for a example, a disposition not to perform cruel acts, or, perhaps, a disposition to reward the virtuous and punish the vicious. We have already seen that there cannot be direct awareness of dispositional characteristics.

(ix)   God's Awareness of Our Thoughts and Feelings

What I have just said seems to indicate that there could be no such thing as being directly aware of the existence of a personal God. (What I have said does not preclude our being directly aware of a non-personal god.) Indeed, I am inclined to think that that one person cannot be aware of another's thoughts is an analytic or conceptual truth – though I wish I could demonstrate this better than I can. Most people take it for granted that our being directly aware of any thought or feeling means that it must be one's own thought or feeling.

God, however, if he is personal, and knows what his creatures think and feel, must be (directly) aware of their thoughts and feelings, without these being his thoughts and feelings. They could not be his because he would then sometimes have evil thoughts and feelings, and very frequently have trivial or otherwise inappropriate ones. However, to suppose that God needed to be told what we are thinking, or to infer what we are feeling from the condition of our body or our overt behaviour, would be absurd. He is supposed (with justice, if there is a personal God) to know our innermost hearts without our needing to reveal it to him, and without the possibility of our keeping anything secret. If this is so, the view that no person can know of another's thoughts without inference must be mistaken, for the word 'person' includes a personal God.

If so, it could be that though God knows everything that we think and feel, we know nothing about what God thinks and feels. But it is perhaps just conceivable that it is just that we know less about what God thinks and feels than he does (everything) about what we think and feel. If one can know directly only about one's own thoughts and feelings, it would follow that we and God share some of the contents of our minds. Sally Beauchamp,[6] a famous case of what is known as multiple personality, had several different persons or 'subpersons' associated with her body. (I do not like the usual word, 'personality', for someone's personality is a set of characteristics, such as being industrious, being punctual and taciturn, and so on. These may change, without the person possessing them at one time but not at another ceasing to be one and the same person.) One of these subpersons which collectively were Sally Beauchamp was aware without inference of everything another subperson sharing her body thought and felt, but this relationship was not reciprocated. The second subperson in the body did not know directly anything about what the first subperson thought and felt, and had to be left messages having these things – distress at having the room they shared left untidy, for example – explained to her.

I cannot say that I take this possibility very seriously, but I throw it out to Christian theologians as a possible model of the relationship between Christ's mind and God's. (It would not enable them to maintain that Christ and God were identical, for then they would have to share *all* their thoughts and feelings, which the Beauchamp girls did not.)

(x)   The Impossibility of a Materialist Account of God's 'Mental Processes'

What I have just said means that any view that reduces propositions about thoughts to propositions about brain activity would make it very difficult to make sense of statements about the mind of God. (This may be why God has no brain processes.) For where human minds are concerned there is actual brain activity, with which their thoughts and feelings could, at a pinch, be identified, whereas with God's mind there are not. A materialist view of God's mental activity would founder on the fact that God does not have a body.

(A materialist view of God's mental processes, incidentally, would be possible if God had a body, and this body were situated in the material world. Empirical investigation of the material world, however, does not reveal any suitable candidates for being the brain of God, and the supposition that there is such a thing as the brain of God is not even remotely plausible. For one thing, it would, I suppose, have to be infinitely big, and there would be no room for it.)

(xi)   Knowing God by the Symbols that are Claimed to Emanate from Him

What I have just said means that the nearest approach we could conceivably have to direct awareness of a personal God would consist in hearing or seeing things which 'emanated' from him in some way analogous to the way in which the written or spoken words produced by other people emanate from them, or in which disarranged furniture can be the sign of the presence of an intruder. We could not witness God's body behaving in a purposive manner, as we can witness human beings' bodies behaving purposively.

The way in which these things emanate from God, of course, would have to be different from the way in which written or spoken words emanate from people. God has no mouth with which to produce spoken words, and no hands with which to write letters, nor arms with which to semaphore; he does not broadcast on the radio or speak over the telephone. His workings on the world would thus resemble those of an omnipotent, omniscient poltergeist who, if there are such things, also have no bodies. (A poltergeist, on some views, is a maliciously disposed personality having the power to direct stones and other missiles in the direction of person it appears to dislike, but has no body or any other physical manifestations.) Even the Bible, if it is the word of God, cannot have been produced by him physically, as we write physically with pen and ink, but must have been the work of amanuenses.

How he could have caused his amanuenses to write at his 'dictation' is an interesting question. It may be that there is no insuperable difficulty – God's alleged timelessness apart – in God's not only producing by an act of will all the symbols or signs he needs immediately by a direct act of volition, but that he can also control in a similar way the hands or the vocal chords of the people whom he is alleged to have created. (I take an act of will to be the manner in which a being with a mind but no body would have to effect changes in the world. It would be analogous to the manner in which we sometimes try and effect changes in the world without using our bodies, for example, by willing someone's to turn and notice us, or (in experiments in telepathy) to make a die, for example, fall one side up rather than another.)

It follows, of course, that awareness of a personal God, if it occurs, would involve, in the first instance, ordinary sense experience of the supposed effects of God's activity which effects are alleged to be mainly visual or auditory, and the most important thing about these auditory or visual experiences ought to be the nature of the messages communicated by them to the people who have them. I do not think it matters that this experience can be classified as hallucinatory, in that it was not caused by the stimulation of the sense organs of the people who claim to have it. Producing suitable hallucinations could be God's way of communicating with us. The fact that Joan of Arc's voices were not produced by sound waves falling upon her ears, and that photons were not responsible for the visions of St Teresa does not itself rule them out from being communications from the deity. Indeed, if Moses really did see a bush that was actually burning that would, to my mind, lower the chances that Moses' experience involved a veridical supernatural communication.

This does not mean that such things as visions – and the auditory equivalent of visions – cannot occur. If, as one ought, one were to accept the sense-datum theory (though few philosophers do) one can say that Joan of Arc experienced auditory sense-data, and St Theresa visual sense-data, which were not caused by the usual physiological changes induced by an external stimulus in their respective perceptual apparatuses. (If one rejects the sense-datum theory, the point can still be made, but in a different way.) The fact, if it is one, that such experiences are more readily obtained after fasting, sexual deprivation, and perhaps after the use of certain drugs, does not necessarily show that they are not veridical. Some people think better on an empty stomach and some drugs may heighten one's sensitivity.

More worrying for a would-be believer should be the fact, if it is one, that sexual deprivation, drugs, etc., can also produce insanity. And the actual content of these experiences is even more worrying. Whatever Joan of Arc may have supposed to the contrary, God is probably not a patriotic Frenchman bent on driving the English back to their own country. The religious experiences of those prone to have them do seem to be much what you would expect them to be from someone brought up in the cultural and religious backgrounds which prevailed in their time. If orthodox Hindus had visions of Christ or the Virgin Mary, one would perhaps be justified in attaching more weight to visions, but one might expect a Christian who was liable to have visions to have visions of Christ and the Virgin Mary, whether these visions were veridical or not. Nevertheless, there may be a common core, which all mystical experience, which claims to be an advanced form of direct acquaintance, shares, and this would tend to indicate that mystical experience was independent of cultural pressures, and so tend to shows that it was veridical.[7] But for the same reason, mystical experience would be unlikely to confirm the tenets of this or that particular religion.

(xii)   The Conditions of Religious Experience being Veridical

Let us suppose, then, that religious experience is not so much a matter of direct acquaintance with the deity as a matter of interpreting symbols. If so, what conditions would visual and auditory experiences have to fulfil for the person who had them to interpret them as his being in communication with God, as certain normal visual and auditory experience – such as seeing flags in certain configurations (semaphore) – are good reasons for the person who has it to believe he is in communication with other people? But since to expect religious experience to be as compelling as ordinary sense experience is to expect too much of it, perhaps we ought to consider rather the question: 'What conditions must such experiences fulfil in order to give some reason which, though less compelling than ordinary sense experience, nevertheless validates to some degree the claims about the deity made on the strength of our having them?'

If we treat what is claimed to be direct experience of the deity as a matter of interpreting symbols, it follows that God's existence is a hypothesis put forward to explain the occurrence of certain 'hallucinatory' sensations – Joan of Arc's voices or St Theresa's visions, for example – just as Tom's existence is a hypothesis to explain why we are hearing certain words on the radio. In this case, that there is a God is not a matter of direct awareness, any more than it is a matter of direct awareness that other people exist.

I cannot see anything in principle impossible about arguing to the existence of a very powerful mind or person from considering messages appearing to emanate from this mind, as we argue to the existence of minds other than our own partly because of messages – in bottles, for example – purporting to emanate from them. However, I am confident that the messages which, if they occurred, would justify us in believing that there was a God, do not actually occur. (In the case of religious experience, it is obvious that we do not usually come across such messages with our external senses. It was not with ears that Joan of Arc heard her voices.)

Arguing to the existence of God from the occurrence of messages from him is not a matter of direct acquaintance with the deity or with the thought processes that caused the messages, but a hypothesis to explain the occurrence of such messages. The theory, therefore, has already been adequately treated of in the chapter on the argument from design (since the messages would be a manifestation of design) and will be reverted to in the chapter on miracles (since their occurrence by God's design would be miraculous). The fundamental point, derived from the argument (in chapters 13 and 14) is that a God who produced religious experience would be one who tinkered with the universe (and, in this case, tinkered with it on a pretty small scale), rather than one who transcended and created it. A God who produced messages would be tinkering with it, as people are when they produce messages. But the existence of God is not a hypothesis, and theology not a kind of super science, whose business it is to explain things like religious experience. All its attempts to explain things that happen in the world have turned out to be failures, and to suppose that it should explain how it comes about that we have religious experience is to make it try to do a job that science can do much better.

(xiii)   Brief Remarks on the Bearing of Religious Experience on Certain Other Christian Doctrines

If religious experience cannot tell us of the existence of a (personal) God, *a fortiori* it cannot tell us of the truth of other Christian doctrines; these commit one to *more* than does the bare assertion that there is a God – and, by and large, are too specific and detailed to be justified by what we can discern by anything so obscure and imponderable as religious experience.

It has been claimed that the doctrine of the Trinity is justified by Christian experience. This claim is ambiguous. It may mean that the doctrine of the Trinity is justified because it explains or accounts for Christian experience. This would not mean that immediate experience was the epistemological justification of Christian doctrine, so much as that Christian doctrine was a theory that explained how it came about that we had the kind of religious experience we do. (I have already commented on this view.) On the other hand, it might mean that religious experience justified Christian doctrine, in the sense that the doctrine was known to be true by immediate experience.

I think what in fact is the case is this.

(a) Many have what purports to be immediate experience of God, which cannot justify us in believing in the existence of God for the reasons already given – mainly because we cannot know by direct experience of the existence of dispositional characteristics like omnipotence.

(b) Christ, the historical person, was crucified 2,000 ago, and we can know about the historical Christ only by normal means, which involves postulating his existence and actions to explain the occurrence of certain meaningful marks on paper or parchment. i.e., the historical records, and of archaeological remains, if any. This activity involves no extraordinary powers whatsoever (though in principle it could involve ordinary powers developed to an extraordinary degree). But history by itself could not, as immediate experience might be claimed to, justify a belief in Christ's *present* existence.

Christians, especially Christian mystics, do undoubtedly have what purports to be immediate experience of Christ, but this experience, too, cannot justify a belief in his present existence. For I suspect that the best that Christian mystics could do would be to have Christ-like imagery. That Christ still exists in whatever form a Christian wishes to suppose that he exists, would have to be a theory to explain the occurrence of these mystical experiences. I have already suggested that this is not a matter for a theologian. It is a difficulty that non-Christian mystics are not as prone as Christian ones to have what purport to be direct experiences of Christ.

(c) One possible theory about experience of that elusive entity, if it is an entity,[8] the Holy Ghost,[9] is that it is experience of what the Holy Ghost does. There is nothing to the Holy Ghost over and above his (or her or its) manifestations. For example, the disciples are supposed to have acquired powers which they did not have before the Holy Ghost descended upon them. There is no reason why the Holy Ghost should not be reduced to the disposition to acquire the powers in appropriate circumstances. In this case to assert the existence of the Holy Ghost would be to assert that certain 'spiritual' powers and experiences come to people either unbidden, or, if they take the necessary steps to acquire them, bidden. Hence I would be inclined to think, though I speak with great diffidence, that experience of the Holy Ghost is not a perceptual or quasi-perceptual experience, the object of which is a person (or any other object) so much as experience of the acquisition of new (spiritual) capacities. However, claiming that Holy Ghost exists does, I suppose, involve claiming that its manifestations do have a divine origin, so it is impossible to believe in the Holy Ghost without believing in God.

(d) Christians, too, speak of having experience of such things as the forgiveness of God. What they can, and I am sure do, have direct awareness of is the experience of feeling themselves to be forgiven. They do not know that they are finally forgiven by direct experience or in any other way,[10] before they attain the afterlife, if they ever do. Since the afterlife – even if it is metaphorical – must still be in the future, it cannot be known about, at least not by humans, by direct experience.

(xiv)   Other Kinds of Religious Experience

Some philosophers have classified certain cognitive experiences other than apparently direct experiences of God as religious experiences. Under this classification have fallen experiences of material objects, dreams and visions. (I have already argued that having feelings cannot give immediate information about anything other than the person who has them.) Insofar as the experiences in question are merely indirect communications from God – as is receiving a letter through the post an indirect communication from a friend – they have already been discussed. There is nothing unusual in the manner of our awareness of the things we are then aware of; that they are communications from God is an interpretation placed upon them, or a theory about them. Even seeing Christ between his resurrection and ascension, if he was seen and had a normal body, may well have been just like seeing anyone else. That what was then seen was the Son of God would be a theory about what was seen, not a matter of direct experience. Indeed, it would in part be a theory about the nature of the mind informing Christ's alleged body, which mind we could not be acquainted with for the reasons given.

Some communications from God are alleged to occur in dreams, while the person having them is asleep, but I do not think that the fact that this person is asleep makes any difference to the philosophical considerations concerning whether these experiences are veridical.

Some people experience the world and see the events in the world as if it and they were God's handiwork. They seem to see the hand of God in the hills, the judgment of God in various natural calamities, and instinctively to interpret natural events as signs of God's presence. One and the same person can do this at some times and not at others. At some times such a person experiences the world as God's handiwork;[11] at other times he does not, much as one would experience a concatenation of marks on paper sometimes as a duck and at other times as a rabbit.

Seeing the world as God's handiwork is not at all the same thing as believing that it is his handiwork, which latter may involve only accepting the theory that it is his handiwork. Psychologically, experiencing a calamity as the judgment of God is quite different from hitting upon the hypothesis that it is produced by God as a judgment. However, I do not think that the apparent direct experience has any more value as justification than the hypothesis. Indeed, I am inclined to think that, though the former might be something we ought to cultivate, if there is a God – and perhaps even if there isn't – its evidential value is nil. To experience a certain concatenation of marks on paper as a duck is no evidence that it is a duck, and even experiencing a duck as a duck is evidence that it is a duck because we have independent tests for what is a duck, which tests, in the case of experiencing the world as God's handiwork, tend to be negative, if there are any such tests at all. I shall assume – I suspect too simply – that what is sometimes called extrovertive mystical experience is, when it is obtained in a Christian context, a species of seeing the world as God's handiwork. When (or if) it is not, I have little that I am competent to say about it.

Experience of such 'objects' as those purporting to be deceased saints or the Virgin Mary is normally classified as religious experience. I assume that, whatever else the experiencer has as well, he often has visual experiences which resemble those of seeing a real saint or a real woman. It seems to me obvious that, in such cases, the experience must be hallucinatory or quasi-hallucinatory. (I say quasi-hallucinatory because to say that they were hallucinatory would be to commit oneself to the view that they were wholly caused by the state of the percipient, which would be to beg the question against the view that the quasi-hallucination was partly caused by, say, the Virgin Mary.) If it is not hallucinatory, there must be a collection of molecules at a certain distance from the observer, from which light waves emanate and which constitute the body of the saint in question. That this should be so seems to me quite incredible. One would not expect someone having experience of the Virgin Mary to have as an object something that left physical traces, which could be detected by measuring instruments, weighed in a balance, or leave an impression on the seat of a chair. (And in general there can be no light waves from the absolute falling upon the organs of a percipient, which means that no direct experience of it can have a physical explanation.)

Not only is it very difficult to believe that there is any suitable collection of molecules present when men have experiences of a saint or of Christ, it is even more difficult to believe that they could be numerically identical with that collection of molecules which was the body of the saint in question or of Christ when either was alive. To suppose, for example, that these bodies were stored up in heaven between the time of the saint's decease and the present, so as to preserve their bodily continuity, would involve an idea of heaven of quite incredible naïvety.

However, I would have thought such religious purposes as such visions serve would not need them to be collections of molecules (material objects). If they were 'quasi-hallucinations', I think the deity would not have to make them veridical by causing light waves to fall on the retina of the person experiencing them. But it might be that, if to be veridical they have to be produced in some other way than by normal experiences, God would have to produce them by interfering with the ordinary workings of this person's brain. (If they were just produced by a naturally occurring brain tumour, and God had not tinkered with our brains, they would not count as veridical religious experience. There are, of course, enormous difficulties with the view that a being beyond space and time can tinker with anything.)

Perceptual experiences should be taken to be veridical if they fit together with other perceptual experiences to give us a coherent unitary picture of the world. Unless the 'religious' experience is experience of an ordinary material object – such as real milk being drunk by real statues of saints – religious experiences will from their very nature not fit with other perceptual experience to make a coherent whole.[12]

(xv) Mysticism

Mystics have a kind of experience which they sometimes claim to be a direct awareness of God. (It has been held (I suspect correctly) that the difference between full-blooded mystical experience and ordinary religious experience is one of degree.)

Though the claims made by mystics may be true, they cannot be direct experiences of an omniscient, omnipotent and perfectly good being, as these are dispositional characteristics. And the description of the objects of their experience made even by Christian mystics often do not look to an outsider to be descriptions of such a being. For example, the object of the experience has been described as a desert, an abyss, darkness, blinding light, measureless heights, or boundless deeps. These do not look like being descriptions of experiences of a personal God.

Mystical experiences do often have as their objects what mystics themselves feel may be appropriately described as 'God', and the attitude that mystics have to them are often ones that it is appropriate one should have to the deity. And when Christian mystics describe the object of their experience as a person – though it is difficult to tell to what extent their language is figurative – it often seems to be a limited and temporal person, which is capable of playing a part in a relationship, which an eternal being would, because of its very temporality, be incapable of doing. The writings of St Theresa and St John of the Cross, for example, often speak of God as if he were – at least in the case of St Theresa – quite a friendly person. To the extent that having what is claimed to be a relationship with God involves having visual imagery, it cannot constitute direct awareness of a person, and that it is awareness of a person at all is, to repeat, a theory to explain the nature of the experience, not something that we can be directly aware of. What is important in the relationship is in any case not the imagery itself, but the mind lying 'behind' the imagery, and it seems very unlikely that one could have direct experience of the minds of others that was not mediated by something like imagery of 'their bodies'.

Christian mystics often have experiences that they regard as involving a relationship with Christ. Even if Christ survived his crucifixion in some way or other, it is obvious, for reasons already hinted at, that the experience in question cannot involve a veridical awareness of a body numerically identical with the body belonging to a person (Christ) who lived many centuries ago. When there is some visual imagery (presumably of a man), awareness of Christ-like imagery could not be the same as awareness of a person who was physically situated in the vicinity of the person having the experience. Awareness of imagery is not the same thing as awareness of a person, even if the imagery resembles the experiences one would have if one were perceiving that person's body. What one is directly aware of is the imagery, not the person. One needs to supplement the direct awareness of the imagery with a *theory* about the nature of the relation between it and the person revealed by the imagery. This brings some alleged mystical knowledge of Christ out of the category of direct awareness and into that of speculation.

A personal God of the kind some mystics claim to be aware of is quite possibly a construction of the mystics' own minds, as the characters of an author are constructions – not necessarily deliberate and controllable constructions – of the author's mind. Hence they are quasi-personal, rather than personal. It seems to me quite possible that they are communications from a part or aspect or subsidiary personality of the person communicated with. This does not mean that it is necessary or even wise to ignore them. I am sure that some ignore them at their peril. If self-knowledge is the beginning of wisdom, knowledge of one's God should be included in self-knowledge.

My criticisms of mystics' claims to have direct awareness of a personal God do not mean that religious experiences are not worth having, or even, if one is courageous, cultivating. But if they are worth cultivating, it is from their intrinsic beauty and their beneficial effects on the person cultivating them, not for the truth they reveal about an omnipotent, omniscient, perfectly good personal deity. If they are direct experiences of God at all, they are experiences of something less than, or at any rate different from, a personal God. This might mean revising one definition of 'God' that I have suggested away from being a perfect person, and perhaps to being not a person. I am not convinced that mystical experience cannot give us knowledge of an non-personal 'God'.

(xvi)   Religious Experience and Insanity

I think it ought to be noted, in case anyone who has religious experience is tempted to take it too uncritically, that there is a strong resemblance between having religious experience and certain types of insanity, in particular, I think, schizophrenia. Schizophrenics not only have hallucinations which resemble the alleged visions of those who claim to have religious experiences; they also have the experience of being guided by forces which are not present to the five senses. I am myself a great believer in listening to one's 'voices', provided one learns from them without prostrating oneself before them uncritically and doing whatever they say. But it should never be overlooked that men have had hallucinations – and been unable to tell the difference between them and religious experiences – which have led them to do all sorts of strange and undesirable things, and have thought they have had guidance to do what has led to disaster both for themselves and others. Hence it is always sensible to allow religious experience to suggest ideas and courses of action to one which one might not otherwise have been able to think of, one's reason, such as it is, should almost always wear the trousers. If there is a God, reason as well as experience would be God-given.

(xvii)   Conclusions

Since no arguments for the existence of God are valid, the only way in which we could come to know of the existence and nature of a personal God would be by direct acquaintance, or on the testimony of someone who had such direct acquaintance. However, we cannot have direct acquaintance of God, partly because we cannot have acquaintance with the contents of minds other than our own, and partly because many of the characteristics of a personal God would have to have would be dispositional ones, with which we could in principle not be acquainted. This leaves open the possibility of there being direct acquaintance with a 'God' that, as some mystics claim, is not personal, or with something like what may be a dramatised aspect of one's own personality that is personal, or quasi-personal. I shall pass a few tentative remarks on this subject later.

Notes

1   The classical treatment of this subject, by William James in *The Varieties of Religious Experience*, is vitiated by the fact that he was a pragmatist, and thought that religious experience must be veridical because it was useful to the person who had it. The most recent treatment known to me is by Alston, 1991. The reader is also referred to W.T. Stace's brilliant *Mysticism and Philosophy*, 1961. Stace's book is discussed by me in Harrison,

1995. The standard account of *Christian* mysticism is Evelyn Underhill, 1993, a learned but somewhat rhapsodic work.

2   *Loc. cit.*

3   The reader is referred to Price, 1932 for a view which accepts the sense-datum theory, but holds that perceiving is not inferring.

4   I criticise the propriety of talking as if minds were substances in 'The Absurdity of the Ego', in Harrison, 1995, but I doubt whether these criticism much affect the argument given here.

5   The reader is referred to my 'Science, Souls and Sense Data', *loc. cit.*

6   See Prince, 1905 and Sizemore, 1977.

7   The point is made by Stace, 1961.

8   It is sometimes said that the third person in the Trinity is the love that holds between the first two. But in that case, it would not be an entity, and to count it as one would be like, if Tom and Mary were married, counting the relationship between them – being spouse of – as a kind of third party in an eternal triangle.

9   Barth defended the doctrine of the Trinity, which he regarded as involving the revealer, the thing revealed, and the revelation. But one would have supposed that only the revealer could be a person. What is revealed would either be a fact, or a thing or person, in which latter case, presumably it would have to be the revealer himself. A revelation is an event of revealing, and so not a person.

10 Unless they know that everybody will be forgiven, a view which seems to make the Christian account of life pointless, like a game in which all the players win.

11 For an elaboration of this view, the reader is referred to Hick, 1957. It is derived from Ludwig Wittgenstein's remarks in *Philosophical Investigations*.

12 I have discussed mystical experience in Harrison, 1995. There I was tempted by the view that since normal criteria of being veridical did not apply to it, it was, so long as the mystic did not use it as a justification for making claims about the observed world, neither veridical nor not veridical.

PART III
GOD'S ATTRIBUTES

14 God's Omnipotence

(i)   How Do We Know that God is Omnipotent?

God is supposed to be able to do everything. The answer to the question 'How do we know that God can do everything?' may be that he is omnipotent by definition. A person who cannot do everything cannot properly be called 'God'. Furthermore, God is perfect by definition, and a person who was not omnipotent would not be perfect. And again, God ought to be an entirely satisfactory object of worship, and a personal God who was not omnipotent would not be one. But from this it follows not that there is a God, but only that if there is a God, he can do everything.

It makes no little difference whether 'God' is regarded as a proper name for the being who governs the universe. If 'God' is a proper name, then, as we have seen, the statement that God is omnipotent cannot be known by definition. God would still be God, even if he were not omnipotent. But this makes no difference to the facts, only to the way in which we should talk about the facts. For were we to discover that the universe was created by only a very powerful being who was not omnipotent, we would, if we insist that a being be omnipotent before we call him 'God', say that there was no God but only an omnipotent creator, whereas, if we used the word 'God' less stringently, we might be prepared to say that there was a God. But the facts would be the same.

Some Christian theologians nowadays do not think of God as being omnipotent. I do not have a great deal of respect for their view. A Christian God must be personal – a God who is a father cannot be anything else – and to suppose that there was a personal God who was less than omnipotent – who could, say, obliterate only half the universe – would be absurd and so aesthetically displeasing. In science one cannot reject a view because it is aesthetically displeasing, but perhaps in theology one can.

It might be argued that the concept of a being who can do everything is incoherent. In that case, if God is by definition such a being, it follows that there could not be a God.

(ii)   Things God Cannot Do

It is not difficult to make a long list of things that God cannot do. Aquinas[1] notes numerous things that it is alleged that God cannot do, some of which it is incoherent to suppose that he should be able to do. If there are such things, this fact will be a reason for thinking that the idea of omnipotence is incoherent. If God by definition possesses an incoherent attribute, there cannot be a God. One may revise one's definition of 'God' so that he does not possess the attribute – in this case omnipotence – in question. Alternatively, one may clarify one's account of omnipotence to make it clear that he does not possess it. But one would suspect that all the things that God cannot do are things which it would be absurd to expect him to do.

Among the things God cannot do are the following.

(a)   God cannot create slithy toves who gyre and gimble.

(b)   God cannot make people sleep more slowly than they do.

(c)   God cannot cause the present king of France to be bald, or to stay bald, or to regain his hair, or to retain his hair.

(d)   God cannot make a thing both be and not be.

(e)   God cannot bring it about that all men are mortal and that Socrates is a man, but that Socrates is not mortal.

(f)   God cannot create both an irresistible force and an immovable object, or bring about a world in which everyone receives help, but no-one gives it.

(g)   God cannot destroy himself.

(h)   God cannot cause himself not to be omnipotent, or change his other characteristics in any way.

(i)   God cannot create something he cannot destroy (or control). Alternatively, if God can create something which he cannot destroy (or control), then he cannot destroy (or control) that thing.

(j)   God cannot forget things, or make mistakes.

(k)   God cannot create something not created by its creator, or create something not created by God.

(l)   God cannot swim (though not because he has not learned to swim).

(m) God cannot tie a bow tie. He cannot form a limited liability company, or marry into the aristocracy,

(n)   God cannot do mental arithmetic.

(o)   God cannot feel pain.

(p)   God cannot alter the past, for example, cause the French Revolution not to have happened. Nor can he do anything that would *involve* altering the past (like making John Major, at the next general election, be elected a Member of Parliament for the first time).

(q)   God cannot act wrongly. He cannot, for example, make his creatures all perish in extreme agony, if it would be wrong of him to do this.

(r)   God cannot bring it about that any of his creatures voluntary decide to do something.

(s)   God cannot make what is right wrong, and what is wrong right.

(t)   God cannot make anyone voluntarily do what is right or abstain from doing what is evil.

It is worth noticing that on the list of things which God cannot do, there are some things which men can do. Men can destroy themselves, can create things they cannot destroy, can swim, tie bow ties, form limited liability companies, marry into the aristocracy, do mental arithmetic, feel pain, forget things, make mistakes and act wrongly. Indeed, they frequently do.

It is also worth noticing, when one is considering whether God can or cannot do something, that it matters how the act in question is described. Man can create things described as 'not created by God', although God cannot create things described as 'not created by God'. Neither man nor God, however, can create something not created by its maker.

There are also some things which God can do at one time, but not at another. Early in the eighteenth century God could quite easily have prevented the French revolution. Now it is too late.

Many things God can do individually or severally, but not collectively. For example, he can make Tom, Dick and Harry receive help without giving it (or give help without receiving it) but he cannot make everybody receive help without giving it. And though he can make either an irresistible force or an immovable object, it is obviously impossible for him to make both.

I shall proceed to discuss these apparent or real limitations to God's omnipotence.

(iii)   God's Inability to do What is Described by a Meaningless Sentence

(a) In some sentences of the form 'God cannot ...', the words following the words 'cannot' are meaningless. Hence they do not describe a class of actions. Hence they do not describe a class of actions which God cannot perform.

Furthermore, if the words following the word 'cannot' are meaningless, the whole sentence must be meaningless, and a meaningless sentence cannot be used to say anything true or false. Hence the sentence 'God cannot ...', when the dots are replaced by a meaningless sequence of words, cannot be used to formulate a true statement asserting that there is something that God cannot do. Meaningless sentences cannot express truths. Hence the fact that God cannot bring about situations described by meaningless words is no reflection on his omnipotence. There can be no such situations.

I have suggested earlier that this fact may enable us to solve the apparent limitation on God's omnipotence imposed by the fact that he cannot alter the moral law. There is no procedure described by the expression 'altering the moral law', which procedure God is unable to carry out.

So far as I know, no theologian has ever explicitly held that God can do things described by meaningless words, or that, if he could not, this would mean that he is not omnipotent. I think it has been held by some theologians, however, that the sentences embodying some items in the Christian faith are meaningless, but that God will manifest (or perhaps already has manifested) his supreme power by making them true.

This latter doctrine is confused. It is impossible to make the proposition expressed by a meaningless sentence true, for a meaningless sentence does not formulate any proposition. It is, however, possible to give a meaning to a meaningless sentence. Even men can do this. Giving meaning (or a different meaning) to a word is, indeed, not even difficult. A synod of bishops could do this quite easily.

(b) Not only can God not do what is described by meaningless words, he cannot make true propositions that involve a 'category mistake'. (A category mistake involves predicating something of a thing in one category that can properly be predicated only of something in a different category. For example, a man cannot be divided by two (though he can be divided into two). For example he cannot make men sleep more (or less) slowly than they do, because sleeping is not the kind of thing that can be done either slowly or quickly. It would be a category mistake to suppose otherwise.) For the same reason God cannot make quadratic equations change in colour, weigh Beethoven's ninth symphony, or multiply £20.31 by $7.93. This, however, is not a genuine limitation upon his omnipotence. We should not blame the deity for the fact that men do not always manage to talk sense when speaking about him.

(c) Nor is it a genuine limitation of God's omnipotence that he cannot do things that could only be done on the supposition that something is true which is false, for example, to heal Tom's children when Tom has no children to heal. To suppose that he could would not be to pay him a greater compliment than to suppose that he could not. The supposition would be just ridiculous.

(iv) God's Inability to do the Logically Impossible

Most items on the above list are things that it is logically impossible for God to do. It is logically impossible for God to do such things as make it the case that all men are mortal and that Socrates is a man, but that Socrates is nevertheless not mortal, or make everybody receive help without anybody's giving it. (The logically impossible is not the same thing as the meaningless, for we have to know what the words in a sentence mean, and that the sentence containing them is properly formulated, and does not involve a category mistake, before we can know whether or not these sentences assert something that is logically possible.)

It seems reasonable to maintain that God cannot bring about the logically impossible. Some theologians, however, have held that God can bring about the logically impossible, and that it would be a genuine limitation to his omnipotence if he could not. This view has nothing to recommend it. If God could bring about anything that was logically impossible, he could bring it about both that he himself did and did not exist, and that I myself did and did not exist. He could make it the case both that he has and has not made promises to man which he both will and will not keep, and that I both will and will not go to Heaven if I do his will. It is only the logical law of noncontradiction (that a proposition cannot be both true and false) that prevents (metaphorically speaking) his being able to do such absurd things. And there is no reason for maintaining that God can perform some logically impossible actions but not others.

Furthermore, it would, if God could do the logically impossible, be pointless to do such things as try to prove that God existed, for God might have made it the case that he could both exist and not exist. And it would be useless to try to demonstrate by argument anything about his nature – or about anything else for that matter – because demonstrations are acceptable only because it is logically impossible for their premises to be true and their conclusions false. If God can do anything, including the logically impossible, he might bring it about that the premises of a valid argument were true and its conclusion false. In that case, an argument's being valid and having true premises would not exclude its conclusion's being false. And God could bring it about both that the premises and the conclusion of a valid argument were both true and false. He could even bring it about that an argument was both valid and invalid at the same time. Worse still, he might have brought it about that the arguments that I have just adduced to show that God cannot bring about the logically impossible were conclusive, although God could bring about the logically impossible nevertheless. Indeed, if all arguments could be both valid and invalid, there would be no point in arguing or trying to think rationally about religion or any other subject.

It might seem that argument is safe, even if God *can* bring about the logically impossible, so long as God *has* not actually brought it about. But if God can bring about the logically impossible, there is no guarantee that he has not actually brought it about (for the only guarantee that he has not is that it is logically impossible that he should). If he had brought about the logically impossible, we could not know that he had. In this case he could both exist and not exist, and a valid argument could have a false conclusion although its premises were true.[2] Hence there would be no point in trying to prove anything, for whatever we succeeded in proving might nevertheless be false.

Hence God cannot bring about the logically impossible, and it is only an apparent limitation on his omnipotence that he cannot. It would be only an apparent limitation on the skill of a golfer that he could not play a round of golf in fewer than 18 strokes. But perhaps there are also logically possible things which God also cannot do.

(v)   Is it a Limitation to God's Omnipotence That He Cannot Do Things That Men Can Do?

The following must be logically possible, because men can do them. Men can destroy themselves, make themselves less powerful than they are, make things they cannot subsequently destroy (or, more frequently, destroy things that they cannot subsequently remake), swim, tie bow ties, form limited liability companies, do mental arithmetic, feel pain, forget things and do evil. But though men can do these things, God cannot.

This is partly because, though men can apply or misapply various skills, like swimming or tying a bow tie, the idea of God being skilful is absurd. This is because the idea of exercising a skill is a spatio-temporal notion, and God is commonly supposed to be eternal and without spatial attributes. It would involve a category mistake to think of God as swimming or tying a bow tie. God can no more do these things than quadratic equations can. This is partly because he does not have a body, and so has no hands or feet.

And, further, God is defined in such a way that he cannot do some of the things which men can do. A being who is by definition indestructible cannot destroy himself, for example, though destructible beings like men can. A perfectly good being cannot act wrongly, because the idea of a perfect being doing so is contradictory. But men can act wrongly because they would still be men, whether they acted wrongly or not.

Some of the things which men are alleged to be able to do, like forget things, are, in man, really limitations masquerading as abilities, on account of the way they are described. The corresponding things that God is alleged to be unable to do, are, in God, abilities masquerading as limitations. To say that men can forget things is not really to attribute to them an ability, but to say that there is nothing in their nature to prevent things going wrong. To say that God cannot forget anything, which superficially looks like a disability, is to say that it must be that he remembers everything, which does not. To say that he cannot make something that he cannot destroy, which looks bad, is to say that he can destroy all things as well as make all things, which looks good. To say that men can make some things that they cannot then destroy is to attribute to them the limitation of not being able to destroy everything they can make. To say that God cannot make something that he cannot destroy is to say, in other words, that he can destroy everything he makes.

In any case, forgetting things is not something that, strictly speaking, men 'do' (in the sense of 'perform'). It is just something that happens to them. Neither is feeling pain something we do. So since feeling pain is not a power or ability, that God cannot feel pain is not to deny him a power or ability. In any case, the sense of 'cannot' involved is not the same that this word has when it is used as a synonym for 'is unable to'. Its being impossible that a bachelor should be married is quite different from a bachelor's inability to get married.

Hence the fact that God cannot feel pain is not a fact to the effect that there is something that God is unable to do. What it means is that the statement that God feels pain is logically contradictory (or at least involves a category mistake), and we have already seen that it is not a limitation on God's omnipotence that he cannot bring such things about. It is the sense of 'cannot' that this word has when we say that if A equals B and B equals C, A cannot not equal C, or when we say that numbers cannot fly. It is a sense of 'cannot' which indicates logical impossibility, not the absence of a power. That God could not bring it about that he himself felt pain would not involve a limitation to his omnipotence if it is logically impossible that he should feel pain, and feeling pain is not an action.

It may be, then that not only must any feat which God can perform be a logically possible feat, it must be a logically possible feat that God can perform, in the sense that there is no logical contradiction or category mistake involved in supposing that he does perform it. God cannot swim, for example, because a category mistake would be involved in supposing that he did. Though swimming, for example, is a logically possible feat, it is not a feat which it is logically possible for God to perform. To assert that God is swimming is to ascribe to God an attribute that he can no more have than a tune can have weight.

(vi)   Doing Something and Bringing it About that it is Done

Perhaps some illusory limitation upon God's omnipotence is suggested by the use of the word 'do' in the sentence 'God can do anything'. God can, it may be supposed, bring about everything that is logically possible. The reason why he cannot tie a bow tie is this. He can bring it about that a bow tie is tied, or bring into existence a tied bow tie, or a tie that is in the shape of a tied bow tie. But he cannot tie a bow tie because to tie a bow tie is not just to bring it about that it is tied. It is to bring it about in a certain manner that it is tied, i.e., by making with one's hands a loop, and putting one end of the tie through this loop, and so on. God cannot do this, if only because he has no hands.

Hence, perhaps, though God can bring about anything that is logically possible, he cannot do everything that it is logically possible for someone to do, for to do something does not always consist in producing some end result (e.g. a tied bow tie); it sometimes consists in undertaking some activity. A non-spatio-temporal being cannot undertake activities, as these are spatio-temporal occurrences. And some activities, like walking in the sunshine, do not necessarily have any end result. Perhaps there is a sense of 'do' in which doing something is always to undertake some spatio-temporal activity, and then, in this restricted sense, God cannot do anything.

There may therefore be a sense in which God can do anything, and a sense in which he cannot. He can bring about every logically possible end result, but he cannot undertake any logically possible performance. Furthermore, he cannot bring about logically possible end results in certain ways, i.e., by indulging in the spatio-temporal activity of bringing these results about in the way normal to people.

Perhaps one can bring the performances God cannot undertake under the formula that God can bring about all and only those things that are logically possible (or do not involve a category mistake) by saying that God's inability to swim is just a special case of his quite excusable inability not to bring about the logically impossible or incoherent situation or state of affairs: God's swimming. Hence we have still not seen sufficient reason to reject the formula that God can bring about all and only those states of affairs that are logically possible, i.e. bring about any contingent fact.

(vii) Things that God by Definition Cannot Do

But perhaps not all the things God cannot do can be brought under the formula that God can bring about all and only logically possible situations, which explains God's being unable to undertake performances as a special case of his inability to bring about the logically impossible For it is alleged that God cannot do evil or alter the past, but this can neither be because doing these things are performances nor because what God cannot bring about is logically impossible. For evil is logically possible, and it is perfectly possible that the past should have been other than it was. (I shall later argue for the view that God can do evil.)

God is defined in such a way that he cannot do some of the things which men can do. An indestructible being cannot destroy himself, for example, though destructible beings like men can. A being who can do anything cannot make something its maker cannot destroy. It cannot be that a being who is by definition good can bring about states of affairs that it is wrong to bring about, and it is presumably wrong for God to bring about evil.

Even if being unable to make something one cannot destroy is not an excellence disguised as a limitation there is no contradiction in supposing that God can make things that he cannot destroy. After he has made such a thing, however, he will be unable to destroy it, but this means that after he has made such a thing, he will no longer be omnipotent. There is no reason why the pronoun 'he' should not be used to refer at one time to an omnipotent being but at a later time, after this being has abrogated his own omnipotence, refer to a being who is not omnipotent.

Whether God can take away his own omnipotence depends upon how the word 'God' is defined. If 'God' is defined as being omnipotent at the moment of speaking, God cannot take away his own omnipotence and remain 'God' at that moment, just as a bachelor cannot get married and remain a bachelor. But he will properly be called 'God' at the time when he was omnipotent. If, on the other hand, a being is properly called 'God' at any time only if he is omnipotent at all times, what will follow is that if the being whom we supposed was God takes away his own omnipotence, this being not only ceases to be God, but never was God in the first place. But this does not mean that God is unable to take away his own omnipotence, in the sense that it is beyond his power to do this. What the being whom we, rightly or wrongly, call 'God' can or cannot do cannot depend upon the rules for the use of the English word 'God'.

An allied question is whether God could bring about his own nonexistence, or cause himself to cease to exist. If he cannot he is not omnipotent; if he can, he would be producing a situation in which God is not eternal (or, at any rate, everlasting, and not a necessary being), which situation is impossible.

One possible answer to this question is that he could bring about his own existence, but that his ability or power to do this does not mean that he is not everlasting; he will be everlasting so long as he has not exercised this power. God can, as we shall see later, have a power which he (logically) cannot exercise, for it is within his power to burn the whole of his creation alive, though logically it cannot be that he will do this, for to do so would be evil.

(viii)   God's Inability to Alter the Past

The view to which the preceding remarks have been leading, but which I shall subsequently reject, is the view that God can bring about any logically possible states of affairs, though not, since he cannot perform spatio-temporal actions, in any possible way. For example, he can cause a house miraculously to appear, or even to be built, but he cannot do it with his own hands. The important thing for his creatures, however, is that he should be able to bring about any logically possible state of affairs. His inability to bring such states of affairs about by an exercise of skill is immaterial. In any case, it is logically impossible that God should have these skills. Other things that it seems impossible that God should do are not so much things that he cannot do at all as things that he cannot do while remaining God. Yet others are powers masquerading as inabilities. Doing things described by meaningless sentences, or things involving a category mistake, are just other instances of God's inability to do the logically impossible.

There are, however, two serious difficulties with this view, which we must now consider. (a) Though the past's being other than it is is a logically possible state of affairs – it is just a contingent fact that the Battle of Hastings was fought in 1066 – it is not possible for God to bring such states of affairs about.

(b) Though evil states of affairs are also logically possible, they, too, are things that it is not possible for God to bring about.

(a) Can God alter the past? If God cannot alter the past, is this any limitation to his omnipotence?

The question 'Can God alter the past?' may mean 'Can God at any time change some proposition about the past (for example, that the French Revolution happened in 1889) from being the case to being not the case?' I think that the answer to this question is that God cannot do this. Nevertheless, since the reason why he cannot is that, even though the past might have been other than it is, *changing* the past is logically impossible, this is no genuine limitation on his omnipotence.

It might be objected (I think wrongly) that, if God cannot alter the truth of propositions about the past, he cannot alter the truth of propositions about the future either. This would impose severe limitations on his omnipotence. This is supposed to be because if once it is true that Oedipus is going to kill his father, it will be true for all time, which means that its truth cannot be altered. But to alter the future does not involve changing the truth of a proposition about the future. The proposition that Oedipus was supposedly going to change, that he was going to kill his father, may always have been true. But we do not, strictly speaking, change the past or change the future, and even if we do, this does not involve our changing the truth of propositions about the past or the future. What we do is to change things or people, or bring new things into existence, or make old things go out of existence. And this does not involve changing the truth value of a proposition about the future. Oedipus killed Laius, but this is compatible with the proposition that he was always going to kill Laius always being true.

The case for holding that it is logically impossible to change the past is this. If the past was altered at any time this must mean that up to that time it was true that, say, a battle had been fought at Hastings in the year 1066, but that after that time it was false. The proposition that a battle was fought in 1066, asserted immediately after the battle, however, *contradicts* the proposition that a battle was not fought in 1066, asserted later than that time. It does not matter when a historian asserts that the Battle of Hastings was fought in 1066. Whenever he asserts it, it contradicts the assertion of another historian who says that it was not fought in 1066, regardless of the date at which these respective assertions were made. Hence it logically cannot be the case that up to a given time it was true that a battle had been fought in 1066, but that after that time it was not.

But perhaps what God would do, if he were to alter the past, would not simply be to cause the proposition that the Battle of Hastings was fought in 1066 to become false. Perhaps what God would do is to cause, at some time or other, this proposition never to have been true. On this second view, he alters the past in a more thoroughgoing way than he does on the first.

Even this latter specification of the change, however, is contradictory. For what it amounts to is this. God could bring into existence a world in which up to the time at which he is alleged to have changed the past it was true that a battle had been fought in 1066, but after that time it was true both before and after this time that there was *not* a battle fought in Hastings in 1066. From this it follows that before the time at which God supposedly changed the past it both was and was not true that a battle was fought in 1066, which is again contradictory.

The only alternative is to suppose that what God does is to make it the case that, before the time at which God changed the past, the proposition that there was a battle fought at Hastings in 1066 is false. But in this event, there will be no difference between those cases in which God has changed the world by causing it not to have ever been the case that a battle was fought at Hastings in 1066, and those cases in which, because no battle ever had been fought at Hastings in 1066, no such change was necessary. But in that case there would be no difference between a battle's not having been fought in Hastings in 1066, and a battle's not having been fought in Cambridge in 1966. God alters the past so thoroughly that, after the time at which the past is allegedly altered, there is no difference between the past having been altered in a certain way, and its never having been like that at all. There would then be nothing that God, by changing the past, had accomplished.

However, these arguments against the possibility of changing the past may be invalid. When we do what may be described as altering the future, we do not do it by changing the truth of a proposition about the future. We have seen that when Oedipus 'altered the future' by killing his father, for example, he did not do it by changing the truth of the proposition, that Oedipus was going to kill his father, from being false to being true. This proposition always had been true. What Oedipus did was to perform some action (putting a sword through Laius's body) which was such that, had he not performed it, Laius would not have died. There is no incompatibility between Oedipus's doing this and the fact that the proposition that Laius was going to die, and at his son's hand, was always true. To generalise, producing changes in things does not involve changing the truth of propositions about the future. Why, then, should changing the past involve altering the truth of propositions about the past?

We can, perhaps, conceive of a way of changing the past that does not involve altering the truth of a proposition about the past. Men and women sometimes pray that God should alter the past. Let us suppose that a woman who has just heard that her son was killed in an aeroplane disaster in which there was only one survivor prays that her son be that survivor. This does not mean that she is praying that God should alter the truth of the proposition that her son did not survive, and make it false when, before she prayed, it was true. Nor is she praying that God should miraculously bring back to life her son, who was not the only survivor. What the woman is trying to do is to perform an action, viz., praying that her son be the only survivor, which is such that it 'brings it about that' her son was not and never had been killed. Is such an activity coherent?

Despite anything that I may have said on other occasions,[3] I think that this activity is not coherent. One can cause only events in the future, and there is linguistic impropriety in speaking of causing events in the past. This is shown by the oddity of the remark of one of the Marx brothers: 'Get him here today' – 'If you give me enough money I'll get him here yesterday'.[4] It is true that the woman's praying may be a necessary condition of her son's being the only survivor, that is, that had she not prayed, he would not have survived. It is conceivable, in fact, that God brought it about both that the woman prayed and that her son survived, and would not have brought it about that the son survived had he not been going to bring it about that the woman prayed. But this does not mean that her praying brought it about that her son survived. The woman could not bring this about, because it had already happened. (Another remote possibility (since, if the prayer was a necessary condition of the son's surviving, the son's surviving must have been a sufficient condition of the woman's praying) is that the son's surviving was the cause of the woman's praying. It would be quite easy to invent a story working out the route.)

But in any case, whether or not doing things in the ordinary way does involve altering the truth of proportions about the future, when we are asking whether God can alter the past we are asking whether he can change the truth of propositions about the past. And the answer to the question is that he can neither change the truth of propositions about the past nor of propositions about the future.

(b) Though God cannot alter the past, this inability involves no limitation on his omnipotence. It is logically impossible to change the past since, as we have seen, doing so involves a contradiction.

I should point out that, if God cannot alter the past, there is a sense in which he cannot annihilate the universe. Though he can cause it no longer to exist, he cannot cause it not to be and never to have been, for this would involve changing the truth of the proposition that it had once been.

(ix)   God's Inability to Do Evil

God's inability to do evil cannot be due to the fact that evil is a logically impossible end result, like a world in which everybody gave help without receiving it, or vice versa. Evil cannot be a logically impossible end result, because it actually occurs. It is more plausible to suggest that what is impossible is that the statement that God does evil should be true, because it involves the contradictory idea of a being who is morally perfect doing evil. God, or so it is argued, obviously cannot bring it about that God does evil if there is a contradiction in the notion of God's doing evil.

However, the formula[5] that God can do all and only those things which are such that there is no contradiction (and no category mistake) involved in the assertion that he does them is not satisfactory. God is able to do evil, although he is unable to bring it about that the statement that evil is done by God should be true, because it is contradictory. It does not follow from the fact that the statement that God does evil is contradictory that evil actions are beyond his power. Since he is omnipotent, he could bring about evil, if he chose, but it is logically impossible that he should ever so choose.

God, of course, can never do evil, though a bachelor can only be unmarried for that length of time during which he is a bachelor. But, if one were stipulatively to define a confirmed bachelor as a man who was, is and always will be unmarried, it would still not follow from the fact that it was contradictory to suppose that a confirmed bachelor ever would get married that he did not have the power to marry. Prime beef cannot ever be anything other than in first class condition, but this does not mean that it cannot degenerate; only that if it does, it ceases to be prime beef. Tom, a 'confirmed' bachelor, might be able to afford a wife, and there might be women who would have him, and the reason why he did not ever get married be simply that he did not want to. The fact that 'confirmed' bachelors are by definition unmarried has not yet stopped anyone from marrying one. The fact that God by definition does not ever do evil does not mean that he is unable to.

(The statement that God might have a power – for example the power to do evil – that he logically cannot exercise looks odd. It may mitigate this oddness to reflect on the fact that what may be impossible for him under one description may be possible under another. God can be described as, among other things, omniscient, omnipotent, perfectly good and the creator of the universe. Though there is a contradiction the assertion that a perfectly good being does evil, there is no contradiction in the assertion that an omnipotent being does evil. Perhaps God can do A if there is at least one description of him according to which the statement that he is actually doing A is not contradictory.)

God's alleged inability to do evil, therefore, does not constitute a difficulty for the formula I have suggested, viz., that God can bring about any logically (and conceptually) possible (future) state of affairs. It is within God's power to bring about evil states of affairs, although it is impossible that he should ever exercise this power. The alleged difficulty, for God's omnipotence, that he is unable to bring about anything other than the best possible world, can be answered in the same way. He could; it is impossible only that he would.

(x) God's Alleged Inability to Make Men Do Things Voluntarily

It has been argued by a large number of philosophers that God cannot bring it about that any of his creatures voluntarily choose to do anything. For if God were to bring it about that they chose to do something, they would either have not done it involuntarily or not done it at all (because God has done it, not they).

(As it stands, if God cannot bring it about that men voluntarily do things, this will be something that men can do but God cannot, for men can bring it about that (other) men voluntarily do things, for example, by persuading them, cheating them, curing them or bringing it about that they have the wants that lead them to perform the actions voluntarily. I shall discuss in the chapters 'Foreknowledge, Will and Fate' and 'The Problem of Evil' whether God can produce voluntary actions in these ways. Here I shall discuss only whether God can cause his creatures to perform voluntary actions 'directly', without producing the states of affairs that result in their doing them involuntarily. (I shall argue later that there is no incompatibility involved in the expression 'cause someone to do something voluntarily'.))

I think it is impossible for God directly to make men do things voluntarily, if 'directly to make' means to make them voluntarily do something by an act of divine fiat, without producing the beliefs and desires, or the causes that produce the beliefs and desires, that normally result in their choosing to do something voluntarily. For if for God to produce an action directly is to make someone do something voluntarily without causing him to want to do it or to believe that it is to his advantage, then, since these people will be doing what they do without wanting to do it or believing that it is to their advantage, their actions will be involuntary. But since it is *logically* impossible to perform a voluntary action without wanting to do it, God's inability to produce a voluntary action directly is a special case of his inability to do the logically impossible, and so no genuine limitation to his omnipotence.

Plantinga, in *The Nature of Necessity*,[6] has held that there are some kinds of possible persons that God cannot actualise; if P is a possible person who will do A and P1 a possible person who will refrain from doing A, God cannot produce both P and P1. But this does not show that there are any possible persons – P and P1 – that God cannot create; only that God cannot actualise both P and P1. All this means is that God cannot bring into existence a person who will both do A and refrain from doing A, though he could easily bring into existence either a person who will do A or one who will not do A. He could also bring into existence a person who is able to do A and able to do -A (though not both). Being unable to produce a person who will do both A and -A is no limitation on God's omnipotence, since what is asked of him is logically contradictory.

(xi) God's Inability to Alter the Moral Law

Some philosophers, for example, Immanuel Kant, have held that it is impossible for God to alter the moral law. That this is so is especially plausible on the view that moral knowledge is a species of knowledge of necessary truth. For God, or so it is often supposed, cannot make necessary truths, such as that things that are equal to a third thing are equal to one another, false.

Of course, God can make it that everybody who thinks that it is wrong to kill should think that it is right to kill. And he could bring about a world in which it was right to kill, for example, by bringing into being a species of men who could not die, but who could only be killed, but who after the age of 300 went into an irreversible, dangerous and expensive decline. What God could not do would be to produce a satisfactory moral code which was very different from our present moral code, given that human beings retained much the same nature and lived in much the same circumstances that they do now.

God could change people so that they disapproved of good tennis players and approved of bad ones, but he could not produce a world in which tennis players who hit the ball often, hard and accurately and won large numbers of points were good tennis players, and tennis players who did the reverse of this were bad ones. At least, he could not do this so long as the object of tennis playing is what it is at present. I argued in the chapter 'God's Commands and Man's Duties' that it was no limitation on God's omnipotence that God could not change the moral law, as the idea of God's changing it does not make sense. And we have already agreed that inability to do things that cannot meaningfully be described is no limitation upon God's omnipotence.

(xii)   God Can Bring About any Logically Possible State of Affairs

The formula that God can do anything, in the sense that he can produce any state of affairs the description of which is not contradictory, is unsatisfactory because the description of unrealised past states of affairs is not contradictory, but God cannot, nevertheless, bring them about. The formula that God can bring about any logically possible state of affairs provided that the description of him as bringing about these states of affairs is not contradictory is also unsatisfactory. It excludes his exercising skills like swimming and altering the past, which things one should want it to exclude, but it does not allow him the power to do evil, which power he has, although it cannot be that he should exercise this power.

None of the considerations we have advanced exclude God's being able to bring about any future state of affairs. (It is really unnecessary to insert the word 'future' in the previous sentence, for it is part of the meaning of the expression 'bring about' that the state of affairs brought about is future.) It is true that God has to bring about these states of affairs by divine fiat, and not, as men do, by exercising spatio-temporal skills. But I have suggested that God's inability to exercise spatio-temporal skills can be brought under the formula that he is able to bring about all and only those future states of affairs that are logically possible in that, if he were to attempt to exercise a skill, this would be tantamount to making true a proposition about the future to the effect that God was exercising this skill on some future occasion, and this is either logically impossible or involves a category mistake.

What is important is that God should have control over everything that happens or has happened. There is nothing in any of the difficulties we have been considering to limit his ability to bring about any conceivable future state of affairs. And though he cannot now change the past (or the present), this does not matter, because he *had* control of it, and the only reason why he should need to change it would be because he had made a mistake in the past which, to the deity, is impossible. He is omnipotent in that he has power over every future state of affairs, and had power over every past (and present) state of affairs. And to have present power over any past state of affairs is impossible.

(xiii)   Three, More Fundamental, Difficulties with God's Omnipotence

There remain three difficulties with the notion of omnipotence, however, though they are not so much difficulties with God's doing everything, as with his being able to do anything at all.

(a) The first difficulty with God's bringing about things is that his bringing about is an invisible, undetectable bringing about that can be inferred only from its effects. With men we sometimes infer that they have done something – say, fire a revolver – from the effects of the firing, such as a corpse; but it is in principle possible on another occasion to see the gun actually being fired. With God this is not possible. This gives rise to a doubt whether the words 'bringing about' mean anything when applied to God.

(b) It has been held that, since God is immaterial, he can have no effect on the material world. It will already be apparent, from what I have said about God's willing things to happen, that I am not greatly moved by this difficulty. As Hume argued,[7] anything may be correlated with, and so cause, anything else; it is just a matter of fact what things cause what. (Finding evidence that God's willing causes things to happen in the world is another matter.)

(c) The things God creates are in time, while he is supposed to be outside time. The idea of an act of a timeless being having effects later in the world is, I think, incoherent. And the timeless act of will by which he produces these affects is also impossible. We have no idea what it would be like for there to be something resembling a human action that does not take place in time. To do so is like trying to conceive something which is like a football pitch, but does not take up any space, or something like a railway journey, but which does not take up any time.[8] Yet that he should be a being capable of exercising timeless acts of will is the only way of reconciling two demands; that he shall be capable of interfering in the course of nature on our behalf, and secondly, that the fact that we do not come across him in the world of space and time should not be a reason for thinking that there is no such being. These two demands cannot be reconciled.

(xiv) Conclusions

I conclude that the concept of a (personal) God who is omnipotent in the way in which we need him to be omnipotent is coherent. He is able to produce any possible future state of affairs, including evil ones, and was able to produce any possible past state of affairs. The other things that it is alleged he cannot do do not limit his omnipotence in any material way. For example, from the formula that he cannot create anything that he cannot destroy it does not follow that there is anything that he cannot create, or anything that he cannot destroy. He cannot exercise skills, but this does not limit his power to create or annihilate everything. If one wishes, this inability can be regarded as a special case of his inability to do the logically impossible (e.g., to produce the logically impossible state of affairs: God's swimming or God's forgetting). His other alleged limitations, such as his inability to alter the past, change the moral law or make men do things against their wills.

But a God who was eternal in the sense that temporal predicates do not apply to him could not be omnipotent, or, indeed, be capable of action at all. (An everlasting God to whom temporal predicates did apply could be omnipotent.)

Notes

1 *Summa Theologica*, Q. 25.
2 It has been argued (by Priest, 1993, to which there is a reply by Timothy Smiley) that there are good and bad contradictions, and that the propositions that contradict one another in good contradictions can both be true, though those that contradict one another in bad ones cannot. In this case, perhaps God can do some kinds of logically impossible things, i.e., those which would be 'ruled out' by good contradictions, but not those that would be ruled out by bad ones.

It is unlikely that this view has any practical importance. Good contradictions are those that are entailed by the premises of arguments which give rise to antinomies, such as that the proposition on the other side of this card is false, when this is written on both sides of this card. I do not know that God's ability to make the proposition on the other side of this card both true and false releases him from the limitation of omnipotence in any significant way, especially as it is part of the way the contradiction is set up that it is not specified what the proposition in question is. If it could be the property that all men would be damned and that all men would be not damned, the conclusion of this rather irresponsible academic exercise might be more exciting.

3 In Harrison, 1971.
4 I am indebted to my former colleague, Mr Michael Clark, for this useful piece of information.
5 Suggested by P.T. Geach in 'An Irrelevance of Omnipotence', 1977.

6   Plantinga, 1974, chapter 9.
7   In *A Treatise of Human Nature*, Book I, Part I.
8   See Pike, 1970.

15 Trouble with the Trinity

(i)   The Trinity

According to the doctrine of the Trinity, God the Father, God the Son, and God the Holy Ghost are three persons, but only one God. (Some mystics have held the view that there is a Godhead, lying behind the three persons of the Trinity, and not identical with any of them (or, indeed, identical collectively with all of them), but I believe this view is regarded as blasphemous.)

There is an alternative view of the Trinity, in which God is not identical with each one of three (different?) persons, but a complex composed of three persons. The Father, the Son and the Holy Ghost would then be three different parts or aspects of one God, who himself was neither Father, Son, nor Holy Ghost. This view, which I understand is heterodox, would not present the difficulties that I shall discuss in this chapter. For it would not even appear to follow that the three persons of the Trinity had their properties in common.

It may be that the orthodox Christian view is not that the three persons of the Trinity are identical, but that they are of the same substance. (As a matter of fact, it would appear to be both, i.e. both that they are identical, and that they are of the same substance.) To me this suggests that they are composed of the (an?) identical substance (or identical substances?), rather than or as well as being identical. If they were identical, they would have to be composed of the same substance. This by itself, however, would not present an adequate defence of monotheism, for they could still be three distinct entities, composed of the same substance. And, though two things may be composed of the same substance at different times, as when one makes two different statues of the same lump of clay, it is difficult to see how two different things can be composed of the same substance at the same time, which is what God the Father, God the Son and God the Holy Ghost are supposed to be. However, since the view that these three entities are of the same substance does not by itself raise the problems I wish to focus on, I shall say no more about it.

(ii)   The Trinity and the Principle of the Indiscernibility of Identicals

Christians, if they take the doctrine of the Trinity literally, believe that Christ is God. (I am assuming for the sake of argument that the Christian view is that Christ and God are literally identical. What I shall say in this chapter cuts no ice as against views to the effect that they are only in a manner of speaking identical.)

There is therefore a difficulty for Christianity brought about by the fact that many of the things, such as walking, which God cannot do, are things which Christ really could do. Although God cannot walk, because he has no legs, and is outside space and perhaps also outside time, Christ could walk, and often did. Yet the three propositions (a) that God cannot walk, (b) that Christ could walk, and (c) that Christ is God, look incompatible. If Christ just is God, everything true of Christ must also be true of God, and vice versa. (If the Son was begotten by the Father, and the Holy Ghost proceeds from the Father, it follows that the Son was begotten by himself and that the Holy Ghost proceeds from himself. And if the Son and the Holy Ghost are identical, it follows that both the Son and the Holy Ghost are both begotten by the Father and proceed from the Father.)

This is because of what might be described as Leibniz's second law. Leibniz's well-known first law, the principle of the indiscernibility of identicals, is that if A and B have all their properties in common they must be (numerically) identical. Leibniz's less well-known second law is that if A and B are numerically identical, they must have all their properties in common. For example, if the author of *Waverley* and the author of *Ivanhoe* are identical, and the author of *Waverley* was sued for debt, then the author of *Ivanhoe* must also have been sued for debt.

However, though Sir Percy Blakeney was, unknown to Marguerite Blakeney (Sir Percy's wife), the Scarlet Pimpernel, and Marguerite greatly admired the Scarlet Pimpernel, she despised poor Sir Percy.[1] If Sir Percy and the Pimpernel had all their properties in common, it would seem to follow that Sir Percy Blakeney and the Scarlet Pimpernel both have and do not have the property of being admired by Marguerite, and both have and do not have the property of being despised by Marguerite. Perhaps, then, Leibniz's second law should be rejected. If so, then perhaps there is no reason why Christ should be able to walk, but God not be able to.

This exception to Leibniz's second law can be shown to be merely apparent if the 'property' of being admired by Marguerite Blakeney is possessed by the Scarlet Pimpernel not *simpliciter*, but merely *qua* Scarlet Pimpernel.[2] Then if Sir Percy really is despised by Marguerite Blakeney *qua* Sir Percy, he nevertheless may also possess the very property the Scarlet Pimpernel possesses, i.e., the property of being admired by Marguerite *qua* Scarlet Pimpernel. Indeed, Sir Percy and the Scarlet Pimpernel, since they are identical, will both possess the property of not being admired *qua* Sir Percy, and the property of being admired *qua* Scarlet Pimpernel. There is no contradiction involved in saying this, for the properties of being admired *qua* Scarlet Pimpernel and not being admired *qua* Sir Percy (unlike the properties of being admired and not being admired, stop) are not incompatible properties.[3]

Hence it might be possible to reconcile the apparently inconsistent propositions (a), (b) and (c) (above) if what we ought to say is not that God cannot walk, but that he cannot walk *qua* God. Again, we should not say that Christ can walk, but only that he can walk *qua* Christ. Hence, though that Christ can walk and Christ is God would entail that God can walk, which is unacceptable, that Christ can walk *qua* Christ and that Christ is God entails only that God can walk *qua* Christ, which may be perfectly all right. The characteristic which God and Christ, since they are one and the same, must both share, is not being: able to walk, but being only: able to walk *qua* Christ.

It could then be argued that the characteristic which God and Christ, since they are one and the same, both share is not, say, being omnipotent, but being omnipotent *qua* God. It follows that it is wrong to say that God is omnipotent, but that Christ is not. The right way of putting the matter is to say that God is omnipotent *qua* God, and that Christ, too, is omnipotent *qua* God. And if Christ *qua* Christ is not omnipotent, all that follows is that God *qua* Christ is not omnipotent, not that God (or God *qua* God) is.

The same would be true, presumably, if you were to substitute 'the Holy Ghost' for 'Christ' in the above argument. For example, if Christ can walk, it follows that the Holy Ghost can walk also, which is, if taken literally, absurd. It looks much more innocuous to say that Christ could walk *qua* Christ, from which it follows, not that the Holy Ghost can walk, but only that the Holy Ghost *qua* Christ could walk. And the same is true if you substitute for 'being able to walk' any other of the properties of either Christ or God or the Holy Ghost. And that God was omniscient but Christ merely inerrant gives rise to a contradiction, but no contradiction is entailed by God's being omniscient *qua* God, but Christ's being *qua* Christ only inerrant.

However, there is no need to take this way of dealing with the apparent inconsistency of the properties of God and Christ. Suppose that God, like Pooh-Bah, is both judge and executioner. He can then, *qua* judge, sentence people, and, *qua* executioner, decapitate them. There is no inconsistency in saying that Pooh-Bah sentences *qua* judge and hangs *qua* executioner. But then there was no inconsistency in supposing one and the same person sentencing and hanging in the first place, so no inconsistencies which adding the word '*qua*' removes. The statements that Pooh-Bah sentences someone, and that he hangs them, are not incompatible, even though they do not contain the word '*qua*'. The analogous theological statements, however, are, at least without some such word as '*qua*', incompatible.

Again, Tom can open a bazaar in his capacity as (or *qua*) mayor, but not in his capacity as (or *qua*) town butcher. There is no inconsistency involved in maintaining that he does this. But this, again, is not a case when Smith can do something *qua* Lord Mayor but do something *qua* town butcher inconsistent with this. It is not the case that, though he cannot both open and not open a bazaar, he can *qua* Lord Mayor open a bazaar but *qua* town butcher not open it. No-one was supposing that *qua* village butcher he was not opening a bazaar, but in his shop selling meat instead. What is the case is that the town butcher does open a bazaar, though he does not open it in his capacity as village butcher. The statement that he opened the bazaar, but in his capacity as Lord Mayor, rather than in his capacity as village butcher, does not entail that he did not open a bazaar. Rather it entails that he did open it. Hence there is no inconsistency that needs to be removed by the insertion of some such word as '*qua*', and so again no parallel with the Trinity.

Let us suppose, however, that the chairman of the finance committee has a duty to spend as little money as possible on everything, including education, that the chairman of the education committee has a duty to spend as much money as possible on education, and that Mary finds herself chairman of both committees. Then, though Mary's having a duty to spend and also having a duty not to spend may *look* inconsistent, one may wish to argue that if one makes the addition of '*qua*', Mary's having *qua* chairman of the finance committee a duty not to spend but *qua* chairman of the education committee having a duty to spend are consistent. It can be argued, then, that this is a case where two attributes were inconsistent if possessed *simpliciter*, but not if possessed *qua* something.

Unfortunately for this attempt to show that the characteristics of Christ, the Holy Ghost and God are compatible, there is again no inconsistency in having a duty to do something, and also having a duty to do the opposite, even if the word '*qua*' is omitted. (If you have a duty to do one thing, and also a duty to do the opposite of that thing, it is probably because you have the first duty in virtue of one of your (conventional) capacities, and the second duty in virtue of another of them.) Though Mary cannot carry out both duties, the statement that she has them both is quite consistent. If one thinks that they are not consistent, this is probably because one has confused the relationship between having a duty to do A and having a duty to do -A (where it is possible to have both duties, though one cannot perform both of them), with having a duty to do A and not having a duty to do A. To say that someone has a duty to do A and also that he has not a duty to do A is inconsistent. (To take another similar example, though wanting something is inconsistent with not wanting it, there is no inconsistency between wanting something and also wanting something incompatible with that thing. Wanting and not wanting something is impossible. Wanting something and also wanting the opposite happens all the time.[4]) Since in these cases there is no inconsistency to be removed, for none of the characteristics discussed were incompatible even without the word *qua*, adding the words *qua* could only make it clear why there was no inconsistency.

However, though it may be possible to find two attributes which would be incompatible without the word '*qua*', but which would be compatible with it, the expedient of adding '*qua*' will not remove apparent contradictions with all characteristics. The word '*qua*' is only useful where the judgments in question have to do with human intentions or with rules, which themselves have to do with intentions. If it is possible for God to have a characteristic *qua* God which he does not possess *qua* Christ, such characteristics can only be of a certain sort. It is not possible for Mary to be a brunette *qua* chairman of the finance committee, but a blonde *qua* chairman of the education committee. It is not possible for her, *qua* chairman of the finance committee, to know of a plan to sack 10 teachers, but to be ignorant of this plan, *qua* chairman of the education committee. (It could be her duty to act as if she were ignorant of it.) And it is not possible for Sir Percy Blakeney to be six feet tall *qua* Scarlet Pimpernel, but *qua* Marguerite's husband only five foot four.

Hence, though it is possible to say that God is worshipped or prayed to by many people who are not worshipping Christ, identical though God and Christ are (because God is worshipped by them *qua* God) and also possible to say that Christ has, *qua* Christ, a duty to intercede on behalf of sinners which he does not have *qua* God, it is not possible to say that *qua* Christ he can walk, which he cannot do *qua* God, or that *qua* God he is omnipotent, though *qua* Christ he is not. This is partly, no doubt, because 'natural' physical and mental attributes, unlike tasks, duties, actions or beliefs (which are all intentional) are not the sort of thing that can be possessed *qua* anything.

(iii)   Change Through Time and the Theory of Relative Identity; Tommy and Thomas Traddles

It is a Christian doctrine that, though the Father, Son and Holy Ghost are three (different) persons, they are all they same God. Though the Father is both a different person from the Son and the Holy Ghost, and the Son is a different person from the Holy Ghost, the Father is nevertheless the same God as the Son and the Holy Ghost, and the Son is the same God as the Holy Ghost. But is it possible for these three entities to be the same and not the same? (It is obviously possible for two things to be the same in some respects, but different in other respects, for example, for two things to be the same in respect of colour but different in respect of shape. But here one is not talking of numerical identity, but only of two different things being similar in that both possess a characteristic.)

(There would be no contradiction if we were to accept an earlier suggestion, that God is a complex entity consisting of three parts, Father, Son and Holy Ghost. For if the Trinity were a complex entity, it could not be identical with its parts individually, nor could its parts be identical with one another.) And it would not itself be a person, any more than a triumvirate, which consists of thee persons, is itself a person.) The word 'God' would also have to be being used ambiguously, for if the parts of the triumvirate were gods, there would be three of them, and so would have to be gods in a different sense from that in which the triumvirate itself was a God, for of that there is only one. This would have the peculiar consequence that the three gods would be persons, but the one God not a person.)

The problem whether there can be three persons but one God is a different problem from the one I discussed in the last section. There is no more any incompatibility between being both a person and being a God, than there is between being both a footballer and a cricketer. (There would only be a problem if it were maintained that Tom, Dick and Harry were all both footballers and cricketers, and that yet there were three footballers but only one cricketer.) Hence the problem whether there can be three persons but only one God, when the persons are supposed to be identical with the God, cannot be solved by the kind of consideration adduced in section (ii), even if it could solve the problem there.

Two Theories about Identity

There are two theories about identity. According to one (the absolute theory) one thing is just identical with another, stop. According to the second (the relative theory), you cannot just say that two things are identical, stop; it is only possible to say that one thing is the same so-and-so as another. For example, you cannot just say that Tommy and Mr Thomas Traddles are the same, stop, as on the absolute view you can. You have to say that they are the same person, or the same man or the same living organism. And, since according to the relative theory, identity is relative to (a class), from the fact that they are the same in relation to the class of persons (e.g., the same person), it is supposed not to follow that they are the same in relation to the class of men (e.g., the same adult male person). If so, it looks as if it would be possible to say that they are the same person, but not the same man.

(It might be regarded as a difficulty in stating the problem that one has to say such things as '*They* are the same man', which appears to beg the question in favour of the view that, since there are two of them, identity is not relative. I do not, however, think that the fact that one has to use the word 'they' has this implication. When one speaks of the morning star and the evening star one says 'They are identical', although it is a known fact there is only one of them. To avoid this problem, one might be tempted to suggest that we ought to speak of two proper names as co-naming, or two descriptions as being co-satisfied, rather than of two entities as being identical. But this would not solve the problem, for in describing what it was to co-name or co-instantiate, one would have to say that what one name or description named or described was identical with what the other did, and the word 'identical' would reappear.)

It is obvious that, if the absolute view of identity is true, it is impossible for the Father, the Son and the Holy Ghost to be different persons, but the same God. They are either the same or not the same, stop. Perhaps, however, it would be possible for them to be different persons, but the same God, if the relative view of identity were correct. They would be different *qua* persons, or relatively to the class of persons, but the same *qua* God, or relatively to the class of Gods.

I myself think that, though the relative theory of identity is in a way true, it does not imply that something can be the same as another thing *qua* member of one class, but, *qua* member of another class, different from that thing. It is not possible for A to be the same X as B, but a different Y from B, even though identity is relative. Indeed, it might be better to describe identity as 'class-referential' than as relative.

The reason why Tommy is the same person as Thomas, though Tommy is not the same man as Thomas, and Thomas is not the same boy as Tommy, is that Tommy is not a man and Thomas is not a boy at all. That A is the same such-and-such (the same *qua* member of the class of such-and-suches) as B presupposes[5] that both A and B are members of the class of such-and-suches. Hence, since Tommy is not a member of the class of men, and Thomas is not a member of the class of boys, they cannot be the same *qua* member of the class of boys or of the class of men. Similarly, when one of Ulysses's men was turned into a pig, he could not have been the same man that he was before, because he was no longer a man, nor the same pig was he was before, because he was previously not a pig.

Hence it is necessary to distinguish between two claims which are being made by those who hold the so-called relative theory of identity. These philosophers are holding first of all that identity is what I have called 'class-referential' (which they confuse with being relative), and that as a result one cannot ask whether A is the same as B, but only whether A is the same X as B. Secondly, there is the view that identity is relative, and that A may be the same X as B, but a different Y from B. If identity is relative, it must, I think, be class-referential, but the converse is not true. Identity could be, and indeed is, class-referential without being relative. I would prefer to reserve the expression 'relative theory' for the view that A can be the same X as B, but a different Y from B.

But what would be the point of identity's being class-referential, if it makes no difference to whether A and B are the same or different things what class you are referring to when you say that they are the same or different? And if it does make a difference, then must not identity be relative?

The answer is, I think, that what class you are referring to does make a difference to whether 'two' things are the same thing or not the same thing, but being not the same does not imply being different things.

Identity is class-referential without being relative, I think, because though A and B can be the same X, but not the same Y, this does not, as we have seen imply that they are the same X, but different Ys. The reason why Tommy and Thomas Traddles, for example, can be the same person, but not the same boy, without identity's being relative is that though both are people, they are neither both boys (because Mr Traddles is not a boy), nor both men (because Tommy is not a man). Their being the same person, but neither the same man nor the same boy, is less than is necessary to imply that they can be the same person, but different men, or the same person, but different boys. Tommy and Thomas are not the same man, because Tommy is not a man, but, for this very reason, they are not different men either. Again, though they are not the same boy, neither are they different boys.

Hence it by no means follows from the fact that A and B can be the same

X, but not the same Y, that A can be the same X as B, but a different Y from B. For A and B to be the same X, but different Ys, A and B must each be member of two classes, X and Y, and A be the same as B *qua* member of the first class (i.e., the same X), but different *qua* member of the second class from B (i.e., a different Y). And it seems to me to be absolutely obvious that this is impossible, i.e., that if Tommy and Thomas are both boys and persons, then, if Tommy is the same person as Thomas he must be the same boy as Thomas.

The Principle of the Indiscernibility of Identicals and Change

There is a difficulty with the view that Tommy and Thomas may be the same person, but not the same man, not because they are different men, but because one of them is not a man at all. It is that, if, as we have seen, A and B are identical, they must, as we have seen, have all their properties in common. Therefore it is not possible for Tommy and Thomas to be the same person, but not the same man, on account of Tommy's not being man. For, according to the principle of the indiscernibility of identicals, which we saw no reason to reject, if one of them is a man, so must the other be.

The answer to the difficulty just stated is that the possibility of A and B being the same X, but not the same Y, has so far arisen only when A or B has a property at one time which it lacks at another. Tommy and Thomas can be the same person because he was the boy who later became the man, Thomas. Nevertheless, Tommy and Thomas do have all their properties in common, because Tommy has, in the 1960s, the property of going to be a man in the 1990s, and Thomas has, in the 1990s, the property of having been a boy in the 1960s. This, of course, is in addition to the fact that Thomas has, in the 1990s, the property of being a man in the 1990s, and Tommy has, in the 1960s, the property of going to be a man in the 1990s.

The Foregoing Remarks Applied to the Trinity

Identity is class-referential, rather than relative, and this fact justifies only the view that A and B can be the same X without being the same Y; it does not justify the view that they can be the same X but different Ys. Hence the most the class-referentiality of identity could do would be to show that Christ and God were the same God, but *not the same* person because one of them was not a person, though both of them were Gods; it could not show that they could be the same God, but *different* persons.

Furthermore, if the only reason why God and Christ could be the same

God but different persons would, on the analogy with Tommy and Thomas Traddles, be that one of them was not a person at all (or one of them not a God at all). This would obviously defeat the whole purpose of the operation. It would not work with Christ, but I commend it to theologians – whom I am sure will not accept the offer – as a way of dealing with the Holy Ghost.

We have here discussed the question whether two things can be the same X but not the same Y only in cases when one of them has at one time a property that later it lacks, or acquires a property that formerly it did not have. Hence the foregoing remarks would show that God and Christ could be the same God, but not the same person, only if the entity 'they' both are has changed. But, if I have understood the matter aright, being Father, Son and Holy Ghost are not properties which God is supposed to have had at one time but lack at a later time. He is supposed to have been Father, Son and Holy Ghost from all eternity. And, though it might be the case that Christ lived for about 30 years at the beginning of the first century AD, the relationship between God the Father and God the Son is not like that between Tommy and Thomas Traddles (unlike the relationship between the young Christ and the older one). For Christ is not supposed to have turned into God, as Tommy turned into a man. He always was and will be God. Since Father, Son and Holy Ghost are supposed to be simultaneously the same God, but different persons, it is still necessary to consider the question whether they can be the same and different at the same time. I shall postpone discussing this question until section (v).

(iv)   Another Alleged Case of Relative Identity Through Time: The Prince and the Cobbler

Locke argued that if the 'soul' of the prince were transferred into the body of a cobbler, the cobbler would not be the same man as the prince, but would be the same person as he. He would not be the same man, because the body of the prince is unequivocally numerically different from that of the cobbler. They would be the same person, however, because all the prince's memories and abilities and character traits and likes and dislikes and so on would, after the transformation, be possessed by the person owning what used to be the cobbler's body. This argument for relative identity cannot be answered by saying that, since the prince and the cobbler are either not both men or not both persons, their not being the same person or the same man does not imply their being different persons or different men. The prince and the cobbler are both men and both persons.

One answer to Locke's case for relative identity has been suggested by Bernard Williams.[6] Williams supposes that two people (one of whom he christens Charles) might each have Guy Fawkes's memories, and in that case they would both have an equal claim to be Guy Fawkes. But they cannot both be Guy Fawkes, for in that case they would have to be identical with one another, which they are not. Hence neither is.

I shall return to this argument in the chapter on survival (chapter 23). But it is worth mentioning that what answer you give to the question whether Charles is Guy Fawkes should depend upon how you regard the transference of the 'soul' from Guy Fawkes to Charles. The transference of a 'soul' may be regarded as (a) the transference of an entity, but it may also be regarded as (b) the transference of a set of 'properties', mostly dispositional ones.[7]

(a) The owner of the body of the cobbler (i.e. the cobbler), before this cataclysmic event happened to him, had none of the prince's recollections, abilities, tastes, etc., but, after this event, acquired them. But, in that case, this transference, from the prince to the cobbler, might be more like the transference of magnetism from one bar of iron to another, or transferring a piece of music from one cassette to another, than like transferring a coin from one pocket to another. One bar of iron loses certain dispositional properties, like the ability to attract iron filings, and another bar gains 'them'.[8]

There is no reason why possessing a soul (or, what is not the same thing, a mind) should not consists in possessing dispositional properties. Possessing (or losing) a soul might (and I think should) be regarded as possessing (or losing) characteristics such as being sensitive to the moral demands made upon by others, to the ostensible presence of the divine, to beauty and to innocent enjoyment. If one were to sell one's soul, one would agree to have these dispositional properties taken away from one in return for wine, or women, or (more sensibly) song. To posses a mind may be regarded as having such dispositional properties as the capacity to think for oneself, to do mental arithmetic, to make plans, to communicate with other people, and so on.

If to possess a soul or mind is to possess dispositional properties, then the word 'person' would be a word like 'magnet', and the difference between an animate and an inanimate body must be like the difference between a magnet and an unmagnetised bar of iron. But if the transference of the mind were like the transference of magnetism, though we would certainly say that there were two bars of iron, we would on the other hand not say that there was just one magnet. If we were to call the first magnet 'Guy Fawkes', and the second magnet 'Charles', Charles would not be Guy Fawkes. He would not be Guy Fawkes, independently of any consideration of whether a second magnet, which also acquired Guy Fawkes's magnetism, was also Guy Fawkes. The possibility of a second magnet also acquiring Charles's magnetism would only make this fact more obvious.

If (a) whether or not one is the same person depends upon whether or not one has the same mind, and (b) transference of the mind is transference of dispositional properties, then the prince and the cobbler cannot be the same person, for the reason that Williams has given. Locke's case then would not be a case where identity is relative, for though the prince and the cobbler might be the same man, they would not be the same person.

It is perhaps more natural, and more in accordance with ordinary ways of thinking, to regard what happened to the prince and the cobbler, or to Charles and Guy Fawkes, as being the transfer of an entity, which might be called the 'mind' or 'soul', from one to the other. In that case, let us suppose that the transference of the soul from one body to another is like the transference of an engine from one car to another. In that case, though the first car is not the same car as the second, there is no word (such as 'carattery') like the word 'person', such that we can say that, though not the same car, they are the same carattery.

Perhaps a better way of looking at the problem is not so much to regard what happened to the prince and the cobbler as the transference of an entity such as a soul or (disembodied) mind might be supposed to be, as to regard a person as having been transferred from one body to another, or as having one body at one time and a different body at another time.[9] In that case, *something* is the same person but not the same man, but it is not the *man* who is the same person but not the same man. The person transferred has a body, but is not a body. (The situation would be like that which would obtain, to pursue the crude analogy already suggested, if one could speak of a battery having one car at one time and another car at a later time.) In that case, nothing would be the same *qua* one thing, but different *qua* another. The person would be unequivocally the same, and the body unequivocally different, but the thing (the person) that was the same would be a different thing from the thing (the body) that was different.

To return to Williams's problem, what are we to say about the two people who each remember being Guy Fawkes? I am a bit inclined to think that – if you regard, as what I have just said implies that you should, each body as being owned by a different persons, each of whom thinks he is Guy Fawkes, and has Guy Fawkes's memories – that we must then say that neither is Guy Fawkes.

Assuming that there has been no person with any claim to be called 'Guy

Fawkes' existing in the interval between Guy Fawkes's death and his double reincarnation, the situation is no different with persons from what it is with material objects. If the Taj Mahal were to disappear, and two buildings precisely similar to it were miraculously to appear a few years later, one in London and the other in New York, neither would be the Taj Mahal. But if neither is the Taj Mahal when there are two 'Taj Mahals', then a new Taj Mahal should not be considered to be identical with the old Taj Mahal in the case where there is only one. This is another reason for thinking that, in the case of the prince who became a cobbler, nothing is both the same person but a different man.

But in that case, Locke has not produced a case for thinking that identity is relative, and so appealing to him does not help us maintain that Father, Son and Holy Ghost are different persons, but the same God.

(v)   Identity and Counting

So far we have been considering arguments designed to show that identity is relative. A positive reason for thinking that identity is not relative concerns counting. It is sometimes supposed that identity must be relative on account of the fact that one cannot ask such things as how many are there in the room, but only such things how many utensils or ornaments, say, there are in the room. And if there are both utensils and ornaments in the room, there is no reason why the number of utensils should be the same as the number of ornaments. There might be seven utensils but only six ornaments. The question 'How many?' and the answer (in terms of number) are both class-referential, as the correct number will always depend upon what class of things one is talking about.

(The statement that two and two are four is not specifically about two men, say, but means that two of anything (any class) plus two more of the same thing (class) make four of that thing (class). It is important not to switch classes. The question how many (blackberries? raspberries?) do two raspberries and two blackberries make does not make sense. (The question how many fruit do two raspberries and two blackberries make does make sense – so long as it is understood that blackberries and raspberries are both fruit, and that raspberries cannot be blackberries.))

However, it does not follow from the fact that number is class-referential that identity is relative. From the fact that there might be seven utensils in the room, but only six ornaments, it does not follow that any of the utensils is the same utensil, but not the same ornament, as one of the ornaments, or vice versa. Number is class-referential, not relative.

(There are examples of class-referentiality which do carry relativity along with it, but identity is not one of them. A large mouse may be a very small mammal – because it may be larger than most mice but smaller than most animals. A good cricketer need not be a good footballer, or, indeed, a good man. (In this respect, being a large man is certainly unlike being the same man.))

Identity must be class-referential, since number is. This is because the question whether or not two members of any class are the same affects how many of that class there are. For example, if one were trying to answer the question 'How many chickens are there?' then, if A is the same chicken as B, A (alias B) should be counted only once. If they are different chickens, then each chicken ought to be counted.

However, there are two reasons for thinking that identity cannot be relative, the first not to do with counting. Even if we are not interested in how many Xs there are, but only in whether what we know about B should be added to what we know about A, and vice versa, we still say 'the same X', though one might think that using a class-referential expression here was unnecessary. (If it were unnecessary, this would be because what we knew about A would still have to be added to what we knew about B, even though they were the same Y, rather than the same X.) But, if A could be the same X as B, but not the same Y as B, even when counting is not an issue, the absurd conclusion would be that we ought to add all the information we possess about B (because it is the same thing as B) to the information we already possess about A, and also (because it is a different thing from B) we ought not to add it.

The second reason, to do with counting, for rejecting the view that identity is relative, is that two classes X and Y have the same number – i.e., there are as many Xs as there are Ys – if and only if there is some relation (a one-one relation) which puts every member of X into one-to-one correspondence with a member of Y, and vice versa. For example, since the relation *spouse of* puts the class of husbands into a one-to-one relation with the class of wives, there must be as many husbands as there are wives. Identity is a one-to-one relation. If every member of class X is identical with a member of class Y, then there must be as many Xs as Ys. But if A and B could be different Xs, but the same Y, then, if one were counting Xs, one would count them as, say, two, but if one were counting Ys, one would count them as, say, one. It is, I suppose, open to those who hold the view that identity is relative to say that identity is not a one-to-one relation. But, in the last resort, the only thing to say is that this leads to conclusions that are incredible.

(vi) Is the Doctrine of the Trinity a Figure of Speech?

Christ is not only supposed to be (identical with) God; he is also supposed to be the Son of God. If he is God, and the statement that the Father and the Son are identical is to be taken literally, it follows that he is his own son.

The reply to this might be that, since they are the same God but not the same person, the one might, *qua* person, be the son of the other, and so different persons, and only *qua* God be the same person. We have already seen reason to doubt the correctness of this reply. It is only intentional characteristics that can be possessed *qua* anything, and being the son of, at least when taken literally, is not an intentional characteristic.

It may be, however, that Christians, when they say Christ is the Son of God, are not speaking literally. Indeed, they cannot be speaking quite literally, since even *qua* person God does not have sexual organs. But this means that it is the word 'father' that is being used metaphorically, not the words 'the same'. God, on this view, must stand in some relation to God the Son analogous to the relation in which an earthly father stands to his son. Quite what it is that is being said in this figurative form I have neither the ability nor the space to enquire. It could be that Christ stands in a loving relation with the Father analogous to that which is supposed to exist, and sometimes does exist, between a literal father and his literal son. But the fact that God the Father and God the Son are father and son only in a metaphorical sense does not enable one to circumvent any difficulties there may be concerning their identity. For even metaphorical fathers are presumably different from metaphorical sons, which means that the difficulty concerning the necessity of their having all their properties in common remains.

It might also be maintained that not only are 'father' and 'son' being used in figurative sense. God is also three persons but one God only in a figurative sense. It is very doubtful what such a figurative sense could be. Is he only figuratively one? Is there, indeed, such a thing as a figurative sense of 'one'. Is there a figurative sense of 'is'? Are God and Christ different persons in a figurative sense of 'different', or the same in a figurative sense of 'the same', or both? I suspect that these questions are simply absurd.

One can at least say this. Either Christianity is a form of monotheism, or it is not. If it is, it is important, if Christ is God, that Christ and God should quite literally be the same. Hence, if metaphor enters into the Trinity, it must be 'different' that is being used metaphorically. But I suspect that neither 'the same' nor 'different' can be being used figuratively in the doctrine of the Trinity, and in any case one would think that the literal status of 'the same' and of 'different' would stand or fall together. We have seen that there is no such thing as a figurative use of the words 'same' and 'different'. Hence the possibility of Christianity being monotheistic must presuppose the erroneous doctrine of relative identity.

(vii)   The Attractiveness of the Trinity

It seems to me that the main advantage of the Trinity is that, (neglecting the Holy Ghost) it offers two different persons for two different 'devotional' needs. It offers us both, in its first person, a 'father' and, in its second person, a friend and guide who actually shows us the way in which we think the former thinks we should go, who will help us on our way and will intercede with the Father on our behalf. It also has the advantage that it can allow us to accept Christ's claim that he was God without accepting, or accepting without qualification, the apparent consequence that God is just a man.

Its disadvantage is that, without the doctrine of relative identity, it is polytheistic, which diminishes each of the persons in it. And it is difficult enough to think that there is one God, let alone three. Hence the doctrine of the Trinity consists of a determined and ingenious attempt to have one's cake and eat it. What would one lose if one dropped the doctrine of the Trinity? The Holy Ghost could be regarded as a disposition. For example, its tendency to descend on people could be regarded as their acquiring certain dispositional properties, for example, powers that they did not know they had, rather than their being fallen upon by an entity. A disposition could not be identical with one person, let alone two. Christ could still be our guide, companion, and intercede with God on our behalf, whether he were identical with God or not. Historically I do not know to what extent it is certain that Christ did claim to be God. But the historicity of Christianity is a great burden to it.

(viii)   Conclusion

I conclude (a) that two things cannot have different attributes, but be (literally) identical and (b) that two things cannot be the same *qua* member of one class, but different *qua* member of another. Hence (a) if the persons of the Trinity have different attributes, they must be numerically different, and (b) there cannot be three persons but one God, if the God is supposed to be identical with each of the persons. This argument shows that the doctrine of the Trinity is false only if this doctrine is taken quite literally.

Notes

1 A characteristic like being despised which is (or which appears to be) such that it applies to something under one description but not under another is said to be 'referentially opaque'. See Quine, 'Reference and Modality', 1953. Quine himself speaks of 'referentially opaque context'.

2 This suggestion was made by Geach, 1973.

3 Other aspects of the problem of referential opacity (which is not really one problem but several) can be dealt with in a similar way. For example, that Tom knows that the Son is God, but does not know that the Holy Ghost is God, although the Son and the Holy Ghost are identical, can be dealt with by saying that the Holy Ghost is identical with something, the Son, whom Tom knows to be God, and that the Son is identical with something, the Holy Ghost, whom Tom does not know to be God. Or, to put it more artificially, both the Son and the Holy Ghost have the two properties of being, *qua* Son, known by Tom to be God, and, *qua* Holy Ghost, not being known by Tom to be God.

4 The difference can be seen most easily if it is put into a more symbolic form as the difference between (a) (A wants X) and -(A wants X) on the one hand, and (b) (A wants X and -X) on the other.

5 I think they presuppose this, rather than assert it, because 'Tom is a boy' presupposes that there is such a person as Tom, rather than asserts it.

6 In 'Personal Identity and Individuation', 1973.

7 A dispositional property is to be defined hypothetically. For example, to say that a bar of iron is magnetic (a dispositional property) is to say that it will attract such things as iron filings, if there are any in the vicinity.

8 I put 'them' in quotes because there is no such question as whether or not the dispositional properties one bar lost are numerically identical with those the other bar acquires. One cannot, and cannot in principle, track properties through time, and see whether the properties possessed by one magnet at one time are or are not spatio-temporally continuous with the properties possessed by the other magnet at a different time.

9 I have suggested the possibility of disembodiment later in this book, and also in Harrison, 1995, Part I, 'Mind Body Problem', and Part II, 'The Blue and Brown Fairy Books'.

16 God's Omniscience

(i)   How We Know that God is Omniscient

I suspect many people will think that it is impious and arrogant to ask the questions about the deity which I shall try to answer in the following pages. If so, I suggest that they phrase them as questions about only the concept of an omniscient being, rather than about God. For though the deity himself may be imponderable and shrouded in mystery, the concept of an omniscient being is a human one. It is about this concept and its implications that I am here talking.

God is commonly supposed to be omniscient. Again, this need not be regarded as a discovery about God. He is omniscient by definition. Because of this definition we know that if there were a God, he would be omniscient. But we would still need to discover whether there was a God who was omniscient.

Even if it does not follow directly from this definition that he is omniscient, it still follows from his being perfect that he is omniscient. And a less than omniscient personal being would be a less than proper object of worship. But, as I have said, if you use the word 'God' as a name for the creator of the universe whether this being is omniscient or not, this makes no difference to the facts.

Though that the word 'God' may not be used to refer to a being who is not omniscient is simply due to a convention about how the word 'God' is to be used, this convention is not arbitrary. For we need the word 'God', or some equivalent word, for a being who is perfect, and a being who fell short of omniscience would not be perfect. (It should be remembered that I think that the function of 'postulating' a God is not to explain what happens in the world, but to elaborate a satisfactory concept of the deity, and since neither an omniscient nor a less than omniscient God can explain anything about the world, we might as well be guided by quasi-aesthetic preference, and allow that God, as he must be to be satisfactory, is omniscient.)

That God is omniscient, then, is not something we discover by investigating the universe. We confer omnipotence upon God, so to speak, in response to a human need, the need to create a concept of a perfect being. This need is partly aesthetic. The concept of an only nearly omnipotent being is less satisfying than the concept of a fully omnipotent being. Indeed, the former concept is somewhat jarring – like beings who do not quite obey the aesthetically pleasing laws of physics. But, if theology were a matter of discovering God's existence, the fact that the existence of a non-omniscient being would jar us would be no guarantee whatsoever that such a being did not exist.

I have just pointed out that it does not follow from the fact that human beings, in response to human needs, have evolved the concept of an omniscient being, that there is anything in reality answering to this concept. It is also the case, conversely, that from the fact that our concept of God is the concept of an omniscient being, it does not follow that reality does not contain a being who is only very, very knowledgable, but not (or not quite) omniscient. All that does follow, if human beings decide to use the word 'God' for an omniscient being, is that, if the universe were to contain a very, very knowledgeable, but not omniscient, being, it would be incorrect to call this being 'God'. But it is as wrong, by a decision about how a word is to be used, to try to legislate things out of existence (in this case a very powerful but not omniscient creator of the universe) as it is to try to legislate them into existence in the same way. But I have explained that I think theology is not a matter of discovering what exists, so much as one of elaborating a satisfactory concept of the deity. If the world were governed by a very powerful and knowledgeable and fairly good being, we would still need the idea of a perfect being to whom we could turn from the former's partial inadequacy, and to remedy his shortcomings.

(ii) The Implications of Omniscience

God's omniscience consists in his knowing everything, i.e., in his knowing the truth of every true proposition. Knowing the truth of every true proposition must be taken to include knowing the falsity of every false proposition, i.e., knowing, about every false proposition, the true proposition that it is false.

God's Knowledge of Negative Propositions

Hence God must know the truth of negative propositions as well as of affirmative ones. For if he knows that it is false that it is raining, it follows that he knows that it is not raining.

Knowing that negative propositions are true involves the capacity to conceive of unrealised possibilities, for one must conceive of an unrealised possibility in order to know that it is not realised. It follows from this that a view about God's creation that is sometimes held, viz., that no sooner does God conceive of something[1] than it comes to pass, must be erroneous. For God must conceive of a thing that has not happened in order to 'disbelieve' the false proposition that it has happened, and so to 'believe' that it is false that it happened. But, just because these propositions are false, the things they describe have *not* come to pass.

God would have to know negative propositions if he were to know universal propositions. He could not know that all men are mortal, for example, without knowing that there were no men who were *not* mortal.

God's Inerrancy

Though it does not logically follow from God's omniscience, it must obviously also be the case that God does not believe any propositions which are false; God must be non-errant as well as omniscient. (If an omniscient being did believe propositions that were false, it would follow that sometimes he believed a proposition that he knew to be false. This is not absolutely impossible in human beings, who are notoriously irrational, but such piece of irrationality could not be ascribed to the deity. It does not follow from the fact that God is omniscient that he is not irrational, but the same motives which lead us to conceive of him as omniscient and inerrant ought also to make us want to conceive of him as not being irrational in this way.)

Omniscience and Knowledge of Hypothetical Propositions

God presumably also must know hypothetical propositions, including unfulfilled conditional propositions. For example, he must know the hypothetical proposition that if an object is an Euclidean triangle its angles must add up to 180°. He must also know some unfulfilled conditional proposition about what would have happened if Churchill had not become Prime Minister in 1940 (although in fact he did), or about what would have happened if the Archduke Franz Ferdinand had not been assassinated at Sarajevo in 1914 (although in fact he was). If he is to interfere intelligently in the affairs of the universe, he must know the truth of unfulfilled conditional propositions about what would have happened were he not to interfere. He must presumably also know disjunctive propositions, for example, that Tom is either a fool or a knave, universal propositions, such as that all God's children go to Heaven, and particular propositions, such as that someone must have yielded to the temptation to plant a bomb at the Conservative Party conference at Brighton.

If God did not know the truth of hypothetical propositions, unfulfilled conditional propositions, and other propositions involving unrealised possibilities he would, though extremely knowledgeable, be also extremely stupid. He would know about everything that is that it is, and what it is like, but he would not know the connection between one thing that is and another thing that is, for he could not know what effect the absence of something that was not absent would have. He would know that Smith had taken arsenic, and that Smith had died, but he could not know that Smith had died because he had taken arsenic, because he could not know that Smith (other things remaining equal) would not have died if he had not taken arsenic. (The qualification 'other things being equal' is necessary, because otherwise that he was woken by the butler does not entail that if the butler had not knocked, he would not have woken, because he might then have been woken by the maid.)

If God could not consider unrealised possibilities he would also find it very difficult to frame a divine plan, for framing a plan involves knowing what would happen if various alternative plans, including ours, which he does not adopt, were to be adopted. This God would not be able to know, unless he can deduce consequences from propositions that are false, for example, the false proposition that if he was going to adopt such-and-such a plan, which in fact he did not adopt.

Omniscience and Conversational Implication

There is an apparent oddity involved in God's knowing some propositions (some of these involving unrealised possibilities), such as that Tom is *either* a fool or a knave, or that *someone* must have been responsible for planting the Brighton bomb, or his knowing that *if* this is an Euclidean triangle, its angles must add up to 180°. This is because, if God is omniscient, he should know whether Tom is a fool or a knave, who was responsible for the planting of the Brighton bomb, and whether or not this is an Euclidean triangle. To say that God knows that at least one man had a sex change in 1990 is to suggest that he does not know how many men had a sex change in that year, and who these men were.

However, that the statement, that God knows that Tom's next grandchild will be a boy or girl does not entail that God does not know whether Tom's next grandchild will be a boy. If it did entail this, then that Tom's next grandchild will be either a boy or a girl would be something God could not know, because he presumably does know which sex Tom's next grandchild will be.

If anyone supposes that the statement that God knows that Tom's next grandchild will be a boy or a girl entails that God does not know which, it may be because he has confused entailment with 'conversational implication'.

There are two important differences between conversational and ordinary implication. First, it is my asserting something, not the statement I assert, that has conversational implications. Secondly, what conversationally implies what is false does not itself have to be false, though what non-conversationally implies what is false does have to be false.

What is implied (about myself) by *the event of my asserting something* is quite different from what is implied (in a different sense of 'imply') by the proposition that I assert. Since my statement that it is raining is about the weather, and not about me, it does not say anything at all about whether I believe that it is raining. Nevertheless, my asserting it conversationally implies that I believe that it is raining, and anyone hearing me say that it is raining is entitled to infer from my saying it that I believe that it is raining. Though it is not contradictory to say 'It is raining, but I do not believe that it is', this is not something that I can properly say (not, at least, to the same person at the same time) because, though the proposition that it is raining is logically consistent with the proposition that I believe that it is not raining, my saying that it is raining is usually done with the intention of producing in the hearer a belief that it is raining, which intention will be defeated if I also say that I myself do not believe that it is raining.

If anyone were to say 'God knows that at least five people in England will have a sex change in England in 1990', this only suggests, and does not imply, that God does not know precisely how many people will have a sex change. This is a suggestion that is impossible to avoid, because we ourselves do not know how many people will have a sex change in 1986, and so to say that God knows that at least five people will have a sex change is the nearest to the whole truth we can get. It does not imply that God can get no nearer. If we were to say that God knows that seven people will have a sex change, this might be true, but would nevertheless contextually imply that we ourselves know, which we do not, and involve a serious risk of our purveying false information.

Two cases involving conversational implication will be discussed later. First there is that case when God's knowing some such thing as that today is Tuesday might seem to imply that he was in time. Secondly, there is the case when anyone's saying (thinking that) certain unfulfilled conditional propositions are true might seem to imply that he was in doubt whether or not their antecedents were true. This might seem to involve a difficulty for God's knowing the truth of unfulfilled conditional propositions when he must always know whether their antecedents are true or not.

Omniscience and Statements Involving Category Mistakes

There are certainly some questions which God cannot answer. He presumably cannot answer questions such as 'What colour are quadratic equations?', 'What is the weight of Beethoven's seventh symphony?', and 'What is five pounds times seven pence?' The reason for this is that these questions are meaningless, and so do not have an answer. A symphony, for example, does not belong to the right category of thing either to have or not have a weight. Hence, from the fact that God cannot answer them, it does not follow that there are answers to some questions which God does not know. There is no deficiency in being unable to answer questions such as these. There would, rather, be a deficiency in thinking that one could answer them. The same remarks apply to meaningless sentences.

Omniscience and Non-propositional Knowledge

There is also the question whether God knows how to do things, as well as knowing that certain propositions are true.[2] Does he, for example, know how to ride a bicycle? My own opinion is that he knows how a bicycle is ridden, but not how to ride one. This is because knowing how a bicycle is ridden is a case of knowing that certain propositions, for example, that you first press one foot down on the pedal and then the other, are true. It is impossible for someone to know how to ride a bicycle, however, unless at some time or other he has been able to ride a bicycle, which involves having legs, which God does not. That God does not know how to do things such as ride a bicycle, however, does not mean that he is not omniscient; omniscience entails only knowing the truth of propositions, not that he knows how to do things. Though knowing how to ride a bicycle is a useful accomplishment in men, I do not think God is any worse, or any the less omniscient, for not being able to ride one.

There are also many other things that men can know, such as people, places, the seven times table, Beethoven's Fifth Symphony, 'To Daffodils', fear, one's onions, one's wife, and one's way. It is questionable which of these God can know. He does not know Mrs Thatcher, because he has not had the privilege of being introduced to her, and he does not know Birmingham, because he has not been there, and cannot find his way about in it, having no feet. He cannot know the seven times table or 'To Daffodils' if this involves being able to recite them, though he doubtless knows all the true propositions reciting the seven times table enables us, if we have been properly taught, systematically to assert, and all the true propositions describing the order of the words in the poem. He cannot know fear because to know fear is to experience it. He does not have a wife, and does not know his way because he does not need to go anywhere, though he might know someone else's way if this involves nothing more than his knowing the truth of propositions describing this person's route.

God is omniscient in that he knows the truth of every true proposition, the only thing that it is important for him to know. Not knowing the things mentioned above does not consist in not knowing propositions. Non-propositional knowledge, with the exception of that acquaintance on which non-inferential propositional knowledge is based, has no epistemological importance.

However, I should have thought that there was a case for holding that God was acquainted with everything there was to be acquainted with, including the thoughts of his creatures if that is possible, even though acquaintance is not propositional knowledge.

Omniscience and False Presupposition

There are also questions which God cannot answer because they involve presuppositions which are false. For example, God does not know the answer to the question 'When did Smith stop beating his wife?' if Smith never has beaten his wife, or has not got a wife to beat. Nor does he know whether or not the King of France is bald when there is no king of France, or whether or not all John's children are asleep when John does not have any children.

Again, the reason why God does not know the answers to these questions is not that they are difficult, or involve the possession of information which God lacks, but because the answer 'Yes' and the answer 'No' would both be equally misleading, and would commit the person saying 'Yes' or 'No' to the truth of a proposition (that Smith has a wife, or that John has children) which is false.

God's Omniscience and Knowledge of 'Self-referential' Propositions

There are also difficulties about God's knowing the truth of propositions that we express in words such as 'My name is "Harrison"', 'Today is Tuesday', 'Mary will soon be here, 'It is icy cold in this room', 'Our destination is not far from here', 'Tom has been dead for several years', 'I have not been here for ages', and 'The end of the world is nigh'. This is because these propositions are expressed in words that tie what they assert to the place and time occupied by the person using them. Words like 'I', 'here' 'today', 'soon', 'here', 'this', 'ages', 'nigh', and past, present and future tenses generally, express what they do by reference to the time and place occupied by the speaker. The word 'I' refers to the person speaking. 'Here' refers to the place at which the person speaking is situated, and 'now' to the time at which he is speaking. The word 'soon' indicates that the events being talked about will occur a short while after the present moment. 'Ago' indicates that the interval between now and the time of the event being talked about is in the past rather than in the future. A person who is speaking in the present tense indicates that the event being mentioned is occurring roughly at the same time that he is speaking, and corresponding things are true of the past and future tenses.

God, however, is supposed to be spaceless and timeless, and as such can be no more closely connected with one place than another, or with one time than another. How, then, can he know propositions such as that there is a cup tie this afternoon? 'This afternoon' means (roughly) 'the afternoon contemporaneous with or shortly after what is happening to me now'; but nothing happens to God, who is outside time, and so 'now' – or so it is said – would not pick out one time, rather than any other, when used by a being who exists at all times. Again, how can God know that there is a thunderstorm here, when 'here' refers to that region of space in the vicinity of the speaker's body, and he does not have a body? I shall return to this problem later in this chapter, and in the chapter 'God's Eternity' (chapter 20).

Omniscience and Fiction

Men sometimes wonder what happened to the characters in novels after the end of the story, or what would have happened to them if they had taken different decisions, or if things that had happened to them had not happened. Examples are 'Did Jane and Darcy have children', and 'What would have happened to Heathcliffe if Catherine had not married Edgar Linton?' Is it possible that these are questions which men cannot answer, but God can?

Since there are no such persons as Jane, Darcy, Heathcliffe and Catherine Linton, questions about what they did after the end of the novel, or questions about what they would have done, cannot arise. People ask such questions because they forget, temporarily at least, that there are no such people for the questions to be about. Hence neither God nor men know the answers to these questions, but the 'ignorance' of both is not genuine ignorance, because there is no real question to answer. God's not knowing such things falls under the heading of false presupposition, discussed above. (There are, of course, questions about what the authors of the novels that contain the characters in question said they would have written, had they finished the story, but anyone asking what these characters really did is confusing fiction with history.)

There is, however, the question: 'What would a person like the character in question in the respects outlined by the novelist have done, if there had been such a person?' The answer to this question is almost always that one has not been given enough information by the novelist, or that one has not sufficient knowledge of the laws by which the past determines the future, or both, to be able to tell what would have happened to a person resembling the characters. (This will be especially difficult in science fiction, for the author may be writing about a world in which the laws of nature that govern this world do not apply.) When there is sufficient information, God will know, and know even when we do not (because he knows more than we about the outcomes of certain situations, for example, the outcome of the situation where a poor conservative American southerner marries a northern feminist orator accustomed to luxury). In favour of speculating about the outcomes of fictional situations it can be said that we can often do little more than guess at the outcomes of similar situations that arise in real life, even when we need to form an opinion in order to act on it.

When the work of fiction in question does not give us enough 'information' to enable the outcome to be determined, I suppose God would know all the possible outcomes, and be able to grade them in the order of their probability.

(iii)   God's Knowledge of Unfulfilled Conditionals

Whether Unfulfilled Conditionals Have a Truth Value

We have seen that God must know – as men must – the truth of at least some unfulfilled conditional propositions.[3] He would not be able intelligently to decide between two courses of action, for example, creating one man instead of another, if he did not know what would have been the consequences of his creating the man that he did not create. And God will have made a mistake if he allows me to go to Heaven, believing that I would not have succumbed to temptation had he seen fit to tempt me, unless the proposition that I would not have succumbed is true. It follows from this that at least some unfulfilled conditionals must have a truth value. But that some unfulfilled conditionals must have a truth value does not mean that all of them must.

I lean to the eccentric view, however, that all unfulfilled conditionals (unless, like 'If the present king of France had not been bald, he would have been more popular', they suffer from one of the kinds of defect discussed earlier) do have a truth value. They must all be either true or false, because, for every unfulfilled conditional such as that if p had been the case, q would not have been the case, one can form a contradictory unfulfilled conditional of the form: if p had been the case, q would have been the case. (That it is not the case that if p had been the case, q would have been the case entails, oddly, that if p had been the case, q would have been the case.) For example, the proposition that if there had been a solar eclipse on the 25 May 1973, my hair would have fallen out, is the contradictory of the proposition that if there had been such an eclipse on this date, my hair would not have fallen out. In this respect, unfulfilled conditionals resemble hypothetical predictions. Just as the proposition that if it rains, England will win, is the contradictory of the proposition that if it rains, England will not win (no commitment having been made in the event of its not raining), so if it had rained, England would have won is the contradictory of if it had rained, England would not have won.[4]

A reason for thinking that all unfulfilled conditional propositions (that are not defective) must be either true or false is that it always might make a difference to somebody's policy of action whether any given unfulfilled conditional proposition was true or not. For example, it will always in principle make a difference whether it is true or false that if there had been an explosion on Jupiter on 7 March I would have sneezed, because, if it had been within my power to produce an explosion on Jupiter, and I did not want to sneeze, this would have been a reason for not producing an explosion on Jupiter. That it is not within my power to produce an explosion on Jupiter makes no difference to the fact that in principle my producing an explosion would make a difference. (It always would be within God's power, and he might or might not want me to sneeze.) If it makes a difference to what policy it is rational to adopt if I accept or do not accept an unfulfilled conditional, this must be because one policy is rational if it is true, and a different policy is rational if it is not true. Hence it must be either true or not true.

What We Ought to Say about God's Omniscience, if Unfulfilled Conditionals Do Not Have a Truth Value

There are two possible things that one might say about God's omniscience if unfulfilled conditionals do not have a truth value (or about those unfulfilled conditionals which do not have a truth value, if some do and others do not).

One possibility, which I shall discuss in more detail later, is that God's not knowing the truth of such propositions is no genuine limitation on his omniscience. It is unreasonable to complain about God's not knowing the truth of propositions that are *not* true.

Another possibility, which I shall also discuss in more detail later (when I come to consider God's knowledge of the future), is that God does know – one cannot in this case say 'know the truth of', though it would be more natural to do so – propositions about the future – in spite of their not having a truth value. This means saying that God knows some things that are not true (though they are not false either), and rejecting the rule that that some person knows something implies that what he knows is true. In that case, that God knows that I would have sneezed, if there had been an explosion on Jupiter, does not imply that it is *true* that I would have sneezed, if there had been an explosion on Jupiter. It just implies that I would have sneezed if there had been an explosion on Jupiter.

I myself do not find it necessary to settle for one or other of these two views, as I think that propositions about the future and unfulfilled conditionals *are* capable of being true or false.

How Men Know the Truth of Unfulfilled Conditionals

There is no difficulty concerning how men – or, I think, God – know unfulfilled conditional propositions in those cases involving logical truth, for example unfulfilled conditionals such as that if the angles of Euclidean triangles add up to 180°, the angles of this object, if it were an Euclidean triangle, would add up to 180°. They know this because it is a necessary truth that the angles of Euclidean triangles add up to 180°.

We sometimes know that this, that and the other piece of Dresden china would have broken, if they had been dropped, because they were dropped, and did break. (The fact that we use the subjunctive does not necessarily imply that they were not dropped; consider 'He would, wouldn't he?') We conclude, on inductive grounds, that other pieces of Dresden china that were not dropped would have broken, if they had been dropped, because the ones that were dropped were broken. In other cases, it is not known what a thing would have done in certain circumstances, because the circumstances have never arisen, or because, though they have arisen, sometimes one thing happened in those circumstances, sometimes another.

Assertions about what would have happened do not imply, as is sometimes supposed, assertions to the effect that anything necessarily happens. It may have been supposed that they do because conversational implication has been confused with implication. If I say that something would have happened, I conversationally imply, rather than assert, that I have some reason for thinking that it would have happened, and such a reason may be that it necessarily happens in the circumstances that would have obtained. (One knows that such things must necessarily happen (a) because they always do, and (b) because attempts to prevent such things from happening always fail.)

It is obvious that there are many cases in which men will not know whether, if one thing had happened, another thing would or would not have happened. There are many unfulfilled conditional propositions that men cannot know, because the relevant situations have never arisen naturally or been produced experimentally. For example, it may not be known what would have happened if certain patients had been given a drug because as yet no men, or not enough men, have been given the drug, which may not yet even have been synthesised.

Men do not know such things as whether, if a large meteor had not burned up while passing through the earth's atmosphere, it would have landed in the northern or southern hemisphere. Not enough is known about the nature of such meteors, and we do not have sufficiently precise information about their mass, direction and velocities, and the forces they will be subject to, to enable us to make any such prediction. But this does not mean that it is neither true nor false that it will fall in the northern hemisphere, and neither true nor false that it will fall in the southern hemisphere. Indeed, since it must, if it reaches the earth's surface at all, fall either in the northern or the southern hemisphere, it must, as I have said, be the case that if it reaches the earth's surface it will fall in the northern hemisphere or that if it reaches the earth's surface it will fall in the southern hemisphere. God, presumably, will know which.

God's Knowledge of Unfulfilled Conditionals

It could be argued that God himself may sometimes not know what would happen in certain circumstances, because the circumstances in which this thing would or would not happen have never arisen. These circumstances could sometimes be produced experimentally, and God could make experiments that man could not make, but it may be that he has chosen not to make some of them. If the only way in which God could find out what would happen were by experiment, there would be things God would not know. It would not be true that he *could* not know such things, because he could make the necessary experiments, if he so wished. Hence this limitation to his omniscience would be self-imposed.

However, it may be that God would know what would or would not happen in such circumstances because, as he is omnipotent as well as omniscient, everything is under his control. If so God, unlike man, *decides* what would happen in the event of circumstances arising that never have arisen. God, presumably, can know what he would have done f he had produced these circumstances, in some such way as that in which we (sometimes) know what we would do in certain circumstances.

In the case of people, there may be ethical limitations on our ability to experiment that mean that there are certain unfulfilled conditionals the truth of which we shall never know. And we may also be limited by our inability to persuade men to do what we need them to do in order for us to ascertain the truth of the unfulfilled conditional in question (e.g., give us funds). I shall discuss whether God is so limited shortly.

God's 'Middle Knowledge'

A reason sometimes given for thinking that unfulfilled conditionals do not have a truth value is that it has been supposed that if certain unfulfilled conditionals were true, I would be unable to help doing the things I do. If I know the truth of the hypothetical proposition that if this were dropped it would break, this suggests that I know this because, if it is dropped, its breaking is inevitable. If its breaking were not inevitable, perhaps, no-one could know that it would break if it were dropped. Hence if God were to know the truth of an unfulfilled conditional such as that if I were tempted I would succumb, my succumbing would have to be the inevitable result of my being tempted, which – or so it has been supposed – would take away my freedom to overcome the temptation. (That if someone had been tempted, he would *probably* not have succumbed is another matter. One can know this without any implication that his resisting temptation is inevitable. But if that were all that we can know, it cannot be known whether he would have succumbed or not, and so there would be something that God cannot, his intentions apart, know.)

I shall argue in chapter 17 ('Foreknowledge, Will and Fate') that, despite appearances, such things as that my succumbing is in a sense the inevitable result of my being tempted do not take away my freedom not to overcome temptation. Freedom and this kind of inevitability are compatible. Hence that it implies inevitability is not a reason for supposing that God cannot know the truth of unfulfilled conditionals about human behaviour.

But the difficulty is more acute if, as I have suggested above, God knows the truth of unfulfilled conditionals because of his knowledge of what he himself would do if certain circumstances were realised. In the case of human beings, God's knowledge of what a human being would do must, if his knowledge of unfulfilled conditionals results from his knowledge of his own intentions, be his knowledge of what he intends that a human being should do. For in that case God does not just produce the circumstances, such as his having the wants and beliefs which necessarily result in Tom's freely choosing to do one thing rather than another. If he knows what will happen in those circumstances because he intended to bring about what happens in them, he must actually 'make' Tom do what he does by an arbitrary fiat that does not make use of causation mediated by the wants and beliefs of the agent.

I shall suggest (again in chapter 17) that God could not by arbitrary fiat cause Tom to stay at his post without interfering with Tom's freedom. But in that case it may be argued – though I think wrongly – that I must be mistaken in thinking that God can know the truth of certain unfulfilled conditionals because of his knowledge of his own intentions, for example, because of his knowledge of such facts as that if he (God) were to put Tom in a situation demanding bravery, he (God) would bring it about that Tom did not run away. For if so, Tom would have no choice but to stay at his post. Hence in certain circumstances, when men never have been in certain situations, God cannot know what they would do were they to be in them, for he could have such knowledge only by removing men's freedom.

This is argument rests on a confusion, however. The true state of affairs is this. Either God brings it about mediately that men perform certain actions, e.g., by producing in them the beliefs and wants which make them freely perform these actions, or he produces these actions immediately by fiat. If it is the former, he knows what men will do because of his knowledge of the laws governing their motives and beliefs, which means – as I shall argue in chapter 17 – that God can have knowledge of men's behaviour which does not interfere with their freedom. These people are then, after all, doing what they want to do, and so must be free. If it is the latter, God's knowledge does interfere with men's freedom, but this does not mean that he does not have the knowledge, merely that, when he does have it, their doing what God knows they will do is, as indeed sometimes happens, not done voluntarily.

God's Knowledge of Unfulfilled Conditionals in an Indeterministic Universe

Recourse must be had to God's knowledge of his own intentions to explain how he could have knowledge of what would happen in the future if the universe were indeterministic, i.e., if some future events were such that they were not determined by and so could not be predicted from knowledge of present and past events. His intentions apart, God knows the truth of some unfulfilled conditional propositions in much the same way that men do. If he knows that if one kind of event were to happen, another kind of event would happen, it is because he knows that such things must happen. This means that if the world is not determined, there would, God's intentions apart, be some things that even God could not know. For example, if quantum theory is true, God would no more be able to know where an electron would hit a screen if it were fired at it than men would. God, however, might be able to know where it would hit the screen because he would know that, if he caused or allowed the electron to be fired at the screen, he would intend that it should land on one part of the screen rather than another. A slight absurdity that seems to me to attach to this idea is, I think, the inevitable result of regarding a personal God as an entity that explains what happens in the universe.

(iv)   Omniscience, Probability and Chance

Men can often know (and say) only that if such and such a thing were to have happened, such and such another thing *probably* would have happened. God, with complete knowledge, will know that such and such a thing, which we think probable, is certain. Men can know (and say) that, if it had rained, England would probably have won (because England usually does win when it rains). But if God were to say what I said, his remark would suggest, falsely, that he did not know whether or not England would have won if it had rained. This raises the question whether God can know such facts as that something or other probably would have happened. If not, the situation would be the odd one in which there was a certain kind of knowledge that God was barred from having by his very omniscience.

There are two kinds of probability judgment. First there are those which are hypothetical, and assert that, on such and such evidence the chances of such and such a thing are so and so. For example, there are judgments such as that, if (or on the evidence that) a card is one of a full pack, the chances of its being the king of spades are one in 52, and the judgment that, if (or on the evidence that) it is a court card the chances of its being the king of spades are one in four. Judgments like these can be known by God, as well as by anyone else. These judgments are compatible with one another, hypothetical, and make no claims about the state of knowledge of the person making the judgment with respect to their antecedents (e.g., that it really is a court card), and so can certainly be known by God, even though he is omniscient.

But there are also categorical judgments such as that a card has a one in 52 chance of being the king of spades, asserted by someone who knows only that it is one of a full pack, and the judgment that it has a one in 12 chance of being the king of spades, asserted by someone who knows that it is a court card. In this case, there would be something very wrong with a person who was in a position to make the latter judgment asserting the former, or *vice versa*. If he possessed the information that it was a court card, he should say that the chances of its being the king of spades were one in 12, though if he possessed only the information that it was a card drawn from a full pack, he should say that these chances are only one in 52. In this case, unlike the former, it might seem that God, whether or not he knows them, ought not to make either probability judgment, for his making them would at least suggest that he did not know, and did not have the information enabling him to say, that it was certainly the king of spades.

There are two ways of dealing with this situation. One is simply to say that God is not omniscient, and does not know these categorical statements about probability. One could add that this is not a deficiency, for it is better to know what is actually the case than to know only what will probably be the case, and God's knowledge of the former makes the latter unnecessary. One could add that God can know such thing as that when Tom acts on the proposition that a card is the king of spades are one in four by refusing to put his shirt on it, he is behaving rationally, which he would not be doing if he knew that it was certainly the king of spades. And God could know such things as that, on the evidence at Tom's disposal, the chances of its being a court card are one in 12, and say this without misleading anyone.

The other way of dealing with the difficulty is to say that God does know such things as that there is a one in 12 chance of a card's being the king of spades, but, were he to say such a thing he would be misleading his hearers into thinking he did not know whether it was the king of spades or not. On this view, God can know what Tom knows, but, unlike Tom, cannot assert this fact 'out loud'. His position with regard to categorical probability statements resembles his position with regard to disjunctive statements. He knows that Tom is either a fool or a liar, but cannot say so without making his hearers think that he does not know which. What he asserts is true, but what he conversationally implies is false.

Perhaps an analogy would help. If someone who said that the chances of a card's being the king of spades were one in 52 was saying that they were at least one in 52, and someone saying that they were one in 12 was saying that they were at least one in 12, their judgments would be compatible. There is no incompatibility between saying that a hill is at least 1,000 feet high and someone else's saying that it is at least 1,500 feet high. (Both judgments will be true if it is 2,000 feet high, and both false if it is 900 feet high. If it is 1,300 feet high, the first judgment will be true and the second false.) But if someone who knew that the hill was 2,000 feet high were to say that it was at least 1,000 feet high, his remark, though true, would be misleading, because it would suggest that he was not in a position to say exactly how high it was. God might then know, but ought not to say, that it was at least 1,000 feet high. If this analogy is correct, perhaps God does know that the chances of the card's being the king of spades are, given that it is a playing card, one in 52, and that these chances are, given that it is a court card, one in 12, though, since he knows that it is the king of spades, he ought not to say either. If a man knowing that it was a court card, were to say that the chances of its being the king of spades were (at least) one in 52, his remark would be true, but he ought not to have made it, his making it suggests that he was not in a position to assess its chances as being higher than this. Hence the reason why God cannot say (though he can know) that the probability of something is, say, one in 12 is like the reason why a man who knows that a hill is 2,000 high cannot say that is at least 1,000 feet high. His remark would be true, and state what he knew to be the case, but might cause unwary hearers to arrive at incorrect beliefs concerning the state of his knowledge. I am very far from being satisfied with this suggestion, but at the moment cannot think of a better one.

Unfulfilled Conditionals Involving Probability

As we have seen, some unfulfilled conditional propositions are to the effect that if such and such were to happen, or to have happened, something else *probably* would happen, or would have happened. There are two cases to be considered, which involve (a) open and (b) closed classes respectively.

(a) If there are 100 balls in a given urn, 60 of which are white and 40 black, one can know that if a ball were to be drawn from the urn it would probably be a black one. (b) We can know that if an unbiased die were to be thrown, it would probably fall six uppermost. (a) The first piece of knowledge involves a closed class; all the balls in the urn. (b) The second involves an open class: all throws of dice without restriction.

(a) On certain assumptions, such as that my fingers have no especial attraction for black paint, knowledge of the first is just a matter of knowing that there are more white balls than black ones. It is no more problematic than knowing that all the men in the room have hearts. I have already toyed with the suggestion that God cannot know that a white ball will *probably* be drawn, though he can know that when I say that a white ball will probably be drawn I can say the most I can on the evidence at my disposal.

(b) Knowing that the next throw of a die will probably be a throw of six is more like knowing that all men have hearts than knowing that all the men in the room have hearts. It conversationally implies that there is some necessity about a die's falling six one-sixth of the time. It is possible that its so falling has the same kind of necessity as does a natural law. We know that it is necessary that objects attract one another 100 per cent of the time, because all attempts to make them deviate from this percentage fail. Perhaps we know that an unbiased die falls six uppermost one-sixth of the time because attempts to make their falling deviate from this percentage always fail. (There are, of course, ways of making the die fall six uppermost more often than this, for example, by tying the coin to the back of a cat and tossing the cat,[5] but these involve, so to speak, 'unbiasing' the die.)

It is not, I think, an ultimate law of nature that dice fall heads one-sixth of the time. It could, I imagine, be deduced from other laws of nature, given enough knowledge of the obstacles the die is going to meet on its way. But this does not mean that it is not also a law of nature of sorts. And it was known to be true long before the laws of nature from which it can possibly be deduced were known.

(v) Omniscience and Constructivism

Mathematical constructivism (or intuitionism) is the doctrine that a mathematical proposition cannot be true unless there is some way of settling the question whether it is true or not, i.e., upon whether or not a proof of it can be 'constructed'. For example, it has been held that since (or if) there is no way of proving or disproving Goldbach's conjecture (that every even number greater than two is the sum of two primes), Goldbach's conjecture is neither true nor false.[6]

The question must then arise: does God himself know such things as whether there is an even number that is not the sum of two primes? But constructivism, whether it is true or not, ought not to make one reject the view that God is omniscient. Not knowing, as we have seen, is not the same thing as being ignorant. It is a deficiency not to know truth; but not to know falsehoods, or propositions which are neither true nor false, is not a deficiency. In cases such as these, presumably, there is, according to constructivism, nothing (no truth) – for example, that there is an even number that is not the sum of two primes – to discover or fail to discover. (One would have thought, although that if there was an even number that was not the sum of two primes, it would in principle (i.e., given enough time) possible to come across it, it would be more difficult to establish that there was not such a number.)

Sometimes constructivists, instead of saying that mathematical propositions which cannot be shown to be true or to be false are neither true nor false, say that there cannot be any numbers except those that can be constructed. It may be that the proper conclusion to be drawn from the fact, if it is one, that infinite numbers, for example, cannot be constructed, would be that sentences containing signs that purport to stand for infinite numbers are meaningless sentences. In that case, too, there would, as meaningless sentences do not express propositions, also be no true propositions for God not to know.

I find constructivism difficult to accept. If there is an infinite number of numbers, it is difficult to see that God could not see all of them laid out in front of him, so to speak, and be able to tell by inspection, rather than by proof, whether or not there was a counter-example to Goldbach's conjecture. (The constructivists can reply that there can be no such thing as seeing an infinite number of numbers unless infinite numbers can be constructed, which they cannot be, so perhaps the argument begs the question.)

If constructivism is true and infinite numbers cannot be constructed, it would follow that God could not have existed for ever – i.e., for an infinitely long period of time, and so either God could not be infinite, or the proposition that God is sempiternal (and perhaps the proposition that he is eternal) would be neither true nor false. I do not think it would follow that God could not exist for ever in the future, for this notion would not involve an infinitely large aggregate's actually existing, but only the more limited idea, which constructivism admits of, that there may be a sequence of operations that never need be terminated.

(vi)   Omniscience and Anti-realism

Constructivism, when transported to philosophy, becomes anti-realism. I shall define anti-realism, narrowly, as the view that propositions (whether mathematical ones or not) that can neither be shown to be true nor shown to be false are neither true nor false. (Presumably 'shown to be true', where what is in question is the truth of an empirical statement, must be taken to include 'increasing or decreasing the probability of'.)

According to realism, what exists or is true is one thing, what we believe or can discover to be true is another. This means that it is possible that there might be a reality about which we could discover nothing. However, according to anti-realism, truth, even in empirical matters, is related to what can be found out, much as, according to constructivism, truth in mathematics is related to that of which a proof can be constructed. It would follow that there could not in principle be any reality 'out there' – a phrase of doubtful meaning – which we cannot find out about, for no propositions purporting to be about such a reality could be true; such propositions would all be neither true nor false.

Ignorance of the truth of propositions which can neither be shown to be true nor to be false is not a matter for regret, for there is no such truths to be discovered. Such propositions are neither true nor false. It should again follow that it is no bar to God's omniscience that there are such propositions.

Anti-realism and Verificationism

Verificationists, with their too casual slogan that the meaning of a statement is (the method of its) its verification, might seem to have a different attitude from anti-realists to there being propositions the truth of which it is in principle impossible to discover. A verificationist would say (or ought to) that the sentences which purport to express propositions answering to this description are, despite appearances, meaningless. The anti-realist would say that the sentences are meaningful, but the truths these sentences claim to express are not truths (though they are not falsehoods either).

When applied to the proposition that there is a God, the supposition that there is no empirical evidence for or against this proposition has lead verificationists to say that the sentence 'God exists' is meaningless. Perhaps it should lead anti-realists to say that the proposition that there is a God is neither true nor false.

This latter view might have the following implication for faith. It normally could not be desirable to cultivate belief in propositions that are not true; this is why it is better to investigate propositions rather than uncritically to believe them. But perhaps it could be desirable to cultivate belief in propositions (for example, the proposition that God exists) if they are not true because they are neither true nor false. It is difficult to see, however, that it could be possible or sensible to cause oneself to believe a proposition one believes to be neither true nor false, for believing something means believing that it is true. Faith may be another matter.

(vii)   Omniscience and Relativism

Relativism is the view that a proposition is not just true or false; it is true relative to something, and so may be true relative to one thing, and false relative to another.

Let us suppose that what the truth a judgment is relative to is the person making the judgment in question, or to his point of view. In that case, something might be true for God, but false for men. Relativism would also have the consequence that knowledge is relative, for knowledge implies truth, so if truth is relative, so must knowledge be. Hence God may know something, because it is true relative to him, but I not know it, not because of my ignorance, but because it is not true relative to me. Indeed, I might know something to be true, because it is true relatively to me, that God knows to be false, but false relatively to God. God's omniscience, presumably, is then reflected not in the fact that he knows the truth of all true judgments, stop, because there are no judgments that are true without qualification, but only in the fact that he knows the truth of all the judgments that are true relatively to him.

One might wish to suggest that perhaps God at least knows that it is true in relation to me that, say Richard III murdered the princes in the Tower, which suggests that, though it is not true in relation to God that he did, it is true in relation to God that it is true in relation to me. But if all truth is relative, truths about truths should also be relative. If so, then it might be true in relation to me that it was true in relation to me that Richard III murdered the princes, but true in relation to God that it was false in relation to me that he did.

However, it is a feature of truth that, if someone asserts something and you agree with him, you must also both be prepared to assert what he asserts, and to agree that what he asserts is true. For example, if someone says that Richard III murdered the princes, and you agree that he did, you must yourself be prepared both to say that Richard III murdered the princes, and that what this person said, when he too said this, was true. (If one uses the past tense, this is not to indicate that that Richard III murdered the princes was true in the past, but to indicate that it was asserted in the past.)

But if truth is only relative to a person, then it ought to be possible to hear someone say that Richard III murdered the princes, and to think that that Richard III murdered the princes is true only in relation to him. Hence, if relativism is true, you ought to be prepared to say that someone else had truly said that Richard III did not murder the princes, and also to hold that that he did murder them is true (because it is true in relation to you). I myself think that consequences such as these show relativism to be absurd. One ought not to entertain possibilities such as that, though in relation to me it is true that I did not sin, in relation to God it is true that I did, and that as a result I am, in relation to God, in Hell, though in relation to myself, I am in Heaven

I suspect that some relativists are confusing holding that truth is relative with certain other views. Some people may have reasons for believing something that other people do not have. Some people have the concepts that enable them to say or think things that other people, without these concepts, cannot say or think. And what one person may permissibly believe without evidence another person may need evidence for. (I do not have space to go through all the possibilities.) Evidence, meaning and justification are relative, though truth itself is not. But relativism is such an enormous subject that I cannot deal with it more than very briefly in the space at my disposal.

Omniscience and the 'Absolute' Point of View

If one accepts relativism, it follows that there is no such thing as the absolute point of view, sometimes supposed to be God's point of view. The absolute point of view is that point of view from which it is supposed to be possible to obtain knowledge that is not relative. If relativism is false, everyone's point of view is the absolute point of view. There is nothing superior, vis-à-vis relativism, about God's point of view, for it is not the case that ours is relative but his is not. Neither point of view is relative; it is just that God knows more than we do – perhaps infinitely more – and knows things in different ways from the ways in which we know what we know them. But our knowledge is just as absolute as God's.

Of course, it is literally true, though not relatively true, that we look out on the world from different points of view. This fact will mean that our knowledge is different, for each will be able to see things that the other cannot see, and to have intercourse with people and ideas that the other cannot have intercourse with. But, though it means that we will have different pieces of knowledge about different things, acquired in different ways, it does not mean that what knowledge we do have is relative.

(viii)   Reasons for Thinking that Propositions about the Future are Neither True nor False

Historically one of the most vexed questions concerning God's omniscience is whether he knows propositions about the future. The reason why it has been supposed that God might not be able to know the truth of such propositions is not that his cognitive capacities are not up to it, but because it has been supposed that such propositions are neither true nor false.

There have been two main reasons why many philosophers have been tempted by this view.

First, it has been thought that to say that a proposition is true is to say that it corresponds to a fact, and there are no future facts for propositions to correspond to. (This difficulty would arise only for a correspondence theory of truth, according to which truth consists in correspondence with fact.)

Secondly, it has been supposed that if propositions about the future are true or false, propositions about the future behaviour and fates of people will be true or false now, and that in that case the people these propositions are about will not be able to avoid their fates, fates which these propositions now say are going to be theirs. To do so would involve changing the truth value of a proposition, which is impossible.[7] If it is true now that Oedipus is going to kill his father and marry his mother, then it must be that, when the time comes, he will kill his father and marry his mother, and there is nothing he or anyone else can do to avoid this being his fate. The only alternative to this unwelcome conclusion is supposed to be to hold that propositions about the future can neither be true nor false. (I shall postpone discussion of this second difficulty in my next chapter (chapter 17).)

(ix)   Can Propositions about the Future Correspond to the Facts?

I am inclined at this point to short-circuit what could be a long discussion of the different theories of truth by endorsing a remark of Aristotle's. Aristotle said that to say of what is that it is not, or of what is not that it is, is false, while to say of what is that it is, or of what is not that it is not, is true.[8] Adapted to apply to propositions about the future this remark becomes: he who says of what will be that it will not be, or of what will not be that it will be, says what is false, but he who says of what will be that it will be, or of what will not be that it will not be, says what is true.

Philosophers may have thought that there were no facts for propositions about the future to correspond to, because they have confused a fact about the future with a future fact. There may be (as yet) no future facts, but this does not mean that there are no facts about the future, and it is facts about the future, rather than future facts, that one would expect propositions about the future to correspond to.[9] Statements about future battles are not made true by future facts about battles, but by facts about future battles. (It could be argued that the word 'fact' is being used ambiguously. In the sense in which one can be an accessory before or after the fact, 'fact' means something like 'deed'. In this sense, there can be future deeds, for some deeds will certainly be performed in the future.)

To my mind the only serious rival to a correspondence theory of truth is the view that the difference between asserting a proposition and asserting that that proposition is true is stylistic. It seems likely that this theory of truth will have no difficulty with propositions about the future.

God's Omniscience and the Third Truth Value

If every proposition is either true or false, then all that is needed is a two-valued logic (the two values in question, naturally, being true and false). If propositions about the future are neither true nor false, two-valued logic will not apply to them. If there is a third truth value (usually called neuter), one possibility is that the proposition that God is omniscient is itself neither true nor false. (The proposition that God knows that he is omniscient may also take truth value neuter.)

The case for saying that the proposition that God is omniscient is neuter is this. To say that God is omniscient is to assert the hypothetical proposition that, if a proposition is true, God knows that it is true. It has been held[10] that, in that case, if the consequent is neuter, the proposition that God knows the antecedent must be false. In that case, it has been suggested that a hypothetical proposition with a false antecedent and a neuter consequent is neuter.

This view, however, begs the question, viz. that God does not know that propositions about the future are neither true nor false. I have already suggested that there is a strong case for holding that God does not need to know the truth of propositions that are not true, including those that are neuter.

But I think that there is an even stronger case for thinking that, if propositions about the future are neither true nor false, and take truth value neuter, God would not be omniscient. For God would be greatly handicapped in framing a satisfactory plan of action if he could not know propositions about the future. For framing such a plan would involve his knowing what would happen in the future if he were to do certain things in the present. And if all proposition about the future were equally neither true nor false, God would never have any good reason for preferring the view that one possible outcome would materialise to the view that it would not. In that case, it seems obvious that there would be things that he would need to know but would not know, and so he would not be omniscient.

(x)   Circumstances in Which God Could be Omniscient Even if Propositions About the Future are Neither True nor False

Even men can have beliefs to the effect that certain things are going to happen in the future, and sometimes these things actually do happen. I can see nothing impossible in supposing that there might be a man whose beliefs, for some extraordinary reason, always turned out to be correct. (Such a man would not be omniscient about the future, for many things would happen which he did not believe were going to happen, and some things, which he believed were not going to happen, might nevertheless happen. (I am having difficulty in avoiding saying that his beliefs about the future always turn out to be true, though they do not amount to knowledge, for this would be question-begging.))

The man we have been envisaging would always be right about the future. It is a fact not usually remarked upon that if someone asserts something, and is right, it does not follow that what he says is true. If I guess that the doll's name is 'Anona', and it is, then I can properly be said to be right (as can my guess), but it does not follow that I am asserting something true. (It may be that this is because to say that what someone said was true would be to offer him congratulations which, in the case of only guessing, he would not deserve.)[11] Hence, even if propositions about the future are nether true nor false, it would not follow that there could not be a person who was always right about the future. If so, it would be very unlikely that it is just coincidence that this person was always right. This suggests that he would not have believed what he did had not the future been what it was going to be. But if that he is right is not a coincidence, it seems wrong to withhold the epithet 'knowledge' from his beliefs.

(The fact that this man's belief that it would rain would be brought about by a future event might suggest backwards causation. I have suggested elsewhere[12] that the future event itself and the belief that this future event was going to occur might be joint effects of the same cause. But if the hypothetical proposition that had if it not been going to rain, I would not have believed that it was, is true, it may be all that is necessary for knowledge. (God's 'beliefs' could be brought about by backwards causation only if he were sempiternal rather than eternal. If he is eternal, the difficulty about his 'beliefs' being 'caused' by the future is no worse than their being caused by the present or the past.))

The propensity of the man I have been talking about always to be right about the future would seem to be an extremely useful accomplishment. Are we then to deny it to God? It may not strictly speaking be implied by his definition, but it would be quite extraordinary to withhold from him any attribute which did not follow from his definition. And I think it would be very odd if God did not possess the capacity to be always right about the future. If a man could possess this capacity God must possess it. A being who did not possess this capacity would be inferior to a being who did, and no being can be superior to God.

It seems to me that it would be quite extraordinary if God's mind were a blank, so to speak, about the future. Even mine is not. And if we suppose that God has some reasonable expectations about the future, as even I have, it is difficult to see how one can stop short of maintaining that he must reasonably expect everything that happens to happen. A reasonable expectation is not the same thing as knowledge, but a reasonable expectation that always turns out to be correct must be counted as knowledge. If we suppose this, then I do not see why we should stop short of maintaining that God knows that everything that will happen will happen. In that case God must be omniscient.

(There is a possibility that God knows the truth only of those propositions about the future that can be inferred from propositions about the present. In that case, but not otherwise, if determinism was true, he would know everything about the future. If he could know only those propositions abut the future that could be inferred from the present, and determinism were false, he could not know everything about the future.)

(xi)   Assessment of the View that Propositions about the Future are Neither True nor False

A great deal of the menace has already gone out of the view that propositions about the future are neither true nor false if – as we have seen that it is – it is quite compatible with people's having correct beliefs about the future, with their being able to have rational expectations about the future which are correct, or even having knowledge of the future.

However, I think that the view that propositions about the future are neither true nor false is not true, though, as we have seen, there is an important element of truth in it. It is not true because we can speak of a person all of whose beliefs about the future turn out to be true. This implies that they were true, even before they turned out to be true, though, until the predicted event occurred, no-one was in a position to say that they were true.[13] Some propositions about the future, such as that there will be an eclipse tomorrow, may even be described as facts.

Nevertheless, I think we are more reluctant to say 'It is true that it will rain tomorrow' than to say simply 'It will rain tomorrow'.[14] Normally, if we ask someone whether a piece of information we have already been given is true, we expect the person we ask to be in a better position to pronounce upon it than was our first informant. This suggests why it is that people are much more reluctant to say 'It is true that it will rain tomorrow' than they are to say 'It will rain tomorrow'. When they say the second, they are just claiming to be able to make predictions which have a reasonable chance of being right. When they say the first, they are (very often) claiming to be in a position to confirm or pronounce judgment upon a prediction that has already been made. In the case of propositions about the future, about which knowledge is notoriously difficult to obtain, people may be so reluctant, before the event at least, to claim to be in a sufficiently superior position, in respect of knowledge, to the person who asserted the proposition about the future in the first place, that they will hardly ever – though I think not never – say, before the event, that these propositions are true.

This does not mean that that it is raining is not (logically) equivalent to that it is true that it is raining. They only seem not to be because they have different conversational implications. Saying 'It is true that it is raining' conversationally implies things about the speaker which are not implied by saying 'It is raining'. It implies this in that sense of 'implies' (conversationally implies) in which my saying 'It is raining' implies that I believe that it is raining, and that (usually) I believe that the person to whom I am speaking does not know that it is raining. That it is raining, said by Tom, and that it is raining, said by Jones, can be logically equivalent even if their utterances have different conversational implications. (They must have different conversational implications, if only because Tom is conversationally implying that he, Tom, believes that it is raining, and Mary is implying that she, Mary, believes it is raining.) Hence that it is raining, asserted by Tom, and that it is true that it is raining, asserted by Mary, can be (logically) equivalent, though the conversational implications of the first about Tom are different from those of the second about Mary.

(xii)   Omniscience and Time

Two Difficulties in Combining Timelessness with Omniscience

There are two difficulties with God's omniscience, each concerning the view that God is eternal in the sense that temporal predicates do not apply to him. One is that a timeless being could not have such knowledge as that today is Friday. For if God believed on Friday, but not on Saturday, that it was Friday and believed on Saturday, but not on Friday, that it was Saturday, his beliefs must have changed. The other difficulty is that God, if he is timeless, cannot know certain truths about time. Knowledge of such truths as that today is Friday could be had only by a person who is in time. For example, God's knowing that today is Friday would imply that he existed on Friday, and so had a temporal position, which he does not have. The function of the word 'today' is to refer to the day contemporaneous with the temporal position of the speaker, which position God does not have.

These Difficulties do not Apply to a Being who is Merely Eternal and Changeless

These difficulties would not apply to God who is in time, but is everlasting, in that he does not have a beginning or an end. (One would have to add that he was also changeless.) Such a God would not have any difficulty in having knowledge of time. He would simply exist at all times. Nevertheless, if the notion of a changeless but everlasting God is too 'mundane' to be wholly satisfactory, the question must arise whether an eternal being could know propositions about time such as those I have mentioned. It is not enough that an everlasting and unchanging one could.

Reply to the Difficulty Concerning Change

One can argue that the first difficulty disappears if one distinguishes between propositions and sentences. All propositions are timelessly true, so his changelessness puts no obstacle in God's knowing any of them. God always knows the proposition that, on Friday, he expresses in the words 'Today is Friday'. It is just that the words in which he has to express this proposition, viz., 'Today is Friday' change. This is because they express a different proposition on Saturday from the one they would have expressed on Friday. But changes to words are not changes to God, for words are just ordinary parts of the universe.

Reply to the Difficulty Concerning Knowledge of Time

If we apply what has been said to the second difficulty, we can say that God can know what I know when I know that Caesar is to be assassinated tomorrow, but that if, for some inscrutable reason, he wished to express this fact, he would have avoid using the word 'tomorrow', and put it in words other than ours. He would have to put it, perhaps, in the words 'Caesar is to be assassinated on the Ides of March'. 'Tomorrow' only refers to the Ides of March if used by a being speaking on the day before the Ides of March, which God, if he is timeless, does not do. But anyone, which includes beings who do not exist in time, can refer to the day of Julius Caesar's assassination with the expression 'the Ides of March'.

However, though this gets rid of the problematic expression 'tomorrow', it leaves us with the words 'is to be assassinated', which also indicate the speaker's position in time in relation to the event talked about. (It indicates that the event in question is, at the time of the utterance, in the speaker's future). Such a temporal position an eternal God would not have.

Timeless Sentences

Some philosophers have held that there is a timeless sense of the verb 'to be', in which, for example, we can say such things as that two and two are four or that objects attract one another in proportion to their mass. The date at which this proposition was asserted in words is irrelevant to its truth.

But, if there is this timeless sense of 'is', it can be used only with propositions, such as the proposition that two and two are four or the proposition that objects attract one another in proportion to their mass, that are not about any specific time. There may be no timeless way of putting something like 'Caesar was assassinated on the Ides of March' (which does refer to a specific time) without either using pidgin English, or revealing the temporal position of the speaker.

Let us try pidgin English. It is, indeed, possible to try to *invent* a way of putting things that does not reveal the temporal position of the speaker. The artificial expression 'Rain on the Ides of March' gets across the fact that there is, was or will be rain on that day, without revealing whether the person speaking is speaking before, simultaneously with or after that event. But it does not look as if 'Rain on the Ides of March' is equivalent to the proposition an ordinary person is asserting when he says 'It will rain on the Ides of March'. In any case, such alleged timeless propositions would not enable us to say everything about time that we need to say. For very often our hearer will need to know whether rain is to be expected, or is occurring or has occurred, and this 'Rain on the Ides of March' does not tell him. And it looks as if there is no way in which such information can reliably be supplied without using either tenses or expressions like 'tomorrow' or 'the day succeeding this utterance'.[15] Hence the difficulty about God's omniscience remains.

The Function of the Problematic Words is to Refer to Events, Not to Make Assertions about Them

There does not seem to be anything necessary to make true any of the four propositions mentioned above – i.e., the supposed timeless truth 'Rain on the Ides of March' and the three tensed truths that it will rain, is raining or has rained on that day – other than that rain should occur on the Ides of March. The function of the tenses and words like 'today' is not so much to determine what is being asserted as to enable the asserter, in order to state some supposed fact about an event, to refer to it by its relation to his own position in time. This will enable his hearer to locate it, if his hearer knows what this position is. It is an obvious corollary of this fact that the speaker, when he refers to an event in this way, must disclose what his position in time is. Indeed, his description would be useless to anyone not knowing what that position was.

Using locutions that depend on knowledge of the speaker's position in time has advantages. If one always knew the date, and knew that one's hearer also knew the date, and also knew that we both knew the date of the event the speaker was talking about, we could use timeless sentences to convey all the information we needed to covey. But since we do not always know these things, using expressions such as 'tomorrow' enables us to avoid this inconvenience. By saying 'Tomorrow' instead of 'On 5 November' we do indicate that the event talked about is future, and how far into the future it is, which the tenseless 'Happens on 5 November' does not do.

But, though the use of tenses and of words that refer to the dates of events by reference to the speaker's time reveals the speaker's temporal position, it does not assert what that temporal position is. (Speaking in a nasal voice reveals the fact that one has a cold, but does not assert that one has a cold.) Nor, when we use such expressions as 'in a week from now' do we *assert* what the speaker's position in time is.

If Tom and Mary are sitting on either side of Jane, a Russian spy, Tom can say 'The lady on my right is a Russian spy' and Mary can say 'The lady on my left is a Russian spy', and the truth of these remarks will stand or fall together. Tom, in using the fact that Jane is on Tom's right to refer to Jane, is not asserting that she is on his right (though anyone hearing him using the expression can infer from his using it that Jane is on his right). That Tom is not asserting that Jane is on his right is shown by the fact that, if Jane were to sit somewhere else, she would cease to be on Tom's right, but remain a Russian spy. What Tom is asserting of Jane would remain true, though Tom would not be able to say it in the words 'The lady on my right is a Russian spy'; the phrase 'the lady on my right' would no longer pick out Jane.[16] What 'the lady on my right is a Russian spy' would suffer from, if there were no lady on Tom's right, would be reference failure, not falsity.[17]

The difficulty for the view that that it was raining yesterday and that it is raining today are equivalent is that one can infer, from the 'truth'[18] of 'It is raining today'[19] that the rain referred to is contemporaneous with the utterance of the sentence, whereas one can infer from the 'truth' of 'It was raining yesterday' the different fact that the rain occurred a day earlier than its utterance. The answer to this difficulty may be that these different propositions are not part of what the person using sentence asserts, but only propositions the truth of which that can be gleaned from hearing these sentences being uttered. From the fact that we can glean from hearing someone say 'Londres est joli' that the speaker is French, but glean from hearing someone say 'London is beautiful' that the speaker is English, it does not follow that what they are asserting is different. Since different things are not inferred from the truth of the assertions, but only from the event of their being asserted, it is wrong to infer that the assertions are different.

It is also no objection to the view that the sentence 'It rained on Tuesday' asserts the same proposition as the sentence 'It rained yesterday' (if yesterday was Tuesday) that you can infer the day on which it rained from the former, but not from the latter. For the first proposition does not *assert* that the day on which it rained was 'Tuesday', and the second does not *assert* that the day on which it rained could be referred to by 'yesterday'. (The proposition that Tom has toothache does not assert that Tom's name is 'Tom', though it can be inferred, from hearing anyone use that particular sentence to assert the fact that Tom has toothache, that Tom's name is 'Tom'.)

God would have to use such words as 'today' and 'now' in order to be understood by us. This does not mean that he commits himself to having a position in time. All that it means is that there are some words that he cannot use to formulate what he knows without there being the possibility of misleading an unthinking hearer into believing that he is in time when he is not. Doubtless courtesy and consideration and the necessity of being understood will demand that God uses temporal words when addressing his creatures, who would have difficulty in understanding him otherwise. If he tells us to prepare to meet our doom, it is enough that our dooms should be future to us: they do not have to be future to God also. I can perfectly well know what Tom knows when he knows that he has a cold, though, if I am addressing Tom, I have to express my knowledge in the sentence 'You have a cold', or, if I am speaking to someone other than Tom, to use the sentence 'He has a cold'. Different inferences can be made from the occurrence of the acts of using these sentences, but this does not affect the truth of what these sentences say. Hence the truth of God's remark that it is now raining is not affected by the fact that it appears to reveal a position in time that God does not have. And the fact that his temporality does not prevent him from asserting temporal facts may also mean that his temporality does not prevent him having knowledge of such facts. (God is in something like the position of a journalist writing for readers who will read what he writes later than he writes it; should he use 'tomorrow' to refer to the day after that on which he writes or the day after that on which he is read?)

Hence God *can* know the truth of the proposition that Tom is asserting when he says such things as 'It is now raining'. For he will know that rain is occurring simultaneously with the time Tom refers to when he uses the word 'now'. The difficulty is only that God cannot express what he knows in English without appearing to reveal a position in time that he does not have. God could not be accused of deception on account of his using English when speaking to the English. What else could he be expected to do? And few Englishmen I hope would believe that he was English because he deigned to communicate with them in English.

(xiii) Omniscience and Space

It would be absurd to suppose that God was located in some one part of space rather than another. Hence the same difficulties for God's omniscience that concern time also arise over space. If Tom is on a journey between London and Cambridge, he can think to himself, as he travels, such things as 'There are some beautiful trees over there' or 'There is a station here'. It could be argued that perhaps an eternal God could not know what Tom knows when Tom knows that there is a station here, for 'here' is a device for referring to the area in the vicinity of the speaker, and since God is not in any place, there can be no places in his vicinity. God could (ignoring the difficulties about tense that we have discussed), know that there is a station at Appleby's End, but to know this is not to know what Tom knows when he knows that there is a station here, even when Tom is at Appleby's End. For one thing, Tom might know that there was a station here, but not know that he was at Appleby's End. (This, incidentally, raises questions concerning Tom's knowing that he is at Appleby's End, and Tom's knowing that the station he is at is called 'Appleby's End'.)

God would, however, always know where on his journey Tom was, for example that he was at Appleby's End, and would always know whether the propositions that Tom believed, and expressed in words like those aforementioned, were true or false.

If there was a word 'ereh' ('here' spelt backwards'), used to refer to the place in the vicinity of the speaker, even when the speaker was not oneself, God could know that Tom was ereh, when Tom knew that Tom was here. Hence God can know what Tom knows when Tom knows that there is a station here. God can know both that there is a station at Appleby's End, and that there is a station ereh.

It looks again as if what Tom knows and what God knows are different. From that there is a station here it looks as if it is possible to deduce something about the whereabouts of the speaker (viz. that he is by the station), whereas from that there is a station at Appleby's End this is not possible. And it looks as if from that there is a station at Appleby's End it is possible to deduce the name of the station, but not from that there is a station here. But one must not confuse deducing something from what is asserted with deducing something from the event of its being asserted (or from deducing something from what is being asserted coupled with facts about the event of its being asserted). From the fact that one can deduce from one occasion of asserting what one cannot deduce from another it does not follow that what is being asserted is

different on the two occasions. Hence what God knows, if God knows that
there is a station ereh at Appleby's End, and what Tom knows, when he knows
that there is a station here, can be the same.

(Though one may sidestep the difficulties presented by an eternal being
having knowledge of time by holding that God is not outside time, but merely
sempiternal, it is not possible to sidestep the difficulties presented by a
non-spatial being's having knowledge of space by saying that he is not outside
space. For to give God a particular spatial location, such as 'on Mars' or 'in
the bathroom' would be absurd. But if, on the other hand, he is at all spatial
locations, then he would be as little able to use words like 'here' and 'there' as
if he were not anywhere at all.)

(xiv)   How Does God Know What he Knows?

The reader's attention is drawn to the remark about impiety that starts this
chapter. What I am doing here can again be regarded as exploring the human
concept of an omniscient being.

Very roughly, men know truths because they are self-evident, because
they can be inferred from what is self-evident, because they can be known by
observation or introspection, because they infer them from what they can
observe or introspect, because they are hypotheses that explain what is
observed or introspected or because (what amounts to much the same thing)
postulating them completes a partial regularity, because they have been told
them by someone who has discovered them in one of these ways, or because
they themselves have previously found them out in one of these ways and
remember them. (We may have some 'implanted' beliefs, and that there is a
God may be one of them, but implanted beliefs, as we have seen, need to be
justified in some other way than by their merely being implanted, i.e., in one
of the ways aforementioned.)

God's Observation of the External World

God's observation can be divided into his perception of the external world
and of the contents of his creature's minds. (I shall prudently say nothing
about his knowledge of the contents of his own mind.) His perception will be
discussed in chapter 22. I shall just mention that there is a difficulty for God's
perception in the fact that perception, to be veridical, must mean that the
perceiver's state of mind depends upon the existence and state of the thing

perceived, which would appear to conflict with God's alleged aseity or independence of the world. But it is possible that his aseity may mean that his existence is not dependent on anything else, not that events (if any) that happen to him are not so dependent.

God's Knowledge of What Men Feel

It has been argued that God cannot be omniscient, because he cannot know what it is like to feel certain emotions, or suffer pain, because he can neither feel nor suffer them, and, unless he does, he cannot have concepts of such emotions.

I am inclined to agree that if (a personal) God was not aware of certain things, he would not have the concepts that applied to them, and that if he did not have these concepts, he could not know truths about the things in question. But it is not obvious to me that God could not be aware of our emotions without having them, and get his concepts from this awareness. Men cannot be aware of others' emotions, or of pain that they do not themselves feel, but it is not obvious to me that God might not be aware of emotions that he does not himself have. (The reader is referred to a case (to be discussed in chapter 20) where one personality of the multiple personality which was Sally Beauchamp could be aware of things felt and thought by other of her personalities, without thinking that she felt or thought them herself.)[20] In that case, one of Sally Beauchamp's personalities might have been directly aware of the emotions of the other without accepting them as her own, and the same might be true of the relationship between God and men. (The distinction between I and thou in a multiple personality is not clear cut, which, I suppose, suggests by analogy a more pantheistic view of God than one to which Europeans are accustomed.)

If one allows that God feels emotions, he could get his concepts of emotion from his own emotions. An eternal God could not feel emotions, but an everlasting one could. People who believe in a personal God think of him as having emotions, for example anger or love. But there are also certain emotions – envy say – that we think that God cannot have, partly because to feel envy is a defect, and partly because God could not have the beliefs that give rise to envy, for example, that someone else is (undeservedly) better off than he is.

God's 'Acquisition' of Concepts

God's acquiring the concepts necessary for omniscience raises another difficulty concerning his eternity. People take time to acquire these concepts, and God is outside time. It is a necessary condition of having a concept that one has a disposition to recognise an instance of it if presented with one, and recognition consists in knowingly using the appropriate word for the thing in question, or behaving appropriately in some other way (e.g., eating it if it is bread and one is hungry, throwing it on fire if it is water and one wants to put the fire out). Since there are difficulties about an eternal being behaving at all, since behaving usually takes time, there would be resultant difficulties about such a being's having a disposition to behave in appropriate circumstances. These difficulties, however, would only apply to an eternal being to whom temporal predicates did not apply; they would not apply to an everlasting being. (Eternity and everlastingness are discussed in chapter 18.) There would also be the difficulty that a person would not really be showing that he possessed a concept of fire unless it were the case that he would not have called fire 'fire' unless there had been fire. This implies a causal connection between what a concept-possessor does and the world, which might seem to conflict with possessing aseity.

Can God Infer?

Where an eternal being is concerned, it may be that though he cannot infer, which takes time, there is a relation of atemporal dependence of some of his 'beliefs' (the 'premises') upon others (the 'conclusions'). A temporal but everlasting being could infer, but the concept of such is excessively anthropomorphic. An omniscient being could not infer.

God's Memory

God presumably will remember everything he once knew. An omniscient being cannot forget, for to forget is to cease to know. In man, remembering involves a causal connection between what he came to know on some previous occasion and his remembering it. Hence an eternal God could not remember, though an everlasting and unchanging one could. An omniscient being, of course, could also not come to know. Hence remembering in this case would have to consist in God's retaining knowledge that he had always had. Again, it is just possible that there might be a non-causal dependence of some of God's beliefs upon others – for example, the 'premises' which he remembers and the 'conclusions' which he 'infers'.

God's Knowledge on Testimony

An omniscient God could not know anything as the result of being told, as he knows everything already. (It follows that we do not need to confess our sins in order to inform him of the fact that we have sinned, but confession may nevertheless be good for us, and improve our relationship with the image of God which many of us have.)

Is God's Knowledge of the Future Obtained by Inference?

Men can observe only what is present, and have to remember, infer or frame hypotheses about the past and the future, which in men is again a temporal process. This raises the question about God's knowledge: can he observe only the (our) present and past, and can he infer – as would seem to be necessary if he can observe only the present – if inference is a temporal process?

God could have 'inferential' knowledge of the future if he is either everlasting rather than eternal, or if there is relation of temporal dependence upon his 'believing' the propositions (about the future) that he infers and his 'believing' those propositions from which he infers them, and which he knows without inference. It is not obvious to me that an eternal God might not see the whole past and present laid out in front of him, as we observe a specious present with which some parts occur after others.[21] His observing the whole of eternity would then be like our observing the motion of the second hand on our watch. (On views of time according to which the apparent change from future to past to present is some kind of illusion, there would still, I think, be the problem of God's understanding the illusion.)[22]

(xv)   Conclusions

There are a large number of things that God cannot know, but this fact does not mean that he is not omniscient. This is often because there is something wrong with the questions to which God does not know the answer. There also is nothing wrong with not knowing the truth of a proposition that is neither true nor false. Some of God's knowledge will depend upon his knowledge of what his intentions about the future are.

Propositions about the future must be either true or false, though it is sometimes improper to say which they are, even when you think you know what is going to happen. In any case, the view that God is inerrant about the future can be retained in the view that all his 'beliefs' about the future will turn out to be true, and the view that he is omniscient about the future retained in the view that nothing can happen in the future without his previously having had a 'belief' that it would happen. It really does not matter whether God knows whether or not it is true that there will be a sea battle tomorrow, so long as he knows whether or not there will be one.

There is no reason, so far as we have yet seen, why an eternal being should not have all the knowledge of time that we have, though he cannot, without misleading his hearers, express this knowledge in the words in which they would express it. I have left the question whether God's omniscience is compatible with human freedom to the following chapter.

Notes

1   This is discussed by Anthony Kenny, 1979.
2   The difference between knowing how (which really should be described as knowing how to) and knowing that was first pointed out by Gilbert Ryle, 1971.
3   It has been suggested that unfulfilled conditionals are plausible, rather than true, but 'plausible' means 'seems true', so what cannot in principle be true also cannot be plausible.
4   J.J.C. Smart, who believes that unfulfilled conditionals have assertion conditions but not truth conditions, asks me whether that if 2+2+5 had been true, there (my example) would have been a crock of gold under the floorboards is the contradictory of if 2+2+5 had been true, there would not have been a crock of gold under the staircase. I suspect that if I discovered, to my surprise, that there had been a crock of gold under the floorboards I would say that the former unfulfilled conditional was true, and the latter false. That there would still have been a crock of gold under the staircase, even if 2+2=5 had been true, is another matter. If there is no connection between 2+2=5 being true and there being a crock of gold under the floorboards, then this unfulfilled conditional would have truth conditions but not assertion conditions.
5   I am told by Elizabeth Anscombe that the example is Hugh Mellor's.
6   If one ties the true to the provable and the false to the disprovable, and some propositions can be neither proved nor disproved, this leads to a rejection of the principle of bivalence, that every proposition must be true or false. The meta-mathematical doctrine known as constructivism leads to the same conclusion.
    I am told that Goldbach's conjecture may have been proved.
7   We have already seen (in chapter 9) that this is impossible in the case of propositions about the past. If it has been supposed to be possible in the case of propositions about the future, this is because it has been wrongly supposed that propositions such as that Tom was going to go, but is going to go no longer, are propositions about the future. In fact they are merely propositions about Tom's present plans or intentions.
8   *Metaphysics* 7 27.
9   But see J.J.C. Smart, 1966.
10   By A.N. Prior, 1957.

11 The view that every proposition is either true or false is better expressed, in the case of guesses, by saying that every guess is either right or wrong. This suggests that the view that propositions about the future must either be true or false may be replaced by the view that all beliefs about the future must either be right or wrong.

12 In Harrison, 1978–9.

13 Incidentally, one should not forget the concessive use of 'true' as it occurs in 'It is true that it will rain tomorrow, but I shall go out all the same'.

14 I have discussed this problem in my 'Mackie's Moral 'Scepticism'', reprinted in *Ethical Essays*, Vol. I, Avebury Series in Philosophy, 1993.

15 Someone can infer from 'Rain on 22 September 2000' that rain is future, but only if he knows what date it is now.

16 It follows that Russell's theory of descriptions, according to which anyone saying 'The lady on my left is a Russian spy' is asserting that there is one and only one lady on his left (and that she (the lady on my left) is a Russian spy), is not only circular, but just wrong.

17 See P.F. Strawson, 1952, especially pp. 184–90.

18 I put 'truth' in quotes because, strictly speaking, I do not think that truth is a property of sentences, but of the propositions that sentences are used to express.

19 It might be more accurate to say, not that it is possible to infer this from the truth of the proposition expressed by the sentence 'It is raining today', but from the truth of this proposition, together with the fact that it is expressed in the words 'It is raining today'.

20 This argument presupposes an old-fashioned distinction between simple and complex ideas, according to which God and other persons could have complex ideas, like that of being a phoenix, without having been aware of any things (phoenixes) to which they applied, but not have simple ideas like azure without such awareness.

21 The specious present is that section of time within which we can observe movement as opposed to inferring it, as we can observe the motion of the second hand of a watch, but have to infer the motion of the hour hand.

22 For such a view the reader is referred to McTaggart, 1934 and Mellor, 1981. An opposite view is put forward by Prior, 1967.

17 Providence, Foreknowledge, Will and Fate[1]

(i) Introduction

It is a further difficulty with God's omniscience that it is not possible for any of God's creatures to do anything other than what he foresees they will do. It has been supposed to follow from this that men cannot help the things they do, so that they ought not to be blamed for doing them. (One ought not to be blamed for what one cannot help.) It would then further follow that God was acting unjustly in sending those who act wickedly to Hell. (It is unjust – and also ineffective – to punish people for doing what they cannot help.) Since it seems more obvious that people *can* help the things they do than that God is omniscient, it might be concluded that God cannot be omniscient, or alternatively that there is no omniscient God.

This argument can be put in a slightly different way. If, provisionally, one defines a free action as one the agent can help, then, if God knows that I am going to perform a free action in the future, it would follow that the action I was going to perform must be a free action (because what God knows to be the case is that I am going to perform a free action). Hence if the fact that God knows that I will perform an action entails that it is not free, the action will be both free and not free, which is a contradiction. But what entails both a proposition and its contradictory must be false. Hence God can never know what free actions I am going to perform.

(ii) Clarifications

Some Preliminary Distinctions

As a preliminary to a discussion of the bearing of God's omniscience (and also his omnipotence) upon the problem of the freedom of the will, it is desirable to consider the bearing of the *truth* of propositions about the future upon man's freedom. (A proposition, of course, can be true without being known to be true.)

To begin with I wish to introduce some distinctions. By '*naïve fatalism*'[2] I shall mean the view that the outcome of man's actions will be the same whatever he does, including whatever he does in order to prevent this outcome. For example, it is a fatalistic view that if a bullet has my name on it, it will kill me, whether I stand up in my trench or take cover, and that, if I am fated to be hanged, some twist of fate will bring to nothing all my attempts to avoid my fate. It may even be that my very attempts to avoid my fate bring that fate about.

By '*sophisticated fatalism*' I shall mean not the view that I am fated to be hanged whether I commit murder or not, but the view that what I am fated to do is to commit murder and as a result be hanged.

A person has 'commonsense freedom' (or 'commonsense free will', or is 'commonsensically free', or just 'free') if, among other things which I shall discuss in more detail later, he can help what he does, if what he does is affected (in the right kind of way)[3] by his wants and beliefs, if threatening to punish him has some deterrent effect, if it is not useless to try to persuade him to do something else, and if, if he had tried hard enough to do something other than what he did, he would have succeeded. These things are true of a free action, like eating one's breakfast, but not true of something we cannot help, like blinking, breathing or growing.

It is also a commonsense view that some actions are right and others wrong, that men have duties, are under an obligation to do some things rather than others, that there are things that they ought (prudentially or otherwise) to do, and that human beings really do deserve to be praised, blamed, punished or rewarded for their actions. (These latter are moral beliefs, as opposed to those mentioned in the previous paragraph, which are factual ones.) And I think that it is a further commonsense view that we are free to do things in a sense (which I think is the sense of the commonsense view) that does not make it either unjust or ineffective to praise people or blame them, to punish them or reward them. If *ought* implies *can*, it is a commonsense view not only that there are things that men ought to do (and avoid doing), but things that they can do (and avoid doing).

By '*metaphysical freedom*' (or 'metaphysical free will') I mean my alleged ability to set aside all the causal forces acting upon me, such as my desires, habits, the state of my brain, my poor upbringing, weak character and dissolute life and, in spite of these forces, do something other than what I actually do. An action that is metaphysically free is uncaused, or not completely caused.

It is caused by an act of will, but the act of will itself is not caused, or not wholly caused, by anything. (A metaphysically free action, however, must have effects, or it would accomplish nothing, but the series of effects would have a 'first cause'; the first cause would be the (allegedly) metaphysically 'free' action of the agent.)

By '*determinism*' I mean the view that everything in the future, including the actions of men, is fixed, either by the fact of its being foreknown, or (more usually and plausibly) by the causal factors knowledge of which enables them to be foreknown. If determinism is true, nothing, including the actions of men, could have happened other than what did happen, any more than, if taking arsenic causes death, anything other than death can happen if one has taken arsenic.

It is worth pointing out immediately that to say that nothing else could have *happened* is not to say that nothing else could have been *done*, even in those cases when what happened was that something was done. To say that nothing else could have happened or been done is to indicate that there are facts about the past that preclude anything happening other than what did happen or was done. (Something's being done is a kind of happening.) To say that nothing else could have been done is (usually) to say that to do anything other than what was done was outside the agent's power. There is, as I shall argue later, no contradiction in saying that one's information (say information about the motivation of the agent) shows that nothing else could have happened or been done other than the agent's freely choosing to do what he did.

The Relationship Between Free Will and Determinism

If you consider the relation between free will (either commonsense or metaphysical free will) and determinism, it is possible to hold that free will is either compatible (this view is known as 'compatibilism'),[4] or is not compatible with determinism. If you think they are compatible, then you can either think (a) that freedom and determinism are both true,[5] (b) that they are both false, or (c) that the view that we have freedom is true and determinism is false or (d) the view that we have freedom is false and that determinism true; but those who think that freedom and determinism are compatible usually also seem to hold that freedom and determinism are both true. If freedom and determinism are incompatible, they cannot both be true, which rules out (a) and one must make up one's mind whether determinism is true and we do not have freedom – which is what is held by the view known as 'hard determinism' – or that we do have freedom and that determinism is consequently false.

I shall call this latter view 'libertarianism', though I am not sure that this is how the word is usually used. It should not be forgotten that, though if two views are incompatible they cannot both be true, they can both be false, which, though it rules out (a), permits (b), (c) or (d). If, however, freedom and determinism are not just incompatible, but contradictories, this also rules out the possibility, (b), of their both being false.

'Soft determinism' is the same thing as compatibilism, with the added claim that determinism and freedom are both true. I shall be more concerned in what follows with whether determinism and freedom are compatible than with whether determinism is true, though I think it is true. That we have commonsense free will seems to me to be just obvious.

Whether Actions are Metaphysically Free: Preliminary Remarks

If actions are free in the metaphysical sense of free, it seems likely that it would be impossible for God or humans to predict them. If they can be predicted only by a knowledge of their causes, and they are not completely caused, they cannot be predicted from knowledge of their causes, though God may know what metaphysically free actions human beings will perform in some way other than basing it on such knowledge. (Perhaps, if he can perceive the future in some way, he can actually perceive our performing them.)

I shall argue that it is not necessary for actions to be free in the metaphysical sense for it to be sensible for human beings to take precautions against possible future mishaps, for them to be to be able to do things other than they do, for men to have duties, and for praise and blame, punishment and reward to be both merited and effective. I shall argue that there is no reason why an action that is commonsensically free should not be both completely determined by its causes and foreseen. An action may be as inevitable as is death after one has taken a large quantity of arsenic, and still be commonsensically free. Indeed, both freedom and determinism are (compatible) commonsense beliefs, and belief in freedom is certainly true.

(iii)   Kantian Compatibilism

According to Kant, there is a noumenal self and a phenomenal self. He was forced into this extraordinary position, he thought, by his attempt to justify synthetic *a priori* knowledge. He thought that all propositions were either analytic or synthetic. Analytic propositions, such as that all bachelors are unmarried, contained their predicate (being unmarried) in their subject (bachelors). Knowledge of analytic truths was justified by logic. We could not deny analytic propositions without contradicting ourselves. For the same reason, they gave us no information about the world, which was why they could be known without observing the world, and so were *a priori*. Synthetic propositions, such as that bachelors do not live as long as married men, since they do give us knowledge of the world, usually have to be justified empirically, by observation and experience (including making experiments.)

But Kant thought that there was a class of synthetic propositions that can be known *a priori*. Since synthetic *a priori* propositions – propositions such as that every event has a cause and that substance is permanent – do give us information about the world, they can be known neither in the way – by logic – that analytic propositions can be, nor in the way – by observation – that synthetic propositions can be, and so stand in need of justification.

Kant's way of justifying them was to say that they could be known *a priori* only because experience conformed to our knowledge, rather than, as was usual, the other way round. We knew that every event must have a cause because a world in which some events had no causes could not be experienced. But it followed from this that the world we experienced was moulded by our own cognitive faculties; being so moulded, it was distorted by our perceiving it, and so was mere appearance or phenomena, and not 'really real'.

But this, or so Kant thought, meant that the self we experienced, the phenomenal self, was itself mere appearance, and that there was a real self which was not the object of experience. This allowed Kant to maintain that, though acts of the phenomenal self were determined – they had to be, because Kant thought he had shown that every event that could be experienced, i.e., every phenomenal event, including human actions, has a cause – acts of the noumenal self could at the same time be free. He was therefore a compatibilist, though a somewhat eccentric one.

The main difficulty with Kant's view is that of explaining how free acts of the noumenal self synchronise with the corresponding acts of the phenomenal self. For if an act of the phenomenal self, say accepting a bribe, were determined, and the corresponding act of the noumenal self were free, this means that, by an act of the noumenal self, I could have refused the bribe. But if I had refused it, my noumenal self would have had, in order to preserve the fact that every event has a cause, to manufacture a whole new set of past causes leading up to my refusing it. This would involve attributing enormous powers to the noumenal self, including the power of altering the past.

But what is even more serious, different acts of one noumenal self, and acts of different noumenal selves, might not synchronise. For the man who was tempted to offer me the bribe could have resisted this temptation, in which case the act of his noumenal self would have had to produce a whole set of past antecedents leading up to his not offering it. In this case his phenomenal self and mine would be out of step; in the event of my rejecting it, which I am supposed to be able to do, I would have rejected a bribe which he would not have offered. This story is preposterous.

(iv)   Fatalism, Determinism and Physicalism; Determinism Taken for Granted by Ordinary Men

According to Lucretius, the universe contained only atoms and the void. According to some more modern versions of materialism, all truths about the universe are entailed by the truths of physics, and could in principle be deduced from them by a being with sufficient intelligence and sufficient knowledge of physics. I do not think that these views are true, but it is a matter of exaggerated importance whether they are true or not. This is because a sensible physicalism is the view that atoms are the only substances there are, and everything else (including, I think, the void) has to be regarded as something other than substance. Numbers, classes, quadratic equations, differential calculus, hurricanes, influenza epidemics, the Aurora Borealis and the equator are all examples. This means that physicalism can allow the existence of almost everything there is by the simple expedient of saying that these things do not belong to the category of substance. Minds, for example, exist, but are not substances, but statements about minds are statements about the ways in which certain substances, viz., the bodies of human beings, behave. But if you allow that there are all these things, it is a matter of relatively minor importance whether physicalism is true or not.

Not only is physicalism of exaggerated importance, it is not true. Indeed, it is the product of man's ineradicable tendency to oversimplify, and is not even plausible. This is an old-fashioned argument, but when we look out on the world, or inside ourselves, what we come across is a universe of expanses of colour, flashes of light, blasts of sound, pervasive odours, images of the aforementioned things, twinges of conscience, pangs of jealousy, and the pains of unrequited love. There is not the remotest resemblance between these and the world of protons and electrons, which are too tiny to be seen, and between which there are (in relation to their size) vast expanses of empty space.

Fortunately for determinists, the case for determinism is independent of the truth of physicalism. Indeed, since in any case the world of electrons and such is not supposed to be deterministic, the case for determinism is actually strengthened by rejecting physicalism. The case for determinism is simply that it is a commonsense assumption – probably biologically favoured by the fact that making this assumption is of great survival value to mankind – that every event has a cause. This assumption is manifested in the commonsense attitude of always expecting that when different things happen on different occasions, there must be some difference in the events leading up to these happenings, which difference is expected to explain why the outcomes are different.

If my car does not start on one occasion, but does on another, we assume that there must be some difference between the two occasions, which explains why it started on one occasion, but not on the other. For example, there might have been sand in the carburettor or petrol in the tank on only one of the two mornings. If Tom is late on one occasion and not on another, one takes it for granted that there will be some difference between the events leading up to the two occasions which explains why he was late on one day but punctual on the other. Perhaps on one day his alarm clock had stopped, but was going on the other. It is facts such as these that enable us to understand and predict (or retrodict) what happens in the universe. And such facts not only enable us to understand the universe, which would be unintelligible otherwise. By being able to produce the causes of things we (sometimes) are at least enabled to produce them, and so to control the universe at least to a limited extent. Common sense not only believes all this, but also believes that the fact that the latter example concerns the behaviour of a person does not mean that he is not able to help performing the action that is explained. If the reason why Tom was late on the second day is that his school had ceased to exact retribution for lateness, it does not follow from the fact that his behaviour is caused that it is not free.

This commonsense belief is very fully confirmed by experience. There is therefore, incidentally, no need for us to bother about the truth of quantum theory. If a commonsense belief in determinism is true, it will be true even if, on account of quantum theory, determinism is not true at the microscopic level. But, incidentally, if determinism is true at a macroscopic level but false at a microscopic one, this is a further reason for thinking that everything that is true cannot be deduced from modern physics. In actual fact, no-one has got very far at all with predicting the behaviour of physical objects, including people, from a knowledge of quantum mechanics; the laws which govern the behaviour of macroscopic objects are accepted because they conform to observed and experimental fact and explain things in their own right. In any case, whether or not an agent could have helped doing what he did can be discovered in a commonsensical way, without any knowledge of whether, among the causal antecedents of his action, some electron in his brain took a path that could not have been predicted. And such things, if quantum theory is true, will occur among the causal antecedents of every action, whether the agent could have helped it or not.

Hard Determinism and Naïve Fatalism must be Rejected

Hard determinism and naïve fatalism must both be rejected, and for much the same reason. If the hard determinist goes to the lengths of denying that we choose, deliberate, hesitate between alternative courses of action, perform acts of moral struggle, and feel justified remorse, the reply must be that we know perfectly well that we do perform acts of choice, i.e., choose some things in preference to others, and that very often such choices are preceded by a process of deliberation, involving hesitation and moral struggle. Furthermore, we know perfectly well that no-one compelled us to do what we did, and very often we know from past experience that we would have done something else had we wanted to. There is an enormous amount of experience that confirms us in thinking that we do have control over our actions. We know that praise, blame, punishment and reward, do affect what we do (though perhaps not as much as strict moralists think). If a philosopher, as the result of a complicated chain of argument, comes to the conclusion that we do not, then it must be replied that what he says flies in the face of common experience, and so must be rejected.

Naïve fatalism must be rejected for the same reason that hard determinism must be rejected. We know perfectly well from past experience that what we do does affect the future. We know that cabbages are more likely to grow if they are watered during droughts than if they are not, that children are more likely to read if they are taught than if they are not, that patients suffering from pneumonia are more likely to survive if they are given antibiotics than if they are not. We know perfectly well that we are more likely to be hanged – or at any rate gassed, injected or electrocuted – if we commit murder than if we do not. Naïve fatalism, according to which there is no point in bothering about the future, like hard determinism, flies perversely in the face of everyday experience of its falsity. For this reason, it is both much more likely that naïve fatalism and hard determinism are false than that the complicated philosophical arguments meant to establish them are valid and have true premises.

Sophisticated Fatalism True

However, sophisticated fatalism, as will appear from what follows, is true. Sophisticated fatalism, be it remembered, was the view that Oedipus was not so much fated to kill his father, whatever he did to prevent it, but to kill his father, but also to perform all the actions that led up to his killing his father and from which his father's death resulted. Hence, if he would not have killed his father if he had not left Corinth, he was fated not only to kill his father, but also to leave Corinth. If he would not have left Corinth if he had not supposed – wrongly – that his father lived in Corinth, then he was fated to believe that his father lived in Corinth. If he would not have killed his father unless the oracle had predicted that he would kill him, then it was fated that the oracle would predict that he would. And so on.

The interesting task, which we shall attempt to accomplish later in this chapter, is to unravel the confusions that produce sophisticated fatalism, and to consider whether its truth has any bearing upon the morality of the fated actions, or upon the morality of the actions, which are also fated, of praising or blaming, punishing or rewarding them. I shall argue later, which should please those who wish to go on doing the latter, that it does not.

Sophisticated fatalism, if you detach it from the view that there are personal or quasi-personal fates who deliberately and perhaps maliciously decide what will happen to us, is very little different from soft determinism, which holds that freedom and determinism are both true.

(v) God's Foreknowledge and Man's Freedom: The Avoidability of Fates

For reasons that will be apparent later, I propose to do something that is seldom done, though it ought always to be, and consider the avoidability of fates and the freedom of actions separately. Let us first consider the avoidability of fates.

Truth Determinism

But first I shall consider briefly fatalism resulting not from alleged determination by knowledge, but from alleged determination by truth. There is an argument for fatalism that goes as follows: every proposition, including propositions about the future fates of human beings, must be true or false.

Hence it must be either true or false that I will, say, be hanged. But, if it is true that I will be hanged, I must, when the time comes, be hanged. There is nothing I can do – for example, avoid committing murder – to make what is already true false. What will be, will be.

This notorious argument, deducing the unavoidability of fates from the fact that it is true that they are going to happen is open to the following objections.

(1) Truths about the future are not among the causes of an event. Astronomers trying to predict eclipses do not predict them from a knowledge of truths to the effect that they are going to occur. Rather, they predict eclipses from facts about the behaviour of the sun, the earth and the moon, knowledge of which facts results in their coming to the conclusion that certain propositions about eclipses are true.

(2) It is not the fact that it is true that an eclipse is going to occur that makes the eclipse occur; rather it is the occurrence of the eclipse that makes true the proposition that it was going to occur.

(3) I discussed in chapter 16 the objection to truth determinism that propositions about the future were neither true nor false. We saw there that there was no need to resort to this view to avoid fatalism. There are other objections to truth determinism, but since they also apply to knowledge determinism, I shall not consider them here.

Knowledge Determinism

The argument to fatalism from knowledge is only slightly different from the argument from truth. It is that every proposition about the future is either known by God to be true or known by God to be false. Since what God knows is going to happen must happen, and what God knows is not going to happen cannot happen, nothing can be done to prevent the things God knows will happen from happening. What is known to be going to be must happen, and what must happen must happen. Hence, if there is going to be an eclipse or I am going to be hanged, God must know that this is so, and so no-one can do anything to prevent the eclipse or my hanging. (There is no difference in principle between what human beings know will happen and what God knows will happen, though human beings, unlike God, do not know everything that is going to happen.)

The fatalistic conclusion of this argument is just as incredible as it was when it was the conclusion of the argument from truth. It will not only follow that, if God knows that I am going to die of cancer, I will die of lung cancer whether I smoke or not; I will be killed by the bullet with my name on it whether I keep my head down or walk about upright in my trench.

This argument cannot be criticised on the grounds that foreknowledge of the future is not possible. Foreknowledge of the future, including foreknowledge of people's actions, is possible. We have a great deal of knowledge of the behaviour of inanimate objects, and of people whom we know well. If we were not for the most part able to predict the behaviour of both, we would not have survived. (We saw in the preceding chapter that foreknowledge of the future would be possible even if propositions about the future are neither true nor false.)

But there are a number of things that may have gone wrong with the argument from knowledge.

(a) Knowledge has no effects The fact that it is known what fate is going to befall someone can, no more than the fact that it is true that this fate is going to befall them, be what causes this fate. My knowledge that the prime minister is going to lose an election is not normally among the causes of his losing it. It is usually the other way round. It is the causes of his losing it that make him lose it, and my knowledge of the causes of his losing it that cause my knowledge that he is going to lose it.

It looks as if, in exceptional circumstances, certain kinds of knowledge that the prime minister will lose the election can cause him to lose it. Perhaps enough people's knowing that other people know that he is going to lose it may cause them to vote against him, and so make him lose it. But this appearance is delusory. (The same problem is raised by the more august problem of whether the knowledge that the dictatorship of the proletariat is inevitable can produce the dictatorship of the proletariat.)

(1) It is not their knowledge, but their belief, that he will lose it that makes him lose it.

(2) It is not the *knowledge* that he will lose it that by itself causes him to lose it, but their *actions* of voting against him, which actions would have the same effect whether they were based on knowledge or not. And if they thought he would lose, but did not vote against him, he would not lose.

(3) In certain cases, it may be someone's belief that other people know that a certain fate is going to befall him that makes him bring about that fate. For example, my belief that my child believes that I am going to bring her a present – her 'fate' – may be what makes me bring her a present. (In fact, it could be argued – I think wrongly, on account of the circularity involved – that she may know that I am going to bring her a present, because she will

argue, correctly, that whenever I believe she believes I am going to bring her a present, I bring her a present.)

(4) If I believe that someone else is going to do something, and communicate this fact to someone else, then what I have, say, written down, may fall into the hands of someone who then makes my prediction come true. For example, someone's predicting that I will be hanged may put the idea of committing murder into my head, and so be a (part) cause of my murdering someone, perhaps because I believe that I will be hanged anyway. But again, this does not mean that my belief that he would do it amounted to knowledge. Nor does it mean that, if it did amount to knowledge, the action was produced by the knowledge; it was rather produced by my having seen it written down. Writing something down, unlike the mere fact of the knowledge that is written down, which cannot have effects, can have effects.

To sum up, beliefs may have effects, but knowledge cannot, for a belief will always have the same effect, whether it amounts to knowledge or not. It looks as if there are two apparent exceptions to this generalisation. (1) If Tom rightly believes that Mary knows that he will do something that results in a certain fate befalling him, then Tom must do what Mary knows he will do, for otherwise it will not be the case that she *knows* he will do it. What I shall shortly say under (b) answers this difficulty. (2) If I act on knowledge, my action must to that extent be successful, but if I act merely on belief my action may be unsuccessful, because the belief may be false. This, since success and failure are different outcomes, means that knowledge may have a different effect from belief. The answer to this difficulty is that it is not the knowledge but the fact that is foreknown that causes my success. For example, if I know that my partner has all the spades I must be successful if I bid a grand slam in spades, whereas, if I only believe that he has them all, I may fail. But it is not the knowledge that he has all the spades, but his having all the spades, that causes my success.

There are, of course, numerous stories in which the very attempts on the part of various people to avoid fates that appeared to be foreseen for them brought those very fates about. But in those cases it is not the foreknowledge of the fate that brings about the fate foreknown, but the attempts to prevent it.

It follows that it is not God's foreknowledge of the fates of his creatures that causes the fates, and so not his foreknowledge of them that prevents his creatures from being unable to avoid them. God's foreknowledge will determine his own actions, and so the actions of others, if he brings these about, but it is not foreknowledge so much as 'forebelief' that determines them, for God would act in the same way if he knows he will if, *per impossibile*, he merely believes that certain fates are going to befall him. And it is not God's foreknowledge or forebelief that are the immediate causes our action, but the actions which God performs as a result of his foreknowledge or forebelief.

(b) The fact that something is foreknown entails that it will happen The fact that, if a man does not do what it is foreknown that he will do it will not have been *foreknown*, is like the fact that if a bachelor marries he is no longer a bachelor. This does not prevent his marrying (except in the exceptional case when the only women he knows do not wish to marry bachelors). All it does mean is that, if he should get married, he will no longer be a bachelor. And all that follows from the fact that what is known must be true is that if the action apparently foreknown were not to come to pass, it would no longer be proper to say that it had been foreknown. This no more prevents anyone from performing the action in question than being a bachelor prevents anyone from getting married.

In the special case when what I foresee is some action of my own, the agent's act is always liable to be affected by the foreknowledge of it. Of course, if I do foresee it, this means that I must do it, because what is not done cannot be foreseen. But if my beliefs about my actions were always to interfere with my actions, this would simply mean that I could never have true beliefs about my future actions. But obviously, I quite often have true beliefs about my future actions. I quite often believe such things as that I will have lunch, and do in fact have lunch, being much too hungry to do anything so silly as to try to falsify my own (or anybody else's) predictions about what I will do. (Doing this would not always be silly.) One might wish to hold that this belief cannot amount to knowledge, because if it did I would be unable not to have lunch. But I can no more be compelled to perform an action by the fact that I know I am going to do it than someone else can be compelled to perform an action by my knowledge that he will do it. And, if I know that I will have lunch because I know that I shall, when the time comes, want to have lunch more than I want to do anything that would mean my not having lunch, my knowledge that I will have lunch does not mean that I am compelled to have it. I am doing what I want to do because I want to, and if I do what I want I am not compelled. Of course, we all believe that we can, if we wish, refute determinism by doing something that it is predicted, even predicted by ourselves, that we will not do. If we do something unpredictable, of course, we cannot have done something that we knew we would not do. But we can think we know that we will have lunch, and decide to refute our own prediction by not having lunch, and then get so hungry that we have lunch despite wanting to refute this prediction – as someone else who knew us better than we knew ourselves knew we would.

(c) Causal connection between belief and what the belief is about Though there need be no causal link between a proposition, such as that the prime minister will call an election, and the event of the election for the prediction that he will call one to be correct, it is arguable that there must be a causal link between the belief that the prime minister will call an election and the election if this belief is to qualify as knowledge. (This is because their conjunction must not just be coincidence.) In the case of a proposition about the past, over and above (1) someone's believing that there was a sea battle in the Aegean two and a half millennia ago and (2) there being a sea battle then, there has to (at least) (3) be a causal connection, between the battle and the belief, such that the believer would not have believed that there was a battle had there not been a battle. Otherwise it will be mere coincidence that his belief is true, and the belief will not amount to knowledge. In the case of the sea battle, there must be a causal route – *via* witnesses recording it, scholars preserving the records of it, historians writing about it, publishers publishing their books and booksellers selling them, from the battle to the belief that there was a battle, if the belief is to count as knowledge. But it is the occurrence of the past battle that produces the knowledge that there was a past battle, not the knowledge that there was a battle that produces the battle.

Could this solution be reversed over future battles, as fatalism would seem to demand? Could the knowledge that a sea captain is going to order a battle be what makes him order the battle, so apparently taking away his freedom to do anything else? I think that, both in the case of knowledge of the past and knowledge of the future the belief in question has to be such that it would not have been held unless the event retrodicted or predicted had happened or was going to happen. In the case of knowledge of the past the event is part cause of the belief, but in the case of knowledge of the future it cannot be, because the future cannot cause the past. Nevertheless, in both cases there is a causal link, though in the case of the knowledge of the future sea battle the battle and the knowledge of the battle are joint effects of the same cause. If I know that there is going to be a battle, then my belief that there is going to be a battle must be based on knowledge of the causal factors that will produce the battle. My belief that these factors obtain must cause my belief that there will be a battle, and my belief that these factors obtain must be caused by the fact that these factors obtain. Hence the factors that produce the battle also produce my belief. This does not mean that the battle is caused by my belief (indeed, it is knowledge, not belief) that there will be a battle, although it is caused by something. Whether the fact that the sea captain's decision to order a battle has causes, even though it is not caused by anyone's knowledge that there will be a battle, will be discussed shortly.

(d) Fatalism and the modal shift fallacy The argument for fatalism from foreknowledge commits the modal shift fallacy. The modal operator 'is necessarily true' governs a different proposition in the conclusion from the one it governs in the premise. In the premise, what it governs, and what is therefore necessarily true, is the whole hypothetical proposition that *if* something is known to be going to happen, it is going to happen. It does not follow from this that the consequent of this proposition is necessarily true, i.e., it does not follow that what is known to be going to happen is necessarily going to happen. For example, from the fact that it is necessarily true that if God knows that Tom is going to be hanged he is going to be hanged, it does not follow that the consequent of this hypothetical proposition, viz., that Tom is going to be hanged, is necessarily true. It would be the necessary truth of the proposition that Tom is going to be hanged that would, if anything does, mean that Tom could not avoid being hanged.[6] The same applies to the statement that what will be will be. It is necessarily true that if something is going to be it is going to be (L(A is going to be -> A is going to be)), but not even true that, if something is going to be, it is necessarily going to be (if A is going to be → L(A is going to be)).

(e) Freedom, hypothetical and subjunctive propositions If Mary has forgotten her dancing shoes, then it follows that, if it is her dancing class today, she has forgotten her dancing shoes. (It also follows, incidentally, that if it is not her dancing class today, she has forgotten her dancing shoes, though making this remark would be pointless, as, if it is not her dancing class today, she will not need her dancing shoes.) It does not follow from the fact that she has forgotten her dancing shoes, however, that if it had been her dancing class today, she *would* have forgotten her dancing shoes. Indeed, if it had been her dancing class today, she might well have remembered them.

Similarly, if Oedipus is going to kill his father (and marry his mother), it follows that if he is going to go to Thebes, he is going to kill his father. It also follows that if he is going to stay in Corinth he is going to kill his father. (Indeed, it follows that if he is going to kill his father, he will kill his father whether he stays in Corinth or not.) But it does not follow from this that it does not matter whether or not he leaves Corinth. For though he is going to go to Thebes and kill his father, the subjunctive that he would kill his father even if he were to stay in Corinth does not follow. And all that follows from the fact that it was foreknown by the oracle that he would kill his father is the former of these two propositions (the indicative), not the latter (the subjunctive). Hence there is no reason to suppose that there was no point in his staying in Corinth, because he would have killed his father anyway. If he had stayed in Corinth, indeed, he would not have killed his father, because his father lived in Thebes.

Philosophers may suppose that Oedipus had to kill his father because it is logically true that nothing can happen which will prevent what is going to happen from happening. If the grass is going to be wet, it can be deduced that, if the grass would not be wet if it were to rain, it cannot rain (i.e., it cannot be that it will rain.) Analogously, if Oedipus is going to kill his father, but would not kill his father if he were to stay in Corinth, it can be deduced that it cannot be that he will stay in Corinth.

It looks as if, if it cannot be that Oedipus will kill his father follows from this that no-one, including Oedipus, can prevent Oedipus's killing his father and marrying his mother, but this does not follow. All that follows is that Oedipus will kill his father for whatever reason, and whether Oedipus can avoid killing his father or not will depend on what this reason is. One thing that follows is the disjunctive proposition that either attempts to prevent his killing his father (like Oedipus's father's attempt) will be made and fail or that no attempts will be made, and from this it does not even seem to follow that Oedipus is unable to avoid killing his father. All that follows from the fact that Jack the Ripper will cut Mary's throat – and some of my readers may think that this is about time – but would not have cut her throat if he had tried not to, is that he will not try not to.

If the reason why Oedipus kills his father is that no-one, including Oedipus himself, tried to prevent this from happening, then it certainly does not follow that if anyone had tried to prevent his killing his father, this person would not have succeeded. Indeed, even if attempts to prevent Oedipus's killing his father made under the impression that his father lived in Corinth, were made, and failed, it still would not follow that the killing could not have been prevented. Different kinds of attempts might have been successful. For example, if Oedipus had tried to avoid killing his father by staying in Corinth instead of going to Thebes – which latter is how he did try to prevent it – he would probably have succeeded. That if he had stayed in Corinth, he would not have killed his father, does not follow from the fact that he did go to Thebes, did kill his father, that it was foreordained that he would do both these things, and foreknown that he would do the latter. Hence from the fact that Oedipus's unfortunate action was foreseen by the oracle it does not follow that nothing could have been done to prevent it.

(f) Avoidability The fact that our future fates can be foreseen does not entail that there is not a perfectly good commonsense distinction between those things in the past which, though they were going to happen and could have been foreseen, could have been prevented, and those which could not have been. The same applies to the future. There is a perfectly good distinction between eclipses, which are going to happen and cannot be prevented, and atomic explosions, which, though they are also going to happen, could be prevented. There is no action such that, if a human being *were* to perform it, it would result in a future eclipse's not occurring. With atomic explosions, however, there are a large number of human actions such that, *if* they were performed, an explosion which is going to occur would not have occurred. Hence if God knows that there is going to be an atomic explosion, it does not follow that there are no steps such that, *if* they had been taken, the explosion would not have occurred.

But, unfortunately, these steps do not have to be taken. Indeed, with knowledge, as we have seen it was with truth, it is a necessarily true proposition that, if something is going to happen, nothing can happen which will result in this thing's not happening. But, to repeat, from the fact that it cannot be that these steps will be taken, i.e., from the fact that nothing can happen other than these steps not being taken, it does not follow that if they *were* to be taken, an atomic explosion *would* be prevented. From the fact that our fates are foreseen it does not follow that they could not be prevented. All that follows is that it cannot be that they will be prevented.

Hence, if God knows that we are going to be hanged, though it does follow that it cannot be that our hanging will be prevented, either by ourselves or by anyone else, it does not follow that our hanging cannot be prevented in the sense that no-one will be able to prevent it. We could have prevented it ourselves by not killing someone, and our parents could have prevented it by bringing us up better, the police by being more vigilant, and the person we killed by hiring a bodyguard. What does follow is that our parents will not in fact bring us up better, that the police will not in fact be more vigilant, and that the person we are going to kill will not hire a bodyguard.

(vi) God's Foreknowledge and Man's Freedom; The Avoidability of *Actions*

It seems cold comfort to be told that there are steps which are such that, if they were to be taken, various fates, disastrous or otherwise, would be avoided, if we are then told that it cannot be that anyone will perform the acts which result in these fates being avoided. This brings us from a discussion of the avoidability of fates to the avoidability of actions.

Any argument for fatalism concerning the fates which are the outcomes of actions, can, since to perform an action is itself a special kind of fate, be applied to the performance of actions, when these actions are themselves outcomes of other actions, as they often, though not necessarily always, are. It would be tedious to repeat all the objections to fatalism concerning fates other than actions, and apply them to fates such as actions. There are, however, since to perform an action is different kind of fate than to be hit by lightning, special considerations for and against the avoidability of actions.

As I have suggested, an omniscient being's foreknowing our future is possible in one of two ways. He can 'infer' it from his knowledge of its causal antecedents and the laws that connect events that take place at one time with those that take place at another. Alternatively, he might be able to 'see' the future laid out in front of him, and know what is going to occur in the same noninferential way that human beings know about some things happening in the present. In either event, the future *seems* inescapable. In the first case it seems to be inescapable because it is determined by the causes that enable an omniscient being to foreknow it. In the second case it seems inescapable because, if an omniscient being can actually 'perceive' it, it must be (going to be) there to be perceived. (In neither case is the action determined by God's foreknowledge of it. We can conceive of a being who is omniscient but impotent, and such a being would foreknow everything that occurred, but would determine none of it.)

However, just as there are reasons for thinking (a) that it does not follow from the fact that fates (including actions) can be foreseen that they cannot be prevented, there are also reasons for thinking (b) that it not does follow from the fact that it could be that the actions that would have prevented the fates are not going to be performed that it is not within the agent's power to avoid these fates.

It has been held that the distinction between those actions we could have performed and those actions that we could not have performed is a distinction between those actions which will be modified by a suitable change in our desires and/or our beliefs, and those actions which cannot. For example, we cannot help breathing, because we will breathe whatever inducements are offered to us to stop breathing, or however harmful to ourselves we believe the consequences of breathing would be. (Perhaps we will be overheard by an enemy searching our house unless we stop breathing, but we go on breathing just the same.) But we can help smoking a cigarette or spitting on the pavement because, if we had wanted not to smoke, or had believed that we would be immediately shot if we were to spit, we would not smoke or spit.

Hence the distinction between actions that are within our power and those that are not is like the distinction between speeds at which a car can be driven and those it cannot. To say that it can reach 100 mph means that if certain conditions – say the accelerator's being pushed further down – which are not fulfilled, were fulfilled, it would be travelling at 100 mph. That it cannot reach 200 mph means that if these same conditions were fulfilled it would still not reach 200 mph. Similarly, the distinction between those loads a rope can carry and those that it cannot is the distinction between those loads which are not heavy enough to make it break, if it were subjected to them, and those loads which, if it were subjected to them, would cause it to break.

Let us suppose for the sake of argument that the above analogy is correct, and an action is one that we can help doing if it is true that we would not be doing it if either our desires or beliefs (or both) were different from what they are. In that case some of the actions which are such that, if they were performed, would result in our avoiding the pleasant or unpleasant fates that are going to befall us, are actions that we can help.

For an action to be one that we do not have to perform it is not necessary that it should be unforeseeable. All that is necessary is that, in order to foresee it, the foreseer must take account of the motives and beliefs of the person who performed it. If one could predict what someone would do without knowing what this person's motives or beliefs were, this could only be because he would do it however badly he wanted not to, or however disadvantageous to himself or those he loved he believed performing it would be. But this would mean that this person was unable to perform the action in question. Indeed, it can be argued that a free action is not an undetermined action, but precisely one that is caused by the motives and beliefs of the agent.

An action that is determined by our wants and beliefs is one we want to do, in a rather wide sense of 'want'. I say 'a wide sense' because we sometimes say, perhaps from a sense of duty or to prevent undesirable consequences, that we do things that we do not want to do. But we are prepared to admit that what we do, in spite of a want not to do it, we really do want to do, because we do want to do our duty, or do want to avoid the disastrous consequences of doing what we want. And doing what we want may involve doing what we do not want, for we may do something, perhaps our duty, because, although we want not to do our duty, we want to do our duty more. But if we would not be doing something if we did not want to do it, then the action must be one we could avoid. But to assert the unfulfilled conditional proposition that if our wants were different we would be doing something different from what we did is compatible with its being foreseen that we would do what we did, and its being foreseen that we were actually going to have the wants that resulted in our doing what we did. On this hypothetical view of human freedom, then, God's foreknowledge of man's future actions is compatible with human freedom. (The hypothetical view of freedom does not mean that an action is free only so long as we want to perform it. To say that an action is free is categorically to assert the hypothetical proposition that we will perform it if we want; just as to say that something is a request bus stop is to assert, categorically, that a bus will stop at it if asked to do so.)

(The fact that one can predict an action from knowledge of the motivation of the agent does not mean that the agent is unable to avoid performing this action. Indeed, the fact that one could not predict the action without such knowledge would often mean that, without this motivation, the agent would perform no action, or some other action, and so mean that he is able not to do it. The fact that I did something because I had a motive for doing something would mean that what I did was free, as when I injure someone from jealousy. (Acting freely from a motive is a special case of my action's being caused by this motive. It would not mean that the action was free in those cases when the motive has other effects than those it has from being the motive from which I act, for example, the effect of making me ill, which actually diminishes my freedom.)

A hypothetical account of freedom very similar to the view that has just been stated is the view that we are able to do something if we would have succeeded in performing this action, if we had tried. There is little difference between these two views, if, if our wants and beliefs were different from what they are, we would try, and if, if we did try, we would succeed.)

(vii)   Difficulties with the Hypothetical Account of Freedom

I shall discuss some major difficulties with the hypothetical account (and remark upon one or two others).

First Difficulty[7]

The first is that actions that, on the hypothetical account of freedom, we are able not to do may be actions that are made inevitable by circumstances that we cannot help. For our beliefs and our desires may be caused by the state of our brain, which we usually cannot help, and the state of our brain caused by our genes, which we also cannot help, and this in turn by our parents' genes, which were fixed long before we were born. It may be inevitable that, if our brain is in a certain state, we will want food, and, if we eat food because we want to, we are doing what we want, and so our action is one which, on the hypothetical account of freedom, we do not have to do. But it is argued that if we have no control over the wants that cause it, the action, despite the hypothetical view, is not free.

The correct reply to this criticism, I think, is to say that it is just false that if what we do is caused by something we cannot help, it must itself be something we cannot help. For example, the fact that I would not have shot a policeman had my parents not, when I was little, instilled in me a fear of the police, a fact which I cannot help, does not mean that I could not help shooting the policeman (though it may mean that my responsibility for this is reduced in some way).

Perhaps it looks as if we cannot help what is caused by what we cannot help because, when we say that an action is produced by our physiological state, it would be true that we *would* be unable to help it if it were produced by our physiological state directly. But our actions are sometimes produced by our physiological states only 'indirectly', because they produce the wants which in their turn immediately produce the actions. In that case, among the causes of the actions there are wants; and any action which we perform from a want must be one that we did not have to perform, and so is free, whether or not we have any control over the factors that produce the wants.

For the same reason, the reason that the fact that an action is determined by events over which we have no control does not mean that it is an action over which we have no control, our powers are not limited by the fact that God has foreseen what we will do and we have no control over what God foresees. (We cannot perform an action if we are unable to perform any action that is a necessary means to performing that action, but in this case causing God not to have known that I am not going to rob a bank is not a *means* to robbing a bank, as is not having a jemmy or dynamite or a skeleton key or an escape car.)

Second Difficulty

The second major difficulty with this hypothetical account of freedom is that there are cases when it is true that I would have done something if my wants or beliefs had been different from what they were, but obviously false that I could have refrained from performing the action in question. For example, if I am unable to give up heroin, it is my very craving (want) for heroin that makes it impossible for me to stop taking it. Hence it is true that if I lost my desire for heroin I would not take it, but nevertheless false that I am able to give it up. It is my intense want for heroin that is the very reason why I cannot give it up. Again, if the reason why I cannot telephone someone is that I do not know his telephone number, then it is true that an alteration of my beliefs (my acquiring a true belief about his telephone number) would result in my telephoning him, but false that I am able to telephone him, given that I do not know his number.

But one may remove this difficulty, so far as it concerns wants, by distinguishing between two kinds of wants; wants which are part of the situation with which one has to deal and the desires from which we deal with it in the way we do. One's craving for heroin is a desire of the former kind, and part of the situation with which we have to deal. This is shown by the fact that what we are trying to do, from some motive or other, is precisely to give up heroin. If we just lost our desire for heroin we would, doubtless, cease taking it, but this does not mean that we would have succeeded in giving it up. Hence we should not be allowed to suppose that the desires that are part of the situation with which we have to deal are different from what they are when we say that an action is (commonsensically) free, and one we could have helped, if we would not have done it if our (internal) desires had been different. And if it is true that, if we had a strong enough (internal) desire to overcome that craving for heroin that is part of the situation with which we have to deal, we would give up heroin, it follows that we are able to give up heroin.

When it comes to belief we must make a similar distinction. The absence of any true belief on my part about someone's telephone number is just what makes it impossible for me to ring him. But again, this belief is part of the situation we have to deal with. In other words, what we are unable to do is to succeed in telephoning this person although we do not know what his telephone number is. Suddenly managing to recall it, getting it from my wife or ringing directory enquiries would not count as success in ringing him without knowing his number. Hence it is beliefs about the advantages and disadvantages of doing certain things, or about whether or not doing them would be conducive to achieving various ends that we are allowed to suppose to be different when we say that a man is able to do something if it is true that if his beliefs had been different, he would do it. Beliefs that are part of the situation with which he has to deal cannot be allowed to vary. Otherwise one is not succeeding in doing something in *this* situation, but succeeding in doing something in a partially or totally different one.

Third Difficulty

Many think that for me to be free it is not enough that my actions should be determined by my wants. I must also be able to control my wants. For example, if I cannot work because of indolence, and indolence consists in having no desire to work, the fact that if I had a desire to work I would work is not enough to make working within my power. I must further be able to make myself want to work. (This objection does not seem to apply to the view that I am able to perform an action if a change in belief would result in my doing it. For example, the view that the fact that I would refuse the cigarette if I believed (rightly or wrongly) that I would be shot if I accepted one does not seem to be open to the objection that I am not able to produce such a *belief*.)

The force of this objection can be reduced somewhat if we consider what has already been said to the effect that an action's being caused by circumstances that one cannot control does not show that it is itself an action that one cannot control. It can be further reduced when it is considered that a desire not to work (i.e., indolence) can also be one of the things that make working difficult. Hence one is not allowed to suppose that one can overcome one's indolence by magically removing one's desire not to work, for that is not to overcome indolence, but simply to make oneself cease to be indolent.

Nevertheless, completely to resolve the difficulty it is necessary to make a distinction between the physical difficulty, of putting pen to paper, say, which is not great, and the difficulty of overcoming one's indolence (or writer's block), which obstacles may be insuperable. Hence a desire to work strong enough to make one put pen to paper, may not be strong enough to make one work. For that one would have to have a strong enough motive to work to overcome one's disinclination to work. But if one would be working if one had a strong enough desire to overcome one's disinclination to work, this does seem to show that it is within one's power to overcome this disinclination.

Similarly, to be able to jump from a dizzying height more is necessary than that one should have the physical ability to jump, which most people have. It is also necessary that one should have a motive strong enough to overcome one's natural fear of jumping. But if one would jump if one had a motive strong enough to overcome one's natural fear of jumping to cause a person to jump does seem to show that one can jump. For example, if one would jump if one wanted to jump badly enough to overcome one's fear, if only from shame or fear of one's sergeant, then one must be able to jump. If, if one had a strong enough motive to make one try to jump one would succeed, then one is able to jump, even if, because one does not actually have such a motive, one's not jumping is inevitable.

Fourth Difficulty

J.L. Austin (in a famous paper)[8] held that the case for a hypothetical account of freedom rested upon confusing a causal 'if' with the kind of 'if' that occurs in 'There are biscuits on the table if you want any'. It is characteristic of this kind of 'if' that it implies that there are biscuits on the table, even if you don't want any, and that it does not contrapose; i.e., it does not imply that if there are no biscuits on the table you do not want any. However, in order for the hypothetical account of freedom to work, the 'if' in 'I can if I choose' must be the kind of 'if' that occurs in 'England would have won, if it had rained', which statement does not imply that England won, and does contrapose, not the kind of 'if' in 'You owe me five pounds, if you remember'.

Austin's argument, however, does not prove what he wanted it to prove. It is true that the 'if' in 'I can if I choose' is the same as the 'if' in 'There are biscuits on the table if you want any'. This is beside the point, however, for the question is whether 'can' can be given a hypothetical interpretation, and it is not shown that it cannot be given one by the fact that it can occur as the consequent of an 'if' statement that cannot be given this interpretation. For example, it would be absurd to maintain that a hypothetical account of fragility could not be given on the grounds that the 'if' in 'That is fragile if you like' is the same kind of 'if' as the one in 'There are biscuits on the table if you want some'. To say that something is fragile is obviously to say that it will break if you drop it, whatever account you give of the 'if' in 'It is fragile if you like'.

(viii)   Willpower and Wants

In saying that I am able to do something if a change in the direction of my wants would result in my doing it, I have not have sufficiently emphasised willpower.

That willpower has been omitted from my account of freedom, however, is partly an illusion due to a manner of talking. When I say that an action is one that I am able to do provided an alteration to the direction of my wants would cause me to do it, I do not mean, as I have said, that the wants cause the action in the way in which my want to eat may cause my salivating, where this happens without any act of will on my part. I mean that if my want to do it were stronger, I would, from this want, (choose to) do it. What is affected by my wants must be something I do, not just something that happens. I may salivate on account of my want for food, but I do not salivate from a want for food, or in order to satisfy a want for food. And though a want may cause an involuntary action, as my want not to die may make me so nervous that I drop my ice pick, I do not drop my ice pick from fear of dying, or in order to satisfy my want not to die. Fear of dying, indeed, should have made me hang on to it.

This fact is better brought out by the variant on the hypothetical view outlined above. According to this variant, I can do something if, if I want to do it badly enough to try, I will succeed. This version makes it more obvious that the difficulty is mistaken, because trying does involve willpower. (I could have said 'if I want badly enough to succeed to struggle against the factors impeding me'.) If I say that I can do it, if I were to attempt to do it, I would succeed in doing it, this does not give the impression that all I am is a spectator of a battle between my desires, and that I await the result of this conflict without being able to influence it.

The necessity of willpower, however, does not mean that willpower can be exercised without my having any want to exercise it, or that actions involving willpower can be explained without investigating their causes. I can do something if, if I exercised my willpower, I would do it, and doing it is a within the range of the power of my will. This recognises that sufficient willpower may be something that I do not have, and cannot by an act of will acquire. Desire comes into the picture in that I must have a desire for something before I exercise what willpower I have in order to obtain it.

Two Effects of Desire

The fact that, if I have a strong enough desire, I have the willpower to do things that I would not be able to do if I did not have the desire, can be accommodated by saying that there are, as we have seen, two kinds of effect of a desire. (a) One effect is straightforwardly causal. For example, my stammering can be caused by an excessively strong desire to talk well, and at the same time prevent me from talking well. A strong desire to remove myself from the presence of a bull can start my adrenaline flowing, and so augment my capacity to run. (b) The other effect of a desire is due to its being the desire from which I act, in which case the desire still causes the action – for without the desire I would not be acting – but causes it in a special kind of way. When I act from desire, I am not made to perform the action by the desire, but, from the desire, I freely choose to perform the action.

It is then possible to say that an effect of a strong desire may not just be to make me stammer or to increase my flow of adrenaline, but also to increase my willpower. Then one must distinguish between two kinds of effect of a desire, one of which is upon willpower. Just as the desire to get away from a bull may enable me to run faster – the kind of effect mentioned under (a) – which does not mean that I can run faster when a bull is not present, so the presence of a desire to do something difficult, despite a weak will, may not only cause me to attempt to overcome my weakness, but also decrease my weakness, i.e., increase my willpower. It seems then possible to say that one effect of punishment may be, by increasing people's willpower, to enable them to avoid committing crimes that they would not have been able to avoid had there been no punishment attached to their committing them. (The other effect, of course, is to make them want to avoid the action from a fear of further punishment, which, may, of course not be strong enough to avoid the punishment. One effect of punishment may be to increase or decrease their ability to avoid committing further acts of crime.)

Willpower, on this view, is like physical strength, a factor only partially within one's control. One may increase the strength of one's will by training, as one can increase one's physical strength by exercise. But the view, which is perhaps fostered by proponents of metaphysical freedom, that one can always, by an exercise of willpower, make oneself do anything that is not outside one's physical or mental capacity, is grossly exaggerated.

(ix)   Duty and Desire

When I say that an action is free if the agent would have done it if, if he had wanted to badly enough to try (perhaps try very hard), he would have succeeded, I am including wanting to do one's duty as one of the wants that can make one try to do something, and which may override conflicting wants. Kant, however, appears to have thought that the sense of duty was not a desire or want. He thought this partly because he thought that an action done from a desire could not be free, and partly because he thought that any action done (only) from desire would be morally valueless.

We have already seen what is wrong with the first of Kant's suppositions. The second can be accommodated by restating Kant's view, and saying not that action done from desire is valueless, but that any action done from a desire other than the desire to do one's duty (for its own sake) is *morally* valueless. But it is certainly not true that actions not done from a sense of duty – one's children may be cared for from love rather than duty – have no kind of value at all.

(x)   An Action's Being Caused Does Not Mean That it is Not Done for a Reason

Some suppose that, if determinism is true, people must do things for reasons other than the ones for which think they are doing them, or perhaps that people do not do things for any reason at all. It is felt that in the event of determinism's being true, all reasons are rationalisations; that I am in the situation of a person who has been hypnotised, and does something because the hypnotist suggested that he should, though the person hypnotised thinks he is doing it for some other reason. For example, a hypnotist may suggests that in five minutes his patient goes to shut the window, and the patient does this, mistakenly thinking that he is shutting it for the reason that he wishes to prevent a draught. Similarly, it is supposed that, if determinism is true, I really do something like go to see my doctor because a neuron has fired in a particular part of my brain, not from the reason I suppose, viz., that I think he can cure my arthritis.

I myself, however, remain convinced that I do do things from reasons, and as a general rule, though not always, do things for the reasons for which I think I do them. For example, I believe I return in time for an evening meal partly from hunger and partly not to upset my wife, and that no amount of neurological speculation will, or should, shake me in this belief. It is this kind of belief, which everybody has and acts on, which has, by producing successful action for millennia, enabled human beings to survive. It would be absurd to suppose that such beliefs are false.

Since it is certain that we sometimes do things for a reason, the view that all our actions are completely caused would have to be rejected if reasons could not be a kind of cause. Hence, if having physical causes is incompatible with having reasons, we must for this reason reject the materialistic view that all our actions have physical causes (physical causes in the form of happenings in our heads).

But, as we have seen, determinism must stand or fall independently of what might be described as physiological determinism, the view that actions have only physical causes. They may also have psychological causes. In any case, it can be argued that an action's – or, at any rate, a series of physical movements – being caused by a neuron's firing does not exclude its also being done for a reason. For example, it can be argued that if I ask my electronic calculator to give me the sum of two and two, and it gives me four, the fact that the symbol '4' appearing on its screen is caused by suitable happenings to electrons does not exclude its producing the symbol '4' for the reason that it 'believed' (correctly) that four is the sum of two and two. (To complete the parallel with a person, however, one would have to add 'and that it wanted to divulge correct information when asked', as some anti-missile missiles might be said to 'want' to destroy their targets.) I do not think that I want to say this of a computer, though may be more sophisticated devices will be produced, of which one might want to say such things.

I myself do not think that there is much similarity between a computer's coming to a correct answer and my coming to a correct answer. Let us consider the things that I do, when reasoning, that a computer does not. I have to concentrate on the sum, if it is a difficult one, and may get irritated when interrupted. I may have mental imagery, relevant (for example, a mental image of two pairs of black dots) or irrelevant (the 'dots' may be in the shape of spades, as on a playing card). And mental events associated with doing something for a reason, such as the agony of making the decision, the process of weighing the pros and cons, the frequent changes of mind, the anxiety in case one has made the wrong decision, are all things that computers cannot as yet experience.

No-one is likely to want to build a 'computer' that does all these things, and perhaps it is just as well. But were a computer to be built that seemed to do them, the following argument is possible. Either what happens to it exactly resembles what happens to a human being when it answers questions and takes decisions, or it does not. If it does not, there is no reason why the difference should not be responsible for the fact that we go through the agony, etc., but the 'computer' does not. But if there is no difference, it must be that the computer goes through the (mental) agony and so on as well as ourselves.[9]

In any case, it is only physical determinism that leads to this difficulty about reasons, and the case I made earlier was a case for determinism, not for physical determinism – the view that every event has a physical cause – which I suspect is false. And even physical determinism may be divided into eliminative materialism (according to which there are no such things as pains, etc.), reductionism, according to which there are such things as pains, but statements about them can be reduced to statements about physical things, identity theory, according to which there are such things, but they are identical with physical things, and epiphenomenalism, according to which there are such things, but they are all caused by physical goings-on in my head. Hence epiphenomenalism does not deny the existence of the non-physical phenomena associated with having a reason for something, and it is open to it to hold that such mental happenings are in fact causes, though they themselves are caused by physiological happenings.

(It is held that according to epiphenomenalism, mental events (they are 'epiphenomena') have no effects, but this remark is ambiguous. Mental events do make a difference, and have effects, in the sense that different physical and mental things would happen were they not to occur. They do not have effects in the sense that no mental happening that would produce these different effects can, given the states of their owner's brain, occur. For example, mental events make a difference in that if the mental event of my trying to move my arm were to occur, my arm would move, which would make a large difference to a lot of physical phenomena. Mental events do not make a difference to what happens in the sense that the event of my trying to move my arm, which would make this difference, cannot, given my physical condition, occur.)[10]

(xi)   Determinism and Moral Struggle

We have seen that the determinist does not have to hold that there is no such thing as deliberation, or as conflict and moral struggle. What the determinist does have to hold is that, if one man struggles against his desires and another does not, or one man succeeds in overcoming his desires but another does not, this fact must have an explanation. Someone knowing both men well enough may even be able to predict that the one will overcome the temptations that beset him and the other succumb to will them. The first man was better brought up, perhaps, or had a stronger sense of right and wrong or a stronger desire for success, which facts will themselves have to have an explanation. There must, the determinist holds, be some reason for the difference in their behaviour, and common sense agrees with him.

Choice is always a choice between alternatives that we suppose to be within, or not certainly without, our power, and if our desires left us no alternative but to do what they prompted us to do, there would be no such thing as choice. The desires which we are trying to inhibit, weigh up or adjudicate between do leave us such an alternative. When we opt for one of the alternatives between which we are trying to choose, we do nevertheless make our choice from some desire or other, though not only from one of the desires that we are dealing with. When all one's desires appear to be laid on the table in front of one, there will be other desires – a desire to do what is right, or a desire for success that would be frustrated by indolence – that may prompt one to side with one desire against another, and prompt us to take action. (I suspect that such things as a desire for success are partly congenital and partly acquired by such things as the example of parents. In either event, they and the degree of their strength will have explanations.) But the 'last desire', which may be no more than a desire not to go on in a state of agonising indecision any longer, that prompts free action is not part of the situation we are faced with, but the one that moves us to deal with the situation in the way we do. It takes us from behind, so to speak, while the ones that are part of the situation lie on the table in front of us. Phenomenologically the last desire has quite a different status from those that are part of the situation. If the desires that are part of the situation that we are trying to deal with determined our action, we would be left without any viable alternatives to choose between, and we would be a mere spectator of a battle between our wants, the outcome of which we would be quite unable to control.

(xii)   Freedom and Causal Necessity

Earlier this century it was supposed that the apparent conflict between freedom and determinism could be solved if one held a regularity theory of causation. On the regularity theory, to say that one event caused another is to say that events like the first are invariably accompanied by events like the second. For example, it was held that to say that taking arsenic in large doses causes death in certain circumstances is to say that taking arsenic in large doses is universally, in these circumstances, followed by death. This seemed to remove the necessitation from causation, and replace it by uniformity. This was supposed to have taken the sting out of determinism, as a neuron's firing being regularly followed by a decision to act did not seem to remove the responsibility of the agent for the decision to the same extent as would the neuron's firing causing the decision by necessitating it.

However, causes do necessitate their effects. I have elsewhere tried to modify the uniformity theory so as to take account of this fact by substituting 'always does and would follow' for 'always does follow' in the definition of the uniformity theory.[11] This is because to say that two events are causally connected is not only to say that one follows invariably upon the other, but to say that it is always the case that if events like the first event had not occurred, the second – other things being equal – would not have occurred either. The account of our knowledge of necessity here presupposed is empirical. We find out that if the first event had not occurred the second event would not have occurred by trying to separate such events in other cases and observing whether we succeed or fail.

On the view of the necessity of causation I have just put forward, a connection, say, between the motives of the agent and his actions, or between some neuron's firing and the agent's doing what he does, is a necessary connection if it cannot be broken, either by human action or by accidental occurrences. Hence if a decision of mine is necessitated by something, there must be some event or set of events preceding it which is such that attempts to break the connection between their occurrence and my decision must fail. Hume's own example was that there is as much necessity between a gaoler's not allowing one to escape from prison without a bribe as there is between being unable to escape through the bars of one's prison without a file.[12] One is as much protected by traffic lights, which make most people of necessity freely decide to stop, as a by a physical barrier. People sometimes do not stop, but physical barriers sometimes fall down. If so, there is as much a cause of the driver's not stopping as there is of the barrier's not standing.

But since it must be attempts by other people to break the connection between motivation and action that fail, it is other people that are circumscribed by the agent's action's being necessitated, not the agent himself. To attempt to break such connections is not something that I myself am unable to do in the sense that, were I myself were to try to break them, I would fail; I myself in principle cannot make an attempt to break the connection between my own action and the causes which necessitate it. To do so I would have to get outside my own skin and, from a motive I do not have, try to bring it about that I perform a different action from the one that in fact proceeded from the ones I did perform.[13] Hence, though necessity implies circumscription, *I myself* cannot be circumscribed by the fact that my actions are necessitated. It is only other people that are so circumscribed. Hence the necessary connection between my actions and the events that cause them puts a limit on the freedom of other people, but does not put one on mine.[14] The prisoner's freedom is limited by the fact that gaoler's will is necessitated in such a way that he will not without a bribe allow the prisoner to escape, but the gaoler's freedom is not itself limited by this fact.

(xiii)   Theories of Mind and Freedom

(a) On one principle of division, that by which theories are classified according to the number of 'fundamental' entities they admit of, theories of mind and matter can be divided into monistic and pluralistic theories.

(1) According to pluralism, there is more than one fundamental kind of thing (or substance). If you are a dualist, there are two kinds of thing, one kind mental and the other kind physical. 'Monism' is ambiguous between the view that there is only one *kind* of thing and the view that there is only one *thing*. Oddly enough, there can be more than one kind of thing, even if there is only one thing. Spinoza, for example, held that there was only one thing (God or nature) which was both a mental and a physical (kind of) thing.

(2) According to monism, there is only one kind of thing, which will be held to be mental, if you are an idealist – in one sense of the word 'idealist' – physical, if you are a materialist, or neither, if you are a neutral monist. (Neutral monists hold that mind and matter are different combinations or arrangements of neutral entities, like sense-data or mental images.).

(b) On another principle of division, concerning causality, there are theories according to which: (1) there is no causal connection between mental and physical events; (2) all mental events are determined only by physical events; (3) all physical events are determined only by mental events; and (4) physical events and mental events interact or partly determine one another. Theory (2) is usually held by physicalists. Theory (3) was held by the idealist Berkeley, who thought that matter was too 'stupid' to cause anything, the only causes being acts of will. Theory (4) is, I think, the commonsense view.

It looks as if, if monistic idealism or monistic materialism were true, the question of the nature of the causal relation between mental and physical events could not arise, because two kinds of event are needed for interaction of the kind at issue (which is conceived of as a causal connection between two fundamentally different kinds of substance). But, in order to be even remotely plausible, both idealism and materialism must admit that in some sense or other there are mental objects (in the case of physicalism) or physical objects (in the case of idealism).

Idealists and materialists can effect such reductions in several ways. They can do it by reducing statements about the mental to statements about the physical, or, less commonly, *vice versa*. They can effect these reductions by identifying certain mental events with certain special kinds of physical events (or, less commonly, *vice versa*.) The most interesting and plausible, though least commonly attempted, way is to admit the things you wish to eliminate as non-substances. For example, materialists can say that statements about minds are not statements about a substance, for the only substance is matter, but about the way that some material substances (animate ones) behave.[15] Idealists can say that statements about material objects are not statements about a substance, for the only substance is mind, but about the manner in which some minds perceive.[16]

If mind and matter can be admitted (or readmitted) to reality as non-substances, or as a species of mental substance, the two above classifications, the one (a) according to number of substance and the other (b) according to causality, become independent of one another. If you are a materialist, minds are non-substances, but, since there is no reason why there should not be a causal connection between a substance and a non-substance, then one could be a materialist and nevertheless think that there is no causal connection between physical events and mental events; that all physical events are determined by mental events; that all mental events are determined by physical events, or that the two kinds of events interact. If you are an idealist, and hold that it is minds that are the only substances, you can nevertheless think that there either was or was not a causal connection between them and substance, all of which substances were material. If you were a neutral monist, you could think that there were no causal connections between those combinations of neutral events that were occurrences to matter and those combinations of neutral events that were occurrences to minds, or that the former determined the latter, the latter the former or that the two interacted. To take a very simple case, one could hold that all mental events were a species of material event, and hold that they were all caused by, but had no effects on, material events outside this species, i.e., on non-mental events.

For this reason I shall absolve myself from the task of discussing in detail the truth of identity theory, according to which mental events are a species of physical event. Identity theory is in any case obviously false. The happenings revealed by introspection of external or internal phenomena do not remotely resemble what we are told by physicists and physiologists is happening to our brain, which happen to entities that underlie and appear to be hidden by the phenomena. We do not even experience what happens to our own brains, which are hidden in our skulls, but we do experience our own thoughts.

And in any case the characteristics of mental events are not suitable to be ascribed to physical events. Pains are supposed to be identical with brain happenings, but brain happenings, unlike pains, can be grey – or, strictly speaking, happenings to grey objects – while pains cannot, and pains can be intense, but brain happenings cannot.

The customary reply to this is that, because of referential opacity (see chapter 15) the fact that brain events are happenings to grey objects, but pains are not coloured, does not prevent them from being identical. My reply to this reply is that referential opacity operates only with intentional characteristics; Sir Percy Blakeney can be despised by his wife *qua* Sir Percy, but admired *qua* Scarlet Pimpernel only because being despised and admired are intentional characteristics. But being grey or intense are not intentional characteristics. Hence mental events cannot be identical with physical ones.

It is supposed to be a question of importance to the problem of freedom whether epiphenomenalism or interactionism is true. This is thought to be because it is easier to reconcile interactionism with freedom than to reconcile epiphenomenalism with freedom. But one would have thought that identity theory would entail *interactionism*, the theory supposed to be the easier to reconcile with freedom; if mental events are identical with a species of physical event, it would be absurd to maintain that there was a species of physical event (namely, those physical events that were (identical with) mental events) which had no effects on other physical events.

It has been held that their being physical is not absurd, because of the aforementioned referential opacity, those events which are both mental and physical can cause things *qua* being physical events but not *qua* being mental events. But it would be poor consolation to suppose that my body's hanging at the end of a rope could be avoided *qua* being the result of the (mental) decision to commit murder, which decision I did not have to take, but not *qua* result of physical happening in my head. I should be dead anyway.

If, on the other hand, one thinks that mental events are something other than physical events, one would obviously not want one's closed physical system to be interfered with from outside (i.e., by mental events). Hence, contrary to what is commonly supposed, identity theory is favourable to interactionism and not a rival to it. For a similar reason, dualism is favourable to epiphenomenalism. I shall not, however, explore this question, because the arguments I have given for commonsense freedom are independent of considerations concerning the truth of materialism. Every event can have a cause, even if every event does not have a material or physical cause.

(xiv) Metaphysical and Commonsense Freedom

Arguments intended to show that we are not to blame for something we do, or less to blame than one might have supposed because we are not fully responsible for what we do, fall into two kinds. There are first of all arguments based on the fact that some actions have certain special features, i.e., features that not all actions possess. Examples of such arguments are that an action is such as that it would not have been performed if the agent had not been either physically or mentally ill, or if he had known all the circumstances, or if he had not been the victim of fraud, or done what he did under duress, or was drunk, or drugged, or in a state of panic, or a minor, or mentally defective, or under great stress, or subjected to irresistible impulses of one kind or another. Such arguments can be, and frequently are, produced in a court of law, and, though not always conceded, are usually listened to. Whether or not they should be accepted depends on the circumstances.

The blanket philosophical arguments for determinism are not like this. They are intended to show that absolutely every action is one which the agent could not have helped and for which he could not be blamed. And they could not be produced in a court of law, not only because, in that context, they would sound absurd, but because their upshot would not be that this particular person accused ought not to be found guilty, or ought not to be so severely punished, for this particular action, but that no one ought to be found guilty, or punished at all, for any action whatsoever.

A jury, rightly, does not consider whether an action is foreknown or not or whether it has causes, in deciding whether to find a prisoner guilty; nor does a judge consider such matters in determining the severity of his sentence. Among the things that might exculpate the accused or reduce his sentence, some but not all of which will mean that he is exculpated because he could not help doing what he did, the facts that an agent's action was foreknown and that it has causes, are rightly never mentioned. This shows that it is commonsense freedom, which some people have and others do not, rather than metaphysical freedom that is relevant to the moral and legal assessment of men's actions.

That when we did it we possessed commonsense freedom is one (but only one) of a number of circumstances relevant to a moral assessment of an action. To the extent that we lack commonsense freedom, the degree of blame deserved to be incurred by performing an action is reduced. And commonsense freedom is compatible with God's foreknowledge and with the determinism on which God's knowledge of the future must (on one view of his knowledge) be based.

Factors That Make us Unable to Do Something

I say 'to the extent that' because commonsense freedom, *pace* Descartes, admits of degrees. We may be totally and completely unable to do something, as we are unable to run a mile in a minute, but, short of that, actions have degrees of difficulty. We may not be totally and completely unable to do something like give up heroin or nicotine, but giving it up may be so difficult that, though we try as hard as we can, our chances of success are small. Or it may be that we can do something, but not without help, or only on a good day, or only if we are lucky and things go right for us. But the amount of help, the number of good days, luck and things going right are all matters of degree.

Among the things that may make us (commonsensically) unable to do something are these.

(a) Lack of physical strength, as when a weight is too heavy to be lifted.

(b) Lack of willpower, as when someone would have won, had he the willpower to persevere just a little longer.

(c) Lack of judgment, as when an administrator is unable successfully to complete some enterprise because he makes wrong assessments of men and situations.

(d) Lack of skill (which does not have to be lack of a physical skill). For example, someone may not succeed in doing something because he could not ride a bicycle, swim, paint a picture, handle people well, or was a poor lover.

(e) Lack of ability, such as the ability to do accounts, make experiments, make speeches, or work for long hours. (There is not a hard and fast line to be drawn between abilities and skills.)

(f) Lack of knowledge, as when someone cannot teach geography because he does not know any, or cannot get into his house because he cannot remember where he put his keys.

(g) Lack of the ability to influence people, the reason why Cassandra failed to prevent the fall of Troy.

(h) Lack of interest, as when a child cannot concentrate because the lessons are so boring.

(i) Lack of opportunity, as when I would like to have fought a duel, but cannot, because I was born too late.

(j) Lack of awareness that there is problem, as when I cannot prevent my children from taking drugs because I do not know that they are taking them. This awareness may or may not be culpable.

(k) Lack of self-control, as when I cannot keep my temper.

(l) Lack of vision, for which reason I might not be able to lead my political party successfully.

(m) Lack of imagination, as when I am unable to avoid making hurtful remarks because I am unable to see that a person hearing them will be hurt, or unable to foresee the likely side-effects of a business enterprise.

(n) Lack of intelligence, as when someone cannot get a job in a bank because he is simply not clever enough to do sums.

(o) Lack of training, as when I cannot write a rescue note because I cannot write, or give someone first aid because I have never learnt any.

(p) Compulsion, either in the sense that someone takes me by the arm and propels me against my wishes, or in the sense that he threatens to shoot me if I do not do what he wants. (In the latter case I am not strictly speaking unable to do something, because I can, and in some circumstances ought to, choose to be shot.)

Possessing all these things will have a causal explanation. All these limitations admit of borderline cases. Some of them may be overcome by willpower. Others may be to some extent overcome by preparation and training over a long period of time, which may be more time than we have at our disposal. Others cannot be overcome at all. Lack of willpower is only one of the things that can produce failure, and its importance has been exaggerated by philosophers and moralists. Moral exhortation is often the cheapest, but also the most effective, remedy for a failing.

The failures that result from the above incapacities may be moral as much as any other kind of failures. For example, I may fail to do my duty from lack of training or lack of willpower or lack of imagination. *Pace* most philosophers, it is not true that I cannot have duties that I am unable to do. Many people resign their posts precisely because they are unable to do the duties that the posts carry with them.

As well as being unable to do my *duty*, I can also fail to do what I *ought* from any of the above reasons. (Hence it is also not true that 'ought' implies 'can'.) One of the functions of education is to enable me to do the things that I ought to do, which implies that, before I was educated, I could not do them. I have driving tuition to enable me to do the things that a good driver ought. And my driving instructor may know perfectly well that I was too flustered to be able to change down before a hazard, but this does not mean that he is wrong to tell me again that that is what I should have done.

Though neither *ought* nor *duty* imply 'can', what may be true is that exhorting, praising, blaming or in some sense or other conversationally implying that the person doing the exhorting or blaming believes that the person exhorted or blamed had the ability to do something other than what he actually did. There is little point in praising someone or blaming him for something he cannot help, or in exhorting him not to do it. But though there is no point in exhorting someone to do what he ought if he is unable to do it, there is some point in informing (rather than exhorting) someone who cannot, at least on this occasion, do anything other than what he did, that he ought to have done something else, or that something else was his duty. The fact that I have lost my voice does not mean that it is not my duty to lecture, though there is no point in blaming me for not lecturing, or exhorting me to lecture. But since all the factors that cause inability (or difficulty) admit of degrees, praise or blame, even without punishment, should admit of degrees. The expectation of praise, blame or punishment also increase our abilities; it is easier not to steal from a department store if we believe we will be found out and reproached for it, even if we do not also think that we will also be punished. And blaming (or punishing) someone for what he could not help on one occasion may enable him to come to help the same kind of thing on later occasions.

It may be that the view that our wills need to be metaphysically free springs from an overemphasis on the importance and effectiveness of willpower and the feeling that willpower can have no causal explanation. But we have seen that only a small proportion of failures are failures in willpower. But experience seems to show that willpower is nearly as much outside one's control as physical strength. Neither are completely outside one's control; one can increase one's strength by exercise and one's willpower by overcoming, or at least trying to overcome, obstacles. (That different people have different amounts of willpower is itself something that admits of a causal explanation.)

(xv)   Empirical Refutation of Metaphysical Freedom

The fact that, if our desires and beliefs had been different, we would have behaved differently, is good enough for us to have commonsense freedom. It would not be necessary for our wills to be metaphysically free, even if there were such a thing.

For example, a manic-depressive woman who is in the manic phase of her illness may go out and buy a racehorse. When she does this, she wants a racehorse, would not have bought a racehorse had she not wanted one, thinks (wrongly perhaps) that she can afford a racehorse or that it does not matter if she cannot, thinks that her husband and children would like her to have racehorse, and is highly impatient of attempts, which she considers irrational and interfering, to persuade her not to buy a racehorse. To prevent her from – among other things – buying too many racehorses she is taken to a doctor, who gives her drugs. As a result, she no longer wants a racehorse, no longer thinks that she can afford one and that her family would like her to have one, and is grateful to her husband for having managed to dispose, for only a little less than she paid for them, of the racehorses she bought. Next time she sees a racehorse for sale, she does not buy it.

Whatever was wrong with this lady's actions, it is not that she could not have helped doing what she did, or that she was not free to do something else. She was free because she was doing what she wanted; no-one compelled her to do what she did, deceived her about the value of the horse, or put any pressure of any kind on her to buy the horse. The pressure, indeed, was all in the opposite direction. That she wanted a horse so badly and thought that she could afford one was, it is true, produced by her abnormal physiological state, but then so were the facts that later she no longer wanted a horse so badly and that she no longer thought she could afford one produced by the return of her normal physiological state. And whether an action is free or not does not depend upon whether or not it is physiologically caused and so not upon whether it is caused by a normal or an abnormal physiological state.

To consider another example, a man who is acutely depressed may think that he is wicked, that other people are condemning him for what he has done, that he is bad at his job and his dismissal from it is imminent, and that his wife and children do not love him and will be better off without him. In consequence he becomes withdrawn, stays in bed instead of going to work, eats little, and becomes incapable of taking even the most minor decisions. He attempts suicide and is taken to hospital, where he is given antidepressant drugs. As a result he comes home, returns to work, and behaves normally. Again, his normal behaviour is as much conditioned by his normal physical state as his aberrant behaviour was caused by his abnormal state. Both kinds of behaviour seem to be determined by the state of his brain, though most of his actions when in both states are voluntary. And one certainly does not suppose that that state, and the actions performed when the people in question are in that state, are uncaused. The fact that one can control, by drugs or conversation, both the normal and the abnormal states, shows that they are not caused.

Hence the view that, despite all the factors acting upon one, one can, by an uncaused act of will, produce one action rather than another, is not born out by the empirical facts. That we have metaphysical freedom is just false.

(xvi)   Metaphysical Freedom Unnecessary[17]

Not only is it an empirical fact that we do not have metaphysical freedom, it is not at all necessary that we should have it. All that is necessary for praise and blame, punishment and reward, is that people should have been able to do something other than the action for which they were punished, and that they should in consequence be capable of responding to the threat of punishment before the event and of modifying their behaviour of a result of punishment afterwards. For this, all that is necessary is that they should have control of their actions. And that they do have control of their actions is shown by the fact that, by and large, the actions they need to perform are within their power, and they can modify their behaviour in response to different circumstances. For example, they need to be able to stop doing something should they no longer want the things that would result from their doing it, and to take different means to their goals in response to obtaining more information, or as different phases in the operation become appropriate, or as circumstances change. This is all they need for successful action, as it is all that is needed by any other kind of mammal. (Even intelligent artefacts need the power to behave differently when given different goals, and for their behaviour to be modified in response to their having different 'beliefs' about these goals and different obstacles being put in the way of their achieving them.)

(xvii)　Free Will as a Gift From God

Free will cannot be any more of a gift from God than any of men's other possessions. There is an excellent evolutionary explanation of how we come to have free will. Men's survival has been to a large extent been dependent on his having the power of reason to a greater degree than other animals, and there would be no point in his having this power if he did not also have the capacity to choose between the alternative courses of action the merits of which his reason had the power of weighing up. Of course, one can say that God presided over the course of evolution, but this hypothesis is either false – if it leads to empirical consequences – or redundant – if it does not. Animals as well as men have free will, as anyone who has tried to stop a dog from barking or jumping up should know.

Man's morality is also something that has evolved because it is of advantage to him, and a morality without freedom would be as useless as a power to reason without freedom.[18]

(xviii) Foreknowledge and Deliberation

God's omniscience is incompatible with one aspect of free action, his power – if it is a power – to deliberate. Men and women cannot deliberate, as opposed to deceiving themselves into thinking that they are deliberating, when in their heart of hearts they know that they have already settled the outcome. Deliberation involves weighing the pros and cons, and it is impossible to weigh the considerations for and against taking a certain decision if one knows, or even believes, that one is going to take it. The fact that God cannot deliberate, however, is no reflection on him, for an omniscient being would not need to balance the reasons for and against doing something; he should know without reflection what these reasons are and without deliberation what weight ought to be attached to them.

Free action does not need to be preceded by deliberation; some actions are impulsive. And there is no reason to suppose that either God or men cannot choose not to do what they themselves know that they are going to do. One often freely does what one knows one is going to do. For example, I know that I am not going to spend the rest of the day without eating, but nevertheless freely decide to eat. Since I would not eat if I did not want to, my action is one that I could have helped; indeed, it is because I know that my want to eat will exceed any want I may have during the day to do something that conflicts with eating that I know that I will eat.

A personal God, incidentally, can no more do something without wanting to do it to than can any other person (though in his case his wants cannot be produced by his physiological state, because he has not got one). And God can no more be governed by pure reason than can any of his creatures; reason alone can no more move him to action than it can any kind of other person.

Man, unlike God, does need to have the power of intelligent deliberation when it is not obvious what line of action he should take. (I suspect that some of the higher mammals deliberate. They certainly have commonsense free will.) But though a man cannot deliberate when he knows what the upshot of his deliberation will be[19] (which has made some philosophers think that events in a world that contains deliberation cannot all be predicted), there is no reason why someone else should not be able to forecast the course and upshot of a man's deliberating. If no-one can forecast the result of his own deliberation, it follows that in a world in which all people deliberate, no one deliberating person would be able to forecast the whole of what was going to happen; no-one could forecast that part of the future which results from the upshot of his own deliberation. There is no reason in principle, however, why everything should not be foreseen by some person or other, though not by the same person.

(xix) Freedom and Predestination

An omniscient God, then, can both foresee and produce everything, and yet be exculpated from the charge of damning men for performing actions that they cannot help. They can help them. There is another charge, however, from which God cannot be exculpated, if exculpation is necessary. This charge is that he himself causes men to perform those actions for which he subsequently damns them. God, by giving men a certain physiological make-up, a certain endocrine balance and certain kinds of brain and nerve cells, brings it about that they are the kind of person who responds in the way they do to the situations with which they are faced. He also brings about these situations.

I have elsewhere[20] likened God to an omnipotent omniscient vice-chancellor, who not only gives people degrees, but the abilities, opportunities and motives that result in people getting degrees. Whatever else such a vice-chancellor might be accused of, he could not be accused of not awarding degrees according to merit.

It could be said that grace (or one sort of grace) is just God's giving people the natures which result in good or bad behaviour in some men but not others. It is not unjust for God to give these natures to some men but not others, for there are no persons, abstracted from the natures God gives them, for God unjustly to give the natures to. (If there is not a God, whether one has these capacities is just a matter of chance, in that sense of chance in which chance consists in the absence of design, not in that sense which involves an absence of necessity.)

Men do not have to do the things they do, because, had their motives or beliefs been different, they would not have done them. But nevertheless, the motives and beliefs that make their actions free are themselves caused by things that (by and large) they cannot help (such as the state of their brains), but which God can help. It would follow from this that God shares with men the responsibility for the performance of these actions, which would, if he sends men to Hell for the wicked things they do, make his doing this nearly as reprehensible by human standards as it would be if he damned them for doing things that they could not help. I myself do not believe that there is a God who sends people to Hell. (A way of attempting to remove this difficulty would be to hold that the kind of God there is, if there is one, does not and cannot interfere in the affairs of men, but I shall say more about this later.)

(xx)   Conclusions: God's Omniscience is Compatible with Human Freedom

God's omniscience is compatible with human freedom. There is no need to hold either that because God is omniscient men must be unable to help doing what they do, or to say that because men are able to help doing what they do, God is not omniscient (or does not exist). Hence it is not necessary, as some think, for God to limit his omniscience in order to act freely. The analogy, or at any rate resemblance, between God's actions and man's indicates, if anything, that God's actions are not free rather than that men's are free, though in fact there is no reason to suppose that both are not free. (It is therefore just false that God's creativity involves his not being omniscient.) Those who think that God is not responsible for everything, including the free actions of human beings, fail, sometimes dismally, to realise the full extent of an omnipotent God's omnipotence.

The conclusion from determinism, together with what is known about brain physiology, is that, if there is a God, the doctrine of predestination is true, and that God brings about each man's destiny, at least sometimes by manipulating his brain. The conclusions that have been deduced from predestination, however, do not follow. God does not predestine men to be damned whether they sin or not. He predestines men first to sin and then to be damned. This does not mean that God is acting unjustly in damning those who sin; he would be unjust only if he damned them for sins they had not committed, and, on the view that God gives men the characters for which he damns them, they not only have committed them, and were able not to commit them. But, since God himself caused or permitted their sinning, what he is guilty of – if there is a personal God – is punishing them for actions for which he is in part responsible. This would be reprehensible in men; whether it is reprehensible in God is another matter.

It will also be true, of course, that God produces, via his control of our brains, our good actions as well as our bad ones. And this may justify one Christian attitude to the omnipotence of God, which involves giving him all the credit for our right-doing, though it seems odd that he is not then ascribed some of the blame for our wrongdoing. But it may be that credit and blame for both ought to be shared between ourselves and the deity. We are to be praised or blamed for the good or bad act, he for permitting it or bringing it about.

This consideration of the implications of omniscience and omnipotence – which will be reinforced in the chapter on the problem of evil – makes it very unlikely that there is a personal God who is omnipotent, omniscient and perfectly good. It will be considered later, however, whether there is any possibility of having something that might be described as faith in a personal god, although believing that there is not one.

Notes

1   I have discussed these topics in a number of papers (1992 and 1993).
2   The strongest case I know for fatalism has been put forward by Richard Taylor, 1963, chapters 4 and 5. I have discussed Taylor's views in Harrison, 1992.
3   I shall explain what the right kind of way is later.
4   Hobbes, Locke, Hume, John Stuart Mill and G.E. Moore were all compatibilists, as was Kant, in an odd sort of way.
5   I think this is the way the word 'compatibilism' is usually used, though this definition would exclude the views that though freedom and determinism were compatible, they were both false, and that determinism was true and freedom false.
6   It is the result of the same confusion (in this case, confusing the necessity of the hypothetical that *if* someone knows something, then that what he knows must be true, with the necessity of what he knows) to maintain (as did Descartes) that only necessary propositions can be known. From this it would follow that propositions such as that my name is Tom, that the Earth is round, that all men are mortal, and that the Battle of Hastings was fought in 1066, cannot be known to be true, because all such propositions, not being necessary propositions, may be false. This would mean that our knowledge was enormously restricted to knowledge of the propositions of mathematics and logic.
7   I have discussed other difficulties to hypothetical accounts in greater detail Harrison, 1993.
8   Austin, 1961.
9   But see J.J.C. Smart, 1995.
10 This point is made more elaborately in my 'Science, Souls and Sense-Data', 1995.
11 In 'Hume on Liberty, Necessity, Uniformity, Causation and Unfulfilled Conditionals' in Harrison, 1995.
12 See Hume, 1976.
13 Something like this appears to have been held by Paul Ree, 1993, p. 86 f. Thomas Nagel seems to think that my inability to achieve this absurdity is something one should regret, but I cannot think why one should regret it. See Nagel, 1986, especially p. 113 f.
14 Some philosophers, for example Nagel, 1986, think that it is especially difficult to reconcile freedom if one is a physicalist, and in consequence think that the universe contains only physical particles governed by the laws of physics. One may, however, as did Hume and most determinists until quite recently, think that man's behaviour is governed by law without holding that physicalism is true. Whether the account of freedom here given enables one to reconcile freedom with physicalism depends upon whether or not the notion of desire can be reduced to something physical. If it can, reducing freedom to the statement that I would have done something different if my desires and beliefs had been different enables physical determinism and freedom to be reconciled. However, doing this accomplishes the reconciliation, even if physicalism is false.
15 Gilbert Ryle, 1947, could be regarded as a materialist of this type.

16 Berkeley can be regarded as this kind of idealist, given his slightly eccentric view of causation (that causes are signs of God's intentions about the future) and given that he thought that statements about material objects were statements either about conglomeration of ideas in the mind of God or statements about what ideas minds would have if they were placed in other circumstances (say, outside the quad instead of inside it). For then changes to conglomeration of ideas or changes in the truth of statements about what ideas minds would perceive, could be signs of, say, whether a mind would later feel pain or distressed, or decide to call a doctor. Phenomenalists could take Berkeley's second way, as suggested by A.J. Ayer, 1954.

17 Though it is an empirical fact that we do not have metaphysical freedom, that this is an empirical fact is not an empirical fact, and it is not an empirical fact that we do not need metaphysical freedom.

18 I have made out a case for this view in Harrison, 1971, 1992 and in 'Sociobiology and Ethics', 1995.

19 It follows from this that an omniscient being cannot deliberate; but whoever would want God to deliberate?

20 In 'Foreknowledge, Will and Fate', 1993.

18 God's Eternity

(i)   Introduction

God is commonly supposed to be eternal. It may well be that God is eternal by definition. It will also be that God is eternal because he is perfect and being eternal is a perfection. It may also be that God is eternal because only an eternal being can be a satisfactory object of worship. And God must in some sense endure for ever, if he is to be always there to give us help.

It does not, as we have seen, follow from the fact that God is eternal by definition that there is a God who is eternal, but merely that, if there is a God, then he is eternal. Nor does it follow that we have a coherent concept of eternity, though if we do not have such a concept and God is eternal by definition, it will follow that our concept of God is at least partially incoherent. From this it should follow that there cannot be such a being as God.

But what is meant by 'eternal'? It is commonly said that it means that temporal predicates do not apply to God. Examples of temporal predicates would be 'born on 22 September', 'listening to the 9.00 news' 'moving', 'changing' and 'accelerating'. Perhaps one can express the fact that God is eternal by saying that no proposition can be true of God at one time which is not true of him at all times. It cannot, for example, be true yesterday, but not today, that he is benevolent, or true yesterday that he was alive, but true today that he is dead. (It does not conflict with God's eternity to say that men have stopped believing in him, or that faith in him is no longer necessary. But, whether true or not, these are temporal statements about men, not temporal statements about God.)

If temporal predicates do not apply to God, it follows that he is 'outside the time stream'. He has no position in time. Further, nothing at all can happen to him. Hence nothing can happen to him to place events in his 'life' before, after, or simultaneously with events which do happen in time, or before, after, or simultaneously with one another.

(ii)   Difficulties with God's Eternity

However, there are enormous difficulties with the view that God is eternal in the sense that temporal predicates do not apply to him.

(a) There are the usual difficulties for Christianity – which will matter only if God and Christ are held to be literally identical – as temporal predicates did apply to Christ. (We have discussed – and rejected – one possible solution of these difficulties.) Christ was born at a certain date and died at another date, and changed considerably between these two dates. I do not want to labour these difficulties concerning Christ, which are obvious. There is just one, however, which is worth special mention. Christ was (allegedly) 'conceived' at one date, and died at another date. Does the fact that Christ was conceived at a certain date and born at a certain date mean that God became incarnate at the first time, although he was not incarnate before? If so, this does seem to imply that God has changed. A timeless being, however, cannot change.

(b) God is omniscient. Hence, if it is raining, he must know that it is raining. But if I say tomorrow that he knows that it is raining, this may well be false, because it may not still be raining by then. God must then have changed in respect of what he knows. (This difficulty has been discussed in the previous chapter.)

(c) It may be true at 7.00 pm on Monday that God has not yet brought about Tom's death, but this may be false by Wednesday. It looks as if this implies that God has done something (permitted or caused him to die) between Monday and Wednesday.

(d) God is frequently spoken of as having emotions; love, righteous anger at man's wickedness, sadness at his folly, etc. Timeless love, anger and sadness, however, are very difficult to conceive. If you are angry, for example, you must be angry at something or with somebody, which implies that your anger occurred after what you are angry at, and was caused by it. Furthermore, anger is by nature not instantaneous (though it may come into being nearly instantly). Even if it were instantaneous, the fact that it had a date (even if it has no duration) would be incompatible with God's eternity. And being instantaneous is a temporal predicate.

(e) God is supposed to forgive man for his wickedness sometimes, if not always. Does this not mean that God forgives men after they have asked forgiveness? Or must he, because temporal predicates do not apply to him, have forgiven them even before they asked for forgiveness? Must he not then, and for the same reason, have forgiven men for their wicked acts even before they have committed them? But surely this is impossible, and in any case, the expression 'before they asked for forgiveness' itself implies that God is not timeless. And if God forgives us because we pray, this implies a causal connection between God's forgiveness and our prayer. Unless causal connections can be outside time, the cause would have to be earlier than or simultaneous with its effect.

(f) God is commonly supposed to have one overall strategic plan for the universe (reconciliation with man) and to have conceived various tactical manoeuvres for realising this plan (e.g., according to Christianity, causing his son to be born as a man). A plan normally involves the thought of doing certain things in the correct logistical order. Hence a timeless plan would be inconceivable or logically impossible.

One may reply that it is the things planned, not the plan, that occur in a temporal order. It is true that the order in which phases in a plan occur to one is not the same as the order in which these phases are to be executed. The last step in the plan may occur to one before the first. But in human beings a plan the thought of which occurs to one at no time at all is not conceivable. Even an instantaneous plan, if such a thing were possible, would have to occur before the things planned were to be done, which implies that the planning would have to be in time. And if the things planned came into existence as a result of the plan, they would have to occur after the plan and be partly caused by its occurring to us, which would be another reason for thinking that God, if he plans things, cannot be eternal.

(g) This same difficulty applies to petitionary prayer in general. If God sometimes gives men what they pray for, he must do this after they have prayed, and 'after' is a temporal 'predicate'. Worse, must he not forgive people because they have prayed, which again puts God 'inside the universe', to the extent at least that he is causally affected by what happens in the universe, in this case, by man's praying?

(h) When Smith acquires his second child, he has a changed in that formerly he was the father of one child, whereas now he is the father of two. God acquires metaphorical children every time a new baby is born, so the number of his children is constantly changing. Hence he must be as much subject to change in this respect as are ordinary human fathers.

(i) At some times, people pray to God, at other times they do not. The proposition 'Smith is praying to God at 11.15 pm on Sunday' logically implies (if there is a God) that God is being prayed to by Smith at 11.15 am on Sunday. The proposition 'Smith is not praying to God at 11.15 am on Monday' logically implies that God is not being prayed to by Smith at 11.15 am on Monday.

Hence God must at one time posses the 'relational property' of being prayed to by Smith, but lack this relational property at another time. Hence he must have changed.

(It is worth remarking, however, that numbers, which are sometimes supposed to be paradigmatic cases of 'objects' that are in some sense or other timeless, can change their relational properties. The number three, for example, can be thought of by Smith at once time, but not at another, and be the number of Tom's children, or Mary's husbands, at one time, but not at another.)

(iii)   God's Changelessness

In view of the last objection especially, it is very difficult to see how God can be timeless in the sense that temporal predicates do not apply to him. However this leaves open the possibility that he may be timeless, if this is a correct use of the word 'timeless', in the much more usual sense that he does not change. That God does change is not implied by the fact that temporal predicates do apply to him. If Mary stops loving Tom, then Tom will no longer be loved by Mary. But we persist in regarding this as a change to Mary, rather than as a change to Tom, though propositions that were true of either at one time are now true of them no longer. If Tom loses his father or acquires a younger brother, he has relations to things which he did not have before, because they did not exist before, but he has not changed.[1] If Tom gets married, loses his umbrella or ceases to live in a house which is being rained on, he acquires or loses 'relational properties', for the things which he is related to have changed. We do not, however, want on this account to say that Tom has changed, as we certainly would if he had put on weight.

Might God be Changeless in the Sense That Only His Relational Properties Change?

Can we then say that God, though not eternal in the sense that temporal predicates do not apply to him, is changeless in the sense that though his relational properties may change, this is the only kind of change possible to him?

In one way, this is not enough, for coming into or going out of existence is not a change.[2] (You cannot say, 'The house I was born in has changed; it does not exist any more.') Hence one could not deduce that God endures for ever from the fact that he is unchanging. His being eternal would imply his being changeless in this sense, but the converse is not true; he could be changeless without being eternal. Nor would his being everlasting imply that he was changeless.

In another way, saying that God is changeless might seem to be saying too much. One may say that being worshipped by Smith at one time, but not at another, is a change in Smith but not a genuine change in God, but only what Professor Geach has called a 'Cambridge change'.[3] (The 'changes' mentioned in sections (b), (c), (g), (h) and (i) above are all Cambridge changes.) But what about God's being angry with Smith at one time, but not at another? Here the positions would seem to be reversed. A genuine change has now happened to God. It is Smith who has changed only his relational properties. Hence the view that God can change only his relational properties would exclude his having many attributes which it is customary to ascribe to him, by ordinary people, at any rate.

Though philosophers tend to regard a thing's changing as consisting in its doing things, or in things happening to it, or in his or its feeling things which he or it did not feel before, ordinary men make a distinction between those things which happen to something which are changes and those which are not. My cat may have been out all night, but come back quite unchanged by the experience. He is no more dirty and no more neurotic as a result than he was before. This does not, of course, mean that nothing happened to him while he was out, or that he did not do things while he was out. My watch may have received hard wear for years and be quite unchanged by this, but, of course, things have been happening to it all the time. (Actually, my watch will have changed a bit, but it is conceivable that it could go on working indefinitely without having changed at all.)

And there is, too, the sense in which we say that the seasons follow one another changelessly, or speak of the changeless breaking of the waves upon the shore, though waves and seasons both involve change. The seasons always take place in the same order and the waves always break in the same way. Abstractions like process, too – for example, the processes by which houses are built or students are educated – can remain unchanged for centuries, though obviously there is nothing atemporal about processes.

Distinction Between Happenings That Count as Changes and Those That Do Not

I find it difficult, however, to elicit the principle which the ordinary person uses to distinguish between happenings to something which count as changes and happenings which do not.

We would usually not say that Mary has changed in the following circumstances.

(a) I have already suggested that (a1) changes in the relational properties of something, or (a2) the coming into existence of something (like a younger brother) to which this thing now acquires relations, or (a3) changes which consist of a thing to which it is related changing, do not count as changes in that thing. (Though we would not normally regard a change in the position of the furniture in the room as a change to the furniture, we might well say that the room has changed, though all that has happened to it is that its relational properties, i.e., its relations to the furniture, have changed. But in this case we must be thinking of the room as including the furniture in it. The room conceived of simply as consisting of four walls, a ceiling and a floor, cannot, strictly speaking, change simply because the furniture in it has moved.)

(b) Mary is older than she was (though, of course, she will almost certainly change as a result of getting older).

(c) Because today she knows that the day is Friday 13, whereas she did not know yesterday (Thursday 12) that the day was Friday 13. (It was not.)

(d) Because today she has kept an appointment which yesterday she had not kept (because it was an appointment for today).

(e) Because she is angry today, when she was not angry yesterday. (I do not claim that this list of occurrences which do not mean that the thing to which they happen is changing is exhaustive.)

Perhaps we say that some person or thing has changed only if his or its characteristics have changed. Being angry today, but not yesterday, does not count as a change, because being angry, though a non-relational fact about the angry person, is not a characteristic of that person. But being irascible (or prone to anger) today, but not yesterday, does count as a change, because being irascible is a characteristic. And, indeed, none of the 'changes' mentioned above (e.g., getting older) involve a change in the characteristics of the thing which 'changes'.

Prescribing that God should be unchanging may be sufficient to rule out his undergoing certain kinds of changes, e.g., changes to relational properties, which we do not wish him to undergo, without ruling out his being subject to other 'changes', the absence of which would give rise to logical difficulties of the kind I have mentioned. It is not enough, however, to prescribe that God be unchanging. Not only does unchangingness not entail that God is everlasting, which he needs to be. Demanding that he be unchanging would not be enough to rule out various temporal features of God that it is necessary to rule out. He could, for example, be both everlasting and everlastingly deteriorate.

Aesthetically Preferable for God to be Outside the Time Order

There does seem to me to be some conflict between the wants which incline us to say that God is inside and those which incline us to say that he is outside the temporal order. The difficulties with saying that he is outside the temporal order have already been mentioned. The main difficulty with supposing that God is inside it is that it detracts from his magnitude, for it means that he does not transcend time – and that makes God more mundane than he ought to be. Indeed, I personally think it makes him very slightly absurd.

I do not know what is the solution of this conflict. Nor can I see how failing to possess an incoherent predicate like timelessness, if it is incoherent, can detract from the grandeur of God. Perhaps it is because a degree of coherence that is necessary for speculating about the world is not necessary for poetry, and when we talk about the divinity, we are quite frequently using language poetically. It should not be forgotten, however, that poetry does not aim to be believed and does not have to be true, whereas most of those who propound theistic views do so because they do believe them to be true and want others to believe them also.

Other Motives for Wanting God to be Timeless

Whether or not God is invented by man, our concept of God certainly is. The motives which have led men to invent the concept of a timeless God are these. God must be omni-accessible, i.e., it must be possible to have access to him at any time. He must always be on hand to answer prayer (or, at any rate, to hear it) or to give solace or consolation. Hence, just as people have supposed that that two and two are four is a timeless truth, partly because it is possible for people to have access to it at any time, so God has been imagined as a timeless being, partly because it has been supposed that he must be capable of being reached at any time that we have need of him.

One reason for wanting it to be the case that there is a God is that we need security. A God who changed would not satisfy this need. For if he could change, he might help us in one mood, but not help us in another; he might not always be just, because he might change from being just to being unjust, or he might be less just than he was before, or less able to implement his just decisions, or to protect us.

But if God were only changeless this would not, as we have seen, preclude his being able to do such things as take decisions, make plans, change his mind, or be aware of something at one time that he was not aware of at another. (Some of these things might be precluded by other parts of his nature, say, by his omniscience.) The desire that God be timeless is partly a desire that he should transcend this petty universe by being 'outside' it. If he is not 'timeless', he is not 'outside time' and so, like everything else in it, subject to change and decay and to modification by prior causes. He is, it is true, prevented by his definition as a perfect being from decaying, but all this means is that if he were to change, he would cease to be perfect, or (if you define God as being always perfect), never have been God. To be incapable of change and decay, he would have to be eternal.

The difficulties with the existence of an eternal God, mentioned in section (ii), are not difficulties with a God who is merely changeless and everlasting. Such a God could have knowledge of time, answer petitionary prayer after it was made, forgive people after they had sinned, and consider plans and take decisions. A God who is changeless and everlasting, however much the idea of such a God is necessary for the devotional life of his creatures, is unduly anthropomorphic. And if there were such a God, there ought to be empirical evidence for his existence, which there is not. And, aesthetically, an eternal God is preferable to one who is merely changeless and everlasting, but nevertheless within the time stream.

An eternal God, however, would be open to most of the objections mentioned in (ii). The conclusion may be, however, not that there is not an eternal God, but the same one that is pointed to by the ontological argument discussed earlier; that there is one, but that he has not created the universe and does not in any way interfere with it. Such a God, though he could give men no more help than could be obtained from contemplating him, could be a satisfactory object of worship.

(iv) God's Eternity and the Unreality of Time

If God is eternal, he is 'outside' time. Hence he will be no 'closer' to the present than to the future or the past. He will view the whole event-series, even if is infinite in time and space, in what might be described, figuratively, as a single instant. Past, present and future will be alike to him. It may even be that he does not understand words like 'past', 'present' and 'future' and words like 'now', 'then', 'earlier', 'later', and so on, which words have a reference to the present. In that case, there will be things man knows but God cannot know, and perhaps cannot even comprehend. (There will, indeed, be two kinds of fact he does not know. He will not know facts about what is happening now, and he will not know facts about the meaning of such words as 'now'.)

It might be that God can evade the charge of being not omniscient if past, present and future are illusory, and not genuine 'features' of reality. In that case, perhaps, it would not be to be expected that God could take cognizance of them. Some of the temporal propositions which we think we know, such as that it is a long time since breakfast, would then turn out to be false – though I myself think it is absurd to suppose such propositions to be false. It is not unnatural – though I think it is wrong – to pass back from the idea that God takes no cognizance of time to the conclusion that all change is mere appearance, that evil, since it involves change, is also unreal, and death an illusion. If God is outside time and cannot be aware of the time-order, and what God cannot be aware of cannot be real, it would follow that change was an illusion, a veil which may one day be drawn aside, to reveal something much more satisfactory and permanent than we might otherwise have supposed.

It might be nice to think so, but the grounds for thinking so are slight. One difficulty is that God, if he is omniscient, must at least know that there is *apparent* change; for no-one disputes that things really do at least seem to change. Death may be an illusion (because it is a change) and, if so, God cannot be aware of it, but at least it is not an illusion that God's creatures have the illusion of death. The illusions themselves may take place in a temporal order; it seems that we have the illusion of being born before the illusion of dying. And the illusion of death may be as bad a thing as death itself. (It is difficult to see how a Christian can hold that death is an illusion, for in that case the Resurrection would have to be illusory also.)

In any case, I doubt whether holding that time is unreal would exonerate God from the charge of not being omniscient. His not knowing such propositions as that I had my breakfast four hours ago will be excusable, for one can know only true propositions, and all such propositions will be false. But, if God is omniscient, he should know that his creatures believe such things as that they had breakfast four hours ago, and this, if he does not understand words like 'ago', he will not be able to do. If he knows everything, he should know about illusions as well as about reality, and so understand what human beings were thinking when they thought, even wrongly, that they had their breakfast four hours ago.

It has been held by some philosophers, in particular by the philosopher McTaggart,[4] that time is not real. I shall present in my own way an argument, that is roughly and predominantly McTaggart's, for this view.

According to McTaggart, there are two series in which events may be 'situated', the A-series and the B-series.[5] Events are ordered in the B-series by the relations of temporal precedence, temporal succession and temporal simultaneity. (To tidy up a little, we could reduce these three relations to one. A temporally succeeds B could be defined as 'B temporally precedes A' and 'A is simultaneous with B' might be defined as 'A neither temporally precedes nor succeeds B'.) The series of events generated by these relations is, according to McTaggart, unchanging. There never was nor ever will be a time when the Battle of Hastings did not precede the Battle of Waterloo, even before either of them had happened, or long after they had both disappeared into the past. Whether both battles are future, the Battle of Waterloo is future and the Battle of Hastings present, the Battle of Waterloo present and the Battle of Hastings past, or both battles are past, the former battle still precedes the latter. Since the passage of time makes no difference to this eternal fact, facts like it do not capture change. It is concluded that if events were ordered in the B-series alone, there would be no such thing as change.

But events are supposed also have a position in the A-series, in which events are ordered by their relation to the present. The third world war is at the moment future, but is getting closer and closer to the present. It will in time become present, and then recede farther and farther into the past. It has been supposed that its position in the A-series cannot be reduced to its position in the B-series, for even before it occurs, and from all eternity, it will temporally succeed the first and second world wars and the Battle of Waterloo.

If this is right, and an event's position in the B-series never changes, change presupposes the A-series. According to McTaggart, however, the existence of the alleged 'A-series changes', changes from future to present to past, would lead to difficulties and so must be illusory. The same events cannot be future, present and past at the same time, for this would be contradictory. An event must therefore be first future, then present and then past at different times. But this, many philosophers have argued, implies that time is itself changing, which implies a second order or hyper-time within which it may change. But this hyper-time would (a) lead to exactly the same problems as did time, which, since they too would have to be solved in the same way, would lead to an infinite vicious regress, and (b) is in any case absurd, for it would lead to such questions as how quickly does the future become present and then past? The idea that an event which is going to happen in two days time should reach the present either quickly or slowly as measured by some nonexistent unit of time other than the ones we have already is held (rightly) to be incomprehensible. There are not, and cannot be, any units in terms of which time can be measured other than the usual ones for measuring the duration of events in time, viz., seconds, minutes, hours, days, weeks, months and years.

Since the A-series is contradictory and the B-series by itself insufficient to constitute change, McTaggart concluded (a little less straightforwardly than has been represented here) that time was unreal. But if time is unreal, it can be no reflection on God's omniscience that he is not aware of the present, the past and the future, because all events are equally temporally 'close' to him. Furthermore, if time is unreal, it can constitute no difficulty for God's existence that, if he exists, he is outside time, or, at any rate, outside the B-series. It is being inside time, not outside it, that gives rise to perplexity and contradiction. And the fact that the Battle of Hastings precedes the Battle of Waterloo is something that God can know, for this fact itself, divested (if this is possible) of its commitment to change from future to present to past, is supposed to be something that God can know while remaining eternal.

(v)   Difficulties with the View that Time is Unreal

Pace McTaggart, however, time is not unreal. As G.E. Moore pointed out, it is as certain as anything can be that we had our breakfast before our lunch. A philosopher's arguments, which are notoriously unreliable, to prove that we did not do this are bound to be less acceptable than our knowledge of what they attempt to disprove. If the statement that time is unreal denies such obvious truths, it must certainly be mistaken. If it does not deny them, then a relatively innocuous doctrine is gaining a spurious air of importance from seeming to do say something much more paradoxical than it really does say.

Hence I shall not attempt to refute McTaggart, though I shall point out that when he says that relations of temporal precedence hold eternally he forgets that it is impossible to express facts about them (i.e. facts about the B-series) in a way that does not actually presuppose the A-series. For if I use English correctly – and it is dangerous, if occasionally illuminating, not to – I have to say that the Battle of Hastings *preceded* (using the past tense) the Battle of Waterloo, which presupposes that the Battle of Hastings is in the past and so presupposes the reality of the A-series. But McTaggart might reply that what presupposes a contradictory fact like the A-series must itself be contradictory.

It might not matter, however, that the B-series presupposes the A-series, if the A-series can be reduced to the B-series. On this view, to say, for example, that the Battle of Waterloo is future, said at the time of the Battle of Hastings, means that the Battle of Hasting succeeds this utterance (when 'this utterance' refers to the uttering of the sentence 'The Battle of Hastings is future'. It would have been better to say 'succeeds the present', for when we say that something is future, we are certainly not talking about an utterance.) And to say that the Battle of Waterloo was past, said at the time of the second world war, means that the Battle of Waterloo precedes this (different) present. Both statements can be true. And God could know both statements, just as he can know that Durham is south of Edinburgh but north of London. No-one has ever thought that there was any illusion involved in the fact that London is further from Durham than Newcastle is.

I myself doubt whether the A-series can be reduced to the B-series. It leads to the conclusion that there is no fundamental difference between our present and, say, Julius Caesar's present, and I suspect that there is such a difference. There is no fundamental difference between Julius Caesar's now, on this theory, and my now, for Julius Caesar's now stands in the same relation to Julius Caesar that my now stands in to me. But common sense thinks, so to speak, that there is a relational present and an absolute present, and thinks that there is more to the present present, which is absolutely present, than there is to Julius Caesar's present, which is merely present relative to Caesar. Common sense, for what this fact is worth, regards my now as (temporarily) unique. According to common sense, my here is just as good a here as the prime minister's, but my now is a much better now than Pitt's. To obliterate an independent A-series is to make time too much like space, something theorists on the subject of time too frequently do.

It might be replied that my present *is* the only one that is unique, in that it is the only one that is my present, but I feel uneasy about this reply. The most natural picture to have of the 'passage' of time is that of a finger,[6] representing the present, moving along a line, representing the series of events in time. It is supposed, as we have seen, that this picture cannot represent the passage of time, because if the present really was like this, it would be possible to ask how fast it moved along the line, which suggests, absurdly, that it might take more or less than a week to get from one Sunday to the next. But the alternative picture, suggested by those who think that the A-series can be reduced to the B-series, is that of a 'stationary' railway line, such that each station represents the present for people at that station, and stations in one direction along the line are future in relation to it and in the other direction past. But change seems to have disappeared, if one views the time series as one views the line, from outside. And even if one imagines oneself at a station on the line, the 'change' from future to present is not adequately illustrated, for other stations on the line, unlike events in the future, never get any closer.

To this extent, it is the analogy of the moving finger that represents time most adequately, for the moving finger does get nearer and nearer to the points on the line representing future events. One could remedy the defect in the railway line analogy by regarding the present as a train moving along the line rather than as a station. In this case the word 'now' would refer to the station at which the train happened to be stopped and future stations would get nearer the train, as future events get nearer the present. But then this analogy would have the same defect as the moving finger analogy; it would again seem to be possible to ask how long the train takes to get to future stations.

I think that the difficulty concerning the speed at which a future event becomes present can be answered by saying that speed is a function of time and distance. Travelling at a 100 miles an hour, for example, means travelling at a speed which is such that one would cover the distance of 100 miles in an hour, if one were to travel at that speed for an hour. But in that case there can be no such thing as the speed at which an event becomes present, for a future event, unlike a car, is not travelling from one point to another, and so it is a category mistake to think that the notion of speed applies to it. Hence it is wrong to think that it is an objection to the existence of an A-series that one must ask the impossible question how fast events become future. The question does not make sense, and so it is not surprising that there is no answer to it.

The aforementioned unfortunate tendency to make time too much like space is helped by regarding time as a fourth dimension, which might also remove any problems there may be concerning God's knowledge of time. There is no reason why one should not regard time as a fourth dimension, provided that one does not then think one has thereby created a static universe. One cannot speak of the four-dimensional world as changing (unless one postulates a fifth dimension in which it could change). One can either speak of an object changing, or of later temporal slices of a four-dimensional object being different from earlier slices. For example, one can either say that London has changed, or say that adjacent temporal slices of the four-dimensional whole that is London are different from the temporal slices preceding and succeeding it. (To say that the cliffs of Dover have not changed is to say that earlier and later temporal slices of this four-dimensional whole are similar.) But the fact that one can speak in the latter way does not mean that London has not changed. For later slices of an object to be different from earlier ones is what it is for an object to have changed. Talking of the temporal parts of unchanging four-dimensional wholes, therefore, is just a way of talking about things changing, and does not deny change. Indeed, I doubt whether it even makes sense to say that anything other than things in the time-series, like people and inanimae objects, change. The time-series itself neither changes nor does not change. In any case, I doubt whether the temporal slice view is wholly satisfactory, for we still need tenses in order to talk about the aforementioned temporal slices. We have to say, for example, that temporal slices of the cliffs of Dover resembled (in the past tense) one another, rather than that they are going to resemble one another in the future.

Time and change, therefore, are not illusions. But, for the reason given, even if they are not illusions, neither the view that the A-series cannot, nor the view that it can, be reduced to the B-series presents an insuperable obstacle in the way of regarding God as omniscient. (Other difficulties, concerning a timeless being's alleged inability to think of anything as being present, have been already discussed in the chapter 'God's omniscience'.)[7]

(vi)   God's Eternity and Eternal Truth

We have seen that it is not enough that God be changeless in the ordinary sense of this word. He could be changeless while he existed, but being changeless while one does exist does not, as we have seen, imply existing for ever. God could also be everlasting.

God could be everlasting without being eternal. If God is eternal in the sense that, if a proposition is true of him at one time it is true of him at all times, then it follows that there is some sense in which he is everlasting. If God is eternal in this sense, there can never have been a time at which it was not true to say that he existed and never will be a time at which it will not be true to say that he exists.

Does this mean that he exists at all times, and therefore that he exists at some time, and therefore that he exists in the time series, for example, now? (This would not matter for an everlasting God, but it would for an eternal one.)

To resist this conclusion one would have to argue that it does not follow from the fact that at all times it is true to say that God exists, that God exists at all times. In the case of ordinary temporal things, however, it *does* follow from the fact that it is true to say at any given time that it exists, that it exists at that time. For example, if on Sunday and every other day it is true to say that there is a man on the moon, then it follows that there is a man on the moon on Sunday and every other day.

Numbers and universals like redness, etc., may be different. It is true to say on Monday, and at any other time, that there is a prime number between three and seven, but it does not seem to make sense to say that there is on Monday a prime number between three and seven, or that there is a prime number between three and seven on Monday. (It may be that the statement that there is always a prime number between three and seven is always true, but falsely suggests something false, viz., that numbers can change.) But if it can be true to say at all times that there is a prime number between three and seven without its being true at all times that there is a prime number between three and seven, then it could be true of God that it is at all times true to say that he exists, without its being true that God exists at all times. In any case, I do not think that God's existing at all times would detract from his timelessness to any extent if he exists at all times only in the way that numbers so exist.

(vii)   Omnipotence and the Everlastingness of God

If God is 'in' time at all, the fact that one can say at all times that he exists means that he exists at all times. It follows that God is ageless, in the sense that the question 'How old is God' does not make sense (unless the answer is that God is infinitely old, and hence always the same age). For there will be no finite number which is the number of years between the time at which he came into existence and the present moment. This is because there was no time at which he did come into existence. (I am assuming for the sake of argument that the year would be a satisfactory unit for measuring time, which it would not in fact be, for it could not be used to measure times before the formation of the solar system.)

That God has no age, is ageless, or infinitely old, will be true at all times, for infinity plus the number of years that have elapsed since the last time we were pondering on the age of God (when even then God was infinitely old) is still infinity. Hence God will never get any 'older', however long we wait, for he will always be infinitely old.

It is possible to argue that God, by definition, always exists. There is something defective about a being who comes into existence or goes out of existence, and a perfect God cannot be defective. Hence that God always exists is a logical or conceptual truth. It would not follow that there actually was a being who existed always, however, but only that if there was a God, he would always have existed.[8] Nor would it follow that there was not a being who, though he did govern the universe, was not everlasting. It would simply follow that if there were such a being, he was not God, if God is by definition timeless. And it is not possible to argue from the fact that there is a god to the fact that he always has and always will exist, for this would be to beg the question. We would first have to establish the fact that the being who governed the universe always had existed and always would exist before we were entitled to describe him as God. (In the same way, we should not be able to convince someone that Smith was unmarried by arguing that he must be unmarried, because he is a bachelor. If anyone is in doubt about whether someone is unmarried, he must be in equal doubt about whether he is a bachelor.)

The fact that God is by definition everlasting and so cannot annihilate himself cannot stop the being who governs the universe from annihilating himself (which he must he able to do, if he is omnipotent), or from being annihilated. All that does follow is that, if the being who governs the universe does annihilate himself, that being was not and never had been God. Similarly, one is not stopped from marrying a man by the fact that he is a confirmed bachelor, though if one does marry him, it cannot ever have been that he was a confirmed bachelor.

Though that God is necessarily everlasting is true if God is everlasting by definition, all this means is that it is necessary that God is in fact everlasting. It does not follow that God is necessarily-everlasting, or that he necessarily possesses necessary-everlastingness, as opposed to possessing (necessarily) everlastingness.

(viii) Are Being Eternal, Changeless, or Everlasting Perfections?

Being changeless is a desirable attribute in God, for we need to be able to rely on him absolutely, and a being who changed could not be relied upon absolutely. The same applies to being everlasting, especially if we believe that we are immortal, for then it would be more likely that we would need there to be a God who was everlasting.

But what about his being eternal (as contrasted with his being everlasting) in the sense that nothing can happen to him because he is outside the time-series? One might argue – indeed, I have argued – that it is more sublime and less mundane to transcend the time order than not and consequently that being eternal is a perfection. On the other hand, one can argue that an incoherent attribute cannot be a perfection and that being eternal is both incoherent and inconsistent – for reasons already given – with the other attributes that some suppose God must have, e.g., forgivingness.

(ix)   The Necessity of God's Eternity

It might be possible that God is not only by definition changeless or everlasting. These attributes might arise out of his other attributes. Numbers are not unchanging because they are by definition unchanging. Their unchangingness arises out of the kind of thing they are. (It may be that the kind of thing they are is the kind of thing they by definition are.) It may be that blackbirds are by definition black. But this is not what prevents birds who are by definition black from changing their colour. What prevents them from doing this is what makes them black, i.e., something about their physical constitution. (The relation between the characteristics that make a blackbird black and its being black is a causal one.)

Hence God may also be necessarily eternal in the sense that his eternity is necessitated by his other characteristics, as a blackbird's blackness is necessitated by its physical nature, or a number's being unchanging is necessitated by something about its nature.

There would be no contradiction in supposing that God was either both eternal by definition and necessarily eternal in that his being so resulted (necessarily) from some of his other characteristics. Blackbirds can be both black by definition and also such that their blackness necessarily results from their physical constitution. It may even be that they have by definition the physical characteristics which necessarily result in their being black, as well as being black by definition. All this being so, it could be that God is not only by definition eternal, but that by definition he is necessarily eternal, in that by definition his eternity necessarily results from other attributes that he by definition has. Two kinds of necessity would then be involved in the concept of God. There would be the logical necessity by which God possessed eternity and some other kind of necessity which made his eternity dependent upon his other characteristics.

But it is difficult both to understand the nature of that necessity which connects God's eternity to his other attributes and also to establish that God is necessarily eternal in this latter sense (that his necessity arises out of his other characteristics). Unlike the connection between the characteristics which determine a blackbird's colour, this relation cannot be established empirically. For it is impossible to observe God's attributes and so to discover by trial and error whether or not they are necessarily connected.

The alternative is that God's unchangingess should arise out of his nature in the way in which the unchangingness of numbers or characteristics arise out of theirs. The sense in which God is eternal should perhaps be that it does not make sense, or involves a category mistake, to speak of his changing. But I suspect that his being unchanging in this way would mean that God would, like numbers and characteristics, have to be an abstraction and so incapable of being personal.

(x)   Conclusions

Nothing, including God and numbers, can be eternal in the sense that a proposition that is true of it at one time must be true of it a all times. It may be possible that God is 'intrinsically eternal', i.e., eternal in the sense that numbers are eternal. However, an eternal being could not have some of the personal characteristics attributed by some religious people (including Christians) to God. The idea that God can change only his relational properties is not compatible with God's being personal. God could be unchanging, but a God who was merely unchanging (and also sempiternal) would, though everlasting, be vulnerable to what happened in the empirical world.

There is thus a conflict between God's being eternal in the sense of being incapable of changing and his being personal. Since there is a variety of reasons for thinking that God cannot be personal, one should opt for the more aesthetically pleasing idea that he is everlasting and incapable of change.

Notes

1   See Plato's *Theaetetus*.
2   As Kant pointed out. However, 'going into' or 'coming out of' existence is a happening; whether it is a something that happens to the house I am not sure.
3   In Geach, 1972.
4   Especially McTaggart, 1934, chapter 5.
5   Though this is a complication that I shall ignore, McTaggart actually thought that there were three series, only the last (the C-series) of which was real.
6   'The moving finger writes'. The reader is referred to Smart, 1966.
7   The reader is referred to the symposium 'Transcendental Tense', Mellor Lucas, 1998.
8   I have made this point in my remarks about Malcolm's ontological argument in chapter 4.

19 God's Infinity, Simplicity, Unity, Impassibility and Holiness

(i)   Introduction

I shall not say much about those attributes of God that will be the topic of this chapter. This is partly because I find the words for some of them difficult to understand. There may be some point in discussing these views even so; for one thing, some may find it helpful if I indicate why I find these words difficult to understand.

(ii)   Infinity

Infinity is not a separate attribute. God is not omnipotent and omniscient and perfectly good *and* infinite. He is, if he is infinite at all, infinitely powerful, infinitely knowledgeable and infinitely good.

The idea of mathematical infinity cannot apply to a personal God. An infinite number is one that is equal to (i.e., can be put into one/one correspondence[1] with) a (proper) part of itself[2] and this idea applies to number, but not to a person. If space is infinite, this fact is irrelevant to the infinity of God, for God is not in space. (It seems moderately obvious that God is not identical with space.)

Since God, if there is a personal God, is omnipotent, he must be so powerful that it is impossible for him to be any more powerful. Since he is omniscient, he must be so knowledgable that it is impossible for him to be any more knowledgable. Since he is good, he must be so good that it is impossible for him to be any better. I doubt, however, whether these statements are best expressed by saying that he is infinitely powerful, knowledgeable and good. Even infinite numbers have other infinite numbers that are bigger than them. Hence to describe God as infinite might not be to pay him as big a compliment as it might seem.

(iii)   God's Simplicity

The doctrine of divine simplicity maintains that God has no parts or components whatsoever. He has no properties, either essential or accidental. He has neither spatial nor temporal extension. There is no division of his life into past and future states, for that would imply temporal compositeness. God's simplicity is allegedly implied by his perfection, which implies independence, which implies his independence of his parts.

However, God must have attributes, if he is omniscient, as omniscience is an attribute. And his existence and his essence (his attributes) must be kept distinct, and not merged into one for the sake of simplicity, for it is the attributes of being omnipotent, omniscient, etc., that may or may not be instantiated. It is true that God can have no spatial parts. But if omniscience, etc., can – misleadingly – be regarded as his parts, he can have parts in an extended sense of 'part'. His omniscience being different from his omnipotence would not *imply* that he was dependent on his omniscience. But since an omnipotent being who was not omniscient could not control the things he did not know about, an omnipotent being would be dependent on being omniscient nevertheless. (It is less than obvious why omniscience should imply omnipotence.)

If God were, as is sometimes said, omniscience rather than omniscient, he would still have something like an attribute, for omniscience would have the quasi-attribute of being instantiated – if there is a God – or not instantiated – if there is not one.

Though simplicity is not a coherent attribute, I feel obscurely that a simple god is a more fitting object of worship or contemplation than a god who is not simple. Mystics have always been attracted by the idea of the One, and a simple god would be more of a one, so to speak, than a god who is not simple.

(iv)   God's Unity

Unity is not, strictly speaking, a *characteristic* of God. To say that God possesses unity is to say that there is only one God. (It is not a characteristic of any wonder of the world that there are seven of them.)

Though there might be more than one omniscient, perfectly good being, there could be only one omnipotent being. If there were two, and one were to try to bring about what the other tried to prevent, it would follow that this thing would both be brought about and not be brought about, which means that the existence of two omnipotent beings would imply a contradiction. In any case, to have more than one god is aesthetically messy. If two gods were exactly alike, there would be no difference between there being one and there being two, and one of them would in any case be redundant. If they were not exactly alike, one would be better than the other, and so only the better one ought to be worshipped.

The only doubt that it is rational to have with God's unity is doubt about whether the number of Gods is as many as one.

(v)   God's Impassibility

God's impassibility is his inability to feel emotion, pain, or to be hurt by what happens in the world. I do not so much have difficulty with understanding this views with seeing that a personal God's possession of this characteristic is (a) a perfection, and (b) consistent with what in practice is the normal Christian conception of God.

(a) Impassibility is not a perfection in a personal God, since such a being ought to suffer on account of man's suffering. It is morally worse not to suffer if others are suffering, especially if one is responsible for that suffering or can relieve it.

(b) It is inconsistent with the Christian idea of God in practice, because a Christian God is supposed to love us and loving implies suffering on account of the suffering of those one loves. Impassibility would not be an imperfection in an impersonal God, however, though perhaps such a God might be better be described as neither passible nor impassible – as quadratic equations are neither heavy nor light – than as passible.

A God outside the time stream would have to be impassible, as he or it could neither affect nor be affected by events within it.

(vi)   Holiness

God is said to be holy. It is very difficult to know what is meant by 'holy'. If one considers people or things that have been said to be holy, it is difficult to believe that there is any characteristic common and peculiar to them, other than people's reactions to what they regard as holy, that might be detected by the five senses or show up on instruments. Hence one is tempted, in the spirit of the logical positivists, to regard 'holy' as a meaningless word, at least if it is meant to be a word for such a characteristic. And though to say that that something is holy – though doing so reveals that the people so describing it regard it as valuable – is a moral judgment is not very plausible. God's goodness is one thing; his holiness quite another.

Though I do not think moral judgments are imperatives, statements about the holiness of things, when they are not confused and impossible attributions of quasi-physical characteristics to them, are something like imperatives. If I may put the matter in my own prosaic way, to say that God is holy is to say that he is not to be taken lightly, not to be approached without care, treated with reverence, and so on.[3] If one says that God is not to be approached lightly, what I say can properly be said to be true by anyone who also thinks that God is to be approached lightly. Though being not to be approached lightly is not exactly a characteristic of anything, the fact that something is not to be approached lightly is independent of whether anyone thinks that it is not to be approached lightly. Whether something is or is not to be approached lightly is dependent upon its other characteristics. In the case of God, if he exists, his omnipotence, omniscience and benevolence alone would make it true that he was not to be approached lightly. Hence God, if he exists, is holy.

I am inclined, peculiar though it may seem, to say that God might be holy even if he does not exist, or if existence is not properly applied to him. For the idea of God is to be treated with reverence. If one even thinks with disrespect of what deserves to be thought of with respect, one is not treating what one is thinking of as God. And God, by definition deserves to be treated with respect, for what does not deserve to be so treated is not God.

I feel sure, however, that, even if the account of holiness which I have given is correct, people do in fact think that, over and above the ways in which God is not to be treated, there is some non-natural characteristic, holiness, which God is not alone in possessing. But, for the reason given, there cannot be any such characteristic.

(vii)   Conclusion

There is at least an appearance of incompatibility between regarding God as personal and regarding him as infinite, simple, unitary and impassible.

This conflict has traditionally been removed by regarding him as possessing personal characteristics only analogically. I have argued in chapter 1 that this attempt to remove the conflict is a failure. If God existed in any straightforward way, he could not be both personal and non-personal.

But if one has some choice about what kind of God one decides to 'have', not on the factual grounds that there is something answering to one description of God but not to another, but because one finds one better satisfies one's needs than the other. But it may be a good idea sometimes to regard God as being personal and at other times to regard him as being non-personal. It may be better to regard him as personal if what one wants is solace, companionship and help; better to regard him as personal for the purposes of contemplation. The more austere may wish to regard God as being only impersonal. (I later refer – in the chapter on faith – to Evelyn Underhill's brilliant description of the contrast between the two attitudes (though she herself does not regard their objects as being incompatible).)

For the purpose of worship God might well be regarded as something like simple, unitary and impassible. Worshipping a non-personal God in preference to a personal one has the advantage that there is not a personal God, and that, since a non-personal God can have no affects, one may worship one without fear of nourishing false expectations of what as a result will happen in the world.

Notes

1   As the fact that (the class of) husbands can be put into one/one correspondence with wives means that there are as many husbands as wives, i.e., the same number of husbands as of wives.

2   As the infinite series of numbers starting with 0 and continued by adding one can be put into one/one correspondence with the infinite series starting with 0, and continued by adding 2, or by doubling (or trebling, or whatever) every member of the first series, or any other of the resulting series.

3   I have put forward a similar view of moral judgments in Harrison, 1971, chapter XIV.

20 God's Embodiment

(i)   God Does Not Have a Body

God is usually supposed not to have a body. It would be indeed extraordinary if, somewhere in the universe, there was something which was the body of God; something which we might come across, if only we knew where to look for it. One thing which must now be very obvious is that examining the universe does not easily discover many, or indeed any, very clear signs of his existence. If there were somewhere in the universe an object which was God's body, then God would, at any rate in principle, be no more hidden than human beings. (Even human beings are partially hidden, in that, even when you find their bodies, inspection of these will not necessarily reveal their thoughts and feelings, especially if they are trying hard not to let others know what these thoughts and feelings are.)

Is it just a matter of fact that God does not have a body, or is it a necessary truth that he does not have one? Before we can answer this question one must say a few words about the relation between ordinary finite persons and their bodies.

One does not ever, in ordinary English, say one *is* a body. One says one *has* a body. Nor, incidentally, does one ever say that one *is* a mind. One says that one *has* a mind. This ought to suggest that people are neither bodies nor minds, though they have both. This leads to the questions 'Is it a contingent fact or a necessary truth that people have bodies?' and 'Is it a necessary or a contingent truth that people have minds?' (It is obvious that the answer to the second question is that people do not have to have minds, as they can suffer brain death, though if they do suffer brain death, they may no longer be persons. I am not very familiar with the use of the rather pretentious word 'persons', but it may well be that persons have to have minds, although people (members of the species *homo sapiens*) do not.)

425

(ii)   The Connection Between Ourselves and Our Bodies[1]

What, then, is the nature of the connection between ourselves and this piece of matter which makes us want to say that it, rather than any other piece of matter, is our body?

We say that a certain body, or material object, is our body if the following propositions are true of our relationship with it.

(a) I feel pain when pins are stuck in this body, but not when pins are stuck in other bodies, whether these other bodies are animate or inanimate. (Part of the meaning of 'animate' may be that a body is animate if pains are felt when pins and such are stuck into it.)

(b) I feel the inside of this body, but not of other bodies. I feel my own stomach, but not other people's. I feel myself breathing, but do not feel other people breathing. I feel tension in my muscles, but not in other people's muscles. There is a mass of bodily sensation, which I suppose is roughly located where I believe my physical body to be.

(c) I see my body in a very different way from the way in which I see the bodies of other people or inanimate objects. I see other people's faces and the backs of their heads, but do not see my own face or the back of my own head (except in a mirror). I believe that, when other people are looking at me, they see something that closely resembles what I see when I am looking at them. When I look at them, I see a face-shaped object in the middle of my visual field, which I take to be a face (or the front surface of a face). I assume that they, too have a face-shaped object in the middle of their visual fields, which object they also unreflectingly take to be a face (my face or the front surface of my face). Without the aid of mirrors, however, I cannot see anything (my own face) like what they can see and I can only infer or hypothesise that something like this is what they see.

Furthermore, I carry my own body about with me wherever I go. I can remain in the vicinity of other people's bodies or I can remove myself from this vicinity, but with my own body I have no choice. This is because the eyes with which I see are fastened to this body, which is also why I cannot see my own face (or my own eyes) or the back of my own head.

(d) I have 'direct control' over the movements of this body, but not over the movements of other bodies. In order to move the glass on the table, which is not part of my body, I have to move my hand and then move the glass with my hand. In order to move my hand, which is part of my body, I do not first have to move anything at all. (I may move one hand with the other hand, but then I am not moving the hand I move in this way directly.)

(e) I look out on the world from a place just behind the nose of this body. I do not look out on the world from a place behind the nose of anyone else's body. The place from which I look out upon the world is situated towards the top of that mass of bodily sensation which I feel when I feel my own body from the inside.[2] What I see, touch, taste, smell and feel is determined by the place where this body is (especially by the position of its eyes, and the direction in which they are looking). It is not determined by the place where other people's bodies are, or by the position of inanimate objects.

(f) If the brain inside the head of this body is hit with a brick, I lose consciousness. If it contains too much alcohol, I see double. If there is a tumour on this brain, I may think I am Charles II or Oliver Cromwell. An excess of certain substances in its blood may cause me to feel depressed or sexually frustrated and a lack of other substances may make me feel hungry. This does not happen to me when other brains are hit with bricks, or contain too much alcohol, or contain tumours, or have the wrong kind of chemistry.

(g) If other people want to communicate with me they have to produce sound waves in the vicinity of this body, make gestures in front of the eyes in this body's head, tap messages in Morse code on the backs of its hands, make noises emanate from wireless or telephone receivers close to this body's ears, etc. It is no good their doing any of these things in the vicinity of bodies other than this body.

Reflections on the Aforementioned Facts

None of these facts entail that I do not also stand in an eighth relationship to my body, that of being identical with it (though I do not think we are identical with our bodies). What these fact do show is that the thought I am having, when I think, for example, that I am related to this body by the fact that I look out upon the world from a place just behind the bridge of this body's nose, is not the thought I am having when I think that this body is me. That these two things are not identical does not show that I am not my body, any more than the fact that the thought that I have when I think that the head of the second oldest member of the Moral Sciences Club is in his room is not the thought I have when I think that I am in my room shows that I am not the second oldest member of the Moral Sciences Club. All it shows is that it is possible that I am not the second oldest member of the Moral Sciences Club.

It is not, I think, an empirical discovery that out of all the material objects in the world there are, that object of which all the seven aforementioned things are true, is my body. It is the fact that these seven things are true of an object that makes it proper to describe it as my body, and any body of which these things are true must be my body. This is because we use the expression 'my body' in such a way that it is properly applied to anything of which these seven things are true. That *if* these seven things are true of a body then it is my body is, therefore, a necessary truth. That this hypothetical proposition is true depends upon the concept of being a body and upon what is meant by saying that a body is my body. However, that the world contains a body of which these seven things are true and so which is my body is an empirical fact.

For each one of the seven relations to my body mentioned above, it is an empirical contingent fact, which might be otherwise, that there is some body, in fact my body, which is related to me by this relation. It is an empirical contingent fact that I feel pains when pins are stuck into my body (for I might be anaesthetised); that I feel the inside of my body (for the same reason); that there is a body of which I cannot see the whole surface; that I have direct control over its movements (for I might be paralysed); that I perceive from behind its eyes (for I might be blind); that I see double when there is too much alcohol in this body's blood stream, for I might be superhumanly resistant to alcohol; and it is also an empirical contingent fact that people have to communicate with me by producing written words or sounds or gestures or other symbols in this body's vicinity.

(iii)   Possible Variants on Normal Embodiment

This gives rise to some interesting possibilities.

(a) Given that I do not have to feel pain when pins are stuck in my body, might I not (i.e., might it not be logically possible for me to) feel pain when pins are stuck in apparently inanimate objects, or in the bodies of other people? (It has been claimed that this actually happens in the case of Siamese twins.) I say 'apparently' inanimate objects, because if pains are felt by me when pins are stuck in this table, it may partially be animated by me. Siamese twins may own parts of their bodies jointly.

(b) Might I not be able to feel the inside of apparently inanimate bodies? There are supposed to be people who suffer from the delusion that they are pieces of Dresden china. If they were pieces of Dresden china these deluded people might know what it would be like to feel the insides of one. Indeed, feeling the inside of a piece of Dresden china might be just what you imagine yourself to be doing when you think, mistakenly, that you are a piece of Dresden china.

(c) Might there not be some other body than mine that I am able to see in the way (i.e., not from all round) that in fact I see my own? If, indeed, I were to grow into my clothes, as a snail is fastened to its shell, I would be able to see my clothes only from the outside.

(d) Might I not be able directly to move material objects other than my own body or parts of my own body? Might I not be able to move a glass without first moving my arm? (This is not what is alleged to happen if the phenomenon known as telekinesis occurs. For telekinesis, if it occurs, consists in my willing objects which are not parts of my body to move and finding that they move. I do not will my arm to move and find that it moves, however, or, if I do will my arm to move, I find that it does not move. I just move it. What I am supposing is that I move the cup on this table without willing it to move, in just the same way that I move my arm without willing it to move. I just try to move the cup and I move it just as I move my arm.)

(e) Might I not see from some body in some place far removed from my own body? H.G. Wells has a story[3] of a man who sees from a place many thousands of miles from the place where his body is. I can see no logical reason why I should not have a visual field just like the visual field of a man many miles from me would have and its contents be determined by what is happening to his eyes and so, indirectly, by the objects which determine what is happening to them.

(f) Perhaps the lump of matter (my brain) which is such that its being hit causes me to lose consciousness, its being disorganised by a brain tumour causes me to lose my sanity, etc., might not be inside this body, but somewhere quite different, in the skull of a body other than mine.

(g) Perhaps, in order to communicate with me, other people might have to make noises not in the vicinity of this body, but in the vicinity of some other body, or of some apparently inanimate object. (I again say 'apparently inanimate', because to the extent that any one of these six things are true of any material object, then that object is not an inanimate object, but an animate one.)

One could even conceive of the possibility of having not one body like the body I have now, but a number of bodies to each of which I am related in all seven of the ways mentioned above. In this case, the normal one/one relationship between body and mind would no longer hold. There would be one mind connected with several 'bodies'.[4]

It might even be that I was related to seven different objects in the world in these seven different ways listed above, so that I felt pain when pins were stuck in one body, could not see the whole of the surface of a second, felt the inside of a third, had direct control over the movements of a fourth, looked out on the world from a fifth, was dependent for my thoughts and feelings on what happened to a sixth, and could be communicated to only in the vicinity of a seventh.

If this were possible, and were actually to happen, it would be very difficult to know how to describe the resultant situation. Would it be better to say that I had seven different bodies, each with a specialised function, or would it be better to say that I had only one body which was composed of seven different material objects and so occupied a region of space more as a platoon occupies a village than as I occupy my armchair? Perhaps in this case, however, though one could speak of me as being embodied, in that the world contains a number of material objects (or bodies) with which I am very intimately connected in the manners described, it would be better not to speak of me as having a *body* at all.

Furthermore, we might be embodied in only six out of the seven ways we have mentioned. This would happen if we were blind, anaesthetised, paralysed, or if we simply did not have a brain. That we have brains at all is an empirical discovery. The ancient Egyptians thought that the seat of thought was in the stomach. It is logically possible that we should cut open someone's head and find just straw, or sawdust, or nothing at all. Very few of us have seen a brain and scarcely anyone has seen his own brain. Hence that we have brains is just a contingent fact, a fact which might have been otherwise.

Then might we not be embodied in only five of these seven ways, or only four, or only three, or two, or even in only one? Again, if this were the case we might, in some cases at least, prefer to speak of our being embodied, rather than of our having a body.

I have suggested that one person might have more than one 'body'.[5] It is also possible, conversely, that several different persons might share one and the same body.[6] (It might be better to say, in the second case, that one person could have more than one mind.) It would be misleading to say that several different *people* – in one sense of 'person', people is the plural of 'person' – might share a body. In one sense of 'person', the sense in which it is the singular of 'people', a person is just a member of the species *homo sapiens*. In another sense of 'person', a person could refer to anything possessing a selection from a list of attributes like being able to think, perceive and act, being sensitive to moral distinctions and being capable of having duties and rights. God and limited liability companies may be persons in almost this sense. Neither are members of the species *homo sapiens*.

More than one person, in this sense of 'person', might share a body. It may even be sometimes a matter for terminological decision how many people we say there are. For example, since all the facts of the matter are the same, it may be simply a matter of how we choose to talk whether we say that there have been two persons alternately occupying a body, or just one person who occasionally suffers from amnesia. In the case of multiple personality – or at least if there are only two 'personalities' in question – it might be just a matter of arbitrary choice whether we say that there are several persons with one body, or one person (but which?) who cannot get access to all the contents of his mind.

There is some empirical evidence (drawn from the phenomenon of hysterical disassociation) that this is possible. Such things appear to happen in the case of alternating personality. For example, a man leaves home and arrives in some other town without the faintest recollection of who he is or what he has been doing or what his past was. He lives there for a while, engaged in normal pursuits, when, after a few months, his former memory returns and he goes back to his home town without the faintest idea of what he has been doing since he lost his memory. This process may be repeated after an interval. During all attacks of amnesia after the first he can remember what he did the last time he suffered from 'amnesia', but recall nothing about what happened to him before the first attack and nothing of the intervals between the two 'attacks'. Similar things are true of his 'normal' periods. One might be tempted to say that, in such cases, two persons occupy the same body alternately.

The case of Sally Beauchamp provides a more striking example. In this case, the personalities exist simultaneously. No less than four 'persons' inhabited the body of Sally Beauchamp and assumed control of this body for intervals of varying lengths. Some of these persons knew of the existence of the others by inference, just as we know of the existence of other people. In order to communicate with one another, such persons usually had to leave messages on pieces of paper, or with 'mutual' friends. One of these persons knew of the existence and thoughts of one of the others without inference, as we know of our own existence, but this knowledge was not reciprocated. These persons had different personalities and generally no memory and nothing but inferential knowledge of what any of the others had done. Treatment eventually fused three of the four persons, so that eventually there was just one person who had the memories of all three and a more stable and integrated personality than any of them had individually. What happened to the fourth makes fascinating speculation.

It is customary to say that there were not four persons inhabiting the body of Sally Beauchamp, but four personalities. In the usual sense of 'personality' this simply is not true. One's personality is a set of characteristics, like kindness, irascibility, honesty and patience, which can be shared by different persons, and which one and the same person can have and not have at different times. But the 'individuals' who owned Sally Beauchamp's body were not characteristics. They possessed personality – and different personalties – rather than were personalities.[7] It might be better to call them 'subpersons'.

(iv)   Disembodied Persons

If disembodied persons are possible or conceivable, then it must be possible or conceivable, problems concerning identity aside, for us to survive the death of our bodies in the form of disembodied persons.

I think it would be conceptually possible for us not to be embodied in any of these seven different ways mentioned above, in which case we would not have a body, and would be a disembodied person. Whether nature, as opposed to logic, is such as to allow the existence of disembodied people, is quite another matter. For not everything that is conceptually possible actually happens.

It would be conceivable for a person not to have a body at all, if that persons have bodies is a matter of contingent fact and not a conceptual truth. (If a person did not have a body, he would still not just *be* a mind. He would have a mind, but not be one.) Some people might not like to describe disembodied 'persons' as persons. And it is all right to refuse to describe them as persons, so long as it is not argued that the things we refuse to describe as persons cannot exist. This would be like arguing that there can be no creatures in Australia that resemble swans except in being black, because swans are by definition white.

The important thing about persons is that they should perceive, think, feel and communicate with other persons. If disembodied persons can do this, then it would be necessary to treat them (if this is possible) much like people, even if we do not quite like calling entities without bodies 'persons'. (They would certainly not, as we have seen, be persons in the sense of 'person' in which persons are individual people, i.e., individual members of the species *homo sapiens*. They might, however, be persons in the sense in which the Trinity is said to be composed of three persons, but not three people.) If they could feel pain, and be caused to feel pain by our actions, we would have an obligation of humanity to them, for our general obligation not to cause (needless) pain is not limited to other human beings, but extends to some extent to all beings capable of feeling pain (e.g., animals). If they could cause us pain by their actions, they might have duties to us as well as our having duties to them.

(v) What It Would be Like to be a Disembodied Person; Further Remarks About the Possibility of Disembodiment

In order to show that disembodied people are possible, one must give a description, which does not fall into any logical contradiction or incoherence, of (a) what it would be like to be a disembodied person and (b) what it would be like to come across a disembodied person.

The Body Image: Phantom People

A disembodied person might feel just as if he, she or it had a body. A man without a leg can feel just as if he had a leg. This is because the brain is deceived by messages precisely resembling those messages which would be sent from this man's leg, if he had one, to the brain from points on the nerve between the place where his leg would have been and his brain. Messages precisely similar to those one would receive from a long distance caller may be sent by the man next door if he has tapped one's telephone. For the same reason, a man with no stomach or heart could feel just as if he had a stomach or heart. A man with a head, but no trunk, might feel just as if he had a trunk. A man with no teeth or ears or cheeks could feel just as if he had teeth and ears and cheeks. Why, then, should not a man without a body feel just as if he had a body? Why should he not have a whole phantom body, just as some people have a phantom limb? One thing Descartes' malicious demon would do, if he existed, would be to make 'people' feel just as if they had bodies, though they did not. This would involve making them feel just as if they had heads, when they did not. The demon would not need to make men feel as if they had brains when they did not, because one does not normally feel one's brain. The fact that one does not feel one's own brain does not mean that brains are not causally necessary for one to exist, but it may mean that having a brain is not conceptually necessary for existence. It was a relatively recent discovery in the history of mankind that we so much as had brains, properly so called.

Perceiving Without a Body

Why should we not see, hear and feel things without a body, just as we can with a body? The propositions that I see only with eyes is not a conceptual truth, but a contingent matter of fact. Indeed, it is not even true. I can see if the visual centres of my brain are appropriately modified, i.e., in the way in which they are normally modified by messages from eyes, whether I have eyes or not. Perhaps one day it will be possible to make artificial eyes, with which men will be able to see as well, or nearly as well, or perhaps even better, than they now can with natural eyes.

There would, of course, have to be a correlation between the visual perceptions of this disembodied person and the nature and behaviour of certain material objects, if a disembodied person is to be able to have any veridical, as opposed to hallucinatory, visual perceptions. For example, for him to be perceiving a boat moving downstream, there would have to be a lawful correlation between his perceptions of the boat and the motion of the boat. It would have to be a true proposition that, had the boat not been moving in such-and-such a way, the man who perceived it would not have had perceptions as of its moving in such-and-such a way. Otherwise it would be just coincidence, and not because he was perceiving the boat, that he had these perceptions.

So far as I can see, there is nothing the matter with Hume's principle that, so far as logic goes, anything can be causally connected with anything else, and it is just a matter of empirical discovery what things are causally connected with what. (Hume thought that a cause would have to be contiguous in space and time with its effect, but I personally think that it is only a matter of experience, not of logic, that action at a distance in space and time does not occur (if it does not occur).)

If Hume is right on this matter, which I think he is, there would then be no *a priori* reason why the perceptions of disembodied spirits should not be causally connected with happenings to the material objects perceived, however unlike one another they are. There might be true hypothetical propositions, established by observation and experience, asserting that the perceptions are dependent upon the object. The two things might be causally connected, however far removed they were in space and time from one another. And even if there is some extra factor to causal connection over and above a constant conjunction between two kinds of events (and, if there is, I think it would have to be the empirical impossibility of separating events of these kinds) there is no reason why this extra factor should not be discovered empirically to hold between material objects and the perceptions of disembodied spirits.

It would be discovered to hold by a process of trying to separate these apparently connected events and finding out whether or not one inevitably failed.

Since one does not observe the perceptions of disembodied spirits, each disembodied spirit would have to establish for himself that there was such a connection. He would have perceptions of, say, an express train approaching and elaborate the theory that he would not be having these perceptions in the absence of the train. He would know that his perceptions were caused by the train in precisely the same way that we know that ours are. Embodied people like ourselves have the theory that their perceptions are caused by what is happening to their brains (as, indeed, they are), but we have to establish a connection between the train and our perceptions before we can establish such a theory, because we cannot normally observe what is happening to our brains. Indeed, our establishing what was real by means of what was caused by our brains would presuppose establishing in some other way than by brain causation that we actually had brains. Since there is no such thing as observing a train without having perceptions of the train, discovering that one's perceptions of a train are veridical involves, as Berkeley pointed out,[8] ascertaining that they stand in suitable relations to other perceptions that also appear to be of trains.

That something is happening to our brains, and what it is, is a matter of (not very daring) speculation (that kind of 'speculation' in which establishing the hypothesis that something exists or is the cause of something confirms a speculation). Two conditions for veridical perception – that the observer's eyes must be open and that his eyes and brain must be in good working order – would not have to be fulfilled in the case of a disembodied spirit, since he does not have eyes and a brain. Where we see with a mechanism, he sees without one. It is just an empirical fact, however, not a matter of logic, that a mechanism is necessary in order for us to be able to see. Since anything may be correlated with anything else, it is possible that there should be a direct correlation between object and perceptions, without the intermediary of the brain. If there are (relatively) simple laws connecting what is happening to the object and what is happening to our brains and then connecting what is happening to our brains with our perceptions of what is happening to the object, there must be more complicated laws connecting directly what is happening to the object with what is happening to our brains. If there is a correlation between the movements of Mars and the sun and the movements of the Earth and the sun, then there must be a (more complicated) correlation between the movements of Mars and movements of the Earth.

Disembodied Feelings

Why should not a disembodied person be able to feel anger and love, etc., like a normally embodied person? Of course, it has been argued that all that anger is is a disposition to hit people, all that fear is is a disposition to run away, all that love is is a disposition to give people presents. If this were so, it would be impossible for someone without a body to feel emotions. For example, a disembodied person will have no legs and so will not be able to run and so will not be able to run away.

But fear is not just a disposition to run away. On this dispositional account of fear, all the really nasty features of fear, the occurrences of feelings of tension, the griping feelings, the hair-standing-on-end feelings, the heart-pounding feelings, have got missed out. Even to run away is not just for one's legs to propel one's body, by alternate motion, in a direction which increases one's distance from some dangerous object or person. It is to do this with the intention of increasing one's distance from the danger and with one's mind constantly occupied with the occurrence of thoughts of the dreadful things which may happen to one if one does not do this quickly enough. And not only is it not enough to say that fear is a disposition to run away, it is not even true. One can feel absolutely terrified without having any tendency to run away at all, if only because one's limbs are rooted to the spot. (The view that these feelings are just brain events will be discussed shortly.)

Thinking Without a Body

There is no reason why one should not be able to think without a body. People who do have bodies may, when they think, think with their bodies in any position or place. They can think standing on their heads, or in the bath. It would also be conceivable that they should think with their bodies in any condition, though there are many conditions in which it is impossible, as a matter of empirical fact, for them to think, e.g., with a big enough iron bar through their skulls. So, if you cannot deduce anything about a man's body from statements describing his thoughts, it looks as if you cannot deduce even that he has a body from statements describing his thoughts. Hence it is conceivable – but not, of course, causally possible – for thought to go on without anything physical going on, and so disembodied thought is possible.

We are, indeed, acquainted with our thoughts, but the existence of our brains is only a well attested (or a conclusively established) hypothesis. Hence logically we do not need brains. Our thoughts (logically) could feel to us exactly as they do now if we did not have brains.

Only we ourselves are acquainted with our own thoughts; others know of them only because they infer them from our behaviour, or because we tell them what they are. (Even this involves hypothesis; we infer what others' thoughts are from the fact that we hear or see certain words, which we believe to have emanated from their bodies.) Such thoughts are private, in the case of ordinary embodied persons. They would be doubly private in the case of disembodied persons. For they would have no body to be found and might choose not to make their existence known. If they were to do this, their existence would be undetectable. (I do not think their having them would be unverifiable, for we know what it would be like, as we shall see later, for disembodied spirits to make their presence known.)

Identity Theory and Topic Neutrality

It has been customary for those philosophers[9] who hold the materialist view that thoughts, feelings, the having of mental images and pains, beliefs and intentions are just identical with physical occurrences, to say that what I have just suggested about the logical independence of the mental from the physical is true, but does not show the independent nature of such things, because statements about them are what is called 'topic neutral'.[10] To say that someone is in pain, for example, is to say that he is in some state which is caused by tissue damage and in its turn causes screaming or aversive behaviour. To say that he is having a yellow after-image is to say that there is something going on in him that resembles what would be going on in him if he were actually seeing something yellow. It is an empirical discovery that these processes are identical with brain processes, much as it was an empirical discovery that those postulated entities which transmitted congenital characteristics from parent to offspring (genes) are in fact identical with the DNA molecule.

The suggestion that descriptions of thoughts, etc., are topic neutral, however, has not the remotest plausibility. When we say we are in pain we are not postulating something with as yet to be discovered characteristics, which is the unknown cause of our pain behaviour. The painfulness of the cause of pain behaviour is only too manifest. Furthermore, it is not a *hypothesis* that we are in pain (as it is a hypothesis that other people are in pain). That there is something that causes our pain-behaviour is, however, a hypothesis. And if it turned out, as in theory it might, that nothing physical caused our pain behaviour, we would not think that we could not be in pain. The pain is obvious, and the hypothesis is not about it, but about what is causing it.

When I have a yellow after-image (and perhaps when I also have yellow mental images other than after-images, as most people do when they are imagining something yellow), it is also, according to identity theorists, a hypothesis (and a correct one, I imagine) that there is something going on in me that resembles what is going on in me when I am actually seeing something yellow. But even if there were nothing going on in me like this, I would still be having a yellow after-image and would know that I was having it.

In any case, it is the after-image that is yellow, not my having it. I know that the after-image is yellow simply by inspecting it. That when I have an after-image, there is something going on in me that resembles what is going in me when I see something yellow, is a plausible hypothesis. Its falsity would not affect the nature and existence of after-images, which is a matter of immediate phenomenological knowledge, not of physiological speculation. Hence I (logically) could go on having images, even if there was nothing other than themselves for them to be identical with, so to speak. I could certainly (conceptually, not causally) go on having them without a brain.

Correlation and Identity

Normally, what makes one decide which brain process a certain mental event is identical with is the fact that there is a constant conjunction between the brain processes and the mental event. We say that pain is identical with certain neurons firing because, if these neurons fire, we are in pain and, if they do not fire, we are not in pain. But though this establishes constant conjunction and makes one suspect a causal connection, it is not an identity. Hence a technique for telling when a coin that was in my pocket is identical with the coin that is now in the pocket of someone suspected of stealing it is not a means of telling whether a pain (to take just one example) is or is not a brain process. There is no such thing as marking the relevant brain process and seeing if the pain bears the same mark, or marking the pain and seeing whether the same mark appears on the pain. What is more, this technique is unavailable in principle, not just in practice. We cannot even conceive of a technique for marking brain processes (by staining the object undergoing the process, perhaps) and finding that the same mark (in this case, the stain) appears on the pain.[11]

When the mind/brain theory was put forward by U.T. Place[12] and J.J.C. Smart,[13] it used as its models of brain/mind identity the identity of the gene with the DNA molecule and the identity of a flash of lightning with an electric discharge. Neither of these analogies is compelling. The identity of a pain with a brain process was supposed to resemble the former because, just as a gene is defined as the transmitter of inherited characteristics, which the DNA molecule is, so pain was supposed to be defined as the unknown cause of pain behaviour. But our concept of pain is not the concept of an unknown (or even a known) cause, for we are all-too-familiar with pain, which has and can be observed to have characteristics which physical causes cannot have. And the relation between observed lightning and that unobserved happening to electrons which is the discharge is not one of identity at all, but that of the observed phenomenon (the flash) to its unobserved physical base. The observed flash could (conceptually could) occur precisely as it does and have the observed non-physical attributes it has, even if the physical phenomena underlying it did not happen. When we talk about flashes of lightning we are not talking about the underlying causes of anything, for the flash is not the unknown cause, but the observed object itself, the cause of which is the happening to unobserved physical objects. If the phenomenal lightning could occur without its physical base, the two cannot be identical. A possible disembodied flash would be a flash which did not have any physical base. It could be seen from a distance, let us suppose, but closer investigation would reveal no further traces of it whatsoever. And if thunder and lightning were both identical with an electrical discharge, instead of being produced by one, they would have to be identical with one another, which they cannot be, since they occur at different times and have quite different characteristics. The same kind of argument shows that the relation between (for example) a rainbow and the physical causes of the rainbow (light being refracted by raindrops) is not one of identity. There could easily be 'disembodied' rainbows, because a rainbow's physical base is nowhere near its apparent or phenomenological location.[14]

A Disembodied World

A disembodied world is also one that it is possible to conceive. For we can imagine a world – among other purely phenomenal worlds – in which nothing is visible of anything from close up. Everything in this world might disappear as we approach closer to it; it is a world in which the only contingently true hypothesis that there are physical entities like atoms and molecules has no experiential support. Even our own bodies, in such a world, would be phenomenal objects only, phantom bodies rather like phantom ships. It is fortunate that, in such an ethereal universe, we would not need food, for that, too, would be disembodied. (I have suggested elsewhere that Heaven might be like this.)

Privacy

Such a universe would not need to be a private universe. Public phantoms, like public hallucinations, are perfectly possible. (The 'Flying Dutchman' was one, if you count fictional objects.) But this world might be private, though it does not have to be, and even if it was not, the pains and the feelings associated (but not identical) with emotions experienced by such creatures would be private. Wittgenstein has argued (on one interpretation of him) that privacy is impossible, because there could be no language to describe such private occurrences (and so no language in which to describe thoughts and feelings, if they were private.) For, according to Wittgenstein, there can only be words for something if there can be rules governing how these words are to be used; and there can be such rules only if it is in principle possible for there to be procedures determining whether or not they are broken.

But other people cannot check whether or not I am using a word for a private occurrence correctly, because they cannot (just because it is private) be aware of the occurrence and so cannot tell whether I am using the word for what I ought to be using it for or not. It might be supposed that I can rely on my memory, but my memory is fallible, and I can check one memory of a private occurrence only by another memory, which must (like checking what is said in one copy of *The Times* with another copy of *The Times*) inevitably lead to the conclusion that this first memory is correct. Hence my deciding for myself whether or not I am using the word correctly is as bad as there being no way of telling whether or not I am using it correctly at all. Hence a rule that can be checked by myself only is not really a rule and so words whose correct use can only be so checked are meaningless.

Wittgenstein's argument (if it is his; I do not wish to get embroiled in often tedious and unprofitable textual exegesis) is mistaken. For one thing, it does not follow that we cannot check whether or not other people are using words for thoughts correctly from the fact that we are not acquainted with their thoughts. There are often the best of reasons for thinking that someone else is, say, in pain, even though we are not acquainted with his pain. Hence we can be sure that if, as he says it is, 'pleasure' is the word he is using for the feeling he has, he is using this word 'pleasure' correctly. And there are many things, over and above how we decided that we would use a word, that we can check *only* by using our memories. What we dreamt of last night, or what we decided yesterday evening that we would do, would be examples. And it is just a mistake to suppose that a first attempt to remember (in this case, how I decided to use a word) and a second more careful and determined attempt at remembering the same thing, must inevitably lead to the same result.

Furthermore, what I mean by a word is not constituted by rules. There are no doubt rules about what I should mean by a word, and, if I do not follow these rules, others will not understand what I say. But what I mean by a word is determined by my intentions and I can have intentions concerning a given word whether I obey rules laid down by others for its use or not, and even without knowing what these rules are. I can have such intentions whether or not there are any such rules and even whether or not there are any people in the universe besides myself to have rules. Meaning something by a word, unlike moving one's pawn – there can be no such thing as a pawn without the rules of chess – is an activity that can occur without rules. (Indeed, the first time someone meant (intended to convey) something by a word, it must have happened without rules.) The rules come into the picture by trying to bring it about that we all mean the same thing by a word; without our doing this, communication would be difficult, if not impossible.

In the last resort it is only I, on the basis of my own private experience, who can test whether or not a word is being used correctly. If one is in doubt about whether a colour is called 'red', one may resolve this doubt by showing someone the colour and seeing whether or not he calls it 'red'. But at this point we have to use our own judgment on the question whether the word 'red' has or has not emanated from the mouth of our informant. It is true that we can ask someone else whether or not he *really has* used the word 'red', but we again have to use our own judgment on the question whether the second person also said 'red'. There is no given point at which it is impossible to check further the word or the colour, but we must stop somewhere, and at this point we must stop with our own unchecked private judgment concerning the word and the colour.[15]

Disembodied Action

We sometimes decide that we will do something on some future occasion. It is very difficult to see what can be deduced about a man's body from a statement to the effect that he has just decided to do something – though one might deduce that he thinks that he has and will continue to have a body from the fact that he has decided to do something like take a walk. Again, we cannot deduce that someone has a body from the fact that he can bring about changes in the world, for it is just an empirical fact that our body is the only thing which we can move without first moving something else. Hence a disembodied person might be able to move things without first moving some part of his body (usually a limb), and so be able to move things without having a body. This view has already been discussed.

Disembodied Persons Possible

Hence it is possible that there should be a being which perceives, feels, thinks and does things, although 'it' does not have a body. If it is as much like a person as this, it seems reasonable to call it a person, even though it does not have a body.

We could not (*ex hypothesi*, for to see someone is to see his body) see a disembodied spirit, which makes some unimaginative people think that it is absurd to suppose that there could be any. As I have already said, when we see another person, we usually see a round face-like patch of colour in the middle of our visual field, which we take to be the surface of his face. (Whether or not it is, as naïve realists suppose it is, actually the surface of his face makes no difference to whether we are acquainted with his internal goings on.) We 'automatically' (or perhaps instinctively or involuntarily) frame the hypothesis that the person we are looking at has, in the middle of his visual field, a patch of colour which he takes to be the surface of our face. We would not come across this patch of colour by looking inside his brain. All we would come across there would be nerve cells. We might, if we were lucky, come across certain modifications to his retina from which we could infer that there was a patch of colour in the middle of his visual field, which he took to be our face. But, all the same, the modified bits of his retina would not be the patch of colour in question and we could infer that he was aware of such a patch only because we had in the past established, by means of testimony in the case of other people, a correlation between the existence of a pattern of neuronal activity and people's seeing such a patch of colour.

(Establishing this is not something we can do ourselves. The correlation would have to be discovered by a person's observing my retina, for example, and reporting what he saw to me and our jointly discovering that what he saw on my retina when I was looking at something like the moon was correlated with what I saw of the moon when I was looking at the moon. More accurately, I would observe that when I saw a silver crescent in the sky, words appeared to emanate from him reporting neurons firing on my retina, and he would observe that when he saw neurons firing on my retina, words appeared to emanate from me, reporting a silver crescent in the sky. The moon (and my image of it) is observed by me and postulated by him, whereas the retinal image (and the image of this image) is observed by him and postulated by me. It is obvious that this establishes only a correlation between the retinal image and the crescent-shaped patch I see when I look at the moon, not an identity between the two. It should be equally obvious that things so different from a retinal image as the silver crescent I see when I look at the sky cannot possibly be identical with a modification to my retina.)

Any person we are communicating with, over and above having an image of our face in the centre of his visual field, is likely to be thinking thoughts, having mental images, experiencing discomfort or pain, aches, tingles in his feet, itches where his woolly vest comes in contact with his skin, hunger pangs if he is late for lunch, or sensations of repletion if he has just had it. He may feel alert, drowsy and have the pleasurable sensation consequent upon anticipating my imminent departure. Since I am not aware of any of these things, that he experiences them at all is a hypothesis over and above the different hypothesis that, when I see the front surface of his face, there lurks behind it an organised conglomeration of brain cells which is responsible for what he thinks and feels. If the former hypothesis is false, as is conceivable, however unlikely, I would be aware of a body that behaved just as if it were animated, but was not (viz., a zombie). One version of solipsism might be that all the bodies that appear to me to be bodies of people are the bodies of zombies.

I have argued that since, even in my own case, happenings to the neurons in the brain is a hypothesis to explain how it comes about that I experience such things as pain, the things explained could logically go on just as they are if the hypothesis were false. If this hypothesis were false in my own case, then I would be a disembodied spirit. If I were a disembodied spirit I would be invisible, for it is only my body and brain that is visible to the outside observer. Hence, if there were any disembodied spirits, it is only to be expected that they would be invisible. (It may be that they are in the wrong category of thing to be either visible or invisible.) But if they could produce effects on the material world (including effects on ourselves) we could know of their existence; but this does not seem to occur.

It is worth remarking that there might not only be disembodied people; there might be phantom people, like phantom ships. A phantom person would not be entirely without a body. He would have a phantom or ghostly body, which, perhaps, might be perceived from some points of view, but not others, by some people but not by others, and obey some of the laws of nature, but not others. (For example it might cast a shadow, which is what it ought to do, but disappear through walls, which it ought not to do.)[16]

I should point out that in what has foregone I have been defending only the conceivability of disembodied 'spirits'. Whether there are in fact any disembodied spirits is quite another matter.[17]

(vi) What It Would be Like to Come Across a Disembodied Person or 'Spirit'

It would be possible to detect the presence of a disembodied person the following way.

The disembodied spirit might bring about changes in the world, by directly moving things as we move parts of our bodies.[18]

How would we know, however, that these changes were brought about by a disembodied spirit? Perhaps we could know this if the changes appeared to be purposive. For example, if stones appeared to hurl themselves in the direction of a human being from a place where no human or animal body was and continued to fly in his direction, whatever avoiding action he took, we might conclude that they were directed by a disembodied spirit having unfriendly intentions towards the person in question. We can certainly imagine this happening. Indeed, one could make a film depicting such an occurrence.

One of the most striking forms of purposive changes of the world a disembodied person could bring about would be the occurrence of meaningful words or symbols. For example, if we saw meaningful messages written on the blackboard in chalk, we could frame the hypothesis that a disembodied person had written them[19] and was trying to communicate with us. The argument we would use would be an argument from analogy. The messages I see on the blackboard resemble the messages I write on the blackboard, which messages I know are produced by a person, namely me. Hence these messages must also resemble the messages I write, in that they too have been produced by a person. Such an argument would resemble the design argument discussed in chapter 7, with the difference that its aim is to prove the existence of a limited being acting within the universe, not one wholly responsible for the universe.

The argument would not be as strong as the argument from analogy to the existence, thoughts, feelings and intentions of an ordinary embodied person. The words I write on a blackboard are produced by a hand, whereas the words a disembodied person writes cannot be. The hand which produces a word when I write is connected by nerves and muscle and bone and sinew to a brain, which, it is natural to believe, controls its movements in such a way that no interruption takes place to ordinary physical laws when happenings to my brain cause my hand to move.

But if there is no interruption to the ordinary physical laws which govern the behaviour of the chalk, supposed to be controlled by a disembodied person, would we not think that it was conclusive evidence that natural physical forces cause the chalk to move in that way and that the fact that it resembled a purposively produced message was just coincidence?

A disembodied person, of course, will be able to hide himself in a way in which an ordinary embodied person cannot. If he chooses to produce effects on the world, these effects will be visible, but he can keep his presence dark, if he wishes, (as God, if there is one, appears to wish) by not producing any effects. If he is an embodied spirit, however, it will always be possible for us to find him, even if he does not want us to.

(vii)   God's Embodiment

In which of the seven ways listed above could God, though he does not have a body, be embodied? It would be quite extraordinary (see (a) above) if there were some part of the material world such that God felt pain when things happened to it. We do not normally suppose God to be capable of feeling pain, and it may be that it would be an imperfection were he able to do so. It would be absurd to suppose that he could feel the inside of anything, as we feel the insides of our body (see b). It would be extraordinary, too (see (c)), if there were parts of his body that God could not see; he could not have a body like ours at all not to see parts of. It would be equally extraordinary if there were some part of the material world which caused God to think and feel as he does (see (f) above), as our brains cause us to think and feel as we do. If there were such a thing, God would then be dependent upon what happened to material things, which would also be an imperfection and incompatible with what is called his aseity.

But it would not be at all odd – indeed it would be an essential part of the concept of an omnipotent God – to suppose that God is embodied (see (d) above) in the sense that he can move or change things in the material world directly, as we can move our bodies directly. This, indeed, would be involved in his having control over the material world, which control he must have if he is to be omnipotent. (He presumably would not have the sensations of stress which human beings have when they control some things, for example, difficult horses.)

Nor would it be at all odd to suppose that God could see everything in the world, as we can see the things in the vicinity of a certain place (see (e) above). To the extent that the fact that a person perceives from a place makes us say that he is embodied in that place or, at any rate, is situated in that place, then, if God perceives from everywhere, then he must in that sense be everywhere, or be omnipresent. (If God is to be capable of perception, as he must be if he is omnipercipient, the world must, as we shall see later, have an effect upon him. For the hypothetical proposition that he would not be having perceptions of the world's being in a certain state if it were not in that state must be true.)

We said earlier (see (g) above) that one of the things which made us want to say that a person was embodied in a certain place was that this was the place where access could be had to him. In order to attract his attention I have to grunt or signal near the place where his body is, or cause there to be such grunts or signals (say, by talking on the telephone). But it seems reasonable to say that, if we can have access to God at all, we can have access to him, as we can to mathematical truth, from any place (and, incidentally, any time) and that, therefore, God is in this sense embodied everywhere (and at all times). If it were not possible to have access to God equally from any place, we would sometimes be unable to ask him for help. A personal God unable to give help would be to that extent inadequate and so imperfect.

It follows that it is not out of the question to suppose that a personal God is embodied. Indeed, if he exists, he must be embodied. It also follows that, if he is embodied, he is embodied equally everywhere in the universe. He can move directly any part of the universe, as we move our bodies. He perceives from everywhere in the universe, as we perceive from behind the bridges of our noses. Access can be had to him (as he can have access to us) from every part of the universe.

It is another question, however, whether it would be absurd to suppose that God is also embodied everywhere in the sense that, just as we see the inside of one material object, namely our body, God feels the inside of all material objects. I think to suppose this would be impossible, because it would be impossible to suppose that God had feelings of indigestion, nausea, tension or muscular stress, and these are the kind of feelings we have of the insides of our bodies.

If God, though he is embodied, does not have, and indeed cannot have, a body anywhere in the universe, I suppose it is just possible that the universe itself might be God's body. This view, however, strikes me as being most implausible. If the relationship between God and the universe were analogous to the relation between ourselves and our bodies, this would again mean that some things which happened to the universe would determine what God thought and felt. In any case, no-one has discovered any part of the universe which even remotely looks as if it might have this function (i.e., the function of the human brain.) If the universe were God's body, this would mean that he perceived everywhere inside his own body and, what is worse, perceived it without eyes, for no-one expects to find anywhere in the universe any eyes which are God's eyes. Nor, of course, could the body of God, if this were the universe, be adapted to its environment, as our bodies are adapted to their environments, for the universe does not have an environment, nor does it have a nervous system and a digestion. It is part of the idea of a body that it is both a tool and a vehicle and the universe as a whole can be neither a tool nor a vehicle, for there would be nothing outside the universe for it to work on (if it were a tool) nor anywhere outside the universe for it to go to (if it were a vehicle).[20]

(viii)   Conclusions

Christianity needs the notion of disembodied existence, even if this is not implied by its doctrine of the resurrection of the body, because God cannot have a body. However, materialism which rejects the possibility of disembodied existence is mistaken. Disembodied 'spirits' or persons are possible, though there is no reason to suppose that there are any. Though God cannot have a body, there is no reason why he should not be embodied. Indeed, an omnipotent omniscient personal God would, by the definition of 'embodiment' have to be embodied.

Notes

1   The argument in the following paragraphs involves a certain amount of borrowing from Harrison, 1973–4, and reprinted in Harrison, 1995.
2   For more about bodily sensation, the reader is referred to Smythies, 1994.
3   'The Case of Jenkinson's Eyes'. 'Where Am I?' in Dennett, 1978, is another example of this clairvoyance.
4   John Wyndham (, 1979) makes this possibility the subject of a piece of science fiction. 'One' child learns mathematics in one class room while 'another' learns French in another classroom and a third geography in another classroom. What each child is taught, they all know. They each know one another's thoughts, as we know our own thoughts, and what any one of them sees or hears, they all see or hear.
5   In 'Doppel-gangers' in Harrison, 1986.
6   In the works cited.

7   *I'm Eve, loc. cit.*, provides another well known example of multiple personality.
8   In *The Principles of Human Knowledge*.
9   For example, by Smart, 1963. The view has also been held by Armstrong, 1968 and by Dennett, 1979 and 1991, and by many others.
10 This idea has also been put forward by Smart, 1963.
11 I have discussed this matter in more detail in Harrison, 1994.
12 See Place, 1956.
13 In Smart, 1963.
14 See Berkeley, 1910.
15 I believe that this argument has been used by A.J. Ayer, but I cannot remember where.
16 I throw out the fanciful suggestion that a resurrection body might be a kind of phantom body. Since Hume was right in thinking that anything may be correlated with anything else, it could have thoughts correlated with its ghostly movements. It would not be normally visible to people on this earth, however.
17 It is conceivable, though not yet achievable, that there might be a person of whom nothing remained but his brain. Such a being would not be a disembodied spirits, because he, she or it would have a brain. The reader is referred to Harrison, 1995.
18 In that case, however, though this spirit would not have a body, he would not be wholly disembodied, as he would fulfil at least one of the criteria laid down earlier in this chapter for having a body. It is possible that action and reaction in that case would not be equal and opposite. Disembodied persons are not the same as invisible persons, for they are intangible, as well as invisible, and there would be no region of space, associated with them, from which (other) objects were excluded.
19 See Putnam, 1981, chapter I.
20 The unwary may assume that the view of the possibility of disembodied persons that I have put forward in this chapter comes from Descartes. In fact it comes from Hume. There are three Humean views that lend support to the possibility of disembodiment. (a) Like Descartes, Hume thought it logically possible that experience might go on just as it does at the moment, without there being any such thing as body, including, presumably, the bodies of persons (*A Treatise of Human Nature*, Book I, Part IV, Section, ii, 'Of scepticism with regard to the senses'). (b) His view that impressions were distinct existences implied that they might exist without bodies (*Treatise*, Book I, Part IV, Section v). (c) It was just a contingent fact that experience was so arranged (i.e. that impressions were constant and coherent) as to cause us to believe in the existence of body (*Treatise*, Book I, Part IV, Section ii). He thought that some impressions were literally nowhere (Book I, Part IV, Section V, 'Of the Immateriality of the Soul').

21 The Body of Christ

(i)   The Body of Christ

It is inconceivable that God should have a body like ours somewhere in the universe; it is not just a matter of fact that he does not have one. If it is inconceivable that God should have a body, then it is unnecessary to look for evidence bearing on the question whether he has one or not.

Of course, it may be a Christian view that God does, or perhaps did, have a body somewhere in the universe, namely the body of Christ. At least, it looks as if the propositions that Christ had a body and that God was Christ logically entail the proposition that God had a body.

I am not sure, however, that Christians, when they say that Christ is God, are using the word 'is' in such a way that it follows that all true propositions about Christ are true propositions about God.[1] (In 'Tom is my bank manager', the word 'is' is being used in such a way that true propositions about Tom are true propositions about my bank manager; apparent exceptions to this rule have already been discussed (in chapter 9.) But Christ is supposed not to be omnipotent and omniscient but nevertheless to be identical with God, who is omnipotent and omniscient.)

The proposition which I wish to maintain, which may or may not be incompatible with Christianity, is that God cannot have a body and that, in consequence, it cannot be that Christ's body is God's body, at least not in a perfectly normal straightforward sense of 'is'. In this straightforward sense of 'is', the statement that Christ's was God would entail that Christ's body was numerically identical with God's body, or that 'Christ's body' and 'God's body' are different descriptions of one and the same thing. However, it may be – and certainly ought to be, if it is to be plausible – that the correct Christian view is that Christ is God in some unusual or esoteric sense of 'is', or that 'is' is being used in the normal way, but is being used 'figuratively'. I put 'figuratively' in quotes because I do not see how there can be a figurative sense of 'is'.) In that case, what I say here is no objection to the statement that Christ is God.

Let us suppose that we come across something that looks like a human body. It is not essential to the argument that it should look like a human body, or even that it should look like an animate body at all). From this body's lips emanate the words 'I am God'. We try to test this apparently extravagant claim by asking the speaker difficult questions. When it always gives the correct answers, we conclude, perhaps a little hastily, that the speaker must be omniscient. We ask it to do seemingly impossible things, like exploding the moon, and when it obligingly does what we ask, we come to the conclusion, again perhaps a little hastily, that the speaker must be omnipotent. Can we then decide that the omnipotent, omniscient being with whom we are speaking must be God? Could the apparently human body in the vicinity of whose ears we ask our questions and from whose mouth issues its replies, be the body of God?

If the body I see is God's body, then presumably God must stand in a relation to it analogous to that in which I stand to my body. That it stands in such a relationship is just what it means to say that something is someone's body. But there are the following reasons for thinking that God does not and cannot stand in this relationship to this (or any other) body.

(a) Surely God does not feel pain when pins are stuck in this body. God is incapable of feeling physical pain. Of course, if pain is felt (by someone) when pins are stuck in this body, God must know that it is felt. This, however, is not enough to constitute a special relation between God and this body, which relation God does not have to any other body, for God must always know when pain is felt when pins are stuck in any body, because he must know whenever pain is felt. (God is sometimes supposed to feel (mental) pain when I act wickedly, but perhaps God can feel mental pain, even if he cannot feel physical pain. It is unnecessary to discuss this matter here.)

(b) Surely God does not feel the inside of this body as I feel the inside of my body? Can God feel its stomach ache, for example, or have pins and needles when the legs of this body have been cramped, or have the sensation of breathing when it breathes, or feel an ache in this body's head? Such a supposition would be absurd.

(c) It would surely also be absurd to suppose that there was a body such that God could not see except in a mirror its face and the back of its head, though he could see the backs of the heads and the faces of other animate bodies. God, if he is percipient at all, must be omnipercipient.

(d) God can move the limbs of this body directly, as I can move my limbs, but so, since he is omnipotent, can he move any other material object, animate or inanimate, directly. Hence the fact, that he can move its limbs directly, does not make him more closely related to this body than to any other body, or to any other part of the material world.

(e) I can see no difficulty in saying that God sees from a place behind the nose of this body. However, though I can see only from a place behind my body's nose, God must perceive from every place. Hence he does not stand in a special relationship to this body, for the place behind the nose of this body is only one of the probably infinite number of places from which he perceives. He would, indeed, perceive from a place behind the eyes of this body whether this body's eyes were in this place or not.

(f) What I think and feel and do is to a very large extent, if not entirely, determined by what happens to my body, especially to the brain inside its skull. But would it not be extraordinary if what God thought, felt and did was determined by what happened to any body at all. Hence God cannot be related to this body as I am to my body. If he were, then, if the head of this body got hit by a sledge hammer, God would lose consciousness, and if it acquired a tumour on its brain God would lose his sanity. And if God cannot change, changes in him cannot be correlated with changes in the brain of this body, and so it cannot be his body.

If God is outside space and time, what happens to this body cannot affect him causally, so again it cannot be his body. If to be causally affected by something is to be dependent on it, and God cannot be dependent on anything, then God cannot be dependent on a body, and so could not be dependent upon this body. God, who is omniscient and omnipotent, could see to it that only those things happened to his body which were consonant with his having the feelings which God decided he would have. But if so, it would not really be the case that what God thinks and feels is determined by what happens to this body, so much as that God has decided to make what happens to this body a sign of what he would think and feel anyway (if he is capable of thinking and feeling, which activities are normally temporal).

(g) We can have access to God, if there is one, by producing noises in the vicinity of the body I see. But this does not constitute a special relationship between God and this body, for it would be ridiculous to suppose that God can hear noises produced only within a certain limited region of space (if God can hear noises, as opposed to knowing that they occur.) To suppose the contrary would be to suppose that he is limited in a way in which God cannot be. Furthermore, a God who could not hear his creatures from wherever they happened to be might not be accessible should they need help. (It follows that access can no more be had to God in special places of worship than anywhere else, but the atmosphere in such place may be more conducive to attaining (or seeming to attain) such access.)

Hence we can have access to God from any place – we presumably do not even need to make audible noises in order to be 'heard' by God – and so this body cannot be especially related to God in that we can have access to him only in its vicinity. Similarly, God could communicate with us wherever we were. Hence this body could not be especially related to God in that he could communicate with us only when we were near it, as we can communicate (without apparatus like telephones) with other people only when we are near enough to their bodies to be able to produce, in these bodies, by manipulating our own body (e.g., by talking), the appropriate physical effects.

Hence this body, from the lips of which emanate the words 'I am God', cannot be the body of God.

This would not mean that these words are being used to say what is false, even when the sentences which emanate from it start with the word 'I'. 'I' (in one of its uses, if not in its only use) is a device to enable the person speaking to refer to himself without having to go to the trouble of repeating his own name. The fact that the body from which these words come is not the body of God does not show that the word 'I' does not refer to God. If 'I' refers to the speaker, they could refer to God, if God is speaking by manipulating the vocal cords of a body which is not his, as when we manipulate a telephone. (When we hear the word 'I' coming from the earpiece of a telephone, we do not suppose that it refers the telephone.) In this case the body I see will not so much be the body of God as a sort of puppet which God manipulates, or a sort of token or representative, which he uses in order to communicate with people. Logically this body may be unnecessary, because God could find other ways of communicating with us, but it might nevertheless be psychologically effective. God would need to have a body to show us by example how to live our lives if this involved such things as being crucified.) It would appear, however, that these interesting views are heretical.

It seems to me that God might communicate with us in this manner without using any material body, but by producing an individual or communal hallucination (a hallucination in the sense that the experiences in question are not caused by sound waves produced by vocal cords). It does not follow from the fact that these words are hallucinatory that they do not make perfectly good sense, nor that they do not enable their user to say what is true. Indeed, there is a sense in which the words are not hallucinatory, for if I have a hallucination of having seen the word 'God', though the material in which it is embodied may be hallucinatory, it is, nevertheless a perfectly good instance of the type-word 'God'. If I see the words 'Prepare to meet thy doom' written in hallucinatory clouds, the clouds may be a hallucination, but the occurrence of the word 'doom' is not. If a group of people were to have a hallucination of seeing, written in the sky, the words 'The end of the world is nigh', it would not follow from the fact that they were having a hallucination that these hallucinatory words did not say that the end of the world was nigh, nor that it was not God who was communicating to us in this interesting way, nor that it was not a fact that the end of the world was nigh.

It also seems to me to be perfectly possible for God to communicate with us by using the body of some quite ordinary non-divine person, a prophet perhaps. The simplest way of explaining this would be if this person were to find from time to time that he had no control over his limbs and vocal cords, which produced edifying messages which he knew did not emanate from him. He would then feel as if he were possessed.

It might even be possible for God to communicate with us by 'putting into the head' of this man the thought that he would say certain things. It would then at least seem to him to be the case that he was saying these things; indeed, it might even be the case that he *was* saying them, for the proposition 'God caused him to say these things' would not entail that he did not himself say them; rather it would entail that he did. If God communicates with us by means of his prophets, this must be the way in which he does it. It is theoretically possible that this is the way in which the bible was written.

It seems to me that the most helpful analogy, (already touched upon) on which to conceive of the relation between God and Christ, providing that we give up the idea that God and Christ are literally one, is that of multiple personality. Sally Beauchamp's four 'personalities' took it in turns to control the body they had the misfortune of sharing, and usually had to communicate with one another by leaving notes, or by leaving messages with friends. One Sally Beauchamp knew of the existence of another without having to infer this from notes or messages, though the first knew of the existence of the second only, as we know of the existence of others as a hypothesis to explain the messages.

The following suggestion is fanciful, but it could be that God and Christ are related in such away that they 'shared' Christ's body as the Beauchamp family shared their body – though God would have to be less intimately related with this body than was Christ. Though either could control it directly, it could be that God forewent his control, as he foregoes controlling our bodies. God would have complete direct knowledge of the contents of the mind of Christ, though Christ would have only partial direct knowledge of the mind of God.

Though Christ could be related to Christ's body in all these ways in which we are related to our bodies, God could be related to this body only indirectly, in that he was related to a person, who had more than average direct access to God's thoughts (if others have such access at all), and this body is the body of that person. (It is not only, however, that God is less closely related to this body than is Christ, so much as that God, unlike Christ, is, as we have seen, equally closely related to other bodies. And Christ could be possessed by God, to the extent that God could control Christ's actions and thoughts, though this could not constitute a special relationship between Christ and God, because God can control anyone's actions and thoughts.)

(ii)   Conclusions

It is inconceivable that God should have a body. Hence it is inconceivable that Christ's body should be God's body, and so inconceivable that Christ should literally be God. However, Christ's mind might be more intimately connected with God's mind than are the minds of his (other) creature's.

Note

1   In what follows I am criticising the view that Christ is quite literally identical with God. I do not attempt to discuss the relationship between the Holy Ghost and God's body. The difficulties with regarding Christ's body as God's body would not be difficulties for heresies such as Arianism and Docetism.

22 God's Omnipercipience[1]

(i)   Perception and God's Dependence

Since we have been discussing God's embodiment and since seeing (since it normally involves having eyes and eyes are material objects) is one aspect of being embodied, perhaps now is a convenient place to discuss whether God is omnipercipient as well as being omniscient, and the nature of his omniscience. If God is omnipercipient, then this might explain a great deal of the knowledge he is alleged to possess of what is happening in the material world. He knows, on this view, such things as that there are two desks in my room because he perceives the desks and perceives the room, and so can perceive that there are two.

If God were omnipercipient he would, since he has no eyes, have to see without eyes. But seeing with eyes has the disadvantage of connecting the seer with some parts of the material world – the place where the eyes are – more closely than with others. Hence seeing with eyes would limit the vision of the seer to objects in their vicinity. Hence God's having eyes would limit him in a way incompatible with his omnipresence. And if God did have eyes, it would be in principle possible for us find them somewhere, which would be a quite extraordinary thing to be able to do.

(Some philosophers[2] have held that seeing is believing. If so, there would be no difficulty in God's seeing if there were no difficulty about his believing. (There would be no difficulty about a sempiternal as opposed to an eternal God's believing.) But seeing is one thing, believing as a result of seeing quite another. If seeing is not just believing, but believing things about an object light waves from which are falling on one's retina (or, more precisely, about that part of an object, light waves from which are falling on one's retina), then God could not see, because he does not have a retina.)

However, whether it actually happens or not, seeing without eyes is perfectly conceivable. Indeed, even as things are, eyes are not necessary for a person to have the experience of seeing, which will happen if the optical centres of the brain are stimulated, artificially or by accident, in the manner in which they are usually stimulated by impulses travelling along the optic nerves from the retina. If an apparatus could be invented for transforming streams of photons into impulses capable of stimulating optic nerves, and later the cerebral cortex, directly, i.e., without first stimulating a retina, it would be possible to see without eyes (though it might be better to say that the subject of this experiment saw with artificial eyes).

It may be that, given that there were to be some other part of one's body which conditions what one sees, as what one sees is conditioned by what happens to one's eyes, this part of one's body is by definition one's eyes, but from this it does not follow that there is some part of one's body which does have this function; i.e., it does not follow that one must have eyes in order to see, even in this extended sense of 'eyes'.

There is another difficulty for the possibility of God's seeing, with eyes or without. If God knows that some proposition about the world is true, it must be the case that he would not have believed it, if it had not been true. For the same reason, seeing must involve a causal connection between our perceptions of a thing and the thing itself. If my perceptions of my desk were not causally determined by what was happening to my desk, then they would not be perceptions of my desk. That I was having perceptions similar to those I would have if I were perceiving a desk, and that there is a desk, would then be only a coincidence. God, however, partly because he is usually thought to be outside time and partly because of his aseity, is normally supposed to be incapable of being causally affected by anything.

Hence God's being able to see would involve some measure of dependence upon those things he saw. Such dependence is often regarded as being an imperfection, but I do not see why it should be one. It is rather the other way round; a percipient God whose perceptions were not dependent in this way would be imperfect, for then his perceptions would not be veridical perceptions of the universe.

If causal connections can hold only between things that are in time (as will be the case if an event must succeed or be simultaneous with, or even earlier than, its cause), God's perceiving would seem to entail that God must be in time.

(ii)   The Nature of God's Visual Perception

If God were omnipercipient, then, in order to see everything and to avoid his being more closely connected with some places than with others (which would limit him) he would have to see from everywhere at once. I can see nothing incoherent about this, though it is difficult to imagine what it would be like to see in this way. Men (and some other animals) see from two places, fairly close together. I can see nothing impossible in God's looking out upon the world from an infinite number of points of view. It may be that Berkeley supposed that God saw everything in this way, for he (sometimes) thought that material objects were perceptions in the mind of God, from which it would follow that God sees the whole of the material world (whether or not it is observed by his creatures) all the time and all at once.

If God is omnipercipient, I can think of two possible theories about the nature of his omnipercipience. (a) According to the first, he sees everything from all round, as opposed to the way in which we see things, which is from some distance and from some angle. God's different views of a tree, for example, must be simultaneous (whereas ours are successive) and (on one view) fit together with one another to enclose that region of space where the tree is situated in the way in which ours might do if we had ours all at once. (Ours cannot do this simultaneously, for we usually have perceptions of a given object only one at a time.) Such a being would not have a visual field like ours, for a visual field limits us to seeing only those objects which are 'reflected' on it.

It could be argued that there would be nothing in God's perception analogous to our experience of visual depth and the slant to our visual fields which results from this. For these two features of our visual experience result from the fact that we see by means of retinas that are roughly flat. And such a being could not have even the experience of moving about – as opposed to actually moving about, which God could not do without a body – because this involves the person (or animal) who has it in first having small portions of his visual field occupied by an object and then large ones, and in his having a view of an object characteristic of his seeing something first from one side and then from another. God, if he saw everything from all round, could not do this. This is just as it should be, however, for if God can move about, he would be more closely linked with one part of space than another.

(b) According to the second possible theory about the nature of God's omnipercipience, God has an infinite number of discrete visual fields, which no more fit together to enclose regions of space than do different photographs of an object taken from different places. From every point in space God would have a view of the world from that point. But there would be no straightforward spatial relations between his view of the world from one place and his view of it from another. To suppose that there were such relations would be like supposing that there could be a spatial relation between my view of Everest from a distance and the view of Everest of a climber actually on Everest.[3] But though there would on this theory be no spatial relations between the views themselves, the places from which these views were had could be, and would indeed have to be, spatially related.

This view of God's perceptions could be endorsed by Russell (if he had believed in God). Russell once held that the physical world consisted entirely of what he called perspectives situated in what he described as perspective space. Russell thought that the contents of the perspectives, sensed or unsensed sensibilia, could exist unperceived. But if this was considered impossible, such a view could hold that sensibilia were ideas in the mind of God, organised in what Russell thought of as a six-dimensional space. (Russell thought it was six-dimensional because he thought that independent coordinates were necessary to fix the position of a sensibilium on its perspective and three more to fix the position of a perspective in perspective space.)

(iii)   Difficulties with God's Omnipercipience

Though there is nothing incoherent about the idea of God's seeing everything from everywhere at once, the view that he does this is nevertheless burdened with nearly overwhelming difficulties. For example, would it not be unacceptably anthropocentric to suppose that God, who has no eyes, nevertheless has a view of the world much like ours in kind (though enormously greater in extent)?

We see the world in the way we do because our eyes are sensitive to light waves with a certain limited range of frequencies. It would be anthropocentric to suppose that God could be limited in his vision by selecting certain light waves in the manner in which our eyes do, let alone by selecting the very light waves that our eyes select. If seeing is (as, among other things, human beings' seeing is) a process of sampling, God cannot do it, for he cannot sample. Sampling is necessary because of the impossibility of examining the whole group from which the sample is taken, and an omniscient being must be familiar with the content of the whole group. And what could God be supposed to see under the surface of earth, or of radio stars, or of areas of the universe which could not hold eyes (because they are too hot, for example)? What could he supposed to see of object when it is simply dark? What could he supposed to see of the insides of things? And why attribute to God a sense of sight, but not a sense of touch or of taste or of hearing or of smell? And why should God be supposed to react in the way in which we react to light waves, and not to wireless waves or X-rays or cosmic rays? Why should God have a visual field that resembles ours (or an infinite number of such visual fields) and not the visual fields of other animals? And what is God supposed to see of protons or electrons, if they are, as I suppose they are, real existences and not just convenient fictions.

I am not sure why it seems natural to suppose that God sees, and perhaps also hears, but not very natural to suppose that he tastes or touches or smells. I suspect that the difference may be that sight and hearing involve distance-receptor organs, which means that those who posses them can be sensitive to objects which are a considerable distance away from us. Taste, however, involves actual parts from the object coming into contact with our mouth and tongue. Smell involves particles (which are just very small parts of the object) falling upon our noses and touch involves parts of our body coming into actual physical contact with whatever it is we touch.

It seems absurd to suppose that something so 'spiritual' as God could be so intimately and corporeally present in the material world as to be able to touch or taste or smell. It is, indeed, logically impossible to touch anything without having a body, for to touch something entails putting part of one's body (one's fingers, say) into actual physical contact with that which is touched. But though it would be impossible (logically impossible) for God to touch anything unless he had a body, it would be possible for a disembodied being to have the sensations as of touching something, without having a body. For, just as we can see without eyes if the appropriate centres of our brain are suitably stimulated, so we can feel without limbs in the same circumstances. Since a head is only causally, and not logically, necessary for having sensations of touch, it is conceivable that there should be a being who had such sensations, without having a brain. It would even be possible for the sensations of such a being to be veridical, although he had neither limbs nor a head. They would be veridical if they were suitably correlated with other sensations. For example, they would be veridical if they enabled the 'person' who had them to predict what other sensations he was going to have. Among these other sensations would be sensations of the words other people would use to describe the sensations they were having.

In spite of all this, however, I feel that it would be absurd to ascribe sensations of touch to God. It may be that sensations of touch are more limiting and less ethereal than sensations of sight. For normally we have to alter something in order to get the appropriate sensations of touching it, which means that we can have such sensations only of things in our immediate vicinity. But since in fact it is arguable that God would have to be as much corporally present in the world to be able to see or hear as to be able to touch, taste or smell, that we are tempted to suppose the contrary is just because we find it easier to overlook the physical aspect of seeing and hearing than to overlook the physical aspects of touching, tasting and smelling. The idea of an omnipercipient God seems problematic, even if God would have to be omnipercipient to explain his omniscience.

(iv)   Omnipercipience and Creation

God's omnipercipience would suggest, though it does not entail, a certain account of the manner of his creating the world. For if God perceives everything from every point of view, there is little need to postulate any unperceived entities (though we will have need to postulate entities unperceived by us). All we need to postulate when we suppose that objects have backs is that God has perceptions of the backs. If one were to postulate such things as protons and electrons as well, then, if God is to have knowledge of them, he will either have to infer their existence and nature, which sounds absurd, or perceive them, if they are the kind of entity that it is in principle possible to perceive, in this case, protons and electrons might be regarded as just a special kind of object of God's perceptions. (I think this is how Berkeley would have regarded them, had he admitted their existence.) All this suggests that God creates the world by deciding to perceive one thing rather than another.

On this view, material objects would be ideas in the mind of God, as Berkeley supposed.[4] Judgments about material objects would be just judgments about what in fact, unknown to us, were ideas in the mind of an omnipercipient being who would, if he were also omnipotent, omniscient and perfectly good, be God. It would not be enough, however, for God just to have a perception of a tree in a quad resembling the one I would have, were I in the quad. His 'mind' would have to contain a whole system of such perceptions, including one from every one of the infinite number of points of view from which the tree would be visible. An infinite being should have no difficulty in doing this.

(v)   God's Omnipresence

If God perceived from everywhere at once, he would be omniaccessible (i.e. accessible from everywhere at once and omnipresent). There would be no escaping his surveillance, and no place from which he could not reward us or wreak vengeance or act upon us should we wish. And there would be no place from which we could not appeal to him, and no place from which he could not hear us.

(vi)   Conclusions

A disembodied omnipercipient being is possible. But, though possible, it would be absurd to suppose that a being of this kind that could properly be called 'God'. For one thing, there would seem to be no hard and fast line that could be drawn between his being able to see everything that there is to be seen and his feeling everything that was to be felt, touching everything that was to be touched and also smelling and tasting everything; but the idea of a divine being who touched and felt would seem to be absurd. (God, since he is omniscient, would have to know that what we tasted and smelt.) For another thing, it would seem anthropocentric to attribute to him visual perceptions just like ours, but if we do not attribute to him perceptions just like ours, equally difficult to know what kind of perceptions we should attribute to him.

There is, however, no difficulty in regarding an omnipercipient being as also omniscient and omnipotent. Indeed, he would have to be omnipercipient to explain how it is that he knows everything that there is to know about the universe. Furthermore, to be omniscient he would, over and above being omnipercipient, have to be acquainted with the thoughts and feelings of his creatures in some way other than by inferring them from his knowledge, obtained by perception, of their bodies, as we infer pain from groans. Otherwise we could hide ourselves from him simply by not groaning. I am not convinced that God's being acquainted with our thoughts and inmost feelings is impossible, but the idea that he infers them is absurd.

These facts further confirm the unwisdom of regarding God as some kind of extra item in the furniture of the world, whom we postulate to explain the existence of the universe and what is happening in it.

Notes

1   I have discussed some of the matters discussed here in 'The Russell Leibniz Theory of Perception' in Harrison, 1975.
2   For example, Armstrong, 1968.

3   I have, I think inconsistently, argued elsewhere, (for example, in 'The Russell/Leibniz Theory of Perception' and 'A Facade Theory of Visual Perception' in Harrison, 1995 that there is such a relationship.

4   It is most unfortunate that Berkeley used the word 'idea' for the (immediate) objects of perception, for this causes him to argue that there cannot be any unperceived ideas and so, if there are ideas unperceived by us, they must be perceived by some other being (in fact, Berkeley thought, by God). It is true that there cannot be ideas that are not the ideas of some person or perhaps 'being', but all that follows from this is that if the (immediate) object of perception should exist unperceived by us, then they cannot properly be described as ideas.

23 Survival of Death

(i) Christianity Needs Disembodied Existence, Even if it is the Body That is Resurrected

Questions concerning the possibility of disembodiment lead naturally to questions concerning human survival of death, for one theory about human survival is that we survive the death of our bodies in a disembodied form; the body may perish, but what might, for the want of a better word, be called the soul is immortal.

Christians sometimes claim that they do not need disembodiment, since they do not believe in the immortality of the soul, but in the resurrection of the body. However, if persons without bodies are not possible, it will not be possible for there to be a (Christian) God, who is alleged to be a person without a body. (I have already suggested that God might be embodied, without having a body.)

(ii) The Idea of a Later Resurrection on Earth

If we survive the death of our bodies, this must be either with a body or without one, or in some form of embodiment, if any such is possible, intermediate between the two.

If we survive our death with bodies, it is necessary to ask 'Where are these bodies? Why do we not see them?' One possible answer to the latter question is that we cannot see them because this survival has not yet happened. But it will happen, and then the bodies we have now will be reassembled and spring from their graves at the sound of the last trumpet, then to be reclothed with flesh. They will again become the bodies of people, who have the characteristics their former owners had and have memories of having done the things their former owners did.

The idea that anything like this should ever happen is preposterous. All the scientific evidence is overwhelmingly against it and good science should always take precedence over bad theology. Nevertheless, the idea has one or two merits. Firstly, it avoids – for men – the difficulties of disembodied existence. Secondly if this event takes place in the not too distant future, before even our bones, as well are our flesh, have totally disintegrated, it just possibly enables us to say that we survive (or some of us do) with the bodies we have now (or, at any rate, a large part of them). This may satisfy those philosophers who say that a man who exists at one time cannot be the same man who exists at an earlier time unless the body of the first man is spatio-temporally continuous, and so identical, with the body of the second.

I say '*may satisfy*' those philosophers who believe in a physical criterion of personal identity' because it is not at all clear that the bodies of these 'two' men would be the same, even though the bones were the same. Since the flesh in all but very recently deceased bodies would have been absent for an interval, it could be argued that what survived was simply the same skeleton, not the same body. The brain, the most important part of the body, would decompose with the flesh. And there would be difficulties about the ownership of the particles which successively comprised the bodies of missionaries and then of cannibals. If the particles in the body of a missionary had been assimilated into the body of the cannibal, it would seem that there were not enough particles to go round.

Furthermore, bodily continuity may be a necessary, but not a sufficient, condition of personal identity, in which case, though a man with a body not spatio-temporally continuous with mine cannot be me, a person with a body that is spatio-temporally continuous with mine does not have to be me. This person would need something else, like having my memories, as well. And a time must come when even our bones perish. To suppose that we are resurrected before this time, if the universe ends on the day of judgment, implies the universe's ending billions of years before scientists predict its eventual heat-death. That this should happen is not something an educated person should take seriously.

The reason why some philosophers have thought that bodily spatio-temporal continuity is a necessary condition of personal identity is this. If I seem to remember having done something wicked on some past occasion, it is normally regarded as a total refutation of my claim to remember this that the body of the person who performed this action has been continuously under observation from the time this act was performed until the present, and is not in fact spatio-temporally continuous with mine, but with that of some other person, say Tom, and the body my body is spatio-temporally continuous with was somewhere far removed from the scene of the crime. If the act I claim to remember having performed is one of murder, it will be Tom who ought to be hanged, if anyone ought, not me. It is not possible, on this view, to get round this difficulty by saying that God can do anything and so can make someone me, even if his body is not spatio-temporally continuous with mine. That bodily continuity is a necessary condition of personal identity is, if true at all, true as a matter of logic (in a wide sense of 'logic'), and matters of logic, as we have seen, are things God cannot do anything about.

(iii)   Heaven a Place not Spatially Related to this World

The same difficulty concerning identity is raised by another possible answer to the questions 'Where is my body, if I survive death in an embodied form? Why cannot my body be seen?' This answer is that there is a place where I find myself after I am dead and meet other people, who have also survived their deaths, in a physical environment which contains material objects – harps, for example – which bodies stand in quite normal spatial relations to my own and others' bodies. But though objects in this other world stand in spatial relations to one another, none of them stand in any spatial relations to any objects in the world we inhabit. Hence, in whatever direction one travels in this world, one will not come across any objects in the other world, and *vice versa*. This explains why we do not come across the other world when we explore this one.

Events in this other world, however, must presumably stand in temporal relations to events in this world, because I 'go' there after my death in this world. Objects in the other world must also stand in causal relations with this world, for presumably I am rewarded in the 'next' world *because* of my virtue in this. Indeed, without causal connection I would not even remember my virtuous acts when I reached the next world, for memory involves a causal relationship between the event that I remember and my remembering it.[1] In other words, what happens to me in the next world is partly determined by what happens to me in this, which means that events in this other world must happen later in the same time than events in this one.

However, the hypothesis of a spatio-temporal world not related to this one also falls foul of those philosophers who think that identity of body is a necessary condition of the identity of the persons to whom these bodies belong and that spatio-temporal continuity of a person's body is a necessary condition of bodily identity. For how can the body I had in this world be spatio-temporally continuous with a body in the other world when bodies in these two worlds do not stand in any spatial relations to one another at all? *Ex hypothesi*, there can be no route which this world's body could have taken to get to the place in the next world occupied by the body of the person who appears to think he is me and who is burdened with and being punished for the recollections of my wicked acts. And since such recollections must be delusive, it will be unjust to punish the person who has them for having committed the crimes he only seems to remember.

(iv)   Disembodied Survival

Another alternative, though I do not think that it is the Christian one, is that I should survive the death of my body in a disembodied form. (Disembodied survival would seem to make Christ's resurrection pointless.) This would explain why, though I still exist after my body has died, I cannot be seen. Seeing someone normally, and perhaps necessarily, consists in seeing his body, which cannot be done if he has not got one. And I will no more be able to see such a disembodied person than I will be able to see someone else's phantom limb, or be directly aware of his thoughts and feelings, his beliefs, emotions, and perceptions.[2]

This theory, too, falls foul of those philosophers who think that bodily identity is a necessary condition of personal identity. A disembodied putative Harrison cannot, if these philosophers are right, be Harrison, for the putative Harrison has not got a body and so, *a fortiori*, his body cannot be spatio-temporally continuous with the body Harrison used to have. Hence, again, if he seems to remember doing the things that Harrison formerly did, this memory must be delusive.

But perhaps bodily spatio-temporal continuity is not a necessary and sufficient condition of personal identity. Perhaps, instead, something like memory is, in which case, perhaps, any person who at some later date remembers or seems to remember doing the things I did and whose memories are caused by my various actions will be me, even though his body is not spatio-temporally continuous with mine and even though he has no body to be spatio-temporally continuous with mine. If so, a person with my bones but new flesh, or with a body in the next world which cannot possibly be mine, or a disembodied person, might be me, because he seems to remember doing the things I did and would not have done so had I not done the things he seems to remember doing.

(v)   Objections to Psychical Criteria of Personal Identity

There is a serious difficulty with this view, however. It is surely very wrong to punish, in this world or the next, for my wicked acts, someone who only seems to remember having done them. Must he not actually have done them before he merits punishment? You can make a case for letting him off if he has totally forgotten doing them, although he has done them in fact. But surely you cannot make out any case at all for punishing him if he seems to remember having done them, but has not. But if you take away bodily continuity and base identity entirely on memory, how can one decide whether he simply seems to remember having done something or whether he really has done it? If he seems to remember having pulled the trigger, it would be plausible to hold that he really does remember doing this if he has a body which is spatio-temporally continuous with the body of the man who did pull the trigger. It would be even more plausible to hold that he must be misremembering if his body is not spatio-temporally continuous with the body of the man who pulled the trigger. But if you think that physical continuity is not the criterion of personal identity, how do you decide whether anyone's memories are veridical or not?

Bizarre cases, too, can be imagined. There could in the next world be two (or more) disembodied people, each of whom seemed to remember doing the things I did.[3] If each of them is me, then, since if two things are each identical with a third thing, they must be identical with one another,[4] they must be identical people, and so just one person, which is contrary to the hypothesis that there are two. But if you cannot say each is me, then you ought to say that neither is, for there can be no good reason for maintaining that one of them is me, but not the other, if these two people are precisely alike. Having my memories, therefore, cannot be what makes a person who exists later than me be the same person as me.

It may be, however, that if other causal connections are added to memory as a condition of personal identity, it can be said that the state of a person who remembers or seems to remember having done the things that I did is a later state of me. If, over and above seeming to remember doing many of the things I did, this person has my mental abilities and character traits and would not have had them had I not had them, this reinforces the case for saying that he is me. (One must again remember Hume's claim that, provided that they are spatially and temporally adjacent, any event may be caused by any other event and it is only a matter of empirical fact what events cause what. But Hume's view must be modified to allow action at a distance in space and time, if the empirical evidence points to it and if there is no physical link between me and the person claiming to be me.)

This answer to the difficulty, if it is the answer, will apply not only to disembodiment, but to states of embodiment, like those in a world that cannot be reached from this one, where spatio-temporal continuity is also impossible. If it must also be the case that the person in this other world would not have seemed to remember having done these things if I had not actually done them, then perhaps if follows that my memories are veridical, and that I am the same person as he, because, were I not the same person as he, there could not be any tendency for what he did to be remembered by me. (This should follow from the definition of being the same person.)

Whether these people are identical or not will depend upon whether the memories the two people, mentioned above, who seemed to remember doing the things that I did, can *both* be effects of the fact that I actually did those things. If the fact that I did the things both these people seem to remember doing can only cause one of them to seem to remember doing these things – the fact that the other also seems to remember doing them being coincidence – this will enable us to say that that one is me and that the other is not me. But if my doing these things can cause each of them to seem to remember doing them, then they will, if that memory is dependent upon the occurrence of the event remembered is a sufficient condition of personal identity, have an equal claim to be me, although only one of them can actually be me. Memory plus causal connection, then, could not in that case be sufficient condition of personal identity, because two different people can both be connected by memory and causation to one and the same person, while two people cannot be numerically identical with one and the same person.

(vi)   Selves and Identity

On one view, two states, for example, are states of the same person if they belong to one and the same self. On this view, to be states of the same person they must both be related to a self and the self to which one is related must be the same self as the self to which the other is related. On this view, I suppose, though I am not sure, only one of the two apparent Guy Fawkeses could be identical with Guy Fawkes, because only one of them could have the self that Guy Fawkes had.

However, I cannot accept the view that a state of a person is state of the same person if and only if it is related to the same self. This presupposes that there are such things as selves. However, I do not accept the existence of selves. This is for the following reasons. (a) Like Hume, I do not come across them when I introspect. (b) The unity of the states (for example) that I introspect is the result of their being all states of me, not on their all being states of my self. (c) 'Me' does not refer to a self. 'Me', like 'I', is a reflexive pronoun, and refers to Harrison when used by Harrison, to Tom when used by Tom, and to Mary when used by Mary. It is to misunderstand the use of this pronoun to suppose that it stands for a self. 'I know myself' is correct. 'I know my self' is not. My states have the unity they have by all being states of Harrison, not by all being states of Harrison's self. Since there are no selves, there can be no disembodied selves, but it is conceivable that there might be disembodied persons. If disembodied persons could talk, they could refer to themselves with personal pronouns. (d) The view does not explain what the relation between a state of me and my self is. (e) It does not answer the question' What makes a self known to exist at one time the same self as a self known to exist at another?' This question is not obviously any easier to answer than the question 'What makes a state a state of the same person as another state?' (f) Not everything I introspect is a state of me. Actions are not states. But it is not my self that acts and believes. I do.[5]

(vii)   Double Bodies

Another way of dealing with this difficulty concerning personal identity would be to say that a person in this world may have one body, but two bodies in the next. (This would obviously not solve the problem as it concerns disembodied survival, for a man without a body could not have two bodies.) And it does seem conceivable to me that one and the same person could have two 'bodies'. Such a person would look out on the world from two points of view, one behind the eyes of one body, the other behind the eyes of the other, and the person owning the first body would see everything seen by the person owning the second. The person owning the first body would also know everything known by the second. Imparting information to the person owning the first body (by making suitable noises in its vicinity) would cause the person owning the second body (who would be the same person) also to have this information and *vice versa*. (Statements imparting this information could emanate from the lips of the either body.) Causing the person owning the first body to feel pain (by sticking pins in the first body) would cause the person owning the second body to feel pain (which might be demonstrated by screams coming from the mouth of the second body). The two bodies would work in systematic harmony to further ends which the one person had. In circumstances like this, the two descriptions, 'owner of the first body' and 'owner of the second body', would be two different descriptions of one and the same person. But it might well be better to say not that one person had two bodies, so much as that the one person had one double body. This person's body would be like a catamaran, which is only one boat though it has two hulls.

I do not, however, think that this will answer the difficulty we are discussing. For obviously there cannot be spatio-temporal continuity of body between the *two* bodies of a person who has two bodies and the *one* body of a person who has only one. The criteria of personal identity, therefore, would have to be psychical, not physical. But if so, there could again be two people, each having a double body, both of whom remembered my experiences and neither of whom would have remembered them had I not had them. Hence we would be back again precisely where we started from. (What I have been saying raises the question whether there is any difference between one person with two bodies and the case where there are two bodies with the same memories?)

(viii)   Can Personal Identity Be a Matter of Terminological Decision?

One possible way of dealing with this problem concerning personal identity is to hold that whether or not two people existing at different times are really one and the same person is a matter for (possibly arbitrary) terminological decision. At the moment brain transplants are not possible. Hence we have no language rules at all – because we do not need them – for deciding questions about personal identity in unusual cases. For example, if Mary suffers serious brain damage in a car accident, but is otherwise unhurt, and her brain is replaced by the brain (and so the memories) of Tom, whose brain is in good order, but is dying of terminal cancer, perhaps there are no rules for the use of 'same person' by reference to which one can decide whether the resulting amalgam should be described as being the same person as Tom or the same person as Mary (or both, or neither).

Maybe the question whether Tom and Mary are the same person is rather like the question 'Is artificial insemination by donor adultery or not?'[6] It can be argued that there is no answer to this question, for the English language has no rules for the use of the word 'adultery' which would cover an unforeseen case like this. Hence, it may be argued, it is not so much a matter for deciding, by application of rules for the use of 'adultery', whether or not artificial insemination by donor is adultery, but of deciding whether or not to call it 'adultery'. That is to say, it is a question of deciding whether to tighten up our rules for the use of 'adultery' in such a way as clearly to include, or, alternatively, clearly to exclude, artificial insemination by donor from the class of adulterous acts. If we decide one way, if could be argued, artificial insemination by donor will be adultery. It we decide in the other way, it will not be. But the actual rules make no pronouncement on this matter. (Similar things might be said about whether a person who is 'brain dead' is dead, or about when a foetus becomes a person.)

However, deciding whether or not to call AID 'adultery' does not settle the question whether adultery is immoral. Indeed, it is hard to see how a material question, an answer to which appears to affect the morality of human action, can be answered simply by a human decision to use a word in one way rather than another. (The same is true of many other cases.) It looks as if such a decision does decide this question, because it looks as if it follows, given that all adultery is immoral, that if we decide to call AID 'adultery', then AID must be immoral. (Of course, if we decide not to call it 'adultery', it certainly does not follow that it is not immoral. Lots of actions which are not adultery – a man's copulating with a girl under 10 years old, for example – are nevertheless at least commonly regarded as immoral.)

But though if all adultery is immoral and all AID is adultery, it follows by a syllogism in Barbara that all AID is immoral, this does not mean that, if all adultery is immoral and we decide to call AID 'adultery', it must thereby become immoral. If AID is not immoral and we decide to call it 'adultery', what follows is that, from the time of this decision's having being taken, anyone saying that all adultery is immoral (i.e., uttering the sentence 'All adultery is immoral', using the word 'adultery' in its new sense) may be saying what is false. (He will not, of course, because the meaning of the word 'adultery' has changed, be saying anything inconsistent with his old view that all adultery was immoral. In the old sense of 'adultery', this statement may still be true.) (We might be tempted to say that we have, by calling artificial insemination by donor 'adultery', created a new category of adulterous acts, which, unlike the others, are not wrong.)

Similarly perhaps, when confronted with a person who has Mary's body but Tom's memories and character traits, we may simply have to take an arbitrary decision upon whether to say she (I say 'she' because her sex, unlike her personality, would be determined by her body, not her brain) is the same person as the former Tom or the former Mary. This might work all right in some cases. If Tom has inherited an estate, it seems quite proper to regard the question, whether the woman with Tom's memories but Mary's body should inherit it, as a matter for arbitrary decision. If Tom quite literally disappears and seems to find himself in Mary's body and Mary has, before this transformation, committed a murder, it would certainly depend upon an arbitrary decision whether or not he is hanged. But can it depend upon an arbitrary decision whether or not he deserves to be hanged? A judge might cause him to be hanged or inherit an estate by ruling that he is Tom, but can we cause him to deserve to be hanged for something that Tom has done by arbitrarily deciding that he is to be called 'the same person' as Tom, or by making more precise the rules for the use of the expression 'the same person as'? How can making decisions about how words are to be used cause someone to have done something that he deserves to be hanged for?

Let us suppose that Tom, before it was decided to have his brain put in Mary's body, feared that the future person having his brain and Mary's body would be imprisoned for life for a murder that Mary had committed, and believed that this person – whom he fears will be he – would be imprisoned for life if the courts decide that 'she' is Tom. It would be rational of him to worry about how the courts would decide to use the expression 'the same person as' only if he thought that, depending on which way they decided it, the person affected by their decision would be him. He is worried from an egotistical point of view about this person's fate – whoever this person may be – only to the extent that it is already the case that Mary is he. He will be worried about how the judge decides to use this expression 'identical with Tom' only because he thinks that how the judge decides to use this expression will determine whether he is sent to prison or not and, for that to worry him, he must have made up his mind that Mary is he, however the judge decides. If he thinks that Mary is he, he must think that Mary is he however the judge decides to use certain words. Hence this question about identity cannot be a matter of terminological decision.

(ix)   Blurring the Distinction Between I and Thou

If we tighten up on the rules for the expression 'the same person', then questions framed by using these words will no longer mean what they meant before the rules for using these words were made more specific. You might then argue that a question which, before the rules were tightened up, was worrying, is worrying no longer. In the old sense it did matter to me whether the man to be hanged was the same person as me. In the new sense it simply does not matter. But then, on the other hand, in the old sense, there would simply be no answer to the question 'Is the person to be hanged the same person as me or not?' and in consequence simply no answer to the question whether or not I ought to worry for prudential reasons about what happens to him.

If so, it ought to follow that there was in principle no way of answering the question whether my concern with the man who was going to be hanged was a matter of altruism or egotism. It might be held[7] that this would be a good thing, for then – because no-one will have a better claim to be me than anyone else – I ought to worry about the future of everyone equally, and it will be no more rational to worry more about the future of someone on the grounds that he is numerically identical with me (i.e., who is me) than about the future of anyone else. Nobody will either be me or not be me.

But this blurring of the distinction between self and others would not apply to everybody, only to certain problem cases, and so would not produce the amount of altruism the world needs. I suspect, too, that the consequences of thinking that there was no answer to the question whether states of a future person were or were not states of oneself would in fact be harmful. For the consequences of there being in principle no-one who could be unequivocally *said to be* me would be much the same as my not knowing whether which of the people who was to be affected *was* me. If I did not know whether it was I who was going to be made happy or unhappy by the actions I perform now, and there was in principle no way of deciding the issue, I would care less about the future of any of the people who are candidates for being me, much as, in the days when the possession of fields rotated in order that the good and bad lands should be equally distributed, no-one bothered to take care of his field because it would not be he, but someone else, who had the use of it in the coming year.

In the imaginary case, where the distinction between one person and another is blurred, it would not be someone else who suffered from my foolish or improvident acts, for, if no-one is me, no-one can be someone other than me either. But it is enough to make me cease to be provident that it will not be I who will suffer from my lack of providence, even if it is not anyone other than me.

Though the motive for providence will normally be primarily egotistical, providence from altruistic motives is also possible, for I may be provident from concern for my dependants as well as for myself (though if there is doubt about whether a person is me, there must be an equal doubt about whether certain dependants are my dependants). But being provident, whether from altruism or egotism, is a good thing and so its impossibility is to be deplored rather than welcomed.

(x)   Caution About the Hereafter

In spite of all that has been said, I do not think I would care, from selfish motives, to believe that, as a result of my wicked acts, there would be a person (or even several persons) in Hell who (a) seemed to remember doing the things I did, (b) would not have remembered doing these things had I not actually done them and (c) had many other characteristics which he would not have had I not once had them, even if there was no answer to the question whether this person was me or not. I would much prefer it if he very clearly was not I, or, better still, if I were sufficiently selfish, if he very clearly was someone else. And if one were to put oneself in the place of such a being, one can see that he (or she), thinking that he was I, would wish that I had not performed these actions, which wish would be stronger if he also felt remorse at having performed them (since remorse would presuppose that he thought that the person who performed these actions really was he). And it would be impossible for him not to feel remorse for having done them, for if he had a clear memory of having done them he could not but think he *had* done them. He could think that *perhaps* he had *not* done them, but the belief that he *had* done them would be presupposed by his memory of having done them.

If this person were sent back to this world, he would be likely to avoid doing the things that I did and he seemed to remember doing, for fear that there would again be a being, in another world, to whom the normal criteria of identity did not apply, but who nevertheless seemed to remember doing the things that this person had done. From the point of view of a deity bent on enforcing morality – if there is one – the fear of there being a person who thought he was me and was *not* clearly *not* me might well be as effective a deterrent as the fear of there being a person who both thought he was me and clearly *was* me. And conversely, the thought that there would be a person who really was me, but who thought he was someone else, might well not be a deterrent at all. So there might be some eccentric point in considering one's fate in Heaven or Hell, if there are such places, even without clear-cut criteria for personal identity.

Again, it is only on a retributive theory of punishment that the person thinking he is me ought not to be punished if he is not me. On a deterrent or reformative theory, it might be necessary to punish him, at least if he has any further opportunities for wrongdoing in the next world. One may object to describing this as punishment if the person punished has not committed the offence for which he is punished, but this terminological nicety will not make the pain any the less.

(xi)   Heaven as an Insubstantial World

Before considering empirical evidence for survival it is necessary to say a few more words about what survival might be like. One way of regarding Heaven is as a 'nonstandard' world. I use the word 'nonstandard' not to denigrate Heaven, but to suggest that it is – perhaps not surprisingly – less fully material than the everyday world. Perhaps it is less material in the way in which mirror images are 'less material' than mirrors. Perhaps we cannot see the environment in which disembodied persons find themselves in something like the way in which one cannot see mirror images from a place behind the mirror.

It is conceivable that an object should be visible from only a limited number of points – only from points beyond a certain distance, say – and that it should disappear when approached more closely than that distance and be incapable of being touched. It might be visible to some but not to others. (It might then be located in something like the way in which rainbows are located.) It is possible that even one's own body should be like this. People in such a world would have what were in themselves normal visual experiences; but the normal physiological base of such experiences – eyes and a brain – would be lacking. Their seeing would consist simply in a correlation between their seeing and the seeing of others, something like a communal hallucination. And Heaven would be invisible to ordinary people; since its inhabitants would not need eyes, quasi-hallucinatory objects in it need emit no light waves to fall upon ordinary people's retinas.

Hell, too, would presumably in this case also have to be regarded as a nonstandard 'receptacle' for the nonstandard bodies of its denizens. But though the devils themselves might be quasi-hallucinatory, one fears that the pain they inflicted would be real.

Another possibility is that the (primarily visual) experiences of those in Heaven could be regarded as being like exceptionally vivid visual images;[8] one's own visual images are invisible to others, who can see only the happenings to the brain by which they are sometimes caused. (I say 'sometimes caused' because it is possible that at other times my deliberately producing an image causes the brain-happenings with which it is associated.) One cannot find a man's visual imagery by looking within his brain. The same is true of his pleasures and pains – which may please those who wish to believe in Hell as well as to believe in Heaven – and the feelings, pangs of jealousy, for example, associated with the emotions.

Instructive though it is to consider such possibilities, I must say that I think that the chances of there being a Heaven (or a Hell) that is actually like this are remote. Perhaps a world like the one I have tried to describe might be more suitable as a picture of the spirit world, if there is one, which I doubt, where reside those who are alleged to communicate with us through the bodies of mediums.

(xii)   Empirical Evidence for Survival[9]

In the preceding pages I have been considering whether it is conceivable that we might survive the death of our bodies and arguing that it is (just) conceivable. Not everything that is conceivable actually happens, however. In order reasonably to believe that sometimes people actually do survive their body's death, empirical evidence is necessary.

Oddly enough there is some evidence for survival, evidence which might be considered quite good were it not for the highly improbable nature of the events which this evidence is supposed to support. These events are improbable because if they occur, then modern physics must be to some extent wrong. The prestige of modern physics is (deservedly) so enormous that one rightly hesitates to believe anything which conflicts with it, and disembodied spirits mucking about with the behaviour of conglomerations of electrons would certainly conflict with modern physics.

The evidence I am thinking of comes from the investigation of allegedly paranormal phenomena carried out by such bodies as the Society for Psychical Research in this country and the American Society of Psychical Research.

For example, messages which purport to come from deceased persons and which contain checkable information which only the deceased could have known are sometimes spelt out by an ouija board, or by table rapping (one knock for 'yes', two knocks for 'no'), by automatic writing or by mediums speaking with what purports to be the ('direct') voice of the departed. (The phenomenon of direct voice occurs when the departed allegedly takes over the body of the medium and communicates to relatives and hangers-on by means of the vocal cords, etc. of the medium.) It is possible that the messages may be produced, consciously or otherwise, by one of the parties to the experiment, or that the medium may be fraudulent. Assuming that this can with adequate safeguards be ruled out, there is the further possibility that the medium simply knows by precognition what the person checking the message will find – although the hypothesis that there really is such a thing as precognition is nearly as much, if not as much, in conflict with modern science as the hypothesis that messages are produced by some deceased person who has survived death in a disembodied state.

I do not think the evidence for the paranormal should simply be ignored on the grounds that it is contrary to the presuppositions of modern science. There is always the possibility, however remote, that some of these presuppositions should be wrong. They became the presuppositions of modern science because they fitted the observed facts, so if the observations of psychical researchers really are facts, the presuppositions of modern science must be rejected because they do not fit them. What stands because of empirical evidence may fall for the same reason, though a very great deal of empirical evidence would be necessary to overthrow something for which so much favourable empirical evidence has already been acquired. I myself do not think enough of such evidence is forthcoming. It is, however, permissible to make the following reflections upon what would be the case, if – and it is a very big if – the evidence for survival of death were accepted.

(a) Firstly, the evidence for survival would not be evidence for the *immortality* of the soul. The cases recorded are usually cases of people who, it is claimed, have survived the death of their bodies only for a few years, or a few centuries at most. Immortality, however, means surviving for ever.

(b) Secondly, it is doubtful whether the state that the people who have survived, if any, find themselves in is a desirable one. Some reports make it seem somewhat bizarre.

(c) Thirdly, there is no evidence at all that survival happens to everybody. If it happens at all, it would appear to happen to some people (the minority), but not others.

(d) Fourthly, there is no connection that I can see between the occurrence of the kind of survival pointed to by the empirical evidence and the existence of God. Survival, if it occurs at all, is not necessarily a religious phenomenon.

(e) Fifthly, there is no reason to suppose that those, if any, who survive the death of their bodies, would be in any better position to answer religious questions than we are. The difficulties concerning acquiring evidence for the existence of God are difficulties of principle, and they would not be any less severe for the persons surviving the death of their bodies, if any, than they are for us. If it is possible to see God face to face, then perhaps one might see God face to face after one's death, but I doubt whether *appearing* to see God face to face after one is dead is any less problematic than seeing him face to face in this world.

(f) Sixthly, there is so far as I know no reason to suppose that the virtuous would find themselves in a happier state after death than the vicious, or that the virtuous would survive more often than do the vicious.

(g) Seventhly, there are no empirically tested recipes either for achieving survival, or for being happy if one achieves it, though one might suspect that an addiction to body-building and rugby football would not be helpful, and that a cultivation of one's inner resources would be the best recipe for living happily in a world in which one did not have sense organs and was deprived of the power of locomotion.

However, that one could have rich inner resources in the absence of a brain seems unlikely. Almost all the empirical evidence, indeed, points to a total dependence of people upon what is happening to their brains. This suggests (the evidence, such as it is, of psychical research apart) that, without brains, people would, as a matter of empirical fact though not of logic, simply be annihilated.

(xiii) Transmigration of the 'Soul'[10]

It is a Buddhist view that the souls of men and animals are trapped in the cycle of birth and rebirth and pass unendingly from the body of one animal (including human animals) to that of another until such time, if there ever is a time, that they can escape to Nirvana. There is some empirical evidence for transmigration, though not nearly enough to outweigh the enormous antecedent improbability of such occurrences, which improbability again results from the fact that they conflict with science.

When there is no evidence for our souls having transmigrated it looks as if, for what this fact is worth, the hypothesis of transmigration seems to become superfluous. For can there be any difference between (1) having been a mouse in a former incarnation, but not having a body that is spatio-temporally continuous with the body of any mouse, nor having any memories of being a mouse, and (2) not having any memories of being a mouse, because one has never been a mouse at all? The consequences of each hypothesis are exactly the same, unless it is held that something like psychotherapy might produce memories of being a mouse, which seems unlikely.

(xiv)   Heaven and Hell as States of Mind

There is a Christian view according to which Heaven and Hell are not places – or realms, if Heaven and Hell are not spatial – in which we find ourselves after death, but states of mind in which we find ourselves in this life. Hell, for example, is a state of separation from God. This view is open to (at least) two very serious objections.

(a) It does not seem to be the case that all the wicked do experience very unpleasant (Hellish) states before they die and hardly any of the virtuous experience very pleasant (Heavenly) ones. And the wicked might not mind being separated from God and the feeling virtuous are probably more likely to feel so separated than the wicked, and to feel this as a result of less serious transgressions, and so be worse off than the more insensitive wicked.

(b) What is painful is not being separated from God, but feeling oneself separated from God. And it would be possible to feel oneself separated from God whether there was a God or not.

To hold that Heaven and Hell are states of mind is to hold a reductionist view, i.e., it reduces what purport to be statements about another world to statements about this one. If one takes reductionism to extremes, then all there is to being separated from God is one's having the experience of being separated from God. But that one can *feel* separated from God is something that even an atheist can believe.

An even more extreme reductionist can hold that all there is to there being a God is people's having such experiences as that of feeling themselves in communication with God, or alternatively feeling themselves separated from God. If this were so, then a person who believes that there are such experiences would not really be an atheist, though he may think that he is. But in fact such experiences purport to be experiences of an object outside the person having the experiences and an atheist may consistently admit the existence of the experiences, but hold that this object does not exist. Reductionists tend to make their views more plausible at the cost of rendering them totally innocuous and banal.

(xv)   Does Religion Need Immortality?

Hence it would be much better to say that there are no such places as Heaven and Hell than to say that they exist only in this life, though their existing in this life may be quite bad (or, in the case of Heaven good) enough for many purposes. Though it would be pleasant – and I think not necessarily dull – to live for ever if one had a sufficiently rich inner life, the claims of religion do not stand or fall by immortality. Indeed, the appeal of immortality is a usually self-interested and unrealistic one which religion ought to be able to do without. If one gets pleasure and sustenance in the devoted contemplation of a deity, this should be good enough in itself, while it lasts, to satisfy those so disposed to indulge in it. Survival of death, if it occurs, is then a bonus, rather than an integral part of religion, and one should be highly suspicious of those who embrace religion only in the hope that they may survive death by embracing it, and one should be still more suspicious of those who advertise it for the same reason.

(xvi)   Personal Identity and Christ's Survival of Death

The problems concerning identity discussed in this chapter are raised in an acute form by the relationship between Christ's earthly body and whatever body, if any, he had after his alleged ascension. It is impossible rationally to believe that, after his ascension, Christ's body took a continuous route – perhaps through a hole in the heavens covered by a cloud – to some place in another world and equally impossible to believe that his body remains somewhere in this world. Hence the ordinary common or garden criteria of personal identity cannot be satisfied in the case of Christ. Still less can they be satisfied if, after his resurrection, he were to *become* identical with God the Father, if he had ever ceased to be identical with him, which latter, of course, would itself pose enormous problems.

(xvii)   Conclusions

There can be no Heaven and Hell in this spatio-temporal system, and, because of lack of spatio-temporal continuity, no being in any other spatio-temporal system could be identical with people in this. Nor could disembodied people be identical with people in this world. (It is sometimes held that Heaven and Hell are states of mind in this world, but I cannot reconcile this inoffensive view with orthodox Christianity.)

Nevertheless, it should be worrying to think that there was to be a person in another world who was going to have the memories of doing the wicked things that I actually did, and who would not have had these memories had I not done these things, even if this being is not linked to me by normal criteria of personal identity. And thinking that there would be such a being, if I did do wicked things, might well prevent me from doing them. But then there is no empirical evidence for the existence of any worlds other than this. But I doubt whether such facts have any genuine religious significance.

Notes

1   A memory is not veridical unless, over and above my having done what I seemed to remember doing, I would not have seemed to remember doing what I did had I not actually done it.
2   For a more detailed treatment of this subject, the reader is referred to my 'Science, Souls and Sense-Data', Harrison, 1994 (reprinted in Harrison, 1995).
3   This case has been put by Bernard Williams in 'Personal Identity and Individuation', 1973.
4   To avoid difficulties concerning time-travel, it might be better to say that if A is a *later* stage in the life of X than is B, and C a later stage than B, then A and C must be stages in the life one and the same person.
5   On this topic I have profited from reading an unpublished thesis, 'The Survival of the Self', by R. Harwood.
6   I have discussed a similar problem concerning whether the foetus is a person in 'Roles, Rules and Relationships' in Harrison, 1995.
7   This has been held by Derek Parfit, 1984.
8   I owe this idea to Henry Habberley Price.
9   For a more detailed treatment of this question the reader is referred to Broad, 1925, chapter XII, 'Empirical Arguments for Human Survival'.
10 I put 'soul' in quotes partly because Buddhists who, as J.J.C. Smart has reminded me, usually believe in reincarnation, do not believe in the soul. But they do believe in an ordered sequence of mental experiences, and reincarnation can be regarded as the last such item attached to one body being causally connected with the first such item attached to a later body. And some philosphers, possibly Hume, have thought that the soul just was an ordered sequence of mental experience.

24 The Problem of Evil[1]

(i) Preliminary Statement of the Problem

It seems that the existence of an omnipotent, omniscient and benevolent God is incompatible with the existence of evil. If God is benevolent, he cannot wish his creatures to suffer evil. If he is omniscient, they cannot suffer evil without his knowing it. If he is omnipotent, he must be able to prevent their suffering evil. But there is evil. Hence God must either be not omnipotent, or not omniscient or not benevolent.[2]

Alternatively, there either is no God, if God is by definition omnipotent, omniscient and benevolent, or the being who created the universe (if there is such a being) and appears to be responsible for evil, is either not omnipotent, or not omniscient or not benevolent, and so is not God.

This is a valid argument in the form of the *modus tollendo tollens*. But it is only as cogent its premises, that there is evil, and that the existence of evil is incompatible with the existence of God.

The obvious way to reply to the argument that, since there is evil, there can be no God, is to say that what God's existence is incompatible with is not evil, but unnecessary evil. There is, I think, no difficulty at all in holding that there is no incompatibility between the existence of God and evil, provided that the evil is necessary.[3] The argument must therefore be restated, with 'unnecessary evil' substituted for 'evil'. The difficulty with this argument consists in showing that the evil is necessary.

It has been argued that God created (unnecessary) evil in order that his existence could not be proved by rational argument (i.e., to make it look as if he did not exist, because believing in him is the more meritorious the more strongly we are tempted not to). But either this is a valid argument for the existence of God or it is not. If it is not, one should pay no attention to it. If it is, then its validity conflicts with one of its premises, for, if it is valid, there *will* be a reason for thinking that there is a God. I do not know why it is so commonly supposed that God has such a strong preference for irrational people.

It has also been said that an omnipotent omniscient God could (or would) have produced consequences from evil which would justify his introducing it, but in a manner that we would not be able to detect. This is another argument that is dangerously reminiscent of the argument: if my wife were a Russian spy, she would not have allowed me to see any evidence of this fact; there is no evidence that she is a Russian spy; therefore she is a Russian spy.

It may be that the conclusion of the above argument is not that there is a God who is responsible for evil, but only that there may be one. But in order for me to be justified in saying that my wife only may be a Russian spy, more is necessary than that there should be no evidence that she is not a Russian spy. There must be at least some positive evidence that she is a Russian spy.

It could be that, though the existence of God is compatible with evil, it is incompatible with the amount of evil the world actually contains. But I think that the existence of God would be compatible with this amount of evil only provided it was necessary evil. (Attempts to show that the evil in the world is necessary evil will be discussed later in the chapter.)

It is said that the problem of evil is not as I have outlined it, but the problem of what to do about evil. (I understand that this is called 'the existential problem'.) There is, of course, such a problem. But the problem of what to do about evil has nothing to do with the academic difficulty concerning the existence of God just outlined. The problem of what to do about evil is something we all have, and have whether we believe in God or not and whether there is a God or not. And the fact that we do not have a *right* that everything should be perfect does not remove the logical difficulty for the existence of God caused by the fact that not everything is perfect. The problem of evil is a problem for God's benevolence, not for his respecting the rights of his creatures, even if, as against him, they can have any rights, which I doubt. But it seems odd to me to say that we do not have a right that everything should be perfect. I may find it odd because the reason why we do not have such a right is that the question whether we have a right to such things as immunity from earthquakes cannot arise.

If no contingent and verifiable consequences follow from the existence of God, then the problem of evil will not arise. The problem of evil can be regarded as just the fact that some of the contingent and empirically verifiable propositions which allegedly can be deduced from the existence of God are not true propositions. And, of course, a proposition or hypothesis that implies what is false must itself be false.

However, if one says that no contingent verifiable consequences follow from the existence of God, one escapes from one difficulty only to be faced with another. If the proposition that God exists is not verifiable, can there be any reasons for thinking that there is a God? Can the sentence 'God exists', which purports to formulate the proposition that there is one, even have any meaning? Will it make any difference to anyone whether there is a God or not? What can be meant by saying 'God is benevolent' or 'God is good', if the words 'benevolent' and 'good', when applied to God, have no connection with their usual significance of being disposed to prevent suffering? (I shall argue later that these difficulties apply only to supposing that there is the kind of God who one would expect to interfere with the world.)

It has been held[4] that if there is an *a priori* proof of the existence of God, the problem of evil is only a minor difficulty for his existence. If the proof in question is an *a priori* proof of a God who does not interfere in the universe, this may be true. But if it is an *a priori* proof of a God who does interfere, then the difficulty is that the existence of evil must make us suspect the correctness of our proof. For it is more certain that there is evil, and that evil would not be permitted by a benevolent God who could interfere in the world, than that any such proof is satisfactory. Indeed, we have seen that no such proof can be satisfactory.

(ii)   The Best of all Possible Worlds

It has been argued that, if there were a God, he would produce the best of all possible worlds – a view of Leibniz's, which has been subjected to much deserved ridicule – from which it follows that, if this is not the best of all possible worlds, there is no God. (If there is no such thing as the best of all possible worlds because there are several possible worlds, each better than all other worlds and as good as one another, then he would have produced one of these. It would not matter which.)

It has been argued in reply that there is no such thing as the best of all possible worlds (as there is no such thing as the largest natural number). In this case, however good the world was, it would always be possible to produce a world that was still better (just as, however, large a number is, it is always possible to produce a still larger number). To produce the best of all possible worlds would then be a logical impossibility and so no limitation to God's omnipotence, omniscience or benevolence.

However, I suspect that if it really is always possible to produce a better world than *any* world that God created, this would be because there would be an unlimited number of small refinements that he could make to its excellence. Happy and good people perhaps, could always be just that little happier and better, though by progressively diminishing degrees. They would approach perfection asymptotically. But this does not mean that a benevolent God would have produced this actual world where there are vast amounts of suffering and moral depravity. Even if it is not possible to produce the best of possible worlds, this is no justification for producing a world as bad as this.

(iii)   Classification of Evils

Numerous attempts have been made by philosophers and theologians to show that the four apparently inconsistent propositions stated above – that God is omnipotent, that he is omniscient, that he is benevolent, but that there is, nevertheless, evil – are in fact consistent. But perhaps, before considering them, we ought to attempt some classification of the various kinds of evil. We shall see that the word 'evil' is a very bad word for some of the things that have been called 'evil'.

(a) First there is what might be called moral evil, though 'evil' will usually be too strong a word. I cannot, however, see that the logical difficulty created by the existence of moral evil is any worse when the evil in question is the moderate idleness from which most of us suffer, or when it is, say, extreme and wanton cruelty, which is comparatively rare. If God exists and has the attributes he is supposed to have, unnecessary evil should not occur at all.

Where moral evil is concerned, evil is usually held to be voluntary. Human beings themselves decide to perform actions which are wrong or wicked, when they might well have decided otherwise. This has been held by many to exculpate God from the charge of being responsible for moral evil. Moral evil is the responsibility of humans, not of God. I shall discuss later in this chapter whether the fact (if it is one) that human beings are responsible for moral evil does exculpate God or not.

(b) The next kind of 'evil' is usually considered to be pain. However, I believe that to include only pain in this class of evils is to make the class unduly narrow. A number of things other than pain present, so far as I can see, exactly the same problem that pain does. Perhaps the fact that we suffer pain can be regarded as just a special case of the problem why, if God is benevolent, we do not have all the things we want or need to have, or which would seem to be good for us, or both, and sometimes have things which we do not want to have, or need not to have, or which would seem to be bad for us. (To say that we simply do not want to suffer acute pain, though true, is of course an understatement. And obviously what we want and what is good for us are not the same.)

Pain, then, is just one of the things we have which we do not want to have – it is not always bad for us, though sometimes it is – but there are others. We might want to be richer, cleverer, more talented, or stronger than we are, for example. It might even be good for us to be some of these things.

The difference between this and moral evil is that 'evils' of this kind are not things people do, and are very often, though not always, things people cannot help. Moral evil is confined to human beings and beings, in other planets, like human beings, if there are any. The latter kind of 'evil' may be suffered by animals. (I believe that some animals, for example chimpanzees, do have rudimentary but nevertheless useful moral codes.)

(c) The third kind of evil might be roughly classified as poor or defective organisation. If the universe were created, the being who created it must obviously be extremely intelligent and powerful. He must be powerful enough to create whole galaxies, since there are galaxies, and intelligent enough to understand the theory of relativity, since he made things in such a way that they are governed by it. Yet it does not seem to have occurred to this very intelligent, very powerful being to have made it rain only at night, or to have given the Sahara a higher rainfall and London less fog, or not to have put carcinogens into tobacco leaves.

(It can be argued that one is not blaspheming if one says that the universe is incompetently governed. For what one is saying is not that God governs it incompetently, but that if it were governed by an intelligent being it would be governed incompetently, so it cannot be governed by God. This looks complimentary to God, rather than the reverse. But from the point of view of the theist, if one said that the world could not be governed by a benevolent God because it was governed incompetently, one would be saying this when in fact it was governed by God, and so implying that God's government was in fact incompetent, which might, I suppose, be blasphemous.)

(d) The fourth kind of evil (of which (3), and perhaps also (2) and (1) may be a species) is imperfection. If everything has been created by God, why is not everything perfect? Human beings, for example, though quite marvellous compared with anything that man can make, are really very defective creatures when you consider what an omnipotent, omniscient being might have done had he wished, and many individual humans are pretty defective even when compared with a not very exacting standard of what it is to be human.

(iv)   Attempted Solutions; Evil Not a Positive Attribute

The first attempt to solve the problem of evil that we shall consider is that evil is not a positive attribute, but merely the privation of good.

It is difficult to see what this means, or why it helps. If someone is in extreme pain, does it really make his pain more acceptable to say that pain is not a positive attribute, but a mere privation?

The idea seems to be this. Poverty, one might say, is not a positive attribute, but merely a privation of money. It could be argued (though not plausibly) that in that case it is unreasonable to complain that we are poor. To do so is to complain that we have not been given more money than we have. We should instead be thankful that we have been given any money at all. Similarly, perhaps, to complain that we are stupid is to complain that we have been given an intelligence quotient of only 70, when we should, instead, be thankful that we have been given even as many points as this.

This answer is not satisfactory. A father who was being charged with neglect of his child could not defend himself on the ground that, though he had not given her enough food to keep her healthy, she ought to be grateful that she had been given any food at all.

And can it be unreasonable to complain that one is in pain, because to be in pain is really just to have a smaller than usual number of units of pleasure? Could moral badness be regarded as a privation on the grounds that a wicked person had at least been 'given' a smaller than usual number of units of good? In that case, perhaps the wicked man might say that he was not really wicked. He was, he might claim, really good, though, he would have to admit, not very good.

The view that evil is a privation presupposes that there is a bottom point on a scale of pleasure (or goodness), which is low enough to enable one to say that pain (and moral badness) are nevertheless a certain distance above it. These points would be like absolute zero, in that even freezing arctic temperatures are a certain number of points above them.

Despite the view that pain is merely a privation, the natural point to take as 0 on the scale of pleasure and pain would be the state in which one was neither suffering pain nor enjoying pleasure. From this it would follow, contrary to the view that evil is a privation, that there could be both positive and negative units of pleasure. Whether there is anything analogous to absolute zero where pain is concerned I very much doubt. Its existence would at least imply that there was something so painful that nothing could be any more painful. I do not know whether there is anything so painful as this. (I am fairly sure that there can be no-one so bad morally that he could not conceivably be morally worse.)

Finally, a man cannot be given his good or bad points in the same way as he is given his income, for there can be no such person as a Smith abstracted from his good and bad qualities, as there is a Smith abstracted from his income, to whom more money may or may not be given. And in any case, money must not be confused with that to which it is a means. While lack of money may be a privation, what results if you do not have enough of it – starvation and misery, for example – is not a privation. And does it make it right to give my child too little pocket money that I might not have given him any at all? In any case, saying that evil is a privation of good, if it helps at all, only helps where the problem of evil arises because of an apparent reflection upon God's benevolence. Where it is a reproach to his capacity as a craftsman or organiser, it does not help at all.

(v) Evil Enhances the Value of the Whole as Does a Discord in Music

It has been held that just as a discord in a piece of music, or an individually ugly colour in a painting, may enhance the beauty of the whole, so evil parts in the universe may enhance the value of the whole. The goodness of a whole, indeed, does not consist in the sum of the goodness or badness of its parts.

Well, I suppose evil parts may increase the value of a whole. Sometimes, indeed, they certainly do increase its value. But, if we cannot see the whole, that they always do so is merely an optimistic (and implausible) surmise. One needs evidence for thinking that this is what actually happens, and there is none. In any case, it needs to be explained just how the evil parts of the universe increase the value of the whole universe.

If the universe were a dramatic performance, it would be quite easy to see how they did this, for 'evil' episodes in a play, i.e., actors acting the parts of people performing evil deeds, or suffering pain or bereavement, may certainly increase the dramatic effect of the play. Indeed, without such incidents there would not be much left for anybody to write plays about. (I doubt however, whether badly written scenes may increase the merits of the play, though of course comic scenes may enhance the effect of tragic ones.)

But there are differences between the universe and a play. Firstly, the audience is problematic. If it is human beings, they, unlike the audiences of most plays, participate in the drama, and run a risk of themselves suffering misfortune, pain and death. This would cause many people not to go the theatre at all were the risk of being subject to such misfortunes the same as it is in real life. Though in a play the actors are not really suffering, in the universe those analogous to actors (i.e., people) playing out the evil episodes really are suffering. Hence, if God is the audience, the comparison with a play would make him rather like Nero, watching tragedies in which actors really were torn to pieces by lions. Hence the analogy with dramatic art works badly. And it is difficult to see how considering visual arts or music helps. For how can suffering make the universe as a whole look either more or less beautiful, or sound either more or less beautiful? Suffering cannot affect the way the universe looks or sounds. Indeed, it may make no sense to talk of the universe as a whole, which cannot be viewed from anywhere outside itself, looking or sounding anything at all.

(vi)   The Existence of Evil is Necessary to the Existence of Good

Another similar solution to the problem of evil is that the existence of evil is necessary, but not aesthetically necessary, to the existence of other and greater goods. If so, it will be impossible for God to produce the good without the evil.

This necessity must be either causal or logical. If it is causal necessity, the impossibility of having the good without the evil is the impossibility of opening a tin without a tin-opener, or of a man's being immortal. If it is logical necessity, then the impossibility of having the good without the evil is like the impossibility of everybody's giving help without anybody's receiving it.

(God might be a utilitarian if he were to cause suffering for the sake of a greater good. I myself do not regard being a utilitarian as a deficiency in the deity. Once upon a time it was not supposed to be an insult to say God was a utilitarian; indeed, some suggested he might be one, because his only concern, like that of a utilitarian, would have been with the happiness or welfare of his creatures.)

(vii)   The Necessity of Evil is Causal

If the impossibility is causal, there are two difficulties with the view that it is impossible for God to produce the good without the evil. We can all think of an enormous number of evils which do not in fact seem to lead to any greater goods. Hence these evils are not justified by the fact that there are greater goods that could not be produced without them. Secondly, God himself must be responsible for the causal laws that make evil a causally necessary condition of these goods. In other words, it must be God himself who made it impossible to have the goods without the evil. Hence he might have produced better causal laws, or in some cases might have abrogated the laws he has produced.

Descartes' Argument

An argument of Descartes' will serve as an example.[5] Descartes thought that it was impossible for God to have made a man who did not suffer acute pain (from cancer, say). The reason was that he needed his nervous system to carry messages from his limbs or instructions to his muscles. Given that a man had such a nervous system, it was impossible that accidents to it happening between the brain and the nerve endings should not cause pain. But even though pain does result when things go wrong, the advantages of having a nervous system outweigh the disadvantages.

But, it can be objected to Descartes, an omniscient, omnipotent being might perhaps have thought of a nervous system that did not break down so easily, or, when it did break down, he might have been more ready than he is to provide a temporary (miraculous?) anaesthetic.

It has been argued that God could not miraculously intervene to prevent suffering, because this would make the world unpredictable and so impossible for men (and animals?) to live in. But God would not have had to make the universe uniformly unpredictable, so to speak; just to make it interfere when necessary. If God did make the world uniform so that man could find his way about in it, he might have given men better brains to predict its behaviour correctly more often.

(If it is a logical truth that the causal laws we have are the best possible ones, as Leibniz must have supposed since he thought this was the best of all possible worlds, then God's inability to improve upon them becomes a special case of his inability to do the logically impossible, but it is difficult to believe they are the best, let alone that it is a logical truth that they are.)

The World as a Moral Training Ground

One reason why it has been held that God must produce evil is that the world is a kind of moral training ground, designed for the moral education and improvement of mankind. Such a view is not entirely without plausibility.

Some pain, for example, though by no means all, does sometimes result in a strengthening of moral character. But if the world is a moral training ground – a depressing thought – it is a rather badly organised one. For example, one would expect easy lessons in endurance to come first and more difficult ones to come later, but this very frequently does not happen. The moral training ground view can give an account only of that tiny fraction of animal suffering that results in some human kindness. Human beings are unaware of most animal suffering and so they cannot show their kindness by relieving it. And the view supposes that man is being trained for the next world, the existence of which is doubtful and about which, if it does exist, we know nothing. But we would need to know at least that there was another world and that man's place in it was determined by his moral stature in this before the moral training ground view of evil will explain even moral evil. Even so, the fact that much evil does not produce any improvement in this world suggests that its function is not to make men sufficiently good to deserve Heaven, if Heaven can be deserved. If Heaven cannot be deserved, there would be no point in producing moral improvement anyway.

Evil Necessary to Produce 'Satisfactory' Souls

John Hick[6] has produced a variant on this view, according to which the function of evil is to produce satisfactory souls. (This is not quite the same thing as producing morally good human beings.)

This view is open to exactly the same objections as the former view. Hick has replied by suggesting that God has produced a universe in which the fact that the function of evil is to produce men with satisfactory souls is disguised, because not knowing that we live in such a universe is itself a means to our having such souls. This suggestion – Hick himself does not regard it as any more than this – can be parodied, as can many other such arguments as we have seen, by the argument: if my wife were a Methodist minister, deeply concerned with my having a satisfactory soul, she would not have told me that she was, as this would be counterproductive; she has not told me that she is; therefore she is a Methodist minister deeply concerned with my having a satisfactory soul. (The same difficulty applies to the view that, if there were a God, it is only to be expected that he would not have divulged to us why there is evil; hence, since there is evil which we cannot explain, there must be a God who has not divulged to us why there is evil.)[7]

Accepting Evil in the Right Spirit

Another reply is that even great evils are a means to good, provided they are accepted in the right spirit. (It is their being accepted in the right spirit that makes them good.)

There are some difficulties with this view. Not all evils are accepted in the right spirit, nor is there any possibility that they should be. It may be better to accept great pain, misfortune, and physical deformity in the right spirit than otherwise, but I myself think that it would often be better not to suffer pain at all. A world in which everybody was unfortunate, deformed and in great pain, but apparently in close contact with the deity, would not be a good world; it would, I think, be a worse world than one in which everybody was healthy, happy and fortunate, even though they were not in close contact with the deity. Further (to anticipate a point I shall make later) the fact that men would accept evil in the right spirit, if they were subject to it, might have as much 'spiritual' value as one in which they actually were subject to evil, which they accepted in the right spirit.

Suffering is something that ought to be accepted with courage and dignity, where this is possible; rejoicing in it is, I think, morbid and mildly repulsive. And people who talk in this way forget that one of the worst kinds of evil is insanity, where the sufferer is attacked from behind; there are certain kinds of insanity where the sufferer has no chance of accepting the resulting suffering with dignity because of the very fact that he is insane. Even if the suffering of the sufferer were more than counterbalanced by the spiritual worth of the way in which he or she bore it, a world in which some people suffered and other people gained spiritually from it would not be one that I should admire. I do not believe that spiritual goods are so good that they outweigh any amount of evil in the life of the spiritual person, let alone that the spiritual goods of some people outweigh evil in the lives of others. The suffering of the Holocaust cannot have resulted in much spiritual good, conceived in the manner of union with Christ, in those who suffered, as those who suffered were mostly Jews.

Some people appear to regard (their) suffering as a welcome means to increasing their intimacy with the God who, in one of his persons, is responsible for it (and who, in another of his persons, suffered it). If they are subject to unavoidable suffering, I do not grudge them any way they can find of supporting it. Suffering may be mitigated if it results (in a small minority of cases) in the beatific vision, but the argument justifying suffering for this reason would need the premise that suffering was the only way of attaining this vision, which I do not think it is.

(viii)   Evil is Logically Necessary

The view that evil is a logically necessary condition of greater goods is more interesting, though not much more plausible, than the view that evil is causally necessary for their existence. There are two ways in which evil might be held to be logically necessary to the existence of a greater good.

(a) Moral goodness is a good of a very high degree. (Some philosophers have held that it is so good that the smallest possible amount of it must outweigh in value the largest possible amount of any other kind of good, but they exaggerate.) If there is to be such a thing as moral goodness, which lies in man's rightly exercising his power of free choice, man must have free will. It is logically impossible for God to have given man free will without man sometimes exercising it wrongly, and so producing moral evil instead of moral good. Actual instances of moral evil are then man's fault, not God's.

If it is held that the consequences of moral evil, as well as moral evil itself, are man's fault, this is open to the difficulty that God could have prevented moral evil from having bad consequences. It could be argued, however, that he could not have done this except at the cost of refusing to allow man to be educated by the realisation that moral evil does have bad consequences. (It does not always have bad consequences.)

There are two difficulties with the view that God (logically) had to make men free in order to give them the opportunity to be morally good.

The first difficulty is that this view will explain only moral evil, not the evil of suffering, and not any of the kinds of evil listed above other than moral badness. Earthquakes, for example, are not the result of man's wrong use of his free will; nor is most animal suffering (though some is). In those cases when animal suffering is the result of man's wrongly exercising his free will, it is the animals, not the men, who suffer. This might be considered unjust.

The second difficulty with the argument is that it assumes as an essential premise that God could not have made man both free and always good. It is true that, as the argument assumes, God (logically) could not have given men free wills without giving them the power to choose wrongly as well as rightly. But could not God have created men who, though they had the power to choose rightly as well as wrongly, exercised this power by always choosing rightly?

There is one argument which suggests that God could have made us both free and always good, or free and better than we are. Our moral character, i.e., whether we usually act rightly or wrongly, depends at least to a very large extent – and some philosophers and physiologists would say that it depends wholly – upon our physiological state. Large quantities of heroin or methylated spirits added to the bloodstream, for example, are not good for us, morally as well as physically and intellectually. Neither are many conditions – brain tumours or thyroid deficiency, for example – that occur naturally. One's moral character, like one's health or happiness, is always at the mercy of a chance blow on the head, or an accidental derangement to the balance of one's endocrine glands.

Hence such physical accidents do not only undermine our health; they undermine our morals as well. But if our moral character depends, as to a large extent it does, upon our physiological state, it ought to be quite easy for God to alter it, because he could, quite easily, alter this state. It involves only altering the state of certain neurons. Even doctors can change it. All that is necessary is for God to change the state of a physical object, viz., the human brain by, say, increasing the supply of those materials which are usually produced by our glands, or putting our brain in the state in which a good enough doctor could put it by operating upon our brain.

The reply, of course, is that an action which was a result of God's controlling the state of our brain would not be a free action. I see no reason, however, why this should be so. As I have argued earlier (chapter 12), so long as it is a true hypothetical proposition that the agent would not have performed the action in question had he not wanted to perform it, it does not matter that the wants from which he performs it have been produced by God's manipulating the state of the agent's brain. If there is no conflict between freedom and determinism, but compatibilism is the correct view, then God could have produced the causal conditions that made men good without in any way interfering with their freedom (see chapter 12).

It has been argued[8] that, even if God could produce an action that was both free and caused by producing the conditions that produced the desires and beliefs that produced the action, he could not *directly* produce the action by an act of divine fiat. I think that this is true, at least if 'directly produce' means 'produce the action *without* giving the agent the desires and beliefs that lead up to it'. For if it was produced without the agent having these wants and beliefs, then it would not be an action that the agent performed because he wanted to, or because he believed that performing it would be to his advantage, or something of the sort. Hence it would not be a free action. But in fact God does not directly produce actions – he has no need to – but produces them *via* producing the desires and beliefs from which they result, so this remark is not relevant and has no tendency to show that God could not have made men both free and good.

(b) The other, less well known, argument to show that God logically could not have produced certain goods without also producing other evils is that some goods logically presuppose evils. Forgiveness, for example, is supposed to be a good of a very high order, but it would be logically impossible for it ever to be exercised unless people sometimes wronged one another. Courage is supposed to be a good, but it could not be exercised without the evil of danger. Sympathy is supposed to be a good, as is helping others in distress or relieving suffering. But sympathy and beneficence logically presuppose suffering, for, were there no suffering, there would be no-one to sympathise with, no-one whose suffering we could relieve, and no-one in distress for us to help.[9] Furthermore, in a world that contains no 'evil', our experience would be extremely narrow. For we could not experience pain, the suffering and death of those we love, defeat and desolation, or the satisfaction of having succeeded in overcoming the enormous obstacles which have beset us in achieving a worthy end.

The above considerations may show that there is some incoherence in the idea of a perfect man or society or world. If some virtues imply other vices and moral goods imply the existence of non-moral ills, then a perfect world is impossible and it can be no reproach to the deity that he has not produced one. It is obvious that not all the virtues can be possessed by one and the same person. Many virtues have their complementary vices. A generous impulsiveness, for example, may be incompatible with meticulous industry. The virtues of an artist are not necessarily compatible with those of a civil servant.[10] Hence God, if he is to make some people generous or impulsive or highly artistic, must also make the same people less careful and industrious than he might otherwise have done. (It may be that this implies that he must make other people more careful and industrious than would have been necessary had he not had to make some people more carefree.) Hence not only is a perfect world not possible, a perfect man or woman is not possible either.

This second attempt to reconcile God and evil by arguing that it is logically impossible for God to avoid evil may be criticised on two counts. First, though forgiveness may entail wrongdoing, wrongdoing does not entail forgiveness, and there is much wrongdoing which does not produce any forgiveness. It could be argued that that some of the wrongdoing produces no forgiveness is something that God cannot help, in that man himself freely chooses not to forgive. We have already seen the difficulty with this answer. Again, benevolence, endurance and sympathy may entail suffering, but suffering does not entail benevolence, endurance or sympathy, and there is a great deal of suffering, especially animal suffering, which does not produce any endurance or any sympathy.

Secondly, it may be argued against this second attempt at reconciliation that what is of value is not actually forgiving people, but having a forgiving disposition. What is of value is being prepared to forgive other people, if they do you wrong. Similarly, what is of value is not actually performing acts of bravery, but being a brave person. One may be a brave person though one has never performed a brave act in one's life, if the reason for this is that one has never had the opportunity to exercise one's bravery. It might be that no-one would ever know that one was a brave person unless one had had the opportunity to perform brave actions, but the value of its being known that one is a brave person in a universe in which there is no need for bravery does not appear to me to be very great.

One can, then, be a brave person in a world in which there is no danger, so long as there is a true hypothetical proposition about one to the effect that one would behaved bravely, if one were to encounter danger. Such a proposition could be true even though one never had any occasion actually to be brave. Again, one can be a sympathetic person even in a universe where there are no distressed people with whom to sympathise, provided one would sympathise with such people, if one were to come across them. Hence pain, danger and being wronged are not logically necessary to there being people of a sympathetic, courageous or forgiving disposition, though they are logically necessary if these character traits are ever actually to be exercised.

I am not, however, entirely convinced by this second criticism of this attempt to show that evil is unavoidable. The universe (logically) could contain forgiving, courageous, sympathetic people who were always asleep. Since being forgiving, courageous, and so on, are dispositional characteristics, there is no more difficulty about being forgiving, courageous and sympathetic while one is asleep than there is about being intelligent or knowing the date of the Battle of Hastings when one is asleep. But would a universe which contained forgiving, courageous and sympathetic people who were always asleep be of any value? Personally I do not think it would be.

But what this reply to the argument that certain kinds of evil are necessary for such things as courage and forgiveness, viz., that courageous and forgiving dispositions may be possessed by people who are always asleep, shows is not that forgivingness, courage and sympathy must be at least occasionally exercised if they are to have any value. What it shows is that some human characteristics or other incompatible with perpetual sleep, not necessarily these ones, must be exercised, if human life is to have any value. Hence all it might show could be that a universe which did not consist of people enjoying themselves, at least sometimes, did not have any value. Though you can be happy while you are asleep, you cannot enjoy yourself while you are asleep. One might think that more was necessary to produce a valuable world than enjoyment, but it is not obvious that this extra factor has to be the manifestation of valuable dispositions like courage. It could be something like intellectual activity or contemplation.

Actual acts of bravery or sympathy, as well as the disposition to perform them, are of value, and these cannot be performed in a world in which there is no danger and no suffering. It is very doubtful, however, whether the total value of the performance of acts of bravery outweigh the dangers which make such acts of bravery necessary. There would appear to be more danger, more suffering, more distress, and more wrongdoing than is necessary to elicit the admittedly valuable qualities of bravery, sympathy, forgiveness and so on. And the danger, suffering, distress and wrongdoing often occur in circumstances in which they do not in fact elicit bravery, sympathy or forgiveness, but in circumstances in which there is no possibility of their doing this.

It is a further difficulty with this reply to the objection we are considering to this solution to the problem of evil that it is possible that, though there would be no need to exercise courage in a world in which there was no danger, and no need for sympathy in a world in which there was no suffering, courage and sympathy would not be useful to us and so would not be virtues. Hence, though these virtues could not exist in a world in which there was no danger or suffering, the reason why God did not make such worlds could not be that they would be deprived of the virtues of courage and sympathy. Though these virtues would not exist in this world, neither would they have any value. They would have as little value as courage, say, would have to a deer. If so, this last attempt to explain the existence of evil we are discussing, like the others, ought to be regarded as a failure. I myself have great difficulty in thinking well of men who are without fortitude, kindness and forgivingness, even if these qualities are not useful to them, but perhaps this is just due to habit and lack of imagination. In any case, attempting to show that evil is logically necessary to a greater good will only work with the problem of moral evil. It will not work, for example, with the problem of defective organisation.

It has been held that non-moral evil is valuable because through suffering we experience God's love and respond with a submissiveness which is itself of great, perhaps supreme, value.

I have a number of difficulties with this view.

(a) Animals cannot exhibit this allegedly valuable response to suffering.

(b) Submissiveness is not a very edifying response to other people's suffering.

(c) The relationship is sadomasochistic, and, though masochism may often be good, if only because it helps people endure the pain which can be an aid to valuable but painful endeavour, I have less confidence in the love of a God who exhibits his love for his creatures by inflicting unnecessary pain on them.

(d) Among the worst evils men suffer are insanity and brain injury, which prevent them from responding to the injury in any appropriate way because they are cabbages, autistic, or suffering from delusions and hallucinations that prevent them from recognising the situation they are in.

(e) This suggestion begs the question, in that though submissiveness to suffering is valuable only if we think the suffering is inflicted for some good purpose, the good purpose cannot itself be to produce submissiveness to suffering. It is true that the satisfaction one gets from a sadomasochistic relationship with a person of the opposite (or indeed the same) sex does not depend on one's friend's inflicting pain on one for the sake of the common good, but it is unduly anthropomorphic to suppose that the universe is constructed partly for the purpose of catering for one's personal desire for a sadomasochistic relationship.

I mentioned earlier the restriction to our experience that there would be in a world which contained no evil. I am not at all sure that evil to others should be welcomed because it widens our experience and gives us the opportunity for experience that we would not otherwise have. But an enormous amount of evil – for example, an animal's being burnt alive in a forest fire – is quite divorced from any possibility of widening the experience of any person or animal, even that of the animal so burnt.

Despite the failure of these attempts to solve the problem of evil, it remains true, for what this fact is worth, that though the more evil there is in the world, the more logically difficult it is to believe in God, the more evil there is in the world, the more psychologically difficult this makes it, for some people at least, *not* to have recourse to belief in God.

(ix)   Plantinga's Defence of the Compatibility of Evil with the Existence of God

Alvin Plantinga[11] has attempted to show that the existence of natural (as opposed to moral) evil is compatible with the existence of God, on the grounds that it is possible (not actual) that the natural evil in the world is produced by non-human beings (e.g., Satan). But this just raises the questions (a) 'Why, if there are non-human beings, does not God keep them properly under control?' and (b) 'Since there is no such person as Satan, is the logical possibility of there being such a person any more helpful in explaining evil than would the logical possibility of there being an additional planet in saving Kepler's laws from being falsified, if there was no such planet?' (Kepler's laws were shown not to be falsified by the postulation of an actual planet, not by a logically possible planet.)

I have already said that what is incompatible with the existence of God is not evil, but unnecessary evil. Plantinga, in arguing (correctly) that the existence of God is compatible with that of evil, is beside the point. But what one would have thought that Plantinga should be doing is to show that the evil in the world *really is* necessary evil.

What Plantinga does instead is to show that there is no contradiction in supposing that the evil in the world is necessary evil. Again, I doubt whether anyone would dispute this. But logical possibility is not good enough. I do not think it would do for a defence council to, say, in order to exculpate his client from the charge of having committed murder, show that it is logically possible that someone other than the accused could have done it. It is logically possible that there should be a fleet of angels who could have enabled some other person both to commit the murder and cover up his traces. But a defence counsel arguing in this way would not impress a jury. (It is possible to make the case for reconciling God and evil seem stronger than it is by using the language of possible worlds which I complained about in chapter 5.)

(x)   What Kind of Idea of God, If Any, Would Survive the Fact of Evil?

But ought one to reject religion because it claims that there is an omnipotent, omniscient and benevolent God, and the existence of such a God is incompatible with that of the unnecessary evil which, nevertheless, exists?

If to make a religious claim is to claim that the universe contains such a God, and that there was such a God was a matter of super-science, the existence of unnecessary evil most certainly would show that such claims are unjustified. If the existence of God was a hypothesis, it would be disconfirmed by the existence of unnecessary evil. Since there is evil, there cannot be a good God who would not tolerate evil. It might seem that God's existence could be preserved by holding that he is not omnipotent. But since, for reasons given earlier, it is contradictory and aesthetically displeasing to suppose that there is a personal God who is anything short of being omnipotent, omniscient and perfectly good, any non-omnipotent being there might be should not be described as 'God'. This would not mean that there is not one, but to claim that there is, as a matter of scientific fact, would be absurd. If there were such a God, scientists would have come across him a long time ago.

But perhaps when one makes claims in favour of a religious life, one is not making a statement about what entities the universe does or does not contain. Indeed, such claims are both unduly limiting of God and unduly anthropomorphic. They are unduly limiting in that they postulate a God whose actions have causes (in his having plans for the universe) and effects on the universe, instead of a God who transcends the universe. They are unduly anthropomorphic in that a God who is or is not responsible for evil must be a being like ourselves, who does things from certain motives, is subject to moral laws, and needs excuses or justifications for apparent aberrations.

I shall later tentatively point out some advantages in accepting a God who is not personal, who is not responsible for the course of nature, and does not interfere with it. The 'existence' of such a God would not, and would not be intended to, explain anything and so would not be refuted by the presence of evil.

I have suggested elsewhere that it is possible to worship a nonexistent God, provided one did not expect anything in return. If one had to choose between worshipping a nonexistent God and the actual God there would have to be to be responsible for the evil the universe contains, perhaps one ought to choose to give one's allegiance to the former rather than the latter.

If there were arguments for the existence of a powerful being who was responsible for the universe, the conclusion of this argument may be that there are two Gods – to put the matter in an Irish way – a nonexistent one and one who exists. The nonexistent one, of whom we have a concept, and is good, demands our utmost respect. But the one who exists, who actually created this cruel and rather unsatisfactory universe, has a lot to answer for and should be opposed, even opposed in the name of the first. The duty of men is not to leave the universe as it is, either in word or deed, but to make a better job of the way it has been made by the first, if there is one, if he will let us.

Most who hold that there is a God hold that the God who exists and the God who deserves our worship are one and the same. In that case, one is maligning the former, albeit unknowingly, by complaining about his handiwork. But if the God who exists really is the God who deserves our worship, then I hope and expect he will understand.

(xi) Conclusion

The nature, quantity of and distribution of evil in the world is incompatible with the existence of a benevolent, omnipotent, omniscient, personal God who created the universe and is responsible for what goes on in it. There may, however, be something left of the claims of religion, even if this is so. For example, we might find that contemplating a God who did not exist helped us face the evils allowed by the 'God' who did.

Notes

1 This chapter, though it has been modified since, was written many years ago, before I had the opportunity of reading J.L. Mackie's *The Miracle of Theism*, from which I have nevertheless profited. I have expressed some views similar to Mackie's in Harrison, 1970.

2 This argument, incidentally, is of the form of the *modus tollendo tollens*: (p.q.r)->s, -s, therefore (-pv-qv-r).

3 Hence Alvin Plantinga, in devoting a paper (1974) to showing that the existence of God is compatible with that of evil is arguing without a sensible antagonist.

4 By Pike, 1963.

5 See *Meditations*.

6 In Hick, 1966.

7 This argument has been put forward by Rowe, 1990.

8 By Alvin Plantinga, *loc. cit.*

9 It is not the case that suffering is a logically necessary condition of sympathy, etc. It would be possible to produce moral good without physical evil if men were to exercise their goodness in relieving what they supposed to be suffering. Relieving supposed suffering is not as valuable as relieving actual suffering, but the complex: relieving supposed suffering without there being suffering is probably more valuable than the complex: relieving actual suffering combined (as it would have to be) with there being actual suffering, especially when there is actual suffering that is not relieved.

10 I discuss this question in greater detail in Harrison, 1985 (reprinted in Harrison, 1993).

11 In Plantinga, *loc. cit.*

25 Miracles

(i) Miracles Would Provide Verification of the Existence of God

It looks as if, if the existence of God is unverifiable, there could be no miracles, or, at least, that *God* can work no miracles. This is because it looks as if a God whose existence is unverifiable would be an undetectable God, and an undetectable God would keep his presence dark and not reveal himself by miracles. In that case, miracles could not provide evidence for the existence of God, for there would be none.

In any case, a God who was a necessary being could not work miracles. That there are (or are not) miracles is a contingent fact, and we have seen that the existence of a necessary being cannot imply any such facts. If it did, this being would not exist in the event of their being false and so could not be a necessary being. It does not follow that the mere occurrence of miracles or what appeared to be a miracle would provide evidence for the existence of God. Miracles would have to occur sufficiently frequently, to be on a sufficiently large scale, and to admit of a single overall purposive explanation, before they could do this.

It is an interesting question whether the fact that there are no miracles would provide proof of the nonexistence of God. The answer is that it would provide disproof of the kind of God who would work miracles, if he existed. I suspect that any God who cared about mankind, had the power to ameliorate the position of mankind, and had let things get into the state they are now, would work miracles.

(ii) The Definition of 'Miracle'

It is sometimes supposed that a miracle is a deliberate interruption or suspension of or overriding of a law of nature by God to serve as a sign to men of his existence, or of some fact about him, for example, of his plans for men, and how he wishes men to live.

If this is intended to be a definition of 'miracle' it will not do. For it seems that there is no contradiction in saying that miracles may be worked by men. (The title of H.G. Wells's story 'The Man who worked Miracles' is not contradictory.) And it is said that there are angels and that angels can work miracles.

And even if miracles do in fact serve as a sign, I can see no contradiction in the suggestion that some are produced for some other reason than the ones just mentioned, or from mere caprice. That they are produced by God is a hypothesis to explain the occurrence of some allegedly miraculous events that have allegedly occurred. That their being God's handiwork is the only explanation of a miracle is not something that follows from the definition of 'miracle'. Hence I shall assume that a miracle is a deliberately produced interruption to a law of nature by some being for some purpose. However, the miracles we shall be interested in here will be those allegedly worked by God.

In the literature of Christianity there are two kinds of miracle; those supposedly worked by God and those supposedly worked by lesser beings, for example, by saints. One may attempt to reduce the latter kind to the former by saying that God also produced the latter miracles, but at the saint's instigation or on his behalf. But this might be to start on a slippery slope at the bottom of which would be the view that God himself performed every action which we appeared to perform. (There would still be a distinction between miracles that men did at least appear to perform, and those that they did not.)

(iii)   Miracles Not Inconceivable

It has been alleged that the statement that miracles occur is either one that it is impossible to prove, or even is meaningless (a) on the grounds that they are produced by an invisible agency. And it has (b) been held that it is impossible for a spiritual object, which is what God is alleged to be, to have any effects on the world.[1]

(a) It is true that one cannot observe a miracle being produced; one can observe only the effects of the action that produced it, say, the water's becoming wine: the action itself is invisible. But when an action is intentionally produced by a human being (other than oneself), one also cannot observe the intentions that produced it (unless they are one's own) and, even if one could, one could not observe that the intentions caused the change and were not just temporally prior to it. (That God should cause miracles assumes that God is everlasting, not eternal.)

(b) Changes to the material world could be produced by the intentions of a non-material being. Causation is a matter of one event's being correlated with another – smoke with fire, for example – and anything can be correlated with anything else; it is just a question or what is correlated with what.

A personal, temporal God, if he existed, could then certainly work miracles. The question is whether he does.

(iv)   Difficulty for Miracles: There Cannot in Principle be Sufficient Evidence for Them

I shall discuss the question whether a miracle has to involve an interruption to a law of nature later in this chapter. (If it does, such things as the birth of a baby cannot literally – but only rhapsodically – be miracles; for one thing, the birth of a baby is certainly not an interruption to the ordinary course of nature.) But if a miracle does involve an interruption to the course of nature, there are difficulties in the way of believing that there are any.

The first and most important is that it will then be extremely difficult, if not impossible, to obtain any satisfactory evidence for miracles. The argument to show that this is so comes from David Hume.[2] Our evidence that water cannot be turned into wine comes from experience. Water's being turned into wine would go against what, as a result of observation, we believe the ordinary course of nature to be. Our evidence that water has been turned into wine is derived from testimony. But we accept the testimony of others only because we have observed that people like our informants, in circumstances such as those in which they were placed, both observe correctly, report their observations accurately, and tell the truth about what they think they have observed. That they should be mistaken in such cases would also go against the ordinary course of nature.

In other words, we are setting two constant conjunctions or regularities against one another, the constant conjunction of people's attempts to do such things as turn water into wine from a distance of a few feet in a brace of shakes being followed by failure, and the constant conjunction of people's reports that such events have happened not turning out to be false. We should accept the testimony of others, that the water has been turned into wine, only if it would be an even greater miracle for them to be lying or mistaken than it would be for the water to be turned into wine.

Hume thought that since human beings are constantly liable to mistake what they see and to deceive themselves and others about it, it would be very,

very unlikely that the testimony's being mistaken would not be the smaller of the two miracles. Hence we ought to disbelieve the testimony. This is especially so since men love marvels (of which miracles are a species) and so want to believe that miracles occur. Since many men, too, often have an interest of one kind or another, which may be commercial, in others believing in miracles, this gives them a strong and constant motive for persuading themselves and others that the evidence for miracles is stronger than it is.

Hume's argument does not show, and is not intended to show, that there can be no miracles. It is intended to show, and does show, that we cannot have sufficient evidence to warrant believing in miracles, if the occurrence of miracles involves an interruption to the normal course of nature. If an Indian were to believe, contrary to his experience of the behaviour of water and the honesty of Europeans, that water could solidify at low temperatures, his belief would be irrational, for all the evidence at his disposal would be against it, but the belief would nevertheless be true. Similarly, if I believe that water was turned into wine, my belief must, if Hume is right, be irrational, but it could, nevertheless, be true.

The difference between the Indian's believing, on testimony, that water naturally solidifies at low temperatures and our believing that a miracle has occurred is that a time may come when he gets better evidence for believing that water solidifies at low temperatures, whereas, from the nature of the case, if a miracle involves an interruption to the course of nature, we can never obtain evidence sufficient to justify us in believing in the miracle. (The Indian may get better evidence by better testimony, or more testimony of the same kind, or by staying in a country where water does freeze.)

Accepting someone's testimony for the occurrence of a miracle involves believing that someone else has actually witnessed a miracle. It is true that we may also accept hearsay evidence – it is not necessarily irrational to believe something on hearsay evidence, though it is disallowed in English courts of law – to the effect that there has been a miracle. (We accept hearsay evidence when A reports what he has seen to B, who reports it to us. There may be an indefinite number of intermediaries, not just one. But a chain of testimony like this would be valueless if it did not, however long it was extended, end with someone who had actually himself observed the event reported.) Accepting hearsay evidence presupposes that the person who started the chain of testimony, and claimed to witness a miracle, was himself justified in believing that the miracle he seemed to witness occurred. If the person who started the chain of testimony could be justified in believing that he had witnessed a miracle it ought to be possible for we ourselves to be this person, actually to witness a miracle, and actually see or seem to see the alleged miraculous occurrence ourselves. Must we not then believe that it really has occurred?

If a scientist seems to observe a ball rolling down a slope with an acceleration of more or less than (roughly) 9.81 metres per second per second[3] is he bound to say 'I have just witnessed a (minor) miracle'? Would he even have to say 'I have just shown that all previous scientists have been wrong in supposing that objects always fall with an acceleration of 9.81 metres per second per second without claiming that there is anything miraculous about this'? Obviously, he would not. He would think that something had gone wrong with the experiment, or with his measuring instruments, or that his senses were deceiving him.

In any case, if he took the apparent result at all seriously, the scientist would probably try to repeat the experiment. If he does, then either the same thing will happen again or it will not. If it does not happen again, then the scientist will believe that it had not really happened the first time. If, on the other hand, it does happen again (and perhaps it will be necessary for it to happen again and again before he believes that it happened on the first occasion) he will look for a natural explanation. He will do this by trying to find out in what circumstances objects do not fall with the usual acceleration. If he finds what these circumstances are, and other scientists find the same, he will in fact have found a new law of nature (and modified an old one). In this case the event will not be a miracle. (The scientist's reluctance to put this aberration down to miracle may partly explained by its not having any obvious purpose.)

Objects not falling with the acceleration that they have in the past could be regarded as a miracle if there was some evidence of purpose behind the change. Such evidence, perhaps, might consist in God's announcing – perhaps by a message written in the sky – that certain laws of nature would change from a certain time, and their changing from that time. But if the change can be explained by God's changing the laws because of changed circumstances, perhaps the change could be explained 'directly' by the changed circumstances themselves, without recourse to God. And it might be possible, instead of saying that a change in circumstances has produced a change in the laws, to say that there has been no change in law; all that has happened is that these circumstances have never previously arisen. To take a homely example, the advent of aeroplanes could make one say that the 'law' that objects heavier than air fall to the ground had been changed so that men might fly, but it would be more sensible and economical to say that it had always been a law that objects heavier than air had fallen to the ground unless they were self-propelled, but there had only recently been any objects that were self-propelled. I suspect that alleged changes in physical laws produced by very high temperatures can be so explained. The new cooler temperatures which are supposed to have produced a change in the laws of physics may then be regarded as analogous to the advent of self-propelled objects heavier than air. I shall return to this topic later.

Even if miracles are in some way law-governed, there is no way of making sure something is a miracle by producing it experimentally. Miracles cannot be produced at will by human beings. And if there were a way in which men could reliably produce them, this fact would *ipso facto* show that they were not miracles, for though their occurrence would interrupt one natural law, there would, as we shall see when we consider magic later in this chapter, be another law in accordance with which they operated.

Incidentally, it might be held that I have made Hume's argument weaker than it is, for there is no law of nature to the effect that testimony cannot be mistaken, whereas there is a law of nature to the effect that water cannot be turned into wine. But that there is a law of nature to the effect that water cannot be changed into wine is not strictly speaking true. There are a number of natural laws which would be violated if water were changed into wine in these circumstances and with this speed. Similarly, though there is no natural law to the effect that testimony cannot be mistaken, that this testimony should be mistaken in these circumstances might conceivably violate some other natural law or set of natural laws.

(v) Second Main Difficulty for Miracles: Laws of Nature Cannot be Interrupted

This brings us to the second difficulty with miracles. If we decide there is sufficient evidence to warrant our accepting that a miracle has occurred, it follows that something that we had supposed to be impossible – water's being turned into wine, for example – has actually happened. But if the miracle has happened it cannot be impossible and so there cannot really be a law of nature ruling out its occurrence. Hence no law of nature can have been violated. If Boyle's 'Law' is a law, then gases must expand when heated, because this is what Boyle's Law (roughly) says they will do. So if some gas does not expand when heated, then Boyle must have been wrong, and so Boyle's 'Law' will not be a law of nature. If not everybody dies there cannot be a law of nature that entails that all men die, and if someone can turn water into wine from a distance of 10 feet, there cannot be any law of nature which prevents people from doing this. Hence a law of nature logically cannot be interrupted and miracles cannot occur. Supposed laws of nature can be interrupted, but nobody considers this to be miraculous. (One should not argue, incidentally, that because Boyle's Law is (by definition) a law, gases cannot do anything other than expand when heated. One should, rather, argue that, if they do not expand, Boyle must have been mistaken in thinking that that gases expand when heated is a law.)

(vi)   Some Other Possible Answers to the Difficulty Concerning Evidence Rejected

It may be said that the trouble with the first difficulty, put as Hume has put it, is that it proves too much. Suppose Hume heard the account of someone who had been so moved by the story of the crucifixion that nail marks had appeared on her hands and feet. Hume would have had to argue that it would be more likely that the testimony of the people reporting this happening was mistaken than that what they said was true and so it would be, given Hume's experience of nature. Yet few nowadays, when we know more than Hume about psychosomatic illness, would suppose that such an occurrence would conflict with a law of nature. Again, the Indian aforementioned might be led by Hume's principle to reject stories told to him by Europeans to the effect that water became solid at low temperatures. His experience of water and his experience of Europeans might make him think it more likely that the Europeans were lying than that the water was solidified.

Hume's principle might lead us to reject anything which is contrary to our experience. (To do this, however, would itself be illogically to ignore experience, for one of the things we have had experience of is that things which we have had no experience of occasionally happen.) So perhaps what Hume's principle would enjoin is that we should disbelieve that a miracle has occurred, but not to such an extent as to shut our minds to the possibility that if there were more evidence – much, much more – then it might be rational to believe it. Hume does allow for this, to the extent that he implies that we should believe the testimony if it would be a greater miracle for the testimony to be wrong than for the alleged miracle to have occurred. However, given certain empirical facts about human beings, that they are credulous, inaccurate and love marvels, our having this amount of evidence is unlikely.

Those who believe in miracles are therefore faced with this dilemma. Either miracles occur very seldom, in which case it is more likely that the testimony for them is mistaken than that they really happened, or they occur fairly frequently, in which case it would be more reasonable to accept the testimony for them, but not very reasonable to regard them as being miracles. The ideal thing, both intellectually and (in this case for those who like wine) practically, would be for us then to discover in what circumstances water could be changed into wine. But if we could do this we would be on the way to discovering a new law of nature, one to the effect that water gets changed into wine whenever these circumstances arise or are produced. Would this in principle be any different from the fact that water gets changed into ice at temperatures of 0° Celsius or lower?, If so, water's being changed into wine in these circumstances would no more involve a miracle than would water's being changed into ice at 0° Celsius.

It has been objected to Hume that he relies on the sciences of his day. But this objection fails; if modern science allows the event, though eighteenth century science did not, it follows that, though it may have occurred, it is not a miracle. (To deny miracles in the name of science is sometimes said to presuppose having faith in science, but this is not so. Science does not need faith, in the sense of needing irrational belief. It may be necessary for some scientists to have an irrational belief in the truth of some hypotheses, in order to make the commitment that was in fact necessary to establish them, but these hypotheses only became accepted after rationally acceptable evidence for them had been found.)

To be more specific, quantum theory is sometimes welcomed by theologians on the grounds that it makes miracles more plausible. It does not in fact do this. According to quantum theory, it is in principle impossible to predict accurately the behaviour of the small particles which compose material objects. The behaviour of an object like a cricket ball can be predicted in the way that the behaviour of a crowd can be predicted. One can say that it is unlikely, though by no means impossible, that Tom will not catch the 8.00 pm to London and the same may be true of all other commuters. But in that case it is very, very unlikely that many of them should all decide not to catch the train to London on the same day, and the behaviour of a coachful of commuters can be predicted with virtual certainty, though the behaviour of any one commuter cannot. According to quantum theory, the same is true of the behaviour of something like a cricket ball, the difference being that since there are many more atoms in a cricket ball than there are commuters on a train, the chances of the cricket ball's behaving aberrantly are even more remote.

It follows that it is theoretically possible for allegedly miraculous events to occur without interrupting laws of nature. It is, or so it is said, only very highly improbable that a saint should remain suspended in mid air for a couple of seconds. But this defence of miracles takes away with one hand what it gives with the other. The very reason that shows that alleged miracles might occur shows that they are not miraculous. If something occurs because of a simultaneous aberration in a vast number of electrons, it is not a miracle.

(vii)   Swinburne on an Example of Hume's

Swinburne has argued that we can set aside a law on the basis of verbal evidence for a miracle and traces of a miracle. (Some points against his view will be made incidentally later in this chapter.) Swinburne[4] partly adumbrates this argument by reference to an example of Hume's, which he quotes, and is worth quoting.

Hume says:

> Thus suppose, all authors in all languages agree, that, from the first of January 1600, there was a total darkness over the *whole* [my italics] earth for eight days: suppose that the tradition of this extraordinary event is still strong and lively among the people: that all travellers, who return from foreign countries, bring us account of the same tradition, without the least variation or contradiction: it is evident, that our present philosophers, instead of doubting the fact, ought to receive it as certain, and ought to search for the cause whence it might be derived.[5]

Swinburne thinks that nowadays, with our greater knowledge of meteorology, we would regard the event testified to as physically impossible if it occurred. (He does not say so, but I think he also thinks that, though physically impossible, we would nevertheless have to accept, if this degree of evidence were available, that the physically impossible actually had occurred.) Hence Swinburne thinks that Hume is wrong in thinking that there could not be sufficient evidence for the occurrence of a miracle. Though again Swinburne does not say so, I think he thinks that the physical impossibility in question would be the earth's stopping turning on its axis.

Hume himself agreed with Swinburne that we would have to accept the evidence for eight days darkness, but that this would not be a miracle, but a non-miraculous 'dissolution' (quantum mechanics or chaos theory?). Here Hume would seem to me to be right and Swinburne wrong, perhaps because of Hume's greater knowledge of meteorology. (Swinburne is wrong because stories of perpetual day on the other side of the earth would also be needed if perpetual darkness on one side of the globe were to be evidence for the cessation of the earth's spinning on its axis.)

Swinburne and those who think like him confuse two contentions. One is that there is a conceivable amount of evidence such that, if it were to occur, it would be good enough to establish a miracle. This statement is, I think, true. We can certainly imagine cases which are such that, *if* there were really to be this amount of evidence, we would have to accept that there was a miracle. Another contention is that this amount of evidence, which is such that it would compel us to accept the occurrence of a miracle, could actually occur. But the fact that the event was impossible would show that this amount of evidence could not occur. That that a horse that thrives though it is not fed is impossible shows that the occurrence of sufficient evidence to establish that there is a horse which thrives without being fed is impossible.[6]

It is conceivable that there should be this amount of evidence, in the sense that it is conceivable that there might be enough evidence to establish that pigs might fly, but, just because pigs cannot fly, there could not in actual fact be enough evidence to establish that they do. The conceivability of the evidence would show the conceivability of the miracle, which no-one disputes, but that does not mean that one should retain an open mind. (It is also the case that there might be enough evidence for a miracle to justify us in accepting that it actually occurred, were it not a miraculous event.) Though imaginary examples have a place in philosophy, for they can, if they are handled with sufficient care, show that something is conceivable, they cannot show that that conceivable thing could actually happen.

There is a further point against Swinburne's argument, which point adds a refinement to Hume's. Those who uphold miracles often argue that the miracle must be accepted because any other explanation involves an impossibility, say the testimony's being mistaken or the wine's being substituted for the water. But in saying this they are being pragmatically inconsistent. They allow themselves to say that the event testified to occurred, but rule out alternative explanations of its occurrence on the grounds that they are impossible. But they are impossible only because they conflict with law, which they themselves say is possible.

Upholders of miracles, like Swinburne, also demand from their opponents some non-miraculous explanation of the occurrence of the false testimony, while allowing themselves to say that there is no non-miraculous explanation of the event testified to. It is true that those of their opponents who are atheists

– which their opponents do not have to be – cannot allow themselves a genuinely miraculous explanation of the failure of the testimony. But the fact that opponents of miracles would be being inconsistent if they appealed to a miraculous alterative to the miracle – which they do not usually do – does not mean that proponents of miracles actually are being inconsistent in ruling out alternative explanations of the miracle on the grounds that they are impossible.

(viii) Possible Answer to the Difficulty Concerning the Definition of 'Miracle'

The second difficulty, that miracles by definition involve an interruption to a law of nature and that laws of nature, by definition, cannot be interrupted (for if they were, they would not be laws of nature, for these state what always happens) is insuperable, so long as we stick to these definitions of 'miracle' and 'law of nature'. But there is this partial answer to it, that though you might deny *a priori*, without evidence, that miracles, as defined above, cannot occur, it would be extraordinary to deny, without evidence, that things such as water's getting changed into wine might happen. All that this argument would show is that if such things did occur, but did not involve an interruption to a law of nature, they could not be properly described as miracles, as defined above. Similarly, black swanlike birds in Australia could not be described as swans, if swans are by definition white, but it would be ridiculous to deny for this reason that there were any such birds. It would involved a similar mistake to deny on *a priori* grounds the existence of albino blackbirds, or that fishlike animals could suckle their young. But to this it may be replied that it may not be of any theological interest that events like water's being changed into wine occur if they do not involve an interruption to a law of nature.

We have seen that the difficulty concerning the *a priori* impossibility of miracles is no better if we regard natural laws as just stating probabilities, as it may be we ought if quantum physics is true. We are then faced with the difficulty that, if nature works according to laws that do not allow exceptions, miracles cannot occur, and that if it works according to rules that do allow exceptions, apparent miracles can occur, but are not miracles (because they do not involve the impossible, but only the unusual). But it should not be supposed that, if natural laws state probabilities, rather than uniformities, anything that occurs contrary to them must be explained by its being improbable. It could be that, even if some particular interruptions to a law of nature were just random, others were miracles deliberately produced by God.

It is a matter for arbitrary terminological decision whether you call probabilistic generalisations laws or not.

If one defines 'miracle' as something which involves a suspension of the laws of nature, and 'laws of nature' as describing what happens except in the event of a miracle being worked, then there is no logical difficulty about the occurrence of miracles, and whether they do occur or not becomes, as it ought to be, an empirical matter of fact. (The reason why we continue to describe something as a law of nature, although not everything that happens can be explained by it, is that in all other circumstances it explains things perfectly well and we cannot think of anything better.) The very expression 'law of nature' (nature as opposed to art) suggests that laws of nature could be suspended by divine fiat and still remain laws of nature, i.e., laws concerning what happens except in the event of artificial divine interference.

(ix)   Occasional Necessity; Nature and Art

The difficulty we are discussing can be reinforced by saying that laws of nature are not just constant conjunctions between events. Two kinds of event are lawfully connected only if they are necessarily connected. But then there is a further reason for thinking that miracles cannot happen, for events that are necessarily connected cannot fail to be connected. If people who have taken arsenic necessarily die, no miracle can cause them not to die. What necessarily always happens cannot ever not happen.

This argument proves that miracles cannot occur only on the assumption, accepted by most (though not all) philosophers from the time of Kant, that what is necessarily connected must be universally connected. I do not, however, think this assumption is true where the necessity of laws of nature is concerned (though it is true of logical and mathematical necessity). For example, I see no reason why it should not necessarily be the case that a decaying carbon atom usually emits a certain number of electrons over a period of time. (Perhaps you might try to reintroduce universality by saying that it is always true that they usually emit so many an hour.)

That something could necessarily happen only a certain proportion of the time is true if you could, as I think you can, define a necessary connection between two events as a connection which is such that attempts to separate the events connected would fail, if they were to be made. It might well be that attempts to prevent a decaying carbon atom from emitting electrons with a certain frequency would all fail.

Not only may two kinds of event be necessarily usually connected, I think it possible for two kinds of event to be usually, but not always, necessarily connected. But if so, there is no reason why events which are normally necessarily connected should not cease to be connected if God were to work a miracle. On this view, all other attempts to prevent men who have taken vast quantities of arsenic from dying are bound to fail, but nevertheless this particular man who has taken a vast quantity of arsenic does not die, and does not die as a result of God's intervention. If a law of nature just states that two events are usually necessarily connected, there is no reason why they should not fail to be necessarily connected in certain cases and therefore no reason why they should not be miraculously separated. Perhaps a similar way of putting the matter would be to say that though man cannot separate the two events, God can. If we were to attempt to separate them we would fail, but if God were to make such an attempt he would succeed. This is because, if he exists, he must responsible for their being necessarily connected in the first place.[7]

(x)   The Possibility that Miracles Themselves are Law-governed

Hence miracles may, and perhaps must, involve the suspension of some laws of nature. It may be that changing water into wine must involve a suspension of the laws of physics or chemistry if it is to be miraculous. Perhaps, however, miracles, if they occur, can be accounted for by, and even demand, laws of nature other than the laws of physics and chemistry.

The same suggestion can be made about magic. Magic involves a departure from normal laws of nature, or what can be deduced from such laws, which entail such things as that people cannot be killed by sticking pins into a wax effigies of them when they themselves are many miles away. But perhaps magic, if it were to occur, would work according to some laws, though not, of course, the established laws of physics or chemistry. Perhaps there are rules about the nature of the substance from which the effigy must be made, the material of the pins, the way in which the pins are stuck and about what preliminary incantations must be made if pin-sticking is to be an effective way of injuring one's enemies. Perhaps if one gets one of these prerequisites wrong, the magic does not work, but, if one gets all of them right, it works, and whoever else can also get the prerequisites right can achieve the same result. In this case, though magic involves a departure from some laws of nature, the ones physicists tell us about, there would be other laws according to which the magic operated. So everything in nature would still work according to laws, though laws more peculiar than most people suppose.

I cannot see why something similar might not be true of miracles; why miracles should not work according to some laws or other, though not according to the laws people suppose govern nature, which latter laws they interrupt, though in a law-governed way. (This would mean that God could no longer, if miracles do occur, be accused of imprudence and lack of foresight in having set up a 'machine', the laws governing which he later had to tinker with.)

But if miracles were law-governed, could they provide evidence for the existence of God? For would they then not consist in an interruption to a law of nature and so not demand to be explained by recourse to God's intervention.

They could provide such evidence if it could be shown that they would not be law-governed unless one postulated a God to explain them, just as the behaviour of a compass needle is a good reason for postulating a magnet in my pocket, if we can show that the needle's apparently eccentric behaviour would not really be eccentric if there were a magnet in my pocket. Postulating the magnet will show that behaviour, the needle's not pointing north, which is apparently not law governed, is law-governed after all. It is an apparent exception to the (erroneous) law that compass needles point north, but not to the law that they point to the strongest magnetic force in the vicinity.

However, the argument that God can be postulated only to explain apparent irregularities in nature has a serious difficulty. If postulating the existence of God would show that apparently irregular occurrences are really regular such a God would, like a ninth planet, have to be a God who existed within nature, rather than one who transcends it. This would make him smaller than our conception of him demands him to be. Such an argument, indeed, has the defects which we saw earlier to belong to the argument from design. It could, if there were sufficient evidence, show that there was a God who was a part of nature, but not that there was a God who transcended nature.

There would, however, be a difference between miracles and magic, in that miracles would be worked by God, and there would be nothing we could do to work them ourselves, or reliably prevail upon God to work them. And there would be nothing, where miracles are concerned, analogous to the rules men can use to secure the efficacy of pin-sticking where magic is concerned, for God would produce each miracle by an act of fiat, not by manipulating nature as we do, by making use of already existing laws.

But if there are miracles, it is an almost irresistible assumption that God himself produces them according to law. We think – and this would appear to be implicit in Christian doctrine – that God produces them for a reason, in which case God's behaviour must be determined by the reasons, as our behaviour is determined by our reasons (see chapter 27). This, too, is presupposed by our belief that God might produce a miracle at our request, for prayer – like prayers for rain – that can be answered only by a miracle presuppose that God has some motive for answering such prayers in the affirmative, that is, that his behaviour is as much subject to the laws of psychology as is that of people. Indeed, it shows how difficult it is to escape anthropomorphism if it is so difficult not to suppose that God is subject to the same psychological laws that we are.

We have just seen that arguments for the existence of God from the occurrence of miracles presuppose the argument from design, which has already been discussed and rejected. Since arguments from design consist in postulating objects in order to turn an apparent irregularity into a regularity, they do not set aside regularity, but maintain it. They assume that alleged miracles have a supernatural explanation, but only to the extent that they presuppose a non-natural object within space and time, having certain (temporal) intentions, with certain ends in view, and wishing to achieve certain results that will occur within the time scale.

Miracles then presuppose that laws apply to God; hence they presuppose supernatural explanation. We take it for granted that miracles must have causes, causes in God's motivation. Miracles are violations of laws of nature, but not of law.

Miracles are interventions in the normal course or nature from 'outside'. They are like the 'interventions' of a new planet upon the courses of the others though a new planet is part of nature. This latter intervention is therefore in principle predictable and the planetary intervener just another part of the universe. Hence either the aberration is caused, in which case it is caused by another part of the universe, or it is not, in which case it is not interesting (because not purposive and so not indicative of the existence and intentions of a being interested in the world). Everything purposive is caused. In any case, God's intervention is either capricious, which it cannot be, or not capricious. If it is not capricious, miracles must be regular.

Hence to explain miracles we would need knowledge of regularities in God's behaviour. We apply what we know of human beings to God. This suggests that it ought to be in principle possible to predict miracles. We presumably think we have some – though not much – ability to predict miracles, for if we do things like pray for rain, this presupposes that we think that God is more disposed to provide rain if we pray for it than if we do not. That in fact we cannot predict miracles is therefore some reason for thinking that there is not a God who works them.

Miracles have to be purposive. The mere fact that objects cease to accelerate at the usual rate is not a miracle unless there is some purpose to be gained by making them fail to do so, as there was some purpose in the water's being changed into wine. In framing the hypothesis that some event is a miracle, we are framing the hypothesis that it is produced by some mind with some end in view; that is to say we are not just postulating an interruption, but a being who produces the interruption and the end for which he produces it. But this postulation manifests a faith in law on the part of the person doing the postulating. The interruption itself is an apparent irregularity, but when a being is postulated who produces the irregularity with some end in view, there ceases to be any irregularity. Postulating such a being is analogous to postulating an unknown planet to explain the aberrant behaviour of the known other planets. When it is postulated the irregularity disappears. The fact that some law of nature is 'broken' remains, but law itself also remains, in that one would expect similar laws of nature to be broken in similar circumstances, if only one could know what these circumstances were.

(xi) Hidden 'Miracles'

I suggested in the last section that the existence of God could be postulated only to explain apparent irregularities in nature, as we postulate magnets to explain apparent irregularities in the behaviour of compass needles. But perhaps miracles could be evidence for the existence of God even if they could be shown to be law-governed without postulating his existence. For perhaps something can be both a manifestation of purposive behaviour on the part of the deity and explicable in physical or physiological terms. Perhaps, analogously, there is no incompatibility between holding both that my arm moves because I try or decide to make it move and that it moves because certain nervous impulses are initiated in my brain and pass messages down afferent nerves, which cause my muscles to expand or contract and so move my arm. If the nervous impulses which produce the movement of my arm also caused me to try to move it, there would be no way of settling experimentally whether the trying could produce the movement without the nervous impulses, or the impulses could produce the movement without the trying. On this view, the movement of my arm would be over-determined. It would be determined both by the neurological happenings and my decision, severally, and each by itself would be sufficient to produce this movement without the other if, *per impossibile*, it were to occur without the other.[8]

If so, the fact that my arm moves because I decided to move it will not be detectable by any interruption to the neural processes investigated by the physiologist exploring the behaviour of my arm, nervous system and brain. Perhaps, similarly, God works miracles which are also undetectable, in that the miracle appears to be (and indeed is) adequately accounted for by antecedent physical events.

In this case it could be both a miracle that someone survives after falling a thousand feet without a parachute and be a normally explicable event. He was held up by a naturally explicable but quite unusual wind eddy, perhaps, or was caught by the seat of his pants by a perfectly ordinary thorn bush, at just the moment that a benevolent God, if there is one, intending to give to man a sign of his presence, would have intervened on his behalf.

(xii)   Difficulties With the View That There are 'Hidden' Miracles

However, there are difficulties with the view just suggested, that there are hidden or disguised 'miracles'.

(a) Many or most or all miracles one reads about are not supposed to be like this. It is usually taken for granted that, if there is a natural explanation for an alleged miracle, it is not a miracle at all. Those who think that an event may both have a natural explanation *and* be a miracle are perhaps trying to have things both ways.

(b) It will follow from this view that both miracles and non-miraculous events will have perfectly normal explanations. But if both miracles and other events have normal explanations, what is the difference between them? God is responsible for everything that happens. Since he is omniscient, he must have known both that, if a miracle occurs, it was going to happen and, since he is omnipotent, he could have prevented it.

We might try to argue that God brought about the miracles, though he simply failed to prevent the other non-miraculous events. And where people are concerned, we certainly draw a distinction between what people bring about and what they fail to prevent. Killing someone and failing to prevent his death are commonly supposed to be different and the latter to be less reprehensible than the latter.

But this distinction cannot be applied to God if it involves either any reference to exertion, or to the alteration of a plan. If the difference between killing someone and failing to prevent his death is that the former involves exertion whereas the latter does not, or the former involves deviating from what one had intended to do, whereas the latter does not, then no distinction can be drawn between what God brings about and what he simply fails to prevent. For example, one might hold (implausibly) that God brings about good, but simply fails to prevent evil. He brings about the death of some, but simply fails to prevent that of others. For it would be very odd to talk of God's either exerting himself or, for that matter, failing to exert himself, and quite impossible for an omniscient being to have conceived a plan which he has to alter on account of circumstances that he had not foreseen. In any case, if miracles are law-governed, it will be quite impossible to tell which events God brought about and which he simply failed to prevent by reference to the fact that the former could not have been predicted, whereas the latter could.

(c) If miracles are supposed to give us some reason, or some extra reason, for believing that there is a God, can they do this if they can be explained by prior events in the world? If the changing of water into wine can be explained in a normal (or even an abnormal) way by means of showing what prior events in the world led up to it and were responsible for it, why do we also need to try to explain the changing of water into wine by saying that God miraculously produced it?

(d) Hidden 'miracles' are contradictory, for a hidden 'miracle' is by definition a 'miracle' that does not involve an interruption to the ordinary course of nature and miracles must, again by definition, involve such an interruption.

This latter objection does not show that what I have described as hidden 'miracles' cannot occur, but only that, if they do occur they cannot properly be described as 'miracles'. The difficulty can be augered by putting quotes round 'miracle'.

(xiii)   A Universe in Which There Were Systematically Produced Hidden 'Miracles'

It seems to me possible that there could be events which need to be explained both by the laws of physics or nature and by reference to God's intentions. (Ordinary miracles would have to be explained only by the latter). Suppose my friend Jones, who has a Chair of Theology, appears to be watched over by a special providence. When he buys shares, on the most inadequate of advice, they always rise and when he is late for an appointment, he is saved from embarrassment by the fact that the person he was to meet is always, quite predictably, just a little later. When he steps off the pavement without looking, the cars that might otherwise have hit him develop punctures and miss. This is to his advantage, but to the amazement of everybody else. One might suppose that he was favoured by the gods, but, whether this is so or not, investigation always shows that there is a perfectly natural explanation for everything favourable that happens to him. There is a perfectly natural explanation, for example, for the puncture that saved his life.

Does the fact that all the good things that happened to our friend were naturally explicable force us to rule out the hypothesis of a providence and plump for coincidence, or is it possible that there might be a special providence which operated by arranging things so that everything worked out well for Jones without the suspension of any natural law? In this case, the universe would have to have been constructed from the beginning so that everything favoured Jones without God's tinkering with the universe at a later date. (The example we are discussing is fanciful, but I suppose there is some resemblance between it and the view that natural selection is God's way of producing man.)

Suppose, to take another example, we see the Ten Commandments written in the sky, or the message 'Prepare to meet thy doom' embodied in the clouds. We investigate the matter, and find that these ostensible messages are conveyed in smoke or cloud formations which can be explained quite naturally, by means of such things as unusual wind current. I see no reason why the fact that these messages can be explained naturally rules out their also being produced by some divine being in order to communicate with us. As we have seen, the fact (if it is one) that the movement of my lips can be explained neuro-physiologically is often supposed, rightly or wrongly, not to rule out their being deliberately produced by me in order to communicate with other people.

The analogy between (a) the fact that certain events can have a 'miraculous' or providential explanation and can also be explained by the laws of physics and (b) the view that the moving of my arm, say, can both (on some views) be explained by neurological occurrences in my head and nervous system and also by the fact that I intended to move it, needs comment.

What is important about miracles, and what distinguishes them from mere marvels, is their purposiveness; the fact, for example, that the water was changed into wine just when it was needed and when wine could not be otherwise obtained. Hence unusual events exhibiting certain purposive features could be regarded as 'miraculous', even if they had a perfectly normal explanation. In that case, their occurrence could not be ruled out for reasons such as Hume's, for they would not go against what we know of nature, and whether they occur or not would be partly a matter for normal empirical investigation and partly a question of whether these 'miracles' show enough of the features of design to admit of their being regarded as purposive.

What might then be described as pseudo-miracles and the universal prevalence of natural law are therefore compatible. But this does not mean that the world really is as it would have to be for 'miracles' of the kind I have been envisaging truly to be said to occur. For a universe like this to be logically possible is one thing. For it actually to exist is another.

Personally, I do not believe that such a universe does exist. Alleged miracles do not occur frequently enough, systematically enough or on a large enough scale to make credible the hypothesis that there are such things, deliberately produced by a God who covers up his traces when he has produced them. They are so far as we know confined to the solar system, which is almost infinitesimal part of the cosmos. Most miracles look like small-scale conjuring tricks when compared with the immensity of the universe. (If they are not confined to the solar system, this suggests the possibility that there have been other incarnations on other planets, a view which may be consistent with Christianity, or at least a heretical version thereof.) Miracles are unacceptably anthropomorphic. The fact that they serve as a sign is dependent upon their being interruption to the normal course of nature; I doubt whether anyone would pay much attention to them otherwise.

Whether or not the universe is like the imaginary universe that I have outlined is matter for empirical investigation rather than for *a priori* argument. It would, I suppose, be a matter for discerning whether there was a pattern in the universe that resembled a pattern in a work of art, with the proviso that the fact that the work of art was informed by the pattern did not rule out there being a causal explanation of the location of each of the paint-blobs that were elements in the pattern. And in any case, the analogy with an artist will not hold, for the now familiar reason that the artist forms his plans before he executes them, which an eternal God cannot do, and has a physical body which visibly interferes with the location of the paint. Even if we conceive of God only as everlasting, the analogy still does not hold. For that the work of art is the result of the design of the artist is testable. There are no ways in which we could test the hypothesis that the kind of universe we are imagining was produced by such a God, even if it there were such a universe.

(xiv)   Christianity and Miracles

Arguments for Christianity *via* an antecedent proof of the occurrence of the resurrection never seem to me to do the work which many Christians require of them. Though Christians use the fact of the resurrection to give plausibility, if not actually to prove, Christianity, in actual fact it is such plausibility that Christianity already has that gives plausibility to the resurrection. If we were not already favourably disposed to thinking that Christ was the son of God, I do not think we should listen to arguments from the resurrection for one moment. The antecedent improbability of the resurrection is so great that it cannot be rendered probable by evidence which would establish any ordinary historical event. And Christians are frequently guilty of a sort of inconsistency in ruling out alternative explanations of the fact – if it is one – on the same grounds (i.e., their extreme improbability) which would, if this were the only thing to be considered, rule out theirs.

The Virgin Birth

The Christian religion seems to need a belief in miracles partly because miracles are in fact recounted in the gospels and one is on a very slippery slope if one tries to accept some of the gospel stories, but not all of them. But it is difficult to see what aspects of the teachings of Christ demand that he should have been born of a virgin. If he had been a great mathematician, none of his teachings would have been made at all more convincing by his mother's having been a virgin at the time of his birth.

If Christ taught that he was the son of God and he could not have been the son of God if he had not been born of a virgin, his teaching must at least partially be rejected if the virgin birth did not occur. It is very difficult to know what the claim to be the son of God amounts to, and consequently difficult to know whether it really does amount to something that entails the occurrence of the virgin birth. If Christ is not supposed to be literally the son of God, there is no need to suppose that he does not have a earthly father for this belief to be true and Christ could not literally have been the son of God. Being the son of is a biological relation in which a non-spatial being such as God cannot stand to anyone. A non-spatial being can no more copulate than he can walk, and Christ could not have had his genes, for God cannot have any genes. Presumably, then, Christ is the son of God in a figurative sense of 'son'. But though God's literally having been Christ's father would exclude any other man's having been his father, God's metaphorically being his father would not exclude a man's being his father. It is therefore not essential to the Christian religion that the virgin birth should have occurred.

The Resurrection

The resurrection might be regarded as the one miracle that Christianity cannot literally do without. If there was not a body which at one time was a dead body (Christ's) and later was not, the resurrection cannot have occurred. But if the resurrection did not occur, there is no reason to believe that we ourselves will be raised and an essential doctrine of Christianity must be discarded. Christ's alleged (implied) promise of resurrection for man[9] might be fulfilled even if his own body had not been raised, but a token, that what Christ had implicitly promised was that we would be raised, would be absent.

Christ would have been defeated by the worldly men who opposed him if his body had not been raised. And though this might have made no difference to his moral and spiritual teaching, though it might be considered to show it to be excessively unworldly, it would have made a difference to his (factual) claim that he was the son of God. No-one could defeat God.

Spiritual welfare is one thing and surviving the death of one's body another. Hence it seems to me that the truth of Christ's spiritual teaching ought to be independent of the occurrence of the resurrection. One could live a 'spiritually appropriate' life in this world and one could, I suppose, ignore spiritual teaching even in a resurrected state.

On the other hand, the resurrection of Christ's body can by itself be no reason for thinking that our bodies will be raised. For the metaphorical kind of resurrection that is the most one could hope for would not be that our bodies would, at some later date in the history of the earth, be raised from their tombs and for a second time be endowed with life, as Christ's was alleged to have been after the (shorter) period of three days. Our resurrection must be less straightforward than this, for reasons already given (in chapter 23). But the occurrence of a less straightforward resurrection could not be substantiated by Christ's allegedly quite straightforward one. Indeed, if Christ's resurrection was straightforward, additional argument would be needed to explain why our resurrection, if it occurs, will not be a straightforward one. For example, the bodily resurrection of Christ would be irrelevant to the question whether our *souls* survived the death of our bodies in a disembodied state. And presumably our bodies are not expected to inhabit the earth for a short time and then be subject to an ascension, as Christ's is alleged to have been.

It remains possible that we are raised in another metaphorical sense. We are raised, perhaps, in that after a conversion experience we become happy and good men, guided by the moral teaching of Jesus, when before we were not, though on this view we go on living in this way only until our normal physical deaths.

But if this is all there is to Christian teaching, it seems to me that the creeds recited in Christian churches ought substantially to be modified or abandoned. (This would not be the only item that ought to be abandoned if certain modern views are right.) What has been taught for 2,000 years is an actual resurrection, not a metaphorical one. In any case, I am sure that adherents of the metaphorical view exaggerate both the extent to which goodness and happiness may be obtained in this world and the extent to which it is necessary to believe in Christ in order to get it. If one looks about one in an unprejudiced way it seems that quite a lot of people are reasonably happy and good without believing in Christ. (There is an odd suggestion of self-verification in the view that goodness and happiness in this world can be obtained only by belief in Christianity, which involves believing that one can obtain goodness and happiness in this world only by believing in Christianity.)

Sometimes it is said that it is the actual resurrection that is symbolic, either of an actual or a metaphorical resurrection. But only what actually occurs can symbolise anything so this view should not be held by anyone who thinks that statements about the resurrection are not literally true.

The Ascension

The ascension, Christ's being taken up into heaven, must have been another miracle. At least, it must have been if his body had been raised and inhabited the world from the date of his resurrection until the ascension and then inhabited it no longer. If the ascension occurred, his body, at this time, whatever else happened to it later, must then be supposed to have disappeared from the face of the earth or, at least, ceased to be the body of Christ in any way analogous to the way in which this is the body of one Harrison. What, if anything, took place at the ascension is a matter for speculation.

It could not have been that Christ transferred from this world to the next in anything like the manner in which one can be transported from Nottingham to Cambridge. For 'Heaven' is not the name for a locality on the earth, or even in the universe, and certainly not a place in this world behind that cloud into which he is alleged to have disappeared. Even if they really witnessed a body disappearing into a cloud, this body must, once in the cloud, have vanished from the earth. Hence what occurred must, if the ascension had any religious significance at all, have been symbolic, representing visually whatever transition did take place, which in principle could not be the kind of transition that could be visible.

There were presumably two sides to the transition, the disappearance of Christ's body in this world and the 'appearance' of something or other, which seems to me to be most unlikely to be Christ's actual body, in the next. The first (the disappearance) is easy to understand, but difficult to believe. The second (the (re)appearance) is both difficult to understand, and difficult to believe. I myself find it difficult to believe that anything at all could have happened in the next world, if there is one, that could be described as Christ's arriving there. This is especially true if the next world is eternal.

The most plausible, though not the most orthodox, view to take of the ascension is to regard it as a collective hallucination. No physical body disappeared even into a cloud, though a number of people had a hallucination of its doing so. What did occur, then, need not have been a miracle, for hallucinations are not miraculous. If, however, this hallucination, as we have seen, was deliberately produced by God to convey a message, it would have had to have a divine cause. But it is an academic possibility that, as we have seen, the ultimate divine cause could have been disguised by its having mediate physical causes; causes, I suppose, of the nature of those that produce hallucinations.

If the ascension was a collective hallucination, there are two possible views about its nature. One view is that the hallucination was pathological, produced by internal mental or physical events and of the kind studied by doctors. In this case it might have been produced by misperception, by frustrated wishes, or by physical happenings to the bloodstream and brain of the kind which may or may not be induced by drugs. Alternatively, it was partly caused by something outside ourselves.[10] This suggests the possibility that Christ's appearances after his death were a series of phantasms of the dead, if he was dead, or of the living, if he was living, if such things occur, which is on the whole unlikely.

Christianity without Christ

I have just mentioned that in an earlier paper I raised the question of what would be left of Christ's teaching if he himself never had existed – and, I should have said, the miracles associated with his existence never occurred. I concluded that nothing need be taken away from those parts of his moral teaching which we could see for ourselves to be true, though we could not accept any moral teaching on the authority of a nonexistent being. (I should have stipulated that this could be true only so long as Christ's moral teaching was not based upon doctrines such as that one is rewarded in the next world, for which there would be less evidence if Christ had never existed.) I should have pointed out that certain factual statements that he is alleged to have made could not be true, if he did not exist. He could not be the son of God, for example, if he did not exist to be the son of God.

Christ's claim that he was 'the way'[11] would have to be rejected, for a nonexistent person cannot be a way, at least not literally so. (Even an existent person cannot literally be a way.)[12] However, a nonexistent person could 'show' one the way, or at lest have correct remarks put into his mouth about what the way was (though he could not actually make these remarks). He could not demonstrate the way by doing the things it appeared he advocated, because nonexistent persons cannot do anything. But it could be that we ought to live as he was described as having lived, even if he never actually existed. Certain spiritual teaching, as well as moral teaching, might remain true. It might be the case, as a matter of wisdom as well as of morality, that we ought not to be excessively worldly, care too much about life, be excessively mean, unloving, unforgiving and self-centred, or ignore one's intimations of the divine, problematic though these are. Perhaps someone who neglects all these precepts will be miserable all his life and lose his soul, in a metaphorical way, and perhaps it really would be better to lose the whole world than to lose that.

(xv)   Does Religion Need Miracles?

There are, then, no miracles. But does religion as, opposed to the Christian variety of religion, need miracles?

Religion satisfies (at least) two needs, a need of many men to contemplate, worship and meditate and a need to think they are watched over and protected by a being superior to ourselves, whose commands they may obey, to whom they may devote ourselves and whose existence gives them a purpose in life. The first need may be satisfied without miracles. (I shall say more about this in my penultimate chapter). The second need might be satisfied by a God who arranges that nature cares for us without his intervention – to the extent that nature cares for us at all – but I suppose it is even more comforting to think that he will intervene when nature does not seem to be doing this. There may even be some solace in thinking of nature as being watched over by a being who wishes us well, even though he does not and cannot intervene in order to care for us. And we might wish to hold – over-optimistically – that the act of communion with God was sufficient to give us all the help and solace we need, without miraculous intervention from him.

(xvi)   Conclusions

Such empirical investigation as has been undertaken suggests either that the miracles that have been alleged to occur had natural causes and were not miracles, or that the alleged miracles did not occur. And one suspects that either miracles do involve an interruption to the course of nature, in which case there can be no good reason for believing in them, or that they do not, in which case there would be little reason to attach any religious significance to them.

One can never have enough evidence to believe in a religiously significant miracle, not only because one ought always to distrust the testimony for a miracle, but also because, if one is going to accept a miracle at all, it is always possible to hold that the desired miracle did not take place, but that laws of nature were 'broken' in some way other than the desired way were they to occur. Miracles would not totally involve interruption to law, because the miraculous interruption to natural laws would take place according to the laws of God's psychology (which we unreflectingly seem to think will resemble and be governed by the same laws as is our own). This would mean that God was within nature to the extent that his actions were caused by some natural happenings – his seeing the need for wine, for example – and caused other natural happenings – say the drinking of wine.

A world in which there were concealed 'miracles' which both display purpose and have natural causes is possible. But we know enough about nature to know that our world does not contain concealed 'miracles' systematically and on a sufficiently large scale for the purposes of religion. And believing in a God who works miracles, as opposed to one that can be contemplated but does not interfere with nature, is involves accepting factual beliefs which ought to be investigated rather than accepted. Religion as such, however, as opposed to orthodox Christianity, does not need miracles.

Notes

1 For example, by Paul Edwards (1967) in his article on miracles.
2 In Hume, Section X, 1975.
3 I am indebted to Matthew Harrison for this useful piece of information.
4 In Swinburne, 1970, p. 47 f.
5 In Hume, 1975, pp. 127–8.
6 The example is R.F. Holland's (see 1989).
7 I have elaborated my views about necessary connection in more detail in 'Hume on liberty, necessity, uniformity, causation and unfulfilled conditionals, in Harrison, 1995. It is often said that Hume weakened his own case against miracles by his view that a law of nature is just a generalisation about what does occur, not about what must occur; but he does have a (rudimentary) account of necessity in Book II, Part I, sections I and II of the *Treatise of Human Nature*. That it is a only a contingent fact that the events connected by law are necessarily connected means that there is no logical contradiction in supposing this necessity to be occasionally suspended by divine necessitation.
8 The enormous amount of over-determination such a view would entail is to my mind a strong reason for rejecting it.
9 St Mark, 9.i.
10 See Gurney, Myers and Podmore, 1918.
11 'I am the way, the truth and the life': St John, xiv, 6.
12 Nicholas Lash (1992) has suggested that the Father, Son and Holy Ghost are three different ways of apprehending one God. This may be so, but the view constitutes an abandonment of the Trinity. For if God is an entity, and one can put ways as well as entities in one list, there should then be four things (not three), one entity apprehended, and three different ways of apprehending it. The Father, Son and Holy Ghost could not possibly be identical, for different ways of apprehending something could not be the same way, or there would only be one way. And none of them can be identical with God, for a way of apprehending an entity cannot be identical with an entity, still less with the entity apprehended.

26 The Efficacy of Prayer[1]

(i) Definition of 'Prayer'[2]

Sometimes people pray for things; sometimes they do not. Sometimes, when they pray for things, what they pray for comes about, at other times it does not. (Sometimes, indeed often, people get the things they might have prayed for, even when they have not prayed for them.) The proposition that if someone prays for something, e.g., health, he will either get it or not get it, is both tautological and trivial. (It is entailed by the trivial and tautological proposition that what he prays for will either come about or not.) Hence that one will either get or not get what one prays for cannot entail that prayer is answered, for the latter proposition is obviously neither trivial nor tautological. It would obviously beg the question to use the fact that all prayers must be answered affirmatively or negatively as a premise to show that there is a God. We would have to show that there was a God before we could show that all prayers were answered either affirmatively or negatively. That all prayers are heard, if there is a God, follows from God's omniscience, and from his omnipercipience, if God is omnipercipient.

It is not, of course, enough to prove that petitionary prayers are answered that sometimes what one prays for happens. At least two further propositions must be true.

(a) It must be that one got what one prayed for because one prayed. What is very nearly (but not quite) the same thing, it must be the case that one would not have got what one prayed for, if one had not prayed for it.

(b) It must also be the case that there is a God, who brought it about that one got what one prayed for.

(c) Furthermore, God must have brought about what one prayed for because one had prayed for it. A causal connection between praying for something that does not work *via* the mediation of God does not count as the answering of prayer. For example, if I my praying to avoid an accident made me miss my bus and the bus had an accident, this could not count as the answering of a prayer unless there was a God who had caused me to pray in order to make me miss my bus.

529

(ii)   Prayer and Miracles

Hence it seems to be the case that answering prayer would always involve a miracle, though perhaps only a minor one. If it rained because I prayed that it should rain, this means that it must have rained for some very unusual reason. Meteorologists do not normally suppose that, in order to predict rain, they need to take into account whether people pray for rain or not. So God must have intervened on one's behalf and brought about rain in spite of the physical conditions which would normally have caused it not to rain. Hence God's answering my prayer must involve his interfering with these conditions and so performing a miracle. (I do not know that minor miracles are any more difficult to bring about than major ones. If it is impossible to move dice without touching them this is just as impossible as to move large mountains or whole galaxies. There are no degrees of impossibility.)

These facts cause difficulties for God's timelessness and his aseity (i.e., his independence of the world). They cause difficulties for his timelessness, because it looks as if he would have had to bring it about that it rained, as we have seen, after I prayed for it, and with his aseity because it looks as if God's 'behaviour' would have to be modified by my praying and so be caused by and dependent upon it. Perhaps it is an adequate answer to the latter difficulty that God's prayer affects God's behaviour only with his consent.

When we consider the relation between prayer and miracles, however, it seems to me to be just possible that the situation might be as follows. God, since he is omniscient, always knows when, in the future, I am going to pray for rain. Hence he can arrange things so that, when I pray for rain, rain is produced in a perfectly normal way. It might even be the case that God has produced a universe in which, sometimes, when I pray from perfectly natural causes, it also rains, from perfectly natural causes. Despite this, it would nevertheless be true that there was a connection between my praying and its raining, such that, had I not prayed, it would not have rained. This is because God would then have a plan which demands that he would not produce the rain (from natural causes) had he not decided to cause me to pray for rain, also from natural causes, even though the prayer was not among the natural causes of the rain.

On this view, there would be a connection between my praying from natural causes and its raining from natural causes. This connection would be rather like the connection between the time told by Tom's watch and the time told by my watch, when I have synchronised mine with his. My watch points to 6.10 pm because his does, although there is no manifest mechanical connection between my watch and his. (I say 'no manifest mechanical connection' because if materialists are right, this connection can be partly reduced to a mechanical, and partly to an electronic, one, because my intentions (to make my watch synchronise with Tom's) and the connection between my intentions and the position of the hands of my watch are both mechanical and electronic.)

Though my control over the hands of my watch is detectable, however, God's control over my praying and its raining will not be. For we are supposing that its raining has a complete set of causes which does not include my praying. I think it follows that the occurrence of the rain is over-determined. It has more causes (if my praying is a cause) than its natural physical causes. On this view, the miracles that occur if petitionary prayer is answered are covered up and hidden. I discussed this matter in my last chapter.

We saw there that there could be (although there was not) a universe in which miracles occurred from perfectly natural causes. God did work miracles, but hid his traces by making it both seem and indeed be that they occurred from natural causes. They occurred in a law-like way. Since answering prayer involves a (usually minor) miracle it would also be possible for God to produce a universe in which prayers were sometimes answered from natural causes. No answering of a prayer would have happened had not God arranged things so that it would be answered, although he arranged things so that prayers would be answered in a perfectly natural way.

Though the universe I have described is a logically possible one, it seems to me to be obvious that it is not the universe that exists in actual fact. For I would be very surprised if there was any statistical connection between praying for rain and rain. If there was I would put it down to the fact that people very seldom get desperate enough to pray for rain until rain is due anyway. I suspect, however, that if a philosopher were to hold that God answered prayers, but that he makes it seem as if what one prayed for came about from natural causes, this would be because one wished to maintain that God answered petitionary prayer, although all the evidence is that he does not.

Prayer obviously has an effect (which does not need to be explained by God's intervention) on the mind and body of the person praying. (It may be that the effect that it has on my body is usually *via* the effect that it has on my mind. Sore knees would not be an important effect.) It seems very unlikely that it would have any direct effect on inanimate objects other than my own body. If it had any effect on other people, which cannot be accounted for in a perfectly normal way, (e.g., by my telling other people what it is that I have prayed for) this could be due to telekinesis, if telekinesis exists. (Telekinesis is the alleged power of people to affect changes on material objects outside the confines of their body without first moving their body.) But in this case it would still not have to be put down to divine agency. For 'telekinesis' would then just be a name for something that was as much a natural phenomenon as anything else.

Petitionary prayer presupposes belief in 'laws' of psychology; for example, the belief that you are more likely to be given something if you ask for it than if you do not and that there are some things one is more likely to get by asking than others. Hence it treats God as the kind of being who is subject to law, and to the same kind of law as is his creatures.

It does not seem inappropriate to ask God for one's daily bread, even though it is a case of petitionary prayer. But it may be that asking this is appropriate only if it is done as a mark of respect and without the expectation that it will make any difference to whether or not we get it.

(iii)   Must the Person who Prays Believe That His Prayer is a Means to His Getting What He Prays For?

It has been held[3] that the person who prays does not necessarily expect this prayer to increase his chances of getting what he prays for and that it is quite proper, indeed, more proper, to pray without than with this expectation. I suspect that holding this rather implausible view is a result of confusing it with the view that an act of prayer is not valuable because of its effects (or only because of its effects). I doubt whether it is any more possible to pray for what one believes to be unattainable than aim to achieve what one believes cannot come about; for example, to run a three minute mile. Petitionary prayer must involve, at the very least, a temporary, and perhaps involuntary, suspension of disbelief in the inefficacy of petitionary prayer.

It may be that people who believe that one ought to indulge in petitionary prayer without thinking that one's chances of getting what one prays for are increased by doing so, think that the alternative is 'automatic' prayer of the kind that can be done by a prayer wheel or by burning a candle, the value of which would have to depend on its effects, if any. Belief that such things as prayer wheels can have anything other than (possibly good) natural effects would certainly be superstitious. It follows that if prayer is to have any value, it must be because of the relationship with what one takes to be God that is involved in it, and the results of this relationship on oneself (and so indirectly on others). But that a relationship with God should take the form of prayer, rather than some other form, does presuppose that there must be a belief on the part of the person praying that it is not impossible that the God with whom he has the relationship should answer his prayer.

Even if petitionary prayer were possible without the belief that there was some chance of its being answered, I do not think that it would be more valuable without than with this belief. If one believed that there was a God who was even metaphorically one's father, praying (in moderation) for what one wanted would at the very least seem to be an entirely natural (though unheroic) way of behaving. If one does not believe that God has the power to answer petitionary prayer, it might be thought valuable not to omit the polite formality of seeming to ask him even for what one believes he cannot give; but God might regard our doing this as a subtle insult.

The remarks I have made apply only to petitionary prayer. There are forms of what might be called 'prayer' other than this. Forms of 'prayer' that have been described as 'higher prayers' – which I shall not discuss here – are supposed to include praise, adoration and thanksgiving. Just as petitionary prayer presupposes the belief that praying may have some effect, so praise, adoration and thanksgiving also normally, though perhaps not necessarily always, presuppose beliefs about the deity. The deity must be believed to be worthy of praise and adoration and to have given us benefits in the past that make thanksgiving appropriate. This, together with the preceding remarks about petitionary prayer, constitutes another reason for rejecting non-belief theories of the kind already discussed (in chapter 11).

(I elsewhere (in chapter 28) claim that it is possible to love God without believing that there is one. The same may be true of some kinds of worship. I suspect that the worship involved is a form of worshipful contemplation (as opposed to bare contemplation) and that it true that worship does not involve belief only when it is nonverbal or non-conceptual.) These kinds of worship would themselves have to be silent and solitary. The remarks I have made about some 'higher prayer' in the form of worship not presupposing belief apply only to private prayer. When prayer is public, it tends to be put in forms of words that have been laid down and so to involve the beliefs these words express. Public worship involves words and so involves the expression of belief.

(iv)   The Morality of Petitionary Prayer

The morality of petitionary prayer has been questioned. Praying seems to suggest that God does not know what one wants without being told, which is impossible in an omniscient being. Whether or not prayer is a manifestation of selfishness or greed depends on what it is one prays for. To pray for something to happen because one thinks it is a good thing that it should happen, is rather like suggesting that God does not know what is best without one's help and advice, or may not do it, if he does know what is best, unless one prays. Praying that God should avoid evil is to suggest that God will not avoid evil unless one intercedes, an attitude of mind which might be considered impertinent. Praying to a God who answers petitionary prayer that one should oneself be delivered from evil is to treat God like a gangster running a protection racket in that, being omniscient and omnipotent, he must himself be partly or wholly responsible – in that he has the power to prevent it – for the harm which you think will come to you if you do not pray. Unlike a gangster, however, God presumably brings about the harm from benevolent motives, though it is often not easy to say what these are. To pray for things that are in short supply would be to invite God to favour oneself at the expense of others.

Eleanor Stump on One Aspect of Petitionary Prayer

In an answer to a variant on one of the problems for the morality of petitionary prayer mentioned above, Stump considers the difficulty – her exposition of which I have abbreviated – that since God will always bring about what is best, he will do what is best whether we pray for it or not; hence prayer can never make any difference to what God does.

Stump's answer – which I have also abbreviated – is that God does not always do what is best when men do not pray that he should, but that the good which consists in man's indulging in petitionary prayer outweighs the loss resulting from this fact and that the loss is a necessary condition of the gain. Hence God really is acting for the best after all.

I have the following difficulties with Stump's answer.

(a) It may be that in principle the world *could* be organised so that the good of prayer outweighed the evil of God's not always doing what is best. The question arises, however, whether that is how the world *is* organised. Leaving aside the difficulty that earthquakes occur whether people pray or not, there is the difficulty that even if prayer did prevent earthquakes, people do not always pray that the earthquakes which do occur should not occur. Hence you have the evil of earthquakes, without the good of prayer.

I think Stump's reply would be that, from the nature of the case, God cannot determine on which occasions men will pray and on which they will not. Hence God has no choice but sometimes to do things like produce earthquakes if men do not pray, as he cannot guarantee that men will pray. Hence producing earthquakes, bad though they are, even when men do not pray, is a necessary condition of prayer. It cannot, however, be a sufficient condition of prayer. God cannot make men pray when it is necessary that they should, because this would be to interfere with their free will.

But we saw in (chapter 14) that God can bring it about that men freely do certain things, for example, that they should freely pray. And to my mind, when one considers the amount and distribution of evil in the world, there is not the slightest support for the proposition that God brings about or allows a worse state of affairs than a good one only when he knows that this harm could be outweighed by the good involved in praying for the better state. All sorts of evil states arise which are so bad that they could not be overweighed in value by petitionary prayer, even if it were effective, and the value of petitionary prayer is in any case problematic. Furthermore, Stump's justification would apply only to ills of a kind which could be avoided by prayer, and earthquakes cannot be so avoided.

My point concerning the possibility of God's making a man who freely prays may best be brought out by considering an example of Stump's, of a man who is so disabled that he cannot even make requests. God, or so one would have supposed, could certainly make him a man who could pray, instead of having made him one who could not. But more than this, God could not only make him a man who was able to pray; he could also give him the motives and beliefs that make men actually pray. In that case, he would pray. Even doctors, who have not the advantage of being omnipotent, can, by suitably treating their patients – giving them drugs, for example – cause them to be the sort of people who freely do things that they would not have done had they not been treated. Medicine, of course, is not yet so far advanced as to determine which actions they will freely decide to do.

There is also the difficulty that a wise God might have organised things for the best, whether people pray or not, and would, since people do in fact pray, have the good of God's doing the best plus the good of prayer. And I think Stump exaggerates the value of petitionary prayer. If the only effects that petitionary prayer can have are natural effects on the person praying – though the value of these effects are not to be despised – then the amount of self-delusion involved in much if not all petitionary prayer must detract substantially from its value. If the universe were created by a benevolent and loving God, who himself brought about the good things in our lives, I think certain responses such as gratitude would be appropriate, and prayer too may be an appropriate response. But whether these would be valuable or appropriate responses to the actual being who governs the universe, if there is one, which being must in some respect be quite wicked, I am much more doubtful. (In my chapter on the problem of evil I suggest that we might need the 'help' of an imaginary good God to help us combat the God who actually exists, if there were one. The 'help', of course, since the God is imaginary, would have to come from our relationship with him, not from his actual intervention.)

(b) I think Stump's answer to the question why petitionary prayer is valuable is unsatisfactory. Petitionary prayer, according to Stump, is valuable because, though it might seem as if, if something were good for a man, God ought to give it him whether he asks for it or not, it is better for God's relationship with men that men should ask, as this preserves men's independence and prevents his being overwhelmed by having benefits he has not asked for thrust upon him by a being immensely wiser and more powerful than he. In any case, some of the things a man needs – for example, prayer itself – in principle cannot be thrust upon him, but require his consent.

This answer is unsatisfactory because, though for the purposes of having a 'dialogue' with what purports to be one's God, limiting his omnipotence in our imaginations is essential, if there really is a God his omnipotence is not limited. We cannot in prayer have a dialogue with God, but only with a little godlet that might simply be another part or aspect of ourselves. In making this answer Stump speaks of God as if he were the boy next door, and does not fully appreciate the immensity of the power involved in his omnipotence. For example, Stump thinks God cannot make men pray, or make men act so that his will is done; but he can. (Incidentally, it was not obvious to me that a man who had showered upon him benefits for which he had not asked would be more spoilt than one who had had to ask for the same benefits. And a boy who got what he wanted simply by asking for it *would* be spoilt, to some extent.)

(c) Stump quite correctly draws a distinction between the first three prayers in the Lord's Prayer – that God's name be hallowed, that his kingdom should come, and that his will be done – and the last four (that God's kingdom should come, that his will should be done, that we should be given our daily bread, and that we should be forgiven our trespasses). She thinks the difference is that between prayers (like those in the first group) that are prayers that other people perform voluntary acts and those which are not.

I think it is true that there is a difference between the two groups of prayers, but it consists in the fact that the first three so-called prayers are, strictly speaking, not prayers at all. (They are not necessarily any the worse for that.)

They resemble remarks like 'O king, live for ever' which does not mean 'O King, I pray that, of the two alternatives open to thee, thou takest the alternative of living for ever'. The expression 'So be it' is similar in that, though it is in the imperative mode, it is not a request to God that things should be as they are or are gong to be, but rather an expression of resignation or acceptance to things being as they are.

(d) Stump touches upon certain problems for petitionary prayer, which problems concern (1) fatalism and (2) God's eternity. I have no space to consider what Stump herself says about these problem, but I should like to take the opportunity of making the following remarks.

(1) If it is true before the event, say, its raining, that God will bring about the event prayed for, it will no more follow from this that God will bring this event about, whether it is prayed for or not, than it follows that, because it is true before the event, that Oedipus is going to kill his father, that he will kill his father whether he decides to leave Corinth or not. (The reader is referred to chapter 17.)

(2) There is the difficulty for God's eternity, mentioned in chapter 18, that though God is supposed to be eternal, his answering a prayer should normally take place *after* the prayer. There is the further difficulty that an eternal being cannot perform temporal actions, like answering prayer. I have already argued that these difficulties are not difficulties for a God who is merely everlasting. And God's answering prayer would not involve God's changing; it would not involve a change to his *characteristics* (again, see chapter 14).) He would remain, both before and after a prayer, the kind of being who was disposed to answer prayers of a certain sort in certain circumstances.)

(e) Stump's paper contains the interesting suggestion that the more people pray, the more effective the prayer. There is even the fascinating idea that the effects of prayer are cumulative, in the sense that though one person's prayer may have no effect, many people's praying may have an effect (much as one person's saving electricity does nothing to stop power cuts, but a large number of people's saving the same amount of electricity may). It follows, that the effects of 1,000 people's praying can be more than 1,000 times the effects of one person's praying, which latter may in principle be nil.) Of course, if one believes that petitionary prayer has effects only on the individual people praying, one must believe the same of collective prayer. But the effects of prayer on the people praying may well be cumulative, though only if each knows that the others are praying (presumably praying for the same thing). (But in her discussion of this point Stump confuses holding that Jimmy Carter's praying may be a logically necessary condition of the kingdom on earth (as it must be if that kingdom is a state in which, among other things, *everybody* prays) with holding that it is a causally necessary condition of such a state, which seems unlikely.)

(v)   The Disguised Answering of Prayer

In the chapter on miracles I discussed the view that there were hidden 'miracles', that is, 'miracles' where the 'miraculous' or apparently miraculous event had natural causes. In this section I shall discuss a similar view about petitionary prayer, that is, the view that prayers are answered, but that there is always a natural explanation of the occurrence of the event prayed for. For example, if rain is prayed for, there may be what I have called a disguised answer to prayer if rain occurs, but has a natural explanation.

Of course, more is necessary for there to be a hidden answer to prayer than that rain should both be prayed for and occur; even an atheist can hold that this happens. What must be necessary, over and above this, is (a) that God should have brought about the rain, (b) that God should have brought about the natural causes of the rain, (c) that the prayer was a prayer for *rain* and (d) that the rain would not have occurred had not the prayer (which is not among the natural causes of the rain) also occurred (and presumably occurred before the rain).

The question is, is (d) compatible with (a) and (b), more particularly with (b), for if the natural causes of rain have occurred, then, surely, there must be rain, whether people pray for rain or not.

However, from the fact that moisture-laden air's rising is sufficient to cause rain it does not *follow* that praying for rain is not also sufficient to cause rain, though it is difficult to believe that the latter is *true*. (That being shot in the head is sufficient to cause death does not show that being shot in the heart is not also sufficient to cause death – or that it is not possible to be shot in the head and in the heart simultaneously.) But for praying for rain to cause rain, it is presumably also necessary that if there had been no prayer for rain there would have been no rain. It looks as if it follows from the fact that damp air's rising is sufficient to cause rain that prayer for rain cannot be necessary for rain; but this does not follows. What does follow is that, if the air's rising is sufficient for rain (p->r) and the prayer is necessary for rain, (-q->-r) then if there were not the prayer, there would also not have been the air's rising (((p->r).(-q->-r))->(p->-q))). If the prayer happened before the air's rising, it would (in these unnatural circumstances) be natural to say that the prayer caused the wind eddies; if the air's rising happened first, it would be natural to say that the air's rising caused the prayer.

If one accepts what I shall call 'Hume's principle', that anything may in principle cause anything else, and it is just a matter of contingent fact, to be discovered by experience and observation, what causes what, bizarre worlds in which air's rising causes prayer and a world in which prayer causes air's rising (or a third world in which it is sometimes the one and sometimes the other) are all perfectly possible. But it seems obvious that such a world is not the world that occurs in fact. And in any case, for our world to be such a world, there would have to be a correlation between such things as prayer and such things as rain, which we all know, wishful thinking and ceremonial occasions apart, does not obtain.

(vi)   The Effects of Prayer on the Person who Prays

If prayer neither has any direct effect on inanimate objects outside my own body nor on other people, it follows that it is irrational to pray for anything other than things for oneself. E.g., it could be rational to pray for one's own health, because it is possible that a causal effect of praying for one's own health is sometimes to make one more healthy, but it would not be rational to pray for the health of others, because there can be no causal connection between what you pray for and what they get. Your praying cannot have any direct effects on them, though it may have indirect effects on them in that it has an effect on you and causes you to do something, e.g., give them medicine, which has an effect on them in the normal way.

It does not follow from this that all prayers must be selfish, because one's motive in praying for a change in one's own body or mind might be a desire to change, albeit indirectly, the state of someone else for the better; one might pray for health, for example, in order to be able to look after one's children.

It does not follow from the fact that prayer has an effect, though in most people this is limited one, on one's own body and mind that prayers are answered. It could have these effects whether there was a God or not. For example, praying for health might, by increasing one's faith that one would recover, make one more healthy, whether there was a God who answered prayer or not.

The belief that a prayer for something could be the result of praying would tend to be self-verifying. For example, if one believed that praying for an improved performance would improve one's performance, the belief (as opposed to the prayer without the belief) that one's performance would be improved by praying would itself tend to improve one's performance. The more sure one was that prayers of this kind would be answered, the more likely it would be that one would get what one prayed for. (I say 'get what one prayed for' rather that 'that one's payer would be answered' because getting what one prayed for, if it was the natural result of praying plus the belief that one's prayer would be answered, would not count as having one's prayer answered. This, as we have seen, would require divine intervention on one's behalf.)

(If it could be established that those who prayed for the strength to work for long hours were more successful in working for longer hours than those who did not, it might be that all this showed would be that those with a greater need to work were more likely to pray. In other words, it would not establish that prayer helped one to work for longer hours so much as that prayer and working longer hours were joint effects of the same cause.)

The beneficial effects of prayer on oneself do not necessarily or even often consist in one's getting what one prays for. One may, for example, pray not to have cancer, which has the effect, say, of relaxing one, which may have beneficial effect on one's health, but not usually the effect of causing one not to have cancer, which one might not have been going to have anyway. Just conceivably, perhaps, since tension is a factor in the causation of many diseases, prayer may have the effect of curing cancer. But this would be a natural effect of prayer and could not count as prayer's being answered.

Petitionary prayer may have an effect upon the person praying for the following reasons. It may increase his expectations of getting what he is praying for, which may or may not make it more likely that he will actually get what he prays for. If he is praying for help in achieving something marginally within his power, it may help him by increasing his confidence in success or his willingness to exert himself. But praying will hinder him if it makes him rely on some other being to do what he ought to be doing himself.

If what he is praying for is not within his power, praying may help him by letting him leave on the lap of the gods something over which he himself has no control anyway, which will save him time and misplaced anxiety. He will at least have nothing to lose (except the time he spends in prayer, which he may consider well spent even if he does not get what he prays for). But if he thinks that he is increasing his chances of what he wants coming about, in a case when his praying can have no such effect, and acts on this expectation, his action will be irrational. He may well bet too heavily on what he has prayed for coming about by taking unwarranted risks, or fail to take necessary or at least desirable precautions. Praying for rain, for example, can be a bad thing if it prevents one from taking steps to irrigate one's crops. It may be too pessimistic a view to say that one should only pray for something when one has exhausted all other possibilities of obtaining it and that one should not pray, instead of adopting other means of getting what one prays for, unless there are no other such means.

Prayer, too, can be a form of communication with what is or what one takes to be another being with whom one can have a relationship, which must very frequently be both pleasant in itself and have a therapeutic effect on one. How beneficial this effect will be will depend upon what one takes to be the nature of the being with whom one thinks one is communicating. By this I do not mean that it will depend on the nature of the being, if any, who exists in fact, but that it will depend upon the nature of one's 'image' of this being.

Whether the effects of petitionary prayer are beneficial or not will depend, obviously, partly on what is prayed for. Praying that one's enemies may be confounded may encourage in oneself an excessively combative disposition, and do harm to other people (one's enemies) if the prayer is answered. The habit of frequent prayer, whether each individual act of praying is beneficial or not, may lead to superstition, lack of realism, excessive dependence, fatalism, and laziness. It might also reduce anxiety, but at too high a price. The biological function of anxiety is to make us avoid unnecessary risks. Individual acts of praying may be harmful because what one is praying for is wrong, because one is communicating with a being of whom one has an 'image' which is evil, or for any of the other reasons mentioned in the preceding paragraph. Petitionary prayers may cancel one another out, as when England prays for victory over France and France for victory over England.

I should like to draw a distinction between petitionary prayer, which I think is of doubtful rationality, and invoking the deity, from which one can expect no more help than can be obtained from the act of invocation itself. Such help need not be negligible and may well be confined to the natural consequence of the act itself. It is not necessarily irrational, may be admirable, and ought often to be encouraged. Its beneficial effects, however, will operate whether there is actually a deity or not.

If the effect of prayer on oneself is beneficial, as it sometimes is, does this mean that it is irrational not to pray? Perhaps it will not be irrational not to pray if prayer involves acquiring beliefs which are false, in which case it will at least be 'objectively irrational'. (It will be 'subjectively irrational' if it involves only acquiring beliefs which seem to one to be false (whether they are so or not).) There are certainly many people who suppose that the belief that there is a God who answers prayer is irrational. Does this mean that they cannot pray without first acquiring a belief that must seem to them to be false? I am not sure whether it does or not.

Petitionary prayer, though it can have no direct effect on anything other than ourselves, will help us to achieve a closer putative relationship with God. Whether there is a God outside of our relationship with him is another matter.

(vii)   The Rationality of Prayer

Whether it is rational to acquire false beliefs (or beliefs that seem to one to be false) because of the beneficial effects of having these beliefs depends upon which is the lesser of two evils. The effects of a belief are of two kinds. There are the effects of having a belief and the effects of acting on it. An example of former would be one's belief that what one is seeing is a ghost causing one's hair to stand on end. An example of the latter would be one's informing the Society for Psychical Research that one had seen a ghost.

The effects of *having* a belief will be the same whether it is true or false. One's hair will stand on end, whether one's belief that one is seeing a ghost is true or not. But the effects of acting on it are likely to be different if it is true from what they will be if it is false. One is more likely to get the things that one was aiming at when one acted on the belief in question if it is true than if it is false. For example, one is more likely to catch one's train if one has a true belief about the time of its departure than if the belief is false. It may be reassuring – an effect of having the belief – to have the belief that one has plenty of time, but if this causes one to act in such a way as to miss it, the reassurance is bought at too high a price. The moral disapproval we feel for people whose beliefs are comfortable, but which lose them the ability to take effective action, is probably due to the fact that such practices are directly harmful to them and indirectly harmful to others. We do not always disapprove of allowing others the comfort of having false belief, however, especially if we know there is no appropriate action they could take if they knew the unpleasant truth.

Whether it is rational to pray if there is no God will depend upon whether the effects of the irrational action one takes on the false belief that there is a God who answers prayer outweigh the good effects on oneself, if any – e.g., in relieving anxiety – of having the belief that they prayer is efficacious.

One may get oneself into difficult situations by praying if one acts on the false beliefs that one's prayers will be answered and then, too late, finds one is in a predicament from which one cannot escape. If there is no God who answers petitionary prayer, it is possible that the most beneficial frame of mind is to have both an irrational belief that there is a God who does answer petitionary prayer and a rational belief that one must rely on one's own actions to get what one wants. These two beliefs are inconsistent, but it is an inconsistency which allows people to make the best of both worlds. This is doubtless why it is so common, but it is difficult to admire it.

Petitionary prayer would be impossible without false belief because what appears to be a petitionary prayer made by someone who does not believe that it can be answered, perhaps because he does not believe that there is a God to answer it, would not count as being petitionary prayer. This must always involve some degree of belief, or at least temporary suspension of disbelief, that there is a being with the power to answer it. One cannot attempt things that one believes to be impossible or virtually impossible (e.g., holing in one).

Perhaps the answer to the problem of succeeding in praying without acquiring false belief is contemplative prayer. Maybe contemplative prayer can produce all or some of the beneficial effects of petitionary prayer without our having to believe that petitionary prayer will be answered.

(viii) The Importance of Petitionary Prayer

Is it necessary to religion that petitionary prayer should be answered? My own feeling, which I shall find difficult to justify, is that it is not important. This does not mean that it would not be a very important fact if petitionary prayer were answered, and a fact we would all have to take account of. But that something is an important fact does not mean that it is necessary to religion.

I have the following reasons for thinking that the answering of petitionary prayer is not important to religion.

(a) *Contemplative* prayer would be possible, even if petitionary prayer was not answered.

(b) It is possible to love God whether petitionary prayer is answered or not. Loving a God who did not answer petitionary prayer would have to be more disinterested than loving one who did, because he did.

(c) Even though petitionary prayers were not answered, they would still sometimes have beneficial effects and might be indulged in for this reason. Sometimes these beneficial effects would consist in one's getting what one prayed for, as when one prays for peace of mind and gets peace of mind as a result of one's prayer. These beneficial effects, even the effect of one's getting what one prayed for, would not count as the answering of petitionary prayer because they would be the natural effects of prayer, effects which it could and would have whether there were a God or not.

(d) There is no reason that I know of why one should not continue to indulge in certain kinds of petitionary prayer even if one thinks that petitionary prayer is not answered. It might be rational, however, to confine oneself to praying for those things which are capable of being the natural results of prayer. In that case, what one is doing might count as invoking the deity rather than as petitionary prayer. Otherwise it may involve a temporary suspension of disbelief.

(e) If prayer can be answered only by one's getting those things which are its natural consequences, the manner and intensity and discipline and regularity with which one prays become all-important. It is not a question of making a request which God, if he is so disposed, will comply with. It is a matter of one's training oneself to do something which will have effects on oneself if done properly – though I suspect that this remark applies better to contemplative prayer than to petitionary prayer. Prayer can increase one's power directly over oneself and so indirectly over others. It is worth repeating that whether the effects of such praying are good or ill depends at least partly on what one is praying for. Doubtless many have been supported by prayer in causes that were totally wrong-headed. Praying to the Devil may increase one's power for ill, even if the Devil does not answer petitionary prayer.

Since the beneficial effects of petitionary prayer are all natural effects and do not depend upon its being answered, these effects will occur whether there is a God to answer petitionary prayer or not. In this event, petitionary prayer becomes optional. There is no reason why those who do not believe that there is a God, and feel no inclination to pray and do not think they will benefit from it, should be under an obligation do so; not everybody seems to need it. And a nonexistent God could not be hurt by one's not praying. And even if there were a God, he could still not be hurt by one's not indulging in petitionary prayer, because he could not be hurt by anything. Hence, if there is a duty to pray at all, it is a part of one's duty to oneself and not (save indirectly, by helping one to help them) part of one's duty to others, nor part of one's duty to God.

(ix)   Contemplative Prayer

Contemplating the deity is sometimes described as prayer, though the word 'prayer' is a misnomer; prayer properly involves making a request or supplication.

It looks as if, in order that one may contemplate something, it must exist. One cannot contemplate one's navel unless one has a navel to contemplate, though perhaps supposing that one has a navel, or that what one is contemplating is one's navel, will do. Hence if one contemplates God, God must exist, whereas one may be thinking about God, or meditating upon the subject of God, whether one thinks that God exists or not. This fact, however, makes possible no argument to the existence of God. For the people who think they are contemplating God cannot really be contemplating him if he does not exist (though maybe they can contemplate a God who, as I shall suggest later, neither exists nor does not exist). One could not deduce the existence of God from the fact that (or so they claim) he can be contemplated; one would have to show that God existed before one could establish that he *really was* being contemplated. I see no reason why the idea of God should not be contemplated, but the idea of God exists.

Contemplative prayer must be law-governed to be of any use. We have to learn empirically how to get in touch with whatever we do get in touch with, and learn by experience what are the (allegedly beneficial) effects of doing so. For us to be able to do this there must be laws governing the effects of whatever steps we may take to achieve contemplation and about the effects of contemplating, just as, to bake a cake, there must be laws about what results from putting heat to something in an oven and laws about the effect upon people of eating it. But the laws we use are laws about us, not – as in the case of petitionary prayer – laws about God. It follows that contemplative prayer may have its beneficial effects whether there is a God or not.

(x)   Meditative Prayer

In what I shall call meditative 'prayer', a subject on which I am also not well qualified to speak, one selects a topic on which to meditate, but the topic does not have to exist. There is no reason why one should not choose as one's theme of meditation God, or the Christian idea of God. I am sure such meditation may have an effect one one's life, which may be a beneficial one believing in the existence of its object or not.

One may meditate discursively, by contemplating certain propositions, which do not have to be true propositions, or 'meditate' by 'focusing' on certain entities, which may be imaginary ones. (In yoga meditation both kinds of meditation are recommended. I put 'meditation' in quotes because I am not sure that it is a correct use of the English word 'meditate' to describe focusing on an object as meditation.) Though we cannot focus on God, because we are not acquainted with him, we could focus on our idea of God, or such alleged manifestations of his presence as we are directly acquainted with, for example, the object, whatever that might be, of an apparent sense of presence. (We saw in chapter 13 that this object could not be God himself.) The fact that such phenomena are not, or not necessarily, manifestations of an independently existing deity is not necessarily a reason for not paying great attention to them.

(xi) Conclusions

Petitionary prayer may have a direct beneficial effect on the person praying, which effect may be, in a minority of cases, the effect prayed for. Petitionary prayer can never directly result in one's getting what one prays for – except indirectly – if this effect lies outside the confines of one's body or – more likely – one's mind. (It may have an indirect effect on other people, if prayer changes the person praying and the person praying changes others.) These facts, however, do not mean that prayer results in divine intervention on one's behalf. When such beneficial effects occur, it may be rational, even for a person who does not believe that there is a God who answers prayers, to pray. It would be difficult, however, to indulge in such prayer without self-deception and self-deception is almost always dangerous. If praying can directly affect only oneself, it would be irrational to pray for others, but one might pray for the strength to enable one to help others. If there is no God, petitionary prayer cannot be answered but, on the other hand, if there is one it is doubtful whether it is complimentary to him to pray. Contemplative 'prayer' and meditation need not involve self-deception and may be both pleasant and useful, though they can be pleasing to God only if there is a God. Since God is responsible for everything we think and feel and do, God himself must decide whether or not we pray.

Notes

1 She slumped into the beat position, and made herself look like a maltreated idiot child. 'What's the use of praying?' 'It keeps the circuits open. Just in case there's ever anybody on the other end of the line', Ross MacDonald, *The Wycherly Woman*.

2 Purists may think that I should say 'definition of 'prayer''. But one can define boundaries, as well as 'boundaries'.

3 For example by D.Z. Phillips, 1971.

PART IV
FAITH AND MORALITY

27 Belief

(i)   Belief

The main ingredient in believing a proposition is having the disposition or tendency to act in a way that would get one what one wanted, if the proposition in question were true. For example, my believing that I have an appointment at 10 o'clock would be manifested in my going to the place of the appointment a little before 10 if I wanted to keep the appointment. It is not a sign that I do not believe that the appointment was at 10 if I do not go to the appointed place at 10, if the reason for my not going is that I do not want to keep the appointment, or want to do something else more. It is also not necessary that the belief on which I act should be true. In addition, my belief that the appointment is at 10 will show itself in my feeling confident that it is at 10, in my using the proposition that it is at 10 as a premise in my internal reasoning, and in such things as my being surprised if I go to the appointed place at 10 and find no-one there.

Inanimate objects can fulfil the first condition of having beliefs. For example, if an anti-missile missile is aiming at the place where its target will be by the time it catches up with it, it can be described as 'believing' that its target will be at that place at that time. If its target will not actually be at that place, the anti-missile missile's belief can be described as being false. Computers, too, can use beliefs as premises. I doubt, however, whether computers or anti-missile missiles have – at least as yet – feelings of confidence, or can feel surprised when their beliefs turn out to be false.

The most important element in a belief is the disposition to act, externally and internally, on the proposition believed. So long as an organism does this, it will – given that its beliefs are true – be doing all that it can, so far as beliefs are concerned, to survive. A feeling of confidence, therefore, is a luxury – though so long as one's beliefs are true, it is better to be confident of them than otherwise. Being disposed to bet heavily on the truth of a proposition is not the same thing as being confident that it is true, though it would be more like it if the qualification 'for a small gain' were added. Normally, however, the reason why one bets heavily is that one feels confident, so confidence and a disposition to bet go together. One would not have survived had they not.

In certain circumstances one can have the feeling of confidence without the disposition to act on what one feels confident of. For example, when one reads fiction one may feel internally much as one would if one thought that the characters one was reading about were real. One does not, however, have the disposition to act on the propositions one reads about. For example, one does not expect actually to come across in the street characters one believes to be fictitious. Our attitude to fiction has been described as the temporary suspension of disbelief, but that this is not true is shown by the fact that we do not intervene to stop a murder enacted on the stage, which we would do if we really had suspended our belief that someone was not being murdered. Our attitude to the fictitious is therefore one of partial or degenerate belief, rather than of temporarily suspended belief.

It is as certain as anything can be that we do have beliefs and to deny that we have them is pragmatically contradictory in that in doing so we express our belief that there are no beliefs, which shows that there are beliefs.

(ii)   Faith and Ordinary Belief; Is Ordinary Belief Morally Neutral?

I should make it clear that, when in this chapter I talk of believing something, I think of it as regarding a proposition as more likely to be true that its negation (i.e., as more probable that it is true than that any of its alternatives are true, taken collectively). Richard Swinburne[1] thinks that there is also something which he calls 'relative belief', which is regarding a proposition as more likely to be true than any given alternative, taken individually.

In his discussion of this matter Swinburne seems to me to be confusing three things. (a) Believing that Protestantism is more likely to be true than Catholicism. This is not a kind of belief, because one may think that both are very unlikely to be true. (b) Thinking that if Christianity is true, Protestantism is more likely to be true than Catholicism. This, too, is not a kind of belief, for one may again think that Christianity is very unlikely to be true. (c) Thinking that a proposition is more likely to be true than any of its individual alternatives, for example, thinking that Christianity is more likely to be true than Buddhism, or more like to be true than Confucianism, etc. None of these imply that it is likely to be true, or more likely to be true than not. (d) Thinking that a proposition is more likely to be true than that one or other of its alternatives indifferently should be true, which is the usual way of believing that something is more probable than not. An example of the difference between (c) and (d) would be believing Christianity to be more likely to be true than is any other religion, no matter which (an example of (d)) and believing that Christianity is more likely to be true than, say, Buddhism (an example of (c)). *Only the former of these latter two* can properly be described as belief.

Philosophers and theologians sometimes distinguish between belief in and belief that. Faith is generally supposed to be more closely connected with the former than with the latter, even if it is not simply a species of belief in.

Faith and belief in are sometimes supposed to be duties, or if not actually duties, something which we ought to have rather than lack, or which we ought to try to inculcate in others and foster in ourselves. Perhaps we can be under an obligation to have faith. If these claims are too strong, it may be held that it is a good thing to have faith or, what is different, that it is something which it is desirable or even admirable to have. It may be a good thing, but not admirable, to be a valetudinarian, for example. If it is not itself admirable, then perhaps it is a sign or manifestation of a good character to have it and the sign of a bad one to lack it.

It would scarcely be necessary to point out that all these things, which we might say of faith, were different, were it not that they are frequently confused. For example, philosophers sometimes say that it is our duty to believe something, or even to know something. But a duty can be a duty only to do things, and believing and knowing are not forms of doing. (Assenting to a proposition, however, is something we do.) It could be, however, that we ought to have believed something, or ought to have known it, even if it could not have been our duty to believe it.[2] For example we might feel that we ought to have known that our friend was to be married, because he had told us and we had insensitively forgotten, but this is not at all the same thing as to say that it was our duty to believe this.

In order to discuss whether faith is a duty, or something we ought to have, or whether it would be a good thing to have it, it is first desirable to examine whether any of these things can be said about ordinary belief. If ordinary belief can be a duty, for example, there will be no particular reason why faith should not be a duty also. On the other hand, if belief (or, if faith is belief, other kinds of belief) cannot be a duty, it will have to be shown how the difference between belief and faith explains why faith can be a duty although ordinary belief cannot be. The same applies to the other moral judgments some people make about faith, other than the judgment that it is a duty. If they can be made about ordinary belief, then there is no reason why they should not also be made about faith. But if such judgments cannot be made about ordinary belief, then the claim that they can be made about faith needs justification.

It is difficult to see that faith could be a *duty*, whatever other moral epithets may be applied to it. For a duty tends to be a task arising from our status or function, and though there may be a class of people, e.g., politicians and undertakers, whose duty it is to pretend to believe (in, say, the success of their party or the merits of the deceased), I do not see how there could be a class of people whose duty it was actually to believe. For one thing, belief is often, though not always, outside our power.

The view that though factual beliefs are morally neutral, moral beliefs are not is not (for what this fact is worth) the view of the ordinary man.[3] The ordinary man has a strong tendency, on certain matters at any rate, to disapprove of people for holding beliefs which are different from his own, whether these beliefs are moral or factual. An extremely heterogenous collection of factual beliefs has been disapproved of at one time or another, for example, that the apparent motion of the sun is produced by the earth's spinning on its axis, that the sale of indulgences does not bring divine pardon; that praying for the dead affects what happens to them; that the mother of Jesus was not a virgin; that the world will not end in (I think) 2000 AD; that Britain would lose the second world war; that men are descended from apes; that telepathy occurs; that women were not meant to suffer pain in childbirth; and that blacks are less intelligent than whites. (It is interesting to speculate on whether this tendency has survival value, which it may have, since it has survived. It may be that we have it because by and large it puts pressure on people to have true beliefs (though it does, perhaps in a minority of cases, also put pressure on them to have beliefs that are false).)

In the case of moral beliefs, a person who has a moral belief different from our own tends to be disapproved of because moral beliefs, even incorrect ones, are a socially unifying force, and dissenting from the view of the majority tends to be disruptive. We need society and cannot live without it. And to a large extent the content of moral beliefs is such that they are ones which it is useful to society that its members should have. Our moral beliefs are beliefs that certain actions, which are in fact socially advantageous, are right. If someone differs from us on a moral matter, then it is possible that he will perform actions which we regard as being socially harmful and so be dangerous to ourselves and those we love. Hence it is understandable that we should be antagonistic to him and his actions. (Having beliefs about what is right that are in fact socially advantageous is not the same thing as believing that what is socially advantageous is right. For example, it is socially advantageous that people believe that murder is wrong, but a belief that murder is wrong is not a belief that what is socially advantageous is wrong, even if murder is socially disadvantageous.)

Factual beliefs, however, can also be and be regarded as socially harmful. A sea captain who believes that the earth is round may evoke the antagonism of his crew because what they regard as his eccentric factual belief may lead him to perform actions that they regard as dangerous, like sailing too near to its edge.

Of course, when we disapprove of others' beliefs, we disapprove of beliefs which we think are false, as we must do, if they are incompatible with what we ourselves believe to be true. I doubt whether anyone at all disapproves of people for holding beliefs that he thinks are true – though one may disapprove of people for saying out loud things which one thinks are true, for example saying to a fat lady that she is fat, or passing certain quite truthful remarks in front of children. We may also disapprove of the means by which we think certain true beliefs have been acquired. And we may wish some people, for example our enemies, to believe what is false. We might wish our enemies to have false beliefs about the disposition of our troops, for example. And we may think that there are things, such as facts about sexual intercourse, that some people, e.g., children, ought not to know, and other things, for example, the state of our bank balance, that other people ought not to have found out.

On the other hand, we do not usually seem to disapprove of people who believe what we believe is false on matters which do not affect action in an important way. For example, academics are usually allowed to believe what they like on supposedly unimportant academic matters, but come to be disapproved of when they hold and express unorthodox views on matters which do have a bearing on action, for example, on politics. It would be very difficult to maintain, however, that people have a duty or are under an obligation to believe what is true, or even, what is more plausible, that they *ought* to believe what is true. It is either true that the next baby born will be male, or true that it will not be male. Obviously, however, no-one has a duty to believe either of these; nor ought they to believe them. Neither can we have a duty to believe what seems to us to be true, for to say that something seems to someone to be true is to imply that he already believes it, and we could hardly have a duty to do what we must already have done.

Hence we can have, in normal cases and faith excluded, no duty in general either to believe what is true, or what seems to us to be true. This does not mean, however, that certain special people do not have such a duty. It may arise from their office, for example. One might hold that an Anglican bishop had a duty to believe that Christ's body had been resurrected (or at least to try to believe that he had) even if other people do not have such a duty. But it may be that all the bishop has is a duty to say out loud that he believes this on certain special occasions, or perhaps to resign his bishopric if he does not believe it.

Nor can we have a duty to believe either what is false or what seems to us to be false, as opposed, perhaps (like cabinet members, who are subject to collective responsibility) to seem to believe what seems to be false, or to assert what seems to be false out loud. But if we have, as we have just seen, neither a duty to believe what is true nor what seems to us to be true, nor a duty to believe what is false or what seems to us to be false, can we have a duty to believe anything at all? For what other possibilities could there be?

Perhaps, although we do not have a duty to believe, nor not to believe, what is true, or what seems to us to be true, we do have a duty to adopt some kind of procedure for forming beliefs, for example the procedure of believing things no more strongly than the evidence warrants or seems to warrant. Alternatively, since not every belief has or needs evidence, perhaps we ought to adopt the procedure of believing in proportion to the strength with which it is justified, or with which it seems to us to be justified. (I am justified in believing that my name is Harrison, or that I am in pain, even if I cannot lay my hands on any evidence for this fact.)

The same difficulty, however, will arise about believing propositions proportionately to the strength of the evidence as arose earlier about belief. Should we believe what the evidence warrants, or what it seems to us to warrant, or (perhaps) to believe what seems to us to be warranted by what seems to us to be the evidence? (The same problem, incidentally, arises about all duties, not just about a duty to believe, if there is one. For example, are we doing our duty with respect to truth-telling when we utter propositions which are true, or ones which seem to us to be true, whether they are so or not? And has a doctor a duty to perform those actions which will result in his patient's recovering, or only those actions which seem to him will result in his patient's recovering? Either answer has serious difficulties.)[4]

However, it would be very odd, for reasons already given, to say that either believing what the evidence warrants, or believing what it seems to warrant, is a *duty*. The most one could maintain would be that one *ought* (or ought to try) to proportion one's belief to the strength, or what seems to one to be the strength, of the evidence, or that it is wise or prudent to do this, or dangerous, either to oneself or others, or a bad thing, not to do this.

On the whole, of course, we will be more likely to succeed in whatever enterprises we have if we have true beliefs, e.g., about the means of attaining our ends, rather than false ones. These ends do not have to be selfish. If one of these enterprises is to do good to others or, at any rate, to avoid doing them harm, we will succeed in this best if we have true beliefs about what is to others' good. Hence our having true beliefs will be best for others (so long as we are well disposed to them) as well as for ourselves.

If we are trying to harm others, it may sometimes be best for them, by and large, that we have false beliefs, for then we are less likely to succeed in doing them harm. Hence it looks as if the most sensible (though not necessarily the most virtuous) policy for us to adopt will be that of believing whatever is likely to be true, or whatever seems to us most likely to be true, and to inculcate true or apparently true beliefs in our friends and false or apparently false ones in our enemies. (This assumes, uncharitably, that our enemies are trying to do us harm all the time.) Of course, this policy will sometimes result in our believing what is false, for that belief which is most strongly supported by the evidence may turn out to be wrong. But the policy of being guided by the weight of the evidence is the policy which will, in the long run, give us fewest false beliefs and most true ones, though not all the beliefs that our adopting this policy provides us with will be true ones. (It is indeed a conceptual truth that the policy of being guided by the evidence produces more successful action than alternative policies. We have most true beliefs when we are guided by the evidence, and whenever action turns out to be successful, this is evidence that the beliefs we were acting on were true ones. If it is unsuccessful, at least one of the beliefs we were acting on must have been false.)

(iii)   Is Belief Voluntary?

There will not be much point in our deciding that sometimes we ought to believe things which seem to us unlikely to be true, or believe such things more strongly than the evidence seems to us to warrant, if belief is never voluntary and we have no control over what we believe. There are certain things that I certainly seem to be unable to believe, for example, that my name is not Harrison, that the earth is not flat, and that I can jump from an upper storey window without hurting myself. But maybe there are other things, things less obviously false, that I can believe if I wish or think I ought to. And even beliefs such as that the earth is flat are beliefs which I can put on a mental list of dubious beliefs, even if I cannot help feeling no doubt about them. If one calls putting a belief on such a list giving assent to it, then such assent is always voluntary, even if belief is not, and we could then assent to anything, even to things we do not believe.

This may be what Descartes was able to do when he decided to disbelieve everything that it seemed possible to doubt. For though he could not actually get himself to doubt that it was a man he could see, he could put it on a (mental) list headed, say, 'doubtful propositions'. Since, if we were careful enough, we could always tell whether a proposition was doubtful or not, it was, according to Descartes, always reprehensible to give our assent to any proposition that was not absolutely certain.[5]

But are there any propositions at all that are within my power to believe? This question splits into two. Are there any propositions which I can decide to believe, here and now, at will? Are there any propositions which I can cause myself to believe at a later date, by taking certain steps which one knows, from past experience or from the experience of others, tend to result in or strengthen belief?

There certainly do seem to be propositions that fall into the latter category. If one associates only with people who are members of the same political party, withholds one's attention from evidence contrary to the desirability of this party, confines oneself to circumstances where holding its beliefs is 'positively reinforced', say, by being given offices, and where lapses from such belief are 'negatively reinforced', say, by being deprived of office, we are quite likely to be rewarded by finding a belief in this party growing up within us by insensible degrees.

It is possible that acquiring belief by such means always involves self-deception. Withholding our attention from unfavourable evidence, for example, must mean that in the first instance we suspect that certain evidence is unfavourable. We must know this, indeed, in order to know what evidence to withhold our attention from. Hence we are taking steps to acquire a belief by means which we must at least suspect of being irrational. This will involve taking steps which we think may lead us to believe at a later date something which we may now believe to be false (though by the time we have acquired the belief in question, we will, of course, believe it to be false no longer and believe that, when formerly we thought it was false, we were mistaken).

Causing ourselves to believe something 'immediately' by a deliberate act of will is always impossible. But the view that we can never *influence* our beliefs by an act of will is too extreme. On this extreme view, I can never influence my beliefs directly, but can only investigate the evidence in favour or against any proposition's being true; belief is then an involuntary consequence of my acquiring or failing to acquire this evidence.

Even on this view, however, our beliefs will be influenced by our decisions. For we will have to decide what evidence to pay attention to and what to neglect and, perhaps most importantly, when to stop investigating the truth of a given proposition, in order to investigate the truth of another proposition which it seems more important to establish. If we decide to stop investigating it, for example, we will be deliberately leaving our beliefs in that degree of firmness which they have by that time reached. Hence we must have control of them at least to the extent that, had we decided to investigate further, which we could have done, we might well have believed them more or less firmly than we in fact did.

There is, however, something resembling deciding what to believe, that is often voluntary. What we often do is to decide that a proposition is one which it is suitable to act on. I think this can be done only with propositions for or against which we have not discovered any evidence that is strong beyond a certain point. Or, at any rate, if we put a proposition, against which we have discovered very strong evidence, into the pigeonhole reserved for propositions that we are going to act on, we will, when the time comes (if it ever does) for acting on it, find we cannot do so.

In any case, the decision whether or not to act upon a proposition is not an all or nothing matter.[6] Whether or not to act as if a proposition is true will depend (a) upon the difference between how much one gains if it is true and we act on it, and how much we lose if we act on it and it is false, and (b) upon what we believe to be the chances of its being true. Hence, though I may decide to put the proposition that my friend is honest on the list of propositions upon which I will in future act, I will in fact only act upon it if what I think I will lose if he is not honest is not large beyond a certain point. The more we stand to lose, the surer we need to be that he is honest before we act as if he is.

According to one main theory of belief, belief consists of having a feeling of confidence that the believed proposition is true. According to another, believing a proposition consists in being disposed to act in a manner which would be successful (in obtaining what one happens to want) if it is true. If the belief is not true, then acting on it does not get us what we want except by a fluke. For example, if I believe that it is Sunday when it is in fact Monday, there are quite a lot of things I want to have or keep that I will not have or keep, including perhaps, my job. (If the same belief can produce very different actions in different people this is because their wants are different.)

It seems fairly obvious that a satisfactory theory of belief would have to combine elements from both these theories and to hold, as we have seen, that one's belief in a proposition was manifested, at the very least, both by one's having a disposition to act on it and by one's feeling confidence in its truth. Belief would also be manifested by such things as our using this proposition as a premise in our (internal) reasoning and by our feeling surprise should it turn out to be false.[7] (It could not consist in behaviour only, for then we would not know whether we believed something until we saw how we behaved, which is absurd.)

(The fact that belief manifested itself in such feelings, as well as in action, would mean that a behaviourist theory of belief was mistaken. It would not, however, mean that *materialism* was wrong. Materialism could still be true, if it could be shown that those feelings of confidence and surprise, which are certainly not behaviour, are, despite appearances, just happenings to the neurons in the brain of the believer. But the truth of materialism is a question into which it is not necessary to enter here.)

It might seem that if belief consists in a disposition to act in a manner which would be successful in satisfying our wants if the proposition upon which we act were true, belief *would* be voluntary. This is because the actions which one performs from belief are (usually) voluntary. However, though all the actions in which a given belief manifests itself are voluntary, it does not follow that the belief itself is involuntary.

When King Canute acted as if he believed that the tide would turn back at his command – he did not actually believe this proposition – it was within his power not to take his courtiers to the beach for them to observe what happened when he ordered it to turn. But if he had decided not to do this, he would have had to have different beliefs from the one he had. He was acting on a conjunction of (salient) propositions that he believed, viz. the propositions that the tide would *not* turn back at his command and that he would achieve the discomfiture of his courtiers when they saw that it did not. Given that he wanted the discomfiture of his courtiers sufficiently to try to achieve it in this uncomfortable way, if he had done something other than what he did, it would have had to be from a different set of beliefs. If he had wanted the discomfiture of his courtiers sufficiently to make him act to produce it if he believed that there was a way of doing so, and did not act in such a way as to produce it, then it must have been because either he did not believe that there was a way of producing it, or did not want to produce it enough to adopt this way. That action on a belief is voluntary, therefore, does not show that the belief itself is voluntary. (Nor does the fact that an action is performed as the result of an involuntary belief and an involuntary desire show that the action so performed is involuntary.)

It could be argued that it is impossible to cause oneself irrationally to believe something, for in that case one will, if one succeeds, know that one believes it merely because one has made oneself irrationally believe it, in which case one will not believe it. I think, however, that making oneself believe something is possible, however difficult or undesirable. For, if I can control my beliefs, I could make myself both believe something and make myself believe that I believed it rationally. Even if I did not make myself forget that I had come to believe it irrationally, and so believed that I believed something for no good reason, this is not an impossible state of mind to be in (though perhaps it ought to be). Many people claim to have beliefs which they believe to be irrational, but which, nevertheless, they cannot easily get rid of. Some people go to psychiatrists to help them to get rid of such beliefs. (Other people go to religious and political leaders to cause themselves to acquire them.)

(iv)   Exceptions to the Desirability of Acquiring True Beliefs

Possible exceptions to the rule that we ought to acquire as many true beliefs as possible (possible in the time at our disposal and given various other considerations such as the strength of our desire for enlightenment on that particular subject, the need for alternative knowledge, or need for leisure) are these.

(a) 'Where Ignorance Is Bliss, 'tis Folly to be Wise'

In some circumstances one may be happier believing what is false than what is true. For example, it may be better to believe that one does not have cancer, when believing that one does have cancer is distressing and unlikely to enable one to take any successful avoiding action. This is, presumably, the assumption people make when they refuse to tell other people that they have cancer. It is more pleasant to believe that you are a good, clever and well-liked person, than to realise the truth that you are none of these things. This may be one reason why we do not gratuitously disillusion other people who have beliefs excessively favourable to themselves, though it may be the duty of some unfortunate people with special responsibilities, for example, schoolmasters, to do this.

(b) Alleged Self-verifying Beliefs

Some beliefs are alleged to be self-verifying. Sometimes a belief that one will be successful makes it more likely that one will be successful and a belief that one will fail more makes it more likely that one will fail. It is very inadvisable, for example, for a tightrope walker to believe that he will fall, at least while he is on the tightrope, and very inadvisable for lecturers to believe that they are lecturing badly, or that their audience is not listening, or that they may dry up in the middle of a sentence. Their having these beliefs will make it more likely that the beliefs will be true, with potentially disastrous results. Beliefs, besides being true or false, have effects, for good or ill, upon the person who believes them and so, indirectly, on others. (It is, incidentally, *what* is believed that is true or false, but *our believing* what is believed that has effects, for good or ill, upon our future success. The reader's attention is drawn to an earlier distinction between the effects of having a belief and the effects of acting on it.)

Some beliefs have desirable effects, even when they are not self-verifying. They will have these latter effects even if we do not act on them and whether they are true beliefs or not.

The effect of a belief in increasing (or decreasing) our confidence is of the latter kind. Some false beliefs have desirable effects, such as making us feel calm, and some true beliefs have undesirable effects, such as paralysing us, and it may be that the desirable effects of a false belief are large enough to outweigh the risk of its leading us to perform actions that are not conducive to our ends, especially if there is no suitable way in which we can act on it.

One effect of having a belief at one time may be to cause that very belief, or something like it, to be true at a later time. (I say 'or something like it' because the belief I have may be the false belief that on Tuesday I am ill, but the belief that is made true thereby is the belief that I have on the following day that on Wednesday I am ill. (As we have seen, the proposition that I assert when I say on Tuesday that I am not ill is a different proposition from the one I assert when on the following day I say that I am ill.))

The belief that something (money) has purchasing power is not a case of a self-verifying belief, for it is the belief that other people will give me goods in exchange for money, which belief, alas, is not self-verifying. The belief that shares that I am considering buying will go up could be a self-verifying belief in the case of a man who can afford to buy enough shares to drive their price up. But all this means is that his belief that the shares will go up is a causal factor in their later going up. It does not mean that the mere belief that they will go up makes this very belief true.

(c) Flukes

Sometimes a false belief may make the believer take the successful policy when a true belief will not. For example, South may falsely believe that West has got the king of spades and so finesse, but, because East is not awake, win the trick. If he had wrongly believed that West had the ace, he would not have finessed and so not have won the trick. His false belief that West has the king of spades in conjunction with his false belief that East is awake causes him to adopt the correct strategy which a true belief that East was asleep would have caused him to adopt, had he had it. The two false beliefs cancel one another out.

(d) False Belief May be Morally Admirable

There may also be some cases where having a false belief, though not in any way advantageous (as it was in the previous three cases), is nevertheless more morally admirable in some way or another than having a true belief, or at least something we ought to have. For example, it is sometimes supposed that we ought to believe people, even when what they say seems to us to be false, or that we ought not to think ill of people, or that we ought to trust them. It might be argued that certain people actually have a *duty* to believe certain things, e.g., that Christian clergymen have a duty to believe in the resurrection, and that men and women sometimes have a duty to believe the false protestations of their spouses.

One preliminary but incidental point may be granted, and so disposed of, immediately. Beliefs, like many other things, are symptoms or manifestations of character. Not believing people may be a symptom of being a suspicious, mistrustful person. Believing them too readily may be a sign of being frank, open and well disposed to others. On the other hand, believing everything others say may itself be a manifestation of a defective character, for example, being naïve, credulous, too easily influenced or just lazy. It should not be forgotten, however, that the fact that a belief is a manifestation of a desirable trait of character does not mean that it is true, and the fact that a belief is a manifestation of an undesirable trait of character does not mean that it is false, or even that one ought to get rid of this belief. I might disbelieve Smith, for example, when a nicer and less suspicious person would believe him, but this does not mean that Smith is telling the truth. Private detectives and policemen may have many beliefs that they would not have had if they had been more innocent people, but this does not mean that these beliefs are not true; such people would not be very useful, or do their jobs successfully, if they tried not to have such beliefs.

(e)   The Virtues of Thought

Another preliminary point is this. If belief were a duty, it must be something we do. Though believing is not something we do (i.e., believing is not an action) it is usually (though not always) the result of thinking, which is one kind of doing. The virtues and vices may be manifested in thinking just as they can in any other kind of behaviour. Laziness, carelessness and slovenliness, lack of imagination, overcautiousness, recklessness or timidity, slavishness, conformity, downright dishonesty, and so on, are all vices and can show themselves in how we think as well as in how we overtly act. And honesty, thoroughness, courage, precision, carefulness, perseverance, industry and imagination are all virtues in thinking as well as in acting.

A timid thinker will not arrive at truth because he is too frightened to take the necessary risks. A reckless or careless thinker will arrive at falsehoods instead of truths because he has not gone to the trouble of taking the necessary precautions against error. An important discovery probably involves a long and heavy commitment, possibly lasting for life, and a cowardly or overcautious or lazy or selfish man, or one who gives up too easily, will not make the commitment and will not make the discovery in consequence. And, whatever may be said of belief, to think carefully may certainly be a duty as well as being usually prudent, or, at any rate, something that we need to do in order to carry out our duties satisfactorily.

I am unable to think of any qualities of character that are virtues in thought that are not also virtues in action. It seems likely that these qualities in thinking and acting are virtues for the same reason in both cases, because they are useful or agreeable to ourselves or others.[8] They are useful in thought, because more than any alternative policy, they produce the true beliefs without which we will be unable to take the correct means to our ends. They are agreeable because they satisfy disinterested curiosity and because truth is often more interesting, as well as more useful, than fiction. And it is useful and biologically advantageous to men to be curious, because it results in their discovering truths and we never know when our knowing something may not be useful.

(v) Are the Four Apparent Exceptions Genuine Exceptions

It is doubtful, however, whether the four cases mentioned above really are exceptions to the rule that I ought to acquire as many true beliefs and as few false ones as possible.

(a) Is Ignorance Bliss?

Ignorance tends to be bliss only in the short run. In the long run reality has a habit of forcing itself on one's attention. It may be bliss, relatively speaking, to believe one has not got cancer when one has, but the result of this may be that one does not see one's doctor and dies, perhaps painfully, in consequence. Let us make further use of the distinction, introduced above, between the consequences of acting on a belief and the consequences of having it. Whether it is wise or not to cause ourselves to believe (or right to cause others to believe) something because it makes one (or them) happier will depend upon a comparison between the consequences of acting on a belief and the consequences of having it. For example, it might be right to cause someone else to have the false belief that he will not shortly die if to believe the truth would make him very unhappy – which is a consequence of *having* the belief – and there is nothing useful he can do to secure his ends if he had it – i.e., there are no consequences of acting on it. On the other hand, if there are important things he needs to do if he knows the truth, it will be better to tell him.

(b) Self-verifying and Other Advantageous Beliefs

The statement that we sometimes perform better when we have a disproportionately strong belief in our chances of succeeding, which tends to make the belief in question self-verifying, must be interpreted with some caution. One would have thought that *before* undertaking some enterprise, say, walking a tightrope, it would be best to have made an accurate assessment of the chances of success. It is after we have started, or are committed to starting and it is too late to turn back, that it does not pay to dwell on the possibility of failure.

It is perhaps important that what we need to do is to distract our attention from the thought that we might fall, rather than to prevent ourselves from believing that we might fall. Indeed, if we actually stop believing that we might fall, we will take risks which may cause us to fall.

The greatest risk may be due to the fact that the very threat of the danger may upset us. We may then reduce the danger by averting our attention from the fact that the path along which we walk has a drop of several thousands of feet on either side of it. (If we are walking along a high ledge, it may be that the physical difficulty of what we do is small. Walking along a band of the same width painted on the pavement would not be remotely difficult.) But averting our attention from the height is not at all the same thing as causing ourselves to believe that the ridge we are walking along is not high. The first is sensible; the second likely to be disastrous. Some people have the gift of being able to withhold their attention from unpleasant possibilities and, if this does not mean actually ignoring these possibilities and so not taking the necessary avoiding action, this gift can be a highly useful and enviable one.

One bearing of this on religious belief is due to the fact that religious belief may sometimes produce a disproportionately strong belief in one's success. This has advantages and disadvantages. The disadvantages occur if our belief that we will be successful, because God is on our side, causes us to commit our forces in circumstances when a rational appreciation of the situation would indicate that we would lose, or if it causes us to neglect obvious precautions, such as keeping our powder dry. (Indeed, if two armies are fighting one another and each believes that they have God on their side, these two beliefs are likely to cancel one another out.)

(c) Rationality and Truth

It is true that if we are not, either deliberately or inadvertently, guided by the evidence, we may sometimes hit on a true belief by accident and so on that occasion be better off than if we had been guided by the evidence. The reason why it is better to believe in proportion to the evidence is that this is the best way of achieving true beliefs and having true beliefs rather than false ones is over a long period of time is the best way of achieving whatever ends one has. (This is so whether these ends are good ones or bad ones). That believing in proportion to the evidence makes it more likely that one will have beliefs that are true is just a tautology, though an important one. Evidence for a belief is just (roughly) that which increases the likelihood of a belief's being true, and good evidence for a belief is just that which makes it more likely than not that the belief will be true.

Hence, though there will sometimes be occasions when we will have more true beliefs if we are irrational than we would have by pursuing a rational policy for forming belief, this is a fluke. There is no way in which, by departing from the policy of being guided by the evidence, we can produce flukes on purpose. This is because there is no way of eliminating from among our rational beliefs those that are rational but false, or of making a selection from among the things we rationally believe to be false of those propositions which are in fact true. Indeed, the suggestion is a contradictory one, for, if it were possible to do it, it would be rational to do it. Hence what we can do is something subtly different from picking out those of our irrational beliefs which are true and believing them. It is going over again the reasons we had for believing and disbelieving certain things and, when we find that we were mistaken, changing the belief in question. But obviously we will not always be successful.

Hence that irrationality occasionally leads to success is no reason for being irrational. That heavy gamblers sometimes win does not mean that it is rational to be a heavy gambler. Over a long period of time they lose. And one may be lucky now and again whether one is irrational or not, so, if one is rational, one will usually have the best of both worlds.

If to be objectively rational is to act on propositions that are true and to be subjectively rational is to act on propositions that seem to one to be true, there can be no conflict between subjective and objective rationality. What one aims at, of course, is to act on propositions that are true. The best one can do, however, is to act on propositions that seem to one to be true. It may or not be the case that the propositions that seem to one to be true really are true. Quite often they are not. But we cannot improve on acting on propositions that seem to be true by acting on propositions that seem to us to be false, and there is no other alternative. And there can be no conflict between objective and subjective rationality, for, although they are not the same, one cannot be faced with a choice between acting on a proposition for which there seems to one to be evidence and one for which there really is evidence. As we have seen, the only way in which we could achieve this enviable feat would be by, absurdly, acting on a proposition that seemed to one to be irrational, hoping, irrationally, that it would turn out to be rational nevertheless. (The same is true of probability.)

(d) The Morality of Acquiring or Retaining False Beliefs

It is doubtful, too, whether it is ever really morally admirable deliberately to acquire a false belief, or inhibit a true one. It may be that one ought to trust someone despite the evidence that they are untrustworthy, but trusting someone is something we do and we can trust people – say, by lending them money – without going to the lengths of believing that they will return the money. The

Victorian women who were alleged to think that they ought to believe, despite contrary evidence, that their husbands were faithful to them, might more safely discharge whatever obligations they had in this direction by simply not investigating too closely whether their husbands were unfaithful to them, by pretending to believe that their husbands were faithful to them, by acting in certain respects as if their husbands were faithful to them, not dwelling unduly on this possibility, or simply allowing themselves to forget what they knew. I say 'more safely discharge whatever obligations they have' because allowing oneself to believe what is false is always to take a risk. A time may come, for example, when the information that their husbands have been unfaithful to them will be useful to them and if they have made themselves believe that this proposition is false they will not have this information when they need it.

People sometimes claim to think that they ought to believe other people, even when they have good reasons for thinking that what they say is false. But perhaps all they ought to do is not to tell these people to their faces that they do not believe them, pretend that they do believe them, not dwell on the fact that what they say is probably untrue, nor probe too deeply into whether what they say is true or not, nor publicise unnecessarily the fact that one thinks they lie, and even to act, in a certain restricted range of circumstances, as if one believed what they said was true. And perhaps a mother does not need to have faith in her children in order to discharge her obligation to them, which she may do by simply pretending to them that she has it, if she thinks this helps. Indeed, if her actually having faith results in her making them irrationally believe that they will be more successful than they are able to be, she will not only do them a disservice, but be unable to discharge her duty of taking precautions against and having alternative lines of action available in the event of, their failure.

(e)   *Ought We to Believe in People?*

The question whether one ever ought to believe *in* somebody or something more strongly than the evidence warrants splits into two questions. We saw that belief in, in secular contexts, involves ordinary belief, as opposed to knowledge, together with a favourable attitude to what one believes being true. For example, a woman's belief *in* her husband implies her believing *that* he will be successful and her wanting him to be successful. A favourable attitude, such as wanting, is not a matter of evidence – one cannot have evidence for wanting, though wanting may be assessed as being appropriate or otherwise in some other way – but evidence for the belief is appropriate.

The question whether one ought to believe in someone depends upon an assessment (a) of the strength of the aforementioned evidence and (b) of the propriety of the aforementioned want. (a) Faith is not desirable if it consists in a stronger belief that someone will succeed than is warranted by the evidence that he will be successful. (It may be that one ought to appear to others to believe in them more than one does, especially if one thinks they will certainly fail if we do not.) (b) Wanting one's wife, one's children or one's country to be successful seems to me more appropriate than wanting other people's wives, children to be successful, especially if their interests are opposed. We tolerate an excessively strong belief that the people concerned will succeed if we approve of the want that they will succeed than if we do not. For example, a stronger than warranted belief that one's children will succeed is tolerated by those who do not share it; during the second world war a stronger than warranted belief in an Englishman that Germany would win would not be approved of, perhaps not even by Germans.

If this looks wrong, I suspect that it is because we are told stories of people who had faith in the success of themselves, their wives and children, which faith contributed to their success. But we would have been less favourably disposed to their faith had the objects of it not been successful and in extolling this virtue we tend to think only of the prominent cases where the people concerned were successful and so do not get a fair sample of cases.

(f) Belief in Oneself

I doubt whether many considerations are raised about faith in oneself that have not already been discussed. There are two differences. (a) The favourable attitude that is an ingredient in belief in looks as if it would always be the same, i.e., a desire for one's own success; but one tolerates more irrational faith if the reason why one wants to be successful oneself is, say, because of the welfare of others than if it is to make oneself rich. (b) One's own faith in one's success is likely often to be a causal factor in one's succeeding, if one does succeed. Where faith in others is concerned it will only sometimes be a help.

If one is inclined to overrate faith in oneself, one should, as with faith in others, remember all the cases where a man's faith in himself has caused him to undertake enterprises in which he has failed, and the fact that we hear more about the successes than the failures. Perseverance is a good thing on the whole, but it needs to be guided by an accurate judgment of the chances of success, otherwise one may be wasting one's time. It should also not be forgotten that faith is not shown to be irrational by the fact that one fails. One may fail from bad luck, in spite of one's determination and of having formed an accurate assessment of the chances of success. One is justified in undertaking something with a lower chance of success if what is gained, either for oneself or others, is large than if it is small.

(vi)   Conclusions

The essential, though not the only, ingredient in belief is the disposition to act, internally as well as externally, in a manner which would be successful in getting one what one wanted if that belief were true. Other elements, like a feeling of confidence in the truth of what one believes and a disposition to feel surprised if it turns out that one is mistaken, are less essential. Belief, in a secular context, is not always altogether involuntary, though acquiring it is usually difficult and takes a long time. Acquiring false beliefs, or beliefs that seem to one to be false, is therefore possible, but hardly ever desirable, as one's true beliefs are more likely to lead to successful policies of action than false ones and rational beliefs more likely to be true; these policies are not necessarily selfish. The occasions on which it might be rational to produce a false belief for oneself or others would be those on which the advantageous consequences of believing something outweighed the probable disadvantageous consequences of *acting* on a belief that was false. Alleged cases where we ought to believe what is false do not survive examination.

Notes

1   In Swinburne, 1981, chapter I, 'The Nature of Belief'.
2   I have argued that we do not have a duty to believe propositions in 'Harrison, 1957. I have also discussed whether we ought to believe things in Harrison, 1987. Both are reprinted in Harrison, 1973.
3   For example by David Hume, 1978, Book III, Part I, Section I.
4   The problem has been discussed by Prichard, 1949, and by Ross, 1939, especially chapter VII.
5   See *Meditation IV*, 'Of Truth and Error'.
6   The reader is referred to Ramsey, 1990, chapter 4, Section (3), 'Degrees of Belief'.
7   The reader is referred to Price, 1969.
8   The view that virtues are qualities of character agreeable to ourselves and others was put forward by David Hume in *A Treatise of Human Nature* and in *An Enquiry Concerning the Principles of Morals*.

28 Faith

(i) Introduction

According to the *Concise Oxford Dictionary*, 'faith' can mean: reliance, trust *in*; belief founded on authority; belief in religious doctrines, especially such as affects character and conduct; spiritual apprehension of divine truth apart from proof; system of religious belief; the faith, the true religion; things to be believed; warrant; promise, engagement; loyalty, fidelity; honesty of intention.

But dictionaries, though good places to start with if one is trying fully to understand a word or clarify a concept, are bad places with which to finish. In what follows, my main interest will be whether there can be anything that can properly be described as faith which is a good thing and ought to be cultivated in oneself and recommended to others. If so, the way in which it differs from ordinary belief, which ought to be investigated rather than cultivated, needs to be clearly drawn out. If faith ought to be cultivated, the question arises whether it ought to be cultivated unconditionally, or only if certain other beliefs are true. For example, is faith something which ought to be cultivated only if there is a God, or ought faith that there is a God to be cultivated even if there is not one?

(ii) A Preliminary Discussion; Some Antitheses Concerning Faith; Some Preliminary Clarifications

I shall start, in an attempt to clarify the distinction between faith and other mental states, by trying to clear up what seem to me to be a number of confusions and false antitheses one finds in writing about faith. Some of the difficulties I confront here will be further explored in this chapter.

(a) There is an antithesis between doubt and certainty. But this antithesis cannot throw much light on the difference between faith and reason; for one can be certain of what one does not have faith in and faith admits of degrees short of certainty.

In cultivating faith, one is supposed to aim at certainty, but if one were to achieve certainty, one would no longer think – rightly or wrongly – that one had faith, but think one had knowledge. There are many things which we are certain of, but which other people would say we do not know, because what we think is not true. But that the proposition in which a man has faith is not true cannot be the reason that others, of the same persuasion as the faithful man himself, have for thinking that the certainty involved in his faith is not knowledge, for they think its object (the proposition of which he is certain) *is* true. And the person who has faith cannot himself think that the proposition in which he has faith is certain, because, if he did, he would think he knew and therefore think he did not have faith. There is a mild paradox involved in cultivating certainty without aiming at knowledge, for if one attains certainty, one is likely to think that one has acquired knowledge.[1]

It is an odd fact, however, about the English tongue that, though one ought not to say that one knows unless one is certain, if one says only that one is certain one suggests that one does not actually know. Hence cultivating faith may involve cultivating that kind of certainty which one claims to have when one was certain, but would not wish to say that one knew what one was certain of. People of great faith do seem to think they know that there is a God; but perhaps they are overconfident.

(b) There is a different antithesis between knowledge and what does not amount to knowledge.

It is often suggested that faith cannot amount to knowledge. (We have seen that this is not the same thing as its not amounting to certainty.) It has also been suggested that it is a good thing that it does not amount to knowledge. This is sometimes said to be because God would be interfering with human freedom – freedom to decide wether he existed or not – if God allowed faith to amount to knowledge.

It is difficult to see why God would be interfering with human freedom if faith were to amount to knowledge. I am not interfering with human freedom if I tell someone – say in a letter – of my existence, though this will normally result in his knowing that I exist. Nor does my telling him that I exist preclude his having to make up his own mind whether I exist or not (e.g., from having to make up his own mind concerning whether having a letter from someone he has never heard of is sufficient reason for thinking that the man who claims to have written it exists).

(c) There is the distinction between beliefs (if any) that are within one's voluntary control and beliefs (if any) which are not. Presumably faith, if it is meritorious, should be the former. But sometimes faith is represented as a gift over which we have no control.

(d) There is the distinction between natural and revealed knowledge of religion. For example, our knowledge that God exists is often said to be natural, on the grounds that we can acquire it without God's having revealed anything to us. It is commonly supposed that knowledge of the divinity of Christ is not natural, in that we can know that Christ is God only because God has revealed this fact.

There is a tendency to suppose that moral epithets can apply only to revealed knowledge (because to disbelieve what has been revealed would be to distrust God, which is supposed to be reprehensible). Moral categories, it sometimes seems to be supposed, cannot apply to natural knowledge, or knowledge that has not been revealed. (It may be conceded that, since it would be question-begging to accept the existence of God on God's own authority, not to believe that God exists cannot be to show distrust of him, though it may be reprehensible for some other reason.)

The difference between revelation and natural reason can have nothing to do with what one ought or ought not to be certain of. There is no reason, however, why we should not be as justified in being as certain of something that we accept on the authority of some other person as of something that we have worked out for ourselves. Hence the antithesis between faith (acceptance of revelation) and reason should not be confused with the antithesis between (so-called natural) reason and acceptance of authority, which latter can be perfectly rational. (Acceptance on authority is in a sense natural, in that testimony is a natural phenomenon and in that we must use our own judgment on whether to accept or reject what appears or claims to be revealed. It would be circular to suppose that not only could some truth be revealed, it could also be revealed that it was revealed.)

I see no reason why faith should be confined to revealed truth. One might need faith in the existence of God, even if that he existed was not a revealed truth.

(e) There is the distinction between knowledge (and/or belief) that is about things seen and knowledge (and/or belief) about things unseen, e.g. electrons. There is no reason why we should not have knowledge of things unseen, or have only probable opinion about things seen. The mere fact that something is unseen does not mean that we need faith that it exists. There is no need to have faith in the existence of electrons, or the other side of the moon.

I see no reason why faith should be confined to the existence of things unseen. Even if we were aware of God in fact, we might need faith that it was God that we were aware of, especially at times when we were not experiencing this awareness.

(f) There is the distinction between propositional knowledge and knowledge of other kinds. For example, faith is sometimes said to be faith that God exists and sometimes said to be personal acquaintance with him. Though the verb 'to know' admits of a distinction between knowing that some proposition is true and knowing a person, I doubt whether it is legitimate to use the word 'faith' for encounter with a person. (This is not to say that encounter with a divine person is not meritorious, or that it does not presuppose having faith in the person with whom we have the encounter or faith in the fact that we are having a genuine encounter.)

(g) There is the distinction between faith in people and faith that certain propositions are true. Having faith in a person is not quite the same thing as trusting him. We might have faith in Smiley and think he will succeed in retrieving the plans stolen by an enemy power, but not be prepared to trust him to repay a loan. Trusting is more a matter of doing something (say, lending someone money, or adopting the way of life he recommends) than of believing something, though one but not the only way of having faith in someone is to believe what he says.

Presumably to *put* our faith in God will normally be to perform an action, not to accept a proposition, but will presuppose that we believe that there is a God, in which proposition we might also have faith.

(h) There is the distinction – mentioned in the previous chapter – between belief that and belief in. Belief in is not quite the same thing as trust, as one may believe in objects incapable of being trusted, such as non-personal entities like cold cures or exercise. (One might trust in a cold cure, though it would not make sense to say one trusted it.) One may believe in abominable snowmen who are not to be trusted. Doubtless God is one of the most important entities to believe in, but perhaps some people do not trust him. Believing in God in the sense of trusting him might well presuppose having faith that there was a God.

(i) There is the distinction between beliefs, if any, that we ought to try to have (or avoid having), for whatever reason, and beliefs that we neither ought to try to have nor try not to have, but simply to investigate. For example, it is not the case that the only things we ought to believe are things told (revealed) to us by other persons. The beliefs we ought to try to have are usually true beliefs. But it could be argued that either we know which these are or we do not. If we know which they are, we believe them already and if we do not, we do not know what to believe. Hence we can never be in the position of trying to cultivate a belief because we believe it to be true. What we ought to do instead is to cultivate true belief in the sense of trying to find out which beliefs are true.

(j) There is the distinction between believing something and acting as if it were true. (If it cannot be a duty to believe that a proposition is true, it could nevertheless be that it was a duty to act as if that proposition was true, or as if we believed that it was true.) It might be our duty to act as if we believed someone, if only from politeness, even if we did not believe him. And it could be the duty of a person who did not believe that there was a God to act – in certain respects, at least – as if there were a God.

The actions springing from genuine belief that there is a God and those springing from a desire to act as if there was one must diverge at some stage, if not in actual situations, at least in possible ones. For example, someone acting as if there were a God but not believing that there was one, might do what a person who really believed that there was a God did only so long as he thought he would gain in some way by doing so. The person who genuinely believed that there was a God might also believe that God would gain something from the action, which the other person could not believe. Hence if circumstances were to arise in which each believed that there was a clash between God's interests and theirs, they would each behave differently. (Both persons might have the same desires, a desire for his own and for God's interests, but only the believer could think he could satisfy the second.)

None of these antitheses is the same as that between faith and reason, though some of them have been confused with it.

(iii)   Faith and Works

There has been an ancient controversy concerning whether faith or works are necessary for salvation. I have not sufficient insight into God's state of mind to know what his intentions are on this matter. The following comments, however, may be helpful.

(a) Both faith and works are matters of degree. It seems unreasonable to hold that any degree of faith, however small, or any degree of works, result in or are a sufficient condition of salvation. (One thing is a sufficient condition of another if the first thing results in the second. One thing is a necessary condition if another if its absence results in the absence of the second thing (see Glossary).)

(b) It may be that some degree of faith and some degree of works are *necessary*, without being sufficient, for salvation, and that both together are *sufficient* for salvation.

(c) It could be that there is a quantity of faith sufficiently large to enable one to be saved without any works and a quantity of works sufficiently large to enable one to be saved without any faith, but that more moderate amounts of either commodity need to be bolstered up with a certain amount of the other. There might be quantities of works and faith so small that even both together were not sufficient for salvation.

(d) It may be that works without faith, or faith without works, are both alike impossible. Faith without works may be impossible because faith inevitably produces works. Works may be impossible without the help of faith. Maybe we cannot achieve salvation without faith because without faith we are not able to achieve enough works to bring our salvation about. But, since people who are not Christians do sometimes seem to achieve quite a lot in the way of overt works, it might be more plausible, if these people are to be excluded from being saved, to say that works must be done in the right spirit to result in salvation. 'He who *through faith* [my italics] is righteous shall live'. Faith, if it is voluntary, could be regarded as a kind of work.

(e) Theologians (e.g., Luther) may dislike holding that works are sufficient for salvation because they think that this view is tied up with the view that works *entitle* us to salvation, or that we can achieve salvation through our own unaided efforts (as we would be able to, on this view, if we could achieve works by our own unaided efforts.) The idea, however, of being entitled to salvation seems to suggest that we might claim salvation from God as of right. This idea these theologians think is both absurd and impious.

However, I do not think that the view that salvation results from works, even without faith, does entail that we are *entitled* to salvation. It could be that no one is entitled to be saved, but that it is God's practice to bestow unentitled salvation upon (or only upon) those with works. (It could be that none of one's children was entitled to pocket money, but that, nevertheless, one gave them pocket money and gave pocket money to those who were good (or more pocket money to those who were good). It is possible that discussions of the relative importance of faith and works confuse salvation's being unmerited with a man's not being entitled to it. But one may merit an estate without being entitled to it and be entitled to it without meriting it.)

I am inclined to think that good men are not entitled to salvation. An entitlement is something conferred upon one by a set of rules, and implies lawyers to argue about the rules and judges to decide when they have been infringed. All these things suggest a body of people of roughly equal power. Rules would be useless in a society whose members had very unequal power, for they could not be enforced upon the more powerful members. The idea of a set of rules binding the omnipotent is absurd. No set of rules can compel

God to save the good and in consequence, the good cannot be entitled to be saved. (The same would be true of faith. Those with faith might in fact be saved, but also not be entitled to be saved.)

(f) Some theologians have held that some men are predestined to be saved; others to be damned. I think it is true that if there is an omniscient, omnipotent God, those men who are saved *will* be predestined to be saved. It does not follow, however, that those who are saved are predestined to be saved whether they have faith or works or not. What God predestines may be that they have faith and so are saved, or alternatively that they perform works and so are saved.

God's omniscience and omnipotence do not favour either the doctrine that one is saved by faith or the doctrine that one is saved by works. For God could predestine one to have faith and so be saved just as easily as he could predestine one to perform works and so be saved. This would not be a matter of moral luck, because luck excludes design, and these would be things that God had designed. (The reader is referred to a fuller discussion of this matter in chapter 12.)

(g) One would have supposed that, if God had decided to save men irrespective of works, he would have been wise enough to keep the fact secret from them – which, indeed, he does seem to have hidden from most of us – for such a view can do nothing to enforce the morality which religion is often supposed to enforce.

(h) Though neither view is plausible, I find the view, if anyone has explicitly held it, that Heaven and Hell are the natural consequences of faith much more plausible than the view that they are the natural consequences of works.

Strictly speaking, I suspect that Heaven and Hell, if they are attainable and the natural consequences of anything at all, are not so much the natural consequences of belief so much as the natural consequences of contemplation and devotion, provided these are pursued with sufficient assiduity. If leading a life of contemplation and devotion could be described as leading a life of faith, Heaven and Hell (regarded at least as temporary states) might in the right circumstances be attained by faith. Happiness is not a natural consequence of virtue and divine interference would be necessary to ensure that the good are happier than the bad. Buddhists seem to hold that what they suppose to be a fact (that there are techniques whereby one can escape from the wheel of birth and rebirth and so achieve Nirvana) *is* a natural fact. In that respect Buddhism seems superior to Christianity, where salvation is usually regarded as a reward.

If salvation is a natural consequence of leading the right kind of life – i.e., not the morally right kind of life, but the appropriate kind of life to lead to achieve salvation – Heaven and Hell, regarded as states of mind in this world, would be affected by one's overall health (including, most importantly, the health of one's brain). Hence leading a life of contemplation and devotion could not be sufficient conditions of salvation or even happiness. Having the right kind of brain activity would also be necessary. Over this we have almost no control. Salvation could be only temporary, for one will eventually die, and our mind is entirely dependent upon our having a brain. It would be surprising if one could get totally disentangled from the condition of one's brain and nervous system by a prolonged course of contemplation.

(i) Unless there is an other-worldly Heaven, the view that Heaven is the *reward* of works is not plausible. Works are not reliably rewarded in this world, though sometimes they are. Even if there *were* a Heaven – say if Heaven were a state of mind in this world – it could not be the *reward* of faith, though it might, as I have suggested, be something one might achieve as a natural result of perseverance in what could perhaps be described as faith. For the same reason, Heaven could not be the reward of faith in this world if faith were just a special kind of work.

(j) In the preceding chapter (chapter 27) I drew a distinction between the effects of believing some proposition (e.g., one's belief that something is a snake making one's hair stand on end) and the results of acting on a proposition (e.g., the death of the snake that made one's hair stand on end). Which of these is supposed to bring about the allegedly beneficial effects of faith?

Let us consider an analogy. If one believes that one's house is insured, and one has peace of mind, then this result is an effect of the belief, not an effect of acting on the belief. But if one deliberately acquired this belief – the simplest way of acquiring it would be to insure one's house – in order to have peace of mind, then one's having peace of mind would also be a consequence of acting on the (different) belief, *about* the first belief, that if one acquired it one would have peace of mind. One's being cured by a faith healer would be the consequences of merely *having* the belief that he was going to cure one but, if one went to a faith healer, one's being cured would be both a consequence of one's *acting* on the belief that one would be cured if at some future time one went to a faith healer and the consequence of, when at the faith healer's, having the belief that he was going to cure one.

I think that salvation by faith would be the consequence of merely having faith rather than a consequence of acting on the proposition (say that God exists) in which one has faith. (The latter might even be impossible if no consequences about the world can be deduced from the existence of God.)

Happiness follows faith as peace of mind follows mere belief that one's house is insured, not as it follows from acting on the proposition that insuring one's house leads to peace of mind.

However, as I have said, in attempting to acquire the benefits of faith, we are nevertheless acting on some proposition or other, though on a proposition about faith, rather than the proposition in which we have faith. If one believes that one is saved by faith, acquires faith for this reason and is saved, one's salvation would be the result of one's acting on the proposition, about faith, that faith leads to salvation (and wanting to be saved). It does not follow that it is the result of acting on the proposition that one is saved by faith alone.

For it to be true that one's being saved was the result of one's acting on the proposition that faith would save one, it must be true that faith will save one. But this in its turn implies, if faith is a belief, that salvation is the consequence of merely having the belief, not the consequence of acting on the belief. If faith is not even a kind of belief, then *a fortiori* salvation through faith cannot be the result of either merely having or of acting on a belief (though one must, in acquiring faith, be acting on other beliefs, e.g., beliefs about faith's desirability and efficacy).

(k) If salvation through faith is the consequence of the belief rather than of acting on the belief, it does not follow that it is a natural consequence of the belief; it may be an 'artificial' consequence which results from the fact that faith is rewarded.

I have little sympathy with the view that salvation is a *reward* of faith. As I have said, it would imply that there exists the kind of God who interferes in the course of events. I have much more sympathy with the view that salvation is a natural consequence of faith. If salvation were the natural consequence of faith, it would have to be a natural consequence in this world of faith, for there is no other. I myself believe that there are in this world beneficial natural consequences of something that one might be tempted to describe as faith, though many people, if not most, seem to manage quite well without it. What is the proper kind of faith, if it is a kind of faith at all, will be discussed later in this chapter. Whether these consequences are so satisfactory, so permanent and so invulnerable as to be described as salvation is another matter. But perhaps half a loaf is better than no bread.

(l) The remark 'He who *through faith* is righteous shall live' suggests, though it does not imply, that he who is righteous, but not through faith, shall not live. The qualification 'who *by faith* is righteous' is one that Luther sometimes seems to omit. When the qualification 'through faith' is not omitted, the remark does not say anything about whether faith without righteousness or righteousness without faith are sufficient conditions of salvation. Luther leaves this an open question. Luther also says that faith is *all* that is necessary to become *righteous*, which may imply that faith is both a necessary and a sufficient condition of righteousness.

It would be consistent for Luther to hold that faith was a sufficient condition both of works and of salvation – as a fall on a jagged surface is a sufficient condition of cuts and of bruises. This would entail what he wanted, that faith was a sufficient condition of salvation. But it would not entail that works were not also a sufficient condition of salvation. Nor would it entail that works were not a necessary condition of salvation. This Lutheran view would also not entail either that there was or that there was not any connection between faith and work, as the fact that though jagged edges cause cutting and bruising, cutting does not cause bruising and bruising does not cause cutting.

Luther, the excellence of whose logic does not reflect the brilliance of his rhetoric, also seems to think it follows from the fact that (as Christ said) man cannot live by bread alone (i.e., bread is not a sufficient condition of living) that he can live by faith alone; but this does not follow (and is not true).

Luther also confuses the doctrine that works can neither be a necessary nor a sufficient condition of salvation at all (because man is justified by faith) with a quite different doctrine, that man is so sinful that he cannot achieve by his own unaided efforts the quantity of works that would be necessary (and perhaps also sufficient) for salvation.

Another possibility is that faith is a sufficient condition of works and that works are a sufficient condition of salvation (as someone's touching a live wire may be a sufficient condition of a large quantity of electricity's running through his body and a large quantity of electricity's running through his body is a sufficient condition of death). This doctrine does not imply that works are not a sufficient condition of salvation. On the contrary, it implies that they are. Nor does it imply that works are not a necessary condition of salvation. All that is implied is the not surprising conclusion that where there is faith there must also be works.

It is perhaps over-optimistic to reflect what an enormous amount of sometimes violent disagreement might have been saved by more careful logical thinking.

(iv)   Faith and Grace

Grace I take to be a collective name for those actions of God which vouchsafe to us the ability to do something that we could not have done by our own unaided efforts. The interesting cases are those in which what we are vouchsafed is to perform an action which we could not have performed without grace. It follows from what I have said in chapter 12 that the fact that God is responsible for our performing a good action, as he will be if it is done though his grace, does not mean that we could not have done anything else. Hence it does not mean that we ourselves do not deserve some praise for doing it.

There has been supposed to be an intimate connection between faith, works and grace. If there is an omniscient and omnipotent God, *everything* we do that is desirable must be the result of grace. This follows from the fact, established among other places in chapter 12, that God is responsible for everything we do, fortunate or unfortunate, good or wicked. We would not, however, describe the wicked or unfortunate action as being the result of *grace*, though these actions must, if there is an omniscient, omnipotent God, be something God himself produces. (There are some who rejoice in the total dependence on God that this dependence signifies.)

This being said, there is a distinction within the things that are the result of grace between those things which we achieve as a result of asking for God's help and those things which we achieve as the result of 'our own unaided efforts'. But the things we achieve as the result of our own unaided efforts will in fact themselves be things we could not have done had God not brought about our doing them. Even our asking for grace will be something which God himself brings about.

God gives grace to some but not others, in the sense that some but not others are permitted to act well, or in the way in which humans regard as acting well. It follows, of course, that, if we are saved only if we ask for grace and receive it, we are saved as a result of something – the ability to ask – which God, possibly but not necessarily arbitrarily, decides to bestow on some but not only others. His decision must be arbitrary in the sense that, if no-one deserves anything without having asked for help to achieve it, then the fact that certain of us are enabled (by grace) to ask for grace cannot be because we deserve it. Until we ask and have been given grace, we will not deserve it. Grace must therefore always be undeserved.

(v) Some Possible Reasons for Having Faith, If Faith is Just Like Ordinary Belief

Let us assume, for the time being, that religious belief is just a kind of ordinary belief, but a belief about divinity rather than one about, say, geography. Then it might be said that we ought to have it more strongly than the evidence warrants, for any one of the four reasons mentioned in the previous chapter.

(a) It could be that belief in God is something that it is pleasant to have and (if we are rational) to encourage (or at least not discourage) in ourselves and in others for this reason. (One must distinguish between a belief's being more pleasant and believing it to have good *consequences*. I pointed out in the preceding chapter that the pleasantness of having a belief had to be weighed against the danger of believing, and so acting upon, a proposition that is *false*.)

It is an interesting point, which I shall have to return to later, that, if the proposition that God exists had no (verifiable) consequences, there would be no danger, or not the usual kind of danger, in believing it if it is false. For the risks attached to believing what is false arise because we expect, and have prepared for, one thing when something else, which we have not prepared for, actually happens. But if belief in God has no (verifiable) consequences, nothing will come about if it is true that will not also come about if it is false. Hence there will be no risk involved in believing what pleases us. (It should not be forgotten, however, that though belief in God had no verifiable consequences, it might be expected by the believer to have such consequences and he might act upon this expectation. In such cases, too, there is the usual risk of his being disappointed. I say 'a *risk* of his being disappointed', for his irrational expectations may nevertheless turn out to be true.)

If belief in God had and was known to have no verifiable consequences, then it would not be a vice to believe in God because it was pleasant to do so. But if belief in God had no verifiable consequences, then belief in him would not be normal belief. For, as we saw in the preceding chapter, normal belief consists partly in a disposition to act in a way that would be successful in achieving one's aims if it were true. But if belief in God had no verifiable consequences, *nothing* could happen if there was a God that would not happen if there was not one. There would be no action that we could take that would be successful if some consequence, deduced from the existence of God, were true, but unsuccessful if it were false. Hence an essential part of normal belief would be absent in religious belief.

It is difficult deliberately to believe something because it makes one happier to believe it, though one does this all the time without trying to. Though it may be sometimes commendable to persuade others to believe things because it makes them happier, it is difficult to see how it could be commendable to believe something because it makes oneself happier. It is questionable whether it is sensible, admirable, or even possible, to believe that there is a God for the reason that it is pleasant to believe that there is one. But if there are no verifiable consequences following from the existence of God, it would be less foolish to believe in God for this reason than otherwise. (Perhaps people sometimes do not try hard enough not to believe in God, considering the strong motives for believing, irrationally, that there is a God.)

(b) It is difficult to see (see preceding chapter) how belief that there is a God could be a self-verifying belief. A Christian God is a transcendent being, outside space and time, who is responsible for the whole spatio-temporal universe. Such a being could not conceivably be brought into existence by our believing that he existed.

Hence it is quite extraordinary that some Christians speak as if he could be brought into existence in this way. But though God himself cannot be brought into existence by our believing that he exists, faith can and does involve having an idea of God and this idea may be brought into existence by faith. If you think that there is nothing of God outside the idea, then all that there is of God is created when we create the idea; but that God is 'created by faith' is precisely what atheists think.

Though belief in God could not itself be a self-verifying belief, there might be some self-verifying beliefs *connected* with belief in God. For example believing that one believed in God might be a self-verifying belief and, if one wanted to believe in God, a first step might be to try to persuade oneself that one already believed in him.

Obviously this would require self-deception, but self-deception is not necessarily a bad thing. Some people could not survive without it. Religion is a sphere which lends itself to a vast amount of self-deception. Sometimes I think that the best thing would be not to try to do without self-deception, but to try to make use of self-deception in a controlled way. It is possible that faith involves doing this. (This matter has already been touched upon in the earlier discussion of whether ignorance is bliss.)

More plausibly, the belief that having faith could enable one more easily to fulfil the demands of faith might make it more likely that one could fulfil these demands. Belief that one might get a response from a prayer for strength might make it more likely that one would get strength. Belief that one would get an affirmative answer to a prayer, as opposed to getting what one prayed for, could not, I think, make it more likely that the prayer would be answered (in the affirmative) for there is not a God who answers petitionary prayer. If something that one prayed for was within one's power, the belief that one would succeed in getting it might well make it more likely that one would get it.

If there were a personal God who answered prayer, I do not know whether he would be more likely to give one what one prayed for if the person making the prayer thought he would be given what he wanted. God might regard this as trusting faith or arrogant overconfidence. Perhaps it would in fact be sometimes the one, sometimes the other.

Ought we to try to acquire irrational belief in God if we rationally believe that this irrational belief will enable us to be more successful in our enterprises – including making us better men, if this is one of our enterprises? It seems fairly clear that belief in a personal God, whether irrational or not, *may* make us more successful in achieving what we want to achieve. We may be more resolute and fearless if we believe that we can rely on his help, and the belief that he is watching over us and cares about what we do may spur us to make efforts that would be beyond our powers if we were unbelievers.

If our irrational belief that God will intervene on our behalf causes us to have an irrational expectation that God will actually intervene – and how could it do otherwise – then, if we undertake enterprises which cannot successfully be completed without divine help and divine help does not come, we will have miscalculated and so fail. But so long as we not only believe in God, but also keep our powder dry (instead of expecting God to dry for us powder which we have carelessly let get wet) we may do quite well. We will do quite well so long as we do not allow our belief in God to produce in us any false beliefs about the outcome, in this world, of the courses of action open to us. But belief in God may in some ways be a handicap. For example, if we believed in a God who did not allow us to fight on Sundays, or to give blood transfusions to our wounded, we would be handicapped in fighting against an enemy whose God did allow this. The instruction to love our enemies might prove an equally severe handicap if it were observed.

I suspect that the answer to the question whether we ought to acquire irrational belief if we find it helpful is that to make a policy of doing this is too dangerous, though it may succeed, through luck, in exceptional circumstances. But perhaps what one needs to acquire in order to strengthen one in one's enterprises is not strictly speaking belief, rational or otherwise, but something simulating belief. I shall say more about this later.

(c) We saw in the preceding chapter that false belief is sometimes useful to its possessor in that it leads one to perform successful actions by accident. Irrational belief is more often useful in this way than false belief, as some irrational beliefs, for example, that my horse will win at long odds, turn out to be true. Irrational belief in God could be advantageous in *this* way only if such belief had, or if we thought it had, verifiable consequences; one must irrationally expect one thing rather than another, in circumstances in which what one irrationally expects actually comes about, before irrational belief can have this kind of advantage. But, if that God exists has no verifiable consequences and we believe that it has not, belief that he exists can never lead to our believing that one thing will come about rather than another. In a world in which the result is the same, however one bets, there can be no rational strategy for betting. (This does not mean that one may not come, as a result of belief in God, *irrationally to expect* things to happen which in fact happen, because one thinks that verifiable consequences do follow from the existence of God.)

(d) Failing to believe religious propositions is held to be morally reprehensible in some way. For example, it has been held – though not in these words – that since God himself has told us that those propositions which are objects of religious belief are true, it would be impious or discourteous and show a reprehensible lack of confidence in him, not to believe them.

But that it showed lack of confidence in God could at most explain why we ought to believe the propositions that God is alleged to have revealed to us, not the proposition (about this proposition) that God *has* revealed it. If God not only revealed to us some such things as that Christ is his only son, but also the proposition that he had revealed to us the proposition that Christ is his only son, the same difficulty would arise about this latter proposition. All beliefs that we believe to be revealed presuppose other beliefs that are not revealed. Assuming, for the sake of argument, that we would have an obligation to believe something if God had revealed it, we could scarcely have an obligation to believe that he had revealed it, or that he existed to reveal it. To believe that there is a God because God has revealed to us that there is a God would be to accept something rather like one of the stock examples of circular argument used in elementary text books of logic, the argument that God exists because it says that he exists in the Bible and the Bible is the word of God.

The same is true of testimony in general. It may be discourteous not to *seem* to believe our friend Tom, if he says he is late because he missed his train. It can hardly be discourteous to him not to believe that he has said this (except in the special case when he himself says that he said it). If, for example, we receive the apology by a friend of his whom we suspect of not telling the truth, it is not discourteous to Tom (though it may be discourteous to the friend) not to believe that he has said what he says that he said.

(vi)   Faith as the Name for a Special Kind of Knowledge

One way in which the word 'faith' is sometimes used by theologians is in one of the senses, already mentioned as being given by the *Concise Oxford Dictionary*, of 'spiritual apprehension of divine truth, apart from proof'. In this sense of 'faith' there is no such thing as faith. If religious experience, which purports to be of a divine entity, were valid, then faith might be a name for this apprehension and it would result in knowledge of truths, but it would itself be (a mystical) awareness of a person or impersonal *entity*, rather than an spiritual apprehension of the truth of a *proposition*.

In contexts other than religious ones, faith (as does belief in) implies (a) belief, (b) a favourable attitude to what is believed's being true, and perhaps also (c) that the person who had the faith or the belief in neither knows that what he had faith in was true nor knows that it is false. If this is so, it supports St Paul's view that we have faith because we 'see through a glass darkly'; if we were *directly aware* of that which we had faith in we might not need to have faith. On the other hand, St Paul's view would not support the view that faith is a name for a special kind of knowledge. If what I have said is right, 'faith' is not a name for any kind of knowledge at all. Nor does what I have said support the view that faith is intermediate between knowledge and belief. There is nothing between knowledge and belief; knowing implies believing (though saying that one knows something often conversationally implies that one does not believe this thing and *vice versa*).

It follows that there is no especial connection between faith and testimony. One way in which our faith in someone shows itself is in our accepting his testimony. But our faith in him may be shown by our expecting him to be successful, reliable, virtuous, honest, and so on. And there is, as I have said elsewhere, nothing irrational about accepting things on testimony. It would quite often be irrational not to accept testimony. Hence the commonly found antithesis between reason and revelation – which latter is a kind of testimony and is often supposed to require faith – is misplaced.

(vii)   Faith and 'Irrationalism'

A number of other Christian theologians and philosophers, notably Kierkegaard and Pascal, have held that the Christian faith should be believed in spite of its irrationality. This is supposed to involve a leap of faith.

However, it is not necessarily irrational to leap. It is not irrational to attempt to jump across a precipice, although one has a rational belief that one will probably fail, if the enemy is behind one and there is no other escape; there is a chance of life if one jumps, and none if one does not. It is more rational to *believe* that one will fall when one jumps that to believe that one will not, but nevertheless rational to *jump*. It might even be rational to persuade oneself to believe that one will succeed in jumping, if there is no alternative but to jump and one's chance of jumping successfully are increased if one believes that one will jump successfully. (In the case of the precipice, though not necessarily in the case of Christian faith, there would not be much time for acquiring belief that one would succeed.)

When one takes a leap of faith, the proposition on which one acts is not the proposition that God exists – which proposition the people advocating the leap themselves say is absurd – but the proposition that acting on such and such an absurd belief gives one a better chance of achieving salvation than is given by acting on more rational beliefs. It is much more rational to believe that God does not exist than that he does, but this does not at all mean that it is not more rational to act as if there were a God, including trying to believe that God exists, than not to act in this way, if there is some chance that to do so is a way of achieving salvation and there is no chance of achieving salvation in any other way. Few suppose that to believe that God does not exist is a way of achieving salvation.

It is usual to object to adopting this procedure that belief is beyond one's power, but in Kierkegaard's case, he had a strong tendency, which he believed to be irrational, to believe and all he had to do was to surrender to it. Allowing oneself to believe what one believes to be irrational is not only a religious phenomenon. A woman who in a Victorian melodrama allowed herself to believe, against what she believed to be the evidence, that her seducer would keep his promises of fidelity, is another instance of the same kind of thing. But in the woman's case, the results were disastrous.

It is worth pointing out that one of the beliefs of the Christian religion is that one attains salvation through believing in the Christian religion. Hence what Kierkegaard may be recommending may involve a double dose of irrationality. He may have thought that the beliefs one has to believe to attain salvation are irrational and the belief that one attains salvation by believing them is also irrational. But this would be absurd.

Tertullian said '*credo quia absurdum est*'. But there are so many apparently absurd religions that the fact that Christianity is absurd would by itself be no great recommendation. But, as we have seen, there would be no irrationality in believing the absurd, if it were really the case that there was some chance, however small, that salvation could be achieved thereby and no chance at all that it could he achieved in no other way.

(viii)   Faith and 'Creativity'

Faith, like belief, has effects in the world and one of these, in secular contexts, can be to bring about that which the believer has faith in. For example, a man's faith that he will become president may be a causal factor in his becoming president. Faith does not, however, 'create its own objects'. My faith in my salvation might be self-verifying by causing me to be saved, but my faith in God cannot be self-verifying by causing God to be trustworthy (as a woman's faith in her husband may cause him to be trustworthy), still less cause there to be a God. (I suppose a man's faith that he will be saved might cause God to save him – which would make faith sometimes self-verifying – if God were the kind of entity upon which faith could have such, or any, effects.)

If a man comes to have faith, there are ideas in his mind that there may not have been before. But, as I have said, faith's creating ideas of God is an entirely different matter from its creating its object, viz. God.

Faith in God no more creates the idea of God, as opposed to creating God, than faith in exercise creates the idea of exercise. And since the same ideas are involved in thinking of God and having faith that there is one that are involved in thinking of God and having no faith that there is one – for exactly the same ideas are involved in an affirmative proposition as in its negation – faith or belief cannot create any ideas that lack of faith or disbelief cannot create.

(ix)   Faith and Subjectivity

None of the remarks I have made about faith involves either subjectivism or relativism, which are views I wish to have no truck with. For example, if it is a fact that faith is different from belief, it is an objective non-relative fact that this is so. If it is a fact that religious people should extend more tolerance to diverse faiths, this view again is neither subjective nor relative, nor does it involve either the beliefs one should tolerate, or one's own incompatible beliefs, or the belief that one should tolerate beliefs incompatible with one's own, being subjective or relative. Indeed, it shows lack of tolerance, rather than the reverse, if one cannot tolerate an opinion until one persuades oneself that it is right from the point of view of the believer. True tolerance demands that one tolerate some opinions that one believes to be absolutely false. It demands that we should tolerate even harmful beliefs (mainly because of the possibility that one might be mistaken in thinking them harmful and because it would be even more harmful to repress them).

It would be to go far too far to think that *all* opinions should be tolerated, let alone taught in school. If one could stop it, it would be wrong to allow children to be taught that Jews should be baited, or that the world was created a few thousand years ago.

(x)   Faith and Groundless Belief

If the object of faith is the proposition that there is a God, believing that there is a God may be a groundless belief. But a groundless belief is a groundless belief; our coming to have faith in it does not mean that there are any more grounds for believing it than there were before. The best we can do, by coming to have faith in it, is to make ourselves unaware of the fact that there our belief is groundless. (I do not think that this is commendable.)

There are indeed certain propositions for which we do not need to have grounds, such as that things which are equal to a third thing are equal to one another. Such propositions are self-evident. But we do not need faith in order to believe these.

There is no resemblance between self-evident propositions and the proposition that God exists, or that Christ was his only son, which propositions are not self-evident unless the ontological argument is valid, in which case the proposition that God exists – though not the proposition that Christ is his only son – should be self-evident. If they were, there would be no more need of faith in order to believe them than to believe that the successor of one is two. Further, the ingredients in faith other than belief mentioned in the preceding chapter are absent from those propositions that are properly believed despite their groundlessness. For example, it is difficult to see why we should have a favourable attitude – love, perhaps – to things which are equal to a third thing's being equal to one another. And that this is so is not something that we neither know to be true nor know to be false. We know it to be true.

(xi)   Faith and Science

Some theologians[2] say that faith is as necessary for science as it is for theology. This is not so. All scientific hypotheses are tested by whether or not they fit the observed or experimental facts. It is not a matter of faith, but of logic, that hypotheses from which false conclusions are drawn are thereby refuted and there is no merit in continuing to believe them after this has happened. (It is a commonly held view that hypotheses from which true conclusions, and no false ones, are drawn are to that extent supported, but this, too, is not a matter of faith. It would be biologically favourable to have, when we were very young, an irrational belief that past regularities were repeated, but they have been repeated so often by now that the belief is now a rational belief.)

I am sure that scientists do need faith. But it is not faith in science that they need, for science is much too secure to need faith, or in the hypothesis which they are testing, in which it would be absurd to have faith, but in themselves and in their own judgment. As much as anyone else, a scientist engaged in a long course of difficult experiments is helped by a more than rational assurance that he will succeed. But this faith may be misplaced and not all scientists engaged in a long course of difficult experiments who persevere on account of their faith in themselves and their own success do succeed. We just do not hear so much about the ones who fail.

(xii)   Faith and Myth[3]

Some have held that faith is a myth to live one's life by. I find this attitude difficult to understand. Myths are (by definition) not true; if one thinks that a story is true, it is wrong to describe it as a myth. (Legends, on the other hand, may or may not be true.) It is true that many people believe what in fact are myths, but the people who claim that they have faith do not just claim to believe myths, they claim to believe myths while at the same time believing them to be myths; they believe Christian doctrine while at the same time believing that Christian doctrine is not a myth.[4] One might reply on their behalf that they do not believe the myth, they just find it helpful to bear it in mind. But if they do not believe it, it is difficult to see how they can find the myth consoling. For example, to believe that God will help one if one is in difficulties, or that one will survive one's bodily death, is consoling, but if one thinks that it is a myth that there is a God to help one, or a myth that one will survive one's bodily death, it is difficult to see how one can be consoled.

(xiii)   The Doctrine of Double Truth[5]

The doctrine of double truth is quite unacceptable. According to this doctrine, one and the same proposition may be scientifically or philosophically false, but religiously true. For example, it is supposed to be possible that it should be scientifically true that miracles cannot occur, but nevertheless religiously true that Christ actually worked miracles. But it is quite obvious that either Christ did or did not work miracles, and that if it is true that he did, it must be false that he did not and *vice versa*. Hence the doctrine of double truth is absurd.

The doctrine of double truth could be held only because it is being confused with a different doctrine, the doctrine that propositions that do not square with science ought to be the object of some attitude different from belief, or perhaps some inferior (or even superior, but nevertheless different) kind of belief. The doctrine may be being confused with the morally questionable view that propositions that ought to be believed in some circumstances – say, in church or when praying – ought not to believed in others. For example, one might hold that one ought, while actually praying, to believe that petitionary prayer may be answered, but not believe that it may be when trying to bring about the things one has prayed for, lest the fact that one has prayed and one believes that prayer succeeds leads one to overlook necessary precautions.

All these doctrines seem to me to be of doubtful honesty. The things recommended really do happen as a matter of psychological fact, but it is difficult to see that one should be in favour of them. The doctrine of double truth was rightly condemned in the thirteenth century.

(xiv)   Faith as a Technique for Dealing with a Sense of Presence

If faith is not a species of belief, it may be that it is a technique for dealing with an experience – if that is the right word – that many have to live with. Many go through life with the feeling – if it is a feeling – that God is directly present to them. They do not appear to perceive him with any of their five senses, but with what some mystics have described as 'ghostly sight'. This sense of direct presence is not a matter of belief; one can believe that there is a God, without having any sense of direct awareness of him at all. (Such people may or may not acquire beliefs as a result of having this sense of presence.) I do not know what are the causes of our having this sense of presence. For the sense to be veridical, one's feeling that the thing was present would have to result from that thing's actually being present.

Many do not acquire beliefs as a result of the feeling of presence. They may have reflected on the experience and decided that it is not veridical, but they go on having it all the same. They feel themselves in the presence of a being other than themselves, a being that perhaps demands obedience, and feel that they have a relationship with 'it', but have decided that an entity of the kind they feel themselves to be acquainted with cannot in fact exist. They may even feel that it would be dangerous to yield to the demands it makes upon them, and they may well be right.

Some such people may be in doubt about whether their experience is veridical or not. In that case, they may decide to treat the experience as if it were veridical. If they decide to persevere in the assumption that it is veridical, they may perhaps be described as having faith. Alternatively, they may decide to suppress the experience. (Many people who decide to suppress the experience appear to live perfectly happy and successful lives.) Some who believe the experience to be delusive may be unable to suppress it; others may decide upon a compromise and pay some provisional and experimental attention to it, though believing or suspecting that it is delusive.

Such people seem to me to be rather like people who hear voices. (Perhaps, indeed, some such people do 'hear' voices, and are possessed of ghostly hearing as well as ghostly sight.) If one hears voices, one may persuade one's psychiatrist to get rid of them – or he may persuade you to let him do this – but others, I believe, do decide to live with their voices. Some of them, I understand, find their voices useful; for example, voices have, literally or metaphorically, often been the manner in which useful inspiration presents itself.

I think it a pity that Christianity is associated with the doctrine that lapses of faith are a bad thing, if only because this insistence upon an all or nothing attitude has prevented many people who do not have faith from taking up a more provisional and experimental attitude to the apparent object of their ghostly sight. How one should live with this experience is a matter of trial and error. But in many cases the sense of presence does demand acceptance and may demand obedience, even absolute obedience. In this case, I suspect, it wants careful watching. God is a good servant, but a bad master. The apparent object of this experience has commanded those who have it to sacrifice their sons, torture heretics, and surrender their lives for trivial causes. Like hearing the voices, having it may be an experience akin to madness, which can cross the border into madness and needs constant vigilance. Used critically, it can be a source of solace, strength and inspiration – though perhaps the more critically it is used, the less the solace and the less the strength and inspiration. On the other hand, if we use it uncritically for strength and solace, there is the danger that it may, as I suspect was what happened in the case with Abraham, demand things that are dangerous, irrational or downright wicked.

What we are aware of cannot be a personal God himself, if only because the problem of evil shows that there cannot be a (benevolent) personal God. A personal God is omnipotent, omniscient and perfectly good. These are characteristics too enormous to be revealed to us in a single ghostly 'view'. At most what we are aware of is a quasi-personal godlet, which may appear immense to us because of our lack of imagination.

I would like to re-emphasise[6] that God neither exists nor does not exist, an odd way of speaking which is perhaps due to the fact that language to some extent breaks down when we try to describe the object of religious experience. (Plotinus held that the One could not properly be said to exist, but he did not think that it did not exist either.)[7] It would be wrong to say that God existed, because this would arouse false expectations about the course of nature, for example, the expectation that God would care for us or answer petitionary prayer. It would be wrong to say that God did not exist, because that would suggest, incorrectly, that one could not obtain religious experiences (which appear to have objects) if one applies the correct recipes for obtaining them and that these experiences are not valuable, useful and repeatable. (One difference between an imaginary God and a God who neither exists nor does not exist is that there are false empirical consequences deducible from the former, as false consequences are deducible from postulating the existence of Pickwick; no such consequences can be deduced from a God who neither exists nor does not exist.)

(xv)   Faith as Kind of Pretence

Faith is in some ways like pretence – I here use the word without any derogatory significance – or like acting as if something were true, or like acting a part.

A child who is pretending to be a lion will behave as a lion behaves in some ways, but not in others. He will roar and walk about on all fours, but he will not wave his tail, because he has no tail to wave, or eat raw antelope, even if there were any raw antelope to eat, because he does not like it. A man acting the part of a murderer will do some of the things a murderer will do, but not others. He will put a liquid in the glass, but not – unless he wants to become a real murderer – put prussic acid in the glass. Some of the differences between what an actor does and what a person really doing the things that an actor simulates will be internal to the minds of actors. A man acting having a quarrel will say the words that a man having a quarrel would say, but with the intention of diverting the audience and furthering his career rather than hurting the person he is addressing,

If having faith in God (or that there is a God) is like pretending that there is a God, a man trying to acquire faith may also try in some ways to behave, internally a well as externally, as if there is a God, though, because he does not really believe that there is one, he cannot, and possibly ought not to, do this in all ways. For example, he may try to act as if there were an afterlife without really thinking that there is an afterlife. He may try to act as if he expected help, without expecting help. He may also try to think as if there were an afterlife, though he does not believe that there is one, or to think as if he were watched over by a loving God, although he does not believe that there is one. This is obviously an uncomfortable attitude which it is difficult to sustain. I doubt whether it is admirable. It has the serious difficulty that the things one pretends are going to happen – such a one's being given help – will often not happen, if faith is only a pretence.

It would not be obviously harmful, and might be beneficial, to pretend in the existence of a God who watched over one but did not interfere on one's behalf.

(xvi)   Christianity, Fundamentalism and the Inerrancy of Christ

There is no way of obtaining knowledge other than by the use of human cognitive capacities, which are frequently liable to error. The only way of finding out whether any claim to knowledge is justified is by checking it oneself. If there is an expert available, one can ask him, but one has to use one's own judgment concerning his reliability. On a matter so imponderable as religion, there are no experts, though some nonexperts may be more reliable than others. In order to decide whether the Bible is true (let alone the whole truth) one has to use one's own judgment. One might argue that, because the Bible or Christ are never wrong, the former is divinely inspired and the latter inerrant, but it is dangerous to argue the other way round.

I think that both fundamentalism and the view that Christ is inerrant have had a harmful effect on Christianity. Instead of religion's being regarded as something that can be improved upon by the collective application of such wisdom in these matters as men possess, it has tended to be ossified. It would have been ossified more than it has if the two doctrines, the inerrancy of the Bible and the inerrancy of Christ, had been taken more seriously than they have been. But what is put in the place of what Christ said is not necessarily an improvement.

Ambiguity of 'Authority'

An authority on early Byzantine architecture is a person who knows more than most people about early Byzantine architecture and whose pronouncements about matters concerning it are likely (though of course not certain) to be true and are commonly accepted and appealed to by people less knowledgeable. But an authority may be a person who has legal *power* – not necessarily actual power – over others, who have a correlative legal duty to obey him.

This ambiguity may lead to confused views concerning the status of authorities in churches, for example, the Pope. The Pope, since he is sovereign in matters of doctrine, can legally lay down what Catholic doctrine should be and what Catholics ought to profess and believe, if they can. But his deciding what ought to be held does not mean that the Pope is an authority on what is true, as would his being an authority on Byzantine architecture. Hence, though it may be that Catholics have a duty to believe, or at least to profess, what the Pope says, because they have been told that they must by someone in authority over them in such matters, this is quite different from their being given information that what the Pope says is true. (To believe what the Pope says will not be a moral duty, but a legal duty imposed on them by the laws of the Roman Catholic church.) If the proposition that they are expected to believe looks to them implausible, they must then have a duty to cause themselves to believe what seems to them to be false.

It would be to beg the question to accept that the Pope is the authority on Christian doctrine because the Pope himself has declared that he is.

(xvii) Faith as Trust

Swinburne and Pascal, among others, have held that faith is a kind of trust. This view has the advantage that trust is in a way voluntary and so can be strengthened in ourselves and inculcated in others, which it is supposed that faith in God can be. Putting our trust in someone is something we do. Feeling trust in God – which is not, strictly speaking, something we do – is unlikely to be something we ought to cultivate, unless our mistrust is pathological. (In that case, we might ourselves know that our mistrust was unfounded, and so rationally try to conquer it without thinking that we were encouraging false belief, to the extent, which is small, that feeling trust lies under our voluntary control.)

Trust in God presupposes belief that there is a God. We could no more trust a nonexistent God than we could trust a nonexistent parent. Hence belief that there is a God cannot be a manifestation of trust. And we normally should not try to alter our beliefs in a person whom we mistrusted in order to make ourselves trust those people. If we decide to put our trust in someone, we must take this risk without altering our belief that he is not altogether trustworthy. For example, we ought not to make ourselves believe that a beggar is trustworthy before we put our trust in him by employing him. We should take the risk with our eyes open. Still less ought we to make ourselves believe that someone existed in order that we might trust him.

It is often held that faith, in the theological sense, is belief in something on the word of God. From the point of view of the person who has faith, he is accepting something on what, rightly or wrongly, he supposes to be the word of God. He cannot, on faith, accept that it is the word of God. Nor could he have a duty (e.g., a duty to God) to try to inculcate in himself the belief that God has said something when all the appearances are that God had not said it.

(xviii)   Faith and Risk-taking

If it makes no difference to what will happen to you whether there is a God or not, then perhaps you are free to believe in God or not without any risk of anything unpleasant happening to you by your acting on a proposition that is false. Something unpleasant might happen to you as a result of your believing a proposition about 'believing' the proposition that there is a God, say, the proposition that believing it helps when it does not.

Let us return to Pascal. If it does make a difference whether there is a God or not, then it may be possible to assess the risks you run and the advantages you gain from believing in God irrationally because you believe that there are long-term advantages resulting from believing that there is a God, should this proposition turn out to be true.

I propose to consider the matter somewhat artificially by assuming that if you decide to act on the proposition that God exists, you stake something – all the good times you might have been having if you paid no attention to what God is alleged to have prohibited – which investment will reap a large return in the shape of future bliss if there is a God. On the other hand, you will lose this stake if there is not a God. If you decide to act on the proposition that there is not a God, you will not give up anything and so will not lose anything if you are right, but if you are wrong it is possible that you will lose your chance of everlasting happiness and perhaps be eternally damned into the bargain. There is in this case no way of not betting, because being undecided on whether there is a God or not has the same results as believing that there is not one. I should re-emphasise that inheriting eternal bliss is the result of having a belief in God, not the result of acting on it. What one does act on is the proposition, about belief, that one will inherit eternal bliss if one does believe the proposition that there is a God.

You can perhaps order the four possible situations, mentioned above, in order of desirability. I rank them as follows.[8]

(a) You bet on there being a God and there is one. (You gain eternal bliss.)

(b) You do not bet on there not being a God and there is not one. (You do not inherit eternal bliss, but at least you do not lose your stake.)

(c) You bet on there being a God, but there is not one. (You do lose your stake.)

(d) You bet on there not being a God, but there is one. (You suffer eternal damnation.)

The rationality of betting on there being a God will depend on the size of the stake and the difference between what you would lose and what you would gain if you won. Also, of course, the relative probabilities of these four alternatives is obviously relevant. The better the chance of there being a God, the smaller the stake, and the greater the gain, the more rational it will be to bet on God's existing.

But Pascal's argument[9] which, roughly, is that the difference between the loss you suffer (eternal damnation) if you bet on there not being a God and are wrong and the gain (eternal bliss) that accrues to you if you bet on there being a God and are right is so enormous that the rational thing to do is to bet on there being a God, however large your stake is likely to be and however great the odds against there being a God are.

Difficulties with Pascal's Argument

There are, however, difficulties with this argument.

(a) However much it is supposed that you might win if you bet on there being a God and are right, or lose if you bet on there not being a God and are wrong, the above argument must presuppose that the chances of there not being a God are not nil. (It could be argued that even if we think that the chances of there being a God are nil, there is always the possibility that we are mistaken, so the chances of there not being a God can never be nil.)

(b) God may not approve of your deciding to believe that he exists from such calculating motives and you may, for this reason, not inherit eternal bliss, even if there is a God and you bet on there being one. One may believe in God because one is very frightened and God may not approve of conformity based on terror. (I do not approve of this and so naturally suppose that God does not approve of it either.) And an academically-minded God might even approve of atheists for being guided by the evidence, which is evidence for the proposition that there is not a God. Even if the conclusion atheists have come to is mistaken, God might approve of deliberately-adopted rationality, which by misfortune leads to error, more than he does of accidentally hitting the truth, and reward them each accordingly.

(c) It may not be within one's power to command genuine belief but only outward conformity, which may deceive one's fellow men but cannot deceive God. But outward conformity may not be good enough to enable us to inherit eternal bliss. Outward conformity, however, may be all that one can produce in response to Pascal's recommendation.

(d) Some Christians believe that God is so benevolent that everyone inherits eternal bliss, whether they believe in God or not. If this is the case and you act as if there is a God in this world, and there is one, you will have wasted your stake, for no harm would have come to you even if you had not so acted.

(e) Different religions make claims which may cancel each other out. The assumption of Pascal's argument is that all you lose if you bet on there being a God when there is not one is your stake. But this assumption may be false. Let us suppose that Jews, Christians and Moslems each suppose that you are not only damned if you do not bet on there being a God; you are also damned if you bet on one of the other rival accounts of God being the correct one. You are saved only if you bet on the truth of their own account. Then, if you plump for Christianity but the Moslem religion is the true one, you do not just lose your stake for being wrong. You are in just as much trouble as you would have been had you bet on there not being a God and been wrong. The claims of the different religions cancel one another out.

Whether or not the rational conclusion from this is that it is not worth betting on any religion for the reason of attaining salvation and avoiding damnation I am not sure. If you are fairly firmly convinced that you will be damned unless you believe one or other of them, but do not know which, then it may seem that the rational thing to do is to believe one of them. If it seems to you that you will die if you do not take one treatment or another, then it will seem rational to you to take one of the treatments. Perhaps it would be rational to take all of them. But the treatments may not be incompatible, although the religions, unfortunately, are.

I am not, incidentally, suggesting that adopting a religion can or ought to be a risk-free enterprise, or that there is anything wrong with taking risks as such. The Duke of Wellington said that probability was the guide of life, which (rightly) suggests that risk-taking is unavoidable. But there are risks and risks, and much depends on the reason why one takes them. Adopting a religious way of life in spite of, or perhaps because of, the risks that it involves is not necessarily contemptible and may be admirable, depending on the kind of religious life that it is and what one's religion enjoins.

The trouble with Pascal's wager is really – since it asks you not to take the slightest risk of going wrong by thinking that there is not a God – that it is overcautious.

(f) Normal betting does not involve the cultivation of irrational beliefs and so does not involve having faith. You may sensibly bet on something when you know perfectly well that the chances of its winning are no more than, say, one in 100, if the difference between what you would lose and what you would win is large enough. (If the bet is in money, what you win will often need to be large enough to justify risking depriving yourself of necessities if you lose in order to gain luxuries if you win. On the other hand, it can be rational to bet on very poor odds if the amount of your stake is so small that you cannot usefully do anything else with it, but you could do a great deal with your winnings, if there are any.)[10] Some religious people speak as if life without God is so worthless that what you are staking if you bet on his existing is not worth keeping. This would make it rational to bet on there being a God even at very long odds.

But in ordinary circumstances you can bet successfully without causing yourself irrationally to believe that you will win, or even to believe that the chances of your winning are very good. With faith, however, you are perhaps not just supposed to bet on the proposition that God exists is true. (Whether you are will depend on whether belief is necessary for salvation, or just such things as churchgoing, alms-giving and bead-telling and other works. These can be done without belief, though they may have no efficacy without belief.) You are supposed actually to believe that it is true, which, oddly, involves believing that you are going to win your bet. It is rather as if, in order to win money on a horse, you not only had to put your money on the winning horse, but had also to convince your bookmaker that you believed that the horse you put your money on was going to win. Indeed, on some Christian views – the view that one is saved by faith alone – it is as if you do not need even to put any money on the horse, in order to win, so long as you believe sufficiently firmly that it is going to win.

The belief in God demanded by an argument like Pascal's must be an irrational belief, as belief acquired as the result of fear of damnation, rather than of seeing the reasons for the belief, must be irrational. This raises the question 'How could I, as well as having this irrational belief, also have a rational opinion that having this irrational belief is the best policy?' (It does not seem that I can both believe that something is true and that it is irrational to believe it.) I suppose I can accomplish the required feat only because I have the second-order rational belief about the advantages of having this irrational belief and this irrational belief itself at different times. At one time I decide that irrational belief is sound policy, and in forming this belief it may be that I ought be as rational as I can. But by the time I have actually acquired the irrational belief, it is both too late and also self-defeating to be rational.

(xix) Differences Between Faith and Ordinary Belief

If I need to believe that there is a God, as well as to act on the proposition that there is a God, in order to gain the benefits from believing, religious belief must be different from ordinary belief. I now want to point out what seem to me to be some of these differences. These will to some extent parallel the discussion in the preceding chapter of the possible cases, if any, when acquiring rational beliefs might be admirable or permissible.

(a) Faith, as we have seen, implies having a favourable attitude to what we have faith in. Ordinary belief does not. I can believe that my husband will be successful, or believe that he will be unsuccessful. I cannot have faith in his failure, unless I have come to have a similar favourable attitude to policies – say my divorcing him and living with my lover – which involve it. This, presumably, must be because I want him to succeed. Hence we could have faith in God only if we had a favourable attitude to God. (This may be why St James refused to say that devils had faith in God, though they did believe there was one.)[11]

(b) As we have also seen, if I bet on a horse and it wins, it really does not matter how firmly I believed that it was going to win, or even whether I believe that it is going to win at all. I get my money just the same. Where religious belief is concerned, however, it is supposed to be the case that the more deeply one believes, the more one benefits. It is not enough that I act in a way that would be rational to act (because conducive to my ends) if there were a God. I am supposed to believe in God as firmly as I can.

(c) Scientists do not meet together to recite the theory of relativity, or the table of elements, however important it is that they should believe them. Christians – or some of them – however, do meet together in groups to recite the creed. Children do publicly recite the multiplication table, or used to, but that is not because they are supposed to have faith in it, but in order that they should remember it. Religious people, however, recite their creeds long after they can remember them quite well. Presumably this is because doing this increases the degree of conviction with which they believe, and also strengthens the favourable attitudes associated with their belief and makes them more likely to stand up for their beliefs under pressure and to adhere to the organisation that feels that it is its duty to propagate and preserve them.

(d) It may well be, as I have already suggested, that the proposition that there is a God has no verifiable consequences. In this case, belief that there is a God *must* be different from belief that any other proposition is true. For an essential part of ordinary belief that an ordinary proposition is true is a disposition to act in a manner that would be successful in getting one what one wants, if that proposition were true. For example, an essential ingredient in the belief that gas is a more efficient way of heating a house than electricity is one's being prepared to instal gas in one's house rather than electricity, if one has the money and wants an efficient heating system more than anything else one thinks one could have procured with the money. If the proposition that there is a God has no verifiable consequences – as, if God is a necessary being, must be the case – then an essential ingredient in ordinary belief must be missing from religious belief.

(This fact about belief is true of *a priori* beliefs as well as of other beliefs. An essential part of one's believing the *a priori* proposition that the square on the hypotenuse of a right-angled triangle is equal to the sum of the squares on the other two sides is one's being disposed to act on this proposition in such ways as testing whether an angle, say, the angle at the corner of a tennis court, is a right angle, if one wants to find out whether the angles on one's tennis court are right angles more than one wants to do anything else that one could to with one's time.)

(e) Where belief in God is concerned, it is supposed to be important constantly to dwell on the fact that God exists and has a certain kind of nature. It is not at all necessary, however, to dwell on such facts as that the Battle of

Hastings was fought in 1066. (It may be important constantly to dwell, in certain circumstances at any rate, on the fact that one is more likely to have an accident if one drinks before one drives, if one is prone to drink before one drives, or to dwell on the fact that smoking causes lung cancer, heart disease and bronchitis if one is prone to smoke. But the benefits just mentioned are the result of the action, not of the constant dwelling, and we constantly dwell in this case in order to make ourselves perform the action.)

(xx)   The Limitations of Ordinary Belief

It is an interesting and relevant fact that dwelling on a possibility may have more effects on one's life than actually believing it. For example, reading fiction may have an effect on one's life, although, since it is fiction, it is not intended to be believed and is usually not believed. The fact that fiction has an effect on one's life may partly be because some people, like those who threw eggs at the villain in a Victorian melodrama, do not clearly distinguish between fact and fiction. But it may also sometimes be because, in fiction, there is often some incidental commentary, which may be intended to be believed – for example, 'You will thus see, dear reader, how a prolonged and excessive addiction to alcohol can harden the heart and blunt the sensitivity of even the strongest of characters'.

   And authors may put true statements and statements that they wish their readers to believe into the mouths of their characters (though doing this does not commit the author to their truth and it is too often wrongly assumed that he believes them). The sentence 'At this point Bishop Fortescue exclaimed "The world would be a much better place if everybody paid more attention to the teachings of the New Testament"' may be a sentence of fiction, but this does not mean that the sentence within the sentence may not express something which the author believed and intended his readers to believe that he believed, and one that he also wanted his readers to believe (perhaps as a result of believing that he believed it).

   Fictional episodes,[12] too, may be, and usually, though not invariably, are, constructed in such a way as to seem to exemplify laws of nature. I suppose that fiction is described as realistic or true to life according to whether the episodes recounted in it could have happened. And fiction may – perhaps better than anything else – suggest possibilities, especially possible ways of living, which may subsequently be thought about, perhaps tested, and then acted upon or rejected.

People, I think, do have an irrational tendency to suppose that fictional episodes do establish or refute beliefs about human nature, whereas this can be done only by actual facts, not by suppositions or fantasies. But there is a way in which everything that occurs in fiction is fact, so to speak. That is to say, everything in fiction is the production of one or more human beings, and therefore, if treated properly, gives the reader insight into the workings of human beings' minds and emotions as exemplified by the mental processes of the author of the fiction, the products of which are open to the reader's examination. Hence they may affect his action by increasing his knowledge of human behaviour

Finally there is the mundane fact that time spent on fiction is time which would otherwise have been spent on something else (perhaps a different kind of fiction) and this alone is bound to affect our lives. And just what kind of fiction we spend our time on will have an effect on our lives and perhaps a great effect, even if we do not believe any of it.

For similar reasons, it is fairly obvious that reading the Bible or the Talmud or the Koran or some other religious book may have an effect on our lives, whether we believe it or not. We might, for example, come to the conclusion that we ought to lead our lives in the way in which Christ is alleged to have lived his, in some respects at any rate, even if we did not believe that there was such a person as Christ, let alone that he was the son of God.

It may be that dwelling on possibilities has more effect on one than believing that these possibilities actually obtain. Let us compare two people, one who believes that there is a God, but never thinks about it, the other of whom does not believe that there is a God, or even believes that there is not a God, but, perhaps partly for this very reason, constantly thinks of God. It seems likely that the first person's belief – if it is belief – that there is a God will have less effect on him than the second person's constantly considering the possibility that there is one. The first person thinks both that God exists, and that God either approves or disapproves of everything he does, but never thinks about this, or wonders, before he does anything, whether or not God approves of it. The second person does not think that there actually is a God, but is constantly speculating, before he does anything, about whether God would approve of it, if there were a God. Perhaps the second person's considering these possibilities would have a greater effect on him than the first person's belief.

Which has the greater effect depends, I think, upon the nature of the belief. Let us return to a preceding example and compare two people, one of whom believes that smoking causes lung cancer and gives up smoking, although he does not think about it very much, the other of whom is always thinking of the connection between smoking and lung cancer, although he does not believe there is a connection and so does not give up smoking. In this case it seems that the first person's belief will have a more beneficial effect on his life than will the second person's obsession with a mere thought. In this case, acting without constantly dwelling is more beneficial than constantly dwelling without acting.

But if nothing about the world can be deduced from the proposition that God exists, it follows that there *is* no action that one can justifiably take on the proposition that God exists (apart, perhaps, from saying 'Yes' rather than 'No' when asked whether one thinks there is a God. But doing this might be acting only on the belief that I would be rewarded for saying 'Yes' and punished for saying 'No', or *vice versa*). (If one *thought* belief in God had verifiable consequences, or rather, *thought* that certain consequences followed from belief, one could act on the proposition that God existed, but, if it had no such consequences in fact, one would not be *justified* in acting on them.) In such a case, that you dwell on the thought that there is a God, or bear in mind what one may consider the remote possibility that there is one and that he has a certain nature, may be more important to one than that one actually believes that there is a God. Indeed, it may be all one can do. In this case, mere belief is dead.

Incidentally, if no consequences follow from the existence of God, it follows that it will be impossible even to act as if there were a God without believing (where 'believing' refers to some straightforward belief) that there is one, which is something we are sometimes recommended to do if we are incapable of actually believing in God. There will be no way in which we can so act. It will, however, not be possible to think as if there was a God, and it is a possible view that it is in this latter that having faith in God consists. All that believing in God will be will in this case consist in acting (internally, for overt actions will be impossible) as if there were one. Thinking as if there were a God would perhaps consist in having a feeling of confidence that there was a God – though I myself do not see how this feeling could be divorced from action, which means that we ought not to try to acquire it – and in having the emotions properly evoked by the kind of God one imagines – if that is the right word – though does not believe, there to be.

(xxi)   Faith Is Not Belief

What I want to provisionally to suggest is that what religious people extol as the virtue of faith, or at least the most essential and valuable ingredient in it, is not so much a kind of belief,[13] for example belief that there is a God, as this constantly dwelling, with a favourable attitude, on the thought of God, coupled with allowing this to have an appropriate effect on one's emotions and actions. (According to Christians, the aforementioned favourable attitude should among other things be one of love. Hating God would presumably not have the desired effects.) It could have this appropriate causal effect even if there were no way of acting on the proposition that God exists, as will be the case if nothing about the world can be deduced from it.) Contemplating a distant star can have an appropriate emotional effect and have effects on our actions, even though there is no obvious way – though in this case there must be some ways that are not obvious – of acting on the proposition that it exists.

Alternatively, I want to suggest that. if it is not what I here suggest it is, faith has been considered to be a 'virtue' because it has been confused with its essential and most important element, this constantly dwelling on the thought of God. If faith is a matter of constantly and devotedly dwelling on the thought of God, then it becomes quite easy to explain why faith can be voluntary while ordinary belief is not. (Religious belief has to be voluntary, if it is something we ought to have and if *ought* implies *can*.)

It might be that if we did not already straightforwardly believe that there was a God we could not make ourselves straightforwardly believe that there was one. In any case, from the point of view of someone who thinks that there is not a God, it must almost inevitably seem to be foolish to try to convince oneself, against the evidence, of the truth of a proposition which one believes to be false or doubtful. But bearing the thought of God in mind is voluntary, to a large extent at any rate, and so can be the kind of thing we ought to cultivate, if there are any good reasons for thinking that we ought. (That one should dwell on the thought of God with a loving attitude may be more difficult to command. Perhaps, however, it may be held that, if we have a correct conception of God, it will be impossible not to love him, or impossible for the good not to love him.)

Since dwelling (favourably) on the thought of God does not necessarily produce any false beliefs, though it may, there is not this particular reason (that it results in false belief) for thinking that cultivating it is likely to make us perform actions which are not conducive to our achieving whatever ends, good or bad, selfish or unselfish, we happen to have. There is no reason, then, why we should not deliberately strengthen our resolution to persevere in our faith, for doing this is not the same thing as irrationally adhering to beliefs when reasons appear for thinking that they are false. It explains, too, why the 'intensity' with which one 'believes' is important, for it seems obvious that this fervour will increase the effects which 'believing', if you call it that, will have on one's life, whereas the intensity with which I believe that tomorrow is Tuesday will not have any important affect on my life at all, so long as I remember that tomorrow is Tuesday and act on the fact. (The very, very optimistic might then hold that an afterlife, or a happy afterlife, was a bonus of both this constantly dwelling with a favourable attitude and appropriate action, for example, acting in a manner appropriate to the idea of God on which one is constantly dwelling.)

(xxii)   More About the Value of Faith

For what I have tentatively and provisionally described as faith – or perhaps only the part of it that can be cultivated – to be a virtue, it must not only be the case (a) that it is both something different from what is normally and rightly regarded as a vice, i.e., believing things without evidence and also (b) something that is possible for us voluntarily to acquire and keep. It must also be the case that faith is valuable.

Hence what I have, rightly or wrongly, described as faith, should have desirable effects, including the immediate satisfaction it gives, on the lives of the people who have faith and those with whom they associate. By its fruits ye shall know it. That it has these effects is, at least in part, a proposition like any other proposition and to that extent a proposition which can be empirically verified.

I say 'at least in part' because the proposition that faith has desirable effects may turn out to be two propositions. (a) Faith has effects (in this world) of such-and-such a kind. (b) Effects of this kind are good. The former is an ordinary factual proposition which can be empirically investigated. The latter is a value judgment. Incidentally, I do not think faith can be a virtue because it is rewarded in another world. It should be shown to be a virtue before it can be shown to be so rewarded, even if there is another world.

If one wants to know whether faith does have good effects, there are two things one can do; one can observe its effects on those who say they have it, or make the experiment of trying to acquire it and seeing for oneself whether having it is beneficial. The proposition that faith in God has good effects is not one of the things in which we must have faith and is not itself part of faith, but a belief about faith. There is thus no reason at all why we should have faith in the proposition that faith has good effects, or believe it any more strongly than the evidence warrants.

David Hume, with a great deal of plausibility, held that virtues were qualities of character (a) useful to ourselves, (b) agreeable to ourselves, (c) useful to others or (d) agreeable to others. Two of the theological virtues, faith and hope, are not qualities of character (as opposed to faithfulness and hopefulness, which are). It does not follow that faith is not a good thing, nor that its value is assessed in the same way as are qualities of character. If so, it may be assessed by its usefulness and agreeableness. (I am using the word 'agreeable' because it is Hume's and I cannot think of a better. It means that faith is to be valued for the immediate satisfaction that it gives and not only for its effects.)

Faith can hardly be a virtue *because* it causes immediate pleasure to God (is agreeable to him), or causes longer-term pleasure to God (is useful to him) as opposed to being useful or agreeable to men. God, being perfect, cannot *benefit* from anything we do. This is not to say, however, that one would not naturally conceive of faith as being agreeable to God. God, if he is personal, might be conceived of as approving of it because it is useful or agreeable to men.

There does not seem to be any difficulty in showing that faith is *agreeable* to many people, i.e., those with religious tendencies, and it may be that everyone or almost everyone has religious tendencies, though these may for some reason or other be latent in many or most people. It does not seem, however, that faith is agreeable to everyone. Faith may also be useful to ourselves, if, for example, it enables us to be more successful in our enterprises.

I doubt however, whether faith could be a 'virtue' because it is agreeable to others. To acquire faith simply because it pleases others (presumably those of the same persuasion as oneself) that we have it would seem to be ignoble. It could be argued that a disposition to please others in such matters, beyond what is required by tact, sympathy and politeness, is harmful, since, pursued indiscriminately, it is as likely as not to encourage people in religions that are wrong-headed.

Faith will be useful to others if it strengthens in us other desirable qualities, such as kindness, loyalty, and integrity in the person who possesses it. Perhaps it strengthens all the desirable qualities there are. (More accurately, faith, or at least Christian faith, is likely to strengthen in us those qualities that we *suppose*, rightly or wrongly, to be desirable.) Faith will be useful to the person having faith for the reasons already given. If it produces bigotry, it will be harmful to self and to others.

Incidentally, these facts about the usefulness, as opposed to the pleasantness, of faith, tend to show faith to be a second-order virtue (which is not the same as a second-rate virtue.). To the extent that it is a second-order virtue, faith is useful only in so far as it strengthens other (first-order) virtues. (Another clearer case of being a second-order virtue is perfectionism, which consists in cultivating the other virtues, the existence of which perfectionism presupposes.) Whether faith is a virtue will depend largely on what sort of god one has faith in, because it is upon this that depends, at least to some extent, what qualities one regards as virtues. We will regard as virtues those qualities which we think the god we have faith in approves of. One could plausibly argue that it is the other way round; what sort of god we have faith in will depend upon the qualities which one regards as being virtues, for we will attribute to that god these qualities in forming our idea of him. It seems likely to me, however, that as a matter of psychological fact the action of our moral beliefs upon our conception of the deity is reciprocal. Sometimes our idea of the god we have faith in will determine our beliefs about what things are our duty; at other times it will be the other way around).

It may be, too, that there are some people who are worse for having faith. There are faiths which are so harsh, demanding and wrong-headed that the people who have them, and those who are affected by them, would be much better without them. And there are people who do not have faith, who are better off for not having it. For they might find having a faith too restrictive and narrowing, find it irksome and unhelpful to go through life with the thought of being watched over, find religious practices restrictive and religious people irrational, severe, censorious, intolerant, hypocritical, intellectually self-indulgent and narrowing, and find that they did not need the support that religion offers.

(xxiii)   Faith and Duty

In my opinion it is not one's duty to adopt either a life of faith or a way of life that does *not* involve faith. Which one does, if there is not actually a personal God enjoining faith, is a matter of personal choice. But, if the account of faith I have given is correct, then faith is something that it is possible voluntarily to acquire and something which one can have without cultivating irrational beliefs, which latter is a vice. To the extent that to cultivate faith is to cultivate a species of belief, it is neither voluntary nor admirable. I think it may be wise for some, but not everyone, to cultivate faith, provided that this is not a matter of cultivating belief.

My own attitude, I think, is that I am glad that some people have faith. And the truth may be that it is perfectly possible to live one's life in a satisfactory way either with faith or without it. One wishes, however, that those without faith were not so insensitive to those who have it, or that those with it were not so anxious to condemn those without it. Faith, on this view, is optional rather than obligatory. Whether one adopts it or not is morally a matter of individual choice. Which choice is most satisfactory for one will depend upon the kind of person one is. (I have already deplored the view that the statement that there is a God is true for those who have faith but false for those who do not have it.)

(xxiv)   Faith and Intolerance

The main reason why different religions have been so intolerant of one another, I think, is fear. One may fear all kinds of groups other than one's own. This is because once upon a time our survival depended upon the survival of our group in competition with other groups and we have, as a result, congenital tendencies to make us prone to treat members of other groups with suspicion and hostility, even when the groups are united spatially, like nations. This fact generates a vicious circle, in that we know that members of other groups have the same fear of us that we have of them and fear the hostile action that may be prompted by their fear of our fear of their fear of us. This tends to make us intolerant of other religions. When the religions are national we fail to tolerate them because they are the religions of possible enemies. When they are international – as they should be – we can fail to tolerate them because they bring with them practices and foreign men who may unite with one another to destroy us and our way of life. Intolerance is wider than religion, and we can be intolerant of groups other than religious groups and of beliefs other than religious beliefs.

Men with charismatic personalities who love power do not hesitate to use our fear of other groups as a means of acquiring and retaining it. They are especially able to do this when they can represent some specific group as an enemy from whom the group they wish to lead needs their leadership and protection, and offer themselves as its protector and leader. This is the way in which Hitler gained power, i.e., by offering himself as a protector against the

Jews, whom he caused to be regarded as a scapegoat. Many communist leaders have gained power by offering themselves as protectors against the bourgeoisie. Intolerance produces a vicious circle when the other group does exactly the same thing. Religious groups are not immune from this proclivity and it is an unfortunate fact about Christianity that the Hebrews' intolerant attitude to other tribes and religions can serve as a model for it, and that certain remarks of Christ's could, rightly or wrongly, be taken to give it support.

(xxv)   Thou Shalt Have None Other Gods But Us

I have several times drawn a contrast between an impersonal and eternal God and a sempiternal personal one. As I have suggested, this parallels a contrast drawn by Evelyn Underhill between the objects of two kinds of mysticism. This contrast is between 'the strange, dark, unfathomable Abyss of Pure Being always dwelt upon by mystics of the metaphysical type' and 'the divine and loved companion of the soul, whose presence is so sharply felt by those which lean to the concept of divine personality'. The first involves what Evelyn Underhill describes as the 'contemplation of transcendence'. The second she describes as 'the contemplation of immanence'. She says that there is all the difference between the two that there is 'between the preparations for a wedding and a journey to the arctic seas'.[14] Exceptionally, she says, the same people may have both attitudes.

The latter is more useful, more intelligible, and more easily prone to empirical refutation. But the companion to the soul can operate only through the men and women who have intercourse with him; there is no other way in which he can work, which puts him on a par (in this respect) with hallucinations. The more austere metaphysical God also cannot work in any other way than through the minds of those who contemplate him, though he, unlike the second God, cannot give encouragement and help. But from an eternal non-personal deity, help other than that obtained by the bare act of contemplating him ought not to be expected, though perhaps from the companion to the soul it should be. Theists can say that both are aspects of the one deity, though I myself find it impossible to reconcile them. But I suggest that there is no harm in having these 'two Gods' alternately.

It has been alleged that God is a jealous God, which might make one think twice before having two Gods. But the eternal, impersonal God is logically incapable of jealousy. The personal one, since he cannot act on the world, could not act in such a way as to do one harm, though one's relationship with him might be harmed by giving him a rival. (Perhaps, however, he would not so much be jealous, as only appear to one as being jealous, if one had another personal god as well as him.)

(xxvi)   The Advantages of a Nonexistent Over an Existent God

'Believing' in a nonexistent God – if I may be forgiven for this Irish way of talking – has advantages over believing in an existent one. One has no control over the demands made by an existent God, which may be too much for one. If God exists, he may lay it down that he is the only god to be worshipped, and that those who worship other gods, or no god at all, are to be ostracised, deprived of jobs, confined to ghettos, or massacred. If there is a God, it may be right or rational to sacrifice men to him, whereas to sacrifice the interests of men to those of a nonexistent God could achieve nothing for God or for man. One may take or leave a God one does not believe to exist, though an existent one may demand that he be not left, however much one may want to; the people I know who claim to have succeeded in eliminating the sense within them of the presence of the divine are all people who started with the advantage, for this purpose, of believing that God does not exist. Even so, it may be dangerous to play with forces that one does not properly understand.

(xxvii)   Conclusions

It may be that faith is a word for nothing clear and that several different things are being confused. Trying to proportion one's beliefs in some other manner than in proportion to the strength of the evidence for them – including the strength of their *self*-evidence – is a vice, as is faith, if it demands this. But there may be some things which are described as faith or are associated with faith or are a part of faith which have merit – though the merit has been exaggerated – and which some people ought to acquire. Bearing the thought of God in mind, trying to explore any possibility there may be of communication, together with contemplation and worship, have all – if this is not to damn with faint praise – much to be said for them, though many people seem to live lives that they find satisfactory without them. Others, however, seem to find these things essential.

All these activities do presuppose having certain beliefs *about* the activities, among which beliefs are value judgments. If one wishes to persevere in having a relationship with what presents itself as the presence of God, one must have certain beliefs about the chances of this relationship being veridical, or the value of maintaining it if it is not. One may do this without having belief in the *existence* of God and it may be possible that one can do it even if one believes in the nonexistence of God, or if we regard the question whether there is a God or not as unreal. Still less does one need to have any more specific views, such as the highly specific views annexed to Christianity, about the nature of God. (It is obvious that the more specific these views are, the more vulnerable is one's position.) The view, which I shall return to later, that God neither exists nor does not exist might, rightly or wrongly, be regarded as a way of accommodating the possibility of having the kind of relationship somewhat cursorily described, involving a concept of God and at the same time considering it of not much importance, nor an insoluble problem, nor a meaningless question, whether there is a God or not.

Since there is not a personal God – though it may be desirable to bear the thought of one constantly and favourably in mind – the 'rewards' of faith must stem from what faith is in itself and from the natural consequences of having it, rather than from any reward a personal God might bestow upon those that have it. Faith cannot literally be rewarded by a personal God if there is not one. In this respect Theravada Buddhism, as I have already suggested, seems to me to be superior to Christianity. Though escape from the wheel of birth and rebirth cannot be a natural consequence of contemplation, for there is no such wheel, one's personal happiness might well be augmented by the practice of Buddhism, though one should not expect too much in the way of bliss. There is no particular reason, however, why the God one contemplates should be personal, and contemplating a non-personal God has the advantage that the God one contemplates is more immune to empirical refutation than is a personal God. (There need be no difficulty about the existence of impersonal things like numbers.) But the situation may well be that questions of existence are meaningless or irrelevant when applied to a God whose 'function' is to be contemplated rather than to explain the universe. As I have said, explaining the universe is a job best left to natural scientists.

One should also bear in mind the possibility that there is no real need at all for faith in God, though I suspect that the truth is that some people need it and others do not. In any case, how much one needs it is a matter of degree. Faith may not be necessary if mystics are right in thinking that some of us have direct awareness of an entity, whether or not this entity can be described as God, of which they have knowledge, rather than faith. But faith may be necessary for those who have not achieved such awareness and, at times when they are not actually having it, for those who think they have achieved it.

I believe one should always listen to one's 'voices', though in a critical and experimental spirit. (One should not necessarily do what they say.) The 'rewards' of doing this are all metaphorical rewards, in that they are the natural consequences of listening. They are not the result of intervention on one's behalf by a personal God who approves of one's listening.

Faith of some kind or other than faith in God may be often be desirable – though not I think necessary – in life as well as, or instead of, faith in God. But all things in this life, not just beliefs, must be tested and weighed in the balance and discarded if found wanting.[15]

Addendum: William James on Faith

James's Argument for Irrational Belief

It is sometimes held[16] that, unless one at first believes in God without evidence for his existence, one will never obtain any evidence. Unless by prayer and devotion one attempts to establish some personal relationship with a personal God, one will not establish such a relationship and so will not obtain the necessary evidence for his existence, which evidence can only come through having this relationship.

Establishing that God exists, in this case, will be unlike establishing that a Loch Ness monster exists, for one can quite easily get evidence that there is a Loch Ness monster without first having to believe that there is one. It could be suggested that one must, even in the case of the Loch Ness monster, first believe something, say, that it is not absolutely impossible that there be a monster in Loch Ness; otherwise one would not bother to look for evidence. But even this is not necessary if one is conducting one's search not in order to find out whether there is a Loch Ness monster or not, but in order to demonstrate to other people (who perhaps are hiring one for this purpose) that there is not one.

It has, presumably, been supposed to be different with God and the Loch Ness monster because it is thought not only that one will not get evidence for his existence unless one embarks upon a devotional life, however rudimentary, and because it is furthermore supposed that one cannot embark upon a devotional life unless one first believes that there is a God. I am not sure whether either of these two propositions are true.

William James' case would not go through if it was possible to have a devotional life without believing that there is a God. (It is obviously true that it is possible to have a devotional life if there is not a God in actual fact.) Granted then, that the statement that someone worships, loves, offers up prayers and so on to God does not entail that there is a God, does it entail that this person believes that there is a God? Can a man still love his wife, although he believes that she is dead, or love Elizabeth Bennet, although he knows that she is a character in one of Jane Austen's novels? If he can, could he not, to begin with, perhaps, and in an experimental way, pray without believing in God, even if he thinks he is unlikely to make this a permanent practice? (It may be that the love one might have for a fictional character is an attenuated kind of love, as I have suggested that belief in God is an attenuated kind of belief. Love of a fictional character cannot be augmented by gratitude, for example, or expectation of favours to come, for fictional characters are impotent. If the existence of God has no (verifiable) consequences, belief that he exists must be attenuated, and one's attitude to fictional characters may be attenuated for such reasons as that one could not feel gratitude to a fictional character, though one could respect one.)

Though a wronged Frenchman cannot petition the king of France for justice, when he knows perfectly well that there is no king of France, one can certainly address letters to Father Christmas without believing that there is a Father Christmas. I have personally done so. You can sing songs of praise without believing that there is a God to praise. Lots of people do this (though whether without this belief they can be described as praising God I am not sure). Anyway, if it is logically possible to love, pray to, or worship a God without believing that he exists, then it should be possible, by doing these things, to try to get the evidence, which one is assured is obtainable, for his existence without first inducing in oneself an irrational belief that he exists. William James must in that case be wrong about this.

What Kind of Evidence for the Existence of God Would One Obtain as a Result of Making James's Experiment?

What is the nature of the evidence that one is supposed to get if one embarks upon a devotional life with or without first believing that there is a God? Perhaps it consists in obtaining some sort of response. One prays for guidance, let us say, and one gets the idea that the best thing would be to do such-and-such, with the feeling that this guidance comes from outside, that God would approve of one's doing so-and-so. One may feel that one is loved by God, or, alternatively that he strongly disapproves of one. One may acquire a sense of his presence. One may feel oneself supported and guided in everything one does. (Perhaps a sense of presence, coupled with the conviction that it is veridical, is what Cardinal Newman meant by 'real assent'.)

Personally, however, I do not see that these responses do give one the necessary evidence that there is a God. If, of course, one has decided to try to have a devotional life although one does not believe that there is a God, God will have the status in one's thoughts of a fictional character – or rather a character which we believe to be fictional – to start with, at any rate. (If we have succeeded in making ourselves straightforwardly believe that there is a God, the response just described may be the same, though if one has succeeded one will not believe the analogy with fiction.)

The trouble, if it is a trouble, with the analogy with fictional characters is that they can quite easily take on a life of their own though remaining fictional. By this I mean not just that they can quickly become very real to one, but that they can develop in ways over which their creator – I say 'creator' because I think that the analogy with faith is closer with writing fiction than with simply reading it – has little voluntary control.

Let us take one well-known example of a fictional character, the imaginary friend. One might suppose that since this friend is an imaginary friend, one could have whatever relationship with it (or him or her) that one wished to pretend one had. This is not, however, the case. The pretence is one which is not wholly deliberate, the direction it takes is not wholly within one's voluntary control, and the nature of the friend and the attitude he or she seems to take up to one are not deliberately decided upon. (Even the expression on the face of a rag dolly is not one that is consciously chosen.) And it is well known that an author's characters and their behaviour are often not laboriously worked out by him, but that they have a will of their own and do and say things of their own accord.

The 'fantasised' people studied by psychiatrists interested in investigating their patients' delusions and hallucinations are not under the conscious control of the patient – but are delusions nevertheless – and belief that there is a God, when it is firmly held, has at least one of the marks of a delusion;[17] it is not amenable to rational persuasion and does not necessarily go away when apparently conclusive reasons have been produced against the reality of its object. It might even be that one of the ways in which this delusion, if it is one, protects itself is by persuading us that it is a *merit* that it is not amenable to rational control. (For the reasons suggested in this paragraph, I do not think that the fact that people have experiences which they regard as genuine encounters with God is any proof of the existence of God. But I am not convinced that their not being veridical necessarily means that it is unwise to cultivate them.)

Hence I think that if one does try to conduct the experiment of keeping the thought of God constantly in mind and encouraging oneself to enter into an ostensibly personal relationship with the God one then constantly thinks of, the fact that this God takes up attitudes to one which one does not deliberately decide upon, so that one gets a response, is not good evidence that there is a God. In other words, that one has not got 100 per cent control over various aspects of one's inner life does not mean that having such an inner life puts one in touch with a reality which is not observable by means of the five senses, but only when one looks inwards and turns one's attention away from the external world.

But this does not necessarily mean that one should not have an inner life, or that certain kinds of inner life are not more desirable than others. Indeed, a case can be made for persevering in having a devotional inner life, even if one thinks that it is unlikely that there is anything in reality corresponding to the idea of God involved in it. (Perhaps faith, however, should not be a word for the inner life itself, but the perseverance in cultivating a devotional inner life despite the apparent lack of any reality corresponding to it.)

It is also possible to pass adverse moral judgments on what I have, rightly or wrongly, described as faith. In trying to acquire it one is at least flirting with the devil of irrationality. If one argues that if one does not take the above-mentioned steps until one first believes that there is a God one will not acquire the evidence, the natural response from someone who has not yet taken these steps is to ask how, if he has to believe in God before he can take them, he can be sure that what he will then appear to have evidence for is not an irrational belief, which he himself has deliberately acquired. If, for some reason or other, you take steps which you are told will result in your believing something that you now believe to be false, it will serve you right if, if you take them, you believe something false as a result.

Even if it is logically possible to acquire faith without also acquiring irrational beliefs, it must be psychologically difficult to do this. And even if, as I have suggested, the proposition that God exists has no verifiable consequences means that it is not a false belief which can manifest itself by your taking mistaken courses of action, this does not mean that it is not false, or that false beliefs are not undesirable. One may be led, too, irrationally to believe that faith has desirable consequences which it does not have. It may be that pretending that there is a God – for faith, on the account of it which I have just given, is little more than pretending – should be regarded as a weak self-indulgence and that we ought to face life without its aid. And the resemblance between the feeling that one is being guided from 'above', and certain symptoms of schizophrenia, when those who have it may also feel that they are being controlled, is alarming. (Faith as pretending has been discussed earlier in this chapter.)

Notes

1   Swinburne, 1981, p. 108, says that if faith does not rule out knowledge, it rules out the kind of knowledge that is incorrigible. But one ought not to claim that one knows if one thinks that there is any possibility at all that one is mistaken.

2   For example, F.R. Tennant in his astute and closely reasoned *The Nature of Belief* (1943).

3   See Braithwaite, 1955.

4   It may be that some such state of mind is similar to that which Kierkegaard describes as a 'paradox', though his paradox is the milder one of believing something with certainty while at the same time believing that the evidence for it is inconclusive.

5   Held by some minor thirteenth century theologians.

6   I have put forward this view in 'The Philosophy of Mysticism' in Harrison, 1995.

7   See Armstrong, 1953.

8   This passage, as indeed was most of this book, was written before J.L. Mackie published *The Miracle of Theism* (1982), to which I am nevertheless indebted.

9   This argument is to be found in his *Pensees*, reprinted in Penelhum, 1989.

10   This argument, incidentally, is dangerous. Though one can argue on one Saturday that the amount of money one will save if one does not bet on the National Lottery is so small that one will not be able to do anything useful with it, though one would benefit greatly from the amount one would win, it can be replied that if one makes a policy of betting every Saturday, the amount one will lose collectively on all the Saturdays on which one bets and loses is something one could do something useful with.

11   James 2:19. Quoted by Aquinas (1963–75), Question Five, Article Two.

12   It should not be forgotten that belief has been likened to fiction by Braithwaite, 1955.

13   The view that religious belief is not a kind of belief has been put forward by Smith, 1979.

14   In Underhill, 1993, p. 346.

15   W.R. Inge, speaking of the intelligence which he holds is enriched by mysticism, says 'it is never a passive spectator of the energies of the will and the raptures of the emotions, but on the contrary is ever active, coordinating, sifting and testing the whole content of experience, and maintaining a mental discipline not less arduous and not less fruitful than the moral discipline which accompanies it'.

16   For example, William James in 'The Will to Believe' (1912) and by F.R. Tennant (1943).

17   Hare once likened religious belief to a delusion in his remarks about 'bliks' in 'Theology and Falsification' (1955).

29 Unchristian Ethics

(i)   Can the Whole of Christian Ethics be Deduced From Two Fundamental Principles?[1]

The two most important principles of Christian ethics are those expressed in the conjunctive command: love the Lord thy God with all thy heart, and with all thy soul, and with all thy strength, and thy neighbour as thyself. It follows that it is a common fallacy to suppose that the Christian ethic can easily be followed by atheists, who will have difficulty with the first of the two commandments, however well they may succeed with the second. It is, I think, just an evasion to say that the former reduces to the latter on the grounds that to love thy neighbour *is* to love God. It is not.

It would be satisfying to think that all other Christian principles could be derived from these two. Whatever might be said about an ideal Christianity, this is not true of actual Christianity. Christians commonly accept, and often think (I think rightly), that they find biblical justification for accepting a heterogeneous collection of rules which they suppose to be obligatory in their own right and not simply because they can be derived from the two would-be ultimate principles aforementioned.

Among these rules are a large number that are not specifically Christian, but belong to the mores of that society which has at some time in its history become more or less Christianised. Christian rules concerning monogamy, for example, seem to have little to do with the two fundamental Christian principles already mentioned, which, taken by themselves, do not obviously prohibit having any number of wives or husbands, or men from marrying men and women marrying women, provided, perhaps, that they love one another and can manage their complicated and eccentric affairs without acrimony. And it is difficult to see that a polygamous or polyandrous people should not love God and their neighbours as much as any other. It is arguable that in fact the rules I have just mentioned have little to do with Christianity, which has simply taken them over from, perhaps, the society in which Christianity first flourished. Indeed, it seems likely that Christ himself would not have approved of some of the rules Christians actually accept.

It is not easy to see what the command to love one another as ourselves amounts to. One danger is to make it acceptable by qualifying it to such an extent that it becomes innocuous and uninteresting; the other danger is to leave it unqualified, in which case it can become fanatical. It ought not to be regarded as demanding (and, indeed, it does not demand) unlimited altruism, for then one's own welfare would count for nothing except as a means to the welfare of others and we would be loving our neighbours more than ourselves. It would be wrong to suppose that it was more than supererogatory, if it is as much as that, to sacrifice oneself for others to the extent of caring for one's own health only in order that one might help others more effectively. (This is not to say that most of us do not help others nearly enough.)

That we should love our neighbours only as much as ourselves is a view which some philosophers have thought could be deduced from utilitarianism. However, even a straightforwardly unmodified utilitarian view, which, since everyone is to count for one, must demand that we 'love' ourselves as much as others, would seem to make unrealistic demands upon most people. For in order to produce the greatest good, one would have to spend time and money on oneself and one's own dependants only when one could not produce more good by spending time and money on other people and their dependants. For most middle class people living in an economically-developed society, this would mean living on only a small fraction of one's salary and giving the rest to those more needy than themselves. It is unrealistic to think that there is any chance of more than a tiny fraction of people behaving in this way, and such saintly behaviour could also only be supererogatory (which is not to say that it would not be commendable). (Those who, like myself, take an interest in sociobiology may be interested to note that a species of men who cared for distant peoples in distress as much as they cared for friends, neighbours and relations when they were in distress would probably not have survived.)

(What I have elsewhere[2] called cumulative-effect utilitarianism, the view that we do not so much have a duty to act in such a manner as to produce good consequences as to act in a manner which would produce good consequences if everyone were to act similarly, is more conservative than utilitarianism in this respect. For example, I may be held to have a special duty to my country, my wife and family and even to myself, on the grounds that more good would be done by everybody's looking after their own countries, their own wives, their families and themselves, than by their looking after other people's countries, wives, families and people other than themselves.)

Not only can the whole of morality not be deduced from the two injunctions to love man and God; these two injunctions may conflict with one another.

(The most notorious example of this would have been provided by the predicament of Abraham, had God really commanded him to sacrifice Isaac, though a god worth worshipping could not have done.) A man having to choose between devoting himself to prayer, contemplation and the welfare of mankind may be faced with the same conflict. In the event of such a conflict, which duty should take precedence will depend upon the circumstances.

Not only cannot all moral *precepts* be deduced from the one precept that we love one another, being loving is not the only *virtue*. Among other virtues are courage, loyalty, industry, honesty, kindness, truthfulness, consideration for others, and moderation in eating and drinking. It is very doubtful whether a man, however much he cultivated being loving, would not be a better man with these other virtues as well. In theory it might seem as if loving one's comrades might make one act in the way a courageous man would act, but in practice genuine spontaneous courage would seem to be easier to draw on in an emergency. And there are many other characteristics, for example, strength and intelligence, which, though not strictly speaking virtues, are nevertheless admirable characteristics that it is well not to be without, but cannot be reduced to being loving.

If I am right in maintaining elsewhere that God cannot be affected by what men do, our duty to God must be regarded as a special case of our duty to ourselves, a duty not to deprive ourselves of the benefits of contemplating him. Since God either does not exist, or does not exist in a way that makes any difference to the world, or cannot, on account of his perfection, be benefited or harmed by what we do, it is impossible to sacrifice people, including oneself, in such a way as to do him any good.

(ii)   Does Sufficient Love Drive Out the Law?

It is an interesting question whether, in a world in which everybody loved one another as themselves, there would be any need for the moral law.[3] (If there were no need for the law, it would not follow that our present moral judgments were false, but only that they would apply only in a world in which there was not unlimited love. It is very unlikely that there ever will be such a world.)

There has been a Christian heresy (antinomianism) that holds that Christians are exempt from the moral law. (This view would have been more plausible if it had explicitly maintained that it was only antinomians who were exempt from the moral law, and then only in respect of their relations with other antinomians belonging to the same community.) Antinomians appear to have held that it was on account of having received grace that Christians were so exempt, rather than on account of the plenitude of their love. I make antinomians, if there still are any, a present of the view that it was grace that gives them the power to love one another to an extent that made the moral law unnecessary for them.

The case for thinking that adequate love exempts one from the moral law has been best made, oddly enough, by 'St' David Hume.[4] (Hume actually said only that it would make justice unnecessary, and he did not think of justice as the whole of morality.) In a world where there was ample love, there would be no need for justice, for no man would purposely injure another, and because each man would willingly give to his neighbour anything his neighbour wanted and so there would be no need for private property.

However, though in a world in which there was unlimited love there would be less need for morals than there is in this world, unlimited love would not make morals totally unnecessary. To produce an ordered society, people would need to be allocated tasks, such as care of children, and stick to those tasks regardless of the more capricious prompting of love, even if that love took the form of universal beneficence. And there would still need to be what might be described as organisational duties. In order for men to cooperate with one another, they would still need to work to set hours and to keep their appointments, and not allow an excess of love to lead them to break them. The statement 'Amo et fac quod vis' is only partially true. They would also need some relief from a duty to love others which duty might become intolerably burdensome, and to be allowed to get on with some valuable activities that are important to them, and which have only a tenuous connection with love. And some of the spice might go out of life without a certain amount of unfriendly competition.

(iii)   Are Christians' Duties More Stringent Than Those of Other People?

Though the antinomians thought that moral rules that were binding upon other people were not binding upon Christians, it is a more common Christian belief that there are moral rules that are binding upon Christians that are not binding upon other people. The duties of Christians, on this view, are more stringent than those of others and the duties of members of certain Christian organisations more stringent than those of ordinary Christians. For example, a Christian might have a duty to evangelise which another man would not have, and a nun a duty to be celibate or what is worse, silent, which another Christian might not have. (Those who think that the best that can be said for marriage is that it is better than to burn may perhaps be inclined to regard the rigours of celibacy as exaggerated.)

One reason for thinking that the duties of Christians are more stringent than those of others is that Christians think that they have more stringent views about what is incumbent upon *everyone* than other people have. If this were true it would imply that the duties of Christians are more stringent than others for two reasons. In the first place, a man is under some obligation to practice what he preaches, which will mean that his duties are more stringent than those of someone else, who – rightly or wrongly – does not profess so great a degree of stringency. In the second place, there is a distinction between objective and subjective duty, and there is some plausibility in the view that if we think that we have certain (objective) duties, we actually do have a (subjective) duty to do the things which we only think, and perhaps think mistakenly, are objective duties. We are to be blamed for doing things we even mistakenly think are wrong. (I am sure, however, that a Thuggee who thinks it is his duty to strangle people is not to be praised for doing things which would, on this view, be subjectively right.) Hence the Christian will have duties that are more stringent than those of other people to the extent that the duties he rightly or wrongly thinks everybody has are more stringent than the duties other people think they have. (I doubt, however, whether Christians are right if they think that Christian duties really are more stringent than those demanded by other religions.)

But in one way, the Christian view of morals is *less* stringent than many non-Christian ones. It is easier for Christians than it is for other people to apply the Christian ethic. It has been for many years customary for people whom I would describe as non-Christians to hold, I think mistakenly, that they can remain Christians if they adopt the Christian ethic, even if they do not adopt Christian religious beliefs. But in trying to observe the Christian ethic atheists are likely to be taking upon themselves the full rigours of the Christian morality without any of the consolations of the Christian religion. And it is very easy for irreligious men, in what religious men might call their arrogance, to expect more of themselves than might have been expected by a loving and forgiving God.

Another way in which Christian morals may be less stringent is that the Christian doctrine of grace, or one element of it, may imply that, without grace, morality is beyond one's power, which doctrine to some extent removes the burden of morality from the shoulders of man to that of God. For it is God who vouchsafes grace; if he refuses there is perhaps no point in worrying excessively about one's inevitable shortcomings, and if he refuses one will not in fact worry. It could be that this is a healthier attitude than one of constant over-anxiety and guilt. But it is not often suggested that, if it really is true that we cannot avoid sinning without grace, we ought not to be punished for what we cannot avoid.

(iv)   Christianity and Forgiveness

Christianity places a very high value on forgivingness and regards forgiveness as a duty that is very stringent. Christ, indeed, seems to have thought that there were no situations in which we ought not to forgive our enemies and it is reasonable to suppose that, *a fortiori*, he thought that we ought to forgive our friends to the same extent.

It has sometimes been supposed that an unlimited duty to forgive people would preclude punishing them, but this is not so. Punishment and mercy, both of which (to avoid partiality and perpetual strife) should be exercised by an authority who has not himself been wronged, should not be confused with revenge and forgiveness which, as a matter of logic, can be exercised only by the injured and perhaps others who, like his dependants, are themselves injured by an injury to him.

Nevertheless, though taking the law into one's own hands by retaliating for injuries is a socially harmful practice which a developed legal system cannot possibly permit, *unlimited* forgiveness – especially in a society in which there is little or no law – is also itself socially harmful.

It is obvious that in a society where there are strong laws forgiveness may be safely practised to a much greater extent than in a society were there are not. But it is unwise for a community to prohibit by law *everything* that is wrong. For example, adultery and fornication are best not dealt with by the law, even when they are wrong, as they sometimes are. Where there is no law, whether because to have a law is undesirable or where the law there is is ineffective, retaliation within certain limits is necessary to prevent there being a race of men who flourish on the misplaced, and possibly fanatical, meekness of others. (Forgiveness should not be practised to an inordinate extent by married couples, who may find otherwise that the consequent resentment spoils their relationship.)

The same is true of many of the other virtues extolled in the Sermon on the Mount. A society in which everybody is meek beyond a certain point would be defenceless and a society in which some people are meek, but others are not, is an open invitation for the meek to be exploited. It can lead to the meek exploiting the less meek by behaviour that is parasitic on their being defended by others when they refuse to defend themselves. If there were another world in which the meek obtained their supposedly just reward, meekness beyond a certain point might then not be a vice, or not a vice for the reason that it harmed the meek person himself. But since we have to make do with the world we have, excessive meekness encourages the bullies, the over-weening and unscrupulously ambitious. (Excessive and prolonged meekness is not only harmful in its consequences, it is also aesthetically displeasing.)

I have no doubt that, since the people who laid down many Christian moral rules and asserted many Christian moral judgments, were giving practical advice to simple people, not writing text books of moral philosophy, they intended what they said to be only for the most part true, or to be only as a general rule obeyed, or were pushing people too far in one direction because of man's natural tendency to lean too far to the opposite one.

(v)   Sociobiology and Forgiveness[5]

Richard Dawkins once envisaged[6] a group of birds who could survive satisfactorily only if they picked harmful ticks off one another's heads. A bird who (not knowing his Kant) did not pick the ticks off other birds' heads, but nevertheless allowed other birds to pick ticks off his, would save time and energy. Hence he and his offspring would tend to survive at other birds' expense. But if all birds were highly 'rational' and benefited from having other birds pick ticks off their heads without wasting time and energy on reciprocation, no birds would go in for tick-picking and all birds would have ticks. Such a race of birds would become extremely miserable and eventually perish.

But though a society of birds none of whom picked ticks off other birds would be temporarily unhappy and finally extinct, a society of birds all of whom picked ticks off one another's heads whether this service was reciprocated or not would be unstable. This is because they would be vulnerable to any bird and its offspring who might, by some chance mutation, come to be born without this tendency. Such birds would gain an advantage over their more virtuous neighbours on account of the time and energy they saved by not tick-picking. Dawkins believes that a stable state would eventually be reached when all or almost all birds pick ticks off other birds heads only so long as their tick-picking is reciprocated, but not otherwise.

(Reflecting on this example suggests that one function of moral sentiment in man is to encourage that altruism which is necessary for cooperation. Perhaps birds pick the ticks off other birds from a love of the individual bird, from an altruistic love of birdkind, because they like the taste, or because they cannot help doing so. But if they felt guilty if they did not pick the ticks off other birds, this would have the same beneficial effect.)

Jesus Christ is said to have told us to forgive our neighbours until 70 times seven.[7] But if Dawkins is right it should be possible for an evolutionary biologist to predict that a belief in unlimited forgiveness – forgiveness in moderation of others in one's community is conducive to the survival of the forgiving species – would not be very prevalent in any society of animals like ourselves. Having this belief would cause its possessors not to survive if they acted on it. (Professing unlimited forgiveness would be harmless enough.) I suspect this shows that unlimited forgiveness is not obligatory and is commendable, if at all, only so long as it does not become a universal rule.

Everything is what it is and not another thing. It does not at all follow from what Dawkins says that all human motivation is selfish (let alone that genes are selfish. Genes are not the kind of thing that can be either literally selfish or unselfish). It may be that we are altruistic because altruism is conducive to the survival of our own genes rather than to the genes of the species *homo sapiens*. If a member of a species helps another, it is in the interest of the member helped to help the member helping and *vice versa*, for by doing so each helps himself. But from this it no more follows that altruism is not a disinterested desire for the welfare of others than it follows from the fact that hunger is also conducive to the survival of our genes that hunger is a *desire* for the survival of our genes, rather than what it in fact is, a desire to eat. (It does not follow that because altruism is a love of others, acting on it is not conducive to the survival of the individual altruist, who may be better off living in an altruistic society than in an egotistical one.) Most of the confusions about sociobiology were pointed out by Bishop Butler in the eighteenth century.

(vi) Christianity and the Golden Rule[8]

Christ is said to have said: 'Therefore all things whatsoever ye would that men should do to you, do you even so to them; for this is the law and the prophets.' I shall refer to this as the 'Golden Rule'.

As it stands, the Golden Rule enjoins giving large quantities of meat to a vegetarian, on the grounds that that is what you would want *him* to give *you*. The reply to this might be that it mentions a want – a want for meat – that is too specific. What my overall desire is is that others should treat me as I want them to treat me, so I should treat others as they want me to treat them. This is not quite the same as to satisfy my wants, for I might desire money, but not to be given money by Tom, who has annoyed me or cannot afford it. (This does not mean that Tom would object to being given money by me.) And they might have desires that were bad desires, or, though not bad, should not be satisfied in the way they want them to be, or, though not bad, were not 'rational', or not sensible, or were desires which it was not in their long-term interest of their possessors that I should satisfy. But one could not say that one should satisfy their good, 'rational', sensible, or desires which were in their long-term interest, for one has to live with people and this can be done only by compromising between satisfying the desires they do not actually have, but would have if they were good or 'rational' or sensible, and those they actually have. Perhaps one should sometimes, though not always, give children or ones wife or one's friends what they actually want, not what one thinks they ought to want, or would be good for them.

One must also consider not only the desires of the person (or persons) one is treating in the way one may think is prescribed by the Golden Rule, but of other people upon whom one's action might have side-effects. If so, perhaps one should not stop short of considering the desires (or the good, sensible, 'rational' or long-sighted desires) of all the people affected by the action. This may lead to some kind of utilitarianism, according to which it is right to produce the maximum satisfaction of desires.

But even this version of the Golden Rule, distant though it seems from the original, leads to what is to my mind its most serious criticism; it applies only to what might be called 'holiday situations' (though the expression is misleading, as some holiday situations, for example, acts of supererogation which involve one's giving enormous sums of money to charity, may involve one's conferring enormous benefits upon, or receiving them from, others).

I recently heard a distinguished speaker going in great detail into the question of, if one preferred to go to meet one's students on foot and they preferred that one should go by bicycle, which preferences one should satisfy. Normally I should say it was no business of theirs how I got to my lecture, but I gather the lecturer's habit of going to his lectures on foot was making him late. Presumably they preferred him to lecture to them and to lecture to them on time rather than not, or they would not have complained. But I myself would only have paid attention to their preferences about how I got there if they had wanted me to lecture on time. Had they preferred me not to lecture, I should (I hope) have ignored their preference. I would have thought that I ought to arrive on time because that was the time appointed for my lecture, that I had contracted with my university to lecture at appointed times, and that it was in consequence my duty to give the lecture. Both my preferences and theirs would have been irrelevant. And I would have considered their preference, that I walk, not so much *qua* preference, but because, if my walking was making me late, there was a rule entitling them to complain and imposing upon me some obligation to attend to their complaint.[9]

In this situation I was applying a rule, and applying it with only a perfunctory consideration, if any, of the preferences of the people affected by my applying it, and the same would have been true if I had been keeping a promise, paying a debt,[10] caring for my wife and children, reporting a felony, attending a meeting, registering a birth, keeping an appointment, or not putting my knife in my mouth when I eat, to take just a few from an enormous range of examples of varying degrees of importance.

My obeying such rules often does not have good consequences and does not maximise preferences. The good is produced by these rules being in general obeyed, even though each individual act of obedience does not do much good, or even does harm. The reason why I should obey such rules, regardless of how much good I could produce or preferences satisfy by departing from them, is that the good the rules produce is produced only if they are obeyed in (most of the) cases when obeying them does no good. (Analogously, since no candidate in a large election ever gets in by one vote, if everybody whose voting made no difference to its result did not vote, a difference would be made to the result.) Of course, applying the rules will have good consequences if the rules are generally applied. But the good consequence in question result only from the performance of enough members of the class of actions to which my action belongs, in which case they will result whether I perform my action or not. Since I should, within reason, obey society's rules even if everybody does not do the same, my duty to obey them cannot be derived from my treating anyone as he wants to be treated and so cannot be derived from the Golden Rule. For example, my not treating a patient in accordance with the Golden Rule by not admitting him to an overcrowded hospital may do no good to the patient or anybody else and by itself make no contribution to the good produced by the rules that such patients be not admitted. It must be obeyed because of the harm that would be done if nonobservance of the rule became universal.

It follows that I ought to apply the Golden Rule, to the extent that I should apply it at all, only when there is no more mundane rule prescribing my behaviour, though doubtless I should not apply any of these rules quite apart from any consideration of how serious the harm done by any individual breach, or without any consideration of whether an accepted rule is one that we might be better off without. What rules actually are useful will vary from one place, time and culture to another, and there are some useful rules, of which Christians might not approve, in other cultures.

The Golden Rule itself is not 'culture-relative' – indeed, the rule, if there was one, that when in Rome one should do as the Romans do would demand culture-relative behaviour, but would not itself be culture-relative. However, the Golden Rule practised in cultures different from our own might demand some such thing as that one give one's wife to a guest who asked for her. (Indeed, I am not sure the Golden Rule itself might not sometimes demand this in this culture.)

One of society's less obvious rules is one allocating to each of its able-bodied members a special responsibility for himself, or to take care of himself. It seems obvious to me that good consequences or preference satisfaction would arise from everybody's obeying this rule, unless one stood in some special relationship to the actor, like being one's spouse, one's child or one's friend. But such a rule is in conflict with the Golden Rule, as it demands that, with the generality of men in the most usual situations, we put ourselves first.

But I suspect that the Golden Rule was never intended to be taken so literally as it has been and that the modifications we have been discussing were far from Christ's mind. His injunction would have been far less effective had it been made more precise.[11]

The Golden Rule and Treating People Alike

The rule, if there is one, to the effect that we ought to treat all similar men similarly is not the same as the Golden Rule, as it does not mention their wants. The former rule entails that we should treat others as (we would that) they should treat us only when there is no difference, or no relevant difference, or no important difference, between the two of us, and usually there is such a difference. And such a rule would have great difficulty in explaining how it could be right to love some people but not others. (The principle that if an action is right, any similar action performed by a similar person in similar circumstances must also be right, also does not entail the Golden Rule.)

The alleged rule that we ought to act as if everybody else were acting rightly, even if they are not, is a different matter from the Golden Rule.[12] In any case, there is no such rule. If there were one, it would entail that we ought not to send criminals to prison, for in a world in which everybody acted rightly there would be no criminals.

(vii) The Ten Commandments

The Ten Commandments are not exclusively Christian, but they have been largely retained by Christianity. I shall make some brief comments, one by one, upon aspects of them which I believe to be of philosophical interest. One rather obvious point I should like to make about all of them is that none of them can hold in all circumstances. For sometimes they clash with one another and it is always possible to imagine a world in which the consequences of obeying one of them would be so disastrous that, in these exceptional circumstances, it ought not to be acted on. The Ten Commandments cannot be ordered in a hierarchy, as which should take precedence would depend upon the circumstances. The Ten Commandments, then, can be regarded as the 10 rules of guidance – and very sensible ones too – rather than as holding and being intended to hold, without any exceptions whatsoever.

1   Thou Shalt Have None Other Gods But Me

This commandment invites the question 'Who's me?' It might be supposed to presupposes polytheism to the extent that it suggests that there are other gods, but that the people being addressed should not 'have' them. But the statement that one should not have gods other than the one God does not imply that there is more than one God, since nonexistent gods may be worshipped. Strictly speaking, an atheist would not be disobeying it, since, normally, he would not have any gods at all.

This commandment does not actually assert that one should as much as worship the one God, but I suppose it may be implied or suggested that one should. If so, the question arises whether one should worship God only if one believes that there is a God, or whether one can, and perhaps should, worship God whether one believes that there is one or not. As I have said, I suspect one can, though perhaps only in a tentative and experimental way. When one sees how much harm can be done by people who worship with full commitment and conviction, perhaps there is something to be said for a more tentative and experimental attitude to worship.

2   *Thou Shalt Not Make to Thyself Any Graven Image, Nor the Likeness of Anything That Is in Heaven Above, or in the Earth Beneath, or in the Water Under the Earth. Thou Shalt Not Bow Down to Them, Nor Worship Them: For the Lord thy God am a Jealous God, and Visit the Sins of the Fathers Upon the Children Unto the Third and Fourth Generation*

One wonders how one can make an image that is a likeness of anything in Heaven, if Heaven is not spatio-temporal. Perhaps 'attempted likeness' is all that is implied.

If the statement that God visits the sins of the fathers upon the children unto the third and fourth generation is simply a medical one, it will sometimes be an underestimate; if the visitation is a punishment, it will, since it is not always exacted, be capricious. I have sympathy with discouraging the worship of graven images if this, as it must usually do, involves endowing them with characteristics which graven images cannot have, such as the capacity to work miracles or intercede on our behalf. But this ban cannot be extended to the length of making worshipping them illegal. For one, thing it would not do any good, as refraining from such worship can only be of any value if it is not enforced. For another thing, it is impracticable.

The yoga practice of contemplating or meditating upon an object in order to alter one's 'spiritual' state, should not be regarded as breaking the first commandment, as it is a matter of fixing one's attention on the object and does not involve endowing what is contemplated with qualities that it does not possess. There is no reason why it should not be the deity that is the object of such contemplation. It does not seem to me to be impermissible to use graven images as an aid to worship rather than as objects of worship, or to worship God through them rather than worshipping them.

3   *Thou Shalt Not Take the Name of the Lord Thy God in Vain*

I feel that taking the name of God in vain shows a certain insensitivity. It will not be punished by God for there is not a God, or not a God the kind who can intervene in the affairs of man. It should not be illegal, for to do so would involve turning many, if not most, respectable citizens into criminals and, since the views of different religions about what is blasphemous differ, also involve either inviting each religion to impose its own views about what is blasphemous on others or giving an unwise preference to the views of one religion (or sect). Religion, like academic belief, ought not to be excessively protected by law, for the result will be religions that are sickly and cannot survive the test of pooled experience.

4   *Remember That Thou Keep Holy the Sabbath-day. Six Days Shalt Thou Labour, and Do All That Thou Hast To Do; But the Seventh Day is the Sabbath of the Lord thy God*

This commandment involves the superstitious idea that out of the seven days of the week there is one that is the Sabbath, whereas, human convention apart, all days are alike except for weather. Proper attention to this fact might enable different religions to celebrate the same day of the week. There is much to be said for keeping one day a week different from the others and even for setting this aside for contemplation of the deity by those so disposed; it might be to expect too much of human nature to contemplate him every day. But I do not know that such Sabbath-day observance should be forced upon those disinclined for it.

5   *Honour Thy Father and Thy Mother, That Thy Days be Long in the Land that the Lord thy God Giveth Thee*

I am, partly as a parent and partly from utilitarian reasons, in favour of this commandment, though it is difficult to see why longevity could result from keeping it, unless parents had been given the power of enforcing it, which, alas, they have not. I say 'partly for utilitarian reasons' as a society which honours its parents, or at least cares for them, will be happier and more stable than one which does not. Some parents do not deserve honour, but one should do one's best. One's 'parent' should not necessarily mean one's biological parent; in some societies children are not reared by their fathers but by their uncles, and in those cases it is their uncles who should be honoured. In these days I suppose 'Honour thy father and thy mother' should be read as 'Honour thy father and/or thy mother', even if stepfathers and stepmothers and one's parent's partner(s) are not also included.

6   *Thou Shalt Do No Murder*

I shall say later (in section xxiii) all I want to say about this commandment.

7   *Thou Shalt Not Commit Adultery*

There are excellent utilitarian reasons for this commandment, on account of the social disruption adultery produces. 'Adultery' should probably be defined as departing from the marriage practices of the society in which one lives, without there being any suggestion that these are either perfect or sacrosanct. It would be to stretch things to regard prohibiting adultery as prohibiting divorce. This, rather than any other commandment, should be regarded as a rule of guidance, as circumstances are so varied and complex, living with other people so difficult, and the sexual urge so strong. Adultery involving the consent of all the parties may sometimes be innocuous, especially if there are no children involved; indeed, the line between it and a marriage guided by unconventional and private rules may be thin. Adultery is not the same thing as fornication, which is a derogatory name for certain relationships which may or may not be immoral, depending on the circumstances.

One bad effect of an attitude to marriage which regards it, as the result of a special kind of vow, as sacrosanct is to make people overlook the real reasons for making marriage permanent, which is the welfare of children and, less importantly, the need for a cooperation between two people which is most effective only if kept up for a long period, and possibly for life. Neither of these are overriding reasons for staying married, even when there are children. I once believed that divorce should be by consent for the childless, totally prohibited to those with children. I now think this attitude too extreme, but not much too extreme.

I myself would like to see the law concerning prostitution in any country similar to this country (i.e., the United Kingdom of Great Britain and Northern Ireland) changed to allow prostitutes to have the protection of the law, especially from exploitation, compelled to work in disease-free environments, reliably to receive an appropriate wage for the service they provide, to be allowed to form an effective trade union, and to be compelled to pay income tax. I feel that the attitude just outlined would be a more 'Christian' (in a wide sense) attitude to prostitution than the one that is prevalent. I do not suppose that resorting to prostitutes or making one's living from those who do is the most admirable way of conducting one's life, but one should not confuse questions about the morality of a practice with questions about the morality of the different ways of regulating it.

8   *Thou Shalt Not Steal*

I feel it unnecessary to discuss this obviously useful commandment in view of what I shall say about the tenth commandment

9   *Thou Shalt Not Bear False Witness Against Thy Neighbour*

There are obvious utilitarian reasons for this commandment. It is of minor interest that it does not forbid lying as such, but I dare say this is an oversight.

10   *Thou Shalt Not Covet Thy Neighbour's Wife, Nor His Servant, Nor His Maid, Nor His Ox, Nor His Ass, Nor Anything That is His*

It has been said that this is the only commandment that prohibits a feeling, rather than an action, but I imagine the feelings are dangerous because liable to produce actions that are dangerous. There are, again, excellent and obvious utilitarian reasons for such a commandment.

One wonders what one's attitude to it should be in a society where property was very unequally distributed. Usually one should work to change the rules of distribution while observing the rules that one's society already has, as some might work for a rule enforcing driving on the right hand side of the road while themselves quite properly driving on the left. Whether force should be used to change them would depend upon how bad these rules were and how much bloodshed would be involved in making the change. It would both be unrealistic and fail to reward talent to have an equal (as opposed to an equitable) distribution of property. It is reprehensible for a society to starve or otherwise denigrate people simply because it does not allow them to work, though it may be very difficult to pinpoint any specific people who are to blame for this situation. If I were really starving, I hope I would steal food, preferably from the rich.

Not only do the Ten Commandments permit of exceptions and need to be interpreted with some latitude; it is obvious that there is a large and heterogenous collection of things that are not prohibited by any of them but which are nevertheless wrong.

A utilitarian like myself must think that the actions allegedly commanded by God are wrong, because harmful, and would remain wrong even if not commanded by him. If one were both a utilitarian and a theist, one would think that God commanded what was useful and prohibited what was harmful. But I doubt whether a utilitarian ought to think that being commanded by

God itself gave one an extra reason for not performing certain actions. Actions prohibited by God are not *per se* harmful, but only because what God prohibits is harmful. A theist who was not a utilitarian could think that there was a superior second-order commandment enjoining obedience to all the others. Then he might think that a sufficient utilitarian explanation could be given of the wrongness of breaking them, but that added to this was the further fact that in breaking them one was also disobeying God (see chapter 8).

(viii)   Some Christian Virtues

Peacemaking

Peacemakers, with certain notable exceptions like Chamberlain at Munich, are undoubtedly blessed; they will not inherit the earth, though they may make it more likely that other people will.

Humility

Humility is a Christian virtue of doubtful merit. One would have thought that it was dangerous to overate oneself, as this would lead one to undertake enterprises for which one was not suited and could not satisfactorily complete. On the other hand, one would have supposed that it was unduly limiting to underrate oneself, as there would then be many desirable enterprises that one would not undertake. One ought indeed have a just assessment of oneself, though modesty may demand that one appears slightly to underrate oneself in public, to one's friends if not to one's constituents. One's mental health and success in action may demand that one slightly overrates one's capacities. Even if the less bad thing is to have an accurate appreciation of them, it is better to err on the side of overestimating than of underestimating them.

But humility may not be a name for an alleged virtue that has to do with self-assessment so much as one that has to do with appropriate behaviour. An agricultural labourer might think he ought to behave with due humility to his betters, even though privately thinking himself abler and cleverer than they. This virtue has to do with behaving according to one's station in life, a virtue which is conducive to the stability of society and in consequence valuable in a society that deserves to be stable (though some undervalued individuals may suffer in such a society). It must be said that even those in higher places in society are supposed to be humble, but I think that all humility in this context entails is not taking advantage of one's superior position to treat others with arrogance, lack of respect, or to ride roughshod over them. A man in a superior position who behaved just as humbly – as opposed to just as politely – as a man in an inferior one would seem absurd. It would not be amiss always to bear in mind one's own insignificance in relation to God, if there is a God and, indeed, even if there is not. But thinking that one is the son of God, whatever else it is, is not a manifestation of humility, even if one is the son of God.

I suspect that much of my criticism of humility may be based on a misunderstanding. This misunderstanding, if I am right in suggesting that there is one, is thinking that 'humility' is a name for an extreme, when in fact it is the name for a mean. What people describe as humility may in fact be simply lack of arrogance and I have no doubt that this is a virtue. Arrogant people undertake tasks that are beyond them because they overestimate their abilities and have poor relations with others because they treat them with lack of respect. I doubt whether there is a name for that extreme which is the opposite of arrogance. 'Humility', however, may be ambiguous and sometimes be a name for the mean and at others a name for the extreme. If or when it is a name for the mean, it is a virtue; otherwise it is a vice.

Faith, Hope and Charity

Faith, hope and charity are the theological virtues. Faith and hope cannot be virtues, for they are not qualities of character, but that does not mean that they may not be admirable. I have said enough about faith in the chapter on faith. Charity is unquestionably a virtue. It is natural to hope for one's salvation, though perhaps one ought not to cling to such hope too strongly if the chances of its being realised are small beyond a certain point.[13]

Piety

I am tempted to regard piety as a virtue, despite the fact that it appears to presuppose God's existence. Though usually the God it presupposes is a fuller-blooded entity that the one I am prepared to countenance (because consequences about the world are supposed to follow from the former's existence), considering how one's conduct would look to a being who overviewed it, and paying 'him' the tribute of being guided by the result, has much to be said for it. (I say 'him' not from feminism, but because of doubt whether you should use the pronoun to refer to a nonexistent God. I have elsewhere said that contemplation of the deity does not provide us with divine access to knowledge of right and wrong, but it might give us access to the results of valuable subconscious ratiocination.)

However, I also regard with admiration that independent attitude which goes through life without asking for help, or considering what any supernatural being would think. These two ways of life may be incompatible, but there is no inconsistency in holding that each is valuable in its different way.

Chastity

I feel that chastity only in moderation can be a virtue. Immoderate chastity can undermine the health of the man or woman who practices it and deprive actual or possible partners of the physical love they need. Naturally, one's sexual arrangements should involve consideration and respect for all the parties involved, whoever they may be. It would be superstitious to suppose that sexual desire is turned into love, or *vice versa*, by a marriage ceremony or its absence (though perhaps it sometimes can be by even erroneous beliefs about the marriage ceremony's efficacy, or, indeed, by the erroneous belief that one has undergone one). The power of a few people may be augmented by chastity, but what they do with the power may be questionable.

Unworldliness

I suspect most people pay at least lip service to this alleged virtue. The problem I find with unworldiness is that it brings with it ignorance of the world and no kind of ignorance can be good, though doubtless knowledge of the world may be bought at too high a price.

But perhaps worldliness does not refer to knowledge of the world, about which one should be realistic, so much as to accepting its standards. The standards of the world are not necessarily wrong, though it is a platitude to say that they can be improved on; but not everybody who tries to improve on them succeeds. I would myself have a preference for a comfortable and benign worldliness over a misguided moral or religious fanaticism, but these are not exclusive alternatives. It is possible, though I suspect difficult, to behave as a moral and religious fanatic would behave, but over causes that are not, as theirs are, misguided.

Obedience

Obedience to one's conscience, or to the voice of God when it appears as one's conscience, is mostly a virtue, provided one does not accept its edicts uncritically, realises that its voice may be no more than the 'internalised' voice of other people, and does not become the slave of conscience to the extent of neglecting other valuable activities or becoming a social pain.

Suffering

One should attempt to avoid suffering, both for oneself and others, rather than make a virtue of it, but if one cannot avoid it one should do one's best to profit from it. A god who does not interfere in the course of nature cannot be responsible for suffering. Hence it is not to be welcomed as a sign of love. It would seem to me to be entirely proper for a suffering person to end his own life, and should be made the duty of those responsible for him to help him, if he so wishes, or when he may be presumed to have such a wish that he is incapable of expressing.

Suicide

Suicide is not a character trait and so not a virtue, but it is convenient to discuss it here. Whether suicide is right or wrong depends entirely upon the circumstances. The Christian view that it is wrong, I think, depends partly upon a misreading of the sixth commandment. I can see no difference in principle between interfering with the course of nature by killing oneself and interfering with it by gardening. In both cases something different will happen if I interfere from what would have happened had I not interfered. If God is not responsible for the course of nature, I am not interfering. Life is neither more nor less a gift from God than plants are.

Final Comment

I should have thought that it was one characteristic of Christianity not so much to have a different list of virtues from other lists – though some items on the lists are different – as to demand that virtuous actions be performed in a different spirit, i.e., in the spirit of one being commanded by a loving God. It cannot be a duty to perform actions in this spirit, as there is not a loving God and it could not be a *duty* to believe that there was one, even if there was one.[14] Whether I ought to act in something like this spirit, even if one thinks that there is not a God, raises issues discussed in other chapters.

(ix)   Characteristic Common to the Virtues

I believe that Hume was roughly correct in holding that virtues are qualities of character useful or agreeable to oneself or to others and holding that the opposite was true of vices. Hume himself was probably an atheist, but if one includes – as Hume himself did not – the deity among the 'others' to whom virtue must be useful or agreeable, then his account of virtues becomes more religiously inclined. If, however, one holds that God would approve only of qualities of character that were useful or agreeable to others of his creatures, the result would be a list of virtues something like Hume's. If, on the other hand, one thought that God's satisfactions might compete with those of his creatures, Hume might have to allow that fasting deleterious to one's health might also be a quality agreeable to 'others', the 'others' in this case being God. But I doubt whether I would approve of having an image of a God who did find behaviour harmful to others pleasing.

(x)   The Seven Deadly Sins

The tradition that pride, covetousness, envy, gluttony, anger, sloth and lust are (deadly) sins is a Christian one and I do not disagree with it. I find it difficult unequivocally to condemn lust when it is satisfied with the consent of both parties, when neither party is exploited and when no undue inconvenience is imposed upon third parties, though doubtless excessive preoccupation with sex is a bad thing. (How much preoccupation is excessive I would not like to say.) It should not be forgotten that a modern industrial society can flourish only if there is a demand for greater and greater luxuries – which tend to be regarded as necessities once we get used to having them – and that art, literature, and science depend upon this society's flourishing. Widespread abstinence can cause unemployment.

(xi)   Christian Lack of Realism

It is interesting to contemplate to what extent the value Christians place on certain virtues is due to a false presupposition, viz., that there is a God, or the kind of God who cares for us as his children and will reward us for virtue, or what Christians regard as a virtue, in an afterlife, and perhaps as a punishment for vice.

The term 'realism', even apart from certain technical uses in philosophy, which uses I shall ignore, is ambiguous. It is usually opposed to 'idealism', but there is a good and a bad sense of 'idealism'. 'Idealism' can mean having high aims, or having unrealistic assessments on matters of fact. There is much to be said for the former, nothing for the latter. (Cynicism involves having a (perhaps) unrealistically low opinion of men's motivation and behaviour and so is compatible with idealism in the sense of having high aims. Indeed, valuing high aims can actually produce cynicism if one feels that people, perhaps including oneself, do not live up to them.)

There is a strand in the New Testament that is idealistic in the bad sense, i.e., unrealistic. We will not, like the lilies of the field, be clothed if we do not spin. We do need to take thought for the morrow (though doubtless many take too much thought for it) and, in a hard climate, we do need to make or procure shoes. God will not help those who do not help themselves. (I have already (in section iii) made some remarks about the lack of realism involved in an excessive commendation of meekness.)

One's Heavenly father will not care for one in this world (though contemplating him may help one care for oneself) and there is no other. If there are not such places as Heaven and Hell, he cannot care for one in the next world either. If there were such places, there seems to be some injustice involved in sending men to Heaven or Hell, for God must himself be responsible for men's having the characteristics that resulted in their going there. But it would not be the kind of injustice involved in rewarding or punishing people for things they had not done. 'Natural' justice might seem to dictate a series of states, graduated in unpleasantness, corresponding to people's graduated degrees of virtue, rather than two extreme ones.

If Heaven were not a *reward* for goodness but its *natural consequence*, the case might be different. But happiness is not invariably the natural consequence of goodness. Though virtue tends to happiness and vice to misery, this tendency can be overridden by other factors such a ill health, stupidity or bad luck.

(xii)   Christian Vices

There are also certain Christian vices, both in the sense that they are held by Christians to be vices and in the sense that they are vices to which Christians are prone. Among the latter are hypocrisy, censoriousness, intolerance, priggishness, and self-righteousness. These vices, however, are not specifically Christian. They are the occupational disease of all who take a more than average interest in morality. The vices one might expect Christians to have, of being excessively meek, humble, forgiving, loving, and of unrealistically expecting God to do for them – for example, clothe them like lilies – what they are not prepared to do for themselves, I have not noticed are ones they often do have. There are minority sects that do have them, for example, the Amish, but they are usually regarded as being eccentric.

(xiii)   Christian Asceticism

The practice of asceticism for the sake of achieving a higher esteem in this or another world is to be deplored. It is to be deplored in the case of the other world because it will be unsuccessful and in the case of this world because it is to be ascetic for a motive that is cheap and hypocritical.

Asceticism, however, can be recommended both for its own sake, as it provides a tension to life that some people need, and as a means to certain ends, such as – or so I am told – excellence in scholarship. It is a challenge and a stimulus that some people need. The amount of asceticism one ought to practice depends upon the temperament of the man who practices it.

I cannot, however, find it in my heart to condemn the man who is not ascetic. It really does take all sorts to make a world. Asceticism cannot be obligatory because it is demanded by personal God, because there is not a God of the sort that can demand asceticism or anything else, but it may well be an aid to contemplation of the deity, which I do not suppose is helped by too many sensual distractions.

(xiv)   Christian Martyrdom

Circumstances may arise in which it is admirable to give one's life for others, though naturally one hopes that they never will. Circumstances cannot arise, however, in which one should give up one's life for a personal God, because such a God either does not exist at all, or cannot be benefited by what one does. There is a sense, however, in which one can use the thought that a sacrifice would be demanded by God as an aid to making it.

Christian martyrs have given up their lives either to succour the sick, which is admirable, or to testify to their faith when it was outlawed by the authorities or was unpopular among those to whom they tried to bring it. On the morality of the latter I have a divided mind. One has a right in most circumstances to express one's opinion, provided the opinion is not too dangerous and one does it with modesty and tact, virtues in which the Christian martyrs may sometimes have been lacking and which they may even have (wrongly) despised. And though one may, by and large, have a duty to say what is true, this can be only a subjective duty if that Christ is God is not true. And one wonders, though I do not have the historical knowledge to pronounce on the matter, what, if any, might be the underlying forces – national or commercial, say – behind what, on the surface, was the propagation of a cult (as also what forces were behind resistance to its propagation).

Christian missionaries have not only spread the Christian faith, but have also spread nationalism, colonialism, business interests, and germs. Again, I do not possess the knowledge to say whether the spread of Christianity has been a bad thing or a good one. It brought with it Western medicine, which is preponderantly a good thing, and mass production, which increases the supply of goods but also increases the need for them. Against the fact that the views they propagated were false must be set the fact that the views they replaced were also false; besides, their views were not wholly false and very often will have been nearer the truth than those they supplanted. With Christianity also sometimes came democracy, but whether the people they converted to this fashionable doctrine – not always for export – were better off in large units ostensibly governed by the people than they were in smaller ones governed by a chief, I do not have the knowledge to say.

One proper way to deal with people who have an erroneous morality would be to make tactful suggestions about how it might be improved. One might, for example suggest to a society who practised fertility rites that, in view of the shortage of virgins, it might be better to adopt more economical and reliable ways of increasing fertility than eating them. (One is bound, if one is to be consistent, to think it wrong for them to eat virgins if one thinks it is wrong to eat virgins. If one thinks only that it is wrong for the English to eat virgins, but not wrong for them, then it is rather difficult to see why one should be a missionary at all.)

(xv)   Morality and Christian Institutions

When Christianity – or any other religion, including communism and some other political parties – is organised into a church, as it will have to be in order to be effective, there is a danger that the church will be regarded as more important than the purposes which it was built to serve and will come to be regarded, perhaps rightly, as an end in itself. Advancement in this institution will attract the same kind of worldliness and be the result of the same political machinations that bring success in more worldly institutions. If it is known that the last will be first and the first last, there will be competition for last place. This attitude to institutions is, I think, inevitable, for excellent socio-biological reasons;[15] men thrive in groups and are built to further the survival of that which, as a general rule, furthers their own survival. The problems concerning the fact that the standards common in private morality may usefully be set aside in public morality will beset a church as well as a government. This may be as it should be in an institution devoted to some end other than the propagation of – among other things – morality, but the Christian church is not such an institution.

If one thinks it not wrong for those responsible for an institution to do some things that would be regarded as wrong if done by a private individual, there is a question why Christian prelates should not be allowed to do them. Perhaps it is because to do so would be inconsistent with what Christians profess – but then, if things are right for institutions that are not right for ordinary people, perhaps it is right for institutions to do things inconsistent with what they profess.

(xvi)   Christianity and Intolerance

Many Christians have been martyred because they refused to forswear their religion and most of us have been brought up to admire their intransigent behaviour. Such behaviour is not an example of Christian intolerance, so much as an example of a deplorable lack of tolerance on the part of others. But in some people the two things are different sides of the same coin. If one regards a belief as sufficiently important to die for, there is a danger that one may also regard it as sufficiently important to kill other people for. Christ said 'I come not to send peace, but a sword'.

What those who died for their faith did was certainly courageous and 'subjectively' right because they supposed, however mistakenly, that it was objectively right.[16] Indeed, many such people showed very great heroism. But was what they did really right? Some of them, it must be remembered, not only deprived themselves of their lives but deprived their families of a breadwinner, and it should not be forgotten that an action that would be wrong if it did not deprive the person who performs it and others of their lives may well be permissible, and perhaps even obligatory, if it does.

If the beliefs from which such people died were erroneous, they were probably (objectively) wrong to die for them, however commendable their behaviour, though to die for an erroneous belief when ruthless and powerful people, who may be unsettled by one's resistance, are trying to force one to abandon it may well be admirable. But Christianity is not all wrong and some of the beliefs for which Christian martyrs died were true ones, and some of the actions they refused to perform – such as hand over Jews to Hitler – really were wrong, though not all Christians did this and Christians were not the only ones to do this.

(xvii) Christianity and Compromise

The topic of martyrdom may make this a not inappropriate place to extol the virtue of compromise. A great many people seem to think that, though one may and often ought to compromise on a matter of policy, which is essential if a group of people are to go in the same or a complementary direction at once, compromise over morals is reprehensible. But compromise over morals, even where these concern religion, is often necessary for the same reason that compromise in other spheres is necessary. Without it people cannot live together.

I think Christianity does encourage, sometimes rightly and sometimes wrongly, an unwillingness to compromise. Christians (as well as many others) think that moral compromise necessarily involves one in doing something that is wrong, for if one person thinks that to do something is wicked and another thinks it is wicked not to do it, and there is no possibility of each going his separate way, it must be that they can live together only if one of them does something he thinks is wrong. (Compromise may involve their both doing something they think wrong.)

In favour of compromise it may be said (a) the parties concerned cannot both be right, so one of them must be persisting in doing something that he only thinks (mistakenly) is wrong. Each, then, should heed Cromwell's advice and consider whether it might not be he and not the other party who is wrong.

(b) There may be clashes of duties and a duty to do something – not to wear a turban, say – may be overridden by a duty to produce harmony. Perhaps some such conflicts can be resolved by adopting the compromise that Tom does something he thinks wrong – and would perhaps be right in thinking it wrong, were it not overridden by a duty to produce harmony – and Mary agreeing, in exchange, to do on another occasion something *she* thinks wrong (and which would be wrong, were it also not overridden for the same reason).

There may, though I do not think so, be some duties that may not in any circumstances be overridden and even duties that do not belong to this category may not be such that they may be overridden by a duty to compromise; but I suspect that any duty may be overridden in the unlikely event of the world's perishing as a result of its being performed, and failure to compromise could sometimes, in these days of atomic warfare, lead to the world's perishing. Hence the feeling that religious duties are sacrosanct may in certain circumstances be extremely dangerous.

The principle, which I think many take for granted, that the party to a dispute who is wrong should give way to the party who is right, would be unworkable. Since both parties think they are right, no-one would ever give way. Adjudication would help, but the parties subject to it would have to agree to do something that they supposed wrong (and which might actually be wrong, were it not for a more stringent duty to accept the adjudication) if the adjudicator found against him.

It is unfortunate that the belief that there is a God who has commanded doing certain things and whose commands ought absolutely always to be obeyed must make compromise more difficult. I can make two suggestions to mitigate the possibly dangerous intransigence demanded by this attitude. In the first place, one might be as liable to be mistaken about what God commands as about one's other duties. In the second place, God might sometimes command compromise.

(xviii)   Was Jesus Perfect?

I think that the moral character and teaching of Christ is less than perfect. I shall give one example of each. The scourging in the temple, if it occurred, seems an extreme way of treating people who may have been trying only to make an honest living. Nowadays one might complain about them to the Dean and Chapter – unless they were doing it to raise money for the fabric – write to a newspaper, or report the matter to English Heritage.

To take an example of the second, in one passage, which is not untypical, Christ says 'And whosoever shall not receive you, nor hear your words, when ye depart out of that house or city, shake off the dust of your feet. Verily I say unto you, It shall be more tolerable for the land of Sodom and Gomorrha in the day of judgment, than for that city.' This seems to be an excessively severe punishment for lack of hospitality and an understandable, even if misplaced, incredulity.

Whether a God-made man should be perfect I do not know. Whether Christ was physically perfect we are not told. We have seen that Christ's moral preaching was flawed, which the moral teaching of a perfect person ought not to be, and not all the imperfections of his teaching can be put down to his speaking inaccurately and saying what is only for the most part true, which one often has to do when not writing academic books on morality. *We are not told about Christ's appreciation of art and literature, though he was fortunate in his translators, nor about his scientific acumen.*

(xix)   Following Christ

There are ways in which we should not follow the example of Christ. If he was celibate, this is no reason why we should try to be. The world would come to an end if everybody were celibate. We should not try to heal the sick in the spectacular ways that Christ did, because we would not succeed. We should not preach in an authoritative way, because we are not entitled to do so. Perhaps we should not preach at all.

Perhaps, however, we ought to follow the same general rules as Christ, but make corrections for the fact that he was divine and we are not, just as an invalid ought to follow the same general rules as a healthy person, but make allowances for the fact that he is an invalid. (Neither an invalid nor an athlete ought to eat too much, but what is too much for an invalid may be not enough for an athlete.) We should not tell people we are the Messiah, because we are not, but in telling people we who we really are, we are applying the same general rule as Christ, who also told people who he was (or who he thought he was). Healing the sick by faith cannot be something in which we ought to imitate Christ, but perhaps we ought to imitate him to the extent that we ought to heal the sick when we are able.

It should not be forgotten that man does not need goodness only; he also needs wisdom, and whether following Christ's teaching is always wise I very much doubt. (He himself did not claim that it was, in this world, at any rate.)

It would be always wise to follow his teaching if damnation resulted otherwise, but there is no literal Hell for the damned and to hold that those who are not good go to a this-worldly Hell presupposes that it is always wise to be good, which I do not think is so. (I think it unquestionable that it is not always *prudent* to be good in this world, and very likely not always wise either.)

If there is a conflict between wisdom and goodness, ought one to be wise or ought one to be good? It would seem tautologous to say that one ought to be good, if being good consists precisely in doing what one ought. However, if asked, I might advise someone to do the wise thing, rather than the good thing.

I would not wish to deny that the estimate of the moral character of Mohammed and the Buddha by their followers was also too high.

(xx)   Christianity and Perfectionism[17]

The Christian attitude to perfectionism is ambiguous. There is a strand in Christianity that regards perfection as impossible to man, which it is, and another strand that regards it as obligatory, which it cannot be if it is impossible. Perhaps what we should do is not to be perfect, but to try to be as nearly perfect as we can. (This accords ill with Christ's injunction 'Be ye therefore perfect, even as your father which is in heaven is perfect',[18] for our heavenly father did not try to be as nearly perfect as he could; he was perfect.) But even trying to be as nearly perfect as we can seems to me to involve an unnecessary morally strenuous attitude to life, an attitude which does not allow enough time for art, literature, science, or recreation and may produce an unacceptably heavy burden of guilt. One might try to defend perfectionism by saying that it is more perfect not to try to be morally perfect than to try to be perfect. But I suspect that there is an overall scale of values on which an extra increment of things other than morality can be weighed against an extra increment of morality, the former sometimes being more valuable than the latter.

Kant, oddly enough, deduced that we were immortal from the fact that we did have a duty to be perfect. His argument went: men have a duty to become perfect; they can become perfect only after an infinite period of time; ought implies can; therefore they will exist for an infinite period of time. This argument is valid, but, even if its premises were true, it is unsatisfactory as a proof of immortality, as it competes with the argument: we do not live for an infinite period of time; doing our duty to become perfect would take an infinite period of time; ought implies can; therefore it is not the case that we have a duty to become perfect. This latter argument is just as good; indeed, it is better, because its premises are true. Furthermore, our having a duty to *become* perfect is not the same thing as our having a duty to be perfect here and now, and holding that the former is our duty suggests that instant perfection is impossible.

Perfectionism might produce an unacceptable level of guilt. The biological function of guilt is, I think, to reinforce laws and other rules that are necessary to human survival and well-being, which is especially useful when they cannot be enforced. Guilt, to the extent that it does this, is a good thing. But excessive amounts of guilt can be counterproductive, produce mental ill health, and turn the person who suffers from them into a miserable slave. Others may take advantage of a person's propensity to guilt to manipulate him for their own ends. Nevertheless, a community that was not liable to suffer from guilt in moderation would be a community of psychopaths. It may be that, though Christianity is liable to produce a higher degree of guilt than atheism, Christians can tolerate a higher degree of guilt than atheists, on account of their believing that there is a God to whom they can turn to be absolved from it.

It is a mistake to think that there is one way of living one's life, from which all other ways divagate. There are many different and incompatible ways of living. For example, there are saints and heroes, who live very different lives, but I personally would not wish the saints to become heroes or the heroes saints.[19] Therefore, if Christianity (among other religions) holds up one such way as the way to be universally followed, it is mistaken. And I myself, though I do not think artists are by their art absolved from morality, would not wish a good artist to spoil his art by worrying too much about morality. ('Artists' in this context includes writers and scientists.)

(xxi) Christianity and Original Sin

The doctrine of original sin is both confused and controversial. If it is no more than the doctrine that some degree of sin or wrongdoing is inevitable in man and that, despite his utmost endeavour, he cannot sometimes avoid acting wrongly, it is true. But with it is sometimes included a diagnosis of this deficiency, viz. that it was caused by man's disobedience to God. Since the story of the Garden of Eden is myth and mythical events, since they have not occurred, cannot cause anything, this doctrine cannot be literally true. Whether the myth is figuratively true depends upon what literal truth is being conveyed. If it is saying that wrongdoing consists in disobedience to God, it is not true, as we saw in chapter 7; in any case, immorality would then not be *caused* by disobedience to God, it would *be* disobedience to God. (But I suppose some acts of disobedience could cause further acts of disobedience, immorality being in part a bad habit.)

A more plausible account of the *origin* of sin than the one suggested above is that man has evolved to have characteristics necessary to his own survival and other characteristics necessary to the survival of others (whose survival will often be necessary to him). If one regards wrongdoing or 'sin' as ignoring the demands of society, as very crudely one can, 'sin' results from a conflict between the demands of society and the wants or needs of the individual and it is difficult to see how wrongdoing can be avoided. Man has evolved partly as a social animal and partly as an individual, and the two aspects of his nature are bound sometimes to conflict, producing inevitable failure to conform. But that immorality cannot be avoided is part of what the doctrine of original sin maintains. (It does not maintain, though it seems to me to be true, that some tendency to resist the demands of society is necessary to most men, and I myself would not like them to be without it.)

The doctrine of original sin is often accompanied by a doctrine, which cannot be deduced from it, that Christ was sent into this world to redeem us from sin (a mission in which he has not as yet been successful). I think it is true that we cannot escape sin by our own unaided efforts and may be strengthened in our attempts at righteousness by appeal to a divinity. But the improvement to our moral characters is a result of the appeal, not of the divinity's intervention; some, even those who have never heard of Christ, seem to manage quite well without making it, and others manage by appealing to gods other than Christ. Those who do appeal are only intermittently and partially successful.

It is one aspect of the doctrine of original sin that men and women would go to Hell rather than to Heaven were it not for Christ's first intervention in the incarnation and his subsequent intercession on their behalf. This doctrine cannot be literally true if there are no such places as Hell and Heaven. If there were such places, it would seem to be an unnecessarily roundabout way of getting us to Heaven for God to have sacrificed his only son (to himself) on our behalf before forgiving our sins; he could have forgiven us anyway. If the view is that God sent Christ to give us an example following which would enable us to achieve that minimum standard of virtue that would merit forgiveness, if forgiveness can be merited, I find it a little surprising that it should be held that we do not know what this minimum standard is without God's having been incarnated. And if, more plausibly, it is held that he was incarnated to show us how to live our lives in a *superlatively* moral way, I am surprised that we need to be saved from the dire consequences of a more mediocre standard of morality; such a view would be quite excessively severe.

I do not think that it is incompatible with Christianity to hold that there is also such a thing as 'original' virtue. At least in the sense in which sin is ineradicable from men, so is virtue. Indeed, I suspect that virtue is more difficult to eradicate than sin; men need virtue, though they do not need sin (which is not the same thing as not needing to sin, which they sometimes do seem to need). We have evolved over a long time as moderately virtuous animals and most of us have a standard of virtue which we would find very difficult deliberately and in normal circumstances to fall below. (I myself think that I would find it fairly difficult to bring myself to perform even certain kinds of quite venial act like stealing from a department store, easy though it looks, but I must admit I have never actually tried.)

(xxii)   Christianity and the Sanctity of Life[20]

It is difficult to see how a duty to treat life as sacred can be deduced from Christ's telling us to love one another, for some people are sometimes so utterly miserable that the kindest thing to do would be to kill them, which sometimes they repeatedly ask one to do. A duty to treat life as 'sacred' could be deduced from the commandment not to kill, if this command were taken literally, which I am sure it should not be.[21] We shall see shortly that it cannot be deduced from the command to do no murder.

More specifically, a duty not to use contraceptives, nor perform abortions, nor kill people in war, nor use killing as a form of punishment, nor kill the elderly and the very young, very deformed or very ill, cannot be deduced from the command to love God and man, which command may positively demand that we do kill in certain obvious circumstances. Nor can it be deduced from the seventh commandment, which I am sure was intended to exclude only the killing of one adult by another adult of the same community or another friendly community. Cain was execrated for killing Abel, but Samson killed a large number of Philistines without anyone's raising an eyebrow. (If this episode is apocryphal, there are others in the Old Testament that are not.) Attempts to extend the command not to kill to exclude other forms of killing take it in too unqualified a way. The rule to treat others as we would they should treat us would sometimes demand killing. I fear that, taken without qualification, this command might sometimes demand the killing of third parties.

Though in the Authorised Version of the Bible we are exhorted not to kill, the Revised Version and the catechism say 'Thou shalt do no murder'. Though the Authorised Version may command too much, it may be that the Revised Version commands too little. This is because murder may be taken to mean 'wrongful killing' and though the command not to kill wrongfully is by no means otiose, it does provide a killer with the defence or excuse that an act of killing is not murder, because it is not wrongful. And it provides no help in borderline cases, for a borderline case is precisely a case when we are in doubt whether to kill someone would be murder or not. (It would not, of course, follow from the fact that the action was *not* murder that it was *not* wrong.)

It is a further difficulty with the principle to treat (human) life as sacred that frequently one cannot avoid killing some people without killing others, for example, a doctor sometimes has to choose between saving the life of a mother or her baby, a commander in the field may have to choose whether or not to lose the lives of some men in order to save the lives of others, the captain of a ship in wartime may have to decide whether to risk his vessel's being torpedoed to save the life of drowning men. There are numerous other examples.

Few of the people faced with such decisions actually kill anyone themselves, though abortion does involve killing a foetus. It seems obvious, however, that one ought actually to kill someone if this results in enough other people being left alive to justify the killing, and to kill them precisely in order that these others shall be left alive. I have no doubt that I ought to kill a man about to pour large quantities of lethal germs into a reservoir, if I could not stop him in any other way. (These actions cannot be justified by the doctrine of double effect – though it is a mercy that double effect should justify some killing – for it can only justify killing only when this is not what one is aiming at doing, but a side-effect of it.)

It is often argued that man, in killing, is usurping the prerogative of God. I have already said that I doubt whether there are any arguments for the view that killing is the prerogative of God which would not preclude fertilizing one's vegetables, which also involves interfering with God's handiwork.

Christianity and War

One would have supposed that an invocation to love would imply pacifism. But it has been suggested that a license to war is implied by Christ's remark 'Render unto Caesar that which is Caesar's', a remark which Christ must, if he knows what it has led to, have bitterly regret having made. (Christ did not actually say *what* things were Caesar's.) I have argued, however, that loving one another may demand killing people, which may even be demanded by love of the person we kill. It can scarcely be pretended, however, that much war falls into a category where killing someone is justified by double effect or the greater good. Most war is waged for the supposed greater good of the participants. An international body to enforce peace, which I believe to be imperative, would have to make war on would-be participants in order to be successful. Enforcement of peace is necessary because it may otherwise be in the interest of each party to make war, whether the other does or not, though it is in the interest of both collectively that there be peace. Hence peace should be enforced. I see no reason why killing to achieve peace should not be held to be consonant with Christian principles. In the absence of any international body with the power to enforce peace, war for other reasons may sometimes be justified, but not, I think, often.

It might be considered a fair deduction from the ultimate principles of Christianity that we should love our neighbour's country as our own, but I think this view would be too extreme. The best interest of everybody is served by each man, as I have said, predominantly serving his own country, as it is by his looking after his own wife and children, caring for his neighbours in a near literal sense of 'neighbours', and taking care of himself. A world in which everybody looked after other people's countries to more than a limited extent at the expense of their own would not be sufficiently well organised to be good.

(xxiii) God and Nature

I have some possibly irrational sympathy for the view that we ought to regard ourselves as stewards of the whole of nature. It is a good way of thinking of nature, even if there does not exist any being whose stewards we are. In any case, we are so dependent on nature that to regard ourselves as her stewards will very often be to the long-term interest of men collectively (but not, alas, individually).

(xxiv) Christianity and Scientific Progress

It is to the great discredit of Christianity that it has so frequently stood in the way of scientific progress and its application for the benefit of mankind. If Christians think they have some divine access to knowledge, they will be likely to distrust apparent knowledge obtained by more earthly (but more successful) methods, should there be a conflict. An institution devoted in part to the propagation of belief cannot easily tolerate beliefs incompatible with those which it is trying to propagate. An institution which thinks that it is in possession of divine truth will not find it easy to test all apparent truth with the rigour that is necessary to root out error. And when Christianity is institutionalised, its members will have a vested interest in Christian truth; the prosperity of the institution that they serve and with which they identify themselves, their livelihood, and perhaps their life, will be built around it, and what better recipe could there be for the retention of error? The fact that Christianity is a historical religion and believes itself in possession of unquestionable truths laid down some considerable time ago helps the mistrust which some Christians have of science. But I suspect that it is more the particular views of Christians than Christianity itself that is a bar to scientific progress, and I am fairly sure that this is true if one is talking about religion instead of about Christianity.

The fault is by no means exclusively that of Christians, but one way in which religion, morals, or erroneous religious or moral beliefs, may impede scientific enquiry is the insistence that all men – perhaps because they are all God's creatures – are equal, when this is not a moral judgment about how men ought to be treated but a factual statement about how men actually are. (It could be, though it is most unlikely, that they ought to be treated in the same way whether they were equal in a factual sense or not.)

For example, the factual question whether 'blacks' are less intelligent than 'whites' needs proper investigation. It is wrong to condemn those who sincerely come to the conclusion that they are less intelligent, even if they are mistaken.[22] If 'blacks' are considerably less intelligent, both they and whites are likely to be harmed if the fact is not known. For example, a policy of positive discrimination must be extremely harmful to both black and white if blacks are less intelligent than whites. The trouble is not caused simply by some people being less intelligent than others, a fact which is almost universally known and does not cause enormous dissention, but by this being correlated with something like colour of skin, which is both highly conspicuous and ineradicable.[23] It seems likely that some kinds of non-whites are more intelligent than whites, others less.

Christianity and the Application of New Scientific Knowledge

Christianity has a long history of opposition to advances in the application of scientific techniques for alleviating human misery. The use of anaesthetics, blood transfusion, contraception, clinical abortion, artificial insemination, eugenics, methods of increasing fertility, the use of human embryos for scientific experiment, euthanasia, electronic tagging, brain surgery to eliminate criminal tendencies, the use of foetuses for experiments, genetic engineering, organ transplants, new ways of increasing fertility or improving children or ending human life and many others, a list which is bound to get unimaginably longer and longer as science evolves, are all found by some to be contrary to the teaching of Christ, who can hardly have been expected to foresee them, or to the law of God, when no-one knows what this law is, or the dignity of man, such as it is. Such new techniques are usually condemned because they are unfamiliar, arouse an unreflecting emotional antagonism, and involve treating human beings as if they are biological objects like animals, though that is what they are. (If men are the children of God, other animals will be also.)

It seems self-evident to many that all sorts of things to do with human life are morally wrong. These principles cannot be self-evident, because nothing in ethics is. All have to be tested by their effects on the welfare of the people concerned.

No-one, of course, disputes that all new techniques can be abused – even old ones can be – in that they can be used for personal gain to the detriment of society and that they may have unforeseen ill effects which should be carefully monitored. But I myself would not have supposed that God would be opposed to anything that would increase the happiness and well-being of his creatures, which many, if not all, such techniques, properly used, are very likely to do.

(xxv)   Medical Ethics

There has grown up recently a subject called medical ethics, which is supposed to be a branch of applied ethics; there have also grown up groups of people whose duty it is to advise doctors on ethical matters. I have no doubt that to discuss ethical problems with intelligent, well-educated, experienced and humane people, versed in law, medicine and philosophy and conversant with a large variety of past cases, can do little but good. One hopes that these people will also be familiar with the attitudes of other places and times to the problems. But it would be idle to pretend that there was any suitable body of agreed ethical knowledge, arrived at by accredited methods, there ready to be applied to difficult cases.

(xxvi)   Art and Christian Ethics

Nothing is said in the Sermon on the Mount, and little anywhere else in the Bible, so far as I know, about art. The result may be a certain philistinism. It is difficult to see how any duty to produce or appreciate art can be deduced from a duty to love God and one's neighbours. (Ordinary non-hedonistic (or agathistic) utilitarianism, which resembles the view that our only duty is to love others, can deal with the morality of art, because ordinary non-hedonistic utilitarianism holds that actions are right if they produce good consequences, and art can be regarded as a good consequence.) Art is valuable to man not from love of others, but from love of art.

Despite the fact that art is not much mentioned in the Bible, Christianity has some extremely beautiful art. But a problem about art is posed by the fact that artists cannot reasonably be expected to devote themselves to art from a strong sense of duty and might well produce bad art if they were to do this. Indeed, it may be that some of the best art is produced by those who care little about their duty to God and, if their art is good enough, one could scarcely wish this to be otherwise. I am not saying, though some would, that artists are exempt from ordinary moral rules on account of their art. But a world in which artists (wrongly) ignore their duty to God and man in order to produce art may be a better world than one in which they do not ignore these duties and produce bad art. It follows that doing one's duty to God and man does not have that insurmountable value which some attribute to it.

Art (with the possible exception of music, which seldom represents anything at all) sometimes depicts what is immoral, is enjoyed despite or perhaps because of depicting what is immoral, and sometimes depicts what it is immoral to enjoy. However, the line between good and bad art is so difficult to delineate, the experimental attitude so necessary to producing good art so easily interfered with, and the idea that immoral episodes depicted well should be allowed but those depicted badly prevented so problematic, that control of art should be kept to the bare minimum.

Love (in a wide sense) might be held to include love of things other than persons, including love of such things as art objects, and the love of producing such things. Dedication to the deity may sometimes help one with art, though I suspect it also sometimes hinders.

This being said, it puzzles me that the contribution of the Christian churches to art has been so enormous. But I suspect that here the ingenuity of men and women has (very properly) filled a deficiency in the Christian religion, at least as it usually was.

(xxvii) Agape and Eros

A crude distinction is often drawn between agape and other forms of love, especially eros. Eros is pagan sexual love. Agape is often supposed by philosophers, though perhaps not by theologians, to be a disinterested benevolence practised from duty, perhaps with the idea that in discharging this duty one is fulfilling one's duty to (a loving Christian) God. It is said that though agape can be commanded, and so can be a duty, eros cannot be. (But though elephants tusks, I understand, are ineffective, I believe more sophisticated methods of commanding eros sometimes work.) It is obvious that Christians are sometimes subject to eros and that agape in the sense just suggested can be practised by pagans. Hence agape is not an exclusively Christian virtue. (Perhaps it not practised by pagans in what is supposed to be in the right spirit, but those who benefit from it ought to be thankful that it is practised in any spirit at all.)

I say that the distinction between agape and eros is crude partly because there are an enormous variety of different kinds of love. (The vocabulary of love is amazingly impoverished.) Though it is commonly said that what Christianity enjoins is agape, reading the work of some Christians – St John of the Cross, for example – makes make me suspect that Christian love is in fact often more like eros. (I do not wish to condemn it for that reason.) At worst eros is a necessary evil. Those who wish to denigrate it should consider what would happen if the presence of chemicals or the absence of kilts caused us to be without it.

It is an unfortunate side-effect of a belief in survival in another world that lack of eros might seem not to matter. Since there is no world other than this, it matters enormously that men and women should have a healthy erotic interest in one another. However, so long as most men and women keep eros, and so the human race, alive, which is not as yet difficult, a few people who devote themselves to other more spiritual forms of love to the exclusion of eros can be tolerated; they might, indeed, sometimes be useful. And affection of parents, offspring and friends, though neither agape nor eros, is probably more necessary to mankind than agape is.

Charity, however, is not quite disinterested benevolence practised from a sense of duty. St Paul said 'Charity suffereth long, and is kind; charity envieth not; charity vaunteth not itself, is not puffed up, doth not behave itself unseemly, seeketh not her own, is not easily provoked, thinketh no evil; rejoiceth not in iniquity, but rejoiceth in the truth; beareth all things, believeth all things, hopeth all things, endureth all things.'[24] I feel he exaggerates a little; otherwise any comment from me would be to paint refined gold.

(xxviii) Christ's Spiritual Teaching

There is a great deal to be said for a certain element of 'spirituality' in one's life, which I shall tentatively define as the practice of giving some weight to those present intimations of the divine which most of us experience, which practice may or may not be accompanied by an (over-optimistic) expectation that these herald something permanent to be gained in an afterlife. Spirituality can to some extent be recommended for its furthering enlightened self-interest in this world. But what I have described as spirituality should not be confused with unworldliness, i.e., the practice of eating and drinking moderately, not seeking fame and fortune, living a quiet life at home, or being dedicated to the good of others, which kind of life one may be fortunate enough to be able to lead. This may be, though not necessarily so, dictated by enlightened self-interest and can be lived without any religious motivation at all.

Unworldliness does not involve the elimination of desire, which is not the same thing as carnal desire. Despite what mystics themselves have said to the contrary, the desire of a mystic who perseveres through the dark night of the soul, or the Christian who gives up the world for the sake of what he may regard as no more than a slim chance of salvation, must be extremely strong.

I have no doubt that to use communion with an imagined Christ as a way of living is often successful – though not as indispensable or successful as it is claimed to be; there are enormous numbers of religious people who find their way satisfactorily through life with quite different 'spiritual' mental furniture from that of Christians, and many find their way without any spiritual mental furniture at all. But a certain amount of unworldliness is in many people, though not all, part of a recipe for happiness. But a spiritual unworldliness is not a recipe for eternal salvation, for nothing is for ever, and unworldliness cannot be an *infallible* recipe for anything, since anyone, however unworldly, may be overtaken by an inoperable brain tumour, producing an insanity which makes the sufferer blind to any spiritual aspirations he may previously have had and which religion itself cannot cure – though medicine sometimes can.

It would not be *believing* or simply accepting that Christ is God that would by itself do anyone any good, so much as following the recipes, or modified versions of them, that Christ recommended. Religious people of other persuasions may follow somewhat similar recipes without believing that Christ is God at all.

It seems to me, though my language is deplorably banal, that love (in a wide sense, to include, over and above love of human and non-human animals, love of engaging in valuable activities and love of beautiful things) is a very important ingredient in a happy life. However, a things's being valuable is not enough for seeking it to offer a satisfactory life to the person who seeks it; he must value it himself and be wise in his choice of what to value, as he cannot pursue all valuable things; life is too short. Not everybody seems to find it necessary to love God in order to live a happy life, but to be happy everyone must love someone or something.

It would be dangerous to try to eliminate from good people that streak of violence that is deeply embedded in human nature. Were one to succeed in eliminating violence in this world – and there is no other – one would be at the mercy of people, who are sometimes religious people, who are also violent but do not observe the constraints which the proper use of force demands. Force is not the same thing as violence, but one needs a streak of violence to exert even legitimate force.

The only sense that I can make of the possibility of surviving the death of our bodies in contemplation and/or worship is the (Eastern, though not exclusively so) idea that we should lose ourselves in contemplating what may be the deity and – having in this manner left our bodies behind, so to speak – survive their wrecking. To do this one would presumably have to have led a life sufficiently spiritual for one to become adept at contemplating. But I regard this escape as virtually impossible. (Again, one's salvation would not be a reward of having led a spiritual life, but the natural consequence of having done so.)

Christians sometimes say that God is love, but love is in the wrong category to be identical with a particular loving being. But if all this means is that happiness lies in loving, there is – provided loving is not confined to loving people – a great deal of truth in the remark, though it is an exaggeration.

(xxx)   Summing Up

I find it virtually impossible to sum up what I have concluded in the preceding sections. The best I can do is to say that the Christian ethic is a very fine one, provided it can be divorced from superstition, dogmatism, intolerance, an unhealthy attitude to sex and excessive conservatism, most of which attitudes, unfortunately, are rooted firmly in the New Testament. Christianity is probably excessively unworldly in the sense that it involves false presuppositions about the world, viz., that we actually are children of a loving God who will care for us in a way that makes a favourable difference to what happens to us in the world. And I think the fact that it is a historical religion makes it insufficiently flexible in adapting to new needs. There is little in Christianity that is much use to artists, scientists, creative writers and philosophers, though it has to some extent been adapted for their benefit. The core of Christianity that is most acceptable, which demands love of others and prohibits excessive worldliness is, I believe, common to all the better parts of the higher religions. (The Christian ethic is similar to the noble eightfold path of Buddhism, for example.)[25] But neither Christianity nor any other religion can give us a way to a permanent and secure salvation, for there is no such way, and no such thing.[26]

Notes

1   Joseph Butler (1897) discussed the problem in his Sermons, XI and XII, and in the 'Dissertation of the Nature of Virtue', which is the second appendix to *The Analogy of Religion*.

2   In 'Utilitarianism, Universalisation and our Duty to be Just' and 'Objections to Cumulative-Effect Utilitarianism', both in Harrison, 1993.

3   See my 'Christian Virtues', *Supplementary Proceedings of the Aristotelian Society*, 1963, and reprinted in Vol. II, 1993.

4   In *An Enquiry Concerning the Principles of Morals*.

5   I am indebted to Collier Macmillan Ltd for permission to adapt a passage from Harrison, 1992. I have in mind Richard Dawkins's deservedly well-known book *The Selfish Gene* (1976).

6   Dawkins, 1976.

7   But though Christ seems to imply approval of the master in the parable of the master and the servant, the master only forgave his servant once (Matthew 18:23–35).

8   See Singer, 1963a and 1963b. An ingenious attempt to defend the Golden Rule has been made by Hare, 1981. I have criticised this attempt in 'Ethics and the Archangelic Prescriber' in Harrison, 1993.

9 Hare makes the same mistake in considering whether, if I want to park in the space occupied by someone else's car, I should be guided by my preference to move her bike or by her preference that it be left where she put it. He forgets that, other things being equal, there is a rule allocating parking space to the person to the first occupier.

10 My debtor or promisee may release me from my promise or absolve me from paying the debt, but if I then do not keep my promise or pay the debt, it is not because he prefers this – indeed, he might prefer me to keep to the bargain in both cases – but because the rules entitle him to release me, in which case the obligation ceases, though I may still pay him as a supererogatory act of friendship or gratitude.

11 I suspect that the Golden Rule could not be modified to demand that it be obeyed provided that everyone else obeyed it, without producing circularity. For if one says that what the Golden Rule enjoins is that I should treat others in a way that I would wish them to treat me, if everyone were to obey the golden rule, the Golden Rule is referred to in its own statement and so the injunction stated cannot be any clearer than the injunction referred to.

12 These matters are discussed in Kant, 1947, especially Part II. See my 'Utilitarianism, Universalization, Heteronomy and Necessity, or Unkantian Ethics', 1993.

13 I have dealt with these topics in more detail in Harrision, 1963. My view has been discussed by Sutherland, 1989. Sutherland objects that, if my account of hope is correct, Mr Micawber would be a typical example of a man having it. But hope is not necessarily a good thing. Stewart Sutherland replaces my account of hope with one that makes it necessarily a good thing, but what is necessarily a good thing cannot be hope.

14 See 'Can I have a duty to believe in God' and 'Some Reflections on the Ethics of Knowledge and Belief' in Harrison, 1993.

15 The reader's attention is drawn to 'Sociobiology and Ethics' in Harrison, 1993, Vol. III.

16 Roughly speaking, an action is subjectively right if the agent, rightly or wrongly, supposes it to be objectively right. He may, however, be mistaken, either because of mistakes on matters of fact or because of moral mistakes. The reader is referred to Prichard, 1949 and Price, 1948.

17 I have discussed perfectionism in 'Be Ye Therefore Perfect' in Harrison, 1993, Vol. III. I have profited from reading McGinn, 1953 and Clark, 1993.

18 Matthew 5:48.

19 The reader is referred to Urmson, 1958.

20 I have discussed this topic in greater detail in 'Roles, rules and relationships, the sanctity of life and the pursuit of knowledge' in Harrison, 1993, Vol. III.

21 The case for its not including suicide has been brilliantly made by Williams, 1958.

22 Louis Pojman has drawn my attention to Herrnstein and Murray, 1994.

23 If one is considering appointing someone to a post, one should, of course, be guided by his intelligence, not by the fact, if it is one, that he belongs to a class of people who, on average, are less intelligent than others.

24 I Corinthians 13

25 There is an interesting element of circularity in Buddhist teaching, in that enlightenment consists in the realisation of the Four Noble Truths, the Fourth Noble Truth recommends the Noble Eightfold Path, which includes right contemplation, which is understanding the Four Noble Truths.

26 Similarly, Buddhism would provide no escape from the cycle of birth and rebirth, even if there were one.

30 Conclusions

(i)   Introduction

This long and sometimes involved book may be regarded as a sustained attempt to investigate the existence of God. If – as seems likely – God does not exist in any straightforward way, it attempts to find some place for religion in a world that shows absolutely no traces of his existing. (There are, of course, for good or for ill, numerous traces of people's believing in God, but God's existence cannot without circularity be reduced to the effects of people's believing that he exists, though this ploy is sometimes attempted.)

I regard my attempt to find a place for religion as largely but not wholly unsuccessful. Almost all the traditional attitudes to God – trust, gratitude, reliance upon his help – must turn out to be misplaced if God does not exist. All that remains is a God whom one can contemplate, love, possibly worship, and from intercourse with whom one may gain strength and consolation. (The kind of worship I am thinking of is silent and wordless; public worship is heavily laden with belief.) However appropriate these attitudes may be, what solace and help one derives from them is the result of the contemplation and worship themselves, not of divine intervention on our behalf.

This book may also be regarded, perhaps too charitably, as an attempt to reconcile the views on religion of Freud and Jung. Freud regarded religion as harmful because it produced false belief. Jung – to oversimplify – regarded religion as beneficial because it augmented man's powers and made him whole. My somewhat pragmatic attitude to religion involves attempting to recommend it as a way of producing wholeness and augmenting man's powers, which Jung thought it did, without producing false belief, which Freud thought it did.

May I say, however, that I do not dispute that the objects of religious experience may have very high aesthetic value. Even if, to put it at its lowest, mystical experience, as I sometimes pessimistically suppose, is only a certain kind of self-induced quasi-hypnagogic[1] imagery, it is doubtless imagery that is extremely beautiful and moving. And though to asses religion partly on account of its usefulness or otherwise, including the usefulness of true belief and the harmfulness of false belief, may seem 'materialistic', the wants false

660

belief prevents us from satisfying are not necessarily physical or 'material'; a desire to save a man may, just as well as a desire to kill him, be thwarted by false beliefs about the effects of the relevant medicines as much as by false beliefs about the efficacy of petitionary prayer. Erroneous belief prevents one from obtaining any of one's want at all, however good, beautiful or otherwise exalted the want may be. The objects that contemplation might help one achieve are not necessarily selfish ones.

(ii) The Advantages and Disadvantages of Christianity

The merits and failings of Christian moral teaching have already been discussed. The other disadvantages of Christianity are not disadvantages of religion as such. Provided we use religion to strengthen our aim to achieve ends which we think are estimable, it can do little other than good, so long as our beliefs about what ends are good are not mistaken. Religion is a proper source of solace, refreshment, inspiration and virtue. The overemphasis by some people on virtue, however, is excessive. Religion is only one good thing among others. One should not get fanatical about it, or think that there is another world that can redress the balance of this one. Religion involves an expenditure of time that may or may not be better spent in other ways, depending on who it is that is trying to be religious.

It would be a serious mistake to try to reduce religion to morality. Cultivating an awareness of God, whether veridical or not, is something over and above doing one's duty to one's fellow creatures, or even to oneself. Religion with morality only is like Hamlet with only the Prince. The blindness of some religious people to the part of God in anything other than morality shows lack of imagination. Religion is a source of emotional satisfaction, consolation, exploration, refreshment or retreat, which, provided it can be detached from the impediment of false or irrational belief, is something some people find valuable or necessary, especially in times of stress.

A disadvantage of a historical religion is that it is unable to react to changes in circumstances, changes in knowledge and increased moral and religious insight, if there are any. Protestantism, with its emphasis on the Bible, may suffer from this defect more than Catholicism, which latter has the defect of placing too much importance on the survival and welfare of an institution and putting too much weight upon the judgment of fallible men in crucial positions. Catholics, in my experience, are more prone to superstition; Protestants to waffle.

Christianity has advantages and disadvantages. Many of its advantages come from its emphasis on love. It has these advantages provided the importance of 'love' is not overemphasised and is taken in a wide enough sense to include love of things other than people, including animals other than man. Many of Christianity's disadvantages would be remedied by a more consistent direct appeal to love as opposed to rigid enforcement of rules based on the authority of a fallible church or an impossible historical revelation. (For example, appeal to love alone would dictate that some be killed and others be prevented from being born.) But the Christian ethic, subject to the criticisms I have made, is a good one, though nothing in this world is perfect. It offers solace, comfort and help and the possibility of 'spiritual' quietness, rest and solace which many sorely need and from which I suspect most would benefit. (It is not the only religion that can provide such benefits.) It is unfortunate that these benefits are usually, and perhaps, though I hope not, inevitably, bought, in their Christian form, at the price of accepting superstition and bad metaphysics.

Its failings come from its tendency to condemn to eternal perdition those who do not accept Christian belief; its habit of inculcating belief – for beliefs ought to be tested rather than inculcated; its tendency to treat members of other religions, or of no religion, as feared or hated enemies; its heavy dependence on an erroneous world view, if not upon outright superstition; its excessive moral conservatism; its distrust of science, which is especially unfortunate when science is used to cure illnesses or remedy biological defects in novel ways; its (sometimes latent) hostility to sex.

Whether these advantages outweigh the disadvantage I would not care to say. But it might be possible to have a religion – though whether it would be a Christian religion is another matter – that retained the advantages, but eliminated the disadvantages.

(iii)   Brief Comparison of Christianity with Other Religions

(a)   'Judaic' religions

These include, in chronological order, Judaism, Christianity, and Islam. (One is tempted to add communism as one of these, but, though it has a church, a sacred doctrine, a scapegoat (the bourgeoisie), and inculcates the duty of faith, it has no object of worship (unless it is Lenin).) These three religions all believe in a personal God and are, with the possible exception of Christianity, monotheistic. Their emphasis on justice and brotherly love and their conception of devotion to an omnipotent, omniscient, transcendent, morally good God who rules over and cares for everybody are admirable. One of their worst defects is to regard their respective sacred book as so inspired by God that what is said in it is bound to be true and unquestioningly obeyed; the more sensible alternative is to regard them as, among other things, a record of the fallible and tentative attempts, which must be treated on their merits, of human beings to reach enlightenment on important but obscure matters. The former attitude both prevents – or would prevent if it were applied more rigorously – learning and progress about religion; in an extreme 'fundamentalist' form it can also encourages a degree of intolerance, unwillingness to compromise, intransigence, stupidity, and sometimes fanaticism to the point of criminal lunacy which, especially when linked to nationalism, is highly dangerous both to believers themselves and to the peace of the world. All three, when the enormous size of the universe is considered, appear parochial.

(b) Hinduism: The Advantages of Polytheism

Hinduism, or popular Hinduism, is polytheistic. Polytheism has advantages, though they are not great. There may be something to be said for dividing our gods in order not be ruled. There may be some psychological merits in having different gods who may be turned to for help by different people in different circumstances. One god cannot possess every admirable characteristic, but all the admirable characteristic might be shared between some god or other. And Hindus may learn from the example of their gods to tolerate those of different persuasions, which I believe they do, and feminists may take encouragement from how many of them are female. The Hindu view that the universe is cyclical is more in accordance with modern physics that the fundamentalist Christian view that it was created quite recently once and for all. The view that Vishnu, Siva and Brahma are a kind of trinity is suspiciously similar to the Christian doctrine of the Trinity, but is metaphysically superior to it in that these three are not supposed to be identical. But they cannot he aspects or manifestations of one god, because aspects cannot be individuals and manifestations are usually events, which they are not. Perhaps they could be regarded as representations or guises of one god

The Hindu doctrine that Brahma – the principle of the universe – is Atman (the self) is best understood, I think, as meaning not that I am identical with the principle of the universe, but that I have a 'self' that is. It resembles the Christian view that one discovers God, as one discovers oneself, by looking within. But a self, if that is an entity, is in the wrong category of thing to be identical with a principle, though the word 'principle' may be being abused, as may be the word 'self'.

Hinduism contains mystical elements that are detached from polytheism and these are worthy of very serious consideration.[2] The Hindu belief in reincarnation is as implausible as the Christian belief in survival, but the belief, embodied for example in Yoga, that escape has to be worked for by meditation and exercise is superior to the belief that it is the miraculous result of faith and/or works. Neither meditation nor exercise will be permanently successful, though both may have shorter-term advantages.[3]

Christianity can itself be regarded as an unfortunate lapse into polytheism. However, it is sometimes alleged that beyond or behind the Trinity there is the Godhead, which is more thoroughly – and according to some, blasphemously – monotheistic.

(c) Buddhism

Ignoring Indian Buddhism, (Vajrayana Buddhism, the Diamond Vehicle) the main contrast in Buddhism is between Theravada Buddhism (called by its opponents the Littler Vehicle) and Mahayana Buddhism (called by themselves the Great Vehicle). Theravada Buddhists do not believe that there exists anything like a personal god. Mahayana Buddhism is less austere and more superstitious than Theravada Buddhism, and the latter's belief that there *is* something like a personal god – a Buddha, who may be identified with the 'absolute' and who can intervene on our behalf – a retrograde step. Both are tied up with implausible beliefs concerning metempsychosis. They hold the belief (enshrined in the Four Noble Truths) that one can escape from the resultant cycle of birth and rebirth by renouncing desire, the source of pain – which doctrine may show that the experience of life of its main adherents has been unfortunate. One must also follow the noble eightfold path, which involves contemplation and good works, but the view that one can escape the cycle that way would be optimistic, if there were a cycle. Extreme physical pain is not, as the Buddha supposed all pain was, the product of frustrated desire, and can only be removed except by drugs, if then. Neither kind of Buddhism has that emphasis on the immorality of disbelief which produces so much contention in the Judaic religions. The ethical teaching of Buddhism is not wholly dissimilar from that of Christianity. But, as Christian ethical teaching is subject to the criticism (along with others) that there is no personal God to reward in another world those who are in this one, say, meek or thoughtless of the morrow beyond a certain point, so Buddhism is subject to the criticism that there is no way of literally escaping from the cycle of birth and rebirth, though we may obtain temporary respite from it in contemplation. Essential tenets of both doctrines, however, can to some extent be disentangled from false metaphysical belief. Critics of Buddhism complain that its adherents spend too much time on their personal salvation and too little on helping others. But contemplation may be regarded as what Plato described as the best thing, an end and means, and it could be and to some extent is used as a means to acquiring greater benevolence.[4] The doctrine that there is no soul, but only a series of states, might not make as much difference as one might suppose if it can be held that a soul just is a series of states.

(iv)   The Non-exclusiveness of Religion

Though each of the main religions claims that it is true and the others false, there is no reason why the demands of different religions should not be compatible if. religion ought not to be believed. Though one ought not to believe incompatible propositions, there is no reason why one should not keep incompatible propositions before one's mind for various purposes. It may be psychologically and socially difficult to adhere to more than one religion, but that is no reason for not recognising the merits of others. (Saying this is not to embrace relativism, a view which I think is absurd. Some propositions involved in different religions are incompatible, cannot all be true, and ought not all to be believed, though they may all be disbelieved or thought about.)

Perhaps I should draw the reader's attention to the advantages of 'believing' in more than one god. An existing god may be a jealous god, but a god whom we 'postulate' for the purpose of contemplation, meditation or worship can to some extent be a matter of choice, so perhaps we may choose one for some purposes, another for others.

(v)   Proper and Improper Ways of Behaving, Thinking and Feeling with Respect to the Deity

There are certain kinds of religious activity that are not ruled out by what for want of a better word I have described – improperly, as it treats nonexistence as an attribute – as a nonexistent God, though it is the best I can do. I should remind the reader that to speak of a God who neither exists nor does not exist is either to say that though God does not exist, one should not ignore what intimations of the deity one has, or to say that, though he does exist, the course of nature goes on just as if he did not and one cannot expect anything from him in the way of help other than that which comes from communing or contemplating him (or it). (Even to speak of communing with *him* or it may be to go to far of a nonexistent God.)

Petitionary prayer is ruled out, partly because it is not answered, partly, perhaps, because it might be considered servile or grasping or just plain silly (like praying for rain). (Strictly speaking, I am not against what might be called prayer when it is a petition for things which may properly be regarded as natural consequences of the act of prayer, made with a view to enhancing one's capacity to achieving those things, and they are worth while. It might be possible to describe doing this as invoking the deity rather than praying. (I think it may be possible to invoke the deity without believing that there is one.))

Acting, or at any rate thinking, as if there were a God, if that is possible, is not ruled out by believing that there is not a God, though whether this is a good thing or a bad one depends very much on the kind of God one acts or thinks as if there were. I am not against what for want of a better word might be described as 'pretending' that one is in contact with a deity, and accepting such suggestions, admonitions, help and companionship as come from this 'pretence'. One should, however, never succumb to the temptation of irrationally persuading oneself, despite the pressures on one to do so, that this is anything more than an expedient, and one should always regard the communications that come from this imaginary source with caution. If this can be described as a modified form of faith, then it is possible to have faith in God and to believe that there is not a God at the same time. One may feel that one should pay attention to what presents itself as God, however obscurely, to what has been described as one's internal sense, though its object is neither visible to external sense nor the subject of rational argument. (To say that God is the object of an internal sense is perhaps to beg a question, which I should not wish to do, in favour of its not being awareness of an object that is only part of oneself.)

I call concentrating with sufficient determination upon this object contemplative prayer, though it is perhaps only one form of contemplation. Contemplative prayer is partly useful because it gives one a sense of proportion and enables one temporarily to lose oneself, which is good for one. It is also aesthetically pleasing and appeals to some deep-seated need which some people have, and which I do not properly understand. It is refreshing and enjoyable.

One reason why some attitudes to God are proper and others improper is that some are based on false belief, others not. (That an attitude is not based on a false belief does not necessarily mean that it is proper.) It is a false belief that there are any manifestations of God's existence other than those which naturally result from our contemplating him or our having a relationship with him. These they would have whether God existed or not.

Proper attitudes to the divinity are: awe, devotion, (silent) worship, love, contemplation, and temporary surrender. (Love of a nonexistent God is the most disinterested kind of love there can be, for it must be its own reward.)

There are also improper ways of acting, thinking and feeling with respect to the deity. We have seen that a nonexistent God cannot answer petitionary prayer. One could not rationally feel gratitude to a nonexistent God. One could not obey him, trust him, or be loyal to him. (It might be equally impossible to be ungrateful, disobedient, mistrustful or disloyal to him.) However, though one cannot let a nonexistent God down, one might be loyal, if that is the right word, in the sense of persevering in doing the things one thought he would ask of one, if he existed. Devotion to the benefit of a nonexistent God would be a waste of time. Making sacrifices to a nonexistent God would be an absurd thing to do. So would making sacrifices to a perfect God, if his perfection meant that he could lack nothing we could give him. A nonexistent God can scarcely be a father, though one might deliberately feign having a father as a heuristic expedient,

A nonexistent God cannot give one a moral code, which means that the moral codes we have cannot be God-given and God-sanctioned. This will have the disadvantage that good moral codes will be less stringently enforced, but the advantage that some of the moral codes that will be less stringently enforced will be bad ones.

I suggested earlier that 'God' may be defined as the proper (or perhaps one proper) object of worship and/or of other appropriate attitudes. An object of worship (or some other attitude or complex of attitudes) does not have to exist; at least, the sentiments involved in worship may be aroused by the mere concept of a being, even though we do not think that anything answers to the concept. And I suppose we can contemplate and perhaps (silently) worship the object of our direct awareness (which, virtually ineffable, and consequently concept-resistant, though it is, I should attempt to describe as sometimes quasi-personal), though we have seen that this object cannot be an omnipotent, omniscient, perfectly good, personal God.

(vi)   The Consequences of Atheism

An atheist is commonly defined as a person who believes that there is not a God. But the word 'atheist' might be defined not so much by what the atheist believes as by what he does. He could be defined as a person who does not in fact worship, or contemplate, or try to seek whatever guidance may be apparently offered by what may seem to be a sense of God's presence. If he has such a sense of the presence of the deity, as I think some atheists do, he pays no attention to it. He could be described as an atheist, in the sense that he does not believe that there is a God, but not be one it the sense of that he does pay attention to the religious aspects of himself, though perhaps without having very high expectations of being successful.

It is a platitude that one may be a theist in the sense that one gives intellectual assent to the proposition that there is a God, but fails to worship him or contemplate him or pay attention to the sense of his presence, if the theist in question has one, which not all theists seem to. Oddly enough, a few modern philosophers seem to be atheists in the sense that they believe that there is not a God, and theists only in the sense that they worship 'him' and devote themselves to 'him'. And a large number of modern theists[5] are covert atheists, in that they hold views that, if clearly expressed, could be seen to be tantamount to atheism, but nevertheless systematically worship God and pay very great attention to the religious part of their natures. Whether they would continue to do this if they saw clearly how atheistic their metaphysical views really were I do not know.

Religious people often recognise that belief to which one pays no attention is as valueless as a mechanical rosary. Perhaps they might, conversely, be prepared to attribute some value to contemplation without belief, to the extent that this is possible.

(vii)   God and the Ontological Argument

The Sterility of Regarding the Existence of God as a Hypothesis

There are no valid deductive arguments with true premises for the existence of God. (An invalid deductive argument does not leave its conclusion with any degree of probability; deductive argument is an all or nothing matter and deductive arguments are either all right or all wrong.) Nor is there any acceptable inductive evidence for God's existence. Nature, so far as one can tell, goes on in just the same way whether there is a God or not. It is impossible to deduce consequences from the existence of God, observe that these consequences obtain, and conclude that he therefore exists. But this should not surprise us if it is improper to regard God's existence as a hypothesis which explains why the course of nature is as it is.

God as a Necessary Being

There are a number of other reasons why the sterility of the existence of God, treated as a hypothesis, should not surprise us. If there is a sense in which God is a necessary being – as there must be if our concept of God is to have its full grandeur and immunity to empirical refutation – then it also follows that no conclusions about the world can be drawn from his existence. Such conclusions are necessarily always contingent. But nothing that might be otherwise than it is can be deduced from something that must be as it is.

Though God cannot be a necessary being in the sense that his existence follows from his essence, he could be an 'incontrovertible' being, in that, since it is not the function of 'postulating' him to explain any contingent matter of fact, his 'postulation', if you call it that, is absolved from having to be withdrawn because of any contingent matter's not turning out to be as it would be if the hypothesis is correct.

It follows from this that 'belief' in God cannot be like any ordinary secular belief. For secular belief includes, among other things, a believer's having a disposition to act in a manner that would be successful in getting him whatever it is that he wants if the course of future experience turns out as he believed it would. One cannot believe that some line of action is a means to obtaining what one wants and not take this line of action, unless one wants something else more. But if no conclusions about the course of future experience, whether in this world or the next, can be deduced from the existence of God, it follows that there is no way of acting on the proposition that God exists. For if the existence of God is unverifiable, in that it entails no consequences about the natural world, one who realises this ought to believe that the course of future experience will be the same whether one believes that there is a God or not. Hence there are no ends which acting as if the proposition that there is a God were true can bring about.

From this it follows that there can be no miracles and that petitionary prayer is not answered (though it may have effects, which may be beneficial effects, upon the person who prays). It also follows that we will not be cared for, that there is no one to intervene on our behalf, that things will not necessarily be all right in the end, and that we have to rely on ourselves to secure our goals. However, invoking the deity may help us do this, providing that 'image' of God which keeps the conduct of some people under constant review is not too hostile to these ends. If it is, the fact that God does not straightforwardly exist should enable one to try to get rid of it.

Christianity is false if it entails, as it would be natural to suppose that it does, the occurrence of miraculous events, such as the Virgin Birth and the Resurrection, the existence of Heaven and Hell and of a divine plan which involves God's systematically controlling the universe, and sporadically intervening in response to petitionary prayer.

Whether miraculous events occur or not, however, has little – I used to think it had none – bearing upon the truth of Christian ethical teaching, which is to a large extent independent of the truth of the Christian metaphysic, though this is not to say that Christian ethical teaching is entirely satisfactory. I say 'little bearing', because there does seem to me to be a certain amount of ethical teaching which is bound up with belief in Heaven and Hell. For example, it would be (objectively) wrong to encourage other people to disbelieve, or not to be baptised, if they were sent to Hell as a result. Even if Hell is only a state of mind in this world, it is presumably one that it is wise to avoid. It may be, however, that this particular branch of Christian teaching is not strictly ethical, but prudential.

(viii)   Some Specifically Christian Religious Teaching is Independent of Metaphysics

Oddly enough, the truth of some (practical) Christian religious teaching is also independent of the truth of the Christian metaphysic. (The view that Christ is God cannot be independent of it.) Some religious teaching consists in propounding a number of recipes or 'implied recipes' – that he that findeth his life shall lose it is a possible example. Some of these recipes can be interpreted as instructions for enabling people to live successfully with the religious part of their natures, which is something many people (though not by any means all) need to be able to do. The usefulness of these recipes is not entirely conditional upon one's freely deciding to make something of this part of one's nature, for there are some people who need so to live, whether they want to or not. Making something of the religious part of one's nature may or may not be an unwise thing to do, depending upon whether or not it is done wisely, upon the kind of person one is, and the kind of religious aspect of oneself one has.

That it may be profitable to lead a spiritual life need not depend on the view that we have an entity called a 'soul' and that there is a world of 'spirits' which we will one day, if we do the right things, join. Living a spiritual life may be regarded as paying adequate attention to such intimations of the divine as one has in this world, without our having thought to any other world. Paying such attention might not suit everybody. I suspect doing so is more a matter of prudence than of morality. To love God, if I am right in thinking that it is possible to love a nonexistent God, cannot benefit him, for he does not, strictly speaking, exist, but to love him may be of benefit to oneself.

(ix)   The Advantages and Disadvantages of Faith

The advantages of faith are not only that it may give one serenity and peace of mind; it may give one a better sense of proportion on account of the relative insignificance of one's own projects as compared with the great 'scheme' of things. It may offer one consolation in times of suffering, and support in adversity. It may make one's conscience more sensitive, or make one more sensitive to one's conscience (a fact from which others are more likely to benefit than oneself). It may have the effect of releasing abilities which are only partially under one's voluntary control, and strengthening one's resolution in pursuing enterprises which one regards, rightly or wrongly, as worth while or important.

These advantages are, however, severely limited. Faith will seldom move mountains, even metaphorically and, literally, will not even move quite small molehills unless it inspires us to dig them up. It will not protect one against everything, and the things that it can protect one against are internal, rather than external dangers; it may, however, enable some to bear more easily the misfortunes which they have been unable to use it to prevent. And it cannot be guaranteed to do even this, not only because to preserve it under severe trial demands more fortitude than most of us possess, but because it itself is not unassailable. So far from being invulnerable, indeed, one's possessing it is risked by any chance injury to one's brain or unforeseen disturbance to one's glands. And like Wittgenstein's duck rabbit, it comes and goes. Though we may often be grateful when we have it, it is not necessarily possible to recover it when it leaves us and we happen to need or want it. Phenomenologically it can feel like an act of grace, extended to us by a being outside ourselves, but we have seen reason to doubt the possibility of such a being.

The main disadvantages of faith consist in the fact that it is nearly, though not, I think, quite, impossible, to disassociate it from irrational belief and even superstition. Irrational belief and superstition may occasionally, from good luck, put one on the correct path, but over a longer period of time the chances are overwhelmingly that they will let one down, and it is both dangerous and ignoble to live one's life in a self-induced cloud-cuckoo-land.

Even irrational beliefs about the *next* world, though they have the advantage that they cannot be discovered to be false before our deaths – after our deaths will be too late – may carry irrational beliefs about this world in their train. Hence, though a man cannot be rudely disappointed by discovering that there is no afterlife, he may waste much time and effort in this world in making sacrifices – perhaps in a monastery – for an other-worldly happiness which does not exist. Much worse, he may compel other people to make such sacrifices, or take risks which would be acceptable only on the assumption that the human race continued to exist in another world and that life on this planet was not the only life. Nor can it be denied that much harm, as well as good, has come to the world through the Christian religion. Much of this harm, I dare say, is because of erroneous beliefs about what Christianity demands, but I doubt whether all of it is. Anathematising unbelief is well founded on the New Testament.

Religion, like morality, is justified by its beauty, which I lack the rhetoric to extol, and its usefulness. It is important not to have religious beliefs that are false. Beliefs *about* religious beliefs are not strictly speaking religious beliefs; it is important that such beliefs should be true. Hence it is important that religion be carefully investigated, both by philosophers, empirical scientists and the individuals who find they possess them.

(x)   God as Transcending Existence and Nonexistence

Once upon a time I thought that God did not exist, but might be the object of favourable attitudes (for example love) in spite of this.[6] I have since revised that view and now hold (very tentatively) that a better way of putting this matter is to say that God neither exists not does not exist.[7] (This is a view that has been held by some mystics.) By saying that God neither exists nor does not exist I hope to do justice to two strands in sensible thought about religion, the fact that there are no traces of God in nature and the fact that at least some men need God, and have experience that presents itself as direct awareness of him.

Saying that God does not exist (or perhaps that God does not-exist) draws attention to the fact that the world goes on just the same whether there is a God or not. The function of 'postulating' God, if you call it that, is not to explain either the universe or anything in it. Theology should not try to compete with science in this respect; if it does, it will inevitably come off worst. It follows from the fact that God does not exist that miracles do not occur, that petitionary prayer is not answered, and that we are not watched over by a benevolent deity who will intervene on our behalf, or who has so arranged the world that, without the necessity of his having to intervene, no permanent harm will come to us. Permanent harm comes to all of us in the long run.

Saying that there is *not* a God, however, suggests unnecessarily that men should not indulge in worship, meditation, contemplation or contemplative prayer, that they should not invoke the deity in face of a challenge, or have resort to intercourse with him when in distress or need, and that people should not consider how our behaviour would look to him if he were to exist (exist in a straightforward way). This latter may involve writing our own moral views large, but there is something to be said for writing them large. It is an advantage of 'postulating' only a nonexistent God that he cannot be responsible for evil (though such a God also could not be responsible for good either).

(xi) Two Views (Among Others) That Divorce Religion from Ordinary Belief

Of the views, discussed in chapter 22, that hold either that faith is not belief, or that what we ought to cultivate, whether it can be described as 'faith' or not, is not belief, the following two are probably the most important.

(a) Entertaining Rather than Believing

According to this view, the function of deistic propositions is to facilitate what appears to be an encounter with what purports to be a personal God; one can embark upon the encounter without first believing in the existence of this God, though one may come to believe, and be justified in believing, in a personal God as a result of this encounter.

Entertaining propositions or having them before one's mind may be a necessary ingredient in some kinds encounter involved in contemplative prayer, as perhaps in contemplation and meditation. Other kinds of experience may also involve what purports to be direct awareness of an entity. One may to some extent continue the aforementioned encounter, as well as contemplation and meditation, even though one does not as a result of it come to believe the propositions involved. This, and other similar attitudes, are pragmatist in that one may continue to foster the experiences because they work in one's life in a helpful way. It is not pragmatist in that it holds, like William James, that this pragmatic or heuristic advantage means that the propositions involved in the attitude must be true.

(b)   Direct Awareness Rather than Belief

Another view is that faith is unnecessary, as we have the direct awareness of an entity aforementioned, an entity which some who claim to have this awareness say is of a personal God. What we then cultivate is not belief, but the awareness – which of course results in, and is claimed to justify, beliefs, though beliefs that it is difficult to communicate.

(xii)   Religion and Mysticism

As I have said, the view that God neither exists nor does not exist, or that the category of existence does not apply to God, or that he transcends existence, has been held by some mystics. This, I think, means that the criteria for distinguishing between what is real and what is imaginary do not apply to the mystical object (and so do not apply to God, if God is the mystical object).

Some mystics claim that the object of mystical experience is personal, others that it is not. I do not see how the existence of a personal God could be revealed by mystical experience; so many untestable consequences follow from supposing that there is a personal God that such a claim has to be rejected. Dispositional propositions such as that God is omnipotent cannot be established by acquaintance (see chapter 13). I myself remain sceptical, though by no means completely so, about claims made by mystics to reveal, by means of direct acquaintance with it, a world that transcends space and time.

The main difficulties I feel with this mystical claim are these. (a) God must be a necessary, in the sense of defined, being and the nature of the world revealed to mystics is just as much a contingent fact as is the nature of the temporal world. (b) To repeat, I have an obscure feeling that religion and factual discovery are two quite different things, and mystics do claim they make factual discoveries, of a sort, though about a world 'beyond' space and time. If the function of religion is not so much to make discoveries, which activity is the function of science rather than religion, as to provide us with a satisfactory object of worship, then providing us with such an object is not a matter of finding an entity lying about the place. But there is no reason why men should not, so to speak, try to create a satisfactory object of worship for themselves.

A reduced concept of God is more likely to have something answering to it, viz. there might be an omniscient but totally impotent being who was in favour of men's being successful in their enterprises, though inadequate because he was powerless. But such a God could not help men when they were in need, though to love God because he could help one might be somewhat ignoble. The existence of such a God would be a matter of celestial geography, but there is no reason why some objects of geography should not be objects of contemplation, for example, Mount Everest.

Rational belief must be, if in anything, in a non-personal God, though if we find it helpful we may entertain soothing propositions about a personal one. Entertaining propositions about a personal God may be a road to acquiring religious experience and so perhaps to belief. But such experience could, because of evil, justify only a belief in a non-personal God.

(xiii)   Verdict

At what is more than a risk of repetition I shall end by making the following observations.

Religion as Science or Metaphysics

One thing religious people have traditionally done is to try to explain the universe, often as the work of a god. There is no *a priori* proof, or empirical evidence for, the universe's being the work of a god, and explaining how the world came to be as it is is properly the work of science – I use science in a wide sense to include such disciplines as astronomy, geology, medicine, psychology, sociology, economics, history, and the life sciences. (I do not think these can all be reduced to physics, and if it could the reduction would be practically useless, as we could not in practice deduce the truth from an anterior knowledge of physics.)

Religious people only bring religion into discredit when they try to compete with science. There are no facts about the world that cannot be established empirically, by ordinary scientific means, including the facts about religion itself. The proper attitude to beliefs about the world is to investigate them and to accept them when they appear to be true and reject them when they appear to be false. Faith, if it conflicts with this attitude, is a vice, not a virtue.

Fully-fledged Religious Belief

There is no personal God who might help us by interfering in the course of the universe, reward us or punish us, or confer upon us life, whether physical or psychical, after death. It follows that, whatever one says about the ultimate assertion that God exists, all the subsidiary doctrines of religion, including those of Christianity, are false. Hence any attitude to God which relies upon his caring for us is misplaced. Contemplating the deity may well help us, but it will help us whether there is a deity or not.

An Unintelligible God

Some theologians, usually of a modernist or post-modernist persuasion, talk in a language which seems to me to be totally unintelligible. This has the advantage that they can talk in way which they seem to find highly satisfying and which doubtless gives them an outlet for their desire to worship, and may cause them to feel protected and cared for, but what they say cannot be refuted because it does not touch ground at any point. This way of reconciling Christianity with science is not to be recommended.

One of the most dangerous ways of making any view more plausible and more interesting than it is is to conflate two contentions, one plausible but platitudinous, the other interesting but paradoxical. Conflating the two may make the unwary think they have just one contention that is both important and plausible. The result is nothing more than a heady confusion.

Diminished 'Belief' or 'Faith'

One might attempt to retain a place for a personal God, in whom one can have trust and who will help one in adversity, by holding that the factual beliefs which this presupposes are not strictly speaking beliefs – which ought not to be accepted without evidence – but propositions (for example, the proposition that one's conduct is being monitored by a morally perfect being) which the 'believer' must keep constantly before his mind in order to enable him to lead a religious life. The trouble with this view is that the propositions in question are not just propositions that have not been established to be true; they are propositions that are in fact false. Hence knowingly attempting to retain some residual and provisional acceptance of them in spite of believing that they are false must lead to an uneasy self-deception and, if they are propounded to others, downright dishonesty.

A Reduced God

It might seem tempting to postulate a God who was reduced in the sense of say, being not eternal, or not omnipotent. It may be, though I do not think so, that the first reduction is acceptable. A God who was not omnipotent could not be responsible for all evil, though he might be responsible for some of it. But a God who is not omnipotent would have the worst of both worlds. All the evidence is against there being such a God, but such a God would lack the grandeur and capacity to inspire awe of an omnipotent God and would be less than perfect. Hence there could be no motives for wanting to think of him as anything short of omnipotent.

A 'Subjective' God

I have suggested that though religious awareness cannot give you knowledge of the existence and attributes of a transcendent God, who is omnipotent, omniscient and perfectly good, it will enable you to explore and have a relationship with a 'godlet' who is probably, in a wide sense of 'part', part of oneself and with whom many have to live, whether they want to or not. Such exploration can tell one nothing about the world outside oneself. Doubtless many who have experience of such a godlet find having it helpful and some could even not do without it. But having such experience does not justify those who have it in making claims about the public world. What one discovers about it applies in the first instance only to oneself; and though others may or may not find that what they experience is similar, it may well be that the similarity is the result of having been brought up in similar religious cultures, rather than by being affected by the same 'objective' entity. Presumably such communication sometimes takes the form of intercourse with an 'objectified' image of Christ, projected on to the universe. It cannot be a veridical communion with Christ, if he did not survive the death of his body.

A Nonexistent God

Though most (Western) attitudes to the deity, including gratitude, awe, trust, faith in the goodness of God and the expectation of help, and the virtue of obedience, demand a personal God who exists and interferes in the universe, meditation, worship and contemplation do not. One can contemplate or worship a being who either does not exist, as I sometimes say, or to whom[8] existence or nonexistence do not apply, as I say at other times. One can worship,[9] as some have been taught to do, an existent omnipotent and omniscient God. (Leading a good and peaceable life may be an aid to such contemplation, but one may not be sufficiently fortunate for the duties one is called upon to perform not to demand unsettling violence, as some duties do.)

But one can also withdraw one's senses both from the external and internal worlds and contemplate what one finds. What one finds may be difficult or impossible to describe, and those mystics who make empirical claims about reality as a result of having it make claims which it is difficult or impossible to test, or even properly to understand. But I suspect that it really does not matter whether what one contemplate exists or not, if even any sense can be attached to the claim that it exists in such dark and imponderable regions. (I believe that it is an advantage of Therevada Buddhism that it offers contemplation that is not contemplation of a personal deity. Unfortunately Buddhism has its own metaphysics and bogus science, though doubtless these can be dispensed with.)

But the attitudes of contemplation, meditation and perhaps worship, though not essential to all but a few, are valuable attitudes, and I cannot find it in my heart to wish them totally to disappear from the face of the world. But 'in my Father's house are many mansions', not all of them Christian ones, and one should not suppose that a life involving contemplation is the only one possible, or that a life not involving it is necessarily, for the person whose life it is, defective.

One has to delineate a fine boundary between religious belief on the one hand – which belief is dangerous because fully-fledged religious belief is simply false – and an insensitive and philistine ignoring of the claims of religion on the other. That boundary I have tried to draw. I do not suppose that my putting it where I have will satisfy anyone, but it is the best I can do. Though so far as one's senses go, the world carries on precisely as if there was no God, and all arguments for his existence are totally invalid, I would not want the idea of God or the practice of contemplating him, however obscure and impotent their object, totally to perish from the world. But if I were forced to make a judgment, and no *via media* could be drawn between religion and science by dissociating religion from belief about the world, I think atheism without religion is probably less harmful than religion with false belief.

Notes

1 Hypnagogic imagery is extremely vivid images, usually visual, which are often experienced when one is dropping off to sleep.

2 J.J.C. Smart tells me that the view that the Advaita Vedanta holds that there is more than one god is an illusion.

3 See Smart, 1992.

4 See Smart, 1958.

5 I have profited from attending Roger Trigg's Stanford Lectures in the University of Cambridge, on the impossibility of divorcing Christianity from metaphysics.

6 In Harrison, 1963.

7 In 'The Philosophy of Mysticism' in Harrison, 1995. A similar view has been brilliantly defended by W.T. Stace (1961) (who holds that God both exists and does not exist).

8 For reasons mentioned in chapter 4 it goes, as I have said, against my philosophical conscience to call existence and nonexistence attributes. So perhaps I ought to say what I have said elsewhere, that when one 'contemplates' that which one is pleased to call 'God', one contemplates something which does not exist, in the sense that it has no effects on the world, but also does not not exist, because it should not be expected to have any effects other than those which arise from the act of contemplation itself.

9 Worship in the form of hymn-singing is too loaded with belief to be of more than therapeutic value; I am thinking of a wordless attitude which can only *faut de mieux* be described as worship.

Epilogue

I feel I ought to explain to my readers why I should have written a book on the philosophy of religion when its conclusions are as negative as most – though not all – of mine have turned out to be. In doing this I may well be taking myself too seriously, but if I do not take myself seriously, who else will?

To some extent this justification should be unnecessary. It would be a bad thing if work on religion were published only by conventional theists. Though atheists may not be any less biased than theists – though it might be said that the latter are inclined to make a virtue (faith) out of their bias – biased atheists might counteract the effect of biased theists, though perhaps unbiased atheists will do this better. If the Devil has had all the good tunes, God may have had all the good write-ups, and perhaps the being who governs this rather unsatisfactory universe does nor deserve some of them. And I suspect that the polite opinion that, even though one is not religious oneself, one should not criticise the religious beliefs of others, can, however much it makes for short-term harmony, in the long run do only harm. A robust religious belief ought to be able to survive criticism and what cannot survive such criticism without protection is not worth preserving.

Hence I should explain that, though I would stake my philosophical reputation on there not being a God, I myself cannot help to some extent doing something that might be described as believing in one in a rudimentary way. (I do not think that I believe that there *is* a God.) I have a religious aspect to my own personality that goes on quite unaffected by the results of rational argument. It is not so much that it will not go away when it finds that it is without rational support, as that it is in the wrong category to need rational support. It is neither rational nor irrational; it is just there. Though it might, on a superficial view, seem rational to try to suppress this aspect of myself, to deprive myself of it would be to close upon myself a window from the world, which might look out on something real, even though what I seem to see through it is, to say the least of it, obscure and quite possibly entirely illusory.

I started this book partly in the hope – but by no means the expectation – of showing such religious experience as I had are, or at least might be, a veridical awareness of the deity. I have failed to do this. Indeed, I am, if anything, more sceptical about the cognitive validity of religious experience than I was before I started. But I have nevertheless decided, somewhat against both what I think is my nonconformist conscience and my better judgment, to allow myself to go on having such religious experience as I have – though perhaps not to encourage myself in having it – even though I cannot show religious experience to be veridical.

As I have already suggested, I have come to be that embarrassing, but not, I think, uncommon thing, an atheist who has what appears to experience of the deity whom he believes not to exist. At intervals I feel myself in contact with a being who seems to watch over me and to care for me. Though it comes in different guises, it sometimes – not always – appears to be a moderately benevolent and not excessively agitated eye which follows me wherever I go and occasionally strengthens my resolve and gives me solace and help when I need it, though to only a limited extent.

It is an interesting fact that I can have the experience of seeming to be in contact with a deity and at the same time be completely unconvinced that this experience is veridical, or that it tells me anything at all about the nature of reality, transcendent or otherwise, outside myself – but perhaps the difference between being inside and outside oneself is not clear-cut. Hence it might be phenomenologically more precise to say not that I am in touch with the vastness of a deity, which I do not think I am, but that I am fortunate enough to be watched over and to some extent guided by a small 'daemon' – in my own case, a good daemon rather than a bad one, though I do not think it perfect and it certainly is not omnipotent. Or to say what is not quite the same thing, what might be described as the phenomenological object of my experience is not an omnipotent, omniscient, perfectly good being who created the universe – how could it be? – but a tiny quasi-personal godlet, which is perhaps no more than a dramatised aspect of my own personality, with the rather limited function of caring for me personally. (Some might wish to think that this was just one aspect of a deity that had many other facets, but I think this would be over-optimistic.)

I doubt very much whether my daemon is independent of me. It will die when I die, thought that is not a reason for not appreciating it while I have it. That it is only a 'subpersonality' of myself might be one reason why the daemon can exist – whatever 'exist' might mean in a this context – even though a creator of the universe does not. In talking of a daemon, rather than of God, I am trying to some extent to counteract what I regard as a prevalent mistake; if a vast number of people have thought that there was a God because they have confused the phenomenological object of their religious experience with an externally existing, omnipotent, omniscient and perfectly good being, I think many others have chosen to ignore the phenomenological object of their experience because they have believed that there was no God.

Part of the reason for the feeling that one ought not to have religious experience if one does not believe that there is a God may be that the language used to describe the phenomenology of religious experience – Western religious experience, at any rate – has been evolved by people of orthodox religious belief convinced that their experience was veridical. As a result, interpretation has been mixed with description and it has been taken for granted that religious experience must be experience of an omnipotent, omniscient and perfectly good being – God the Father – or of Christ, his son, or perhaps even of the Holy Ghost. Hence normal Christian religious language is for certain purposes unhelpful when it comes to talking about the experience that I, and I suspect many other people, actually have, and which in any case are probably all different.

I do not infer the presence of such a 'being', if my daemon can be called a being, from the occurrence of the experience. As I have said, I do not think that any being independent of or 'outside' myself is there either to be inferred or directly presented. But I seem to myself to be in immediate contact with the apparent object of my experience. It feels to me as if I were immediately acquainted with this 'entity' and I do not need to produce for myself arguments, with premises and conclusions, for its existence, any more than I need arguments for my own existence.

I regard the experience I am talking about, however, as needing careful watching. It could so easily get out of hand. Though it offers guidance, I am sure that any suggestions it seems to make about what I do should be scrutinised with care. The demands it makes on me are fairly small, but this is partly because I see to it that they are small. I fear that, were I not careful, they could grow to become an obsession and I would cease to be in control of my own life. Though there are some who regard being controlled in this way as a virtue – and even recommend religion because it enables one to surrender control of one's life to it – I am not one of them. I like to feel that I am in charge of my life – at least as much as anyone is, which is not very much. I do not want my life to fall into the hands of forces which I do not properly understand. The risk of this is all the more frightening because having ostensible contact with the deity can so closely resemble the symptoms of schizophrenia, when the schizophrenic patient often feels that he is controlled from without. (Indeed, its resemblance to schizophrenia is one of the things that makes me sometimes distrust it.)

Though most men who feel themselves in direct contact with the deity, if this is what I feel myself to be in contact with, appear to be proud of this fact – though perhaps it is only the ones who talk about it who are proud – I am in fact a little ashamed of it and admit to it only on very rare occasions like the present, when there seem to me to be compelling reasons of common honesty for doing so. Though I shall say nothing in the following pages that is incompatible with my having (and indeed valuing) religious experience, what I say could well give the false impression to a careless reader that either I did not have it or did not value it, whereas I both have it and value it. But my reason for writing this is also partly that I should not like to deprive, by my arguments, anyone who has it the solace of seeming to be acquainted with such a being, even if this acquaintance is illusory. It might, however, help him get his logic straight.

On the other hand, I should not like the people who have religious experience to be too confident that their experience is objective. The result of such confidence might well be, though it does not have to be, to produce an unfounded assurance about the nature of the universe and the demands of morality. This in its turn might produce an intolerant refusal to allow liberty to people whose religious experience, if they have any, is different from their own, or which are nonexistent – fortunately for them, I sometimes think, because it makes their lives so much more straightforward. And there are already far too many forces impelling men to kill one another or worse. Those who feel that God demands that they kill people who disagree with them are sometimes put in mental hospitals, but unfortunately others become great religious leaders.

I think that fear is the most potent force in producing religious intolerance – which is not the only kind of intolerance – and I wish I could say that I thought it was unjustified fear. Religious and nationalist intolerance probably have their roots in attitudes which were of advantage to our remote ancestors, but it would, in view of such things as the fate of the American Indians, be rash to hold that it cannot still be of advantage to the people who still practice it, though it is likely to get more and more dangerous with the advancement of science.

The reason why I think that my experience is valuable to me – and I assume that at least some other people are similar – is that it sometimes makes me calm when I am not calm and more confident when I am not confident at all. Sometimes it enables me to look at things from more detached and less self-centred point of view than I would otherwise. I am not sure why it is better not to be self-centred, but I suspect it is because the self-centred person cannot have the pleasure of losing himself in something he thinks bigger than himself. It is important to me to keep on good terms with its object. In my case, and I am sure in the case of most others, religious experience, though connected with morality, is not inescapably so, and I suspect moral religious people exaggerate the connection. Not only is morality just a small part of religion, it is not even necessarily a part of it. Religion often offers, though the offer is sometimes spurious, help with most of one's enterprises. If I were to try to rob a bank, I would assuredly ask for the assistance of my daemon before doing so, and I am not confident that I would not get it. On the negative side – though it is perhaps just as well that there is a negative side – there also are things my daemon will not let me do, or at any rate does not wish me to do. But keeping on good terms with my daemon seems to demand only an average standard of good behaviour, though I understand that other people are less fortunate in this respect than I am. And I find I can ignore what I regard as its more overexacting demands with near impunity.

I value such religious experience as I have not only for its results. The experience I am talking about is not only (up to a point) useful, it is also enjoyable. Having it has some of the characteristics of certain kinds of (predominantly visual) art. I imagine that in others more fortunate than me it can occasionally be sublime. Even in myself it can partly resemble a clap of thunder or the view of a distant mountain range. But I am sure that the objects of everybody's religious experience are different and, though this may well be as it should be, it makes it unwise to generalise.

However, in order not to follow in this respect the example of religious people, who exaggerate its benefits – for what man is on his oath when he praises his Lord – I think it important not to overrate the benefits of what I myself experience. It would be wrong to say that I could not live without religious experience. Indeed, I have lived most of my life almost without it and have not yet come to disaster, though there is still time. Religious experience is an added amenity, rather than a necessity, to the furniture of my inner life. And such faith as I have, if, indeed, such a tentative and experimental attitude can be called faith, will not move mountains, or even quite small molehills without a spade. It does not enable me to take no thought for the morrow, though sometimes it causes me to take, rightly or wrongly, less thought.

What I have as a result of having religious experience I have usually had to work for, though perhaps not as hard as I might have done otherwise; its benefits have not been acquired in any supernatural way. Though having religious experience seems to ease the parts of my life, like access to the fruits of inspiration, which are only partly, if at all, under one's voluntary control, it would be quite wrong to suppose that I would be entirely uninspired without it. Very often I am uninspired even with it. But even if inspiration is the product of unconscious brain activity, this does not mean that, by invoking the deity, one might not both expedite this activity and get better access to its result.

I fear that I am here taking up a characteristically cautious attitude to faith, if faith is what I am talking about. But it may be that those who exaggerate the benefits of faith, with more eye to good salesmanship than is entirely proper, are doing their religion a disservice. It may, like advertising, secure converts but make faith vulnerable to those sufficiently sceptical to see that the more exaggerated claims made for it are most unlikely to be true. That we survive death as a result of acquiring religion seems to me to be the most exaggerated of these claims.

It is not the business of a philosopher to investigate anything beyond the point, if there is one, when reason ceases to be helpful. But I must at least point out that I am not at all in favour of what might be described as irrationalism. If one is to take leaps of faith, they must be calculated ones. They should be taken only if the size of the benefits and the risk of getting them justifies the expenditure of time and effort that could have been used in some other useful way. There is nothing irrational about acting on a proposition which it would be irrational to believe. One may sensibly do so if the benefit one gets from acting on this proposition, if it is true, is sufficiently large to justify risking what one would lose if one were right in thinking that it is false. But I suspect that this attitude to religion, regarding it as something like a risky investment that will pay enormous dividends in a next world in the unlikely event of its coming off, is totally and completely wrong. The benefits must be in this world if religion is to be worth pursuing, since there is no other, though this does not mean that it is risk free.

I myself, however, do not take great risks or make great sacrifices for the privilege of going on having what religious experience I do have, and in general it seems that most other people exaggerate the sacrifices they themselves make. Such sacrifices are often alleged to be enormous, and I am sure that they sometimes are, but more usually, looked at from the outside, they seem fairly small. And there is no merit in mortifying the flesh for its own sake. Self-discipline is a trait of character that would not be a virtue unless one oneself or somebody else benefited from one's having it. Hence the benefits of having religious experience must outweigh such sacrifices as are involved in paying attention to its claims.

I feel, too, that the benefits of religion must be in this world rather than the next, for the existence of the next is so very, very doubtful as to make sacrificing oneself for the sake of happiness therein a bad risk and perhaps one that it is ignoble to take. And there is no merit in persuading oneself that the chances of there being a next world are greater than they are, i.e., negligible. For, whatever may be said of 'belief' in God, belief that there is a life after death is a factual belief like any others and should not be believed more strongly than the evidence suggests.

Hence not only must the benefits of being religious belong to this world rather than the next, these benefits are in the first instance entirely confined to the religious person himself. Only I can benefit from my own contemplation. Hence the motivation for being religious is, and properly is, primarily selfish. These benefits can, if there are no miracles, fall only on the religious person himself in the first instance and only indirectly, if at all, through him upon others. And God himself, if there is one, cannot profit from any of the things that I can do, for either he is perfect, or is incapable of being affected by human action, or both, and has no need of them.

It could be argued that one ought not, even prudentially, to let oneself believe that there is an object in reality corresponding to one's experience. The feeling that there is such a being would be too terrifying to bear. And that the feeling should be entirely out of one's control and subject one to demands which might mean total slavery, welcome though some claim this to be, is too dreadful to contemplate. Some claim that the service of the Lord is perfect freedom, but if they do not exaggerate, this is presumably because their only want is to obey, and normal people have and should have more wants than this. God is by definition perfect, but the 'God' of one's experience is a good servant but a bad master. Hence, religion, like most or all other things, should, except perhaps by an elite few, be taken only in moderation.

Institutionalised religion, and perhaps also a creed, is essential if any religious practice or doctrine is to be preserved in a relatively unadulterated form, adequately advertised, its adherents given mutual support, its views heard in the right places, and its teaching handed down from one generation to the next. This, of course, involves compromise, a hierarchy of power, and careerist churchmen, who perform a necessary function from not necessarily the noblest of motives. But institutionalised religion must inevitably be second best to genuine feeling and belief resulting from one's own experience and thought. Religion requires more than occasional churchgoing and notional assent to a belief, which institutionalised religion tends to perpetuate. It also tends to discourage, or not necessarily to encourage, experiment and unorthodoxy, which are the lifeblood of all artistic and intellectual activity. Though it offers much more than the joys of conformity, there is inevitably a do-it-yourself element in genuine religion, and it should not be relegated to the status of a spectator sport. But for myself I find public religion too encumbered with false belief to indulge in it frequently, though I flatter myself that I would go to any service of any denomination, and even a Thuggee ceremony, provided I was not expected to participate.

Some may regard this book as the manifestation of an unfortunate tendency to run with the hare and hunt with the hounds, with the result that it will, like a swallowed filling, fall between two (very large) stools. But running with the hare and hunting with the hounds, though someone unaware of the risk of incurring the wrath of believer and unbeliever alike may regard it as cowardly, is not an unintelligent thing to do. For one thing, it enables one better to understand the point of view of both animals. And the trouble with wanting to have one's cake and eat it is not so much that it is wrong as that it looks impossible. If a way could be found of having both, what sensible man would refuse to take it?

Part of my object in this book, over and above simply trying to illuminate its subject, may be said to be to find a place – albeit a small one and not one for everybody – for religion in an alien world, a religion stripped of false theology, exploded science, and meaningless metaphysics. But I would not wish to encourage religion beyond a certain point, either in myself or in others. Religion is an excellent thing when one's attitude to it is provisional and experimental and when it is informed by that due intellectual humility which must respect the doubts of others and put oneself in their place. But carried to excess religion can produce an arrogant and interfering dogmatism which can be an enemy of the religious man himself and all with whom he comes into contact. All man's enterprises, including his religions, are his own fallible products. Forgetting this may discourage freedom of thought and the courage to experiment practically. But self-satisfied and unimaginative atheism, without any insight into or sympathy with religion, or at least the forces that produce it, is also a kind of blindness. But religion, to be of proper service to mankind, must be completely free of superstition.

I have little doubt that I shall die as I have lived, having found no resolution to the practical conflict between on the one hand the demands of the image of God which I could never quite banish from my mind even if I wanted to and my reason, which tells me that if a personal God is meant to be an item in the furniture of the universe, or even beyond it, the universe contains no such thing. Indeed, I do not think any resolution of my conflict is possible, and having achieved a *modus vivendi*, however self-deluded, I no longer even want to find one. Perhaps age has made me take myself as I find myself.

I know that there are those in my predicament who have an 'awareness' of the deity which they do not consider to be veridical and who have had the courage and determination to extirpate this awareness. I cannot bring myself to do this, partly because I suspect that religion, like sex, gets dangerous when swept under the carpet. One unexpected result of writing this book and here conducting, though in only a perfunctory way, the phenomenological investigation that should not be left only to believers, has been to bring me 'closer to God', in the sense that it makes me more aware of the ostensible presence of the divine. But this increased awareness is not altogether welcome. I fear it is becoming too demanding. By its fruits ye shall know it, and if it causes me fruitlessly to do lose my peace, religious experience is no good. When I have finished the book, I feel that I may be forced to make a decision. I shall either have to accept its demands, or extirpate it if I can – as have some of my friends – though I may have left the latter too late. If thy god offend you, cast him out, for a nonexistent God must stand or fall by his usefulness to man (not necessarily by his usefulness to the man whose God he is). If I have to wrestle with the angel to escape, I hope that, though the angel is usually quoted as odds-on favourite, I shall win. What I shall do if I am forced to decide I do not know but, unless I am forced by self-preservation, I hope I may, ignoble though this may be, go on as I have in the past and continue to sit on the fence. (Intimations of divinity as a background to my consciousness are welcome.) One reason why I hope that I am not forced to make a choice is that I am in the odd position of having both a need to do what I think is right, and follow the argument, which makes me think that I ought to believe that there is not a God, and a need for the support of God in order, by following the argument, to do what I think is right.

Even in those days, which for all I know will return, when I was more atheistic than I am now, I would have been sorry to have seen the idea of God disappear from the *imaginations*, if that is the right word, of men. But belief is another matter.

Glossary Mainly of Logical Words

I have frequently heard people complain that they cannot read books on philosophy because they contain too much technical terminology. Since I would like this book to be capable of being read by theologians and the general reader as well as by philosophers, I have included a glossary of some of the more central logical terms used in it, incidentally trying to give a very, very brief and very, very elementary introduction to logic. Without any knowledge of logic at all one is constantly prone to make mistakes such as thinking that to show that an argument is fallacious is the same thing as to disprove its conclusion. I would suggest that the glossary can be read as a whole, preferably before reading the book.

For more detailed and much wider information, the reader is referred to the excellent *The Oxford Dictionary of Philosophy*, by Simon Blackburn, Oxford University Press, 1994.

Absolute/relative: a judgment is absolute if it is true regardless of who asserts it, where he is when he asserts it, what language he uses to assert it in, whatever his beliefs and attitudes to its truth, and whatever the culture of the locality in which he was brought up or lives. If its truth depends on one or other of these factors, it is relative to that factor. Being relative is frequently confused with being 'self-referential'. For example, the sentence 'I have a cold' said by Tom and the same sentence said by Mary do not assert one proposition that is relative, but two different propositions, one about Tom and the other about Mary, both of which may be absolute.

Abstract/concrete: it once used to be considered to be sufficient to determine whether something was abstract to ask whether it had weight. 'Abstract' entities like numbers, parliamentary government, and differential equations cannot have it. But since some physical particles are now also supposed not to have mass, this test is inapplicable. See 'substance'.

Acquaintance, direct acquaintance: knowledge by acquaintance is contrasted with knowledge by description. For example, one is directly acquainted with one's own thoughts, but knows of the existence of others' thoughts only by description. More loosely, one is acquainted with one's wife, but probably not with the prime minister. The author believes that a number of distinctions are here being confused, but has not space to demonstrate this.

Affirming the consequent: in an argument of the form of the *modus ponendo ponens*, it is a fallacy to affirm the consequent and conclude that the antecedent must be true. For example, the argument: if there were a God, he would have created a universe; there is a universe, therefore there is a God, commits this fallacy.

A fortiori: an *a fortiori* argument argues from the fact that if a strong claim – for example, that all men will be punished – is true, a weaker form of it – say, that all murderers will be punished – must be.

Analogy: in an argument from analogy, one proceeds from a known resemblance to an unknown one. For example, Mars resembles Earth in being a planet of the sun, therefore there will be life on Mars as there is on Earth is a (weak until more resemblances are mentioned or found) analogical argument.

Analytic: a proposition is analytic if (speaking loosely) its truth follows from the definitions of the words in the sentence that expresses it; for example, that vixens are female is an analytic proposition. Analytic propositions cannot be denied without self-contradiction and their truth is said to follow from the meanings of the words in the sentence that formulates them. In those which are of subject/predicate form, such as that vixens are female, the predicate is 'contained' in the subject. With certain exceptions, a proposition that is not analytic is synthetic.

Antecedent: in the hypothetical proposition: if that's a Messerschmitt, I'm a goner, that that's a Messerschmitt is the antecedent (and that I'm a goner the consequent).

Apodeictic: the premises of an apodeictic argument necessitate its conclusion.

A posteriori: see '*a priori*'.

A priori: a proposition is *a priori* if it can be known to be true without any empirical investigation of what the world in fact is like. For example, one needs empirical investigation to find out whether Mars contains men, but one can know without such investigation that if all Martians are mortal and Tom is a Martian, Tom must be mortal.

Argument: in one sense an argument consists of at least two propositions, a premise and a conclusion, and the premise either supports, or has been given by someone as a reason for, the conclusion. Arguments in this sense are 'abstract' entities. Two or more people may also argue concerning whether a proposition is true. In this sense an argument is an event. (These people may or may not use various rhetorical devices to win the argument without having proved the proposition which is in dispute, their doing which may tend to disguise the fact that the argument is fallacious, if it is.) There can also be arguments – which are also events – that do not so much concern the *truth* of a proposition, as what to *do*.

Assertion: if I say that God exists, *that* God exists is what I assert, and is an assertion, or a proposition that is asserted. Such propositions are true or false, founded or unfounded, wild or considered, etc. They should not be confused with acts of asserting, which can also be called assertions and which are things people do, that is, events that occur at a certain place and time.

Barbara: the name of a valid syllogism with two universal affirmative premises and a universal conclusion, for example: all men are mortal and all Greeks are men, therefore all Greeks are mortal.

Begging the question: one begs the question if one assumes the very point at issue, for example if one argues that God exists because it says so in the Bible, which is the word of God.

Belief: belief is one of a number of 'propositional attitudes', which include doubt and disbelief, hope and fear, that may be taken up to propositions. One believes a proposition if one feels confident in its truth and is prepared to act on it, i.e., to act in a way that would succeed in getting what one wants if it were true.

Bivalence, principle of: the (questionable) principle that every proposition must be either true or false.

Categorical: a categorical proposition, for example, that it will break, is sometimes contrasted with a hypothetical one, for example, if you drop it, it will break. A proposition is asserted categorically if it is asserted. A proposition that is a constituent of a compound proposition – for example, a hypothetical proposition – that is asserted is not itself asserted. For example, someone who says it will break if you drop it is not asserting that you will drop it, nor that it will break. But a hypothetical proposition can be asserted categorically just like any other proposition. It would be a good idea to distinguish between the question whether a proposition is compound – as hypothetical propositions are – or not and whether it is asserted or not.

Categories: there are not only different classes of things, such as reptiles and mammals, there are also different categories of things, such as substances and events. When things belong to different categories, there are usually things that can meaningfully be predicated of the one but not of the other. For example, battles, which are a species of event, can be prolonged, but whales, a kind of substance, cannot be.

Category mistake: the mistake of attributing a property to something when it does not belong to a category that could possess that property.

Causally possible: see 'logically possible'.

Cause: an almost circular definition of cause is that it is that which produces an effect, but this definition is good enough for our purposes. The fallacy of *post hoc ergo propter hoc* is the fallacy of supposing that because one thing happens after another, it happens because of the other. The usual, but not an infallible, way of avoiding this fallacy is to try to repeat the alleged causal sequence in question and find out if you can separate the two events allegedly causally connected. For example if you shut the refrigerator door and this appears to cause a loud explosion next door, one must suspect the belief that the former caused the latter if one shuts it again and notes whether or not on this occasion too there was an explosion.

Certainty: one ought not to say that something is certain if one is oneself not certain of it, but usually when one says that something is certain one is claiming in addition that other people are certain of it, and perhaps also that they are justified in being so certain. If I say that I am or that he is certain of something, this does not imply that it is true. If I say that it is certain, this *does* imply that what we are certain of is true.

Chance: something happens by chance if it does not happen by design. For example, a chance meeting is a meeting where neither of the parties intended to meet. It is often supposed by philosophers that a chance happening is an uncaused happening, but there may be perfectly good causes of my meeting Tom when and where I did. Games of chance are games where it is difficult – and if the game is one of pure chance, without divine prescience, impossible – to predict what will be the outcome of various strategies. The chances of something's happening or of a proposition's being true are the same as the probability of these things.

Characteristic: a property or feature, such as being red or round, possessed by something. There may be characteristics of characteristics; for example, being possessed by something is a characteristic of the characteristic: being a man. A thing's characteristics include the relations in which it stands to other things as well as its properties.

Circularity: an argument is circular if its premises cannot be established without first establishing its conclusion. A definition is circular if the word to be defined is defined indirectly in terms of itself, for example, the useful definition 'A horse is a thoroughbred horse if both of its parents are thoroughbred horses'.

Class: a class is all the things which possess some characteristic (in a wide sense of 'characteristic'). For example, the class of curates consists of all those men and women who possess the characteristic of being a curate. The null class, of which there can be only one, is that class which has no members, and is determined by attributes such as being a chimera or an abominable snowman.

Compatibility: one proposition is compatible with another if they can both be true. Two propositions are incompatible if they cannot both be true. There are two species of incompatibility, contrariety and contradiction. Two propositions are contrary if, though they cannot both be true, they can both be false. They are contradictory if they cannot both be true and cannot both be false. For example, it is my duty to kill her and it is my duty to keep her alive are contraries, because it may be my duty to do neither. That it is my duty to keep her alive and that it is not my duty not to keep her alive are contradictories.

Compound proposition: a proposition composed of two or more (atomic) propositions, e.g. if it rains, it pours, the constituents of which are (a) it rains and (b) it pours.

Conceivability: something is conceivable if it can be conceived or imagined as happening, even if there is no reason to suppose that it does happen and perhaps every reason to suppose that it does not.

Concept: we have a concept of a man if we can use some such word as 'man', or some private symbol, for men, recognise men when we come across them, behave correctly with respect to them (treat a man as a man which an animal like a dog can do) and think about them either in their presence or in their absence. Concepts should not be confused with universals. All yellow things will have it in common that they are instances of the universal yellowness, whether there are any intelligent beings in the universe or not, but the concept of yellow is dependent upon the existence of intelligent beings to have the concept.

Conjunction: the conjunction of two statements is a statement which asserts both of them, for example, he is a fool and he is a knave.

Connotation: a word like 'men' is applied to individual men, which are what it denotes, because they have those attributes – allegedly rationality and animality – which 'men' connotes.

Consistent: two or more propositions are consistent if they can all be true. There is a different sense, which is difficult to elucidate, in which a *policy* can be consistent.

Contrary: see 'compatibility'.

Conversational implication: that all men are mortal and Socrates is a man implies that Socrates is mortal. *My saying* that all men are mortal conversationally implies a large number of things about me; that I believe it, that I believe that it is something my speaker wants to know, that I believe that it is not too obvious to be worth remarking upon, that I believe that it is relevant to our previous discussion, and so on. Whereas it is the proposition that all men are mortal and that Socrates is a man that implies that Socrates is mortal, it is my asserting that all men are mortal that has conversational implications about me. And though what implies a false proposition must be false, asserting something that conversationally implies something false about the judger does not make what he asserts false. For example, my saying that all men are mortal conversationally implies that I believe that they are, but this does not mean that that all men are mortal is false if I do not believe that they are.

Conceptual truth: something is conceptually true if it is inconceivable that it should be false. For example, that quadratic equations cannot swim is a conceptual truth. The idea of conceptual truth is rather wider than that of analyticity. Some philosophers, impressed by the fact that the factual study of reality is apportioned among the empirical sciences, have thought that philosophers can discover only conceptual truths, which are truths about second-order propositions about reality.

Conceptual possibility: a proposition is conceptually possible if asserting it does not involve a contradiction or a category mistake. It is a conceptual possibility that Tom should sleep more soundly than he does, but not that he should sleep more slowly than he does.

Conclusion: what one is seeking to show to be the case by adducing certain premises is the conclusion of the argument which consists of those premises and the conclusion. ('Conclusion' is ambiguous between *what* is concluded, which is abstract, and the *concluding* of what is concluded, which is an event.)

Consequent: that if 'ifs' and 'ans' were pots and pans, there'd be no need for tinkers is a hypothetical proposition. That there would be no need for tinkers is its consequent, i.e., the consequence of 'if' and 'ans' being pots and pans. (See 'antecedent'.)

Contingent: a truth (a true proposition) is contingent if it just so happens that it is true and neither its being so nor its not being so is necessary. For example, it is just a contingent fact that more boys are born than girls.

Contradiction, contradictory: see 'compatibility'.

Contrapositive, contraposition: the contrapositive of that if 'ifs' and 'ans' were pots and pans, there'd be no need for tinkers is that if there is a need for tinkers, 'ifs' and 'ans' are not pots and pans. A contrapositive is formed from the proposition contraposed by interchanging the negations of the original antecedent and the original consequent.

Corollary: one thing is a corollary of another if it can be deduced from the other.

Correspondence theory of truth: the not very daring view that a proposition – for example, the proposition that Tony Blair is prime minister – is true if it corresponds to a fact – in this case, the fact that Tony Blair is prime minister.

Counterfactual conditional: see 'unfulfilled conditional'.

Cross-division: if a class is subdivided on more than one principle, the result may be a cross-division. For example, if you divide the class of apples into Cox's Orange Pippins, Golden Delicious, Worcester Permains and French apples, you are dividing the class of apples on two principles, species and place of origin, and the result may be that there are some applies that do not belong to any of these classes and others that belong to more than one of them.

Deductive argument: a deductive argument (as opposed to an inductive argument) is one in which the premises entail the conclusion and in which it is consequently impossible for the premises to be true and the conclusion false.

Definition: the most elementary kinds of definition are (a) those that stipulate how a word is to be used and (b) those that state how a word is in fact used. In a logical system a definition tells you that a symbol may be substituted for another symbol, or defines a term by putting forward principles that involve using it (implicit definition). There are also recursive definitions.

In a wide sense, a definition can be given by explaining the logical relations between the proposition expressed by the sentence in which it occurs and other propositions. For example, the statement that the average man has 2.4 children can be elucidated by saying that all it means is that the number of children divided by the number of men is 2.4. This prevents one from regarding 'the average man' as a strange metaphysical entity, capable of having more than two but fewer than three children. This is the sense in which analytic philosophers are so much concerned – though not exclusively so – with definitions.

Definite description: a description like 'the man in the iron mask. '*A* man in an iron mask' is an indefinite description.

Demonstration: to demonstrate something in philosophy is usually to prove it. A demonstrator, however, does not prove things, but shows how things are done.

Denying the antecedent: in hypothetical arguments of the form of the *modus ponendo ponens* it is a fallacy to suppose that from the fact that the antecedent is false, it follows that the consequent is also false. For example, to argue: if he had measles, he would have spots; he does not have measles; therefore he does not have spots, would be to commit this fallacy.

Dilemma: the simplest kind of dilemma is of the form: if I confess I will be hanged and if I do not confess I will be hanged; but I will either confess or not confess: therefore I will be hanged.

Disjunction, disjunctive: a disjunctive proposition, for example, that he is a fool or a knave, asserts that either of two or more propositions must be true, but does not tell you which.

Disposition, dispositional characteristic: a dispositional characteristic is a characteristic like being soluble, which consists in the fact that a soluble substance will dissolve if put in water. Dispositions must be distinguished from their manifestations, e.g., actually dissolving because put in water. It is obviously impossible to tell whether something is soluble just by inspecting it. One has to put a substance that is possibly soluble into water and see whether it dissolves. An object cannot possess dispositional characteristics alone; the fact that two substances have different dispositions must be due to some further difference between them, say, to a difference in their molecular structure.

Double negation: two 'nots' cancel one another out, except in Somerset and one or two other places, where they are used for emphasis.

Empirical (contrasted with *a priori*): knowledge is empirical if it is acquired by observation. Very roughly, there are two ways of acquiring empirical knowledge, by observation, as when we know that the substance in front of us is turning red, and by inferring it from what we observe or putting it forward as a hypothesis to explain what we observe, as we when know that the substance in front of us is an acid, or that the stars we observe are moving away from us. I believe that that someone is in pain is known because it explains why screams are coming from his lips and that that the Battle of Hastings was fought in 1066 because it explains why the appropriate words are to be found in manuscripts and history books.

Entails, entailment: one proposition entails another if the second can be deduced from the first. For example, that all men are mortal and that Socrates is a man entails that Socrates is mortal. Defining entailment by saying that it is impossible for the entailing proposition to be true and the entailed proposition false, or in terms of saying that the truth of the first proposition makes it impossible for the second proposition to be false, is less satisfactory, for reasons that I shall not go into.

Entertain: to entertain a proposition is an old-fashioned but useful word for having a proposition before one's mind without necessarily either believing it or disbelieving it.

Enthymeme: an argument – in practice most arguments – where one or more of its premises is not stated.

Epistemology: roughly, the study of knowledge and the way in which we acquire it. Some would say that it includes the question whether we have knowledge at all.

Equivalence: two propositions are equivalent if the first implies or entails the second and the second implies or entails the first. (See 'if and only if'.)

Excluded middle: the principle that there is no alternative intermediate between a proposition and its negation.

Ex hypothesi: as a consequence of the hypothesis that is being considered.

Existential import: the existential import of a subject predicate proposition is what it implies or presupposes about the existence of the objects mentioned by its subject and predicate. For example, it has been held that that no men are mortal does not imply that there are any men, but that some men are mortal does.

Existential propositions: a proposition is existential if it asserts that something exists. It is usually held that existential propositions do not assert a predicate of a subject. 'Dodos do not exist' cannot attribute a property to dodos, because there are none, but asserts that there are no members of the class of dodos. Some existential propositions are empirical and contingent, but others, for example that there is a prime number between seven and 13, are *a priori* and necessary.

External relations: the doctrine of external relations maintains that everything in the universe so interpenetrates every other thing that nothing can change its relation to another thing without also changing its 'nature'.

Fact: facts can be opposed to judgments about the facts, theories, falsehoods, moral and aesthetic judgments, and statements about law; to myth, legend and fiction. Truthful people try to make their judgments correspond to the facts. It may be a theory that Tom is the murderer, though a fact that his handkerchief was found near the scene of the crime. It is a fact that Dickens wrote Pickwick, though not that Pickwick was sued for breach of promise. That Mary shot Tom is a factual judgment – though possibly not a fact – but that she was right to do so a moral one. Whether or not it was murder or manslaughter is a question of law rather than of fact. (But in 'before (or after) the fact', 'fact' means event or deed.)

Fallacy: a fallacy occurs when something is deduced from one or more other propositions that do not in fact entail it; for example, the argument: all men are mortal, Socrates is a mortal, therefore Socrates is a man is fallacious (although in this case its premises and its conclusion are both true). Certain fallacies, for example, the undistributed middle (which fallacy the above argument exemplifies), affirming the antecedent, denying the consequent, *ignoratio elenchi*, or *post hoc ergo proper hoc*, have names, but most ways of going wrong are subtle, difficult to detect and nameless. (The gambler's fallacy is the fallacy of supposing that, for example, a long run of heads increases the probability of the next toss being a tail.)

False: see 'true'.

Falsifiable: capable of being shown to be false by empirical disconfirmation. Entailing only one false consequence shows that a proposition is false, whereas a number of confirming instances are usually necessary to show that it is true.

Usually what something that apparently disconfirms a hypothesis shows is that one or other of a conjunction of hypotheses must be false. It is often held that an allegedly empirical proposition that cannot be disconfirmed or falsified by empirical tests – for example the proposition that bread and wine turn into the body and blood of Christ during the communion service – is vacuous.

First-order: it is sometimes convenient to distinguish first-order propositions, for example, the proposition that dogs bark, from second-order propositions about such propositions, for example, that that dogs bark is true, false, easily ascertainable, believed, known, based upon perception, universal, incontrovertible, synthetic, contingent, and empirical. (It has been held that philosophy is a second-order subject, which does not deal with reality directly but only with judgments about reality, but one's second-order views about such things as whether certain first-order judgments can be ascertained will make a difference to which first-order judgments one holds.) A meta-subject, is the same as a second- (or perhaps an nth-) order subject.

Follows from: one proposition follows from another if it is entailed by that proposition. (See 'entails'.)

Form, logical: that if this is a triangle it will have three sides and that if this is a whale it will be a mammal have the same form – they are both hypothetical – but different matter, as one is about triangles and the other about whales. (Similarly $2 \times 3 = 6$ and $7 \times 11 = 77$ have the same form, but different matter.) The validity of an argument depends upon its form, for any argument of the form: if this is a whale, it will suckle its young; it does not suckle its young; therefore it is not a whale; will be valid, whether or not it is about whales. This fact makes it possible to make generalisations about the validity of arguments. If one uses one kind of symbol for form and a different kind of symbol for matter, one can say that all hypothetical propositions have the form, p->q. 'P' and 'q' (for the matter) are called variable symbols, because different propositions may be substituted for them. '->' (for the form) is called a constant, as one always substitutes 'implies' (or 'if ... then') for it. One may then generalise the fact that all arguments having the same form as that if this is a mammal, it suckles its young; it does not suckle its young; therefore it is not a mammal, by: p->q, -q, therefore -p (where '-' is a logical constant meaning 'not'). Whatever propositions are substituted for variables such as 'p', 'q' and 'r', the result will be a valid argument, so long as '->' means 'implies'. Appropriately combining constant and variable symbols enables one to make logically true generalisations such as ((p->q).(-q))->-p (where '.' is a logical constant meaning 'and'). An argument is valid if the statement that its premises imply its conclusion is *logically true*.

Foundationalism: the view that propositions can be divided into those that can be known without inference and those that cannot, the latter being derived from the former. There is no reason why propositions that can be known without inference should be certainly true, or why a proposition should not be believed both because it can be inferred from propositions that can be known without inference and because it is 'coherent' with or supported by other beliefs.

Genus: that of which a species is a species, for example, crocodiles are a species of reptile. ('Genus' has a more technical meaning in botany and zoology.)

Hypotheses: a hypothesis is a proposition that is advanced tentatively to explain some fact or facts. For example, the hypothesis that things like stars are moving away from us is advanced to explain why they look more red than they would if they kept their distance. General hypotheses tend to get described as 'laws' when they get sufficiently well confirmed.

Hypothetical proposition: a hypothetical proposition is a species of compound proposition that asserts that one proposition (called the consequent) is true if another proposition (called the antecedent) is true. The kind of hypothetical proposition most commonly recognised, e.g. if all men are mortal, Socrates must be, asserts a connection between its antecedent and its consequent, without committing the speaker to the truth of either. But 'if I did not plant peas in this row, I planted beans in it' is true simply so long as I did not plant peas, but beans, in it and saying that there are biscuits on the table if you want some is little more than a way of asserting its 'consequent', that there are biscuits on the table.

Ideal/real: the antithesis between 'ideal' and 'real' is a false one. Idealists are a species of monist who hold that the only substances are minds and that matter is just a 'modification' of mind. It is a mistake, which idealists themselves may unwittingly encourage, to suppose that they do not think that material objects are real.

Idealists like Berkeley sometimes thought that material things were combinations of ideas, in Berkeley's case ideas in the mind of God. It is a mistake to think that Berkeley thought that propositions about objects could not be established, or that they were neither true nor false, or that things were not real. (He did think that words for 'what physicists call matter' were meaningless.)

Identity: 'two' things are properly identical only if they are one and the same thing. 'Identical' twins are not one and the same twin, but only precisely similar.

Identity of indiscernibles: Leibniz held, wrongly, that no two things could have all their properties in common; if they did, there was just one thing. The principle of the identity of indiscernibles must not be confused with the principle of the indiscernibility of identicals, which holds (correctly) that that if two things are identical, they must have all their properties in common.

If: 'if' is usually used to indicate that something that the speaker is not committing himself to is being supposed so that he may say what would be the result if it were so. If the supposition is known to be false, the question may be of only academic interest, but if it is not known whether it is true or not, it may be of immense practical importance to decide, say, what the results of certain courses of action would be, if they were taken, or what the consequences of certain hypotheses would be, if it were held. Hence the frequent complaint that what someone says is only hypothetical is misplaced.

If and only if: that you can join if you have a large income means that if you have a large income you can join; you can join only if you have a large income means that if you do *not* have a large income, you *cannot* join. You can join if and only if you have a large income combines these two assertions.

Illicit process: the fallacy of arguing from information about some of a class to a conclusion about all of it.

Imperative: a sentence (usually) expresses an imperative if it is in the imperative mood. Imperatives, unlike propositions, are incapable of being true or false, believed or disbelieved, asserted or denied, and so on.

Implication: one proposition implies another if, if the first proposition is true, the second proposition is also true. For example, that all Ancient Greeks were unbelievers implies that some among unbelievers were Ancient Greeks.

'Implies' is usually used more widely than 'entails'; for example, one can say that smoke implies fire, although the existence of smoke does not logically entail the existence of fire. (Implication also includes conversational implication, which see.)

Inductive, induction: an argument is inductive if it argues from what happens in observed cases to what happens in all cases whether observed or not. For example, it is an inductive argument that because objects are always observed to attract one another with a force proportional to their mass and have never been observed not to, they always do. Inductive arguments include those to the effect that because something is observed to happen a certain percentage of the time, it will always happen that percentage of the time. Arguments that conclude that a hypothesis or theory is true because its consequences are found to be true are also called inductive.

One reason why accumulating inductive evidence in favour of a generalisation strengthens one's belief in it may well be that the more times a hypothesis is tested, the more likely it is that the circumstances surrounding each test are different from those surrounding previous tests, thus serving, though only incidentally, to eliminate alternative hypotheses. For example, if on a large number of occasions arsenic is followed by death, this serves to eliminate the possibility that factors other than arsenic caused these deaths, if these factors were not all present on all the occasions.

More widely, inductive arguments aim to complete partial regularities by postulating entities or events – for example, unobserved fireplaces and unobserved chimneys to complete the partial regularity connecting smoke with fire – in such a manner as to complete these regularities. Testing hypotheses presupposes induction, in that it is assumed that if a hypothesis is once refuted, it will be refuted again the next time the refuting experiment is made.

Inductive arguments are invalid by the standards of deductive logic. For example, since observed instances of a class are only some of its instances, inductive arguments commit the fallacy of illicit process. If one concludes that a hypothesis is correct because it leads to conclusions that are true, one is committing the deductive fallacy of affirming the consequent. This, however, does not mean that deductive arguments do not have their own standards of validity.

Karl Popper has held that induction is invalid and that hypotheses are established by eliminating their alternatives, but induction is needed to establish that a hypothesis, once eliminated, stays so.

Ineffable: something is ineffable if it can be experienced but nothing can be said about it. It should follow that it is impossible to say what can be experienced or what cannot have anything said about it, as this would be to talk about it. There may, however, be some experiences the objects of which are very difficult to describe.

Inference: the process of passing from the supposed truth of one's premises to the supposed truth of a conclusion, which may or may not follow from it. Inference should be distinguished from implication; it is *because* A is the father of B implies that B is the son of A that one can validly infer the latter from the former. Mistaken inferences occur because one thinks that one's premises imply one's conclusion when they do not.

Intuition: one knows something – for example, that things that are equal to a third thing are equal to one another – intuitively if one can just see without argument that it is so. Only *a priori* necessary truths can be known in this way.

Invalid: an argument is invalid if its conclusion does not follow from its premises. It is possible for an argument to have conclusions and premises that are both true and nevertheless be invalid, though a valid argument cannot have true premises and a false conclusion. One should not suppose that showing an argument to be invalid means that its conclusion is false.

Knowledge: the difference between knowledge and other cognitive attitudes such as belief is that what is known must be true, though one may believe what is false. It may also be the case that, if one knows something, one has come to believe it by a method that necessitates that what one believes is true.

L: the symbol usually used for necessity. Hence L(vixens are female) means that, necessarily, vixens are female. One must take great care in deciding what proposition the necessity operator 'L' governs. For example, L(If Tom knows p, then p) is a quite different proposition from if Tom knows p, then Lp. The first is true. The second would imply that we could know only necessary propositions such as that two and two are four and so is false. 'M' is used for possibility.

Logic: roughly, the study of arguments. This divides into the study of terms (such as 'men'), the study of propositions (such as that all men are mortal) of arguments (all men are mortal and all Greeks are men, so all Greeks are mortal). Partly because an argument is valid only if the statement that its premises imply its conclusion is logically true, logic also studies logical truth. It is possible to make generalisations to the effect that certain kinds of argument – i.e. those that have the same logical form – are valid; for example, any argument which asserts that because one class is included in another and an individual is a member of the first class, this individual must be a member of the second, must be valid. The premises of a deductive argument, such as the one just discussed, entail their conclusion, whereas the premises of an inductive argument – say, all observed crows are black and no observed crows are any other colour, so all crows must be black – support their conclusion without entailing it. (The premises of this latter argument, incidentally, are not true, which (again) does not mean that it is not valid.)

The reader is referred to the appendix on logical symbols at the back of *The Oxford Dictionary of Philosophy* (see above).

Logical positivism: the view that a sentence is meaningless unless it expresses either a statement that is tautologous (either this is an acid or it is not an acid) or empirically verifiable, or (a qualification that is frequently forgotten) one of the statements that verify the latter. For example, the sentence 'That is an acid' is empirically verifiable because from it can be deduced that if this is litmus paper, this will turn it red. That this is turning red is verifiable by direct inspection. It could be that the supposition that everything is daily doubling in size is meaningless because there is no way of establishing it; if everything were doubling in size, one's measuring instruments would also be doubling in size.

Logical possibility: something is logically possible, as opposed to being causally or technically possible, if it is not logically contradictory; for example, it is logically impossible to end a journey before one starts it. Something is causally possible if its being true or occurring would not infringe the laws of nature, for example, man's leaving the solar system. It is technically possible if it is something that man has the technical resources to do, for example, to build a tunnel under the Atlantic. What is logically or causally impossible at one time will remain so – unless, perhaps the laws of nature changed after the big bang – but something that is technically impossible at one time may be technically possible later, or *vice versa*. But to say that something is possible may be to say that the person making the judgment is in possession of no evidence that excludes the proposition that he says is possible from being true.

Logic, symbolic or mathematical: logicians have always used symbols, but symbolic or mathematical logic dates from the vast extension of their use when logic was taken over and greatly advanced by mathematicians in the middle of the nineteenth century.

Logical symbolism: just occasionally it will be helpful if I use logical symbols for propositions. The usual ones are p, q and r, etc. These can be negated (-p, -q, -r) and joined by and (.) to make p.q; by either (v) to make pvq, or implication (->) to make p->q (if p, then q) and by equivalence to make p<->q (p if and only if q). The negations of propositions may themselves be negated (-p) and compound propositions can be negated -(p.q), or not both (p and q), and conjoined with other propositions in the aforesaid ways (p.-q)->-(p->q) (if p is true and q false, it cannot be that p implies q). For a fuller but still elementary treatment of symbols, again see the appendix of logical symbols in *The Oxford Dictionary of Philosophy*.

The symbols 'p', 'q' and 'r', and so on, are used by logicians in order to make generalisations about propositions, as the symbols 'x', 'y' and 'z', and so on, are used by mathematicians to make generalisations about numbers. Hence, just as axb = bxa is a law in mathematics, pvp->p is a law in logic. (Naturally there are more interesting laws in both subjects.)

But it is not the case that he is both a fool and a knave with -p and q (e.g. it is not the case that he is a fool, but he is a knave), just as one should not confuse -(a+b) with -a+b.

Logical truth: that there was a sea battle yesterday is not a logical truth; but that either there was or was not a sea battle yesterday is a logical truth, for it will be true whether there was a sea battle yesterday or not. But problems arise about the statement that there will be a sea battle tomorrow.

Many-valued logic: logic modified to fit the possibility that there are more than two truth values, for example, truth value neuter as well as true and false.

Matter of fact: a fact that is not a necessary truth.

Meta-: see first-order/second-order.

Modal logic: that branch of logic which deals with the relations between propositions which assert that something is possible or necessary, as well as those propositions that assert that something is contingent or just happens to be so. See 'L'. An example of a statement of modal logic is that if a proposition is true, it must be possible for it to be true (p->Mp).

Modal operators: a proposition, besides just being true, may be true, possibly true (often symbolised by 'M') or necessarily true (often symbolised by 'L'). In the sense in which 'possible' is used by logicians, to say that a proposition is possible neither excludes its being true nor its being necessarily true. To say that a proposition is true entails that it is possible and does not exclude its being necessarily true.

There is a modern view to the effect that to say that a proposition is possibly true is to say that there is a possible world in which it is true. On this view, to say that a proposition is necessary is to say that it is true in all possible worlds. To say that it is true is to say that it is true in this world.

Modal shift fallacy: the fallacy resulting from thinking that a modal operator, usually necessity, governs a different proposition from the one it does govern. For example, if one says, as if one were expressing a necessary truth, 'What will be will be', it may be that one is confusing its being a necessary truth that if it is going to be then it is going to be, with if it is going to be, then it is a necessary truth that it is going to be.

Monist: a monist is a philosopher who thinks that there is only one kind of substance. If he is an idealist, he thinks that this substance is mind; if he is a materialist, he thinks it is matter; if he is a neutral monist he thinks that mind and matter are both composed of neutral entities. There is also a sense of 'monist' in which a monist – for example Spinoza – holds that there is only one substance (as opposed to one kind of substance).

Naturalism: the view that there is nothing over and above nature. Naturalism must lead either to pantheism (God is nature), to reductionism (statements about God can be reduced to statements about nature), or to atheism.

Necessary: a proposition is necessary if it must be true. For example, the proposition that 2 + 2 = 4 is necessary, because two and two must make four and cannot make anything else. There are also senses of 'necessary' in which things other than propositions, for example, tin-openers, can be necessary. In this sense, causal connections can be necessary, though propositions saying that some things cause other things are contingent. Necessity is usually symbolised by 'L' preceding the statement that is said to be necessary, when necessity is a property of a statement at all.

Necessary and sufficient conditions: there being petrol in the tank is a necessary condition of my car's starting, because if there is no petrol in the tank, my car will not start. There being petrol in the tank, the engine's being switched on, the self-starter's working, etc., are jointly (but not independently), sufficient conditions of its starting, because if all these condition obtain, my car will start.

Noncontradiction, principle of: the principle that a proposition and its negation cannot both be true.

Nothing: to say that there is nothing in the larder is to say that there is not anything in the larder. One is not asserting the existence of some ethereal entity about which it is possible to write long and tedious metaphysical treatises.

Objective/subjective: something is 'objectively' true if it is true independently of the state of the person who asserts it. It is subjective if it is not objective. Being subjective should not be confused with being about the subject (or judger). For example, the judgment that the judger himself is ill can be made true by his being ill, but not by his attitude to his being ill. Hence a judgment can be about the subject without being made true by his attitude to it. 'Objective' is often, wrongly, opposed to 'relative' or 'ideal'.

Ockham's razor: one should not multiply entities (or hypotheses) unnecessarily. But being too illiberal in this respect is one way of being too uncritically tender-minded.

One-one: a relation is one-one, as opposed to being one-many or many-one, if it holds between only one term and only one other term. 'Father of' is one-many, 'son of' is many-one, and spouse of is one-one. If there is a one-one relation between each member of two classes of terms, there must be as many terms in the first class as there are in the second.

P: 'p', 'q' and 'r', etc.: symbols for propositions, just as 'x', 'y' and 'z' are symbols for numbers.

Ponendo ponens: the argument: if there is a God, there is no evil; there is a

God; so there is no evil, is an argument in the form of the *modus ponendo ponens*.

Positivism: the view that the only things about reality that we can know are things that are discoverable about the natural world in a broadly scientific way. Logical positivism is the more extreme view that sentences that do not express any verifiable facts about the natural world are not even meaningful.

Possible: see 'logical possibility'.

Pragmatism: the view that what makes a proposition true is the fact that it is useful to believe it or, more plausibly, that acting on it leads to success.

Predicate: if I say that all men are damned, then 'men' is the subject of my sentence, and being damned the predicate. Predicates must not be confused with attributes, though the function of a predicate is often to attribute some attribute to something picked out by a subject.

Premise(s): the premise or premises of an argument are the propositions that are adduced for believing a conclusion. The argument is valid if the reasons really are good reasons for that conclusion; it is a proof if the premises are also true. There are often supposed to be two kinds of argument, deductive and inductive arguments.

From the premise that Tom's first client is a murderer and the premise that Mary is Tom's first client, one can deduce the conclusion that Mary is a murderer. This is a piece of information that could not be deduced from either premise without the other.

Presupposition: one thing presupposes another if, if it were not true, the second thing could not be true (though it might be neither true nor false). For example, that all men are wicked presupposes that there are men.

Probability: in ordinary parlance, something (a proposition?) is said to be probable if it is more likely to be true than not. As used by logicians and mathematicians, a proposition is said to be probable if it has any degree of probability, from 0 to 1. The notion of probability is closely connected with that of frequency. For example, heads and tails are said to be equally probable because in a long run of tosses they occur roughly in equal proportions and this proportion approximates more and more closely to equality the more tosses there are.

It is a common mistake to suppose that probability statements are refuted by citing just a few contrary instances. For example, when someone says that smoking increases the probability of one's getting lung cancer, it does not refute this statement to say that one's grandmother smoked and lived to be 90 without getting it.

Proof: something is a proof if it establishes a conclusion beyond reasonable doubt. Hence the conclusions of proofs must be true and it is improper to do such things as talk of the ontological proof of the existence of God if you do not think that its conclusion does follow from its premises, or do not think that its conclusion is true. In a proof something is deduced from true propositions by means of a valid argument. It is sometimes added that the premises should be known, by the person using this argument, to be true and that it should be possible to establish the premises without first establishing the conclusion. If it is not possible to establish the premises without first establishing the conclusion, an argument that purports to be a proof is circular. (See 'premises'.)

Property: see 'characteristic'.

Proposition: a proposition is that which is true or false, where 'is the case' can be substituted for 'true'. (True Thomas is not a proposition, nor is a true whale or a true line.) For example it is true that the Earth is round and false that it is flat. Many philosophers think that what is true or false is a sentence (i.e., the sentence which I would say formulated the proposition). But it is in fact a solecism to say 'It is true "the Earth is round"' rather than 'It is true (that) the Earth is round'.

Quotes: normally a word or phrase or sentence is put in quotation marks to indicate that one is talking about that word or phrase or sentence. For example, one shouts 'Fire', not fire, eats dirt, not 'dirt', and spells 'Constantinople', not Constantinople. 'Shit', but not shit, is a four letter word, and 'shit', but not '"shit"' is a rude word.

Rationalist, opposed to empiricist: just as an extreme empiricist thinks that everything we know we know by observation, experience, and experiment, so an extreme rationalist thinks that everything we know can be worked out by reason alone. (He may think that, though we in fact know many things empirically, everything we know could in principle be worked out by reason alone.) The difference between rationalists and empiricists is a matter of degree. Even the arch-empiricist David Hume thought that there was scope for *a priori* argument (in determining what he called the relation between ideas, i.e., such facts as that if one has two groups of two, one has a group of four). Probably the only philosopher to think that we could know everything only by observation was John Stuart Mill.

Some philosophers have thought that it is irrational to be immoral, but I cannot see that this is so.

Real: see 'ideal/real'. In ordinary English 'real' is used in opposition to such expressions as 'imaginary', 'imitation', 'fictional', 'genuine', 'contrary to appearances', 'pretended', 'virtual', 'so-called', 'exaggerated', 'fake', 'forged', 'counterfeit' or 'borderline'. The controversy in philosophy concerns the extent to which the things we perceive and know about are independent of our knowing and perceiving them, but I cannot for myself see what this has to do with their being real.

Reasons: one's reasons for believing that something is so should be propositions that support it. There are reasons for doing things as well as reasons for believing things. Reasons are sometimes contrasted with causes, for example, his reason for believing in democracy may be that he thinks that no-one ought to be governed without his own consent, but the cause of his believing in democracy may be that he was brought up in Hong Kong. The cause of his killing himself – that he was depressed – may be different from his reason for killing himself – that he thought that there was a conspiracy against him. But in fact reasons are a species of cause. He could have killed himself both because he was depressed, which would not have made him kill himself had he not also thought that there was a conspiracy against him, and because he thought there was a conspiracy against him, which would not have made him kill himself had he not also been depressed.

Reductio ad absurdum: to show that something is false by deducing a preposterous consequence from it; more narrowly, to show that something is false by showing that it implies its own falsity.

Reduction: one class of statements is reduced to another if statements belonging to the first class are shown to be equivalent to statements belonging to the second. This is usually done because the first class of statement involves problematic notions and the second class is thought, sometimes mistakenly, not to. For example, it has been attempted (successfully) to reduce statements about the average man to statements about individual men; with dubious success to reduce statements about states to statements about individual citizens; and with no success at all to reduce statements about the deity to statements about the natural world.

Refute: a proposition is refuted if it is shown to be false; an argument is refuted if it is shown to be invalid. The conclusion of an argument that has been refuted does not have to be false. (Refuting must not be confused with rebutting, which consists in merely asserting that something someone else has asserted is false. One can only refute a false proposition or invalid argument.)

Relations: a relation holds between two or more terms, unless you count identity as a relation, in which case a relation can hold between a term and itself. The two-term relation: being the father of, holds between Abraham and Jacob; the three-term relation: being on the left of, holds between two objects and a person (so that what is on one person's left may be on another person's right). Relations have certain logical properties; for example, a two-term relation (for example, larger than) has the property of being transitive if, if a term A has it to a term B and the term B has it to a term C, A must have it to C. Relations – for example that of being the successor of, which applies to numbers – are important in the study of mathematics.

Relative/absolute: see 'absolute/relative'.

Second-order: see 'first-order'.

Self-contradictory: a proposition is self-contradictory if one 'part' of it contradicts another. For example, the statement that some Christians do not believe that Christ is God is self-contradictory, if a Christian just is a person who believes that Christ is God.

Sentence: a sentence is a form of words or other symbols which expresses or formulates a proposition, question, command, wish, hope, belief, supposition, thought, etc.

Statement: if someone states that the Earth is flat, then that the Earth is flat is a statement. That the Earth is flat is also a proposition, but though there is an infinite number of unstated propositions, it looks odd to speak of unstated statements. Hence it is usually better to speak of propositions than of statements.

Solipsism: the view that one is oneself the only person or mind in the universe. If one seriously believed it, one would not bother to write books proving to others that it is true.

Subject: if I say that all men are damned, then 'men' is the subject of my sentence, and being damned the predicate. It was once supposed that all propositions ascribed a subject to a predicate, but this is not true of compound propositions, existential propositions, propositions ascribing identity, relational propositions, and others.

Subjective/objective: see 'objective/subjective'.

Substance: the word 'substance' is a very tricky one in philosophy and I find most philosophical conversation about it incomprehensible. It can mean 'that which has attributes', which is all right so long a one does not suppose that saying this implies that there can be something stripped of all its attributes. It can mean 'that which lies behind appearances', i.e., in fact, protons and electrons and such – which use I think results from confusing appearances with attributes. This is the sense in which Berkeley thought there was no such thing as substance, though he himself confused it with the former sense. Sometimes 'substance' means 'that which persists through change' which has been taken to imply that there must be some respect in which anything that changes must remain the same. One is also inclined to say that such things as impulses or waves are not substances, but reducible to such things as the way trucks (in the case of impulses) or water molecules (in the case of waves) or electrons behave; but physicists appear to disagree about this.

Something – such as a cat – is a substance if it is theoretically capable of existing all by itself. Substances are thus opposed to such things as events or characteristics or grins which, or so it is said, can exist only by happening to or characterising or being had by substances. An example of an important controversy surrounding the idea of substance is whether space and time are substances. See 'abstract'.

Syllogism: a form of argument in which a relation between two classes (called the extreme terms) is deduced from their common relation to a third class (called the middle term). For example, if the class of ancient Greeks is included in the class of unbelievers and the class of unbelievers included in the class of the damned, it can be deduced that the class of ancient Greeks is included in the class of the damned, i.e., that all ancient Greeks are damned.

Synthetic: see 'analytic'.

Systematic ambiguity: a word is systematically ambiguous if it is ambiguous and its two (or more) different senses are systematically related to one another. For example, urine, complexions, food and people can all be healthy in different, but connected, senses of 'healthy'.

Tautology: that she received a mortal wound from which she died is a tautology, because it has already been said that she died from the wound when it was said to be mortal. One knows *a priori*, without any empirical investigation of what actually happens, that men and women die from mortal wounds and, of course, people necessarily die from mortal wounds. Strictly speaking, the word 'tautology' should be reserved for solecisms, but philosophers use it in a wide sense to include quite elegant expressions that can be said to be true on account of the way in which words are used. It has been held that mathematics and logic is a set of interrelated tautologies in this wide sense. That God is omniscient may well be a tautology and, if the ontological argument is valid, that God exists is also a tautology.

Technically possible: see 'logical possibility'.

Then: 'then' indicates that one thing that is been said or has happened is dependent upon another thing that has been said or has happened. 'Then', 'so' and 'because' have much the same function as 'therefore', though 'then' can just mean 'afterwards'.

Theory: a theory is a proposition advanced to explain something, for example, the theory that there is no petrol in my tank is advanced to explain why it will not start and the theory that measuring instruments contract in the direction in which they are pointing was advanced to explain why the Earth's motion through the ether could not be detected.

Therefore: to say that so-and-so, therefore such-and-such, indicates that so-and-so is both true and a conclusive reason for such and such; from which it follows that such-and-such must also be true.

Tollendo tollens: one may accept the hypothetical premise in a *ponendo ponens* but deny its consequent, and so conclude that its antecedent is false. For example, one may argue: if there is a God, there is no evil; there is evil; therefore there is no God.

Transcendental: a transcendental argument is of the form (a *modus tollendo tollens*): we would not have experience if not p (unless p), we do have experience, therefore p.

True: a proposition is said to be true if things are as it says they are. For example, if I say that God exists, and he does, that God exists is true. If I say that God exists, and he does not, that God exists is false. It is a disputed question in philosophy whether there are any propositions that are neither true nor false.

Truth-value: the usual truth-values are true, false and perhaps also neuter. The truth-value of a proposition, would you believe, is determined by whether it is true or false.

Type and token word: in the token sense of word, the word 'Guardian' may appear millions of times on newspapers every morning. In the type sense, it appears just once.

Unfulfilled (or subjunctive) conditionals: an unfulfilled conditional proposition asserts a relation between one proposition and another, while at the same time suggesting that either the antecedent or the consequent or both are false. Since we could not usually know that an unfulfilled conditional was true without knowing something about the relation between antecedent and consequent, our asserting something such as 'If it had been an Euclidean triangle, its angles would have added up to 180°' suggests that we believe that the angles of Euclidean triangles add up to 180°. Saying 'If this patient had been given antibiotics, he would have recovered' suggests that we believe that patients with bronchitis given antibiotics usually do recover.

Uniformity of nature: to say that nature is uniform is to say that the same thing always happens in the same (similar) circumstances. Therefore if one thing happens in one set of circumstances and something different in another, there must be some difference between what leads up to these happenings to explain this fact.

Universal: universal propositions, for example: that all God's chillun got wings, as opposed to that some of God's chillun got wings, are about the whole of a class, or every member of it.

Universals: see 'concepts'.

Validity: validity is something arguments have if their conclusions follow from their premises. It is possible for a valid argument to have true premises and a true conclusion, false premises and a false conclusion, and false premises and a true conclusion. It is not possible for a valid argument to have true premises but a false conclusion, which is why valid arguments with true premises must have true conclusions. One should not confuse validity with truth; it makes sense to speak of valid arguments but not of true ones and of true premises or conclusions but not of valid ones. If the only arguments to show that Tom is guilty of murder are invalid it does not follow that Tom is not the murderer, merely that there is no reason, or not enough reason, for supposing that he is.

Veridical: a perception is veridical if it is not delusive. There is no reason, however, why a veridical perception should not involve illusion or perspectival distortion.

Verification: black crows verify the hypothesis that all crows are black and her having spots verifies the hypothesis that she has measles, if a symptom of measles is spots.

Vicious regress: the statement that every proposition is known by inference generates a regress of propositions inferred from other propositions inferred from yet other propositions and so *ad infinitum*. This regress is benign if there is no reason why it should have a first member, vicious if there is.

Why?: the question 'Why?' can mean 'From what cause?', 'From what motive?' 'With what end in view?' 'For what reason?' or 'From what explanation?' 'Why' questions can be regarded as asking that the blanks in sentences such as 'She left because ...' be filled. Filling this blank would answer the question 'Why did she leave?'

Select Bibliography

Chapter 1: Meaning and the Word 'God'

Alston, William P., *Divine Nature and Human Language*, Cornell University Press, 1989.

Aquinas, Thomas, *Summa Theologiae*, ed. Thomas Gilby, Eyre and Spottiswoode and McGraw Hill Publishing Company, 1963–75, Prima Pars, Question 13.

Ayer, A.J., *Language, Truth and Logic*, Victor Gollancz, 2nd edn, 1946.

Berkeley, George, *The Principles of Human Knowledge*, J.M. Dent and Sons, 1910.

Black, Max, 'Metaphor', *Proceedings of the Aristotelian Society*, 1954–5;

Black, Max, 'More about Metaphor' in ed. Andrew Ortony, *Metaphor and Thought*, Cambridge University Press, 1979.

Cajetan, Thomas, *The Analogy of Names and the Concept of Being*, tr. Edward A. Bushniski and Henry J. Koren, Dusquesne University, 1959.

Chomsky, Avram Noam, *Knowledge of Language: its Nature, Origins and Use*, Praeger, 1986.

Cohen, Jonathan, 'Philosophy of Language and Ontology', *Sprachphilosophie*, 1996.

Cooper, David, *Metaphor*, Basil Blackwell, 1986.

Davidson, Donald, *Inquiries into Truth and Interpretation*, Oxford University Press, 1984.

Fodor, Jerry, *The Language of Thought*, Harvester, 1976.

Fodor, Jerry, *Psychosemantics, The Problem of Meaning in the Philosophy of Mind*, M.I.T. Press, 1987.

Frege, G., *Foundations of Arithmetic*, tr. J.L. Austin, Basil Blackwell, 1950.

Grice, Paul, *Studies in the Way of Words*, Harvard University Press, 1989.

Harrison, Jonathan, *Hume's Moral Epistemology*, Oxford University Press, 1976.

Harrison, Jonathan, *Essays in Metaphysics and the Theory of Knowledge*, Vols I and II, Avebury Series in Philosophy, 1995.

Hume, David, *A Treatise of Human Nature*, ed. L.A. Selby-Bigge, revised P.H. Nidditch, Oxford University Press, 1976, Book I, Part I.

Katz, Jerrold J., *Language and Other Abstract Objects*, Basil Blackwell, 1981.

Kripke, Saul, *Naming and Necessity*, Blackwell, 1972.

Kripke, Saul, *Wittgenstein on Rules and Private Language*, Basil Blackwell, 1982.

Locke, John, *An Essay Concerning Human Understanding*, ed. P.H. Nidditch, Oxford University Press, 1975.

Pike, Nelson, *God and Timelessness*, Routledge and Kegan Paul, 1970.

Price, H.H., *Thinking and Experience*, Hutchinson's University Library, 1953, chapter XVIII.

Putnam, Hilary, 'The Meaning of Meaning', *Mind, Language and Reality, Philosophical Papers*, Vol. II, Cambridge University Press, 1975.

Quine, W.V.O., *Word and Object*, Harvard University Press, 1960.

Russell, Bertrand, *Introduction to Mathematical Philosophy*, George Allen and Unwin, 1919.

Wittgenstein, Ludwig, *Philosophical Investigations*, eds G.E.M. Anscombe and R. Rees, tr. G.E.M. Anscombe, Blackwell, 1953.

Wittgenstein, Ludwig, *Tractatus Logico-Philosophicus*, tr. D.F. Pears and Brian McGuinness, with the introduction by Bertrand Russell, Routledge and Kegan Paul, 1961.

Chapter 2:   The Impossibility of Rational Theology

Ayer, A.J., *Language, Truth and Logic*, 2nd edn, Victor Gollancz, 1946.

Bennett, Jonathan, *A Study in Spinoza's Ethics*, Cambridge University Press, 1984.

Harrison, Jonathan, 'Some Reflections on the Ethics of Knowledge and Belief', *Religious Studies*, Vol. 23, 1987.

Harrison, Jonathan, *Essays in Metaphysics and the Theory of Knowledge*, Vols I and II, Avebury Series in Philosophy, 1995.

Hume, David, *Enquiry Concerning Human Understanding*, ed. L.A. Selby-Bigge, revised P.H. Nidditch, Oxford University Press, 1975.

Hume, David, *A Treatise of Human Nature*, ed. L.A. Selby-Bigge, revised P.H. Nidditch, Oxford University Press, 1976, Book I, Part I.

Spinoza, Baruch, *Ethics*, ed. Andrew Boyle, revised with an introduction and notes by G.H.R. Parkinson, J.M. Dent, 1989.

Chapter 3:   Objections to Empiricism

Ayer, A.J., *The Foundations of Empirical Knowledge*, Macmillan, 1940.

Ayer, A.J., *Language, Truth and Logic*, Victor Gollancz, 1947.

Baker, G.P. and Hacker, P.M.S., *An Analytic Commentary on the Philosophical Investigations, ii, Wittgenstein: Rules of Grammar and Necessity*, Blackwell, 1980.

Berkeley, George, *The Principles of Human Knowledge* and *Two Dialogues Between Hylas and Philonous*, J.M. Dent and Sons, 1910.

Bradley, F.H., *Appearance and Reality*, Oxford University Press, 1893.

Broad, C.D., *Scientific Thought*, Routledge and Kegan Paul, 1923.

Broad, C.D., *The Mind and its Place in Nature*, Kegan Paul, 1925.

Fodor, Jerry, *Psychosemantics, The Problem of Meaning in the Philosophy of Mind*, M.I.T. Press, 1987.

Gödel, Kurt, *Works*, Clarendon Press and Oxford University Press, 1986–95.

Harrison, Jonathan, 'Science, Souls and Sense-data' in *New Representationalisms*, ed. Edmund Wright, Avebury Series in Philosophy, 1993.

Harrison, Jonathan, *Essays in Metaphysics and the Theory of Knowledge*, Vols I and II, Avebury Series in Philosophy, 1995.

Harrison, Jonathan, 'The Trouble with Tarski, or sentences and Propositions, Pragmatic Contradiction, Analyticity, Linguistic Relativism, Conventionalism, "convention" T and More', *The Philosophical Quarterly*, forthcoming.

Hume, David, *A Treatise of Human Nature*, ed. L.A. Selby-Bigge, revised P.H. Nidditch, Oxford University Press, 1976, Book I, Part I.

Kant, Immanuel, *Critique of Pure Reason*, tr. Norman Kemp Smith, Macmillan, 1929.

Kenny, Anthony, 'Mystical Experience, St. John of the Cross', *Reason and Religion*, Blackwell 1987.

Kripke, Saul, *Naming and Necessity*, Blackwell, 1980.

Locke, John, *Essay Concerning Human Understanding*, edited with an introduction, critical apparatus and glossary by P.H. Nidditch, Oxford University Press, 1975.

Mill, John Stuart, *System of Logic, rationative and inductive, being a connected view of the principles of evidence and the methods of scientific investigation*, ed. J.M. Robson, introduction by R.F. McRae, University of Toronto Press, 1973–4.

Moore, G.E., 'External and Internal Relations', *The Proceedings of the Aristotelian Society*, 1919–20 (reprinted in *Philosophical Studies*, Routledge and Kegan Paul, 1922).

Morick, *Challenges to Empiricism*, Methuen, 1980.

Plantinga, Alvin, *God and Other Minds*, Cornell University Press, 1967.

Popper, Karl, *The Logic of Scientific Discovery*, Hutchinson, 1959.

Price, H.H., *Perception*, Methuen, 1932.

Quine, W.V.O., *Two Dogmas of Empiricism*, Harvard University Press, 1941.

Quine, W.V.O., *Word and Object*, Harvard University Press, 1960.

Russell, Bertrand and Whitehead, A.N., *Principia Mathematica*, Cambridge University Press, 1910–13.

Ryle, Gilbert, *The Concept of Mind*, Hutchinson, 1947.

Schwartz, S.P. , ed., *Naming, Necessity and Natural Kinds*, Cornell University Press, 1977.

Sellars, Wilfrid, *Science, Perception and Reality*, 1963.

Swinburne, Richard, *The Coherence of Theism*, Oxford University Press, 1977.

Wilkerson, T.E., *Natural Kinds*, Avebury, 1995.

Wittgenstein, Ludwig, *Philosophical Investigations*, eds G.E.M. Anscombe and R. Rees, tr. G.E.M. Anscombe, Blackwell, 1953.

Wittgenstein, Ludwig, *Tractatus Logico-Philosophicus*, translated by D.F. Pears and B.F. McGuiness, Routledge, 1961 (first German edition, 1921).

Chapter 4: The Ontological Argument

Anselm, St, *St. Anselm's Proslogion*, with a reply on behalf of the fool by Gaunilo and the author's reply to Gaunilo, translated with an introduction and philosophical commentary by M.J. Charlesworth, various publications, e.g. Hackett Publishing Co., c1996.

Barnes, Jonathan, *The Ontologial Argument*, Macmillan, 1972.

Descartes, Rene, *Meditations*, J.M. Dent and Sons, 1912, Meditation V, 'Of the essence of Material things; and again of God, that he exists'.

Findlay, J.N., 'Can God's Existence be Disproved', *Mind*, 1948.

Flew, Antony and MacIntyre, Alasdair, eds, *New Essays in Philosophical Theology*, Part IV, 'Can God's Existence Be Disproved?', S.C.M. Press, 1955.

Gale, Richard, *The Nature and Existence of God*, Cambridge University Press, 1991.

Harrison, Jonathan, *Ethical Essays*, Vol. III, Avebury, 1993.

Harrison, Jonathan, *Essays in Metaphysics and the Theory of Knowledge*, Vols I and II, Avebury Series in Philosophy, 1995.

Hume, David, *A Treatise of Human Nature*, ed. L.A. Selby-Bigge, revised P.H. Nidditch, Oxford University Press, 1976, Book I, Part II, Section VI.

Kant, Immanuel, *Critique of Pure Reason*, tr. Norman Kemp Smith, Macmillan, 1929.

Kenny, Anthony, 'God and Necessity', *Reason and Religion*, Blackwell, 1987.

Kripke, Saul, *Naming and Necessity*, Blackwell, 1988.

Mackie, J.L., *The Miracle of Theism*, Oxford University Press, 1982.

Malcolm, Norman, *Anselm's Ontological Arguments*, first published in the *Journal of Philosophy*, 1960 (reprinted in *The Ontological Argument from St. Anselm to Contemporary Philosophers*, Macmillan, 1968).

Moore, G.E., 'Is Existence a Predicate?', *Proceedings of the Aristotelian Society*, 1936 (reprinted in his *Philosophical Papers*, Allen and Unwin, 1959).

Oppy, Graham, *Ontological Arguments and Belief in God*, Cambridge University Press, 1995.

Plantinga, Alvin, *The Ontolgical Argument*, Macmillan, 1965.

Plantinga, Alvin, *The Nature of Necessity*, Oxford University Press, 1974.

Quine, W.V.O., 'On What There Is' in *From A Logical Point of View*, Harvard University Press, 1953.

Spinoza, Baruch, *Ethics*, ed. Andrew Boyle, revised with an introduction and notes by G.H.R. Parkinson, J.M. Dent, 1989.

Swinburne, Richard, 'Analyticity, Necessity and A Priority', *Mind*, 1975; *Is there a God?*, Oxford University Press, 1966.

Swinburne, Richard, *The Coherence of Theism*, Oxford University Press, 1977.

Williams, C.J.F. *What is Existence?*, Oxford University Press, 1981.

Chapter 5: Possible Worlds and the Ontological Argument

Hughes, G.E. and Cresswell, M.J., *An Introduction to Modal Logic*, Methuen, 1968.

Ingwaden, Peter, 'Ontological Arguments', *Nous*, 11, 1977.

Ingwagen, Peter van, *God, Knowledge and Mystery, Essays in Philosophic Theology*, Cornell University Press, 1995.

Kripke, Saul, *Naming and Necessity*, Blackwell, 1980.

Lewis, David, *On the Plurality of Worlds*, Oxford University Press, 1986.

Lewis, David, 'The Impossibility of Possible Worlds', *Philosophy*, forthcoming.

Otto, Rudolf, *The Idea of the Holy*, Oxford University Press, 1923.

Plantinga, Alvin, *The Ontological Argument*, Macmillan, 1968.

Plantinga, Alvin, *God, Freedom and Evil*, George Allen and Unwin, 1975.

Plantinga, Alvin, *The Nature of Necessity*, Oxford University Press, 1978.

Read, Stephen, *Thinking about Logic*, Oxford University Press, 1994.

Ryle, Gilbert, *The Concept of Mind*, Hutchinson, 1947.

Stalnaker, Sydney, 'Possible Worlds', *Nous*, X, 1976 (reprinted in Burnyeat, Miles, and Honderich, Ted, *Philosophy as it is*, Penguin Books, 1979).

Chapter 6: The Cosmological Argument

Aquinas, Thomas, *Summa Theologiae*, ed. Thomas Gilby, Eyre and Spottiswoode and McGraw Hill Publishing Company, 1963–75, 1963–75, Prima Pars, Question 3, Article 2.

Ayer, A.J., *The Central Questions of Philosophy*, Weidenfelt and Nicolson, 1973.

Broad, C.D., 'Arguments for the Existence of God', *Religion, Philosophy and Psychical Research*, Routledge and Kegan Paul, 1953.

Butler, Joseph, *The Analogy of Religion, Butler's Works*, Vol. II, ed. W.E. Gladstone, Oxford University Press, 1897.

Butler, Joseph, 'Of the Nature of Virtue', Appendix to *The Analogy of Religion*, Everyman's Library, London, 1936.

Edwards, Paul ,'Why?' in *The Encyclopedia of Philosophy*, ed. Paul Edwards, The Macmillan Company and the Free Press, 1967.

Haldane, J.J. and Smart, J.J.C., *Atheism and Theism*, Blackwell, 1996.

Heidegger, M. *Being and Time*, tr. J. Macquarrie and E. Robinson, Oxford University Press, 1967.

Ingwagen, Peter and Lowe, Jonathan, 'Why is there anything at all?', *The Aristotelian Society Supplementary Proceedings*, 1996.

Kant, Immanuel, 'Transcendental Dialectic', Book II, chapter 3, Section 5 ('The Impossibility of a Cosmological Proof of the Existence of God'), *Critique of Pure Reason*, tr. Norman Kemp Smith, Macmillan, 1929.

Kenny, Anthony, *The God of the Philosophers*, Oxford University Press, 1979.

Lipton, Peter, 'Contrastive Explanation', ed. David-Hillel Ruben, *Explanation*, Oxford University Press, 1993.

Mackie, J.L., *The Miracle of Theism*, Oxford University Press, 1981.

Mill, John Stuart, *System of Logic, rationative and inductive, being a connected view of the principles of evidence and the methods of scientific investigation*, ed. J.M. Robson, introduction by R.F. McRae, University of Toronto Press, 1973–4.

Nozick, Richard, *Philosophical Explanations*, Oxford University Press, 1981.

Parfit, Derek, 'The Puzzle of Reality; Why does the Universe Exist?', *The Times Literary Supplement*, 3 July 1992.

Quine, W.V.O., 'Necessary Truth' in *The Ways of Paradise*, Harvard University Press, 1966.

Russell, Bertrand, *Introduction to Mathematical Philosophy*, George Allen and Unwin, 1919.

Russell, Bertrand and Whitehead, A.N., *Principia Mathematica*, Cambridge University Press, 1910–13.

Smart, J.J.C., and Haldane, J.J., *Atheism and Theism*, Blackwell, 1996.

Swinburne, Richard, *The Coherence of Theism*, Oxford University Press, 1977.

Swinburne, Richard, *The Existence of God*, Oxford University Press, 1979, chapter 7.

Chapter 7: The Argument from Design

Aquinas, Thomas, *Summa Theologiae*, ed. Thomas Gilby, Eyre and Spottiswoode and McGraw Hill Publishing Company, 1963–75, Prima Pars, Question 2, Article 3.

Broad, C.D., *Religion, Philosophy and Psychical Research*, Routledge and Kegan Paul, 1953, 'Arguments for the Existence of God'.

Butler, Joseph, *The Analogy of Religion, Butler's Works*, Vol. II, ed. W.E. Gladstone, Oxford University Press, 1987.

Darwin, Charles, *The Origin of Species by means of Natural Selection,* with an introduction by J.W. Burrow, Penguin Books, 1968.

Dawkins, Richard, *The Blind Watchmaker*, Longmans, 1986.

Dennett, D.C., *Darwin's Dangerous Idea*, Simon and Schuster, 1995.

Gale, Richard, *On the Nature and Existence of God*, Cambridge University Press, 1991.

Grice, H.P., 'Utterers Meaning, Sentence Meaning and Word Meaning', *Foundations of Language* 4, 1968 (reprinted in *The Philosophy of Language*, ed. J.R. Searle, Oxford Readings in Philosophy, 1971).

Harrison, Jonathan, *Our Knowledge of Right and Wrong*, Allen and Unwin, 1971.

Harrison, Jonathan, *Challenges to Morality*, Macmillan Publishing Company, New York, 1992.

Harrison, Jonathan, 'Evolution and Sociobiology', *Ethical Essays*, Vol. III, Avebury Series in Philosophy, 1993.

Hume, David, *Dialogues Concerning Natural Religion*, ed.with introduction by Stanley Tweyman, Routledge, 1979.

Huxley, Thomas, T.H., *T.H.Huxley's 'Evolution and Ethics', with new essays in its Victorian and socio-biological context*, ed. James Paradis and George C. Williams, Princeton Univeristy Press, 1989,

Kant, Immanuel, *Critique of Pure Reason*, tr. Norman Kemp Smith, Macmillan, 1929.

Keynes, John Maynard, *A Treatise of Probability*, in *The Collected Writings of John Maynard Keynes*, Vol. XII, published for The Royal Economic Society by St. Martin's Press, chapter XIX.

Mackie, J.L., *The Miracle of Theism*, Oxford University Press, 1982.

Mellor, Hugh, *The Facts of Causation*, Cambridge University Press, 1995.

Mill, John Stuart, 'The Argument from Marks of Design in Nature' in *Theism*, The Library of Liberal Arts, 1957.

Morris, Thomas V., ed., *The Concept of God*, Oxford, 1987.

Morris, Thomas V., *Our Idea of God*, Notre Dame, Indiana, 1991.

Paley, William, *Natural Theology, or evidences of the existence and nature of the Deity, collected from the appearances Nature*, London, 1802.

Popper, Karl, *The Logic of Scientific Discovery*, Hutchinson, 1959.

Putnam, Hilary, *Reason, Truth and History*, Cambridge University Press, 1981, chapter I.

Read, Stephen, *Thinking about Logic*, Oxford University Press, 1994.

Ridley, Matt, *The Origins of Virtue*, Viking, 1996.

Ryle, Gilbert, 'Imaginary Objects' in *Collected Papers*, Hutchinson, 1971.

Swinburne, Richard, *The Existence of God*, Oxford University Press, 1979, chapter 8.

Wittgenstein, Ludwig, *Lectures and Conversations on Aesthetics, Psychology and Religious Belief*, ed. C. Barrett, Oxford, 1966.

Chapter 8: God and Morality: Ethical Arguments for the Existence of God

Adams, Robert Merrihew, 'A Modified Divine Command Theory of Ethical Wrongness' and 'Divine Command Metaethics as Necessary a Posteriori' in ed. Paul Helm, *Divine Commands and Morality*, Oxford University Press, 1981.

Berg, Jonathan, 'How Could Ethics Depend on Religion?' in ed. Peter Singer, *A Companion to Ethics*, Blackwell, 1991.

Broad, C.D., *The Mind and its Place in Nature*, Kegan Paul, Trench, Trubner and Co. Ltd, 1925.

Butler, Joseph, 'Fifteen Sermons' (especially Sermons II and III) in ed. W.E. Gladstone, *Butler's Works, Vol. II*, Oxford University Press, 1897.

Butler, Joseph, Dissertation II, 'Of the Nature of Virtue', 'The Analogy of Religion' in ed. W.E. Gladstone, *Butler's Works, Vol. II*, Oxford University Press, 1897.

Geach, P.T., 'The Moral Law and the Law of God' in *God and the Soul*, Routledge and Kegan Paul, 1969.

Harrison, Jonathan, *Our Knowledge of Right and Wrong*, Allen and Unwin, 1971.

Harrison, Jonathan, 'Geach on God's Inability to do Evil', *Philosophy*, 1976.

Harrison, Jonathan, *Challenges to Morality*, Collier-Macmillan, 1993a.

Harrison, Jonathan, *Ethical Essays*, Vol. III, Avebury Series in Philosophy, 1993b.

Harrison, Jonathan, *Our Knowledge of Right and Wrong*, Gregg Revivals, 1994.

Harrison, Jonathan, 'The Philosophy of Mysticism', in *Essays in Metaphysics and the Theory of Knowledge*, Vol. II, Avebury Series in Philosophy, 1995.

Helm, Paul, *Divine Commands and Morality*, Oxford University Press, 1981.

Kant, Immanuel, *Critique of Practical Reason*, tr. Norman Kemp Smith, Macmillan, 1929.

Kant, Immanuel, 'Fundamental Principles of the Metaphysics of Morals' in *The Moral Law*, by H.J. Paton, Hutchinson, 1947.

Moore, G.E., *Principia Ethica*, Cambridge University Press, 1903.

Morris,Thomas V., 'Duty and Divine Goodness', *The Concept of God*, Oxford University Press, 1987.

Murdoch, Iris, 'On God and Good' in ed. Mary Warnock, *Women Philosophers*, Dent, 1996.

Plato, *Plato's Euthyphro, text with introduction, commentary and vocabulary*, by Chris Emlyn Jones, Bristol Classical Texts, 1991.

Price, Richard, *A Review of the Principal Questions in Morals*, ed. D. Daiches Raphael, Oxford Press, 1948.

Sartre, J.P., *Existentialism and Humanism*, tr. Philip Mairet, Methuen, London, 1948.

Ward, Keith, *Ethics and Christianity*, George Allen and Unwin, 1970.

Chapter 9: Theology without Propositions

Alston, William, *Divine Nature and Human Language*, Cornell University Press, 1987.

Ayer, A.J., *Language, Truth and Logic*, Victor Gollancz, 1936.

Ayer, A.J., *Ludwig Wittgenstein*, Penguin Books, 1985, especially chapter 7, 'On Magic and Religion'.

Buren, Paul van, *The Secular Meaning of the Gospel*, S.C.M.Press, 1963.

Davis, B., *An Introduction to the Philosophy of Religion*, Oxford University Press, 1993, chapter 2.

Hare, R.M., *Language of Morals*, Oxford University Press, 1952.

Hudson, Donald, *Ludwig Wittgenstein, The Bearing of his Philosophy upon Religious Belief*, Lutterworth Press, 1968.

Lash, Nicholas, *Believing Three Ways in One God*, SCM Press Ltd, 1992.

O'Hear, Anthony, *Experience, Explanation and Faith*, Routledge and Kegan Paul, 1984.

Wisdom, John, 'Gods' in *Philosophy and Psycho-Analysis*, Oxford University Press, 1957.

Wittgenstein, Ludwig, *Philosophical Investigations*, eds G.E.M. Anscombe and R. Rees, tr. G.E.M. Anscombe, Blackwell, 1953.

Wittgenstein, Ludwig, *Tractatus Logico-Philosophicus*, tr. D.F. Pears and Brian McGuinness, with the introduction by Bertrand Russell, Routledge and Kegan Paul, 1961.

Wittgenstein, Ludwig, *Lectures and Conversations on Aesthetics, Psychology and Religious Belief*, ed. C.K. Barrett, Oxford University Press, 1966.

Chapter 10: Deistic Phenomenalism: A Reductionist Account of the Existence of God

Arnold, Matthew, *Arnold: Poetical Works*, ed. C.B. Tinker and H.F. Lowry, Oxford University Press, 1950.

Ayer, A.J. *Philosophical Essays*, Macmillan, 1954.

Berkeley, George, *The Principles of Human Knowledge; Three Dialogues between Hylas and Philonous*, J.M. Dent and Sons, 1910.

Harrison, Jonathan, 'In Defence of the Demon' in ed. J.R. Smythies, *The Case for Dualism*, University of Virginia Press, 1989.

Mill, John Stuart, *An Examination of Sir William Hamilton's Philosophy*, University of Toronto Press, 1979.

Chapter 11: Religion without Belief

Braithwaite, R.B., *An Empiricist's View of the Nature of Religious Belief*, Arthur Stanley Eddington Lecture, Cambridge University Press, 1955 (reprinted in ed. Basil Mitchell, *The Philosophy of Religion*, Oxford University Press, 1971).

Hudson, Donald, *Ludwig Wittgenstein*, Lutterworth Press, 1968.

Lash, Nicholas, *Believing Three Ways in One God, A Reading of the Apostle's Creed*, S.C.M. Press, Ltd, 1992.

Mackie, J.L., *The Miracle of Theism*, Oxford University Press, 1982.

Phillips, D.Z., 'Religious Beliefs and Language Games' (reprinted in ed. Basil Mitchell, *The Philosophy of Religion*, Oxford University Press, 1971).

Smith, Wilfred Cantwell, *Faith and Belief*, Princeton University Press, 1979.

Wittgenstein, Ludwig, *Lectures and Conversations on Aesthetics, Psychology and Religious Belief*, ed. C.K. Barrett, Blackwell, 1966.

Chapter 12: Minor Arguments for the Existence of God

Aquinas, Thomas, *Summa Theologiae*, ed. Thomas Gilby, Eyre and Spottiwoode and McGraw Hill Publishing Company, 1963–5, Prima Pars, Question 2, Article 3.

Butler, Joseph, *Sermons, chiefly on the Theory of Religious Belief, preached before the University of Oxford*, C.J.F. and J. Rivington, 1843.

Butler, Joseph, *Butler's Works*, ed. W.E. Gladstone, Oxford University Press, 1897.

Descartes, Rene, *Meditations*, J.M. Dent and Sons, 1912, Meditation III.

Harrison, Jonathan, *Our Knowledge of Right and Wrong*, Allen and Unwin, 1971.

Lovejoy, Arthur O., *The Great Chain of Being, a Study in the History of an Idea*, Harvard University Press, 1936.

Newman, John Henry, *An Essay in Aid of a Grammar of Assent*, ed. I.T. Ker, Oxford University Press, 1985.

Plantinga, Alvin, *God and Other Minds*, Cornell University Press, 1967.

Swinburne, Richard, *The Existence of God*, Oxford University Press, 1979, especially chapter 9.

Chapter 13: The 'Argument' from Religious Experience

Alston, William, *God, The Epistemology of Religious Experience*, Cornell University Press, 1991.

Audi, Robert and Wainwright, William J., *Rationality, Religious Belief and Moral Commitment*, Cornell University Press, 1986.

Ayer, A.J., *Language, Truth and Logic*, Victor Gollancz, 1936.

Bailie, John, *Our Knowledge of God*, New York, 1959.

Broad, C.D., 'The Validity of Belief in a Personal God' in *Religion Philosophy and Psychical Research*, Routledge and Kegan Paul, 1953.

Buber, Martin, *Ich and Du*, Leipzig, 1923 (tr. R. Gregor Smith as *I and Thou*, T. and T. Clarke, 1937).

Gale, Richard, *On the Nature and Existence of God*, Cambridge University Press, 1991.

Happold, F.C., *Mysticism, A Study and an Anthology*, Penguin, 1963.

Harrison, Jonathan, 'The Philosophy of Mysticism', *Essays on Metaphysics and the Theory of Knowledge*, Vol. I, Avebury, 1995.

Hick, John, *Faith and Knowledge*, Cornell University Press, 1957.

Huxley, Aldous, *The Doors of Perception*, Grafton, 1954.

James, William, *The Varieties of Religious Experience*, Longmans, Green and Company, 1902.

Lewis, H.D., *Our Experience of God*, George Allen and Unwin, 1965.

Mackie, J.L. *The Miracle of Theism*, Oxford University Press, 1982, chapter 10.

O'Hear, Anthony, *Experience, Expalanation and Faith*, Routledge and Kegan Paul, 1984.

Otto, Rudolf, *The Idea of the Holy*, Oxford University Press, 1923.

Price, H.H., *Perception*, Methuen, 1932, chapters VII and VIII.

Price, H.H., *Some Aspects of the Conflict between Science and Religion*, Arthur Stanley Eddington Lecture, Cambridge University Press, 1953.

Prince, Morton, *The Dissociation of a Personality*, Oxford University Press, 1905.

Plantinga, Alvin, *God and Other Minds*, Cornell University Press, 1967.

Schleiermacher, Friedrich, *The Christian Faith*, tr. H.R. Mackintosh and J.S. Stewart, Edinburgh University Press, 1948.

Sizemore, C., *I'm Eve*, Doubleday, 1977.

Stace, W.T., *Philosophy and Mysticism*, Macmillan, 1961.

Swinburne, R., *The Existence of God*, Oxford University Press, 1979, chapter 13.

Underhill, Evelyn, *Mysticism, the Nature and Development of Spiritual Consciousness* (reprinted by Oneworld Publications Ltd, 1993).

Chapter 14: God's Omnipotence

Aquinas, Thomas, *Summa Theologiae*, ed. Thomas Gilby, Eyre and Spottiswoode and McGraw Hill Publishing Company, 1963–75, Prima Pars, Question 25.

Geach, P.T., *Providence and Evil*, Cambridge University Press, 1973.

Geach, P.T., 'Can God Fail to Keep Promises?', *Philosophy*, 1977.

Harrison, Jonathan, 'Geach on God's Alleged Inability to do Evil' and 'Geach on Harrison on Geach on God', *Philosophy*, 1976 (reprinted in *Ethical Essays*, Vol. III, Avebury, 1993).

Harrison, Jonathan, 'Geach on Harrison on Geach on God', *Philosophy*, 1977 (reprinted in *Ethical Essays*, Vol. III, Avebury, 1993).

Harrison, Jonathan, 'Dr. Who and the Philosophers', *The Aristotelian Society Supplementary Proceedings*, Vol. XLV, 1971 (reprinted in *Essays on Metaphysics and the Theory of Knowledge*, Vol. I, Avebury, 1995).

Hume, David, *A Treatise of Human Nature*, ed. L.A. Selby-Bigge, revised P.H. Nidditch, Oxford University Press, 1976, Book I, Part I.

Kenny, Anthony, *The God of the Philosophers*, Oxford University Press, 1979.

Mackie, J.L., *The Miracle of Theism*, Oxford University Press, 1982.

Pike, Nelson, *God and Timelessness*, Routledge and Kegan Paul, 1970.

Plantinga, Alvin, *The Nature of Necessity*, Oxford University Press, 1974.

Priest, Graham, 'Can Contradictions be true?', *Supplementary Proceedings of the Aristotelian Society*, 1993.

Swinburne, Richard, *The Coherence of Theism*, Oxford University Press, 1977.

Chapter 15: Trouble with the Trinity

Aquinas, Thomas, *Summa Theologiae*, ed. Thomas Gilby, Eyre and Spottiswoode and McGraw Hill Publishing Company, 1963–75, Prima Pars, Questions 27–32.

Geach, P.T., *Providence and Evil*, Cambridge University Press, 1973.

Griffin, Nicholas, *Relative Identity*, Oxford University Press, 1977.

Harrison, Jonathan, *Essays in Metaphysics and the Theory of Knowledge*, Vol. I, Avebury Series in Philosophy, 1995.

Kripke, Saul, *Naming and Necessity*, Blackwell, 1980.

Lash, Nicholas, *Believing Three Ways in One God, a Reading of the Apostles*, S.C.M. Press, 1992.

Noonan, Harold, *Objects and Identity, an Examination of the Relative Identity Thesis and its Consequences*, Martinus Nijhoff, 1980.

Noonan, Harold, ed., *Personal Identity*, International Reserach Library of Philosophy, 1993.

Noonan, Harold, *Personal Identity*, Routledge, 1989.

Parfit, Derek, *Reason and Persons*, Oxford University Press, 1984.

Quine, W.V.O., *From a Logical Point of View*, Harvard University Press, 1953.

Shoemaker, S. and Swinburne, R., *Personal Identity*, Blackwell, 1984.

Wiggins, David, *Sameness and Substance*, Oxford University Press, 1980.

Williams, Bernard, *Problems of the Self*, Cambridge University Press, 1973.

Chapter 16: God's Omniscience

Aquinas, Thomas, *Summa Theologiae*, ed. Thomas Gilby, Eyre and Spottiswoode and McGraw Hill Publishing Company, 1963–75, Prima Pars, Question 14.

Gale, Richard, *On the Nature and Existence of God*, Cambridge University Press, 1991.

Harrison, Jonathan, 'Mackie's Moral "Scepticism"' in *Ethical Essays*, Vol. I, Avebury Series in Philosophy, 1993.

Harrison, Jonathan, 'If I know I cannot be wrong', *Aristotelian Society Proceedings*, 1978–9 (reprinted in *Essays in Metaphysics and the Theory of Knowledge*, Avebury Series in Philosophy, 1995).

Kenny, Anthony, *The God of the Philosophers*, Oxford University Press, 1979.

Kneale, William and Martha, *The Development of Logic*, Oxford University Press, 1962, especially chapter I.

McTaggart, John McTaggart Ellis, 'The Unreality of Time' , *Philosophical Studies*, Cambridge University Press, 1934.

Mellor, D.H., *Real Time*, Cambridge University Press, 1981.

Plantinga, Alvin, 'On Ockham's Way Out', *Faith and Philosophy*, Vol. III, 1986.

Prior, A.N., *Formal Logic*, Oxford University Press, 1957.

Prior, A.N., *Past, Present and Future*, Oxford University Press, 1967.

Ryle, Gilbert, 'Imaginary Objects' in *Collected Papers*, Vol. II of *Collected Essays, 1929–1968*, Hutchinson, 1971.

Smart, J.J.C., 'The River of Time' in *Essays on Conceptual Analysis*, ed. A.G.N. Flew, Macmillan, 1966.

Strawson, P.F., *Introduction to Logical Theory*, Methuen, 1952.

Swinburne, R., *The Coherence of Theism*, Oxford University Press, 1977, chapter 10.

White, Alan, *Truth*, Macmillan, 1970.

Chapter 17: Providence, Foreknowledge, Will and Fate

Adams, John Merrihew, 'God's Middle Knowledge and the Problem of Evil', *American Philosophical Quarterly*, Vol. 14, 1977.

Aquinas, Thomas, *Summa Theologiae*, ed. Thomas Gilby, Eyre and Spottiswoode and McGraw Hill Publishing Company, 1963–75, Question 19.

Austin. J.L., 'Ifs and Cans' in *Collected Papers*, Oxford University Press, 1961.

Ayer, A.J., 'Freedom and Necessity' in *Philosophical Essays*, Macmillan, 1954, chapter 12.

Boethius, *Consolations of Philosophy*, with the English translation of 'L.T.' (1609), revised by H.F. Stewart, Loeb Classical Library, William Heinemann Ltd, and Harvard University Press, 1918, The Fifth Book of Boethius, II.

Broad, C.D., 'Determinism, Indeterminism and Libertarianism', *Ethics and the History of Philosophy*, Routledge and Kegan Paul, 1952.

Dennett, Daniel, *Elbow Room*, Oxford University Press, 1984.

Descartes, Rene, *Meditations*, J.M. Dent and Sons, 1912, Meditation IV, 'Of Truth and Error'.

Gale, Richard, *On the Nature and Existence of God*, Cambridge University Press, 1991, especially chapter 4.

Harrison, Jonathan, *Challenges to Morality*, The Macmillan Publishing Company (now Collier Macmillan), 1992.

Harrison, Jonathan, 'Tom and Jerry, or What Price Pelagius?', 'Foreknowledge, Will and Fate' and 'Some Reflections on Hypothetical Accounts of Freedom of the Will' in *Ethical Essays*, Vols I and II, Avebury, 1993.

Harrison, Jonathan, *Essays in Metaphysics and the Theory of Knowledge*, Vols I and II, Avebury Series in Philosophy, 1995.

Hobart. R.E., 'Free Will as Presupposing Determinism, and not Incompatible with it', *Mind*, 1934.

Hobbes, Thomas, *Hobbes's Leviathan*, ed. Richard Tuck, Cambridge University Press, 1996, chapter 21.

Honderich, Ted, *A Theory of Determinism*, Oxford University Press, 1988.

Hume, *A Treatise of Human Nature*, ed. L.A. Selby-Bigge, revised P.H. Nidditch, Oxford University Press, 1976, Book II, Part I, Sections 1 and 2.

Ingwaden, Peter, *An Essay on Free Will*, Oxford University Press, 1983.

Kant, Immanuel, Fundamental Principles of the Metaphysics of Morals in *The Moral Law*, by H.J. Paton, Hutchinson, 1947.

Kenny, Anthony, 'Aquinas on Divine Knowledge and Freedom' in *Reason and Religion*, Blackwell, 1987.

Lucas, J.R. *Responsibility*, Oxford University Press, 1993.

Moore, G.E., *Ethics*, Williams and Norgate, chapter 6.

Nagel, Thomas, *The View from Nowhere*, Oxford University Press, 1986.

Nowell-Smith, *Ethics*, Penguin Books, 1954, chapters 19 and 20.

Pelagius, *Pelagius's Expositions of the 13 Epistles of St. Paul*, Alexander Souter, ed. *Texts and Studies*, Vol. IX, Cambridge University Press, 1926.

Pink, Thomas, *The Psychology of Freedom*, Cambridge University Press, 1996.

Plantinga, Alvin, *God and Other Minds*, Cornell University Press, 1967.

Ree, Paul, 'We are not responsible for what we do' in Jonathan Harrison, ed., *Challenges to Morality*, The Macmillan Publishing Company (now Collier Macmillan), 1993.

Ryle, Gilbert, *The Concept of Mind*, Hutchinson, 1947.

Smart, J.J.C., '"Looks Red" and Dangerous Talk', *Philosophy*, 1995.

Strawson, Galen, *Freedom and Belief*, Oxford University Press, 1986.

Taylor, Richard, *Metaphysics*, Prentice Hall, 1963.

Watson, Gary, ed., *Free Will and Determinism*, Oxford University Press, 1982.

Chapter 18: God's Eternity

Augustine, *Confessions*, translated with an introduction by R.S. Pine-Coffin, Harmondsworth, 1961, Book XI.

Gale, Richard, *The Philosophy of Time*, Macmillan, 1968.

Gale, Richard, *On the Nature and Existence of God*, Cambridge University Press, 1991

Gale, Richard, 'Indexical Reference, Egocentric Particulars and Token-Reflexive Words' in ed.-in-chief Paul Edwards, *The Encyclopedia of Philosophy*, Macmillan, 1967.

Geach, P.T., 'God's Relation to the World', *Logic Matters*, 10.3, Blackwell, 1972

McTaggart, John McTaggart Ellis, *Philosophical Studies*, Cambridge University Press, 1934 (re-printed by Books for Libraries Press, 1968).

Mellor, Hugh, *Real Time II*, Routledge, 1998.

Mellor, Hugh and Lucas, John, 'Transcendental Tense', *Supplementary Proceedings of the Aristotelian Society*, Vol. LXXII, 1998.

Morris, Thomas V, *The Logic of God Incarnate*, Cornell University Press, 1986.

Pike, Nelson, *God and Timelessness*, Routledge and Kegan Paul, 1970.

Prior, Arthur, *Past, Present and Future*, Oxford University Press, 1967.

Smart, J.J.C., ed., *Problems of Space and Time*, The Macmillan Company, 1964.

Smart, J.J.C., 'The River of Time' in *Essays in Conceptual Analysis*, ed. A.G.N. Flew, Macmillan, 1966.

Stump, Eleanor and Kretzman, Norman, 'Eternity', *Journal of Philosophy*, 1981.

Swinburne, Richard, *The Coherence of Theism*, Oxford University Press, 1977, chapter 12.

Chapter 19: God's Infinity, Simplicity, Unity, Impassibility and Holiness

Anselm, St, Monologian, 21, Proslogian, 20.

Aquinas, Thomas, *Summa Theologiae*, ed. Thomas Gilby, Eyre and Spottiswoode and McGraw Hill Publishing Company, 1963–75, Prima Pars, Question 3.

Creel, R., *Divine Impassibility*, Cambridge University Press, 1985.

Harrison, Jonathan, *Our Knowledge of Right and Wrong*, George Allen and Unwin, 1971.

Kretzman, Norman and Stump, Eleanor, 'Absolute Simplicity', *Faith and Philosophy*, 2, 1985.

Mann, William E., 'Simplicity and Immutability in God', *International Philosophical Quarterly*, Vol. 23, 1983.

Chapter 20: God's Embodiment

Aquinas, Thomas, *Summa Theologiae*, ed. Thomas Gilby, Eyre and Spottiswoode and McGraw Hill Publishing Company, 1963–75, Prima Pars, Question 3, Article 1.

Armstrong, D.M., *A Materialist Theory of Mind*, Routledge and Kegan Paul, 1968.

Berkeley, George, *The Principles of Human Knowledge*, J.M. Dent and Son, 1910.

Danto, Arthur: *Analytic Philosophy of Action*, Cambridge University Press, 1973.

Dennett, Daniel, *Brainstorms: Philosophy, Mind, Psychology*, Harvester, 1978.

Dennett, Daniel, *Consciousness Explained*, Penguin Books and Viking, 1991.

Descartes, Rene, *Meditations*, J.M. Dent and Sons, 1912, Meditation II, 'Of the existence of the human mind, and that it is more easily known than the body'.

Geach, P.T., *Mental Acts*, Routledge and Kegan Paul, no date of publication given.

Harrison, Jonathan, 'The Embodiment of Mind, or What use is Having a Body', *Aristotelian Society Proceedings*, Vol. LXXIV, 1973–4 (reprinted in *Essays on Metaphysics and the Theory of Knowledge*, Avebury Series in Philosophy, 1995).

Harrison, Jonathan, *A Philosophers Nightmare, or the Ghost not Laid*, Nottingham University Monographs Series, 1986 (reprinted in Vol. I of *Essays in Metaphysics and the Theory of Knowledge*, Avebury Series in Philosophy, 1995).

Harrison, Jonathan, 'Science, Souls and Sense-Data' in *New Representationalisms*, ed. J.R. Smythies, Avebury Series in Philosophy, 1994 (reprinted in Vol. II of *Essays in Metaphysics and the Theory of Knowledge*, Avebury Series in Philosophy, 1995).

Harrison, Jonathan, *Essays on Metaphysics and the Theory of Kowledge*, Avebury, 1995, Part I, 'Mind and Body Problem', Part II, 'The Blue and Brown Fairy Books'.

Hume, David, *A Treatise of Human Nature*, ed. L.A. Selby-Bigge, revised P.H. Nidditch, Oxford University Press, 1976.

Jantzen, G., 'On Worshipping an Embodied God', *Canadian Journal of Philosophy*, 8, 1978.

Penelhum, T., *Survival and Disembodied Existence*, Routledge and Kegan Paul, 1970.

Penelhum, T., *Immortality*, Wadsworth Publishing Company, 1973.

Place, U.T., 'Is Consciousness a Brain Process?', *The British Journal of Psychology*, 1956.

Puccetti, Roland, *Survival and Disembodied Existence*, Macmillan, 1968.

Putnam, Hilary, *Reason, Truth and History*, Cambridge University Press, 1981.

Smart, J.J.C., *Philosophy and Scientific Realism*, Routledge and Kegan Paul, 1963.

Smythies, J.R., *The Walls of Plato's Cave*, Avebury Series in Philosophy, 1994.

Strawson, Peter, *Individuals*, Methuen, 1959.

Swinburne, R., *The Coherence of Theism*, Oxford University Press, 1977, chapter 7.

Wells, H.G., 'The Case of Jenkinson's Eyes' in *The Short Stories of H.G.Wells*, Ernest Benn, Ltd, 1927.

Wyndham, John, *The Midwich Cuckoos*, Penguin Books, 1979.

Chapter 21: The Body of Christ

Morris, Thomas V., *The Logic of God Incarnate*, Cornell University Press, New York, 1986.

Morton Prince, *The Dissociation of a Personality*, Oxford University Press, 1905.

Chapter 22: God's Omnipercipience

Alexander, Samuel, *Space, Time and Deity*, Macmillan and Co. 1920.

Armstrong, D.M., *A Materialist Theory of Mind*, Routledge and Kegan Paul, 1968.

Berkeley, George, *The Principles of Human Knowledge*, J.M. Dent and Son, 1910.

Descartes, Rene, *Meditations*, J.M. Dent and Son, 1912.

Everitt, Nicholas, 'Quasi Berkeleyan Idealism as Perspicacious Theism', *Philosophical Theology*, University of East Anglia Papers in Theology, 1995.

Harrison, Jonathan, *Essays on Metaphysics and the Theory of Knowledge*, Avebury, 1995.

Leibniz, *Monadology*, an edition for students, ed. Nicholas Rescher, Routledge, 1991.

Mackie, J.L., *The Miracle of Theism*, Oxford University Press, 1982.

Russell, Bertrand, 'On Our Knowledge of the External World' and 'The World of Physics and the World of Sense' in *Our Knowledge of the External World*, Allen and Unwin, 1914.

Russell, Bertrand, 'The Ultimate Constituents of Matter' and 'The Relation of Sense-Data to Physics' in *Mysticism and Logic*, Longmans, Green and Co., 1918.

Chapter 23: Survival of Death

Blakemore, C. and Greenfield, S., *Mindwaves*, Blackwell, 1982.

Broad, C.D., *The Mind and its Place in Nature*, Kegan Paul, London, 1925.

Broad, C.D., *Lectures on Psychical Research*, Routledge and Kegan Paul, 1962.

Butler, Joseph, *The Analogy of Religion, Butler's Works*, Vol. II, ed. W.E. Gladstone, Oxford University Press, 1897, Dissertation I, 'Of Personal Identity'.

Edwards, Paul, *Reincarnation: a Critical Examination*, Prometheus Books, 1996.

Flew, Antony, *Body, Mind and Death*, The Macmillan Company, New York, 1964

Geach, P.T., *God and the Soul*, Routledge and Kegan Paul, London, 1969.

Harrison, Jonathan, 'Science, Souls and Sense-Data' in *New Representationalisms*, ed. J.R. Smythies, Avebury Series in Philosophy, 1994.

Harrison, Jonathan, *Essays in Metaphysics and the Theory of Knowledge*, Avebury Series in Philosophy, 1995.

Hume, David, *A Treatise of Human Nature*, ed. L.A. Selby-Bigge, revised P.H. Nidditch, Oxford University Press, 1976, Book I, Part IV, Section VI, 'Of Personal Identity'.

Locke, John, *An Essay Concerning Human Understanding*, ed. P.H. Nidditch, Oxford University Press, 1975, chapter XXVII, 'Of Identity and Diversity'.

Lowe, E.J., *Subjects of Experience*, Cambridge University Press, 1997.

Noonan, Harold, *Personal Identity*, Routledge, 1989.

Noonan, Harold, *Objects and Identity, an Examination of the Relative Identity Thesis and its Consequences*, Martinus Nijhoff, 1980.

Noonan, Harold, *Personal Identity*, ed., International Research Library of Philosophy, 1993.

Parfit, Derek, *Reasons and Persons*, Oxford University Press, 1984.

Penelhum, Terence, *Survival and Disembodied Existence*, Routledge and Kegan Paul, 1970.

Penelhum, Terence, *Immortality*, Wadsworth Publishing Company, 1973.

Quinton, A.M., 'Spaces and Times', *Philosophy*, 1962.

Shoemaker, S. and Swinburne, Richard, *Personal Identity*, Blackwell, 1984.

Swinburne, Richard, *The Evolution of the Soul*, Oxford University Press 1986.

Wiggins, David, *Identity and Spatio-Temporal Continuity*, Basil Blackwell, Oxford, 1971.

Wiggins, David, *Sameness and Substance*, Oxford University Press, 1980.

Williams, Bernard, *Problems of the Self*, Cambridge University Press, 1973.

Chapter 24: The Problem of Evil

Adams, Marilyn McCord and Adams, Robert Merrihew, eds., *The Problem of Evil*, Oxford Readings in Philosophy, Oxford University Press, 1990.

Ahern, M.B., *The Problem of Evil*, Routledge and Kegan Paul, 1971.

Aquinas, Thomas, *Summa Theologiae*, ed. Thomas Gilby, Eyre and Spottiswoode and McGraw Hill Publishing Company, 1963–75, Prima Pars, Questions 47–49.

Augustine, St, *Confessions*, translated with an introduction by R.S. Pine-Coffin, Harmondsworth, 1961, Book VII, 3–5.

Augustine, St, *The City of God*, ed. translated by Henry Bettenson, with an introduction by David Knowles, Book XI, chapters 16–18 and Book XII, chapters 1–9.

Descartes, Rene, *Meditations*, Meditation VI, J.M. Dent and Sons Ltd., 1912, especially pp. 139–40.

Harrison, Jonathan, 'The Place of Virtue in a Teleological Ethical Theory', *Australasian Journal of Philosophy*, 1970.

Harrison, Jonathan, 'Be Ye Therefore Perfect', *Religious Studies*, 1985 (reprinted in *Ethical Essays*, Vol. II, Avebury, 1993).

Hick, John, 'Soul Making and Suffering' in *Evil and the God of Love*, Macmillan, 1966.

Hume, David, *Dialogues Concerning Natural Religion*, ed. with introduction by Stanley Tweyman, Routledge, 1979.

Leibniz, Gottfried William, *Theodicy; Essays on the goodness of God, the freedom of man and the origin of evil*, tr. E.M. Huggard, London, 1951.

Mackie, J.L., *The Miracle of Theism*. Oxford University Press, 1982, chapter 9.

Pike, Nelson, 'Hume on Evil', *The Philosophical Review*, 1963.

Plantinga, Alvin, *God, Freedom and Evil*, George Allen and Unwin, 1965.

Plantinga, Alvin, 'God, Evil and the Metaphysics of Freedom' in *The Nature of Necessity*, Oxford University Press, 1974, chapter 9.

Rowe, William L., 'The Problem of Evil and Some Varieties of Atheism', *The Problem of Evil*, eds Marilyn McCord Adams and Robert Merrihew Adams, Oxford University Press, 1990.

Wisdom, John, 'God and Evil', *Mind*, Vol. 44, 1935.

Chapter 25: Miracles

Aquinas, Thomas, *Summa Theologiae*, ed. Thomas Gilby, Eyre and Spottiswoode and McGraw Hill Publishing Company, 1963–75, Prima Pars, Question 105.

Augustine, St, *The City of God*, translated by Henry Bettenson, with an introduction by David Knowles, Harmondsworth, 1967, Book IX, chapters 16–18 and Book XII, chapters 1–9.

Edwards, Paul, *The Encyclopedia of Philosophy*, Collier-Macmillan, 1967.

Flew, Antony, *David Hume: Philosopher of Moral Science*, Blackwell, 1986, chapter V.

Galton, Francis, *An Enquiry Concerning Human Faculty*, Macmillan, 1983.

Gurney, Edmund, Myers, Frederick W.H. and Podmore, Frank, *Phantasms of the Living*, by abridged edition prepared by Mrs Henry Sidgwick, Kegan Paul, Trench, Trubner and Co. Ltd, 1918.

Harrison, Jonathan, *Essays in Metaphysics and the Theory of Knowledge*, Vol. II, Avebury Series in Philosophy, 1995.

Holland, R.F., 'The Miraculous' in *Miracles*, ed. Richard Swinburne, Collier Macmillan, in the series Philosophical Topics, general editor Paul Edwards, 1989.

Hume, David, *An Enquiry Concerning Human Understanding*, ed. L.A. Selby-Bigge, revised P.H. Nidditch, Oxford University Press, 1975.

Lash, Nicholas, *Believing Three Ways in One God*, S.C.M. Press, 1992.

Mackie, J.L. *The Miracle of Theism*, Oxford University Press, 1982.

Paley, William, *A View of the Evidences of Christianity*, R. Faulkner, 1794.

Paley, William, *Natural Theology, or evidences of the existence and nature of the Deity, collected from the appearances Nature*, London, 1802.

Swinburne, Richard, *The Concept of Miracle*, Macmillan, 1970.

Swinburne, Richard, ed., *Miracles*, Prentice Hall, 1989.

Voltaire, 'Miracles', *Philosophical Dictionary*, 1764.

Chapter 26: The Efficacy of Prayer

Aquinas, Thomas, *Summa Theologiae*, ed. Thomas Gilby, Eyre and Spottiswoode and McGraw Hill Publishing Company, 1963–75, Secunda secundae, 83, articles 1–17.

Galton, *Enquiry into Human Faculty*, Macmillan, 1983 (the chapter 'Statistical Enquires into the Efficacy of Prayer', omitted from later editions, has been reprinted in Sir Francis Galton, *Three Memoirs*, printed for the Eugenics Society, 1951).

Geach, Peter, 'Praying for Things to Happen' in *God and the Soul*, Routledge and Kegan Paul, 1969.

Penelhum, Terence, *Religion and Rationality*, Random House, 1971.

Phillips, D.Z. *The Concept of Prayer*, Routledge, 1965.

Phillips, D.Z., 'Religious Beliefs and Language Games', reprinted in *The Philosophy of Religion*, ed. Basil Mitchell, Oxford University Press, 1971.

Poulain, A, *The Graces of Interior Prayer, A Treatise of Mystical Theology*, translated from the sixth edition by Leonora Yorke Smith, and corrected to conform with the tenth French edition with an introduction by J.V. Bainvell an appendix on the discernment of spirits, with a preface by the Rev. D. Considine, S.J. Routledge and Kegan Paul Ltd, enlarged edition 1950.

Stump, Eleanor, 'Petitionary Prayer', *American Philosophical Quarterly*, 1979.

Underhill, Evelyn, *Worship*, Nisbet and Co., 1929.

Chapter 27: Belief

Audi, Robert, *The Structure of Justification*, Cambridge University Press, 1993.

Audi, Robert, and Wainwright, William J., *Rationality, Religious Belief and Moral Commitment*, Cornell University Press, 1986.

Clifford, W.K., 'The Ethics of Belief' in *The Ethics of Belief and Other Essays*, eds Leslie Stephen and Sir Frederick Pollock, with an introduction by Arthur Robertson, Thinker's Library, 1947.

Cohen, Jonathan, *An Essay on Belief and Acceptance*, Oxford University Press, 1992.

Descartes, *Meditations*, J.M. Dent and Sons, 1912, Meditation IV, 'Of Truth and Error'.

Harrison, Jonathan, 'Can I have a Duty to Believe in God?', *Philosophy*, Vol. 32, 1957 (reprinted in *Ethical Essays* Vol. I, Avebury, 1973).

Harrison, Jonathan, 'Some Reflections on the Ethics of Knowledge and Belief' in *Religious Studies*, Vol. 23, 1987 (reprinted in *Ethical Essays* Vol. I, Avebury, 1973).

Hume, David, *A Treatise of Human Nature*, Book I, Part III, ed. L.A. Selby-Bigge, revised P.H. Nidditch, Oxford University Press, 1978.

James, William, 'The Will to Believe', *The Will to Believe and Other Essays in Popular Philosophy*, Longmans Green and Co., 1896.

Meiland, Jack W., 'What ought we to believe?, or The Ethics of Belief Revisited', *American Philosophical Quarterly*, 1980.

Pascal, Blaise, *Pensees and Other Writings*, tr. Honor Levi, with introduction and notes by Hulbony Levi, Oxford University Press, 1995.

Phillips, Griffiths, ed., 'Knowledge and Belief' in *Philosophy*, Oxford University Press, 1967.

Price, H.H., *Belief*, George Allen and Unwin, 1969.

Prichard, H.H., 'Duty and Ignorance of Fact' in *Moral Obligation*, Oxford University Press, 1949

Ramsey, Frank, chapter 4 in ed. D.H. Mellor, *Philosophical Papers*, Cambridge University Press, 1990.

Rawls, John, *The Theory of Justice*, Oxford University Press, 1971, especially Section 26.

Ross, W.D., *The Foundations of Ethics*, Oxford University Press, 1939.

Stich, Stephen, *Folk Psychology in Cognitive Science; the Case Against Belief*, Clarendon Library of Logic and Philosophy, Oxford University Press, 1975.

Swinburne, Richard, *Faith and Reason*, Oxford University Press, 1981.

Chapter 28: Faith

Aquinas, Thomas, *Summa Theologiae*, ed. Thomas Gilby, Eyre and Spottiswoode and McGraw Hill Publishing Company, 1963–75, Secunda Secundae, Questions 1–7.

Armstrong, A.H., *Plotinus*, George Allen and Unwin, 1953.

Ayer, A.J., *Wittgenstein*, Penguin Books, 1985.

Braithwaite, Richard, *An Empiricist's View of the Nature of Religious Belief*, Cambridge University Press, 1955.

Freud, Sigmund, *The Future of an Illusion*, tr. W.D. Robson-Scot, The Hogarth Press, 1953.

Hare, Richard, *New Essays in Philosophical Theology*, eds A. Flew and A. MacIntyre, S.C.M. Press, 1955.

Harrison, Jonathan, *Essays on Metaphysics and the Theory of Knowledge*, Avebury Series in Philosophy, 1995.

Hick, John, *Faith and Knowledge*, Cornell University Press, 1967.

Hudson, Donald, *Ludwig Wittgenstein*, Lutterworth Press, 1968.

James, William, *The Varieties of Religious Experience*, Longmans, Green and Co., 1902.

James, William, *The Will to Believe and Other Essays in Popular Philosophy*, Longmans, Green and Co., 1912.

Kenny, Anthony, *What is Faith?*, Oxford University Press, 1992.

Kierkegaard, Søren, *Philosophical Fragments, or a Fragment of Philosophy*, tr. D.F. Svenson, Princeton University Press, 1936.

Kierkegaard, Søren, *Concluding Scientific Postscript*, tr. D.F. Svenson, and W. Lowrie, Princeton University Press, 1941.

Mackie. J.L., *The Miracle of Theism*, Oxford University Press, 1982.

Newman, John Henry, *An Essay in Aid of a Grammar of Assent*, ed. I.T. Ker, Oxford University Press, 1985.

Pascal, Blaise, *Pensees and Other Writings*, tr. Honor Levi, with introduction and notes by Hulbony Levi, Oxford University Press, 1995.

Penelhum, Terence. ed., *Faith*, in the series *Philosophical Topics*, general editor Paul Edwards, The Macmillan Company of New York and Collier Macmillan, 1989.

Plotinus, *Enneads*, with an English translation, by A.H. Armstrong, The President and Fellows of Harvard College, 1966

Plotinus, *The Enneads of Plotinus*, tr. Stephen McKenna, abridged with an introduction and notes by John Dillon, Penguin Books, 1991.

Pojman, Louis, *Religious Belief and the Will*, Routledge and Kegan Paul, 1986.

Price, H.H., *Belief*, Allen and Unwin, especially chapters 9 and 10.

Smith, Wilfred Cantwell, *Faith and Belief*, Princeton University Press, 1979.

Swinburne, Richard, *Faith and Reason*, Oxford University Press, 1981.

Tennant, F.R., *The Nature of Belief*, Centenary Press, London, 1943.

Underhill, Evelyn, *Mysticism, The Nature and Development of Spiritual Consciousness*, Oneworld, Oxford University Press, 1993

Wittgenstein, Ludwig, *Lectures and Conversations*, ed. C.K. Barret, Oxford University Press, 1966.

Chapter 29: Unchristian Ethics

Aquinas, Thomas, *Summa Theologiae*, ed. Thomas Gilby, Eyre and Spottiswoode and McGraw Hill Publishing Company, 1963–75, especially Secunda Secundae, Questions 23–27.

Butler, Joseph, *The Analogy of Religion*, *Butler's Works*, Vol. II, ed. W.E. Gladstone, Oxford University Press, 1897.

Butler, Samuel, *The Way of all Flesh*, ed. R.A. Streatfield, Grant Richards, 1903.

Clark, Michael, 'On Wanting to be Morally Perfect', *Analysis*, 1993.

Dawkins, Richard, *The Selfish Gene*, Oxford University Press, 1976.

Hare, R.M., *Moral Thinking, its Levels, Methods and Point*, Oxford University Press, 1981.

Harrision, Jonathan, 'Christian Virtues', *Supplementary Proceedings of the Aristotelian Society*, 1963 9reprinted in *Ethical Essays*, Avebury Series in Philosophy, 1993).

Harrison, Jonathan, *Challenges to Morality*, Macmillan Publishing Company, New York, 1992.

Harrison, Jonathan, *Ethical Essays*, Avebury Series in Philosophy, 1993.

Herrnstein, Hard J. and Murray, Charles, 'The Ethnic Differences in Cognitive Ability' in *Bell Curve: Intelligence and Class Structure in American Life*, Free Press, 1994.

Hume, David, *An Enquiry Concerning the Principles of Morals*.

Kant, Immanuel, 'Fundamental Principles of the Metaphysics of Morals' in *The Moral Law*, by H.J. Paton, Hutchinson, 1947.

Mackie, J.L., *The Miracle of Theism*, Oxford University Press, 1982.

McGinn, Colin, 'Must I be Perfect', *Analysis*, 1953.

Price, Richard, *Review of the Principal Questions in Morals*, ed. D. Daiches Raphael, Oxford University Press, 1948.

Prichard, H.H., 'Duty and Ignorance of Fact' in *Moral Obligation*, Oxford University Press, 1949.

Robinson, R., *An Atheist's Values*, Oxford University Press, 1964.

Russell, Bertrand, *Why I am not a Christian*, George Allen and Unwin, 1957.

Singer, Marcus, The Golden Rule', *Philosophy*, Vol. 38, 1963a.

Singer, Marcus, *Generalisation in Ethics*, Eyre and Spottiswoode, 1963b.

Sutherland, Stewart, 'Hope' in *The Philosophy of Christianity,* ed. Godfrey Vesey, Cambridge University Press, 1989.

Thielicke, H., *Theological Ethics*, A. and C. Black, Vol. I, 1968, Vol. II, 1969.

Urmson, J.O., 'Saints and Heroes' in *Essays in Moral Philosophy*, ed. A.I. Melden, University of Washington Press, 1958.

Williams, Glanville, *The Sanctity of Life and the Criminal Law*, Faber and Faber, 1958.

Chapter 30: Conclusions

Harrision, Jonathan, 'Christian Virtues', *Supplementary Proceedings of the Aristotelian Society*, 1963 (reprinted in *Ethical Essays*, Avebury Series in Philosophy, 1993).
Harrision, Jonathan, *Essays on Metaphysics and the Theory of Knowledge*, Avebury Series in Philosophy, 1995.
Smart, Ninian, *Reasons and Faiths*, Routledge, 1958.
Smart, Ninian, *Doctrine and Argument in Indian Philosophy*, E.J. Brill, 1992.
Stace, W.T., *Philosophy and Mysticism*, Macmillan, 1961.

Index